The Selected Journals of
L.M. Montgomery

VOLUME I

In 1981 the University of Guelph acquired the journals and scrapbooks of Lucy Maud Montgomery (1874–1942): ten large legal-size volumes containing almost two million words and spanning the years 1889 to 1942. Montgomery willed her journals to her son, Dr. E. Stuart Macdonald, a Toronto physician, requesting that he use his own judgement concerning their publication. For personal reasons he sheltered them from scrutiny until, two years before his death, they became the property of the University of Guelph. They will not be opened to the public until 1992.

This volume contains a selection from these journals covering the years 1889 to 1910.

1.   *L.M. Montgomery aet. 30 (1904)*

The Selected Journals of
L.M. Montgomery

VOLUME I: 1889–1910

EDITED BY
Mary Rubio & Elizabeth Waterston

TORONTO
OXFORD UNIVERSITY PRESS
1985

DRAWINGS BY ERICH BARTH

CANADIAN CATALOGUING IN PUBLICATION DATA
Montgomery, L. M. (Lucy Maud), 1874–1942.
The selected journals of L. M. Montgomery

Includes index.
Partial contents: v. 1. 1889–1910.
ISBN 0-19-540503-X (v. 1)

1. Montgomery, L. M. (Lucy Maud), 1874–1942 – Diaries.
2. Novelists, Canadian (English) – 20th century – Diaries.* I. Rubio, Mary, 1939–
II. Waterston, Elizabeth, 1922– III. Title.

PS8526.045Z53 1985   C813′.52   C85-099705-4
PR9199.2.M6Z468 1985

2 3 4 – 8 7 6

Printed in Canada by
Webcom Limited

TO THE MEMORY OF
Dr. E. Stuart Macdonald

AND TO
Ruth Macdonald

Contents

Illustrations

Drawings

Acknowledgements

I wish to express my appreciation for the trust confided in me by the late Dr. E. Stuart Macdonald, the son of L. M. Montgomery (Macdonald), who gave me exclusive access to the journals, until 1992, for the purpose of editing and overseeing publication in the form I deemed best. Until his sudden death in 1982 he offered generous assistance and the greatest possible encouragement. His widow, Ruth Macdonald, has also been unfailingly generous with her time, help, and encouragement.   MARY RUBIO

We wish to acknowledge gratefully the support of the University of Guelph and of many of our colleagues. The late President, Donald Forster, enabled us to begin the project with financial assistance from the University's Research Advisory Board. David Murray, Dean of Arts, procured funds that made it possible for us to proceed with our work until major grant assistance became available, and provided constant encouragement. From Douglas Killam, Chairman of the Department of English, we have received much valuable advice. Margaret Beckman, former Chief Librarian, arranged with her staff for the acquisition of Montgomery's journals and papers as a major addition to the University's Scottish and Scottish-Canadian Archives. Nancy Sadek, Archivist, and the library staff have been continuously helpful. Finally, the Institute of Computer Science, and Illustration and Information Services, supported us with great efficiency.

In the Atlantic Provinces, and particularly in Prince Edward Island, we owe our gratitude to archivists, genealogists, and scholars: Malcolm Ross of Dalhousie University; Patricia Townsend of Acadia University; Mary Beth Harris and Francis W. P. Bolger of the University of Prince Edward Island; Orlo Jones of the Prince Edward Island Heritage Foundation; and at the Confederation Centre, Charlottetown, Eleanor Lamont and Mark Holton.

Further research assistance was provided by Chris Beaver, Heather McKend, and Nick Whistler. The accuracy of Erich Barth's birdseye view of Cavendish was confirmed by Marion (Webb) Laird and Anita Webb—whose parents, Ernest and Myrtle (Macneill) Webb, were the owners of the house Montgomery used as her model for the one in *Anne of Green Gables*. (In Montgomery's childhood it had been owned by David and Margaret Macneill, a brother and sister who raised their grandniece Myrtle and were said to have borne a resemblance to Matthew and Marilla Cuthbert.) Restored by Parks Canada, this is now the "Anne of Green Gables House" in Cavendish.

We received assistance in ways that are much appreciated, but too numerous to mention, from Barbara Conolly, Bonnie Hulse, Jennie Rubio, Evan Siddall,

Patricia Sillers, and Dan Waterston. We are also grateful for the help extended by Barbara Filshie, Rae Fleming, Marian Hebb, Henri Pilon, Tracy Rubio, Jan Walker, and the late Dr. John B. Woodger.

In the preparation of this first volume of the Montgomery journals, William Toye has assisted us not only as the publisher's editor but as a valued collaborator at every stage of the book's development, from the selection of entries to the choice of illustrations.

Above all, we wish to acknowledge gratefully the long and patient support of our husbands, Gerald J. Rubio and Douglas Waterston.

The Research Grant Division of the Social Sciences and Humanities Research Council of Canada provided an exploratory grant in April 1982 and generous assistance in May 1985, which we gratefully acknowledge.

MARY RUBIO & ELIZABETH WATERSTON

Introduction

Lucy Maud Montgomery was born in Clifton (now New London), Prince Edward Island, on 30 November 1874, one year after the Island had entered the Confederation of Canada. Thirty-four years later, in 1908, her first novel, *Anne of Green Gables*, put Prince Edward Island on the literary map of the world. When she died in 1942 Montgomery had published over twenty books, hundreds of short stories and poems, and her name was known far beyond the English-speaking world. Her books were mostly "juveniles" in the technical sense, but they are unusual in that they have remained popular with children all over the world—and with many adults as well, who have retained a love for them throughout their lives. Her descriptions of the feelings of childhood, the quirkiness of human behaviour, and the landscape of her childhood haunts have immortalized the Island, which is visited by increasing numbers of her readers from all around the world.

Both branches of the family into which L. M. Montgomery was born had been settled on Prince Edward Island since the 1700s and were closely identified with its historical development—political, social, and educational. By family legend, the first English-speaking settler in Princetown (Malpeque) had been her great great-grandfather, Hugh Montgomery of Scotland, who settled there with his wife, Mary McShannon Montgomery, in 1769. On her maternal side, her great great-grandfather John Macneill was one of the founders of Cavendish, and her great-grandfather, William Simpson Macneill (1782-1870), who laid claim to having been the first male child born in Charlottetown, served as a Speaker of the House in PEI and was very prominent in the province as a politician and businessman. From these early roots both sides of the family established themselves on the Island as successful and influential businessmen, farmers, and politicians. Alexander Marquis Macneill (1820-98), L. M. Montgomery's maternal grandfather, was a farmer and the postmaster in Cavendish. Her paternal grandfather, Senator Donald Montgomery (1808-93), was both a good friend of the first Prime Minister of Canada, Sir John A. Macdonald, and represented PEI in Ottawa from 1874 to 1893, the year of his death.

Needless to say, the family derived feelings of superiority from their early associations with the history of PEI. But Montgomery herself took great pride as well in having an ancient lineage that she traced back to the Norman Conquest. According to genealogical papers she prepared, the Montgomerys originally came from Normandy, in the train of William the Conqueror, and moved on to Scotland. The title of Earl of Eglinton has been held by the Scottish family of Montgomerie since 1508. Montgomery's descent through the Earls of Eglinton gave her a sense of being rooted in a romantic and legendary past.

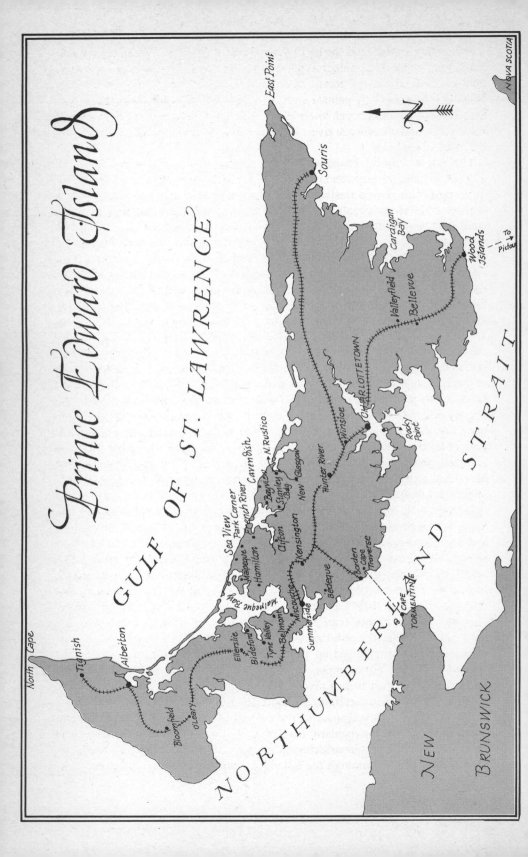

Prince Edward Island is the smallest province of Canada, with an area of only 2,184 square miles. In summer its meadows, fields, and woodlands become a rich quilt of many shades of green, made more dramatic by its contrast with the Island's red earth. Tidy painted wooden houses are set off by flower gardens. Small brooks bubble through lowlands, connecting with larger ponds. The gently rolling hills and picturesque rivers run down to pale sand beaches that slope into the blue Atlantic Ocean.

The Prince Edward Island of Montgomery's childhood was home to over 100,000 people. (Its population fell steadily through the early part of this century, as young people moved westward, and it regained its former population only in the late 1950s.) Most people were of Scots or English descent, but there were also some who were of Irish and Acadian French stock, a few Micmac Indians, and some American Loyalists who had moved there during the American Revolution. (Montgomery herself was primarily of Scottish stock, though she had some Loyalist and English blood.) In her childhood the PEI communities—linked by a newly built railway—were self-contained and picturesque settlements whose inhabitants had known each others' families for generations and who formed a close-knit unit of inter-married clans. Montgomery's hometown, Cavendish, was a small rural settlement near the coast, with neat houses facing each other up and down the main road. Many of them belonged to the three families who had first settled the area: the Macneills, the Clarks, and the Simpsons. "From the conceit of the Simpsons, the pride of the Macneills, and the vainglory of the Clarks, good Lord deliver us," ran the local Island joke. Nevertheless, in 1912, after Montgomery became famous and began reflecting on her formative years, she described her Cavendish folk as "loyal, clannish, upright, God-fearing, inheriting traditions of faith and simplicity and aspiration". They valued high moral purpose and a settled, industrious life, and they were intelligent. "The old Simpsons and Macneills, whatever their faults, were intellectual people with a keen interest in intellectual things."

Though the Cavendish settlement was rural, it was no cultural backwater. The Scots in Canada are noted for their efforts at setting up schools and universities, and the Scots character of Cavendish, and of PEI in general, ensured that children were educated and that they learned to express themselves well in public. The adults read newspapers and magazines to keep up with events outside the Island, and they imported books from the United States and Britain, circulating and discussing them in their Cavendish Literary Society. Children put on "school concerts" to display their learning and their mastery of oral expression, and men held public debates on such topics as "Free-trade vs. Protectionism". Women read magazines that flowed up from the States, and these furnished a strong cultural influence. For example, Montgomery's spelling in her journals reflects American rather than British practice. And she tells us that she first visualized Anne when she saw a picture of a young girl in an American magazine.

The world also reached small PEI settlements like Cavendish through sources other than print. Ships regularly docked on the Island, bringing an infusion of outside influences. Missionaries spoke of their adventures among the "heathen". Evangelists travelled through the Island, and secular speakers, politicians, and

Lucy Maud Montgomery: GENERATIONS & CONNECTIONS
in Prince Edward Island

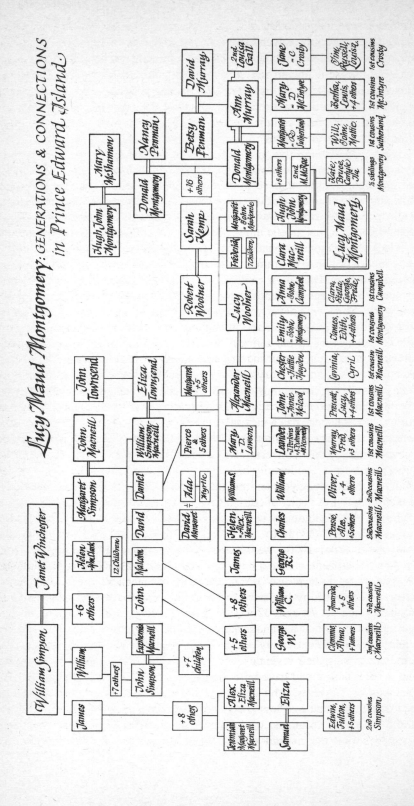

performing artists (elocutionists, singers, and other musicians) drew large audiences.

The long winters in Cavendish were conducive to visiting, gossiping, and honing one's skills as a raconteur. Summers brought the return of vacationing relatives from the mainland and the opportunity for trading stories. The women enjoyed making afternoon visits, and the church provided many occasions for "socials". It was a time when people enlivened social gatherings with their own stories about family and community and, more publicly, with recitations of memorized poems and "set pieces".

Possessing good narrative, oratorical, and conversational skills was as much a mark of social caste on the Island as claiming ancestry with the first settlers in the area. Montgomery says that she inherited her literary abilities and tastes from the Macneills, who claimed relationship to the minor Scottish poet Hector Macneill, a contemporary of Robert Burns. Of her grandfather, Alexander Macneill, she wrote: "He had a rich, poetic mind, a keen intelligence and a refined perception. He was a good conversationalist and a lover of nature." She spoke also of the poetic ability of "Cousin Jimmie" Macneill, her grandfather's older brother: "a most eccentric individual—a curious compound of child and genius. He was a born poet. He composed hundreds of poems and would recite them to favored individuals. They were never written down and not a line of them is now extant. But I have heard grandfather repeat some of them and they were real poetry— most of them being of the satirical and mock-heroic order. They were witty, pointed, dramatic and picturesque" (journal entry of 28 January 1912). She was particularly drawn to the storytelling powers of her grandfather's sister: "Aunt Mary Lawson is really the most wonderful woman of her age I have ever known. In her youth she had no educational advantages save a few weeks each year at the district school, but she had a naturally powerful mind, a keen intelligence, and a remarkable memory, which retains to this day everything she has ever heard and read. She is a splendid conversationalist and it is a great treat to get Aunt Mary started on tales and recollections of her youth, and all the vivid doings and sayings of folks in those young years of the colony. She is a stately old lady, with a nice amusing little bit of vanity about her yet" (5 June 1911).

When L. M. Montgomery was only twenty-one months old her mother, Clara Woolner Macneill (1853-76), died; shortly afterwards her father, Hugh John Montgomery (1841-1900), went west, where he remarried and stayed. Young Maud—she had been named Lucy after her grandmother Macneill, and Maud ("without an 'e' if you please") after a daughter of Queen Victoria—was left to be raised in Cavendish by her stern maternal grandparents, Alexander and Lucy Woolner Macneill. At ages 52 and 56, having already raised six children, they were faced with raising a granddaughter whose exceptional intellectual gifts were accompanied by an extremely sensitive, emotional, and excitable nature. They were approaching their seventies when Maud became a teenager, and her head-long enthusiasms would have been a trial even for flexible young parents. The grandparents, however, who kept the local post office, were rigid and dour, becoming more dour and less sociable as they aged. They liked a quiet life of carefully regulated routines, while young Maud—whose boundless imagination was fuelled by the natural energy of youth and by books that she read

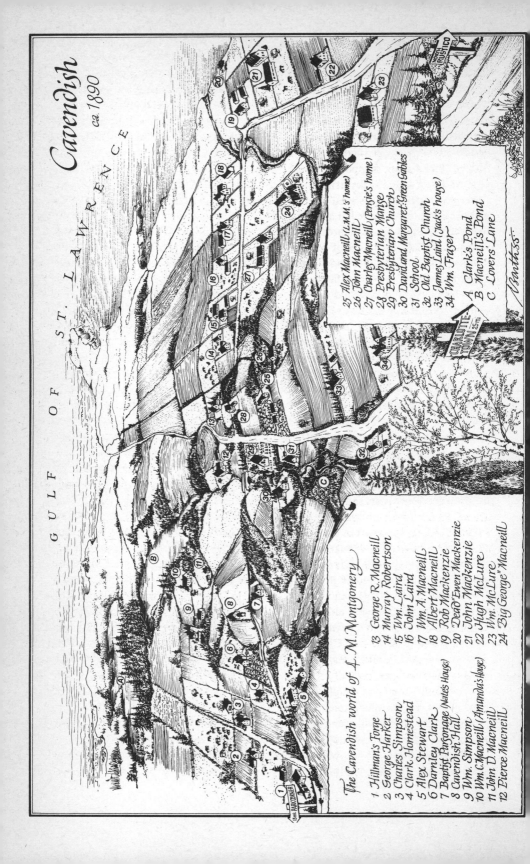

Cavendish
ca. 1890

GULF OF ST. LAWRENCE

The Cavendish world of L.M. Montgomery

1 Hillman's Forge
2 George Harker
3 Charles Simpson
4 Clark Homestead
5 Alex Stewart
6 Darnley Clark
7 Baptist Parsonage (Nate's House)
8 Cavendish Hall
9 Wm. Simpson
10 Wm. C. Macneill (Amanda's House)
11 John D. Macneill
12 Pierce Macneill

13 George R. Macneill
14 Murray Robertson
15 Wm. Laird
16 John Laird
17 Wm. A. Macneill
18 Albert Macneill
19 "Dead" Ewen Mackenzie
20 John Mackenzie
21 Rob Mackenzie
22 Hugh McLure
23 Wm. McLure
24 "Big George" Macneill

25 Alex Macneill (L.M.M.'s home)
26 John Macneill
27 Charles' Macneill (Pensie's home)
28 Presbyterian Manse
29 Presbyterian Church
30 David and Margaret "Green Gables"
31 School
32 Old Baptist Church
33 James Laird (Jack's house)
34 Wm. Fraser

A Clark's Pond
B Macneill's Pond
C Lovers' Lane

Barth 85

surreptitiously—was talkative and impulsive. Because her grandparents were strict and judgemental, old beyond their years, requiring her to be quiet, well behaved, and respectful, Maud began to live more and more in her imagination, where she was safe from censure. This no doubt was an important factor in the development of her writing habits: her bubbly, expressive nature craved an audience. But her Macneill grandparents' ears were tired, if not closed—their emotions were perhaps calcified by their rigid beliefs and unyielding dispositions—and they provided scant sympathy for their granddaughter. They did, however, provide ideals. Good Presbyterians that they were, the Macneills believed in the "examined life" and fostered in Maud an overly active conscience as well as an inclination to re-examine her actions and her life and to show disapproval of those who did not meet her standards. These were traits that endured in her character.

While the Macneill side of her family provided Montgomery with moral and intellectual fare, she was indebted for much emotional sustenance to her Park Corner relatives: her Grandfather Montgomery and the family of her Uncle John Campbell, who had married her mother's sister, "Aunt Annie". Trips to Park Corner (thirteen miles away), where both families lived, furnished good food, companionship, warmth, and gaiety. Her Grandfather Montgomery was interested in his sparkling little granddaughter (though too deaf to engage in meaningful conversation), and the hospitality at the John Campbell house was legendary. Maud naturally preferred her jolly Park Corner cousins to the Macneill group. In her journal entry of 22 January 1898, however, she claimed to have inherited both "the passionate Montgomery blood and the Puritan Macneill conscience". These uneasy opposites are evident in her journals, as well as in her novels, where there is constant tension between the restraint of age and the energy of youth, between the strictures of proper social customs and human spontaneity.

Montgomery says that she began keeping journals when she was a "tot of nine", but she destroyed the earliest ones. Surviving are ten handwritten volumes that were begun when she was fourteen and that date from 1889 to 1942. The selection that follows represents the first two and covers Montgomery's life in Prince Edward Island from ages 14 to 36 (1889 to 1910), with flashbacks to her very early memories. It takes her through her childhood and school days in Cavendish; through one year as a student at Prince of Wales College in Charlottetown (1893-4) and another in Halifax at Dalhousie University (1895-6); three years of being an Island schoolmarm in Bideford, Belmont, and Bedeque; and through a long and largely unhappy period, beginning in 1898, of keeping house for her grandmother in Cavendish, broken only by a stint on the Halifax *Echo* in 1901-2. During these last Cavendish years—she left PEI after she married in 1911—she had her first small successes in writing, selling poems and stories, until in 1908 she unexpectedly reached bestsellerdom with *Anne of Green Gables*. We see Montgomery as a high-spirited schoolgirl and serious student, a youthful teacher, a young woman much admired by men, a harassed working journalist, and a dutiful and kind granddaughter—all roles that she transmuted into her fiction in stories about Anne, Emily, Valancy, and her other heroines.

What compelled L. M. Montgomery to write her voluminous journals, in addition to her prodigious literary output? Even she was fascinated by her need for them. "Only lonely people keep diaries," she wrote in January 1904, and indeed her childhood was often lonely, in spite of the many schoolmates she was fond of and her continual enjoyment of her beautiful environment. Like so many highly gifted children, Montgomery developed quite early the awareness that she was somehow "different" from her peers, and that her imaginative and emotional life had dimensions that theirs lacked. Her sense of isolation was heightened by the deaths, between 1893 and 1900, of several close relatives and friends with whom she had strong emotional bonds. Her childhood girlfriends married and grew away from her; some of her nearest relatives patronized, insulted, or exploited her; numerous suitors pursued her, proposed, and were hurt when she had to refuse them; and her grandmother grew increasingly demanding and difficult. The journals gave her a necessary outlet and eventually became a safety valve that served Montgomery all her life.

They present a wide range of feelings. Bored, Montgomery scribbled for amusement; happy, she scribbled to capture moments of pleasure to relive later; angry, she wrote to release her tension; lonely, she turned to the journals as a listening ear. Providing an easy means of expressing her many moods, and a place to examine the patterns they created in her life, the journals enabled Montgomery to develop stratagems for coping with both her wildly fluctuating emotions—there are vivid accounts of her various psychological states, from depression to almost manic elation—and her creativity. She had unusually deep emotional responses to everything around her; capturing them in words gave her control over her feelings. From time to time she reread entries—looking for new insights into her life and its meaning, and for evidence of patterns that pointed to her destiny—and then reflected on them. Her journals also reveal, from the beginning, her intellectual curiosity, her impressionability and sensitivity, her independence of spirit, her sense of her own dignity, her dislike of pettiness in others, her love of nature, and her devotion to reading and writing—all traits that appeared in many of her fictional characterizations.

Montgomery viewed her journals as a "personal confidant in whom I can repose absolute trust". There were many times when, brought up to value loyalty to her clan, yet resentful of unkind treatment by some of them, she could not voice her conflicting emotions to anyone. After she married, and was unable to discuss her deepest fears and frustrations with her husband or with anyone in the community where she was the minister's wife, the journals became her best friend. In the beginning she enjoyed the experience of pouring out her feelings, as many young girls do; but a later need to record steadily her most private and intimate thoughts and impressions motivated her until her journals became an essential part of her life, both a duty and a joy. She fantasized that they were resentful whenever she neglected them. If she had nothing to write, or felt "flat", she apologetically tried to whip up more enthusiasm; if she wrote too long in a depressing vein, she chided the journal for failing to reflect the real Maud. Beginning her Volume 3 (selections from which will be in the next Oxford volume), she says:

I have just been reading over my first two volumes; and the thought uppermost in my mind is that, after all, in spite of my free confessions and self-analysis, a stranger perusing these journals would receive from them a quite misleading impression of my real character and life.

The first volume seems—I think—to have been written by a rather shallow girl, whose sole aim was to "have a good time" and who thought of little else than the surface play of life. Yet nothing could be falser to the reality. As a child and young girl I had a strange, deep hidden inner life of dreams and aspiration, of which hardly a hint appears in the written record. This was partly because I had not then learned the art of self-analysis—of putting my real thoughts and feelings into words; and partly because I did not then feel the need of a confidant in my journal. I looked upon it merely as a record of my doings which might be interesting to me in after years. Hence, I kept to the surface of existence and thought, in the writing of it, and never attempted to sound the deeps below.

Again, the second volume gives the impression of a morbid temperament, generally in the throes of nervousness and gloom. Yet this, too, is false. It arises from the fact that of late years I have made my journal the refuge of my sick spirit in its unbearable agonies. The record of pain seems thus almost unbroken; yet in reality these spasms came at long intervals, when loneliness and solitude had broken down my powers of endurance. Between these times I was quite tolerably happy, hopeful and interested in life. (11 February 1910.)

This appraisal is typical of Montgomery's constant desire to be realistic and truthful—though the "misleading" impressions she cites are only to be expected in a long-term, sometimes daily, outpouring of entries. One senses that already Montgomery was aware that she was creating in her journals a significant life history, a richly detailed social document: her intelligence demanded objectivity.

The young Maud had a passion for words—she often speaks of being drunk on words—and, like Anne, enjoyed using big words and writing purple passages. (As she grew older, she saw these for what they were and liked "deflating" her overwritten passages.) As a child she loved sentimental "pot-boilers", and such novels never failed to charm her; but she also developed mature literary tastes that were wide-ranging and intellectual. She studied Latin, French, and Greek and kept up a reading program that encompassed many of the great works of literature. For instance, she read and re-read Gibbon's *Decline and Fall of the Roman Empire* and other classic works. Her first income from writing was spent on books by Byron, Whittier, Longfellow, Milton, and Tennyson. The picturesque landscape that surrounded her gave rise to descriptions whose cadences echo passages in the King James Bible and in the romantic poets of Britain and America. Living in an age when people learned long poems by heart and recited them at social gatherings, as she often did, Montgomery had an uncommonly retentive memory and laced her journals and her novels with phrases and lines from Shakespeare and other writers, both ancient and modern. In spite of such knowledge, however, her mode of writing and her sensibility were too deeply rooted in her romantic storytelling heritage to be much influenced by the serious literature she read.

The journals reveal the same literary qualities, in a relatively artless form, that have endeared Montgomery's fiction to generations of readers: narrative interest,

and natural affections — bonds, not of the
intellect, which sees and admits the flaw
and drawback, but of the heart which
cries, "Yes, I see there but I love in spite-
of them."

Saturday. June 20. 1908

Cavendish. P.E.I

To-day has been, as _Anne_ herself
would say "an epoch in my life". My book
came to-day, fresh from
the publishers. I candidly
confess that it was for
me a proud, wonderful,
thrilling moment! There in
my hand lay the material
realization of all the dreams
and hopes and ambitions
and struggles of my whole
conscious existence — my
first book! Not a great
book at all — but mine,
mine, mine — something
to which I had given
birth — something which,

Cover design of
"Anne"

but for me, could never
have existed.

As far as appearance goes the
book is all I could desire — lovely cover
design, well bound, well printed. Anne
will not fail for lack of suitable garbing
at all events.

On the dedication page was the
inscription "To the memory of my father
and mother". Oh, if they were but living
to be glad and proud! When I think of
now father's eyes would have shone!

2. *A page from the journal.*
[*Half size*]

sentiment, humour, wit, and a realistic view of human nature. What is perhaps most remarkable about them is that they were maintained with an apparently effortless narrative flow that sustains the reader's interest even through trivia. Incidents, emotional confidences, objective commentary, and vivid descriptions are related with the ease and the flair of someone who likes a good read and is herself a gifted storyteller. Montgomery instinctively creates moods and word-pictures that dramatize and colour the text, and provides all necessary narrative links and embellishments. Frequently written in the heat of strong feelings, and embracing a wide range of styles according to her mood—arch, flippant, brisk, languorous, sentimental, stern, thoughtful, matter-of-fact—her journals are never dull.

As editors of the journals we have made it our first concern to provide a more-or-less complete portrait of Montgomery's life—her interests, her most memorable experiences, her deepest feelings—and at the same time to retain narrative threads and the many allusions to events that were later used in her fiction. We have attempted to reproduce the handwritten entries exactly. However, omissions (listed at the back) have been necessary in the interests of producing a book of manageable size and saleable price: these are entries that are either repetitive or non-essential to the unfolding drama of Montgomery's life. A few short deletions within entries are indicated by spaced ellipsis marks. (Non-spaced ellipses are Montgomery's own.) The journals of this period contain three long sections—mature reflections on earlier events—of which only the third has been included as the penultimate entry in our selection. Long portions of the other sections were used in the articles that were published posthumously in Montgomery's *The Alpine Path: The Story of My Career* (1974).

In the interests of typographical style all headings have been moved from the right side to the left, and the first paragraph of each entry begins flush left. We have almost always retained Montgomery's inconsistencies, both in the spelling of names that begin with "Mc" and "Mac" (these are legion) and in punctuation. We have of course retained her American spelling, which reflects the strong cultural influence of the New England and other seaboard states. A few misspellings have been corrected lest they cause confusion, and these are cited in the notes—unless, in our judgement, the error was made solely in the haste of copying (such cases are very few). Late in life Montgomery prepared a typed and greatly abridged version of her journals (to 1936), apparently for publication. (In this typescript she predictably deleted some of the most interesting and psychologically revealing sections, and toned down criticism of people who were still living.) She usually corrected her errors: but if she perpetuated a spelling mistake in the typed version, we have noted this in making our correction. When we could not make out a word in the handwritten manuscript, or when (rarely) a necessary word was clearly missing, we turned to the typescript for assistance. However, we have refrained from changing any words in the handwritten version as the result of consulting her later edited version, feeling that the integrity of the original document should prevail. Anyone who wishes to make comparisons with Montgomery's typed document may do so after 1992.

Montgomery wrote her journals between 1889 and 1918 in "blank books" of varying shapes and sizes. In 1919 she began recopying these journals into the legal-size ledgers that now house them. She wrote that her policy was to be "careful to copy it exactly as it is written", and to "illustrate it" as she went along "with such photos of the scenes and people who figure in it" as she possessed.* We cannot of course be sure that Montgomery copied her text exactly as it was first written, for the original books are apparently lost or destroyed.** In style, the early entries might seem more polished in diction than would be usual for a fourteen-year-old diarist; but if we compare the earliest entries with the essays she was already beginning to publish, we see a comparable ease and polish. (However, her letters to Pensie Macneill—reproduced in Francis W. P. Bolger's *The Years Before Anne*— are written in a loose, colloquial style that she obviously adopted for her friend.) Even before 1919 L. M. Montgomery was using her journals to re-enter the world of childhood and to create its voices and textures: she therefore had good reason to leave her record as it stood. She knew that if she ever wished to publish her journals, she could adapt and polish them later (as in fact she did in the typescript). It is worth noting, however, that several pages of the handwritten volumes were carefully cut out and replacements just as carefully inserted. For instance, in the entry in which she first described her future husband, the Reverend Ewan Macdonald, she removed the page and inserted a replacement. Unless the earliest journal-books turn up somewhere, we can never be sure whether the first entries, written when she was fourteen, were copied exactly.

Because the journals are so full and frank and cover such a long period, and because they are the work of a successful professional writer, they provide a degree of information, anecdote, and personal history that makes them unique in Canadian letters. The interest attached to the autobiographical content is obvious. What may not appear so obvious in this first volume is that the complete journals of L. M. Montgomery provide a fund of engrossing social history covering more than half a century and draw the reader surprisingly far into the depths of one woman's life.

---

* We have selected approximately 100 from over 400 photographs Montgomery inserted in the first two handwritten volumes. Some of these photographs were taken years later than the date of the passage they illustrate.
** Montgomery's son, Dr. E. Stuart Macdonald, said that in her last few years she burned quantities of letters and papers she considered unimportant, and that after her death other materials mysteriously disappeared before he was able to have them removed from the house.

1889

Cavendish, P.E. Island
Sept. 21, 1889

I am going to begin a new kind of diary. I have kept one of a kind for years—ever since I was a tot of nine. But I burned it to-day. It was so silly I was ashamed of it. And it was also very dull. I wrote in it religiously every day and told what kind of weather it was. Most of the time I hadn't much else to tell but I would have thought it a kind of crime not to write daily in it—nearly as bad as not saying my prayers or washing my face.

But I'm going to start out all over new and write only when I have something worth writing about. Life is beginning to get interesting for me—I will soon be fifteen—the last day of November. And in *this* journal I am never going to tell what kind of a day it is—unless the weather has something to do worth while. *And*—last but *not* least—I am going to keep this book locked up!!

To be sure, there isn't much to write about to-day. There wasn't any school, so I amused myself repotting all my geraniums. Dear things, how I love them! The "mother" of them all is a matronly old geranium called "Bonny." I got Bonny ages ago—it must be as much as two or three years—when I was up spending the winter with Aunt Emily in Malpeque. Maggie Abbott, a girl who lived there, had a little geranium slip in a can and when I came home she gave it to me. I called it Bonny—I like things to have handles even if they are only geraniums—and I've loved it next to my cats. It has grown to be a great big plant with the cunningest little leaves with a curly brown stripe around them. And it blooms as if it *meant* it. I believe that old geranium has a soul!

Sunday, Sept. 22, 1889
Cavendish, P.E. Island, Can.

From sheer force of habit I was just going to write "a dark cold day with frequent showers of rain."

But I won't!

Last night Pensie came up and asked me to go down and stay all night with her. Pensie Macneill—almost everybody in Cavendish who isn't a Simpson is a Macneill and mostly they are both—is a girl who lives about a mile from here and is my second cousin. She is a good bit older than me—she is nearly eighteen—but we have always been great chums. It is fine fun to go down there to stay all night. We've had some dandy old times together—coasting and berrying and picking gum and going to the shore and playing with the cats in the barns.

Today we came up to church together and after dinner we went to Miss Clemmie Macneill's funeral.

1

Tuesday, Sept. 24, 1889

We have lots of fun in school these days. Mollie wasn't there to-day and I was terribly lonesome. Mollie is my greatest chum. Her real name is Amanda Macneill but the boys always call her "Mollie" and me "Pollie." I liked being called "Pollie." Mollie and I have always sat together in school ever since we were teeny-weeny tots.

Clemmie Macneill—not the one who was buried yesterday but another—and Nellie Macneill sit behind us. They are hateful girls. I fell out with them a spell ago and we have never spoken since. I don't want to speak, either. They would like to make up again though. They told Lucy—Lucy is my cousin. She lives just across our field. *She* is a Macneill, too—that they would speak to me if I would speak first. Well, I will not! They got mad first and they can get over it first or stay mad—*I* don't care which. They are not the sort of girls I care to be very friendly with anyhow. They are not to be trusted.

Snip was in school, too, and we had some fun. Snip—dear me, if I hadn't burned all my other journals I wouldn't have to explain all over again who everybody is—is Nathan Lockhart. He is the Baptist minister's step-son and lives in the parsonage. Mollie and I call him "Snip" and John Laird, who sits with him and is *his* chum, we call "Snap." Snip is a very nice boy and we are great friends. He is crazy about books and so am I. We exchange those we've got and talk about them. And the other scholars don't like it because we talk of things they don't understand.

Wednesday, Sept. 25, 1889
Cavendish

This has been such a perfectly exquisite day that I've just got to say something about it. It was so bright and crisp, with an exhilarating air and *such* a lovely sky—brilliantly blue, with lacy trails of misty white cloud straying over it. But I hadn't much time to enjoy it. We were picking potatoes all day up in our hill field. I don't think anybody ever got to such a pitch of virtue as to like potato-picking. I hate it! But since pick I had to I was glad it was up in the hill field because I love that field. There is such a glorious view from it—the deep blue sea, the pond as blue as a sapphire, the groves of maple and birch just turning to scarlet and gold, the yellow stubble-lands and the sere pastures. I just love to look at such things. But glory be that we are done with the potatoes! To be sure, potato-picking has its funny side. It would have made a hermit laugh to have seen Lu and me as we trudged home tonight, in tattered, beclayed old dresses, nondescript hats and faces plastered with dirt and mud. But we didn't *feel* funny—no, indeed!

Friday, October 11, 1889

After school I took a basket and set off to "Sam Wyand's field." This is a lovely field away back behind Jimmy Laird's woods—now, never mind who Jimmy Laird is!—where we go to pick strawberries in summer. It is all surrounded by maple woods and it is just lovely. And we go through such beautiful lanes to get there, all trees overhead and ferns underfoot. The maple leaves are just splendid now. I picked my basket full and then just roamed around, having a fine time in spite of an impertinent little shower that came pattering down, making the maples overhead rustle like silvery music. I just love the woods and those woods in particular.

Tuesday, October 22, 1889
Oh dear, we have an examination in arithmetic tomorrow. I don't like arithmetic. I had to write a composition on Cleopatra tonight. But I like writing compositions. Miss Gordon makes us write them every week. Miss Gordon is our teacher. She is a good one and I like her splendidly.

Thursday, October 24, 1889
Nate brought me "Undine" to-day and I read it under the lid of my desk while Miss Gordon thought I was studying history. It was delicious—"Undine", I mean, not history. You don't catch me calling history delicious! I love books. I hope when I grow up to be able to have lots of them.

I went to prayer-meeting tonight and had such fun. Topsy followed me—Topsy is my cat—and all my efforts to send her home were unavailing. She went under the church and I sat through the meeting on pins lest she should take it into her perverse little head to come in and attend the services.

Wednesday, November 13, 1889
It seems a long while since I've written in my journal but there has been nothing much to write about until last night when Rev. Mr. Carruthers of Charlottetown lectured in the hall. With much difficulty I got grandpa's and grandma's leave to go. I went over to stay all night with Mollie and we went to the lecture. The hall was crowded and the lecture was splendid. I never laughed so much. When it ended Mollie and I began to edge our way out. We had to go slowly because of the crowd. I could see Snip behind us, pushing ahead with all his might. He appeared to be in a great hurry but when he got behind Mollie and me he stopped forging ahead and seemed content to take things a little easier. Out on the platform we met Miss Gordon and Mollie asked her if she were walking.

"Oh, no," she responded. "We have a first-class cart."

Humph! A few minutes later we saw her perched in Toff McKenzie's buggy, as composed as if first-class carts were never heard of. The boys tormented Toff by hanging on to his wheels to keep him from turning and all the time Miss Gordon sat there, while poor Toff, reins in hand, was vainly trying to get into the buggy and saying "Comeah, comeeah," to the plunging and terrified horse!

Mollie and I decided not to start until all the buggies had gone, because it is so awfully dark on the hall hill. When we did start Nate and Neil Simpson were just behind us. At the top of the hill Neil turned in at his own gate. Snip also turned in at his, but said to us as he did so,

"I don't suppose there will be any *white horses* on the road tonight, will there?"

"No, I guess not", I said.

"If I thought there would be I'd go with you," he said.

Mollie laughed and I said, "No necessity" but Snip said meditatively,

"I guess I'll go anyhow."

"He's coming," whispered Mollie excitedly.

And come he did, right home with us. You don't know how silly I felt, walking down that road arm in arm with Nate. We had lots of fun and rehearsed all our private jokes, for the road seemed deserted, except for our three gay selves. What was our dismay therefore, on going down the slope by Wm. Simpson's lower gate to discover two girls just ahead of us—Clemmie Macneill and Emma Tobin. Emma Tobin is Mrs. Spurr's servant girl. Mrs. Spurr is Nate's mother. These explanations will be the death of me, especially when they come at such a breathless moment.

We were furious. Clem and Em were just crawling along—on purpose, as we knew very well—and as Mollie and I could not summon up enough courage to pass them we had to fall into step behind.

"Oh dear me," I whispered "that hateful creature will have this all over Cavendish tomorrow."

"Oh, well, what's the difference?" said Snip easily. "They must have something to talk about, you know."

This was undoubtedly true but I did not relish them talking about *us*. At last C. and E. reached John Macneill's gate and had to turn in. They stood there watching us as we walked past—gnashing their teeth, I've no doubt, for they are both crazy over Nate. We walked faster then, anxious to escape a crowd of boys coming behind, until we reached the shelter of Mollie's lane, down which we sauntered at a more leisurely pace. Of course, after Mollie and I went to bed we talked for *hours* and just *couldn't* get to sleep. I suppose we were a pair of fools; but then it was the very first time we had had an escort home; and we knew Clemmie and Nellie would be wild with rage over it. They *were*, too. They did nothing but talk about it all day in school. Nate was not there at all; perhaps Clemmie and Emma waylaid and murdered him on the way home last night!

Saturday, Nov. 23, 1889
Last night there was a Literary concert at the hall. Miss Gordon asked Mollie and me some time ago if we would recite. I consented but I was dreadfully nervous for I've never recited in public before. But I learned a piece, "The Child Martyr", and have been practising it right along.

Well, yesterday morning it was pouring rain and we felt very blue. I tried to cheer everybody up by assuring them that it would certainly clear up at sunset—a theory that was rather laughed at by the other scholars, most of whom, with the exception of Charlie Mackenzie—who also *would* be hopeful—had resigned themselves to the collapse of the whole enterprize.

There was no school in the afternoon on account of a funeral, so Mollie came up to stay with me until we saw how the weather turned out. At four it *had* stopped raining, though it was very foggy, so we went over to her place.

It *did* clear up at sunset, as I had so faithfully believed it would. We went up to the hall early. There were only a few there when we arrived and all was confusion and excitement—men going and coming, singing out orders, arranging seats, and running hither and thither. At last all was ready—the choir and organ in place,

George Simpson in the chair, and the hall well filled.

Jamie Simpson opened the programme with a march. Then came a recitation, then a song, then Mollie's recitation. She got through with it all right and could then settle herself down to enjoy the concert but I could only sit there in nervous suspense. At last my turn came. George Simpson looked down at me and said,

"The next is a recitation by Miss Maud Montgomery."

Feeling myself grow cold all over, I rose. Clemmie Macneill, who sat behind me remarked to Emma Tobin in a sneering whisper "There she goes!" I *did* go, but how I got out and up to the platform I don't know and will never be able to tell. And how I trembled! My voice seemed to be something coming through my lips that did not belong to me at all. And I had the most curious sensation of being an enormous size—as if I filled the hall! But I got through at last and Miss Gordon whispered to me as I sat down "You did *very* well"!

I enjoyed the rest of the programme splendidly and felt sorry when it was concluded. Of course we then had to listen to several prosy speeches by "the old chaps" and finally they gave us a vote of thanks and let us go.

Mollie and I at once started up the hill. Nate was standing by his gate as we passed. He opened and shut it with an ostentatious bang for the benefit of stragglers but he *stayed outside*. Soon he came sneaking up and said,

"Will you try me again tonight, girls?"

We *did* try him and I may say that the experiment was successful. We had a scrumptious walk home. I expect Clemmie will take a conniption when she hears of this second "escapade."

Tuesday, Nov. 26, 1889
There is going to be a big ruction in school to-morrow. Clemmie Macneill and Annie Stewart have been fighting for weeks and it has been getting worse and worse. Mamie Simpson and Clara Mckenzie are in it too—on Annie's side of course, while Nellie naturally sides with Clemmie. Well, to-night Clemmie and Nellie went to Miss Gordon with a dismal tale of how the girls were treating them. I am mixed up in the affair since Annie intends to call on me as a witness because I was unlucky enough to be present one day when she and Clemmie were having a wordy scrap and heard all that Clemmie said—and Annie, too, for the matter of that, for Annie can take her own part in any affair that comes to a question of *tongue*. Now, I know too well what Clemmie Macneill is and she is especially keyed up just now. If she thinks I give evidence in Annie's favor she is quite liable to blaze out about *our* quarrel and Nate will be dragged into it and the mischief to pay all round. Clemmie got mad at me because Nate and I are such good friends, that is just the plain truth of it. If it comes out, as it probably will—for Miss G. has a genius for ferretting—that this is why Miss Clem and I fell out—well, it is too awful for anything.

Wednesday, Nov. 27, 1889
The court held its first sitting to-day. Miss Gordon was as cross as X all day with everyone. When school was over we knew by her expression what was coming. It came. As Nellie was not there the proceedings could not be thorough. Annie, of

course, called upon me to prove the truth of a part of her defence and I had to admit that I heard Clemmie say certain things. Miss Gordon wrote all the evidence down—Miss Gordon has rather terrifying ways by times—and the trial was adjourned until Nellie should be there. What is to come I wonder.

Monday, December 2, 1889
I'm perfectly savage to-night!!!

All the parties concerned in the "grand row" were in school to-day. I had begun to hope that Miss G. intended to let the matter blow over without further investigation; but evidently she is not one who will turn her back after putting her hand to the plough.

So when school was dismissed she said,

"Clemmie, Nellie, Annie, Mamie, and Clara will remain after school. Also Maud and Lucy, as their testimony is required. Amanda, do *you* know anything about this?"

Amanda said "no" and got clear. I can't for my life see how she could tell such a fib and look so innocent. She knew as much about it as I did. But she was bound not to get mixed up in the fuss and a lie or two was an ever-present help in time of trouble.

Then Miss G. began. She ought to have been a criminal lawyer. She didn't extract much from me, though, for I just kept as fast a hold on my information as I could and all her cross-questioning didn't elicit much beyond some general admission of facts which everybody knew already.

Then Mamie's turn came and she began to tell how the squabble between *her* and Clemmie began—for it seems that Clemmie has a row on hand with her, too. One day, some time ago, Clemmie had remarked to Mamie,

"Isn't it absurd, the way Maud and Nate go on?"

Mamie said—or *says* she said, which is not necessarily the same thing—

"Well, I don't suppose it is anybody's business but their own."

And then Clemmie flew into Mamie and called *her* names. That dear Clemmie must be an amiable soul!

Miss Gordon pricked up her ears.

"*The way Maud and Nate act!* Why, how *do* they act?"

Clemmie gave her head a toss and said with volumes of malice in her tone,

"Well, they are always passing notes to each other in school, and walking round together at recess—and *talking*!"

Miss Gordon looked rather blank. I think she had been expecting to hear that Nate and I broke all the ten commandments all at once every day. As for me, I was too angry to speak—and a little uncomfortable as well. For of course it was true enough about the notes and the strolls and I didn't know just what view Miss Gordon might take of it in her present exasperated mood. But Nate is a favorite of hers and more over, I fancy she didn't want another investigation on her hands. So she merely said,

"I have never thought that either Maud or Nate required watching, nor do I think so now. This has no connection with the present case."

Fancy my relief! The examination of the others went on while I sat there and tried to regain my composure. Annie defended herself vigorously and I fancy Miss Gordon got her eyes opened a bit. At last she got all the evidence she could drag out of anybody and then she "summed up". Both parties got an impartial drubbing and she solemnly adjured them to cease from quarrelling and be at rest or they would be expelled from the school. Then the welcome word of dismissal was given and I hurried out and home in a red-hot rage. Wait till I tell Nate!

Tuesday, Dec. 3, 1889

What can be going to happen? Well, something sufficiently surprising *has* happened for Clemmie actually *apologized* to me to-day for saying what she did. It is the first time she has spoken to me for months. I answered coldly but politely. I cannot believe her apology was sincere—she is simply not that sort of a girl! I know her real reason. She is badly gone on Nate herself and does not wish to incur his anger.

He is furious. Last night I wrote him a stormy letter in which I poured out an indignant account of the famous interview and all my resentment regarding it. I don't believe he will ever speak to Clemmie again. As for me, I'm beginning to cool down. After all, it was all rather funny!

Monday, Dec. 23, 1889

I am all cooled down long ago. We have been having a great time in school lately preparing for our Xmas examination, which comes off to-morrow. We have been learning songs and practising dialogues galore. Annie and Clara are still fighting with Clemmie and Nellie. It is apparently too good fun to give up. Clemmie and Nellie persist in trying to sing and they are poor singers. Annie and Clara, who *can* sing, are cranky too, and sulk if anything happens that doesn't suit them. They made a regular kick against Clemmie's singing to-night and there was a lively spat. Well, I can't sing and don't pretend to, so I'm not in this scrap, thanks be!

Nate slipped a French grammar across the aisle to me to-day and in it I found a long "poem" he had made about the night of Mr. Carruther's lecture. It was awfully funny. At least, I thought so. I don't suppose Clemmie or Emma Tobin would. It all depends on the point of view.

Thursday, December 26, 1889

I went to prayer-meeting this evening. Prayer-meeting is about the only amusement we have. Mollie and I sat together and made our plans for to-morrow night. There is another lecture at the hall and I am going over to go up with her. When we got out it was very dark and Annie Jack and I started off together. There were four or five sleighs on the ground and we had to dodge through them. As we went down the bank to the road a boy came running up and collided with us. My hat fell off and we had to claw around in the snow for it, laughing until we could scarcely breathe. Then we tried to get off on the side of the road, out of the way of the sleighs and got into deep snow and Annie fell and my hat came off again and my shawl, too, and we could hardly regain our feet for laughing. One of the boys in the sleighs jumped out and careered up and down the road, acting the clown. Of course he was only in fun but I really believe Annie was scared to death for whenever he came near she would cling to me and scream. I suppose Mr. Archibald would think the noise was shocking but we couldn't help it.

Now, I suppose someone might say,

"And what was there in all this that was so exhilarating? You fell in the snow—and your hat came off—and a boor cut up capers. What was so funny in all that?"

Really, I don't know. But it seemed funny at the time and we got a good laugh out of it anyhow.

Tuesday, Dec. 31, 1889

Well, journal, this is the last day of the old year. To-night we will say farewell to '89, with all its record of joy and sorrow, pleasure and pain, and bid the New Year welcome. God grant that it may never record unfulfilled aspirations, unsatisfied longings, or ungathered flowers. Good-bye, dear old year. You have been on the whole a very happy one for me.

3. The old home
[*The house of Alexander Macneill, LMM's grandfather*]

4. The shore
[*Cavendish*]

5. *Cavendish school*

6. *Snip's home*
[*The Baptist parsonage where Nate Lockhart lived*]

7. *The Presbyterian Church, Cavendish*

8. *Cavendish Hall*
[*A community centre*]

9. *Miss Gordon*

10. Amanda's house
[Amanda's father was William C. Macneill]

1890

Mollie and I have made a decidedly startling discovery about some of our little personal affairs. I am not going to write it down because it is a dead secret. We have refused to tell Nate what it is but we have just hinted at enough to fire his curiosity to the blazing point. I presume we'll have to tell him later but not till we tantalize him a wee bit.

Max is up on the table bothering me fearfully. Max is one of my cats and he is just a beauty—a gray, tiger-stripe fellow. I do love cats. I have another named Topsy—a motherly old gray-and-white.

Saturday, Jan. 25, 1890
I feel cross and horrid! Yesterday I went over with Mollie from school. There was to be a lecture at the hall and Hamilton drove us up. Then we were greeted by the unwelcome intelligence that the lecturer had not come. However, they got up a debate which was fairly interesting.

But I do heartily hate that Ham Macneill. He is simply odious. If he were not Mollie's brother I would not be even civil to him. But I don't want to offend her so I put up with him outwardly. He teased and tormented me to-day until I was ready to scratch his eyes out. I have just arrived home in a very disgruntled mood.

Nate and I don't have much to say to each other just now. We have had a bit of a tiff. But I guess it will soon wear off. I hope so anyhow, for I miss Nate when he is sulking.

Tuesday, Feb. 4, 1890
Nate and I are good friends again. He is certainly a nice boy—clever and intellectual, and that is more than can be said of the other Cavendish boys, although they are a nice enough set of lads. I love to talk to Nate about books. There is nobody else in Cavendish who cares to talk about them.

Saturday, Feb. 8, 1890
I feel rather *blue* to-night. I am a horrid little goose, I know—but the trouble is, I can't help being a horrid little goose.

Yesterday night Mr. Archibald lectured at the hall, so I went over with Mollie from school. We walked up alone. The hall was filled and the lecture was very good, but of course all those musty old Simpson speakers—oh, don't they *just* think they are *It*!—had to get up after it and say it all over again.

When we got out at last we started home and had got a good bit past the parsonage gate when Nate came running up.

13

"Will you tell me that secret discovery of yours tonight, girls?" he said.

I just made some saucy rejoinder, never dreaming that he would take it seriously, for I thought Nate was too well used to my little speeches to take them for more than they were worth. But I guess he was in one of his moods tonight for he simply turned on his heel and went off—mad, I suppose.

It was just too mean. But I don't care. If Nate is so huffy he can sulk all he likes! I didn't sleep much last night, though goodness knows I tried hard enough to. This morning was so stormy that I could not get home and I was vexed for several reasons, but principally because I wanted to get away by myself and have a good cry.

In the evening it cleared up a little and Ham drove me home.

Oh, dear, I feel glum. I know Nate is mad at me and I didn't mean to say anything to vex him.

Monday, February 10, 1890

I went to school this morning, still feeling cross and blue. Nate was there but not a word did he say about Friday night and appeared the same as usual. I think he was feeling a little ashamed of himself. But I am glad we are good friends again. It was so dreadfully lonesome the last time we quarrelled.

We have splendid fun now, coasting on Pierce's hill. The boys bring their sleds and it is so exciting. Nate always takes Mollie and me.

Monday, Feb. 17, 1890

In school to-day I got a note from Nate, smuggled over in his Latin grammar, that is going to be a nuisance. I must make a long explanation why.

One of our school superstitions is that if you count nine stars for nine continuous nights the first boy you shake hands with afterwards is to be your future husband. It is very hard to get the nine continuous nights. Mollie and I began about the first of November but we've never got them yet although if it keeps fine I really will get mine out tonight. But Nate got his out long ago. Mollie and I tried to coax him to tell us who he shook hands with. We thought it was Zella Clark, a great, gawky thing who lives at Bay View. Nate wouldn't tell then but he agreed with me that if I, when I got mine out, would tell him with whom I shook hands, he would tell me.

But I soon came to see that if I waited until I got mine out I might wait a long while and still be no wiser. So I began to tease Nate again. And just then Mollie and I made that "discovery" of ours.

So I told Nate that if he would tell me *right away* the name of his Fair Unknown, I would tell him the mysterious secret, besides keeping to my agreement of telling him with whom I shook hands if I ever got my stars out.

Nate squirmed a good deal and wouldn't come to heel for a long time. At last, however, he agreed, but only on condition that I was *to answer, fair and square, without any evasion, any one* question he might ask me. In return, *I* might ask *him* any one question I pleased and he would pledge himself to answer it.

I hesitated at first, but curiosity got the better of my prudence and finally I agreed for I was wild to know what his mysterious question was. So I wrote down my information last Friday and in return received his letter. When I read that it was *I* with whom he had shaken hands I nearly had a fit for I had never suspected *that*. But I forgot surprise and everything else when I saw that fatal question. "Angels and ministers of grace defend us."

It was:— *"Which of your boy friends do you like best?"*

Horrors! I had never dreamed of this! *What* was I to do! Of course, I liked Nate best—nothing very extraordinary in that. He is very nice and we have always been chummy. But owning up to it in plain English is quite another thing. Besides, he may think the admission means a great deal more than it really does.

In my perplexity a brilliant idea struck me—at least I thought it was a brilliant idea then. Why not ask him the *same question* in regard to his girl friends? I *was* sure he wouldn't want to answer such a question and rather than do so would let me off and consent to let the whole thing drop. So I wrote him my decision and the next day—Saturday—when he came for the mail, I gave him my letter. He went off to read it and came back looking as foolish as a flat-fish. As I had hoped, he at once proposed to let the whole thing drop.

So I was quite at ease until this morning, when another "awful revelation came", in the shape of a letter from Nate in which he said he had *reconsidered his decision*. He would answer *my* question and I must answer *his*.

I was fairly in for it. And I thought savagely that it served me right for being fool enough to agree to answer a question I was ignorant of. I tried to escape but in vain—Nate held me to my bargain. If I had been certain that he would say he liked *me* best—I wouldn't have minded so much but I was very far from certain. In fact, I suspected Mollie would be the chosen one, because she has always been as good as gold to him, whereas I have teased his life half out.

At last I agreed to fulfil my bargain but only on condition that he would let me see his note *first*. I could see Nate didn't like the idea and I suppose he suspected my little game but he finally agreed.

So here I am in rather a plight. I've taken a sheet of paper and written this highly graceful statement.

"*You* have a little more brains than the other Cavendish boys and I like brains—as I suppose I like *you* best—though I don't see why I should, after the trick you have played on me."

If Nate likes *me* best—I'll give him that and he may take all the comfort he can get out of it. If he doesn't I'll tear it up and write Jack's name—true or not true! "Desperate diseases require desperate remedies."

Besides, it *will* be true. If Nate says he likes anybody else best I'll hate him!

Tuesday, Feb. 18, 1890
I am sure I shall never forget this date! I went to school this morning in an unutterable state of mind. Nate gave me his note during the forenoon—and he looked uncommonly foolish. After the reading lesson I asked permission to go out and ran down to my favorite old spot under a big maple tree in the school woods. I always go there to read Nate's letters or else to a dear little sprucy corner down the road.

The first thing I saw was my own name! And the next—well, I don't know what

I felt like, for hadn't that absurd boy gone and written down that he not only *liked* me best—but loved me!

I felt like a perfect idiot when I went back to the school and I have no doubt I looked like one. I never so much as glanced at Nate but plunged into fractions as if my whole soul was wrapped up in them.

At noon I passed my French grammar over to Nate, with *my* confession in it and hurried off home. He seemed in high spirits all the afternoon but I was as frigid as a glacier.

I *am* sorry, when all is said and done, that this has happened. I feel that it is going to spoil our friendship. Besides, I don't care a bit for Nate *that* way—I really don't. I only just like him splendidly as a chum. I don't mean to take any further notice of his nonsense.

And yet I admit I *do* feel a queer, foolish triumphant little feeling about it. I've often wondered if anyone would ever care for *me*—*that* way—and now someone really does.

Here is a copy of Nate's letter—my first love-letter and so worthy of being enshrined in this journal.

"Well, Polly, it must be done. I at first intended to write quite a lengthy epistle, setting forth my poor opinion of myself, my very inferior *personal* endowments, my happiness, or rather ecstasy if your note proved favorable to my wishes etc. etc. etc. But I have altered my plan of arrangement and resolved to give you *hard, dry, plain* facts, for they may possibly appear as such to you, but they are nevertheless as true as gospel. Here goes:—Of all my feminine friends the one whom I most admire—no, I'm growing reckless—the one whom I *love* (if the authorities allow that word to come under the school boy's vocabulary) is L. M. Montgomery, the girl I shook hands with, the girl after my own heart.

Yes, Polly it is true. I always liked you better than any other girl and it has kept on increasing till it has obtained "prodigious" proportions. Oh, *wouldn't* I like to see you reading this. But I must conclude or you will say it is very lengthy after all. Remember I am waiting for you to fulfil your part of the transaction with ever-increasing impatience.

from
Nate.

P.S. I suppose you'll say I'm very sentimental. Well, perhaps, *rather*. However, it's not much difference. I was just laughing over the tenacity with which we cling to our diverse manner of spelling Polly (Pollie). I'm going to cling to my manner *ad finem*, because it's right. I expect you'll prove stubborn too.

N. J. L."

Wednesday, Feb. 19, 1890
After school I went up to take my music lesson. I go twice a week to Mrs. Spurr. Past Mollie's gate I was alone with Nate. I felt rather frightened and silly but thank goodness he didn't say a word about our letters of yesterday. He gave me a letter however, just before we turned in at his gate. I read it after I came home, sitting curled up before the fire in the sitting room. There was a lot of nonsense in it. I don't know whether I liked it or not. In some ways I did—and in others I didn't.

We are all busy in school these days writing essays for the *Montreal Witness* school competition. There was one last year. I was the only one from this school who tried. I wrote up the story of Cape Leforce and got honorable mention. This year Nate and Asher are trying, too. They are both writing about the famous "Yankee Storm". I am writing about the wreck of the Marcopolo. The Marcopolo was a Norwegian ship which came ashore here about seven years ago. I remember it well and all the excitement of that summer.

I am not afraid of Asher but Nate will run me close. He is a good writer. I read his essay to-day and I am afraid it is better than mine. But I thought it a trifle too florid in style.

Thursday, Feb. 27, 1890

Last night we went to Minnie's. We found the house full of company—Mr. & Mrs. Wallace Toombs, Maud, Herbert and Hammond Toombs, Mr. Rogerson, the Rustico school-teacher, Miss Gordon, and Nina and Stanton Macneill. We had a glorious time. We played all kinds of games and laughed until the house echoed. After lunch we all went out to the kitchen. Joe, the French boy, played a tune on his jewsharp and we danced an eight-hand reel. It was my first attempt at dancing and I danced with Stanton Macneill. I stayed all night with Pensie again. Oh, I've had such a good time this week! It must be awfully nice to live in a house where there are lots of people.

My mother died when I was a baby. I have always lived with Grandpa and Grandma Macneill. Father is away out west in Prince Albert, Saskatchewan. He is married again. I have never seen my stepmother or my two-and-a-half-year old sister, Kate. I have always had a good home here but sometimes it is very lonesome. Grandpa and Grandma always seem so averse to my going anywhere or having my friends here.

Saturday, March 4, 1890

I'm so tired, and I ache all over. The school has never been cleaned since last winter and since the pipe was taken down it has been disgracefully dirty. The trustees wouldn't bestir themselves to have it cleaned so a lot of us girls agreed to do it ourselves if the boys would help. So Nate, Jack, Chesley, Clemmie, Nellie, Maggie and I met there this morning. As it was pouring rain we couldn't light a fire outside and had to heat water over the stove—a slow job but only one of our difficulties. The boys brought water in a cask from the brook and while it was heating we took down the blinds and maps and cleaned out the inside of the desks. When the water got hot we wiped off the blinds with damp cloths but the maps were too greasy for that so we just laid them on the floor and scrubbed them with soap and water. Then we scrubbed the desks, windows, doors, and wainscotting. After that came the floor. *It* ought to be spelled in capitals. A shovel would have been the best thing to tackle it with. But in the end we got it done. Nothing more remained but the stove which we wanted to blacken before leaving. But there was a big fire on so John got a bucket of water to put it out. He opened the door and poured in nearly the whole bucketful "at one fell swoop", and oh, such a cloud of boiling water, ashes, steam and soot burst out in Jack's face. He gave an unearthly whoop and fell over backward, spilling what water was left in the bucket all over himself, while the awful swell of the gas was what somebody has called "deafening." I thought Jack was killed but when he picked himself up with a real live "cuss word" I concluded he wasn't. But his face was all spattered with soot and he did look so funny.

We all rushed to open the windows, while Jack, nothing daunted, got another bucket and went at the fire again. This time he took the precaution of lifting the damper off the top and pouring the water in there. Poof! Up flew another cloud right to the ceiling which it spattered all over with drops of water and soot. The fire seemed to burn all the brighter so we decided to leave it alone and clean the stove some other day. We wiped up the wet floor and departed. When we told the folks about the fire they were horrified and said it was a perfect marvel the stove didn't explode and kill us all. But I shall *never* forget the look of Jack!

Thursday, April 10, 1890
I hadn't been to the shore this spring yet, so this evening after school I went. The shore is about two thirds of a mile from here. Away down beyond the brown fields lay the sea, blue and sparkling, dotted by crests of foam. The walk in the fresh moist spring air was lovely and when I got down to the shore and climbed out on a big rock I just held my breath with delight. The sea was an expanse of silvery gray. Afar I saw the purple slopes of New London scarfed in silvery hazes. To my left extended the shining curve of the sandshore; and on my right were rugged rocks with little coves, where the waves swished on the pebbles. I could have lingered there for hours and watched the sea with the gulls soaring over it.

Friday, April 18, 1890
This morning Pensie sent up word that she would go to the hall tonight if I would go with her. When she came it looked so like rain that we concluded not to go after all. So we went down to the school woods instead and hunted for gum. Our search was not very successful and we soon came up and went into the school, where we stayed a long time looking over my scrap-book which was there. Then Pensie said she must go home and I went a piece with her. We met Stanton and Alec and Russell on their way to the hall. Nothing would do but we must turn back and go with them, so we did and a right jolly walk we had. The debate was on reciprocity and was awfully dry.

Tuesday, Apr. 22, 1890
This morning Mollie and I concluded that it was really too fine to spend the whole forenoon cooped up in school so we decided to try to get out together. I got Emma Simpson to ask out and a few minutes later, when Miss Gordon had forgotten that Emma was out I asked out and got permission. Then, when Emma went in, Mollie stuck up her finger at once, and Miss G. seeing one girl just come in, forgot, as we had hoped, that I was just out, and let her go. We flew down the road and into the woods where we rambled about for a quarter of an hour and had a fine time. Miss G. was never a bit the wiser—or if she were, she didn't let on. I think she is a little "skeered" of running up against us big girls.

We had more fun to-night. Mollie, Lottie, Nate, John and I have been trying to get up a dialogue for Friday evening and we resolved to remain after school and practice it a bit. As John wasn't there we got Ches to read his part and Emma was also allowed to stay as she and Lottie were the only girls going west. But Everett, Prescott, Charlie, Asher, Russell and Austin persisted in hanging around and we couldn't get rid of them. We were bound they should not hear us practicing and they were bound they would. As reason and coaxing were of no avail we decided to resort to strategy. At a given signal we dialoguees rushed out and slammed to the porch door. In spite of their efforts we got it shut and locked. Then we cleared the fence and tore down through the woods, for we knew we must hide while we had the chance as they would be out of the window in a minute. We thought we were safe and were just beginning our dialogue when an exultant shout told us we were discovered and we saw the boys rushing down through the trees with Everett at their head. In our confusion no plan was made. Each of us flew in the handiest direction. I tore down the brook road, followed by Mollie and Emma and finally stopped before Cyrus Macneill's old house. We had fled so quickly that our pursuers had not seen us. Nate and Lottie were nowhere to be seen at first but presently Ches came tearing down the hill and soon after Nate and Lottie came gliding along under the big spruces by the brook. We scrambled over the brook—Nate in gallantly trying to help us girls over fell kerplunk in up to his knees—and climbed the fence beyond. Then we ran along Pierce Macneill's field to the back end. No one was in sight so we perched ourselves on a nice convenient longer platform where a haystack had been and for a second time began our rehearsal. Just at that very moment Charlie loomed in sight down in the hollow. He caught sight of us and dashed back into the woods, presumably to call the others. Over the fence we scrambled once more and fled to a thick copse of young spruces away across the brook. This time we really had baffled our pursuers and we managed to practice our dialogue in a kind of way, although we were so breathless and excited we hardly knew what we were saying. Then we started back and after jumping I don't know how many brooks—or rather, jumping the brook I don't know how many times, for it does nothing but double and twist down there—we at last reached familiar haunts. All was quiet and we slipped up to the school, got our books and went home without interference. We have since found out that the boys were still prowling about the woods in pursuit of us but we had baffled them completely.

Do you know, journal mine, I may take a trip out west to see father this summer. Grandpa Montgomery is talking of going and if he does he will take me. It has been talked of vaguely all winter but it is about settled now. I expect we will go in August; I feel so excited about it. It will be such a splendid trip. And then to see darling father again! I am frightened to think or say much about it for fear I will not get there after all.

Tuesday, May 6, 1890
We have been playing ball in school all the spring and such fun as we do have! A good game of ball is just glorious. It isn't baseball—don't know that it has any particular name—just "ball", that's enough. The thing itself is all right. We have

some most exciting contests. Asher and Nate are the best players among the boys, while Annie Stewart and I are considered to be the best among the girls, principally because of our ability to slant the bat in one direction and send the ball in another, thereby throwing the scouts out of their reckoning.

To-day at dinner hour, however, it was really too hot to play, so Annie, Clara and I betook ourselves to the woods. Those dear old woods down there are so pretty—all shadowy nooks, carpeted with moss, or paths with ferns and wildflowers nodding along them. We sauntered down under the trees and flung ourselves down on a mossy bank by the brook. And there fanned by the cool breezes, we lay and gazed through half-shut-lids at the blue sky, smiling through the traceries of the spruce boughs, or explored by the eye the intersecting glades and dreamed idly of long, delicious summer days to come, when we might wander at will through those ferny depths and gather all the joys of Nature's bridal hours.

But at last we heard Maggie Clark's voice calling, "Teacher's coming, girls." So we sprang up from our mossy couches and fled towards the dusty realm of sums and books. I like school in winter but when spring comes I don't like it.

Tuesday, May 13, 1890

We had a "mayflower picnic" to-day, and a splendid time. After school came out we started for the barrens. Jack and Nate were the only boys who went. The girls were Mollie, Lucy, Lottie, Maggie, Annie, Mamie, Emma and I, with Miss Gordon as mistress of ceremonies. Of course, Mollie and I paired off together and had our own private and particular fun. On the road up we had a comical adventure with Clarks' cows but finally reached Charlie Simpson's—Shady Lane Farm—where we had all been invited to tea. After tea we went over to the barrens, joined by Bessie and Lalie Fraser. We found all the mayflowers we wanted—such beauties, too. Then a party of us set off to hunt up an old well which Mamie declared to exist somewhere in the woods. After much merry seeking we found it in a boggy fir hollow and had a sort of victorious war-dance around it.

Finally we all sat down under the firs on a mossy hill and made our flowers up into wreaths and bouquets. When going home time came we all formed in procession, Nate and Jack at the head, Mollie and I next, and so on, two by two, with our hats all wreathed and big bouquets in our hands. I assure you we made quite a show. We marched down to George Harker's, singing all our school songs and then we went in and had some music. After that we all went home and had lots of fun on the road.

We scholars are going to have a concert about the last of June, and we are preparing for it now, getting up songs and recitations and dialogues.

Saturday, May 31st, 1890

The *Montreal Witness* came to-day and in it was the essay report for P.E. Island. As I expected, Nate's ranked higher than mine, but I came next and was third for the county. Asher wasn't mentioned at all.

Pensie came up for the mail this evening and we had a walk. The country is very beautiful now. The young leaves are such a bright, tender green, and the opening apple buds are pink and white. The grass is green and velvety, starred with hundreds of dandelions.

Saturday, June 7, 1890
Yesterday was a glorious day. At dinner time Nate and Mollie and I were larking about the school and I said to Mollie,

"I believe I'll go down to the shore to-night."

"Oh", she said, "come over and stay all night with me and we'll go to the shore together."

I agreed to this on the spot. Nate looked at us askance, as much as to say, "Why don't you ask me, too?"—but we didn't, for all his beseeching looks.

After school we went over and had our tea. We could not go directly to the shore as Mollie had some sewing to do. She didn't hurry any, until Ham came in and began to tease us, saying he had seen Nate going down to the shore. Although we entirely disclaimed any interest in Nate's designs or whereabouts, it was curious to see how quickly Mollie despatched her sewing, and how quickly we walked when we were out of sight of the house! As we went through the gate behind the barns we saw a black figure away down on the crest of a sand-hill but it disappeared like a flash, having no doubt been on the look-out for our appearance. We were sure it was Nate but when we reached the shore not a sign of him could we see far and wide. We guessed he was hiding somewhere among the sand-hills, trying to play a trick on us, so we resolved to get ahead of him. Mollie went down to gather dulse, but I ran up to the hills to ferret him out. I nosed around for a time without discovering him but at last I saw him, hat in hand, sneaking along behind a hill and watching Mollie. The next minute he caught sight of me and went down among the long grasses like a shot, but I ran over and soon found him. We then rejoined Mollie and wandered merrily along the shore, gathering dulse and shells, and laughing and talking in sheer light-heartedness. It was a glorious evening. The sea was a rippling expanse of sparkling blue, the air was soft and clear, the sky full of brightness.

When we came to the rocks we sat down to rest and watch the beautiful scene before us. We talked of many things, we three, soberly but not sadly—we were all too happy for sadness. The sea changed from blue to gray and the little waves plashed at our feet. The sunset was not brilliant but there was a sort of savage, sullen, fascinating grandeur about it. The sun sank in a low bank of black cloud, leaving a wake of rosy gold, while below the cloud ran a strip of fiery crimson, flecked here and there with tiny cloudlets of gold and scarlet. When it grew dark we sauntered back and wandered homeward through the dewy, gloaming fields, and past the tranquil starlit pond.

Tuesday, July 1, 1890
School closed last Friday and we had our concert last night. It was a great success. Yesterday we all met at the hall and a busy time we had, hanging the curtains, arranging the seats, writing out our programme and finally having a grand "dress rehearsal."

I am really sorry it is over for we have had lots of fun getting it up. I have enjoyed it all, although, as usual, it was somewhat embittered for me by the fact that grandpa and grandma did not approve of it—why, I cannot say. It just seems that they never do approve of anything which means the assembling of young folks together. I suppose they would not have let me take part at all if it had not been for Miss Gordon.

When, away back in the winter, Miss Gordon began to talk of a concert for the end of the term we did not think it would ever come to anything; and even after we were really embarked in the enterprise there were times and times when it seemed as if the whole thing would fizzle out. There was seemingly no end to the quarrels and complaints and jealousies. Some *wouldn't* do their parts right and then when the good things were given to those who would, the snubbed got their backs up and declared that they would have nothing more to do with it—a resolution that generally lasted until the next day! Those who hadn't important parts were jealous of those who had; some wanted things arranged one way, some another. In short, we quarrelled over anything and everything and were miserable if we hadn't a row on hand. We were mostly employed in fighting among ourselves, but sometimes we all banded together and made common cause against poor Miss Gordon, and in this—for there is strength in numbers—we generally got what we wanted.

But somehow or other, goodness only knows how, everything smoothed itself out in the long run and the concert came to completion as if we had never had but one mind about the matter. As spring came on we began to have great fun practising. Every evening after school we would go over our recitations and dialogues. At first we liked this, but we soon got fearfully tired of it and *so* sick of the pieces. They came at last to have no more meaning for us than the alphabet.

Still we managed to get a lot of amusement out of the business. At recesses we would generally repair to the brook and discuss every pro and con with as much zeal as if the fate of nations were involved therein.

Last night we met at the hall at six, all in our best bib-and-tucker. We did not go in, however, as we all intended to march in in procession when the time came, so we all scampered into the birch woods behind the hall lest a premature eye should get a glimpse of our glories. There under the birches and maples we clustered and chattered like parrots and betrayed our whereabouts to everybody by the noise we made.

At last Miss Gordon called us and we ran up the slope, scrambled over the fence and assembled by the platform. Oh, how excited we all were—really it was delicious! Emma slipped in and played a march and we all paraded in, two by two, the smallest first, and so on up to the tallest. Nate and Jack were the last, before them Ches and Charlie, then Mollie and I, and so on, down to the tots who never *would* march right. The doors were opened and in we went proudly and took our seats on the platform, facing a goodly audience.

The first number was "An Opening Speech" by "Master John Laird." Snap rose and made his way rather sheepishly to the front. Such a time as Miss Gordon had training Jack to give that speech and teaching him to bow properly. Jack gave the speech well and it made a hit but Miss G's pains with his bow were all lost for he just gave a little duck of his head as if it worked on wires.

Then the programme went smoothly on with choruses and recitations until Neil Simpson's reading came on. Neil always read as if he had a hot potato in his mouth and this time was no exception—or so they said. I never noticed for I was occupied in screwing up my courage for the next number. I had to play and I had never played in public before. It was ten times worse than reciting. I was cold with fright. When my name was called I rose and stumbled blindly to the organ. The room was just reeling all about me. Somehow I got on the stool, placed my music before me and plunged into "The Swedish Wedding March." I know I must have made an appalling number of mistakes but I got through at last and crept back to my seat in deep Thanksgiving.

Mollie and I sat together and of course had our fun out of it all, besides keeping the kids nerved up. The last number was a recitation by the whole school, called "The Ship On Fire." We stood in two rows and each one had two verses to recite in turn. At the end of each verse we all had to shout "Ay, ay!" and some of the verses were recited by two performers like a dialogue. The last verse we all recited together. I think we had more fun practising that than anything else.

Well, it is all over and I fear we will never *all* be together again. But no matter where we roam, a tie of common friendship will always bind us in memory—a tie that can never be utterly broken. All these little festals of ours, our concerts, practices, picnics and games, tend to make the tie closer. Perchance in after years, when a lifetime has intervened between us and last night, a chance song or verse may recall the whole scene to mind and we will pause to smile or sigh over the memory of our concert.

Monday, July 14, 1890
Cavendish, P.E.I.
Early this morning Lu, Murray Macneill—Uncle Leander's son who is here for his vacation—Pres, Frank—Lu's brothers—and I went back to "Montana" to pick berries. "Montana" is a big leafy stumpy waste away back of Charles Macneill's farm, and we always have splendid expeditions there every summer. After we had picked our jugs full Lu and I took a walk down a lovely old lane we call the "C.P.R." It is all arched over by maples. We went to "Indiana" which is a big clearing in the heart of the spruce woods where we go to pick raspberries. The woods were beautiful. The path was bordered by ferns, pink-pinks and "ladies-lips." The last have the sweetest perfume in the world and the pink-pinks come next.

I enjoyed the day—for I do so love the woods and fields. But I would have enjoyed it much more if the boys had not been along. I like most boys and can always get along well with them; but I do *not* like either Murray or Pres or Frank and am miserable when I am in their company. There is such a mean, *petty* streak in every one of them. Frank I particularly detest.

I am sitting on the kitchen doorstep as I write. It is a lovely evening. Everything is so clear and beautiful and I feel almost sad when I reflect that soon I shall be far away from those dear hillslopes and clover fields—for it is all settled that I am to go for a trip west and will probably stay there a year. We will leave in August I expect. I am looking forward to it with great delight.

Saturday, July 26, 1890

Yesterday afternoon I went over to Mollie's and after tea we went to the shore. Nate had promised to meet us there but there was no sign of him when we arrived. A set of Hunter River people were having a picnic at Cawnpore, so we did not like to go there, but we went as near as we could and then sat down and had a merry little chat all by ourselves. We had sat there nearly two hours and were just concluding to go home when away upshore we saw Nate at last. Just at the same time two H.R. boys came up and asked us to go over to the picnic grounds. Just for fun we went and about half way there Nate overtook us. He seemed to be in an ill-humor over something—perhaps over the presence of the other boys. We invited him to go along with us but he complied so grumpily and was so curt that I felt annoyed and let him severely alone.

When we reached Cawnpore the boys got the piper to play the bagpipes for our edification and we had some fun but soon left for home. Nate thawed out when we were alone but *I* didn't. The fact is, Nate is absurdly sentimental these days—or would be if I would allow it. I hate that sort of thing. He has just spoiled our lovely, old comradeship completely. He is *so* nice when he is sensible and *so* horrid when he isn't!

Thursday, July 31, 1890

This morning I had a book spree—reading a novel Uncle Leander brought home with him. Uncle Leander is "Rev. L. G. Macneill" who ministers to souls in St. John, N.B. The novel was "Devereux" and is by my favorite author, Bulwer Lytton.

Pensie came up in the afternoon and after tea, Lu, Pen and I took the men's tea to the shore. While we were there Uncle L. came down and got Pen and me to help him row a little trouting boat from our shore to Cawnpore. We had such a time! The boat was a villainous old tub—leaky as a basket, and the water half filled her. Pen and I were complete novices in the art of rowing, so that, what with making mistakes and correcting them, we had no time to protect ourselves, and our feet and the tails of our dresses got soaked to the core. But we had great fun.

Friday, Aug. 8, 1890

This morning I went picking raspberries down in the school woods. Nate happened along and we had our last chat and said good-bye, for I expect to go to Park Corner to-morrow. I was sorry to say good-bye to Nate—who goes to Acadia College in September—but not so sorry as I would have been if he had not spoiled our friendship by falling in love with me. I've been rather stiff with him of late, just on this account, and as he resented this, our relations have been a little strained.

I feel excited about starting away to-morrow—and a little blue, too. I've never travelled any but I think I'll like *that*; but what about Prince Albert? Shall I like it? And my stepmother? I do not know. She seems nice from her letters and I mean to love her if I can, just as if she were really my mother.

Park Corner, P.E. Island
Aug. 9, 1890

Well, here I am! This morning Uncle Charles Crosby—Aunt Jane's husband—came down for me. Thus brought up against the realization that I was really leaving home, I didn't feel at all exultant. I was relieved when all the farewells were over and we got away.

We had a hot, dusty drive to Park Corner. At Clifton Uncle C.—part of whose creed is certainly to take things easy—stopped at a certain Mrs. McKay's, of whose existence I was never before aware but who is, it seems, a remote relation of mine. I was taken into the parlor and introduced to several ladies. That was just it exactly—*I* was introduced to *them* but *their* names were not mentioned to *me*. How I hate that way! How in the world am I to know who people are, even if they are my relatives, if I've never seen them before? It does make me feel so awkward. By dint of holding my tongue I got through our call without any bad breaks but I felt decidedly relieved when we were once more on our way, even if Uncle C. did begin an abstruse discussion on the probability of the spirits of the departed ever returning to revisit the scenes of their earthly pilgrimage and kept it up with variations until we reached Grandpa Montgomery's.

And here I am, sitting all alone in this strange bedroom, writing in my journal for comfort because I feel a bit lonely. I am all ready to hop into bed, so goodnight and as there is no one else here to do it for me, I will wish myself "pleasant dreams and sweet repose" and seek my maiden couch.

Monday, Aug. 11, 1890

This has been *such* an exciting day. It was pouring rain when we got up this morning and I felt real sick, too, so the outlook was not cheerful. I couldn't eat any breakfast, which greatly alarmed Grandpa Montgomery. He thinks if a person can't *eat* she must be dying. That is just his besetting sin. I believe if he hadn't persisted in stuffing me so yesterday I wouldn't have been sick to-day. I am sure he imagines I am hollow all the way down to my boots!

But he is the dearest old soul! Although I've lived all my life with grandfather Macneill I haven't anything like the affection for him that I have for Grandpa Montgomery. And the latter is *such* a handsome old man—just like a grandfather out of a story. I love him. He is always so good and kind and gentle to me.

At last we got off. It wasn't a very pleasant drive for it drizzled rain all the way. Finally we reached Kensington where we were informed that a special containing Sir John and Lady Macdonald—who are touring the Island—would be along in an hour; so Grandpa—who is a Senator and a great crony of Sir John's— telegraphed to Hunter River for Sir John to stop at Kensington and take us on. I assure you I was quite excited over the prospect of seeing the Premier of Canada. When the special came I followed grandpa on board and the next moment was in the presence of the great man himself. He was very genial and motioned me to a seat between himself and Lady M. where I sat demurely and scrutinized them both out of the tail of my eye.

Sir John is a spry-looking old man—not handsome but pleasant-faced. Lady M. is quite stately and imposing, with very beautiful silver hair, but not at all good looking and dressed, as I thought, very dowdily.

I never was on a train before but I enjoyed this, my first ride, very much. We reached Summerside in about thirty minutes and went to Aunt Nancy Campbell's where I was warmly welcomed by my aunt and cousins. After dinner I attended Sir John's reception in the Market Hall. I went with a Miss Cairns from Freetown. The stage and hall were beautifully decorated. An address was read to Sir John who replied to it in an interesting speech.

Later on, Miss C. and I strolled down to the wharf to see the St. Lawrence, the boat which was to take the Premier and his suite across to Pointe du Chene. In the evening we all went to the Salvation Army "Barracks". I never was in such an old rookery. The dirt was enough to terrify one had not the danger to one's bones from rotten boards, ricketty steps, projecting cornices and loose plaster served as a counter irritant. I don't like the "Army" at all. I can't see any real religion in such performances.

Tuesday, Aug. 12, 1890

This morning I woke up with my heels on the pillow and my head where my heels should have been. After breakfast Uncle Dan drove us down to the wharf and we were soon on board the boat. The day was fine but cool and cloudy and the sea had by no means a glassy appearance. I was afraid I would be seasick but I wasn't and we had a fine trip over to Pointe du Chene. We got on the train and we have just started. We are flying along at a great rate and I have all I can do to take in the new sights. I "journalize" in a little notebook and will copy it into my regular journal later on.

Night, Aug. 12, 1890

Here we are in St. John. We have had a splendid trip so far. The scenery was so picturesque. The road went through high wooded hills. Here and there they would sweep around to disclose a beautiful lake or river curve, like a mirror set in an emerald frame.

We are at the Belmont House. We learned while at supper that our train would not leave until 11.20 so I came up to the waiting-room while grandpa went to get our tickets. The only other occupant was a tall, thin lady who was for a time severely silent. At last, however, we drifted into conversation and I found her to be very nice. She was "Yankee" to the core—hails from Providence, R.I., and talks with a big accent. We went out for a walk and had a very nice time. Soon after she left on the Halifax train.

Wednesday, Aug. 13, 1890

We are on our way to Montreal. Last night after I finished writing I yawned away a dull hour and was very glad when at last Grandpa came in and said our train was due. We then went over to the depot where we found it was half an hour late. But I did not find the time long—there was so much to see. At last the headlight of our train flashed like a fiery red eye through the outer darkness and a few seconds later the long line of cars thundered in. We went on board and soon were flying through the night.

When the sleeping berths were made up I crawled into mine. The upper berths are not at all nice. They are so small you don't dare to move in them and if you forget once in a while and sit up *whack* goes your head against the roof.

When morning dawned we were among the wooded hills of Maine. I got up—or rather I got *down*—and I've had a splendid time so far. I love travelling. We are now passing through a rough country. There is nothing but steep, wooded hills. Now and then we pass a little clearing where a log cabin stands with a cluster of ragged children around it. The banks along the track are yellow and purple with billows of golden-rod and fireweed. The scenery about Moosehead Lake is enchanting.

Same day. Montreal
Here we are in the big St. Lawrence Hall. The views you see when crossing the St. Lawrence River on the C.P.R. suspension bridge are magnificent. We got there about 5.30. The thronged streets were brilliantly lighted by electricity. You hear as much French as English here.

Thursday, Aug. 14, 1890
This morning after breakfast I felt rather lonesome and, as grandpa was out, I formed the somewhat daring resolution of going out for a walk by myself. I was very careful not to lose my way and I enjoyed myself very much and all the more from the little spice of adventure in it. After lunch Grandpa took me for a five mile ride in a street car. Montreal is a fine city but I am sure I wouldn't like to live here.

Friday, Aug. 15, 1890
We are now whirling across Ontario. Last night after I finished writing I went down to the balcony of the Ladies' Parlor. The only other occupant was an old lady who did not seem at all companionable and I was soon making up my mind to go back to my room when she suddenly said,

"Are you staying here?"

I believe I really jumped I was so startled but I was dying for someone to talk to and I soon found myself engaged in a very animated conversation. I have seen some people who could ask a pretty decent lot of questions but I never saw anything to equal her. However, we got on very well until the time came for me to go so I bade her good-bye, probably for all time and, in *her* opinion, doubtless for all eternity, for she had discovered that I was a Presbyterian and she, being High Church, seemed to regard me as little less than a pagan and entirely outside the pale of Christianity.

We left at eight, but had to wait at the junction an hour and a half for a belated Boston express. A long freight train stopped beside us for a quarter of an hour. It was loaded with live pigs and the odor which blew in therefrom could never have been mistaken for those spicy breezes that are reputed to "blow soft o'er Ceylon's Isle."

I had a lower berth last night and slept like a top—though why a top should be supposed to sleep sounder than anything else I could never understand. But I don't feel at all well to-day. My head aches horribly. We are passing through a very bleak, desolate country. There is absolutely nothing to be seen but stumps—and goodness knows there is enough of them.

Seven O'Clock
We are still in the region of stumps and rocks. *Sam Slick* in "The Clockmaker" says they have all the ballast out of Noah's Ark on the east coast of Nova Scotia, but if he had ever travelled over the C.P.R. he would have changed the locality to the northern wilds of Ontario. Rocks are all well enough in their way—"in moderation" as Everett Laird says of girls—but they pall on the taste finally. At some of the stations we all get out and pick blueberries which are very abundant.

I read and doze by turns. I wish I had somebody to talk to. Grandpa is rather deaf to be of much use in that respect. If only Mollie were here what fun we would have!

Saturday, Aug. 16, 1890
I have enjoyed myself immensely to-day. When I woke up this morning and pulled aside the curtains of my berth I almost imagined I was down on the shore at home. Below me lay a line of rugged brown rocks with foam-crested waves dashing against them, while far as eye could reach was an expanse of tossing water. I knew that this must be "cold Superior's rock-bound shore" and all day I have been revelling in the exquisite views which every turn reveals.

Sunday Evening, Aug. 17, 1890
This has been a dull day. We saw the last of the rocks this morning and all day we have been whirling over the prairies of Manitoba. They are beautiful but monotonous. Acres of ground are covered with sunflowers as with sheets of light. They remind me of a certain boggy field at home where buttercups abound. We reached Winnipeg at 12.30 and had to wait four hours. It was dreary for I had no one to talk to and grandpa did not leave the train. I did take a little walk by myself but there was nothing to see, as we were somewhere in the outskirts. I don't admire Winnipeg. It looks as if someone had thrown a big handful of streets and houses down and forgotten to sort them out afterwards. But no doubt the centre of the city is better.

Monday, Aug. 18, 1890
This has been a most surprising, delightful, exciting day. We got to Regina at five this morning. It was cold and dim and foggy. We went to the Windsor Hotel and got rooms. Then grandpa went out, saying he would go up to the Lansdowne Hotel and see if there was a letter from father there. In a short time a knock came at my door. I opened it—there stood grandpa, smiling broadly:

"I have brought a friend to see you," he said, stepping aside.

And there was father!

I can't describe the time we had! I laughed and cried. Oh, it was so delightful to see dear father again. He hasn't changed at all, although it is five years since I saw him. Such a day as this has been! Father took us out for a drive in the afternoon. Regina itself is not a bad little place but the country around it is the nearest approach to a desert of anything I have ever seen. We leave to-morrow morning. There are no passenger trains running on the new branch line to P.A. yet, so we will have to go in something they call a "caboose". That sounds bad!

Prince Albert, Saskatchewan
Wed. Aug. 20, 1890
Here I am at my destination at last—in this little town on the Saskatchewan, 3,000 miles from home.

Yesterday's ride in the "caboose" was dreadful and I was almost played out when we reached Duck Lake at eleven at night. We then drove a mile and a half in a "buckboard" to a Mr. Cameron's house where we spent the night. When morning came I got a good look at the country and was delighted to see that it was fair and green and fertile-looking—altogether unlike those dreary wastes around Regina.

Father had telegraphed to P.A. for a team and Mr. McTaggart, his father-in-law—or rather, the second husband of his mother-in-law—was along bright and early. I enjoyed our drive very much. The prairies are jammed with flowers. I thought the prettiest were the exquisite little bluebells, as abundant as they are beautiful.

We reached Prince Albert at four. It is quite a pretty little town—rather "straggly", built along the river bank. Father's house is a nice one on Church Street. Mamma seems quite nice and friendly and my two-year-old half sister Kate is a very pretty child. There is also a girl staying here and going to school—Edith Skelton. She belongs to Battleford, and is just my age. I have met so many strangers that I feel bewildered—and very tired.

Saturday, Aug. 23, 1890
I am desperately homesick! I have fought it off as long as I could but to-day I succumbed and had a fierce cry all to myself. I'd give anything to see dear old Cavendish for half an hour. Oh, for a glimpse of the old hills and woods and shore! There, the very thought of them makes me cry!

I am to go to the High School here. It opens Monday week. I don't know how I shall like it. I suppose it will be very different from Cavendish School. But I mean to study hard and do P.E. Island all the credit I can.

It is lovely to be with father again, though. He is *such* a darling. His eyes just *shine* with love when he looks at me. I never saw anyone look at me with such eyes before.

But, to speak plainly I am afraid I am *not* going to like his wife. I came here prepared to love her warmly and look upon her as a real mother, but I fear it will prove impossible. I have been here only three days and already my eyes have been opened by several little things. For instance this morning at breakfast she did not pour any tea for me. Of course I knew this was just an over sight and waited for a minute or two after the others had begun eating before asking for it, as grandpa was speaking and I did not want to interrupt, but before I could speak she turned to me and said, in the most cutting and insulting tone of voice I ever heard and with the *blackest* look, "What are *you* waiting for, Maud?"

I suppose she must have imagined that I was expecting something to be on the table that was not on it. But what a way to speak on mere suspicion! I shall *never* forget that tone and the look that accompanied it! I answered quietly, "my tea, please" and she looked silly enough, poured out the tea, slammed it down before me with such force that the tea spilled out of the cup in the saucer and hardly spoke a word to anyone the rest of the meal.

She also informed father yesterday that she wanted him to stop calling me "Maudie", as it was entirely too childish. I believe it is the affection implied in the diminutive of which she disapproves. In my short sojourn here I have already seen several displays of temper and sulkiness on her part towards father which were utterly unprovoked. She seems to have a dreadful disposition—sulky, jealous, underhanded, and *mean*. Why, she never goes out of the house without locking the pantry door—for fear, I suppose that Edith or I would help ourselves to a bite to eat in her absence. I *know* I am not going to be happy here. I have been as nice and respectful to her as I could be but already I find myself disliking and fearing her, and that is not a pleasant prospect.

I am sitting here alone at my bedroom window. In the next house a lot of children live and it is *so* funny to hear them when they are out playing. They quarrel pretty often—they are at it now and one lad is howling at the top of his voice while another is angrily and repeatedly demanding, "Where is my hat?" A third is flinging biting taunts at the "baby" for crying, and a fourth, who seems to be a neighbor's boy, has beaten a retreat with his hands in his pockets and a very lordly air.

My only comfort here is Edie. She is such a lovely girl. We room together and have any amount of fun.

Tuesday, Aug. 26, 1890
I had a letter from Lucy to-day and it was very welcome. It was full of home news. I read it over half a dozen times and then had a good homesick cry after which I felt much better.

This afternoon Edie and I, together with Jennie and Will McTaggart—mamma's half sister and brother—went hazelnutting up on the hills and had lots of fun. P.A. is built on several natural "terraces" along the river bank, with "bluffs", as the hills are called, behind it, sloping back to wide, rolling prairies dotted with groves of willow and poplar and countless tiny blue lakelets. Across the river are great pine forests and the views upstream are very beautiful.

Edie and I had a confidential talk that evening over various things. I found out that she does not like mamma at all, either; and she told me several things that made me feel very sorry for poor father. He himself told me that he finds it hard to get along with his wife and asked me to put up with some things for his sake. I notice that she picks and nags at him unceasingly and on some days he cannot make the simplest, most harmless remark but she snubs him for it. For example—at dinner time to-day father and I were talking about Aunt Emily and Uncle John Montgomery. Father said he did not think Aunt Emily cared a great deal for Uncle John when she married him.

"Oh, I suppose you think she wanted you," sneered Mrs. Montgomery, in her most insulting tone.

It seems to put her in a rage to hear father talking to me of any of his old friends and haunts. She will go around for days at a time without speaking a word to anyone when she gets into one of her tantrums. I could bear the way she treats me but I *cannot* bear the way she uses father. He is so good and kind to her as he is to everybody, and there isn't a shadow of justification for the way she behaves— unless the fact that he is not rich is a justification. She seems to resent that most bitterly.

Monday, Sept. 1, 1890
This cold, wet morning Edie and I scrambled out of bed at dawn and dressed ourselves for school. Annie McTaggart called for us. She is a young half-sister of mamma's and I do not care much for her so far. Away we went, myself trying to look as if I liked it. The High School is not far away but it is in a very bleak place and when we went in things didn't look very cheerful. The room looked as if hadn't been swept or dusted since the year one. There were only nine pupils there—we three girls and six boys. The teacher, Mr. *Mustard*—what a funny name!—seems fairly nice and I think I shall get along all right, when I get the hang of the studies. The text-books and methods are all new to me and I find them rather bewildering. I am going to study for a teacher's certificate.

Tuesday, Sept. 2, 1890
It rained cats and dogs all day. Edie had to stay home to do the washing, so I ploughed off to school alone through the mud, with tears running down my nose when I was going through vacant lots where nobody could see me. I felt so homesick for dear old Cavendish school with all my chums and our jolly goings-on. But when school went in we got a good fire on and things began to be cheerful. I was the only girl there to-day but I didn't mind that, and we had a real nice time over our lessons.

Wednesday, Sept. 3, 1890
Company came last night—Mrs. McKenzie of Toronto and her two daughters. Her husband, William McKenzie is my step mother's uncle, and is a railroad king and millionaire, I understand.
   I like school here now pretty well. When the room is warm and tidied up a bit it is rather cosy. We actually have an open fire place in it. There are eight boys going now and I must say they are a rather queer assortment. Arthur Jardine and Willard Goodfellow seem quite nice. Frank Robertson and Willy McBeath are not half bad either. But Tom Clark, Joe McDonald, Douglas Maveety and Henry Oram are detestable. They are "nitchie"—which means that they have Indian blood in them—and are as homely as stump fences, especially poor Douglas, who looks as if he had ten times too many teeth for his mouth.

Friday, Sept. 19, 1890
We had quite an exciting time in school to-day. This afternoon Mr. Mustard had a cranky fit on—he takes these occasionally although between times he never makes any attempt to secure order—and nearly snapped our heads off if we spoke a

word, so Edie and I resorted to the old device of writing on our slates. We were thus carrying on quite an animated conversation about our own personal affairs, when I became aware that that little sneak of a Bertie Jardine, who sits behind us, was looking over my shoulder and reading all I wrote. So, just to "give him a run for his money" I began to write rather caustic comments on all the boys present, fully aware as I did so that Master Bertie was copying everything I wrote down on a piece of paper. I didn't say a word about him or his brother, however, so that he had no excuse for what he did at recess. He showed the other boys the paper with all my comments and they were furious and went to Mr. Mustard. I explained the whole affair and Mr. M. took my part and gave Bertie a good drubbing. So after awhile they all cooled down. Bertie J. is a meddling little sneak, anyhow, and nobody can bear him. Arthur is so different—such a nice gentlemanly little chap.

The country around town is very beautiful now for every tree is purest yellow. The view from the schoolroom window is just lovely. You can see away up the blue river between its golden banks. But oh, I'd rather look out into an old spruce wood with ferns growing in its glades and a sea-wind purring in the treetops.

However, it can't be denied that school here is rather good fun, although very different from old Cavendish school days. There are a lot of rooms in the building—it was formerly a hotel—and they are all utilized for various purposes. The one above ours is a public ballroom and on the occasion of a ball our room is used as a ladies' dressing room. On the next morning we generally find numerous hairpins, feathers, flowers etc. strewn over the floor, and sometimes a hand mirror or two. On the other side of a big dusty, cobwebby hall is the Town Council Room and above it is the Free Mason's Room. In the back of the building are the patrol quarters, where two or three mounted policemen are stationed to patrol the town. When they arrest a drunken man they bring him in there, haling him through the hall and locking him up in one of the row of small dark cells, which runs directly back to our room.

Mr. Mustard has a pretty hot temper and as several of the boys have a fair share of "nitchie" in them, we have lively times occasionally. When Mr. Mustard starts in to thrash anyone he locks the door and uses a murderous-looking rawhide whip as long as himself.

Our amusements are very limited. At recess we girls wander around the dusty old place or sit out on the verandah and watch the boys playing football. Or perhaps we idly watch the passers-by—Indians for the most part—"braves" with their dirty blankets over their shoulders or chattering dark-eyed squaws with their glossy blue-black hair and probably a small-faced papoose strapped to the back.

As for our studies I am not satisfied at all. Mr. Mustard is not a good teacher and the work seems to drift along without any "go" or life in it.

Friday, Oct. 3, 1890
Well, the Bible assures us that we shall never have another deluge and it is very consoling that it does, for otherwise I fear me we should have had uneasy minds to-day. It has simply poured down since daylight and tonight I was really terrified. The water seemed to descend in sheets, while vivid bolts of lightning went hurtling through the darkness and thunder crashed incessantly overhead.

School was quite brilliant to-day. When Mr. M. was hearing the Junior Latin we all somehow got going laughing—I'm sure I don't know what at. The very imp of laughter seemed to take possession of us and it was impossible to stop. We saw a joke in everything and even Mr. Mustard seemed to catch the infection.

Monday, Oct. 6, 1890

School was very dull to-day but we had some excitement in the afternoon. At dinner hour Douglas Maveety had killed, or aided in killing a *skunk* over at the public school and when school went in after dinner the smell was dreadful. There we all sat, with our noses buried in our hankies, while poor D. sat dejectedly in one corner, as much avoided and shunned as if he had been a leper or a smallpox patient. At last Mr. Mustard sent him home to change his clothes but the odor pervaded the place for the rest of the day.

I am feeling lonely and dejected to-night, for father is away and I miss him so. He is all that makes life livable here at all for me. Otherwise it would be intolerable. Mrs. Montgomery—I *cannot* call her anything else, except before others for father's sake—has, I think, the most dreadful disposition ever put into the heart of a woman. She is sulky, jealous, utterly unreasonable. She just makes father's life miserable, continually carping, complaining, and fault-finding. But there is no use in writing anything more about her. Besides, I am constantly afraid she will sometime find and read this journal, although I keep it locked up. She reads all my letters and everything else she can find in my room when I am out. I suspected that very soon after I came here and I laid traps for her which proved it to me. I did not, however, let her know that I found it out for I am determined I will not make a fuss, for father's sake. He has enough to bear as it is.

Monday, Oct. 20, 1890

Edie went this morning and I felt dreadfully. It has been a dismal day. I am up here in Southview now and I feel so lonely. I missed Edie bad enough all day but it is tenfold worse now because this was always the time when we had the most fun, when we got up here away from Mrs. Montgomery's eye. She hated my intimacy with Edie and would have put a stop to it if she could. If Edie and I laughed together over some little innocent, mutual joke she seemed to take it as a personal insult. She even descended low enough to try to make my friend a spy upon me, too, but Edie was too loyal to me for that.

When I came to P.A. Mrs. M. did not approve of my wearing my hair up. She said I was too young for it. I admit I was, but her reason for disapproving of it was that she was afraid an apparently grown-up step-daughter would make *her* seem older. I was willing to please her and I have always worn it down since I came. But last Saturday morning I was dressing in a big hurry and, hunt high or low, I couldn't find a hair-ribbon. So at last I twisted it up in a knot behind, poked a handy hair-pin or two through it and thought no more about it. I was not out of the house all day, so didn't suppose it mattered. I never thought about Mrs. M. in connection with it. She was in a vile temper all day, but that is too common to excite wonder and I never dreamed of connecting it with my hair. But that night Edie came up to our room where I was studying, and said, "Why did you put your *hair up to-day, Maud?"* "I couldn't find a hair-ribbon," I answered indifferently. "Oh, I'm so glad you said that," said Edie. "Why," I asked in amazement. "Because," said Edie, "Mrs. Montgomery *told me to ask you if you put it up to annoy her.* Now, when she asks me what you said I can tell her the truth."

I think it showed her own disposition when she attributes such motives to other people. It must be the sort of thing she would do herself. And then to stoop to ask such a thing of a girl in Edie's position—household help. It has made me feel absolute contempt for her.

To-day I got a letter from home with some pressed flowers in it—red poppies and purple pansies. It just seemed as if they *spoke* to me and whispered a loving message of a far-off land where blue skies are bending over maple-crimsoned hills and spruce glens are still green and dim in their balsamic recesses.

Tuesday, Nov. 11, 1890

When I came home at noon to-day I found four letters awaiting me, from Lu, Mollie, Pensie—and Nate. I felt a little dubious as to what might be in his letter but it was all right. There was a little sentimental nonsense in it but not much and the rest was in a pleasant, friendly strain. I can heartily respond to *that* and I have written him a long letter full of fun. He is at Acadia College, Wolfville, and stands high in his classes. I think he is likely to do well for he is very clever.

Sunday, Nov. 16, 1890

A Mr. McLeod preached for us this morning. I don't think I ever in my life heard a minister I liked so much. He was a benevolent looking old Scotchman and although he could not be called eloquent there was such a touching *earnestness* about all he said and every word held so much. His address went straight to the heart and made one want to be better and live better just because goodness was so beautiful.

To-night I have been writing a composition on Evangeline. Nice Sunday evening's work. Not quite a logical outcome of Mr. MacLeod's sermon. But we have to hand them in tomorrow and as I have no Longfellow I had to wait until Annie had finished hers and could lend me the book.

Wednesday, Nov. 19, 1890

To-night I went to a concert in St. Alban's church and I never enjoyed such a treat in my life before. The chief features of the entertainment were eight recitations by Miss Agnes Knox, a Toronto elocutionist. It was a pleasure to look at her as well as listen for she is a very beautiful woman and looked like a queen in her dress of black velvet, with an exquisite bouquet fastened at her shoulder.

Monday, Dec. 1, 1890

Oh, oh, winter is upon us at last. No making a mistake about *that.* It was *sixty degrees below zero* to-day. And yet there are people who will tell you that this climate is no colder than down east! Of course, we don't really *feel* the cold so much. I was a funny-looking object going to school to-day. I had on a big buffalo coat—the *real* buffalo—with its collar turned up around my head, so that nothing of me was visible but nose and legs—all the rest was fur. But I didn't care a cent for appearances. What I was after was to keep from freezing to death!

Mr. Mustard has been in the doleful dumps for a week and you can't get a word out of him. He takes these spells frequently. He says he doesn't know what is the matter with him. Well, neither do I, but I *do* know that he is abominably cranky.

Thursday, Dec. 4, 1890

This evening papa was out and Mrs. M. was upstairs, so I was alone. Presently a knock came at the door and when I opened it there stood Mr. Mustard himself. He comes now and then to call on Mrs. M. as they were old High Schoolmates in Ontario. So I showed him into the room and skipped upstairs to inform her. But she was in bed or pretended to be—I think she had rolled in, clothes and all, when she heard his voice—so I went reluctantly down to make her excuses, hoping with all my heart he would go away when informed that she could not see him. But such an idea evidently did not enter into his head so there I had to sit the whole evening and entertain him. And he is *such* a bore! He stayed until I thought he would never go. When the door finally shut behind him I gave a tremendous sigh of relief.

Friday, Dec. 5, 1890

We have lots of fun in school these days. A new boy is going now—Willie Pritchard. He has red hair, green eyes and a crooked mouth! *That* doesn't sound attractive and he certainly isn't handsome—but he's splendid. I have lots of fun with him.

To-day we were all a little hilarious and poor Mr. Mustard lost his patience, kept a lot of us in after four, and gave us a sum in compound interest, a yard long, to work. The rest of them did it, or tried to, but I was just bound I *wouldn't*. If he had kept me there until midnight I wouldn't have made a figure. But he couldn't exactly rawhide a girl, so he had to let me go with the rest. Annie and I hurried home and went to a concert practice at the church. Willie P. was also there and we had lots of fun. I was introduced to his sister Laura. She seems like a lovely girl. She and I and Willie and Annie are going to have a dialogue called "Trapped". I don't care for it—it's such a mushy kind of thing but Mary McK. has settled on it so I suppose we must go ahead with it.

Sunday, Dec. 7, 1890

Well, this has really been the proudest day of my life! I *feel* at least three inches taller than I did yesterday. About three weeks ago I wrote a poem on the legend of Cape Leforce and sent it down home to the Charlottetown *Patriot*. I did not dare hope it would be printed, so I never squeaked a word about it to anyone. To-day when I came down, ready for Sunday School father came in with last night's mail and among it a *Patriot*. I seized it with a beating heart and trembling fingers and opened it. I grew dizzy—the letters danced before my eyes and I felt a curious sensation of choking—for there in one of the columns was my poem! I was just too delighted to speak. Father was *so* pleased and I am so glad and elated and happy. I can't find words to express my feelings.

Mrs. Montgomery looks as if she considered the whole thing a personal insult to *her* and has never mentioned the poem at all.

Monday, Dec. 8, 1890
Was at practice to-night and went through our dialogue but Laura and Willie and I dislike it so much that we are trying to have "The Census Taker" instead. But Annie is cranky—because she would have "too little to say in it"—and Mary seems awfully offended because we don't like the dialogue *she* selected. So I don't know what it will be yet.

Wednesday, Dec. 10, 1890
Annie came down off her high horse to-day and we agreed to have the *Census Taker* and meet at Mr. McTaggart's at seven to-night to practice it. School dragged along as usual until evening. When Senior Caesar came on we all got rather unruly. We laughed and whispered too much and Mr. Mustard lost his patience completely and threatened to keep us all in if we didn't keep quiet. We weren't any quieter than before so he did keep us in—Annie, Willie P. and me, who had been the worst offenders. In a few minutes a man came along in red-hot haste for Willie P. to go up to the M.P. barracks to identify a steer, so he got off, leaving Annie and me to our fate. Meanwhile, although we had to sit in separate seats we kept talking to each other. Mr. Mustard gravely announced that we would have to be silent for a certain length of time before we could get out. This statement he repeated every four or five minutes but we thought we could stand it as long as he could and kept on talking. When we couldn't think of anything to say we whispered verses of poetry which served the purpose just as well. Mr. Mustard lit a wax candle and took to writing at a terrific rate. He looked as solemn as an owl but he *had* to grin once in a while when one of us said something funny in a pig's whisper. Then I'd whisper, also according to piggy, "He's relenting, Annie." He *didn't* relent however. I found a scrap of candle in my desk, lit it, and began reading but by his order had to put out the one and consequently stop the other. But Annie and I still kept on talking, for we were bound we wouldn't give in.

"Leave hope behind all ye who enter here", I groaned at last. Mr. Mustard had to smile and then he rose.

"Well," he said, "I see it is of no use to keep you any longer. You can go."

We did not stand upon the order of our going but went at once. We hurried home, got our teas, and went up the hill to practice. Our dialogue went on swimmingly. For me it had many old memories—for we had it at home last summer at our school concert, Mollie, Ches, Annie Stewart, Nate and I. We stayed at Mr. McTaggart's till nine and then Laura and Willie and I came home together. We had lots of fun, too. (Snakes). They are both so nice—they are "my style" and I am right at home with them. We are kindred spirits.

Thursday, Dec. 11, 1890
When school came out we all went direct to Mr. Pritchard's to practice our dialogue. Then I came home to find that father and Mrs. M. were going out for the evening. This scared me, for Mr. Mustard had said something in school to-day

about calling this evening. I didn't care then, but *now* if he came when they were out *I* would have to entertain him and I didn't pine for *that*. So, when they went, I blew out all the downstair lights, came up to Southview, pulled down both blinds, pinned a heavy shawl over the window to keep out any ray of light and then I resolved if he came not to answer his knock but just let him think there was no one at home. He hasn't come so far—at least, I haven't heard any knock—so I hope he won't. I don't want to see *him* but I would welcome almost anybody else for I'm awfully lonesome. I've been very lonely and homesick of late. Oh, for one glimpse of Cavendish! Of course I know it is winter down there now, just as here, but in thinking of it I always remember it just as I left it in the prime of summer with buttercups and asters blooming by the brooks, ferns blowing spicily in the woods, lazy sunshine sleeping on the hills, with the beautiful sea beyond, blue and bright and far-reaching. There is no spot on earth more lovely.

Sunday, Dec. 14, 1890
Went to S.S. and unexpectedly found myself transformed from a pupil into a teacher. Kate McGregor was not there, so I was asked to take her class. I did so with a great deal of inward "sinking awayness." My class was of little girls and not one of them knew a single thing about the lesson, not even its name, but they had a fearful knack of asking awkward and irrelevant questions. It all seemed like a chapter out of a "Pansy" book—but I did not feel at all like a "Pansy" heroine!

Wednesday, Dec. 24, 1890
Cold enough to freeze your marrow—40 below zero. I've been more than busy to-day, however, for this was our concert night.

When father came in last night and woke me up to give me a letter I was too sleepy to care much about it and so didn't read it until this morning. When I woke up I looked at it and in the dim light could not see the writing very plainly but something in its bold outlines reminded me of Nate's and I thought it was from him. So I jumped out of bed and pulled up the blind. Then I saw it wasn't Nate's writing and whose it was I didn't know, so I very sensibly concluded to open it and see. It turned out to be from Asher Robertson, the very last person in the world from whom I would have expected a letter. But I was pleased to hear from him for I always liked him. The letter was Asher all over—very commonplace but friendly and nice.

Our concert came off tonight and we had a pretty good audience in spite of the cold. Everything "behind the scenes" was turmoil and confusion for our "dressing room" was only about four feet square and everybody piled their wraps in it. Such a mess as we had! We performers *couldn't* find our things and were all the time hunting and puffing, for it was awfully warm in that corner and so jammed I don't know how we ever managed at all. But we continued to keep the confusion pretty well out of sight. One of our tableaux fell through altogether and other things were just pulled through by the skin of their teeth. I got on all right with my recitation "The Child Martyr" and our dialogue was a big success. Our tableau "The Five Foolish Virgins" was also very pretty. We were all dressed in white with shawls on our heads and empty lamps in our hands.

Laura P. and I were down to see the train come in last night and had great fun. She is a lovely girl. Willy was there and walked home with me, and Andrew Agnew came home with Laura. Willy is *awfully* nice—the nicest boy I ever met.

Monday, Dec. 29, 1890

Somebody has been trying to play a joke on me I guess! When father brought up the mail yesterday there was a parcel for me and as it was addressed to "Miss Montgomery, *Town*", I knew it must be from somebody in P.A. When I opened it I found a nice little memorandum book and a cute pencil, also a slip of paper with the name of William McBeath on it.

Now, you wouldn't imagine that Willy McBeath ever sent it. I know Willy P. sent it for a joke and I am going to talk to him about it. Willy McBeath is, or tries to be, a regular little lady-killer, and always deluges us girls at school and practices with candy. I get my share of it and Willy P. sees fit to tease me about him. So I know that he is at the bottom of this but he has not succeeded in hoaxing me for all that. I suppose he thought it would be great fun if I wrote a note to Willy M. thanking him for a present he never sent. No, no, Master Willy P. Try someone else.

Wednesday, Dec. 31, 1890

This is the last day of the old year. As I look back over the past year—the most eventful one in my life so far—I cannot help feeling sad. What a year it has been—so full of change and joy and grief! But there has been a lot of pleasure mixed up with it too. Altogether, I don't grumble at the old year. All I ask of the new year is that it will take me back home.

11. Pensie [Macneill]

12. Down in school woods
[Cavendish]

13. Cavendish School scholars
Eight boys in back row from left to right: Robbie McKenzie, Johnny Simpson, Charlie McKenzie,
Chesley Clark, Austin Laird, Arty Macneill, Frank Macneill, Fred Clark.
Eight girls and teacher in second row: Maggie Clark, Lottie Simpson, Mattie McKenzie, Emma Simpson,
Clara McKenzie, Lucy Macneill, Nellie Macneill, Annie Stewart, Miss Gordon.
Children in next row: Ada McKenzie, Aileen Laird, Myrtle Laird (standing), Edith Spurr, Kate Macneill,
Lena Simpson, Bessie McKenzie, Ruby Simpson, Ellice Laird, Lisle Archibald, Helen Archibald,
Ernest Macneill, Harry McKenzie, Wilbur Clark, Milton McKenzie.
Children on ground: Ethel McKenzie, Laura McKenzie, Campsie Clark, Jean Laird, Jennie Archibald,
F. Stewart, Garfield Stewart, Gordon Robertson, Ernest Spurr, Winchester Simpson.

14. View from kitchen doorstep
[of Alexander Macneill's house]

15. *Grandpa Montgomery*
[Donald Montgomery]

16. *Father's house in Prince Albert*

17. Father and his second wife
[Hugh John and Mary McRae Montgomery]

18. Willie Pritchard

19. Cape Leforce
[Cavendish]

1891

Monday, Jan. 5, 1891

We are in the council-room for good now and have our desks moved in. Two new girls are going—Martha and Aggie Thompson—both nice girls but not especially "my kind." I sit with Martha.

Mind you, Willy P. has declared himself innocent of that joke. I was very cool to him all day and coming home he asked me what was the matter. I flared out, of course, but he stoutly declared he hadn't a thing to do with it, so I got left there.

I am afraid it really was Willy M. that sent the book, for Willy P. says Willy M. told him he sent a book to a girl for a Christmas present. *I* feel kind of cheap over the way I went for Willy P. about it. However, I don't think he bears me any grudge. We are just the best of friends. He always walks home from school with me and carries my books.

Wednesday, Jan. 7, 1891

Mr. Mustard has been dreadfully cranky for a week and to-day his ill-humor reached a climax. He quarrelled with Annie this morning and she wouldn't go to school this afternoon. I came in for my share of it, too, as he kept me in at dinner-time to lecture me on my "haughty manner of speaking" and my use of "slang"—to which last, however, I am *not* notably addicted, Mustard to the contrary notwithstanding. But he affects to be a great purist in regard to English undefiled. As for my "haughtiness"—alas and alack! So much for what I had flattered myself was a dignified reserve!

I might have taken the reproof amiably enough from some men, but *not* from him, for I have no respect for him. I froze up and was as chilly as an iceberg to him all the afternoon, while taking particular care to keep all the rules. I can tell you he found me "haughty" with a vengeance!

Thursday, Jan. 8, 1891

Annie McT. declares she won't go to school to Mustard again and is going out to teach in the Lindsay district. I didn't thaw out towards Mustard at all and he kept me in again to "explain", saying that his action had been prompted by his "sincere friendship" for me. I do not want his "friendship" and I listened in stony silence, for I was angry clear through. I did not say *one* word and *that* seemed to discomfit him more than anything else. When we came out Willy P. was waiting patiently in the cold hall and as he took my books and helped me on with my coat he got some very black looks from Mr. M. I confided my grievances to him as we went home over the cold snows, and I got enough sympathy to soothe my ruffled feelings.

This evening I went down with Laura to see the train come in. Oh, I forgot to say that last night I got another parcel from that horrid little Willy McBeath enclosing an illustrated booklet. He didn't sign his name this time but wrote "From a Friend in the Junior Class". I shall just have to snub that kid!

Monday, Jan. 26, 1891
I seem to have budded into a regular S.S. teacher now, as for the last two Sundays I have had to take Annie's class of boys and from present indications I fancy I shall have to keep them. Such little imps as they are too, full to the lips with mischief. But I like them for all. I'd far rather have a class of boys than one of girls.

To-day in school I still kept up my reserve towards Mr. M., never speaking to him unless spoken to, and then most freezingly polite. But alas for my dignity! This evening when I went to answer the door, who should stand there but he himself smiling and bowing most amiably. Of course, I had to be civil and then, as father was away at a council meeting and Mrs. M. took excellent care not to come down stairs I had to sit there the whole evening to entertain him. And that is no enviable occupation for he is a fearful poke. Whatever did he want to come here again to-night for, when he was here only Friday?

There was a heavy white frost to-night and this morning the town looked beautiful. All the trees were dreams of mist, looking as if a breath would demolish them, and across the river the forest looked like fairyland.

By the way I believe it was not Willy McB who sent that last booklet, after all, but—worse and worse—Frank Robertson. Willy P. has found out all about it. He is a regular detective.

Tuesday, Feb. 1, 1891
To-day was a son and heir born unto the house of Montgomery. The baby is a pretty little fellow and father is pleased as Punch over having a boy. I'm glad it is a boy, too, somehow. I always like boy babies better than girls.

Friday, Feb. 13, 1891
School is really quite lively nowadays. We have great times in it over the elections. Father is going to run on the Liberal ticket and as Willy P. is a rabid *Tory* we have interesting debates. He and I have adopted a cipher alphabet. He is constantly writing notes to me and sometimes they go astray and fall into the hands of the other boys who show no mercy. So Will suggested we employ a cipher and we are going to use the one Nate and I used to use. It comes in very useful. Poor "Snip" and "Snap". How I'd like to see them again—perhaps meet them on the dear old school playground when the trees cast long shadows, and the golden light fell across the old spruces that rustled and crooned so softly!

Monday, Feb. 23, 1891
Mr. Mustard was furious with me to-day because he caught me exchanging notes with Will. What *does* make him act so? The note which riled him so proved to be an invitation to go with Will and Laura to a toboggan slide up at the barracks

tonight. At about seven this evening Laura came over and soon after Will drove up with a dandy turn-out. As we were too early we went for a drive away out into the country. When we got back the fun was just beginning. The chute had arches all over it at regular intervals hung with Chinese lanterns and it looked like fairyland. As I had never been on a toboggan before I was very nervous and hung back for some time. But finally Laura and I summoned up enough spunk to go. All I was conscious of was an arrow's speed, a whirl of fine snow in our faces, a dazzle of colored lights overhead, two or three awful "dips", and then a long level spin. It was splendid, and after that we went often. Spills were numerous and lots of funny things occurred. Once my hat blew off going down and fell right on the slide and how it escaped being crushed flat by the next toboggan I don't know. Will rescued it from the scrimmage and we went off merrily again. Another time Laura, Katie Fulcher and I went down with two of the soldiers. It was a very narrow toboggan and I knew the minute we started that we were "in for it". Down we shot until we reached the first "dip". There was an awful bounce and over we went in one grand spill. I was dragged for several yards with my face in the snow and really thought I'd be smothered. But on the whole it was a jolly evening.

Saturday, March 7, 1891
Father has lost his election I am sorry to say. But I never expected anything else. This is a confirmed Tory riding—and so Gov't money has been spent in showers. I am glad it is over for this past month has been nothing but excitement and worry. I have not been in school for a week and am going to start again now, as we have got a servant girl—Fannie McLauchlin, a "breed" girl. I had to give up my dear little "Southview" to her and sleep in the spare room. It is too bad. I just loved Southview. It was my haven of rest where I could fly with all my troubles.

Monday, Mar. 9, 1891
Went to school to-day and found things pretty much the same. Mr. Mustard was terribly cross and had a sickening hand-to-hand fight with Frank Robertson. If Will P. and I ventured to say a word to each other he pounced on us, though everyone else seemed at liberty to talk as they pleased. This evening I went over to see Laura. She is a lovely girl and we are devoted chums. She and I were alone in the earlier part of the evening but later on Will came in and of course his advent didn't exactly depress us any.

Tuesday, Mar. 10, 1891
Prince Albert
Fannie has skipped out—left us unceremoniously in the lurch, giving as a reason that Mrs. M. was "too cross and particular"—which is too true to be funny. So there is no more school for me until we get another girl.

The Temperance Concert came off tonight. I recited "The Christening," was encored, and gave "The Other side." I had a fine time all round.

Friday, Mar. 20, 1891
Prince Albert
This evening as I was sitting, swinging Baby Bruce in his hammock Laura popped in to ask if I would go for a drive with her and Will. I didn't need to be coaxed and soon we were speeding down the street with the bells jingling a merry chorus. Oh, such a jolly time as we had! We went away up the river for miles, then back and away down to Goschen. It was a glorious night—bright moonlight, with brilliant stars shining in the dark blue sky and a rare splendor in the air, clear, crisp, exhilarating. A merry trio we were, laughing, talking, joking and star-hunting, the last named being especially amusing.

I had a letter from Nate to-day—very jolly and interesting. He enclosed a small photo of himself—a very good one. He seems to be doing finely at college.

Saturday, Mar. 28, 1891
To-night I felt horribly ill with a cold and intended to go to bed right after tea—or rather right after I had finished the dishes. But alas, by that time Mr. Mustard arrived and stayed till eleven. I thought he would *never* go and I was so dull and sleepy I could hardly sit up straight in my chair.

I have never been in school since the first week in March and have come to conclusion that I am not to get any more. Mrs. M. is not trying to get a girl, I can plainly see that, and I have to stay home and do the work. She does nothing but attend to her children. I do really think it is too bad. I came out here in the hope of getting to a good school and this is the result. I do not say a word, however, because it would make father feel so bad. I would put up with anything to save him trouble.

Monday, Mar. 30, 1891
Prince Albert
Got an invitation to Mary McKenzie's wedding to-night. She is to be married to Mr. Stovel on April 8. "Such is life," as Asher Robertson used to say every time he heard of Stewart Simpson going home with Mamie.

I am here in my room, sitting up in bed scribbling in my journal, as I used to do down home. Dear old Cavendish! I can just imagine how it looks at this moment....

Monday, Apr. 6, 1891
Prince Albert
This evening Laura came over and we had a jolly talk which was interrupted by the advent of Mustard at nine o'clock. I don't know how it came about but we got up to our ears in theology and began to debate about the doctrine of predestination. I denied it; Mustard upheld it. Laura sat on the fence and shot arrows impartially at both sides. We had an argument worthy of the name, for theology is one of the few things Mr. Mustard can really talk well on. In the end we both agreed to retain our own convictions on the subject. As for me, a million Mustards could never make me believe that God ordains any of his creatures to eternal torture for "his own good-will and pleasure."

Thursday, Apr. 9, 1891

That detestable Mustard came again to-night and stayed until 11.30. To be able to keep up a conversation with him one ought to be posted on every subject from Adam down, to be blessed with a large supply of patience in order to listen to all the stale anecdotes he never fails to rehash at every call, and, in brief, to assume interest in *everything*. Let me just see! I will recount the subjects I have scratched over this evening for morsels of conversation: Mary's wedding—which, by the way, came off yesterday—weddings in general—rather risky topic, say you?—card-playing and dancing—M. is down upon them of course—education, civil-engineering, Montreal, autographs and auto-hunters, school days, various personal likes and dislikes, ancestry, nomenclature—Mustard thinks *his* name "was assumed for political reasons"!!!—genealogy, various events about town—no, *not* gossip. M. never indulges in anything so interesting!—school-teaching, letter writing, another whack at predestination and—but oh, if that wasn't all it ought to be! My poor brain is in a state of collapse. I must go to bed straight off and get my "beauty sleep" and if Mr. Mustard calls again for a fortnight I will even fall upon him and rend him limb from limb!!!!

Monday, Apr. 13, 1891

Well, it is nearly 12 o'clock and I am just boiling over with rage. *Mr. Mustard was here again* to-night. That is the fatal secret! He stayed till 11.30, too. What possesses the man? I can't, of course, pretend to be ignorant that it is I whom he comes to see but surely he doesn't mean anything by it. I certainly hope not, anyhow. But pshaw! He'd surely never dream of getting foolish over a chit of sixteen, especially since I've led him such a life of it.

Monday, Apr. 20, 1891

This is the night Mr. Mustard generally comes—I suppose because father is always away at Council meeting. I did my best to escape him. First, I thought I would run over to Kennedy's and see Laura. (Pritchards have moved out to their farm now but Laura, who goes to the convent school, is staying until vacation with her aunt, Mrs. Kennedy, who lives right next door to us.) But I couldn't get away. So then I ran over and got Laura to come over with me and help me out. We tormented poor Mustard terribly to-night—it *is* such fun to tease him—he gets so confused and sheepish. Laura had to go at nine but father was home by then and he stayed in the room and read, for which I was very thankful. I *hate* to be alone with Mustard!

I must admit that his attentions are becoming rather serious. All the town is talking about them. I am teased to distraction about him and all sorts of jokes on his *name* are fired off at me. Even father can't ask me to pass him the *mustard* at the table without a grin! It makes me simply furious!

Thursday, Apr. 23, 1891
Prince Albert
This evening Laura and I went for a walk in the delicious spring twilight. These western twilights are remarkably beautiful. We went up to the cricket grounds where Will was playing and watched the game for awhile. Then we came back and walked up Church St. as far as McColl's. Just by Judge McGuire's house we met Willy who had a huge parcel of vanilla creams for us. We strolled around for an hour and had a delightful time. It was bright moonlight and the little town was sheathed in misty silver light, dreamy and lustrous.

It is so delightful to have Laura living right next door. She and I are always having delightful chats in the back yard.

Monday, Apr. 27, 1891
Anticipating Mr. Mustard's arrival to-night I got Laura over. You may be sure we led him a pretty dance of it. Father and Mrs. M. were both out so we tormented him to our heart's content. In the course of the evening I found a chance to put the clock on half an hour, so M. left at what he fondly believed to be 10.30, whereas it was only 10.

I am going to get home all right this summer. I have been very hopeless of it for some time but it is all settled now. I shall be sorry to leave father and Laura and Will and a few other friends, but that will certainly be all my regret. It will be so wonderful to escape from the atmosphere of suspicion and petty malice and persecution which Mrs. Montgomery seems to exhale wherever she is. Sometimes I feel as if I were literally smothering in it. I work my fingers to the bone for her and her children and I am not even civilly treated for it. I do all the work of this house, except the washing, which she gets in a squaw to do. She herself is never happy unless she is gadding out somewhere. However I don't complain of *this* last, for the only hours I *live* in this house are when she is out of it. I *love* it when father and I are alone together for a meal. We can be as jolly and chummy as we like then, with no one to cast black looks and sneers at us.

This evening at sunset Mr. and Mrs. McTaggart called and took Katie and me for a drive in the phaeton. We had just a lovely time. We drove away down to Goschen in the soft, sweet twilight with the pale hues of sunset lingering in the west and reflection in the broad river.

Saturday, May 8, 1891
This evening Laura ran in to invite me over, as two of her schoolmates, Lula and Maggie Taylor, were at Mrs. Kennedy's. We had fine fun. Will dropped in at nine and we all went down to meet the train and had no end of a good time. We always get a bit of a ride on her when she is shunting.

In a letter from Pensie to-night she said that Will Spear had been killed by a falling tree in B.C. He was an English boy who stayed at Darnley Clark's a winter long ago and went to school. He was a dark, nice-looking boy, much given to teasing the girls, especially Mollie and me, who sat in front of him. Poor Will, he is the first of my schoolmates to go. It has begun I suppose—the first bead on the string has slipped off and one by one sooner or later, all the rest must follow.

Sitting alone in the twilight this evening before Laura came, swinging Bruce in his hammock, I fell to thinking of my early schoolmates and among others of Maud Woodside who was my seat-mate and devoted chum when I first began to go to school before Mollie went. We used to have lots of fun together. Maud W. was a nice little girl and we were two small, happy, thoughtless mites with a world of our own behind that old brown desk at school, shared also by Minie Kesley, another of my early mates. Maud and I sat together for only one summer. Then we formed new combinations. Mollie began to go to school. It was always thought a great thing among the older scholars to have a new pupil sit with them. Pensie and Emma Stuart had corralled Mollie and kept her for two days. I was sitting alone in the seat just ahead. I offered Pensie and Emma four big sweet apples if they would let Amanda sit with me. We had almost the only orchard in C. at that time and I was a power in school because of this. Apples would purchase almost anything, from "chews" of gum up to "new girls." They bought me Mollie. Pensie and Emma took the apples and Mollie was transferred chattel-wise from their seat to mine. We were never again separated from that day until we left school last summer. Mollie and I sat together through thick and thin, through evil report and good report. It was not a bad bargain for four apples!!!

Wednesday, May 13, 1891
Prince Albert
After tea I went over to see Laura. Will was there, too, so we all went over to their town house to feed a cat he has there, and then we sauntered down the street to Goodfellow's. Will went in there to invest for our benefit and Laura and I went down to the river to pick up pebbles. The evening was lovely and the river perfectly exquisite. Presently Will rejoined us, loaded with candies, and we sauntered down the Goschen sidewalk as far as Strachan's photo gallery. While Will and I were looking at the photos Laura ran down to the river to get a drink and during her absence Will asked me to give him my photo when I should have some taken and I agreed on the principle of a fair exchange. Then Laura came back and we walked home slowly and got to Kennedy's at 8. We sat down on their steps until 10, and had just a jolly time, laughing, talking, and telling stories, while the air grew duskier and sweeter and the eastern sky was lurid with a prairie fire and the frogs chorused faintly in the distance. Will stole my little gold ring and put it on his finger. He wouldn't give it back but then I didn't coax *very* hard.

Thursday, May 14, 1891
....This morning at breakfast father was relating to me some of the incidents of his life in Boston. I really know so little of father's life—and it has been a life full of incident and adventure too. First, on the farm at Park Corner where he was brought up, then a young sea-captain, cruising to England, the West Indies and South America, then a merchant at Clifton—where I was born—then a clerk in Boston, then a Government clerk in Battleford and P.A. He has had all sorts of adventures, especially in the Indian rebellion here in 1885 when he was a volunteer. It has not been a very successful life. Father is a poor man to-day. Yet he is one of those men who are loved by everyone. And I—I love him with all my heart—better than anyone else in the whole world—dear, darling father!

May 25, 1891
Prince Albert
Have had a lovely time to-day. It is the Queen's Birthday—or rather the birthday itself was yesterday and was celebrated to-day. We, with several other families, were all invited to spend the day out at Mr. McArthur's ranch. It was a tip-top day, cool, clear and—for a wonder—calm. We left at 9.30 this morning. It is about 12 miles out to the farm, over a very pretty trail. We all got lost on the road and were some time finding our way again but that only added to the fun. We got there about twelve. After we were rested Lottie Stewart and I went for a walk. She is fearfully quiet and slow however. There was a rough bridge built over the dried bed of a lake and beyond it was a beautiful prairie, miles long, dotted with white-stemmed poplars. After dinner Mr. Stovel made some bats and we all went over to the lake and had a game of baseball. It was glorious. Mr. S. and I were on the same side and we just made things hum. We won the game, too.

We left for home at seven and I came home in Mayor Johnson's rig and drove the team all the way. When I told father this when I got home Mrs. M. remarked in her amiable fashion, "It is a wonder Mrs. Johnson would feel safe if *you* were driving."

I suspect that Mrs. Johnson, having a better temper, has also better nerves than Mrs. Montgomery.

Sunday, May 31, 1891
Had a letter from Nate last night. His year at the Academy will soon be up. It closes on June 4 and he expects to be in C. by the 10th. Wish I could be there too. I've no idea just when I'll be going as I have to wait until Parliament adjourns. I'm going down to Ottawa to go home with Grandpa Montgomery.

I sent down to the *Patriot* to-day a little poem called "June". I remember so well the time I composed it—two years ago one lovely June day when I was sitting on the banks of the brook under the maple tree up by the hill spring, while the sky was blue and the air sweet.

Was in to see Mrs. Kennedy this evening. She is such a dear little woman. Lolla was out. Will is away to Battleford now on a business trip and we miss him dreadfully.

I've moved back into dear old Southview again and I'm so glad.

Saturday, June 6, 1891
Will is back and looks fine after his trip. I saw him to-day for a few minutes before he went out home. This evening Mr. Mustard came shuffling along at nine and stayed till eleven. I wished the cats had him. He was quite confidential and said he was going down east to go to college. He then asked me what profession I thought he'd better follow! I felt like snickering but managed to keep a straight face and said very gravely,

"Oh, Mr. Mustard, I couldn't advise, not knowing what you are best fitted for. Follow your own inclination if you wish to succeed."

And then Mr. M. sheepishly informed me that he was thinking of going to Knox College and meant to be a minister. I don't know how I kept from laughing right out in his face. Mustard a minister!! Oh Lordy—how it will sound—Rev. Mr. Mustard. I pity the poor woman whose fate it will be to write "Mrs." before such a combination. I have a dim suspicion that Mr. M. intends asking *me* to accept that honor but I may be mistaken. I think I see him in a pulpit! Well, I suppose as far as looks go he'll do well enough; he isn't bad looking, being tall and fair, with blue eyes and a golden moustache which he cultivates very carefully. But if he couldn't find something more interesting to say than he does in *our* conversations he'd be anything but a brilliant preacher.

Now, I must go and look up my Bible class lesson. We have Bible class in the manse now every Sunday afternoon after S.S. and it is very interesting.

I am writing an article on Saskatchewan for *The Times* here, and have it nearly done. I've given a description of the prairies and scenery and the characteristics of the Indians and will finish up with a flowery peroration on the possibilities of the country as a whole.

Tuesday, June 16, 1891
Prince Albert, Sask.
I was invited to spend the evening at the Kennedy's and of course we had a scrumptious time. Andrew Agnew, Mr. Sinclair, and Willie were there and we had such fun making a table rap. Willie asked me to go with him to the convent school closing to-morrow night and I agreed. Mrs. K. got us lunch and we all sat around the table and told ghost stories until I vow when I got home I sneaked upstairs in mortal terror and stood with my back to the wall all the time I was undressing so I couldn't fancy there was anything behind me!

Thursday, June 18, 1891
Prince Albert
Mr. Mustard was here this evening and was as limp as usual. He is going back to Ontario in three weeks time. He asked me to go with him to an ice-cream social to-morrow night at the manse, but as I have to stay home with the kiddies I had a good excuse for declining. I had been feeling a little disappointed because I was not going to go but I would rather stay home and look after a whole orphan asylum than go anywhere with him. He also asked me to correspond with him and I consented rather stiffly because I didn't know how to refuse. Anyhow, I can drop it gradually.

My article is out in *The Times* and is making quite a bit of sensation.
"T'is pleasant sure to see one's name in print,
A book's a book although there's nothing in it."
Laura has gone out to the farm now and I simply feel lost without her.

Monday, June 22, 1891
This evening was lovely—too lovely, indeed, since it put a wretched idea into Mustard's pate. I was busy washing the tea dishes when he came shuffling along to ask "if I would mind"—he always prefaces his requests with this graceful please—"going out for a walk?" I *did* mind very much indeed, but I couldn't think of any valid excuse on the spur of the moment, so I consented rather grimly

and told him to call at 7.30. I also felt properly scared. He is going away in a fortnight's time and I was terrified lest he were looking for an opportunity to say something I didn't want to hear.

We started at 7.30 and I managed to tow him through the back streets and away up the river trail where I thought I'd run no risk of meeting acquaintances. But it's always the case that you are sure to meet the very people you most want to avoid and in the most unlikely places. And so of course we met Mr. and Mrs. McTaggart and Min Wheeler—a girl who is visiting them—square in the teeth. Just imagine my feelings. I hope they didn't show too plainly in my face. Such a grimace as Min made at me as the carriage passed! Won't I catch it when I see her!

I talked on nervously, uttering I don't know what silly nonsense, so as not to give M. any chance of saying anything embarrassing. I'm firmly convinced that that was just his aim and object for he was silent and pre-occupied all the time and acted as if he were trying to screw his courage up to some sticking point or other; and once he picked some wild roses and sheepishly—oh, he is *so* sheepish *always*— asked if I would wear them! I took the roses—but I didn't wear them! Instead I picked them deliberately to pieces and scattered them over the trail as we walked along. I didn't give him the ghost of a chance but hurried back as soon as I decently could. On the way back he said,

"Oh, say, *would you mind* going out for a drive some evening soon?"

I nearly took a fit. Cooped up in a buggy with Mustard where I couldn't get away from him! *No*, thank you! So I told him I would be too busy to go driving *any* evening. He must have thought me a most hard-working mortal!

When we got back he came in and sat for two hours! *What* possesses the man! He *must* think something of me when he is so persistent and yet how *can* he? Why, I've never been half decent to him. I've snubbed him times without number! I've made fun of him to his very face and he knows it—and yet he comes and comes! Thank goodness, he's going soon!

Friday, June 26, 1891
Prince Albert
After dinner I took a jug and went away out to the east flats to pick berries. I was away two hours and had such a lovely time. It was clear and cool and I was all alone among the sweet grasses and leaves, with the birds singing in the poplars. At such time the charm of this north land comes home to me and I felt that I could have loved it and been contented here if Mrs. Montgomery had been a different woman.

Mustard did another of his queer things to-day. He called in the afternoon and asked for me. I squirmed darkly into the parlor and he gave me my set of book-keeping books he had brought from the high school. Then, as he rose to go, he asked me if I'd be in to-night. As I was expecting to go up to Mrs. McTaggart's I said "no".

"To-morrow night then?" he insisted.

As I had unfortunately no engagement on hand I had to say yes.

"May I come and see you?" he asked.

Now, considering the fact that he has been coming here two and three times a week all winter, to see me—or papa?—without troubling himself about the formality of asking if he might, this question struck me as unique.

"If you wish to, Mr. Mustard," I said ungraciously. He turned a shade or two redder and showed himself out. *I* felt like a perfect fool. Oh, I'm mortally afraid he's going to say something yet.

Sunday, June 28, 1891
Prince Albert
Last night it simply poured and I was comfortably sure that Mustard would never venture out in such a deluge. But come he did—"to see me." I suppose he "saw" me, for I sat in front of him for two mortal hours, and talked or tried to talk. But that blessed pater of mine was home and sat reading in the room all the evening, so Mustard couldn't say anything if he wanted to. I was *so* thankful. If I can *only* head him off until he gets away! I don't care what he says by letter—I can manage *that*—but I shall die if he says anything by word of mouth. There is something about the man which makes me feel so self-conscious and positively *ashamed*.

In the *Patriot* to-day was a list of those who had passed the exam for Second Class license and Jack Laird's name was in it. I suppose he will be teaching now. How *funny* to think of "Snap" being a teacher!

Tuesday, June 30, 1891
To-night Annie McTaggart had a school concert out at Lindsay where she has been teaching ever since her quarrel with Mustard. Mary Stovel and I had promised to assist her, so we drove out this morning. The prairies are just one blush with wild roses now and we had a charming drive. We had dinner at Mr. Millar's, where Annie boards, and then drove down to the log schoolhouse. It was in a state of glorious confusion, with loads of poplar boughs, wild roses, and orange lilies heaped about. And the children—*such* faces, *such* costumes! But some of them were pretty and they sang wonderfully well. We set to work to decorate. Annie had got the lend of an organ—the only one in Lindsay—and we banked it up with poplar boughs and those lovely orange lilies. We wreathed windows and blackboard with poplar and piled up lilies and roses and wild peas wherever we could. When all was swept and garnished that school looked quite gorgeous. It was four by this time, so we went back to Mr. Millar's, had our teas and donned our war-paint, which we had brought out with us in a valise. Then we went to the school. Mr. Stovel came out and was chairman. Quite a number of our town friends were also out but the rest of the audience were the queerest assortment I've ever seen. After it was all over—about nine—Mr. McNiven, one of the trustees, got up to make a speech and upon my word I laughed until I was nearly sick. He was so drunk that he could hardly stand—but *that* was not what I was laughing at—and he spoke for *a whole hour*. He would begin,

"Gentlemen, chairman, gentlemen and ladies"—he would repeat this four or five times, with variations—such as "lairmen and chadies"—and then he'd say, referring to Annie's pluck in taking a hard school like Lindsay, "that darling little *lion*, Miss McTaggart, with the courage and the abilities of a *tager*." When he referred to the concert words failed him. "I regret my *un*ability to express my thoughts on *this grand subject*. It's in this poor human critter"—patting himself with both hands on the breast—"but he can't get it out."

They finally induced him to stop and we started for home. Mr. Stovel came with us and we sang comic songs all the way. It was a cold night with a white fog and the mirages were wonderful. At times you seemed to be driving down to an ice-covered bay. Then it would change to a sunset lake dotted with islands. We got home at 3 o'clock after a very amusing but fatiguing jaunt.

Wednesday, July 1, 1891

The first thing on to-day's programme was going this forenoon to see the laying of the cornerstone of the new Presbyterian church. When I came home from it I found Mrs. Montgomery indulging in a fit of hysterical crying and raking father down for something he had done or left undone—I couldn't make out which—during the progress of the ceremonies. What that woman needs is a good spanking.

After dinner I went to see the Dominion Day sports. Laura and I were together as usual. The athletic sports were fine and the horse races were splendid. Will rode a horse and won easily. He did look so cute on horseback with his little jockey cap on. Laura asked father if I could go out and stay a few days with her next week and to my great delight he consented. I had been afraid he would not, for of course Mrs. M. will make a fuss about doing her own work while I am away.

Ten O'Clock

I feel like shrieking. It would be a great relief but it might make too much of a sensation in the neighborhood, so I'll have to exercise some self restraint.

Mustard actually *mustered*—oh, forgive the pun. It just *made itself*—up enough courage to put his fate to the test this evening. He did it about as awkwardly as possible but he did it.

Now, I've been expecting it for some time and I thought I'd be awfully confused and nervous, but I wasn't—not a bit. Instead, I wanted to laugh all the time. Well, perhaps *that* was a phase of nervousness because there really wasn't anything at all funny about it. In fact, the only truly descriptive word I knew of to apply to the whole interview is *sickening*.

There was an excursion down the river to-night and father and Mrs. M. went on it, so Mr. Mustard and I were left alone in the twilight—a very dangerous time. I was sitting in a corner of the sofa, rocking my snoozing and unconscious baby brother, and Mr. M. was sitting opposite me on a rocker. He talked very jerkily for some time and then ensued a period of uncomfortable silence. I had what Laura calls "a creepy, crawly presentiment," that something was just on the point of happening. He looked out of the window while I glared at a piece of yellow yarn on the carpet—I shall remember the shape and location of that yarn as long as I live—and wished myself a thousand miles away.

Finally Mr. Mustard turned with a very ghastly sort of smile and stammered out painfully,

"Do you think, Miss Montgomery, that our friendship will ever develop into *anything else*?"

And his look and tone plainly revealed what he meant by "anything else."

Well, I had to say something, so I said,

"I don't see what else it *can* develop into, Mr. Mustard."

I said it very well and composedly, too. I had expected to be flustered—but I wasn't. It all depends on the person, I suppose. Now, when Will says anything significant to me I color up and look foolish and lose my voice instantly. But I wasn't troubled with any such symptoms in poor M's case.

"It's just as *you* think," he said slowly.

Just at this point the gate banged and Mrs. McTaggart's hearty old face appeared in the doorway, little dreaming, good woman, what she was so unwittingly interrupting. On finding that Mrs. Montgomery was out she went away again and another *awful* silence ensued. I stared steadily at the aforesaid piece of yarn and held my tongue for I was determined not to speak until he did, if I sat there for a thousand years. At last he stammered out that he "hoped I wasn't offended—he did not wish any misunderstanding—"

This was my chance so I dashed in nobly and blurted out, "Certainly not, Mr. Mustard. And I shall always be your friend but nothing more."

Then—silence! Oh, dear, it was really dreadful. And there were actually tears in his eyes. But *I* didn't cry or feel like crying. He has brought it all on himself, for any sane man might have taken the hint that I had no use for him long ago. I just wanted to laugh but at last the situation got so unbearable that I explained,

"I'm very sorry that this has happened, Mr. Mustard. I hope you won't feel hardly to me because of it"—Here I floundered helplessly again and he broke in with an assurance that he would not and that, I am glad to say, ended it. He stayed a little while longer and carried on a jerky conversation on several subjects. I continued to feel like a fool, and I suppose it is likely Mr. M. felt like one too. Anyway, he soon went away. And I am devoutly thankful that the dreaded ordeal is over.

Sunday, July 5, 1891
Laurel Hill Farm

This has been a most delightful day. I was to come out here to-day. Willy came in to Bible Class and said he would call for me after it was over. Shortly after I got home Mustard also called to say good-bye, as he leaves tomorrow. Really, I was never so heartily glad to see the last of anyone in my life before.

Soon after Will came and we set off. I was glad to get out of the house for Mrs. Montgomery was in a white fury over my going at all. Will and I had a lovely drive and got here at six. Mr. Pritchard's house is in such a pretty place. Lolla and I had such an enthusiastic meeting. Mr. Agnew and Mr. Gunn—a pair of Laura's admirers—were also here. We had such fun. After tea Willy and I and Laura and Mr. A.—poor Gunn wasn't in it—went for a long, delightful ramble through the green fields just starred with all kinds of flowers. Then we came back and sat at the front-door until dark. Presently another gentleman came along—a Mr. Weir who is likewise all broke up on Laura—and we adjourned to the parlor to finish up our Sunday evening with some hymns. I sat down on one corner of the sofa and Will sat down on the other—a very proper arrangement to be sure. But there must

have been something queer about that sofa because the space between us grad-
ually narrowed in the most mysterious manner until it wasn't there at all! I'm sure
I never moved. There I just sat in my corner! Laura sat on the organ stool and Mr.
A. hung over her, bending down very close at times—to turn the music of course!
They sang *for* the rest of us and *to* each other. Willy and I had such fun watching
them and intercepting numberless kiss-and-let-me-die-love looks. We snickered
to ourselves under cover of the music—but didn't spend *all* our time watching
Laura and Andrew. I daresay if anybody had been watching *us* they wouldn't have
found it bad fun either—but of that deponent sayeth nothing.

Finally the gentlemen took their departure and Laura and I came upstairs where
we are now, all ready for bed. But we don't expect to do a great deal of sleeping
tonight. We are just going to *talk*.

To-night on the sofa I got Will to give me back my ring but I promised to give it
to him for "keeps" tomorrow. He also asked me to give him a lock of my hair and
although I pretended to refuse I *may* change my mind.

It's all rather funny, isn't it? I wonder if this will ever come to anything. No, of
course it won't. We will just be good friends. I *like* Will better than any boy I ever
met but I *know* I don't love him—he just seems like a brother or a jolly good
comrade to me.

Tuesday, July 7, 1891

Laura and I didn't talk *quite* as late last night but our eyes rebelled this morning.
We wrote a "ten-year" letter to each other in the forenoon and spent the afternoon picking berries with Will. It is so delightful here—just like home. And it is
so strange and lovely to feel that I can move around and talk without feeling
myself constantly under the espionage of a hostile and malevolent eye, ever on the
alert for anything that can be twisted and interpreted to my disadvantage.

Tuesday, July 21, 1891
Prince Albert

I've been sick, off and on, ever since writing last, with some kind of intermittent
fever. I've really had a miserable time and have swallowed enough horrible
medicine to kill or cure anyone. The truth of the matter is I've been working like a
slave for the past eight months and I've just gone beyond my strength. I've had to
do all the work of this house, except the washing, and help tend the baby, besides,
while Mrs. Montgomery parades the streets or visits with her relatives.

I spent a couple of days after my worst attack up on the hill with the McTaggarts.
Mrs. McTaggart is such a dear old soul. Her daughter does not resemble her in
any respect. I had a good rest and a lovely time while up there. One morning I was
a little amused. Mrs. McTaggart, out in the kitchen, told her youngest son Willy,
a bright lad of twelve, that he must go down town and stay for the day at our place,
since father had to be away. "I just won't," said Willy. "I hate going down
there—Mary is so cross."

"Hold your tongue and don't talk so," said his mother. But I noticed she didn't
say that "Mary" *wasn't* cross. It would seem that her young half-brothers have
pretty much the same opinion of Mrs. Mary Ann Montgomery as I have.

I'm better now and beginning to enjoy life again after a fashion. I was in to see Mrs. Kennedy tonight. Mrs. and Miss Gunn were there and Willy also dropped in—he seems to have contracted a chronic habit of "dropping in" places where I am! We went down to the station, but finding that the train was two hours late we didn't wait for it.

Friday, July 24, 1891

I was out to the Methodist S.S. picnic at Maiden Lake to-day and had a scrumptious time. We all went out in trams. Mrs. McLeod, Mr. & Mrs. Rochester, Mrs. Coombs and I were in the same tram and we had a very jolly drive. It is four miles out over such a beautiful trail, and Maiden Lake is a perfectly lovely spot—a long sloping hill dotted with white stemmed poplars, and at the foot a big blue lake. At first I prowled around with Aggie and Martha Thompson, although out of the corner of my eye I saw quite plainly that Will P. was shadowing us.

"Oh," you said—didn't you?—"*now* I begin to see why you had a good time." Don't be impertinent, you journal, you!

After wandering around for some time Miss T. and I sat down under a tree and were chatting away when a shadow fell over us and looking up I saw Will. He coolly sat down beside me. Miss T. evidently concluded that three was a huge crowd just then and left us alone. Will and I went for ice-cream, heard a recitation given by a school-teacher—a capital one it was, too—and then Will suggested a walk. So off we went, followed by several encouraging remarks from his chums. We had a delightful walk of over a mile. The prairies were just abloom with asters, bluebells and daisies. Will picked a bunch of daisies and sweet clover and remarking that their language was "innocence and beauty" he pinned it on my dress. He also produced a parcel of delicious candies and I nibbled at them as we walked.

When we got back we had tea. A lot of our chums were at the same table— Holdenby and Stevie and Miss Cassie and the McGregor girls—and we had no end of fun, especially over some Scotch shortbread that was nearly all dough and sandwiches minus any filling. I'm sure I hope the builders thereof weren't about or they must have writhed at our remarks.

After tea we had some jolly swings and then Will and I wandered away to a big poplar down by the lake. I cut my initials on the bark and he cut his right under and then we conjointly cut the date over them.

When going home time came I had to hustle off to catch the last tram. It was so full I had to wedge down on the floor with half a dozen others as tight as a sardine, and so had a very uncomfortable ride back to town. But then, I had the loveliest time at the picnic.

"Just because Willy walked with you," you remarked scornfully—didn't you?— "and said pretty things to you and generally made a fool of himself, over you"!!!!

Well, and what if that was why?

Friday, July 31, 1891

Picnics are all the "go" now. The Bible-class one came off to-day and was rather slow until the wind-up came. We all met at the manse in the morning. There were 17 in our tram going out and we had a very jolly time. When we got out to the place we had dinner but after that things dragged dolefully. We did try a game of baseball but it was too hot. We had some fun at tea, though Charlie Newitt and Alexina and I sat together. Newitt is an Englishman and the oddest thing that ever happened. He talks so funnily and acts so absurdly that he is as good as a play.

We left for home at 8. I sat between Laura and Will. Newitt was on the other side of Laura and he kept things stirred up. We had a most hilarious drive. About a mile from Goschen a thunderstorm came up and there was a skirmish for cloaks and umbrellas. I muffled myself in mine and Will held my umbrella over us— quite *low*—and then, as it was getting dark and everyone else was likewise lost under umbrellas I leaned back, cuddled up against him and we had a nice little talk. Among other things, we were talking of writing each other a "ten year letter." I said dreamily, "Dear me, ten years is a long time. I wonder where we'll be when we read them."

"Perhaps we'll be reading them *together*," he whispered.

I didn't say anything, only laughed rather awkwardly. It gave me a pleasant little thrill—but still, I can't quite see *that*.

Laura came home with me to stay all night. She is here now and we are just going to have a good-night's talk.

Saturday, Aug. 1, 1891

We had it—I rather guess! We *talked* and *talked* and *talked*. I never met a girl I could confide in as I can in Laura. I can tell her *everything*—the thoughts of my very inmost soul—and she is the same with me. We are twin spirits in every way. We talked until 2.30. Fancy!

Once we had a glum fit on and were squeezing each other and lamenting our approaching separation.

"Do you know," whispered Laura, "I believe Willy will just break his heart when you go away. Look here, I never say anything but I know this—he just worships the ground you tread on."

I laughed and said "nonsense". But I smiled a wee bit to myself in the darkness. It's nice to be—liked!

Sunday, Aug. 2, 1891

Had such fun in Sunday School to-day. My class is right up by the bookcase and as Will is librarian he sits there, too, and we have lots of fun on the sly. I took my "ten year letter" with me and he brought his and we exchanged. That absurd boy had directed his to "Mrs.—-". Said he didn't know what my name would be when I opened it!

Thursday, Aug. 13, 1891

There is no use in talking—such another day I never did spend in my life and—although it was good fun on the whole—I'm quite certain I never want to spend such another again. My feet feel—oh, now they *do* feel! And every bone in my body is letting me know it is there!

This morning I was up at five and flew over, according to agreement, to waken the Kennedy's who were all sleeping soundly. My pounding on the door soon dispelled their dreams and I came home and got my breakfast. My costume, when ready for a start, was certainly striking. I had on an old cotton skirt that barely reached below my knees, an old blue jersey, and a straw hat in the last stages of decrepitude. But as over all I wore my long gray mackintosh I wouldn't have looked so awfully terrificable if it hadn't have been for the hat.

We set off carrying enough cans and buckets for an army. We started for Goshen as it is down there the squaws cross and we hoped to get some of them to row us over. Our plans were rather hazy and when we did get down we had a terrific time trying to get across. A dozen times at least we raced along that river back through the thick shrubs dripping with dew until we were wet to the skin. There was no sign of any boat or squaw and though we shrieked "watoo" and "minnecossa" to the breeds in the tepee across the river until we were hoarse it was all in vain. At last we found a squaw's "dug-out" on the shore and Mrs. K. and Laura declared they could paddle it over themselves but I refused to go on the grounds that I hadn't made my will before leaving home. I was wet to the ears, mud to the knees and tired all over, so I sat down on the bank in a disconsolate heap while Mrs. K. and Laura held a council of war. It resulted in Laura's going up to a Mr. Macdonald's house near by to see if she could get a man to paddle us over. She came back without that desirable biped, however, and with her came Bella Macdonald who declared that she could paddle us over as well as any man. After much hesitation Mrs. K. and Laura decided to risk it and the three of them got into the dug-out. I told them I'd meet them in the happy land later on, as I didn't intend to drown myself just now, and they pushed off. About five yards from the shore a panic seized them all. Mrs. K. stood up and jumped clear out of the boat. Fortunately the water was only up to her knees, and she dragged the dug-out back to shore. The rest of us laughed frantically and Mrs. K. stood on a stone and wrung the water out of her skirt.

At this juncture a man came rowing down the river and took us across!

Once landed on the opposite shore we took the road to the Indian camp. It was a pretty walk and the breath of that pine wilderness was delicious. But we were getting awfully tired. It was three miles to the camp, when we inquired of a breed the way to the berry barrens. Then we sat off again with renewed faith and courage. We trudged two more weary miles until we came to where the breed had told us we would find berries. Alas for the breeds! They are truly "the fathers of lies." The berries were few and far between, and although we extracted a lot of fun out of our search fun didn't fill our gaping buckets.

At last we gave up in disgust and scrambled down the steep banks of the Little Red River to see if we could find any raspberries in default of our blueberries. What a wilderness it was! Steep banks covered with mighty, heaven-sweeping pines, weird with age; below, a thick undergrowth of poplar through which we forced our way to a most romantic little spot. In a little hollow stood a rude, deserted lumberman's hut. On all sides rose the wooded banks. We were tired out, so we sat down at the root of a huge old pine stump and ate our lunch as well as the mosquitoes would let us. A picturesque spot it was—that wild, yet beautiful wilderness, where nature ran riot in untrained luxuriance. If ever I write a novel I must put that scene in.

After lunch we resumed our hunt for blueberries but found none, and at last, wearied out, we resolved to start for home. Our feet were so sore that we had to take off our shoes and walk our five miles barefoot. When we reached the river bank we had no end of a time coaxing the squaws to take us over. They didn't want to and at one time I really feared we'd have to stay there all night. In the end they relented and took us over. We had to make three trips of it—Laura first, I next, and Mrs. K. last. When we were all safely landed at Goshen we gave a huge sigh of relief and trudged home. No more over the river excursions for me if you please!

Sunday, Aug. 16, 1891

I have felt quite mixed up to-day—sad and glad in about equal proportions. When father came downstairs this morning he kissed me and said, with a tremble in his voice,

"I had a letter from father last night and I expect you'll have to start on Monday or Thursday week."

I felt dreadfully over the thought of leaving father and just ran upstairs and cried. But then, to go back to dear old Cavendish—I just *had* to feel glad over that. And to escape from Mrs. Montgomery's ceaseless petty tyranny and underhand persecution—what a relief that will be!

I went to church this morning and after dinner went to S.S. Will, as usual, was at his post. When I told him I was going away next week he looked dreadfully glum all the rest of the service. Well, I felt glum, too.

We have had it pretty well understood that we were to correspond but he has never asked me to in just so many words. So when *he* said,

"You'll write us from Ottawa, won't you?"

I said demurely, "Who's us?"

He laughed and said, "Well, write to *me* then. How will that do?"

"It's much less ambiguous," I answered and of course I said I would.

After Bible Class Annie McTaggart came over with me to tea, as father had gone down to Colleston for Mrs. M. and the children who have been there for several days. After tea it came up a fearful thunderstorm and it is pouring rain now. Annie and I are going to church but it doesn't look as if there would be too many there.

Wednesday, Aug. 26, 1891

It has come at last—my last day in P.A. And a weary, fatiguing, heart-breaking day it has been. In the morning I packed up and spent the day making good-bye calls. After tea Mrs. Davies and Miss Patterson called to bid me good-bye, and after they had gone Mrs. Pritchard came. I was so sorry to part with her—she has been so kind to me. Laura and Willy were at Mrs. Kennedy's and Laura soon came over. Father and Mrs. M. went out and Laura and I washed up the tea dishes together. We then went into the garden where we each picked a bouquet of mignonnette, petunias and sweet peas and exchanged them for farewell keep-sakes. Will came along as we lingered at the gate in the red glow of the sunset and we all chatted very sadly. Previously, Laura had told me that Will had been in a fine worry all day for fear he wouldn't be able to get in to bid me good-bye—Mr. P. being away—and that he had written a letter to send to me in case he couldn't.

Presently Mr. and Mrs. Rochester came over and we all went in. Mr. R. gave me a letter to his people in Ottawa, bade me good-bye and went off with father to a lecture. Katie Fulcher and Lottie Stewart also dropped in and then came Fred Porter and Miss Wheeler. We were quite a roomful and were very merry but the fun all seemed a little bit strained—to me, anyhow, and Will didn't look as if he were enjoying himself extremely.

Presently the girls went and then Laura tackled Porter—who couldn't seem to see that he wasn't exactly wanted—while Will and I had a confidential chat in the corner. Will produced the letter, explained how it came to be written, and said I might as well have it anyway. After awhile it did dawn on Freddie's brain that four was a tremendous crowd just then, so he made his adieux and left. Then we three had the room to ourselves. Laura amused herself at the piano and was discreetly deaf and blind to all that went on in the corner behind her.

About ten we all went over to Mrs. Kennedy's. Laura was going to stay in to see me off but Will had to go out. He and I walked back in silence. At the steps we paused. Above us the stars were shining tranquilly in the clear August sky. About us was the soft, dewy dusk. Down the slope glimmered the lights of the town. It all looked dream-like and I felt as if I were in a dream.

"Well", he said, holding out his hand—and his voice wasn't *very* steady— "good-bye. I hope you will have a very happy time—and don't forget me."

"I'll never forget you, you may be sure," I said, as we shook hands. "Good-bye."

"Bi-bi," said he. Our hands fell apart and he was gone. I felt so badly I couldn't cry—I just felt stupid. I went up to my room and read his letter. He said in it that he loved me and always would. I curled up on my bed after I had read it and had a good cry. I felt so lonesome and horrid. If I hadn't known that Will had left town I believe I'd have run out after him.

I am very glad I came to P.A. although once I did not think I could ever say so. I have been a whole year with dear father, I have made a few good true friends whose friendship has enriched my life and I have had a very pleasant social time this summer. I will have had two fine trips and seen a good deal of Canada. Yes, indeed, I shall always be glad that I came to P.A. and I shall look back to it kindly in the years to come. I wonder if I shall ever come back to it. Perhaps I shall, if Will—but no, somehow, in spite of all, I can't think *that*—at least, not yet.

And this is the last night I shall sleep in Southview. Poor little room! How bare and desolate it seems now with all my things gone!

Thursday, Aug. 27, 1891

It's all over—the dreadful parting and all—and here I am flying along the rails to Regina and feeling fearfully lost and lonely. This morning we were all up early. After breakfast we heard the train whistle and I went slowly upstairs, put on my hat and cloak and bade farewell to little Southview. Mrs. M. did not go to the station so I said good-bye to her at the house. I could not pretend that I felt sorry for she has used me very badly indeed and I shall never be able to think of her with anything but aversion.

On our way to the station we overtook Alexina. It was a sad walk and I could hardly keep back the tears. When we got down to the station there was quite a crowd to see me off—Mr. Stovel, all the McTaggarts, Mrs. Kennedy, Laura, and the Jardines. We stood around and talked until "all aboard" was shouted.

I'm going to skip the next ten minutes. I shall not forget them if I live to be a hundred. At last they were over and the train pulled slowly out in the fresh morning sunshine. One by one my dear P.A. friends vanished and as Laura's face passed out of sight I realized that I was really off and "homeward bound."

I rushed to my seat in an agony of tears and cried for the first three miles. Then I sat up, wiped away my tears, and determined to grin! Eddie Jardine was in the seat before me; all the rest in the car were strangers. To-day has not been very interesting. Eddie is no company; he doesn't seem to know he has a tongue; and I don't think he has any ideas either. We don't get to Regina until nine and it is now seven. It is growing dark and the country is as flat as a pancake and as featureless. I feel forty different ways at once—and I do wish I could see father and Laura and Will!!

Saturday, Aug. 29, 1891
Somewhere In The Woods

It is raining and foggy. We expect to be in Fort William at one o'clock and have to wait there over night for the boat—I am making faces over this. We are in a rough country—all woods; but oh, it does my heart good to see the spruces again!

9 o'clock P.M.

Have been through a lot of fuss and worry. When we got to Fort William and disembarked I felt dreadfully at sea. Eddie is no earthly good in an emergency evidently. A gentleman on board, whose name is Porter and who belongs to the Island, advised us to go to the *Avenue Hotel*, as it is considered the best—or rather, the *least worst*! So we came here. If it *is* the best I am glad we did not strike the worst!

As the place is crowded I had to be satisfied with a wretched little room right at the head of the stairs. It is about as big as a closet and utterly destitute of conveniences—except a cracked basin and pitcher. There wasn't even a match wherewith to light a smoky lamp to curl my demoralized "bangs." However, it was Hobson's choice for I couldn't camp in the street. After a poor dinner I went to this charming apartment and tried to fight off the blues. It was pouring rain outside but anything was preferable to that dreary room, so I put on my coat and cap and sallied out. For about an hour I rambled around and in spite of the rain I rather enjoyed it. Fort William is a pretty place. The mountain scenery around it is very beautiful and there are some nice houses. But it is all as yet pretty rough; the streets are full of charred unsightly stumps among which promenade numerous pigs!

After tea I went out again, for that room got on my nerves. How lonely I felt! Last Saturday night I was in Prince Albert with Laura and Will, and now here I was, a thousand miles away, prowling alone about the streets of Fort William. If only Will and Laura had been with me what a jolly time we could have had! Then the rain and grime and discomfort could only have been a joke for us.

Sunday, Aug. 30, 1891
One O'Clock
Fort William, Ontario
This is a perfectly lovely day—couldn't be finer. This morning after breakfast I concluded to go to church so, after inquiring my way to a Presbyterian church I sallied out. As it was not yet church time, however, I prowled around a bit to see the sunny side of Fort William. In my ramblings I fell in with Eddie J. and we walked about a mile down the railroad track to get a good look at "the mountain". When we stopped it didn't seem to be any nearer than before—the distances in regard to these mountains are very deceptive. When we got back to the church we heard singing and thought we were late. I was quite taken aback to find only about a dozen people in the building. I slipped into a back pew where I looked around and wondered if that were all the Presbyterians Fort William could scare up. But I soon found it was not a regular service. We had strayed into some sort of a Bible class and it was decidedly dull. After it was over we hurried back to the hotel and got our dinner. We are just ready to leave and I am thankful for this hotel is the dirtiest and most uncomfortable place I ever was in.

Sunday Evening
Ten O'Clock
Have been having a lovely time. We came to the boat at one. It is the "Manitoba" and she is a dandy. The promenade deck is the favorite resort. The sunset on the lake this evening was superb. I am writing this in the saloon under the brilliant electric light, while a hum of conversation rises from the groups around me. I am very sleepy. This hasn't seemed like Sunday at all. I wonder how poor Will got on teaching my class to-day.

Monday, Aug. 31, 1891
A glorious day—fresh breezes, blue skies, blue waters. I have enjoyed every minute of it, haunting the promenade deck, reading and writing at intervals. At noon we got to the "Soo" and went through the "locks" of the canal, a very interesting experience. We were there until 3 o'clock. The American side of the "Soo" is very pretty but I must admit the Canadian side is very scrubby-looking. When we got out of the locks we passed down the St. Mary River. The scenery was exquisite. Then we emerged into Lake Huron.

Tuesday, Sept. 1, 1891
3 O'Clock P.M.

Am on my way to Toronto. This morning we were in the Georgian bay and at noon we sighted Owen Sound—the jumping-off place. The train was waiting for us and off we went at a dizzy rate. The country is lovely. Ontario is a beautiful place.

Evening 11 O'Clock

We reached Toronto at 4 and as I had 5 hours to stay there I decided to go and see the McKenzies'. Eddie's cousin met him and we took a street car and drove three miles up Sherbourne St. to Mr. McKenzie's house. I was delighted with Toronto. It is a beautiful city. When we got to my destination I got off, bade Eddie good-bye—not at all regretfully—and ran up the steps. To my disappointment I found that Mr. and Mrs. McKenzie, Gertie and Mabel were out in the country. However, the governess and a Miss Campbell who was there were exceedingly kind and so were the children. I had a lovely time. Later on Rod McK. came in. He is very nice and I spent a delightful evening. At 8.30 Rod drove me to the depot and put me on board the train. I am to be in Ottawa in the morning but I have to change cars at Smith's Falls during the night.

Wednesday, Sept. 2, 1891

Arrived in Ottawa at 5 this morning. Not a trace could I see of Grandpa Montgomery so I took a street car and went to the Windsor Hotel where I knew he was staying. Here I found that he had gone down to meet me. He soon came back in a great flurry, bless his dear old heart, but calmed down when he saw me safe and sound. When he had to go to the senate I went out to do a bit of shopping. Ottawa is nice but not nearly so nice as Toronto. When Grandpa came back he said he had met a Mr. and Mrs. Hooper of Ch'Town who were going to leave for home tomorrow and he thought I had better go down with them, as he cannot go for some time yet.

After dinner Grandpa took me all through the Parliament buildings. They are magnificent. I sat down for a minute in the Governor General's chair and felt at least two inches taller after that, of course! The library is fine. Wouldn't I like to ransack it!

Then we attended a session of the Senate. The Senate Chamber is beautiful. We met the Hoopers there and we all went up to the gallery of the House of Commons and heard Sir Richard Cartwright speak on the Census. Then Grandpa showed us all around Parliament Square. It is beautiful and we saw the Chaudiere Falls in the distance.

Thursday, Sept. 3, 1891
Ten O'Clock
Montreal

....We left Ottawa this afternoon and here we are at the St. Lawrence Hall. We came by the Intercolonial. I am simply tired out and am going straight to bed.

Friday, Sept. 4, 1891

We left Montreal early this morning. It was very wet and dismal. We passed through the Victoria Bridge—the longest iron tubular bridge in the world. All day we have travelled through Quebec. The scenery didn't amount to much. At noon we reached Point Levis, opposite the city of Quebec. I saw the famous plains of Abraham and the Montmorency Falls. Mrs. Hooper is very nice but the same can't be said of her lord and master. I don't like him at all. It is dark now and we are somewhere near Miramichi. This time to-morrow night I shall be in dear old P.E.I. Isn't that good to think about?

Saturday, Sept. 5, 1891
3 O'Clock P.M. Northumberland Strait

A beautiful day—and here I am in sight of the Island! We will be there in another hour and meanwhile I am feasting my eyes on its distant green hills. This morning we got into Moncton at 5 after a very miserable, cold, sleepless night. We had to stay in Moncton till ten, so went to the Brunswick Hotel. At 10 we left and at one we reached Pointe du Chene, where we took the boat. It has been very rough but I have not been at all seasick. I kept an eager look-out for land and the minute I saw it I flew like the wind to get a good look at the "ould sod".

Eleven O'Clock
Park Corner, P.E. Island

Here I am!!! We got to Summerside at four this afternoon. It *did* seem a rather chilly home-coming for there was not a face in all the crowd that I knew. Never mind—it was home and that was enough. Still, I *was* tired and lonely; and I had to wait two dreary hours in the station for the train. I got to Kensington about sunset, trudged up to the Commercial House and hired a team to take me to Park Corner.

How I did enjoy that drive! It was all so lovely—the beautiful sunset, the rich harvest scenery, and the aroma of the firs along the road. I just gazed my eyes out. And when we came in sight of the sea I could not speak for emotion. I listened to its hollow roar in unspeakable delight. It was quite dark when we drove up to the Senator's door. The first face I saw was Lucy Pickering's and then Uncle Jim and Uncle Cuthbert came running up. They hardly knew me at first—they thought I had changed so much. After tea I hastened over to Uncle John Campbell's. Aunt Annie and Uncle John were sitting in the kitchen and they actually did not know me until I told them who I was. *Such* a time as we had! The girls were in bed but they got up and came tearing down. Clara and Stella have both grown so tall I wouldn't have known them either. I am going to stay here all night.

Tuesday, Sept. 8, 1891
Cavendish, P.E.I.

I am at home—actually at home in dear old C. and it is jolly. Uncle Crosby brought me down this afternoon. It was such a delightful drive. When we got to Stanley I began to feel pretty well excited and my excitement increased all the rest of the way as I gazed my eyes out on all the familiar spots until Uncle Crosby must have thought he had a crazy girl on his hands.

When we got here, I sprang down, tore in, hugged everybody, and ran through every room in the house. Then I ran over to Uncle John's. All the children have grown especially Kate.

At dusk Lu and I set out for a walk. We went to the school first, then to Uncle Jimmy's and the manse. Then we ran down to Robertson's to see Miss Gordon but found her away. On our way back whom should we meet but Pensie and hadn't we a time!

Wednesday, Sept. 9, 1891
After dinner to-day Lu and I went to the shore and along to the old "Hole in the Wall." There was quite a surf on and it was so lovely to see the big waves rushing up into the old cave and flinging showers of foam to the very top of the cliff. To-morrow is dear Mollie's birthday and I am going over as I am dying to see her.

Friday, Sept. 11, 1891
Yesterday afternoon I set off. I went to the school first and saw all the girls. The old school is unchanged. There were the old desks where Mollie and I and Nate and Jack sat—how long ago was it? It seems *ages*. There were the initials cut into the porch, there was the old nail I used to hang my hat on—we girls all had our own particular "nail" and woe betide a trespasser—there written above it by Nate my nickname in our old cipher " ꙅꙩλλꞑ ";   there on the walls the scribbled names of dozens of flirting couples, and then the old hacked door. What memories haunt that poor old school!

When I got over to Mollie's I found, much to my disappointment, that she and her mother had gone to Rustico and would not be back until evening. As Lillie was home however I waited for them and at 8 they came. Mollie and I had a most enthusiastic meeting. I stayed all night and we talked until nearly morning. Bessie Fraser is away in Nova Scotia and Jack and Nate are both off to college again.

Saturday, Sept. 12, 1891
Mollie came over this afternoon and we had a high old time. After tea we put on our hats, linked our arms, and sallied forth in old time fashion, down the lane, under the birches, until we reached the school, wrapped in drowsy September sunshine. We pushed up a window and climbed in. How deserted the poor old school looked with its rows of empty seats! We finally climbed out again and found our way down the path to the brook. We loitered around familiar spots for awhile and talked over old times. We finally pulled up in "Pierce's Woods," where we sat down to rest and fell into a reverie. I gazed dreamily down the vistas. The yellow sunshine fell lazily athwart the tall gray spruces and the gossamers glimmered like threads of silver among the trees. The crickets were chirping and all the air was full of music. How jolly it would have been to have seen Jack or Nate come whistling through the woods as they were wont to do of yore. At last, recalling ourselves to realities, we sauntered home, with a lonely sort of feeling, as if we somehow belonged to those past days and had no business in the present at all.

Sunday, Sept. 20, 1891

Went to church to-day and saw a lot more old acquaintances, including the famous Clemmie, who actually flung her arms about me and kissed and hugged me until I almost gasped for breath. Clemmie can "put on" when she likes. I suppose that is uncharitable. But I cannot easily forget all that girl has done and said against me in times past.

But, speaking of kissing, I must tell you of my meeting yesterday with old Mrs. John Wyand. It was too funny for any use. She came for the mail and I went out to see her. I held out my hand for a cordial handshake with the poor old soul but lo, she opened her capacious arms and gave me an embrace and kiss that almost overwhelmed me. Then, backing up to sit down on her chair, she mistook the place and sat plump down on the floor instead! You should just have seen her!

Tuesday, Sept. 22, 1891

Had a letter from Will to-day and I consider the event to be worth recording. It was a long letter and very interesting. I was so glad to hear from him. He seems pretty *lonesome*!

Monday, Oct. 4, 1891
Cavendish, P.E.I.

This morning I drove grandpa to the station, as he was going to town to attend an Exhibition. Just as I left Hunter River for home it began to rain and was soon a very dirty day. The rain simply poured down—but I rather enjoyed it. I must have some duck in my composition for I always love to be out in a rainstorm. At tea-time Aunt Emily and Uncle John Montgomery arrived, likewise on their way to the Exhibition.

Thursday, Oct. 22, 1891

I finished writing a sketch of my trip home to-day and sent it to the *Patriot*. I have been working at it for a good while. I wrote it because Grandpa wanted me to.

This afternoon Lu and I set off for Sam Wyand's field, with a basket of apples. The "Intercolonial" is beautiful now and we found loads of delicious gum along it. When we got through we had some excitement dodging Laird's cows and climbing the breakneck fences that abound back there. We broke a longer on every fence we climbed to-day and sometimes more than one. The lane to the field is as pretty as ever and as is the dear old field as it lay bathed in amber sunshine, amid its crimson maple trees. We loitered around it for awhile and then went on. In the next field were Wyand's cows and as they had an unfriendly look we had to make a wide detour through thick woods and over *awful* fences to avoid them. I don't know how it is that we have got to be such cowards over strange cows. We never used to be so. Finally we reached the fence below "Montana." It is one of old Mrs. John Wyand's construction so you may be sure we destroyed some of its symmetry in getting over it. Then we went up the path but when we reached the top—oh, horrors! There right before us were two cows and they *looked* simply savage. In a panic we turned and flew down that path headlong. We struck against the worst panel in the lot and over it went with a crash! We ran until we got to the corner. Such idiots! To go any further was out of the question for nothing could induce us to face those cows again. So we took to exploring all the fields around and had no end of fun in spite of the fences. Then we went back to Sam Wyand's field, sat down under the maples and demolished the rest of our apples. We had no end of a time getting home, in deadly fear of cows, and smashed some more fences of course.

Miss Gordon is going to get up another school concert for Xmas and wants all her old pupils to help in it also.

Tuesday, Nov. 3, 1891
Cavendish, P.E.I.
When the mail came to-day I got an invitation to a wedding—Uncle Cuthbert Montgomery's, no less. He is to be married tomorrow night to Miss Mary McLeod. I have never met her. They say she is a very nice girl. It is high time Uncle Cuthbert was married. He is not overly young now.

Saturday, Nov. 7, 1891
Grandpa drove me up to Park Corner Wednesday morning. Just by Stanley we met a young man in a buggy who looked very intently at us as he passed but we took no account of the circumstances then. We got to Aunt Annie's in due time and after dinner I went over to the Senator's. Aunt Maggie Sutherland and Aunt Mary McIntyre were there, "baking and brewing and boiling and stewing." And now I discovered that the young man we had met was my cousin, James McIntyre on his way to Cavendish to bring me up. When he got back we had a hearty laugh over our hit—or—missing. He is quite nice and nice-looking. When we went to Long River he drove me over. It was a glorious evening and we had no end of fun. There was a white frost and a beautiful young moon "with the old one on her arm".

The bride was dressed in white muslin with a tulle veil. Uncle Jim was best man and her sister, Miss Lizzie McLeod, was bridesmaid. In a few minutes Uncle Cuthbert had crossed his Rubicon and I had a new aunt.

I must say the rest of the evening was frightfully dull. We just sat in a row around the parlor and stared at each other like simpletons. Nobody seemed to be acquainted with anybody else. I was very glad when it was all over. But Jim and I had another merry drive home through the keen starlit night.

….I have been reading my various printed articles over to-night. I wonder if I shall ever be able to do anything with my pen. Dr. Stovel assured me that I would but that was only a guess. If I could only manage to get a little more education! But that seems impossible. I wish I could peep into my future for a moment—and yet no! What if it were gloomy!

Monday, Nov. 16, 1891
This evening I went down to the school as we are beginning our practice for the concert. Dear me, it seemed at once so strange and yet so natural to be in that school again. But there were so many familiar faces missing—Charlie, Asher, John, Everett, Mollie, Ella, Mamie and Nate. Their seats were filled by a lot of

"kids" who knew and cared nothing about those old days. We got underway with recitations and dialogues and made a fair start. Nellie is as cranky as ever.

Thursday, Nov. 19, 1891
This afternoon I went to see Mrs. Spurr and had a very nice time. She showed me Nate's class picture. He is not at all well taken. Still it is like him.
....After dark to-night I set to work to study. I can't quite give up the hope that I may get to college yet and meanwhile I don't want to forget all I've learned. So I have mapped out a course of studies for the winter. To-night I began with English history, Physical Geography, Latin, geometry and English literature.

Thursday, Dec. 3, 1891
Spent this afternoon at Mollie's and had a fine time. We came over to prayer-meeting and sat with Pensie. Of course it was dreadful but Pen and I got to laughing at several things and stop we could not. We shook with smothered mirth the whole time. Fortunately we were away in the back seat so we escaped notice.

I had a letter from Mr. Mustard to-day. It was a frightfully dry epistle. He also sent me a Knox College magazine—very exciting literature!

Friday, Dec. 4, 1891
Everett Laird came down to the school to practice this evening. He is the "teacher" in our dialogue "The Country School". He is the same old Everett with his dry, funny remarks, and we had lots of fun. I was up to Literary to-night. There was a programme. I recited and played a couple of pieces—much to the rage of Deacon Arthur Simpson who hates me almost as much as he hates music. He hates music because he was born that way; and he hates me because I belong to a family who have never given any indication of thinking Deacon Arthur the most wonderful man in the world. The Deacon is known to irreverent young Cavendish as "Pa" and his pallid, malicious wife as "Ma" because of their habit of addressing each other thus upon all occasions. I think Arthur Simpson is the one and only man in the world I hate with an undiluted hatred. I hate him so much that it is nice and stimulating. And it is such fun to do things—perfectly innocent things which other people like, such as playing on the Hall organ etc.—which infuriate him!

Saturday, Dec. 19, 1891
Cavendish, P.E.I.
Really, it's a wonder I'm alive to tell the tale! In fact, I'm not quite sure I *am* alive—I'm so tired and stiff and generally petered out. We all met at the hall this morning to get it ready for our concert which is to come off Monday night. Lu and I went up early to find Ches and a good fire awaiting us. Most of the others soon arrived and we fell to work in good earnest. We first put up a big fir motto "Welcome" in the centre of the wall, high up, and decorated it with pink and white tissue roses. Then we put up another motto, "We Delight In Our School" and just as we were struggling with it along came Austin and Everett—and guess who else! Why, Jack himself—"Snap" in the flesh, home for his Xmas holidays from Prince of Wales. You may be sure we had an enthusiastic meeting. Jack is

the same old sixpence. He is tall and slim and very nice-looking.

After we got the curtain hung we had a "dress rehearsal," and then finished with the decorations. On one side of the "Division" charter we hung a Union Jack and on the other a scarlet banner with a Latin motto *"Non scholae sed vitae discimus,"* on it, ornamented with ferns and moss rosebuds. Then we put a triple arch of fir sprays over the banners and charter. Ches and I built this and were all puffed up with earthly pride over our success. Then everybody went home except Annie, Mamie, Everett, Ches and I. We cleaned things up, arranged the seats and swept the floor, raising a most tremendous dust in the process. Will Stewart came along about 8 with a buggy and drove us all home. We had a lively drive.

Tuesday, Dec. 22, 1891
Our wonderful concert is over and everyone, up to latest accounts, has survived. Yesterday was growly; it spit snow all day but cleared up beautifully at night. We had stacks of fun behind the curtain, peering out at the arrivals or prinking before the glass in our improvised dressing room. There was a good audience and the programme went off slickly. There wasn't a hitch or breakdown from beginning to end. Our dialogue brought down the house. I am glad it is so well over but I am sorry it is past. I shall feel quite lost having no pleasant practices to go to. We've had so much fun at them.

This evening I have been reading Washington Irving's "Sketch Book". He is delightful—his style is so easy and graceful. "Rip Van Winkle" is charming.

Thursday, Dec. 31, 1891
The old year did not slip away in a green twilight and a pinky-yellow sunset. Instead, it is going out in a wild white bluster and blow. It doesn't seem possible that another year has gone. Taken all around, it has been a very happy year for me.

I am cosily tucked up in bed now, sitting up to write this. It is a wild night out—one of the nights when the storm spirit hustles over the bare frozen meadows and black hollows and the wind moans around the house like a lost soul and the snow drives sharply against the shaking panes—and people like to cuddle down and count their mercies.

20. *River Street, P.A.* [*Prince Albert*]

21. *Laura Pritchard*

22. *Father*

23. *Birches above the Trouting Pool*
[*Cavendish*]

24. *"Hole in the wall"*
[Cavendish shore]

25. *Grandpa Montgomery's house*
[Park Corner]

1892

Tuesday, Jan. 10, 1892

I went to church this morning like a dutiful Presbyterian, and spent the afternoon and evening reading Emerson's Essays. To be interested in Emerson you must get right into the groove of his thought and keep steadily in it. Then you can enjoy him. There can be no skipping or culling if you want to get at his meaning. I admire and appreciate Emerson, although I do not always understand him—I suppose I am too young. His style is clean, precise, and cold, with all its beauty. I think his ideals are rather impracticable in this sort of a world. He doesn't seem to take "human nature" sufficiently into account.

What a difference there is between Emerson and Irving. Yet each is a fine writer in his own way. Emerson had the great *intellect*, Irving the greater *heart*— "which is the better the gods alone know." But for my own part I go in for the *heart*. I like the jolly, *lovable* folks ten times better than the clever, brainy folks who are not lovable—and *livable*.

Friday. Afternoon. Feb. 13, 1892

Grandma went up to Park Corner last Tuesday and I've been head cook and chief bottle washer ever since—not the most enviable position in the world where a man like grandfather is concerned. Nothing I do pleases him when grandma is away.

Last night was stormy and Lu came over with me from prayer-meeting to stay all night. We went to bed and were just dropping off to sleep when suddenly the kitchen door opened and a minute after I heard Uncle John asking if we were in bed. Grandpa called out "yes" and then Uncle J. said "There's two young McIntyres from town stuck out here in a snow bank."

Lu and I sprang up, dressed and hastened out to get on a fire. I did not mind that in the least, but grandpa acted so crankily and disagreeably that I felt dreadfully bad. He is always so unjust and insulting when any of my friends come to the house and this time he was worse than I have ever seen him before.

Uncle John brought them in all covered with snow and it turned out that it was James McIntyre and some Mr. Mytton from town on their way to Uncle John's with a "trial" organ. They had got upset in a snowdrift behind our barn. I was glad to see James, or would have been if I could have made him welcome. Mytton was a case! He was a thin little Englishman, dressed as if for a party in light summer clothes and patent leather shoes and he was half frozen.

We got them down to the fire and thawed them out. Grandpa had not got up at all and—although it was not just easy for me to arrange for them and show them to their room etc.—I was very thankful for this, for I knew he would only have made a show of himself if he had.

Finally, Lu and I got back to bed. We decided that we must get up at six in the morning to get breakfast for them and be on hand if they should wander down too early and fall into the clutches of grandfather. So we two geese determined to stay awake all night for fear that if we went to sleep we wouldn't wake early enough. Now *wasn't* that a brilliant idea! We lay and laughed for about two hours over Mytton—who had had a spasm of toothache when he came in and who would have had a spasm of another kind if he had known all the fun we were making of him with the laudable purpose of keeping ourselves awake. Then, do our best, we began to get alarmingly sleepy, so we sat up, lit a candle and played parchesi until we were too cold to play anymore. Then we put out the light and fell to talking again. We extracted a good deal more fun out of Mytton and fought off our drowsiness heroically. I never knew I was asleep until I was conscious that it was broad daylight and that Lu was bending over me saying, "It's half past seven." Perhaps I didn't jump!

But fortunately the boys were not up. When they came down I had breakfast ready for them and although Grandpa was very surly to them he at least refrained from insulting them openly, as I had dreaded he would do. After breakfast he simply turned them out, for he told them to go on up to Stewart's and they might sell their organ there. So they went and under the circumstances I was heartily relieved to see them go, for I felt bitterly mortified....

Tuesday, Feb. 16, 1892
Park Corner, P.E.I.
Here I am, a somewhat weary mortal. I have come up to give Clara, George and Stella a quarter's music lessons. I rather guess we are going to have some fun. I am too dead tired to write anymore.

Monday, Feb. 22, 1892
Park Corner
I'm really half dead from laughing. Clara and I talked most of the night last night. When the girls came home from school to-day we began to make and eat pancakes and we laughed until the pancakes nearly choked us. My head is splitting from the racket. It is all very foolish I suppose but it is delightful foolishness.

This New London is really a dreadful place for gossip and "fights". "Eye hath not seen, nor ear heard, neither hath it entered into the heart of man to conceive" what the New Londoners, and especially the natives of that section of it known as French River, can do when they get started. Most of them seem to spend half their time deliberately inventing pure, unmixed fiction and the other half in diligently circulating the same for Gospel truth. Every day I am treated to some harrowing account of a quarrel or a feud. Even Aunt and Uncle indulge entirely too much in gossip. I have vowed a deep and solemn vow that during my stay in Park Corner my conversation will be yea, yea, and nay, nay, only.

Saturday, Feb. 27, 1892
Although it was freezing cold to-night Cade, Stell and I went to the Literary Society in French River Hall. Quite a crowd was there. Capt. Geo. McLeod came up to me and we had quite a talk. He asked me for a recitation for their programme and then paid me some compliments on my writings—"told me to be sure and keep on." Ta-ta, Capt. George, that is just what I mean to do.

Then we drifted into an interesting discussion about books, especially "Robert Elsmere" which is setting the literary world by the ears just now. As I have not read it Capt. George got it out of the library for me.

Cade and I sat together. Edwin Simpson sat right across from us. He is attending school here and although we've never been introduced I've seen him several times and heard a good deal of him. He is very nice-looking and has fine eyes.

Midway in the programme was a "social intermission", in which everybody talked. Lem McLeod came over to me and we had a nice little chat. Also Edwin S. came up and spoke to me. I had a nice time all round.

Sunday, Feb. 28, 1892
This has been a very lazy Sunday. It was too cold to go to church, so after breakfast Cade and I betook ourselves upstairs and went to bed again, where we talked and napped till dinner time. We got up then, helped devour a roast goose, went back to bed and slept till tea-time....

Monday, Mar. 7, 1892
....I am invited to a wedding next Wednesday night. Uncle Jim Montgomery is to be married to Mrs. Eliza Johnson of Clifton.

Thursday, Mar. 10, 1892
Park Corner, P.E.I.
I feel so sleepy I don't know whether I can write connectedly or not. Yesterday it poured rain but after dinner I went over to the Senator's. James McIntyre was out and drove me over to Clifton. Quite a long procession of us went and such roads I never was on before. We went by the ice, although it was very bad, and passed over some pretty risky places. Just below Clifton we were brought to a dead stop by open water ahead. So we had to turn and go all the way back to Anderson's, where we took the road again and it was wilder than ever. But we got over at last and had a very pleasant evening. Addie Johnson was bridesmaid and James McIntyre was best man.

At eleven we all started for Park Corner and came around by the Long River road. I shall never forget that awful drive as long as I live. The night was pitchy dark and our horse did nothing but rear and plunge and balk in the slush and soft snow, falling down now and then by way of variation. I got deathly sick from sheer nervous terror and was almost demoralized by the time we got to the Senator's. However, after I had recovered, I had a fine time. We had tea and played games for several hours. As the Clifton people could not go back before daylight there were not enough beds in the house to go around so Jim McIntyre, Jim Crosby, Lewis McIntyre, Russell Crosby, Will Sutherland, Louise Crosby (all cousins of mine) Addie Johnson and I said we'd sit up the rest of the night in the parlor. We sat around the fire, told ghost stories galore, and kept up a racket of jest and laughter all night. When morning dawned we were a pretty seedy-looking lot. I nearly fell asleep at the breakfast table and I actually did at prayers. After breakfast I came straight over home and went to bed—never woke up until 4 o'clock and then felt as if I wanted to sleep half a dozen weeks longer. However, a wild frolic with Clara this evening has pretty well wakened me up.

Saturday, Mar. 12, 1892
Park Corner, P.E.I.
....This evening the girls and I went down to our pet dissipation, "Literary". They had a debate on that venerable conundrum "Which was the greater general, Napoleon or Wellington!" Wellington carried the day and then we adjourned. When Clara and I got out Lem McLeod asked us if he and Jack Sims might drive us home. They had a nice comfy pung so we scrambled in, along with Jim Crosby who invited himself, and had a merry drive of it.

Wednesday, Mar. 16, 1892
A glorious day this—mild and sunny; moreover, it has been one of those rare ones when everything goes exactly right and life seems bright and serene. This morning I took a walk through the woods down to the spring—the loveliest spot. Oh, it was all so beautiful! The calm, fresh loveliness of the woods seemed to enter into my very spirit with voiceless harmony—the harmony of clear blue skies, mossy trees and gleaming snow. All the little fears and chafings shrank into nothing and vanished. Standing there beneath that endless blue dome, deep with the breathing of universal space, I felt as if all the world had a claim on my love—as if there were nothing of good I could not assimilate—no noble thought I could not re-echo. I put my arm around a lichened old spruce and laid my cheek against its rough side—it seemed like an old friend.

Saturday, Mar. 26, 1892
Uncle Cuthbert, Aunt Mary and I went down to Cavendish this morning and had a lovely drive. We came back this evening and stopped off at the hall for Literary. We had quite a nice little programme and Ed Simpson walked home with me. Such a time as we had! The girls and George and the Hiltzes and Jim Crosby and Lucy Pickering kept behind us all the way and tormented our lives out. I'm sure Ed must have been secretly furious. We talked about books etc. all the way home and pretended to ignore the racket behind. I don't know whether I like Ed or not. He is clever and can talk about everything, but he *is* awfully conceited—and worse still, *Simpsony*. To anyone who knows the Simpsons a definition of that quality is unnecessary; and to anyone who doesn't it is impossible.

Saturday, April 9, 1892
Park Corner
We had a hooking here to-day and Jean and Annie Howatt, Edie Pillman, Hannah, Beatrice and Eveline McLeod, Blanch and Mrs. Donald, Sue Stewart, Mamie Cameron and Josie Hiltz were here. We had such fun. In the evening we all went down to Literary and the walking was simply dreadful. The first thing at Literary was a big "row" between Captain George and Albert Simpson over some constitutional clause. They squabbled until nearly nine and we didn't get out till ten. It was pitch dark and the mud was awful. Stell and I were standing by the steps when Lem came slyly up. I made some original remark about the mud and he made some brilliant comment on the rain; then he managed to get up enough spunk to ask if he might see me home and we slipped away. We came home a different way from the others and had lots of fun. Lem is a rather nice, jolly boy but there's nothing much in him.

Saturday, May 7, 1892
Literary to-night and everybody and his brother were there. First and foremost the powers that be had another lively skirmish which occupied so much time that the programme was cut severely short. Meanwhile, I was wondering how I could escape from Lem and Ed—for it makes so much gossip when there are two of them trying to rival each other in that fashion, and besides I am sick and tired of being teased about them. So I made up my mind to rush right out the moment Literary adjourned and get away up the road before the boys could get out. Accordingly, I made a dive for the door—but so did everyone else apparently and I found myself packed in a crowded, squirming mass below the stove. I pushed frantically on, flattering myself that I was far ahead of the boys, when I discovered Lem right behind me and Ed right beside me. I was as mad as a wasp. I made another wild effort to get through the crowd and as a result got jammed in between the two of them! But at last we got to that blessed door. I clutched Clara's arm, bolted headlong down the steps, and gained the road in safety. But I hadn't got my breath before Lem had caught up with us; he gasped out a request to see me home and whisked me off before I could answer yea or nay. Since it had to be one of them I was glad it was Lem. Ed is much cleverer but somehow I never feel at ease in his company. Lem and I had lots of fun coming home, although the crowd of factory boys on the road kept up a terrific racket just behind us.

Tuesday, June 7, 1892
I feel rather disgruntled to-night. We went to prayer meeting at French River to-night and as I'm going home to-morrow I wanted to have a nice little racket to finish up with. Ella Johnson of Long River and her cousin Dan McKay were there and when we came out they came up and offered to drive me home. I didn't want to go because I could see Lem waiting out on the moonlit road, but I had no excuse for not going. Or rather, to refuse to go and then to walk home with Lem would have seemed too silly. So I assented reluctantly for very shame's sake. Lem waited till the very last and I'm sure he would be vexed when he saw me drive away with Ella and Dan. I'm not a bit "struck" on Lem and I don't care about this

on that account; but we have been good friends and have had lots of fun together this spring, and I wanted to have a farewell walk to-night and say good-bye decently by way of a pleasant wind-up; but it's all spoiled now.

Monday, June 20, 1892
Cavendish, P.E.I.
I've been home ever since the 8th. I was dreadfully lonesome at first but I am getting over it now and beginning to enjoy myself again. I went to prayer meeting to-night—Mr. Archibald is holding revival meetings now—and as Pensie and I were too early we went for a walk to the school where we crawled in at a window and enjoyed a good long chat about various matters. Miny Robertson passed and we called her in too. We saw a crowd of boys coming up the hill and had to lie low till they passed for we didn't want them to see us. Then, afraid we would be too late we rushed to the window, flung it up, and Miny and I sprang out. "Hold the sash," cried Pen—but she let go and jumped before we could catch it. It came down with a fearful bang and a piece split clear out of one of the panes; besides, nearly all the putty fell off. If the trustees get on our trail they'll make us repent in sackcloth and ashes.

Friday, June 21, 1892
Who should pop in for the mail to-day but—Nate? I ran out to see him, feeling silly—but I didn't let him see I felt so. He hasn't changed a bit except that he has grown a lot taller. He doesn't expect to be home long. Jack Laird is also home from town. It's such fun to see the boys again and have a good chat over old times.

Wednesday, June 22, 1892
I took a prowl away back to Montana this morning, to see if there was going to be any strawberries. I had a lovely walk.

Went to prayer-meeting this evening, met Pen, and we again went down to the school. We didn't go in but leaned against the northeast window for some time, talking about a lot of little matters dear to our hearts. Presently we heard a buggy coming up the hill and as we didn't want to be seen we pushed up the window to get in and hide. And then—well, I just didn't know whether I stood on my heels or my head, for there in the corner stood Miss Gordon!!! All the nonsense Pen and I had talked flashed back in naked horror over my mind. She must have heard every word we said. But I think she felt as foolish as we did at being caught. Whatever could she have been there for, all alone—and it was as dark as anything? We talked lamely to her for a few minutes to hide our confusion, and then went, gasping at each other up the road, laughing and lamenting by turns, and thanking our stars that among all the things we *had* said, we had *not* said anything about her and Geo. R. Macneill, who is going with her. I suppose we *would* have come to them sooner or later, if it hadn't have been for that providential buggy coming up the hill.

I wish Junius Simpson *would* clear his throat out before he begins to pray. Perhaps one could make out a word once in a while then, and anyhow he'd get through quicker.

Jack Laird came home with me and we had a jolly chat. College has smartened Jack up a good bit and he is very nice, although there is not a great deal in him.

Thursday, June 30, 1892
Miss Gordon was here this evening to say good-bye. She is going to Oregon. Oh, how sorry I am to part with her! I have lost a true friend—the only one in Cavendish who sympathized with me in my ambitions and efforts. I shall miss her dreadfully and I feel too blue to write anything more about anything.

Sunday, July 17, 1892
Murray is here for his vacation and yesterday he and Lu and I drove over to New London. I had a scrumptious time. Grandpa Montgomery was telling me that he had met Lieutenant Governor Schultz of the Territories in Ottawa and that he had read my article on Saskatchewan and admired it very much; and he told grandpa to ask me for my photo and anything I might have written since. Quite a compliment for little me, isn't it?...

Friday, July 22, 1892
Cavendish, P.E.I.
After sunset this evening Murray, Lu and I started off for a walk with no particular object in view save to have a good time anyway that might turn up. I do not go looking for good times with Murray by choice, for he has a tendency to rather spoil good times, unless he is the centre of them, with everybody else revolving around him, like obedient and adoring little satellites. I am not one of his satellites and consequently I am no favorite of his. Lu is, because she flatters him to the top of his head—and then ridicules him behind his back. He eats up the flattery and is happily ignorant of the ridicule.

We went in along the road. It was a lovely twilight, cool and breezy, with tones of blue and amber, green and gold, threading its dusk.

We went as far as the Baptist church and then came back. On the hill a sulky passed us with Don McKay and Jack Laird on it. Jack is teaching school at North Rustico now. At the foot of the hill Jack sprang off and joined us. We all stood there about half an hour and laughed and chatted—at least Jack and Lu and I did, while Murray glowered in silence. To Murray, it was a deadly insult that any girls, even one he disliked should take any notice of another boy when HE was around. Finally Jack and I came home by the road, while Lu and Murray went across the fields. It was very jolly to be walking up that old road with Jack again. We talked over all our old rackets and school jokes, and had a fine time.

Saturday, July 30, 1892
Little twilight "rackets" are the order of the day now. Mollie came over for the mail at dusk and we took a walk in along the road. On our way back Jack pounced out on us from among the trees, as suddenly as his namesake in a box and came along with us. We both went home with Mollie and had fine fun. Then Jack and I came back in the moonlight and Jack began to simmer; but the more sentimental *he* got the more saucy and independent I got. When he said he "loved" me I

laughed at him so much that he got sulky and and sulked for ten minutes. Then, seeing that *that* didn't worry me any he got friendly and sensible again. Jack doesn't "love" me any more than I love him. It was just the moonlight.

Monday, Aug. 1, 1892
....Who do you think came after dinner? Why, Well and Dave Nelson! You may be sure I was glad to see them. Well has changed very much and has grown stout but not tall. Dave has changed less in the face but has shot up into a slim, leggy fellow. We had no end of fun revisiting the scenes of our early life together and recalling the events, comic and tragic, of our lang-syne playdays.

Wellington and David Nelson were two orphan boys who boarded here and went to school, when I was seven to ten.
....Since I was nine I had kept a childish diary—long ago committed to the flames—in which all my small transactions were faithfully recorded every day. I was always in a state of chronic terror lest someone—the boys in particular— should see it. I generally kept it on a little secret shelf under the sitting room sofa. One winter Well began to keep a diary also and in his turn would never let me see it although of course I was devoured with curiosity. At last, in an evil hour, I chanced to discover where he hid it—between the end of the kitchen cupboard and the wall—and one night after the boys had gone to bed I went and read them—half a dozen little yellow notebooks! If you imagine that I was at rest then you are much mistaken. Satisfied curiosity counted for nothing at all and for weeks my conscience pointed the finger of scorn at me. Nine years cannot draw a very fine distinction between an honorable and a dishonorable action. Nevertheless, I was haunted unceasingly by the galling conviction that I had done something *mean*. What worse could befall me? For in our code the epithet of "mean" was to us what "nithing" was to the Saxons of old. To call a boy "a mean coward" was to offer him a deadly insult. Judge then what I suffered when I *felt* "mean" in my inmost soul. That is one of the little mistakes of my childhood which I would gladly blot out if I could and yet it was one that taught me a valuable lesson. Never since have I read anything not intended for my eyes.

I was a week older than Well. Dave was a year younger. The brothers were totally dissimilar in looks. Dave was fair, with mild blue eyes and a pouting mouth. Well was a dark handsome lad with laughing eyes and a merry face. Both boys were very hot-tempered and many a fight they had. Well was bright at his books but Dave was a born mechanic, never happier than when tinkering away with the scraps of old iron and wood in our "table drawer". Dave always got the worst of their fights for he generally lost his wits entirely. His temper was the quicker of the two and he used to get so red in the face that Well and I—I always sided with Well in right or wrong—nicknamed him "The Rooster". The application of this never failed to bring on a fight between the two boys; yet they were affectionate little fellows and would be hugging each other ten minutes after a grapple with teeth and nails. A fight was a positive enjoyment to them. Grandpa usually put a summary stop to this kind of pleasure when he was round. But one winter or autumn evening Grace Macneill got married. Aunt Annie and Aunt Emily came down to go and grandmother went with them. Aunt Annie left Clara, then a girl of about six with me and Grandpa stayed home to look after us all. He told the boys that they could fight the whole evening, if they wanted to. They took him at his word. From eight to ten the kitchen resounded with howls, yells, and thumps, as they rolled in a clinch around the floor. Clara and I stayed in the bedroom off the sitting room and played calmly there, safe from the racket and din out in the kitchen. At ten o'clock grandpa sent everybody to bed. Well and Dave were black and blue for a week but they had had the time of their lives. I'm sure they wished Grace Macneill could have got married nightly.

In the long winter evenings we would play "dominoes", "keep your temper," "tit-tat-x" and other age-old games. The boys were always very kind to me and many happy hours we had together. But one day the boys went away suddenly for good and all—so suddenly and unexpectedly that there was little time for good-byes or grief. I was sorry and lonely too, for I had few other companions. But youth forgets speedily.

They went away this evening. Well talks of going out west.

Tuesday, Aug. 9, 1892
I feel happier and more contented to-day than I have felt for a long time. It was decided to-day that I am to go to school here again and study for Prince of Wales and a teacher's license. I am delighted. I have always longed for this. I realize that I must do something for myself and this seems the only thing possible but grandpa and grandma have always been so bitterly against it that I was getting discour-aged. They have given in at last however and I am to begin school when it opens next Monday. A Miss West is the teacher. I mean to study very hard for I *must* get some more education.

Monday, Aug. 15, 1892
I went to school this morning and it seemed so natural to be there again. And yet I missed the "old crowd" so much. There are not many of them left. I got in a lot of work and had a good time. It was delicious to sit in my old seat and look through the window away down into the old spruce woods, with their shadows and sunlight and whispering. At recess I took a ramble through them by myself. They are deserted now. None of the small fry ever think of playing there. When the "old crowd" and I were small we fairly lived in the woods. Dear me, the summer is nearly gone. The asters and golden-rod are blooming and the twilights are pink and chilly.

Monday, Nov. 21, 1892
Miss West left a week ago and to-day our new teacher, Miss Selena Robinson, came. It is to be hoped that in this case at least, appearances *are* deceptive, or I much fear me that Cavendish educational institution will *not* go forward this winter by leaps and bounds. She is a short, dumpy little person, with brown eyes, excessively red cheeks, and a very expressionless face.

I am going to take up Greek. I expect it will be tough, especially the verb. I have heard a few things about the Greek verb.

Thursday, Dec. 10, 1892
Went to a magic lantern show in the hall to-night and had a fine time. Miss Robinson and I were the only girls coming east. She is quite a jolly girl when you get to know her—though she certainly isn't much of a teacher—and we had quite a gay time. Jack Laird and Elton Robertson drove us home.

Saturday, Dec. 31, 1892
Cavendish, P.E.I.
This is the last of the old year. '92 dies to-night—a glorious death, for the white earth floats in aerial silver of frost and moonshine and the sky is powdered with thousands of stars to watch its deathbed. I am sorry to see it go for it has been a very happy year for me. Will '93 be as good, I wonder. What does it hold for me in its upsealed days and months?

26. Uncle John Campbell's house going up from the bridge
[Park Corner]

27. Clara Campbell
[Park Corner]

28. *Myself at 17*
[1891]

29. *Park Corner scholars, 1892*
Back row: Mr. McIntyre, Clara Campbell, Louise Crosby, Addie McLeod, Jack Sims, Edwin Simpson,
Bessie Cameron, Stanley Bernard, Josie Hiltz, Lem McLeod, Irving Howatt.
Middle row: Maurice Cameron, Stella Campbell, Hannah McLeod, Nettie Palmer, Unknown,
Beatrice McLeod, Unknown, Edie Pillman.
Front row: George Campbell, Mel Donald, Unknown, Ev McLeod, Annie Howatt,
Kate Bernard, Jean Howatt.

30. *Wellington and David Nelson and their sister*

31. *A photo of Miss Robinson, taken 17 years later*

1893

So far the new year hasn't been dangerously exciting. Had a jolly letter from Will to-day. I wish I could see him and just chatter nonsense for an hour or so.

Ches and I are clubbing together to send for books. I am going to get "Scottish Chiefs", "Valentine Vox" and "Midshipman Easy". How I do love books! Not merely to read once but over and over again. I enjoy the tenth reading of a book as much as the first. Books are a delightful world in themselves. Their characters seem as real to me as my friends of actual life.

We have lots of fun in school these days. Austin Laird and Ches Clark are going and we keep things stirred up.

Thursday, Feb. 15, 1893
Cavendish, P.E.I.
The funniest thing happened in school to-day. Lu had slipped over to my seat to discuss a scheme and I was whispering behind a book. Jim Wyand was up in his class and the last word in my sentence was "Jim"—referring to quite another Jim. Just as I got to it Austin Laird leaned across the aisle and gave me a vicious punch in the side. As a result I involuntarily screamed out "Jim" at the top of my voice. The sensation produced was enormous and poor Jim Wyand looked flabbergasted, as well he might.

Went to prayer meeting this evening. Don took Lu and Pen driving and Alec walked home with me. When I got home I found a thumb and finger frozen white and stiff.

Friday, Feb. 17, 1893
Made Austin awfully mad in school to-day writing a piece of poetry about him called "The Boy With the Auburn Hair". He dared me to do it, so he needn't have got his fur up so about it....

Thursday, Feb. 23, 1893
School was very dull to-day for Ches wasn't there. Austin was, but no fun was to be had out of him, for it is a sad and sorrowful fact that nowadays Austin and I "never speak as we pass by". He has not yet forgiven me for burlesquing him in that unlucky rhyme and persists in treating me with what he doubtless imagines to be lofty disdain.

The mailman didn't get along, and tonight being prayer-meeting night, our evil genius had to brew up a storm and prevent it. Too bad, when prayer-meeting is the only "social function" we poor "kids" have!

Wednesday, Mar. 15, 1893
Austin is very anxious to make up now, but I never take any notice of him. His dignity will not let him address me directly but he talks *to* others and *at* me. I am apparently deaf, however.

I went to the Missionary Sewing Circle this afternoon. They are making quilts for the Indians so I chipped in to do my mite for the poor heathen. Mollie was there and she and I sat together and sewed a long pleasant chat into our gay seams.

Tuesday, April 25, 1893
Cavendish, P.E.I.
I had a really fearful time with Austin to-day. He has been trying several ways of making up recently but I've never taken the least notice. This afternoon he kept making remarks to Jim who was sitting between him and me on the back seat. Poor A. would say in his solemn way,

"Jim, I don't know how you can resist the temptation to sit over closer to that girl"—here he would give Jim a fierce shove in my direction—"I'm sure I couldn't if I were in your place. 'Watch and pray lest ye enter into temptation'—that is what *I* have to do. 'The spirit is willing but the flesh is weak' "—and so on, until in spite of my efforts to appear deaf I *had* to laugh. This seemed to encourage Austin—he evidently thought I was relenting at last. So he got Jim to exchange places with him and then he slid right over to my desk.

"Look, Jim," he said, "This is for old acquaintance sake. This little girl and I are old friends."

But I got up and marched to another seat. Austin need not suppose for a minute that I'm going to make up in that fashion. He got mad over a joke and said very nasty things; and if he isn't man enough to apologize for it he can just go. Ches was in this evening and told me that Austin had told him a long yarn to the effect that he and I had made up and were better friends than ever and that we had signed a written contract never to quarrel again!!! Did you *ever*! Well, Austin may romance all he likes. *I* shall stick to facts.

Sunday, June 4, 1893
Selena and I went in to Baptist preaching to-day. Nate was there, sitting up in the corner of the choir pew. He looked over my way a good deal—and so did other people, to see how I was taking it. When church came out I hurried away at once for I didn't care about speaking to him under all the eyes of the "Jesuits". He looks just as usual and hasn't changed a bit.

Thursday, June 8, 1893
Cavendish, P.E.I.
I had a letter from Mr. Mustard to-day. It was a very incomprehensible epistle. He seems to be tired of life—or the life he is living—and says he is thinking seriously of "retiring and becoming a sort of college recluse and celibate"—and he wants *my* advice to "steer him past the rocks of his delusion, if delusion it is."

Fancy giddy *me* advising an embryo Presbyterian minister what to do!!! Poor Mustard, I can't think it would be a great loss to the world if he did "retire" from it. But I shan't say so. Instead, I'll preach away just so-so and give him heaps of good advice, if that is what he wants....

Friday, June 9, 1893
Eight O'Clock in the morning
It's such a beautiful day and such a beautiful world that I must "bubble over" to someone and you, old journal, are the only one I dare bubble over to. Oh, the world is so lovely now. It is the very prime of glorious springtide. The apple orchards are a pinky blush, the cherry trees are wreaths of perfumed snow; and in the mornings the fresh moist air is dizzily sweet with their delicious odors and resinous breaths of fir. The fields are like breadths of green velvet and birches and maples swing heavy curtains of green leaves. Oh, it's a dear beautiful world!

Friday, June 30, 1893
Two O'Clock P.M.
I'm off in another hour to town to put my fate to the test. Oh, I wish the entrance exams were over! I've studied very hard all the year. But Selena, though a jolly girl and good friend, isn't any kind of a teacher. I might just as well have stayed home this past year and studied, for all the good going to school every day did me. So I don't know how I'll come out and I'm much afraid of some things.

I went to school this morning. It was the last day and I felt sorry. Of course it was nothing to what it would have been if it were the "old crowd" I was parting with but still I felt many a twinge of regret at leaving the old school forever. When we were dismissed at noon I bade good-bye to every old corner but I wouldn't let even one weeny-teeny tear come to my eye, because Austin was looking at me! Pres is to drive Selena and me to the station and we leave shortly.

Saturday, July 1, 1893
Charlottetown, P.E.I.
10.30 P.M.
Here I am, a stranger in a strange land. We got in about 8.30 and I came up to Selena's as I am to be her guest during the exams. After tea we went out for a walk and had a very enjoyable time. To-day being Dominion Day we all went out to the Park after dinner. It is a pretty place but I found the afternoon very dull, having nothing to do but sit on a bench and watch a crowd of people I didn't know. This evening Selena and I went over the ferry to Southport and had an enjoyable little trip.

Sunday, July 2, 1893
This morning we went to St. Paul's (Episcopal) church, as Selena is an Episcopalian. I found the service very interesting but the seats were extremely uncomfortable—narrow box seats whose back took one—or took me, anyhow—just across the neck. After dinner we took a walk to the cemetery but the heat and dust rendered it anything but pleasant. This evening we went to St. Peter's Church—the "highest" of the "high"—Roman Catholic in all but name. I felt devoutly thankful that I was a Presbyterian. If I went to that church a year I'd have

nervous prostration—that is, if they always go through all the kididoes they went through to-night.

Tuesday, July 4, 1893
I am still alive but so tired I don't know if it is worth while!

This morning Selena and I went down to the college. The crowd of candidates was huge. Austin was there, too, smiling expansively—but *I* didn't smile—at least not at him. It was 10.30 before we got to work. I found myself in Professor Caven's room, with about 60 others, not one of whom I knew. The French professor, Arsenault, had charge of our room. When he put the English paper on my desk I trembled like a leaf; but when I had glanced wildly over it I knew I could do *it* all right. I finished it in an hour and a half and feel sure I did pretty well. To be sure, I was frightfully provoked to discover, after I had come home, that I had simply overlooked the second division of the second question entirely— so maddening when I could have answered it in full.

In the afternoon we had history and a hard paper it was but I think I did fairly well in it. I was awfully tired when I came back, but there was no rest for the wicked, for to-morrow we have Agriculture, Geography, French and arithmetic. I plunged into the latter for I'm desperately anxious about it, as it is one of the vital subjects. I worked the problems till I was dizzy. I can do well enough in arithmetic when I know I have plenty of time and that nothing very important depends on the result. But otherwise I lose my wits and do silly things.

Wednesday, July 5, 1893
The arithmetic paper was terrible—it fairly made my hair stand on end. I don't know whether I made a pass in it or not. The problems were "catchy". They seemed to be deliberately designed to trip candidates up, instead of to discover what their grasp of the subject was. As for the other three subjects I think I got along all right. Tomorrow is the last day for which glory be! It is also the worst, for we have Latin, Geometry and Algebra. I dread the geometry but am not afraid of the others. I am dreadfully tired but must go and revise the Latin.

Thursday, July 6, 1893
I'm *free*! Hallelujah!

When the papers were passed around this morning I quaked from my toes to my crown. But they were all easy; even the geometry wasn't half bad. Reviewing all the papers I think I'll get through all right if the arithmetic doesn't knock me out. I shiver when I think of it.

Tuesday, July 18, 1893
The date is worthy of capitals for I am truly—as Selena prophesied in her last letter I would be—the happiest girl in Cavendish. The pass list came out to-day and I am fifth in a list of 264 candidates. If I had not made that silly mistake in the English paper and another one equally silly in the arithmetic I would likely have led, or nearly, as the highest was only 21 marks more. But I am well content. The relief from the suspense of the past ten days is enormous. I had worried so much

over that arithmetic paper that I had begun to believe I had surely failed.

Poor Austin did not pass. Selena has gone to teach in Flat River.

To-night I went to the shore. It was a glorious evening. The sea was gleaming blue, the western sky a poem of rose and gold, emerald and azure. The sea's blue changed to silver gray, with the boats gliding over its shimmering glory, homeward bound. When our boat came in I came home through the purple dusk, with lurid bolts of lightning hurtling over the dark clouds on the south-east horizon.

Wednesday, Aug. 3, 1893

Yesterday word came that Grandpa Montgomery was dead. It was no surprise for he has been very ill for a long time. I feel so badly. He was such a dear, lovable old man and I have loved him dearly. He was always very, very kind to me and I shall miss him very much when I go to Park Corner.

To-day Grandpa Macneill took me up to the funeral. It was a very large one and the Rev. J. M. MacLeod preached a beautiful sermon. Poor grandfather was sadly changed. The dear old face was wasted but had a singularly peaceful look.

We came home this evening and I feel very tired. Uncle Leander is here now for a visit.

Friday, Sept. 2, 1893

I was collecting my traps together to-day for emigration—a rather dismal task for I simply hate the thought of leaving Cavendish. We had prayer-meeting to-night instead of last night. Don McKay took me driving afterwards and the way that wild mare of his flew over the road made me dizzy. It was moonlight and we had lots of fun.

So ends the long list of jolly drives for me. Many a pleasant time I've had this past year on prayer-meeting nights. It is over for me though not for others. Prayer-meetings will go on, the girls will hurry down the dark roads when it is out, go driving with the boys, sit in the back seats, and laugh at the Simpsons. But I'll be far away, among strange new faces and ways of life. It makes me blue to think of it.

Monday, Sept. 4, 1893
Charlottetown, P.E. Island

At four this morning I was roused from a most interesting dream that some girl in Melbourne, Australia, had written me a letter in which she wanted to know if she couldn't "send me one of those delightful little auburn-haired *sheep*". I think Austin must have been haunting my pillow.

Grandma drove me into town. We reached here about nine and came to a Mrs. Alexander MacMillan's, she having been mentioned to us as wanting boarders. I am to board here but I don't know whether I shall like it or not. Mrs. M. is a widow, living quite near the college on a very ugly block on Hillsboro Street. She has a daughter Mary, about my age, a son, Jim, about 20, and another, Dan, of 12. Miss Florrie Murchison, a pronounced "strawberry blonde", is the only other boarder here. I felt pretty lonely when grandma went home but I guess I shall get on all right.

Tuesday, Sept. 5, 1893

Well, the first day is over and I have got off with rather more than my life, although I feel dreadfully tired. At nine this morning I went to college. At ten Dr. Anderson called all the girls in and registered us one by one. That over, I went out and had a chat with Irv Howatt whom I met in the hall. Then I went out and sat down under the trees of the campus with some of the college girls and had a good deal of fun, although we were ravenously hungry. We had to "grin and bear it", however, as we do not get out until two. When the boys had all been enrolled we girls were called in to Professor Caven's room where the sheep were divided from the goats—that is to say, all of us who were going in for "First Class" were "sorted out" from those who were to take second class work. The latter were let off at once but we poor F. Cs. were kept there until nearly three before Dr. Anderson came in to interview us. We have to take an extra arithmetic exam next week before being allowed to skip the first year's work and meanwhile we begin First Class work tomorrow by 20 lines of Virgil. Also we have to be there at 8 every morning to take Agriculture.

Wednesday, Sept. 6, 1893
Charlottetown, P.E. Island

The first thing this morning was Agriculture in Prof. Harcourt's room over at the Normal. Then we went to Dr. A's room for roll-call, then upstairs to Prof. Shaw's room for mathematics, then down to Prof. Caven's room for French. Then we had a 15 min. recess. First-class English came next and then third-year English which I am taking as a substitute for Trigonometry.

The First Class girls seem rather stiff. I find the second-class girls more approachable—perhaps because they are strangers like myself.

Monday, Sept. 11, 1893

I love going to college. It is simply delightful. To be sure, I don't believe I will ever get acquainted with the First Class girls. They seem to be an "unacquaintable" lot, with the exception of Annie Moore who is not quite so stand-offish—perhaps because she, too, is a newcomer. I only sit with her in Mathematics though. In Dr. A's room I sit with a Miss Huestis, who has no more animation than a statue, and in Prof. Caven's room with Clara Lawson who is fearfully quiet and slow.

I am all alone in my room now. I am not homesick—I have never been a bit homesick since I came to town—but I *am* rather lonesome to-night and would like very well to see some of my Cavendish friends—girls preferably but boys would *do*—and have a good jolly chat.

Monday, Sept. 18, 1893

We had our extra Arithmetic exam last week and this morning after prayers Dr. A. came in with a folded paper in his hand. My heart began to thump violently, for the exam had been very hard and I was badly frightened that I had not made a pass—which would mean dropping back to Second-Class work. Dr. A. opened the fatal document with awful deliberation and began to read with as much composure as if a score of half-stilled hearts were not awaiting their owners' names in order to beat again. "There was silence deep as death", as one by one the names were called and at last mine *did* come. I made only 68—but that was 19 marks higher than I had feared. What a huge relief it was!

Thursday, Sept. 28, 1893

Selena and I went out to the Exhibition grounds this afternoon but as it poured rain the whole time we did not enjoy ourselves frantically. The rain also spoiled our project for going out to a concert this evening.

I had quite an exciting letter to-day. Soon after I came to town I wrote a little poem called "The Violet's Spell" and sent it to *The Ladies' World* of New York. And it has really been accepted! They offer me two subscriptions in payment. It is a start and I mean to keep on. Oh, I wonder if I shall ever be able to do anything worth while in the way of writing. It is my dearest ambition.

Tuesday, Oct. 3, 1893

This evening Nell R. and I started for the social in Zion Church—I attend Zion church, by the way. We picked up seven other college girls on the way, so that we were quite an imposing procession when we finally reached there. We had a splendid time at the social but it was spoiled for me by the fact that Wallace Ellis, a second class booby, whom I despise, walked home with me.

Everything is in unholy confusion here at present for Mrs. MacMillan is moving to another house down on Fitzroy Street. The new house is a double tenement and the rooms are just boxes. Besides, it is quite a long way from college. I don't care very much for boarding with these folks, anyhow, but I must just put up with it.

Friday, Oct. 6, 1893

We are settled down at last in a very *un*settled condition. My room is a back one on the third floor. At present, in the terrible jumble of things belonging to Mrs. M. which are piled into it, it is a work of art to navigate around with anything like safety to myself or the surrounding articles.

Friday, Oct. 13, 1893
Ch'Town, P.E. Island

This evening I went with Nell, Lucetta. Mary and Ida to a social in "The Kirk", as St. James Presbyterian church is always called. The college students were out in great force and we had quite a nice time. Wallace Ellis was there and was determined to join us and we were equally determined he should not and we dodged him until I was breathless from laughter. Finally he gave up in despair and took his stand by the door, ready, I suppose, to pounce on me when I went out. So I made the girls promise they'd go right to my door with me and as soon as we got out I made a frantic dive between Mary and Ida and there I stuck like a burr the whole way home. Soon as we got to the door I whisked in like a shot and reached my own sanctum sanctorum in safety.

I am to have a room-mate henceforth—Bertie Bell of Hope River who is coming in to learn the dressmaking. I am not overjoyed at the prospect as she is a stranger to me. However, she looks quiet and harmless. She and Mary MacMillan are very chummy—which is a pretty sure sign that she and I will *not* be. I cannot bear Mary McMillan. She is precisely the style of girl I detest—pert, shallow, ignorant, with a furious temper.

Tuesday, Oct. 17, 1893
I'm really too furious to say my prayers, so must calm myself by "writing it out" before I go to bed. After tea this evening I was down in the sitting room studying my Greek when the door-bell rang. Mrs. MacMillan answered it and I heard a voice asking for me—the voice of that *unutterable*—Wallace Ellis. I gazed wildly around for some loophole of escape but none presented itself and I heard her showing him into the parlor. I was meditating retreating out of the back door and hiding in the yard, leaving Mrs. M. to explain my disappearance as best she might, when she sailed in, beaming significantly. I took her by the shoulders and said with awful impressiveness,

"Mrs. McMillan, if that *creature* ever *dares* to call on me again, remember that I'm not in. *Remember*!"

And, leaving the solemnity of that final "Remember" to sink deep into her soul, I went in to the parlor. *Such* an evening! I tried to be decently civil while all the while I was wishing him in Jericho. He is a fearful bore. He stayed until 9.30, thereby demoralizing my whole evening's work and exasperating me to my present pitch of fury. The horrid pig!!!

Thursday, Oct. 19, 1893
After Greek this morning, as the boys were passing out—they always take precedence of us in Dr. A's classes because the blessed man says they take less time to get out than the girls do —Irv Howatt stopped at my seat long enough to whisper that Lem was in town. So when I went out for a walk this evening I was not surprised to meet him and Stewart Simpson on the street. I stopped to speak and Stewart S. evidently thought three was too much of a crowd just then for he whisked himself out of the way while Lem and I had a walk and chat together.

Sunday, Oct. 22, 1893
At dinner to-day Mrs. McMillan proposed to Bertie Bell and me that we go over to Southport on the ferry boat for an outing, so we went. We got our tickets and Mrs. M. marched us down a dock and on board a ferry. I had been over to Southport in the summer with Selena and I was sure we were on the wrong boat but I couldn't convince Mrs. M. of this because the old tub—I mean the boat not Mrs. M.—had "Southport" painted on her. So we started and in about ten minutes Mrs. M. and Bertie came around to my views, with gratifying completeness. There was no doubt that we were on the wrong boat—the one that went to Rocky Point! Here was a pickle! They would certainly have to take us there, since they couldn't very well dump us off in mid-harbor but suppose we didn't get back in time to keep our several engagements for the evening! Or, worse still, suppose we couldn't get back that night at all! We were busy supposing all sorts of complications when the captain came around and relieved our minds by accepting

our tickets, plus an extra cent all round, and stating that they left for home at five. We got over at 2.30 and while Mrs. M. went to call on some friends Bertie and I, on the strength of some rather vague directions, set off across the fields to hunt up the remains of the old French fort. We went down lanes and across scrubby commons, along steep cliffs and over sandy bogs, and finally climbed a fearfully steep hill. There was the fort—no great sight for so much trouble—just a square grass-grown mound, surrounded by a deep ditch. The view from it is, however, very beautiful.

We had a lovely sail home. I went to tea at Mrs. Young's, had a rather dull time and attended the Big Brick Methodist with her. The music was fine—they have the best choir in town. Lem was there and we strolled about until nine, as is the custom in this goodly town. Upper Prince is the favorite promenade and a very pretty street.

Thursday, Oct. 26, 1893
Ch'Town, P.E.I.
In School-Management class to-day Professor Caven read out the names of all those appointed to give an object lesson to the Normal kids next week and I was quite startled to hear mine as I had not expected it so soon. I am to go on Tuesday. I intend to take the Prince Albert Indians for my subject. I feel fearfully nervous. I wouldn't mind it so much if Prof. Caven didn't have to go with us and criticize our performances before the School Management class next day.

I had a letter from Mr. Mustard to-day. He is back at Knox again and is more utterly utter than ever. Poor mortal—he seems to have an uncomfortable sort of temperament—always torturing himself and others on the rack of self-analysis.

Tuesday, Oct. 31, 1893
This has been quite an exciting day. This morning in Latin Composition Class everything was going smoothly and we were drinking in the rules about the relative when Dr. A. suddenly paused in his harangue, looked out of the window and said "How do you do?" to some invisible person below. "Is Miss Montgomery in your room?" called out the invisible person, and I recognized grandfather's voice. Dr. A. motioned me to go and I raced up the aisle, scuttled over the bare space and slid out of the door, conscious that I was being as closely scrutinized by some 60 pairs of eyes as if the reason for my summons might be read in the appearance of my back. I found grandfather and grandmother outside. We put in a busy morning shopping and at 12 I went back to the college, as I had to be there at one to teach. I followed Prof. Caven quakingly over and saw a roomful of children, from ten to twelve. I advanced to the front, announced my subject and plunged headlong in. Then I warmed up, forgot to be nervous and got on swimmingly. The subject was new, so it took the children's fancy and they kept good order. At the close when I questioned them about the lesson I had given, they shouted out the answers with gratifying promptness and vigor. I am very thankful that the ordeal is over. Prof. Caven gave me quite a puff in class about it.

Saturday, Nov. 11, 1893
Ch'Town, P.E.I.
Lem was down to-night as *usual* and we discussed many subjects and talked nonsense about most of them. Once Lem said he was going out west when he got through Business College and I said I thought he'd be a goose if he did.

"Why, wouldn't you go with me?" he said.

"No, indeed, I wouldn't," I remarked decidedly. "I've had enough of the west, thank you."

I meant it, too. I haven't the least intention of going anywhere with Lem McLeod. He's a nice, jolly lad, but if I see him for an hour once a week for a newsy chat that is quite enough for me.

Monday, Nov. 27, 1893
O—o—o—o! "From Greenland's icy mountains"! It has been awfully cold to-day. In consequence of last night's late hours I overslept myself this morning and great was my consternation on hopping out of bed to find it twenty minutes past seven. Well, exactly forty minutes from that I was in my seat at agriculture class, so imagine how I wiggled!

Mary Campbell and her brother Norman are coming here to board. She came to-night. We are to room together in the big front room. I am very glad she is here for she is so jolly.

Saturday, Dec. 2, 1893
I'm "going to the dogs" completely I fear. Here are exams coming on apace and I've never opened a book to-day! Bertie McIntyre and I were invited up to tea at Mrs. Sutherland's. We had a pretty nice time, and loads of fun when John and Will came home. They board there, Mrs. Sutherland being their aunt. I am getting really acquainted with my two tall cousins now and fine nice fellows they are. At 7.30 Bertie and I started home, escorted by Jack's six feet of young manhood. At Judge Young's corner we met Hedley Buntain looking for me to go to the opera again—so we went. The play was "Arrah-na-pogue" and was even better than last night. I laughed and cried and enjoyed it enormously.

Tuesday, Dec. 5, 1893
We had our Latin Composition Exam to-day and it was dreadfully hard. I began to revise Chemistry to-night, for we have the exam Thursday and I'm very much befogged in it, owing to not having had the first year's work. But just as I got well started John and Will S. came in and stayed till nine. That meant no more chemistry of course but it meant lots of fun.

There is some Mr. McDonald here to-night—an acquaintance of Mother Mac's. He is a tall and lank old fellow with a considerable "jag" on, and they have put him to sleep in the spare bedroom. I'm really frightened to go to sleep with such a creature in the house. Mrs. McMillan might exercise charity in some other fashion, I think—for instance, in giving us a decent meal now and then. She keeps a wretched table—and worse than that the food isn't even *clean*. Why, Mary found a piece of *soap* in her slice of bread last night at supper.

Wednesday, Dec. 6, 1893

I hardly know whether our recent adventures belong to yesterday or to-day but I think they might piece in with both, since the racket began before twelve and lasted after it. Mary and I went to bed before eleven. She was soon sound asleep and I was nearly so when suddenly I saw a light—the door opened softly and a tall gaunt form appeared on the threshold! Stricken dumb with terror I simply stared at this apparition with dilated eyes and couldn't utter a sound but began to dig frantically into Mary with my elbow.

Then he spoke. I have since come to the conclusion that what he really said was, "Will you come and unlock the door?" but at the time I took it to be, "Did you hear me knock at the door?" and I gasped out "No" plump and plain.

"O—o—o—h", he said softly and was apparently about to close the door when Mary came awake and gave a howl that might have wakened the dead. We jumped up in a panic, lit a lamp, and bolted into Florrie's room. She and Mary M. were scared, too, and when we heard him coming upstairs again we held the door. He called out several times for Mary M. to "come and unfasten the door" but she, thinking he meant the bedroom door, wouldn't stir, so he lumbered downstairs again. Then Mary C. and I went in and wakened Norman, who had slept calmly through it all. He and I then went downstairs to see what the disturber of the peace wanted. He said he wanted to go to the boat for fear he would miss it—it was only twelve then and the boat was due to leave at seven! So we let him out, re-locked the door and came up again. Mary and I, between excitement, fright, and cold hardly closed an eye the rest of the night and I felt like "something made in Germany" all day.

Wednesday, Dec. 13, 1893

Freezingly cold. We had our algebra exam to-day and it was hard but I dare to think I didn't do too badly. I felt awfully tired all the rest of the day and was nearly frozen coming home. It wasn't much better when I got here for I never saw such a cold house. The wind seems to blow through it like paper; besides, Mrs. M. is *very VERY V-E-R-Y* economical in regard to coal. We are *never* warm except when we are in bed and not always then unless we pile every stitch of clothes we own on the bed and sometimes even the mats from the floor!

I was busy cramming agriculture to-night when Jack S. and James M. called. They stayed about an hour and we had such fun. Before they came I had been feeling blue and worried and as if agriculture would press me down all my life but their visit cheered me right up. They are two such nice boys.

Friday, Dec. 22, 1893
Cavendish, P.E.I.

Here I am in dear old Cavendish again and a good place it is after the wear and tear of much "examining". Our English exam began at 11 to-day and was a snap. Shaw also gave us back our geometry papers. I had been sure I had not passed but I just made it out by 52. When I got home I found that grandpa was in for me. John S. came down before I left and brought me a sweetly pretty Xmas card. We left at 2.00 and it was fearfully cold. For awhile I enjoyed the drive but soon began to suffer keenly from the cold. At last we got to the "Halfway House" and I went in and got thoroughly thawed out. Then we set off again and I could once more enjoy the cold pure beauty of the landscape. The sun set, throwing long rose-lights over the snowy hills. A pale, chilly moon looked out from behind a fringe of purple clouds in the east. The west was a pinkish yellow shading up into crushed raspberry and from that into ethereal blue, while thin veils of cloud floated across and caught the tints of that shining arch. The snow crackled and snapped under the runners. The sky faded out but the strip of yellow along the west got brighter and fierier, as if all the stray gleams of light were concentrating in one spot, and the long running curves of the distant hills stood out against it in dark distinctness and bare birches hung their slender boughs against the gold with the very perfection of grace.

32. Interior of Baptist Church
[Cavendish]

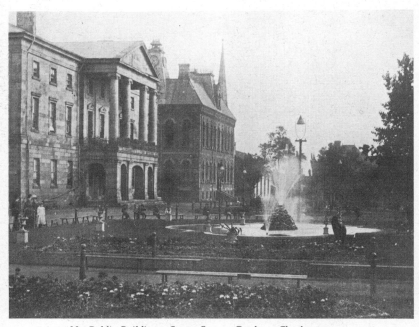

33. Public Buildings, Queen Square Gardens, Charlottetown

34. *Old P.W.C.* [*Prince of Wales College, Charlottetown*]

35. *Jack Sutherland* [*on left*]

36. *Mary Campbell*

1894

Saturday, Jan. 6, 1894
I had a letter from Miss West to-day, saying that there is to be a concert in Winsloe
Hall next Monday night and that she wants me to go down to her uncle's, where
she lives, next Monday and recite for them. It is to be a basket social also. Guess
I'll go. It will be a jamboree to wind up the holidays with. College opens Tuesday.

Tuesday, Jan. 9, 1894
Ch'Town, P.E.I.
Here I am back at "the old stand"—and I can't say I think it has improved much
in my absence! We left home yesterday morning at 4.30. It was quite dark and not
a bit cold and I enjoyed the drive very much. We reached Mr. Holman's at 8 and I
stayed there while grandpa went on to town. Mr. and Mrs. Holman seemed nice
and Miss West was there—also her brother Fred West, B.A. who is quite a
famosity in a not altogether desirable way. The Methodist choir from town was
coming out to give the music and were to have a goose supper at Mr. Holman's. I
found I was expected to give two recitations and take part in a dialogue from
Shakespeare with Fred West. Just imagine how silly I felt over the latter performance! I had never seen the selection before but I studied it up through the day
and finally concluded I could do it as well as West could—if that was anything to
boast of. They fixed up a basket for me also. It was bitterly cold at night but all the
folks came out and after supper we drove to the hall which was packed full. I gave
my recitations which were well received and West and I had our "dialogue". *It*
didn't take at all enormously. I fancy Winsloe audiences don't altogether appreciate Shakespeare especially when interpreted by "Freddy". The sale of baskets
was very amusing. Mine went highest at four dollars. Fred West bought it, which
didn't please me at all—I don't like him. We didn't get to bed till 2 o'clock and I
was so tired that not even the awful coldness of the room could keep me awake.
West drove a lot of us into town after breakfast and it was bitterly cold. Things are
much as usual here. Mary and Norman and I had a joyful reunion.

Wednesday, Jan. 10, 1894
Still bitterly cold. Mary and I almost froze while dressing this morning. As
Agriculture is done we do not have to go until 9 this term—fortunately. As soon as
I got to college I was surrounded by my chums and it was so nice to be back again.
Prof. Caven gave us back our English papers to-day. Dave Shaw and I led, tied
at 98 marks....

Tuesday, Feb. 13, 1894

"Oh, mi dere diry," as saith the famous "Bad Boy", this is awful! Mary and I were almost frozen last night and this morning the ice on our jug was two inches thick. It was very cold in college also, especially in the Normal where I simply felt my nose turning blue. When we got out we hurried home and after another dinner of "ditto"—as Mary and I call the lean boiled mutton which has formed our constant mid-day repast for the last three weeks—I sat down to those unfailing studies. But about three who should appear but Selena who is in town on a visit. We had a delightful confab.

Thursday, Feb. 15, 1894

It is really worth while to record that we *didn't* have "ditto" for dinner to-day. Instead, some fried potatoes and antique bacon. Mrs. MacMillan really keeps a wretched table. We are half starved most of the time.

The college boys have started a college paper and to-day Tal MacMillan—no relation of *our* MacMillans—asked me to write something for it. I have built a "pome" and will send it in.

Jim McIntyre was up this afternoon to bid me good-bye. He was going on the night train and I have just heard it blow, so he is off. I am awfully sorry and will miss him muchly.

Fannie Wise and I had no end of fun in the Byron class to-day. We have finished "Childe Harold" and I suppose the next thing will be an exam in it, although old Prof. Caven, bless his heart, hates giving them, I really believe, as much as we hate taking them.

Thursday, Mar. 1, 1894

Certainly March has made its debut in the character of the meekest and mildest of lambs. To-day was a spring poem. To be sure, the streets were far from perfect, but that is only the beginning of the end.

The "College Record" was out to-day. It is quite cute and well edited. My "pome" came in for a good deal of notice and even Prof. Caven himself told me, pulling his long gray beard the while, that it was "excellent". At least, he said "There was some excellent poetry in the *Record*", and as mine was the only verse in it I appropriated the compliment!...

Thursday, Mar. 8, 1894
Ch'Town, P.E.I.

In college and had a gay racket during chemistry hour. We had previously voted to get up a "peanut party" and all of us subscribed two cents each. At School Management hour the First Class girls, who do not take it, sneaked off uptown and got four pounds of peanuts. After recess we all went over feeling pretty mutinous. We got the peanuts distributed, cracked, ate them and threw the shells at one another. The air was thick with flying shells and beans, while a big carrot and a red herring also passed and repassed. Harcourt was furious but powerless. He took down—or pretended to—a lot of names and I expect we'll hear something more of it yet: but they can't kill us and Dr. A., who dislikes Harcourt, never pays much attention to the latter's complaints. Harcourt is no good whatever as a teacher and is not respected in his classes at all.

Tuesday, March 13, 1894

Lem came down for a farewell call tonight as his term at the B.C. is ended and he is going home tomorrow. Mary C. was in with us until nine and we had oceans of fun and teased poor Lem unmercifully. After she went I kept it up, for I was in mortal terror lest he should become sentimental. He *did* come perilously near it once or twice, on perceiving which I would immediately utter some wild speech and so side-track him. We hadn't an affecting parting at all for I was frosty in the extreme. Still, I was sorry to see him go and I shall miss him a good deal. But we are not exactly boy and girl now and our harmless little affair is beginning to assume a shade of seriousness that does not please me at all, so it is best that he is going.

I am invited out to Mary's home in Darlington for the Easter holidays. We are to have two weeks and won't we make Rome howl!

April 2, 1894

In Cicero class this morning Dr. A. appeared with a handful of papers and was greeted with a vigorous clapping, for these were our long-unheard-from Virgil papers. I made 82 and Dr. A. added that it was a good paper. Words of commendation from the doctor are like angel's visits and hence are muchly appreciated. Prof. Caven also gave us back our Byron papers. John Riley led with 97 and I followed with 96. I ought to have had 98 but Caven took two marks off for the expression "humble pie" which he said was "slang". Mean old thing! Besides, I do not agree with him that it is slang. It is an old proverb or rather old colloquial metaphor.

Mary and I intend to stay up until eleven to-night and study. This is our new programme as we want to get used to staying up late against the fatal day of exams.

Wednesday, April 4, 1894

At recess to-day we First Class girls, being ripe for mischief, went to work and changed all the books in Caven's room. We had just finished our performance and began to look innocent when the bell rang and the boys trooped in. Of course the scene of confusion we had counted upon took place. Everybody was tearing frantically around searching for books while Caven, fairly foaming with rage, stood upon the platform and shouted orders until he was black in the face, but all to no effect. It was a good half hour before we got settled down to work and even then there were ripples of disturbance all through the rest of the time when someone found a book among his belonging to someone else and passed it to its rightful owner with much ostentation. Caven was furious of course but never thought of blaming us guilty ones as we had mixed up our books among the rest.

Saturday, April 7, 1894
Mary and I were out for our customary "constitutional" this evening and on our way home we met James Stevenson and Stuart Simpson at Crabbe's Corner; they smiled with such unusual expansiveness that we wondered what on earth was wrong with us. On arriving here however we discovered the cause—they were coming here to board. We are rather glad as it will likely be good fun.

Wednesday, May 2, 1894
B. Faye Mills, a noted evangelist, is at present holding meetings here and the place seems wild with excitement. I had not been to hear him before but to-day Mary and I went. The meeting was held in the opera house this afternoon. The house was packed: we had to sit behind the speaker on the stage. Mr. Mills did not impress me as being much of a speaker but there is something very magnetic about him. Ida "got converted", as they say—how I hate the expression!—and I imagine Mary C. was pretty hard hit.

I went up town after the meeting and met Selena who is in for her vacation. Mary whisked off to the meeting again this evening but I declined to go and spent the time reviewing Greek instead.

Sunday, May 6, 1894
This afternoon Mary and I went to the Big Brick for the 2.30 service. We got there early enough to secure a seat in the gallery, just below "the Prince" from whom we got several very broad smiles. Mr. Mills' address was very fine and made me do some thinking. I have been feeling rather dissatisfied with my life this past week or so. Besides, I knew Mary Campbell really wanted to "come out" but was a little afraid of me—my sarcastic tongue and unfailing and unsparing raillery. I knew if I came out she would, too; if I turned away so would she. The responsibility was one I did not care to assume and the result was that we both signed the prayer cards when they were passed around.

After all, I hardly know whether I've done a wise thing. There are some things I find it very hard to believe.

The farewell service was held to-night in the Big Brick and 2700 people were present. The meeting was certainly very thrilling. But *feeling* and *belief* are such very different things —at least, after we begin *really* to think.

When we struggled out through the crowd we discovered to our dismay that it was raining. We had on our new spring hats—and we had no umbrella; a nice predicament! But John Sutherland came gallantly to the rescue of two such distressed damsels with a stout arm and a sheltering umbrella and brought us safely and dryly home—bless his heart!

Monday, May 7, 1894
Mary and I sacrificed our dearly beloved morning nap this morning in order to get down to the station to see B. Faye Mills off. A huge crowd was there for the same purpose.

College to-day was quite lively. We have an exam in English Thursday. *That* doesn't frighten me much but next week may some benign fate watch over me for we have French, Roman History, Xenophon and Latin Composition! Just imagine how we'll have to hustle!

Monday, May 14, 1894
Ch'Town, P.E. Island

I went to college this morning with anything but a good conscience, seeing that I had never looked at the French. The exam began at eleven in Dr. A's room and was pretty hard but I think I'll be all right in it if an accident that occurred doesn't get me in wrong with Caven.

Will Sutherland sat across from me on the other side. He sent a note over to me asking a question *re* the 4th section of the paper. While I was scribbling an answer Dr. A. came in and sat down at his desk where he was concealed from my view as I from his by the blackboard. I finished the note, folded it carefully up and passed it to Sam Willis who in turn passed it to Ethelbert McDuff. Then the catastrophe came. The doc pounced like a hawk on the unfortunate McDuff and ordered him to bring the missive to his desk instanter. I don't say of course that the doc expressed himself in just such classical language but that was the gist of it. McDuff had to prance up with the note, while Will and I exchanged horrified glances. I expected nothing short of an earthquake but the blessed old doc simply threw the note into the waste basket without so much as looking at it and sent McDuff back to his seat. I drew a long breath of relief and went to work again. But alas! As soon as the doc went out that old sneak of a Caven hunted out that note and read it. Of course no name was on it, and the writing was so atrociously bad that I hope he won't recognize it as mine. He cross-questioned McDuff closely but got small satisfaction from him. McD. assumed his blankest look and didn't appear to know anything—where the paper came from or where it was going. I don't know what the outcome of it will be I'm sure. Nobody, except Willis and McDuff, and two or three girls in my immediate vicinity, knows anything about it and they won't tell, but I'm afraid Caven won't rest until he has ferretted the matter out. Stewart and Jim nearly drove me frantic with suppressed laughter at dinner time discussing the rumpus and wondering who had written the note. I didn't give it away for I think the fewer who know of it the better.

Tuesday, May 15, 1894

Our exam in Roman History began at 9 to-day and lasted till 2—five mortal hours. That sounds pretty bad—but it wasn't so hard after all, in spite of its quantity.

Just imagine, we have another boarder—a Mr. McMann. He is a middle-aged man and a Catholic and has a wife somewhere down west whom he expects here soon. He is an Irishman and a carpenter and altogether seems to be a very rough and boorish sort of person.

Thursday, May 17, 1894

We had our Latin Compo exam this morning and it was quite easy. I think I'm all right in it—surely at least I did better than last time. *That* was too disgraceful.

But after the exam came my long-expected earthquake. I had heard no more of that unlucky note since Monday and had almost forgotten it and hoped everyone else had, too. But alas, when I came over from the Normal, after chemistry, Caven met me in the hall with a brow like the traditional thundercloud and whirled me into the doctor's room. I saw that wretched note in his hand and knew what was coming.

"Did you write this?" he demanded, dramatically holding out the accusing scrawl.

"Yes, sir, I did," I answered humbly, for I knew my wisest course was to throw myself on his mercy.

"You did! Well, you are the last girl on this side of the grave I would have suspected of doing such a thing," he said violently. "I would *never* have thought it of you. Now, who was it for?"

I had employed the time of this outburst by rapidly thinking what to do. I was bound I wouldn't betray Will. He was working for a diploma and to lose it would be serious. I could not get a diploma, owing to being here only the one year, so Caven might pour out the vials of his wrath upon me if he choose.

"I cannot tell you," I said firmly.

"Had it reached its destination?" demanded Caven.

"No, sir," I replied promptly, glad that I could at least exculpate poor McDuff.

Caven cross-questioned me severely but I would not tell him and at last he said,

"Well, then I will punish you since you will not tell me the real culprit. How will you like to have that whole section struck out of your paper?"

I wouldn't like it at all, that was flat. It would mean a loss of at least 25 marks. But I stood firm and then he dismissed me. I felt blue all the rest of the day. But after all I think Caven will forgive me when his anger cools. I have been his favorite pupil and I don't think the old man will harden his heart against me for long. At least I hope not.

Friday, May 18, 1894
I think Prof. Caven has got over the crisis. He was quite nice to me in French class to-day.

I wrote several drafts of applications for schools this evening but didn't write any real ones as Jim was in here all the evening writing an application for a position in the bank and driving us half distracted with his nonsense.

Oh dear, just think! A month from to-day all will be over. I cannot realize it. In one way it seems barely yesterday since I came to P.W.C. and in another it seems an age. I've had so much fun and made so many nice, new friends.

Mr. McMann's wife arrived on the scene to-day. She is an odd-looking personage.

Jack S. was down to-night and we had such a nice chat. Dear old Jack, he is simply the nicest fellow in the world—so chummy and simple and jolly, without any sentimental nonsense about him.

Wednesday, May 22, 1894
No exam to-day—but we shall pay up for that on Friday when we have both Chemistry and Greek Composition. I am dreadfully frightened of the Chemistry.

Caven informed me to-day that he had decided to "forgive me completely" and I am quite reinstated in his good graces.

Thursday, May 24, 1894
As this is our "Gracious Queen's" birthday we were blessed with a holiday from exams—and I wish I could add from studies as well but they seem to be irrepressible. I "crammed" Greek Composition and chemistry all the forenoon. After dinner Mary, Nell and Ida went to the park. They coaxed me to go too but I said, "Get thee behind me, Satan", and buried myself in formulas and chemical properties until three o'clock. Then I hopped up, threw the chemistry across the room, dressed on the double quick and set off for the park. Everybody and his sister were there and I had quite a hunt before I found the girls. We went and sat down on the harbor shore. It was charming. The water was such a pale, ethereal blue and the little capes and headlands were hazy purple. Professor Shaw and a Mr. Matheson came along after awhile and sat down beside us and we had such fun, discussing exams and such agreeable topics in a very light-hearted way. When we came home we had tea—such as it was—and then Mary and I came up here and had a snack of candy. I finally finished up my loyal celebration by studying English literature.

Friday, May 25, 1894
Ch'Town, P. E. Island
We had our Greek Composition exam this morning and it was quite easy. I made at least three pretty awful mistakes, though. Still, I think my average in Greek will be fair.

But if the Greek was easy the chemistry more than paid up for it. Such a horrible paper! It is a wonder my hair did not stand straight up on end. It *was* pretty badly disordered before I got through. I answered all the questions in some sort of a way but goodness only knows what I put down—*I* don't. Thanks be, it's over anyway.

Old McMann and his wife are a terrible couple. They fight like cat and dog. All the time he is home she is quarrelling with him and when he isn't she stays in her room and cries. She has just had a spell of it now.

As I was too tired to study to-night and was all alone I recruited my shattered nerves by getting out and reading over a lot of old trash—old time rhymes, such as "Dahlias", "A Concert" etc. How vividly they seemed to bring back all those dear old schooldays! They recalled memories of Mollie and Nate and Jack. Dear old Mollie, what chums we were! If Nate, loitering along the green roads on his way home from the post-office, saw "Mollie" coming around the corner he knew "Pollie" wasn't far off and if "Snip" came whistling up the hill "Snap" was generally within earshot.

Mary is out to-night and I miss her so. Dear me, we have very little longer to be together—a brief three weeks. Thus it goes. Just as soon as I meet and learn to love a friend we must part and go our separate ways, never to meet on quite the same ground again. For, disguise the fact as we will, when friends, even the closest—and perhaps the more so on account of that very closeness—meet again after a separation there is always a chill, lesser or greater, of change. Neither finds the other *quite* the same. This is only natural. Human nature is ever growing or retrograding—never stationary. But still, with all our philosophy who of us can repress a little feeling of bewildered disappointment when we realize that our friend is not and never can be just the same as before—even although the change may be an improvement?

Monday, May 28th, 1894
Ch'Town, P.E.I., Can.
I went to college with chill forebodings which were more than fulfilled when I saw the algebra paper. It was a *beast*! I did all the sums except two but I can't for the life of me say whether I did them right or not. The exam lasted four hours and left me feeling limp.

The climax of the McMann-MacMillan affair came tonight. Old McMann and Mrs. MacMillan had a really dreadful fight. He said everything to her—and gave her some pretty good hits, too, it must be confessed, although they were not conveyed in very classical language; then he discarded his weeping wife altogether, packed up his goods and chattels and departed, his last words to Mrs. MacMillan being some curt advice to change her ways and "do the square thing by her boarders." I am really not a bit sorry for Mrs. MacMillan. She deserved all she got for taking in such people in the first place.

Mrs. McMann soon sneaked out also, bawling down the stairs, and it is to be hoped we have seen the last of the amiable couple.

Tuesday, May 29, 1894
I verily believe that 187 Fitzroy has a monopoly of the queer things that happen in this town. Last night, just as Mary and I were getting ready for bed, the bell rang. I lifted the blind and peeped out. Below was that forlorn Mrs. McMann, in company with a strange man.

"Who is there?" I asked.

"It's me. Mrs. Mullen," she wailed, evidently taking me for our gracious landlady whom she invariably called "Mullen"—and the unknown escort supplemented this by saying,

"I found this lady wandering around lost in the park and I brought her home as she said she lived here."

Meanwhile, Jim Stevenson, having heard the commotion, had run down and let her in and she came upstairs sobbing and wringing her hands and said she would have to stay here all night. I went into her room and she was going on at a fearful rate. Mrs. MacMillan refused to get up and Mary C. wouldn't go near her, so I had to do the best I could to calm her. She had followed McMann, she said, "far into the woods," and only turned back when he threatened to kill her. Then she lost her way and was found by some man and brought home.

Well, *such* a time as I had trying to soothe her and get her to go to bed! She hadn't a cent or a friend in the world she declared. I said everything I could to cheer her up, gave her lots of good advice about how to manage men—Jim and Stewart, who were listening to it all on the stairs, have never given me any peace since!—got her to bathe her face and go to bed. Then I left her. Of course, after all this excitement I didn't sleep for half the night. Mrs. McMann decamped this morning before we got up and it is to be hoped we have seen the last of her.

To-day was beautiful. Summer is really here now and all the trees have donned a misty green. But this spring I have no time to enjoy the beauty of nature. Nothing but exams for me! I'm so tired of them. We had our geometry to-day and it was rotten as Shaw's exams always are. Tomorrow School Management will finish the college exams.

Thursday, May 31, 1894
Ch'Town, P.E.I.
We had our college groups photographed to-day and took the School Management exam in the afternoon. It was very long—8 questions and all with several divisions. I answered them all in some sort of way, making up what I didn't know. I have been revising Cicero all the evening for the License, although continually interrupted by Stewart and Jim who have had one of their wild fits on. Jim has won the medal. It has been a stiff pull between him and John Riley, a lank, ugly, unpopular academic but Jimmy has won out at last.

I have to write an essay to read at Commencement and feel rather creepy over the thought. I am going to write it on the character of *Portia* in the play we have been studying.

Everything is now in a continual flutter at college over the License exams. I have got back most of my college papers and have led in several subjects.

Tuesday, June 5, 1894
Five more days of worriment over! To-day was perfect, with blue skies and sunshine and the tender sheen of young leaves. But all this beauty was lost on us poor miserable creatures.

This afternoon while I was revising Latin Jim came up and began tormenting me about the valedictory. He wants me to write it for him, simply because he is too lazy to do it himself. I don't feel as if I had the time to waste on it. But I wanted to oblige Jim so I finally took a sheet of paper and scribbled down a few standard platitudes.

Wednesday, June 6, 1894
Had toothache all night and when I got up this morning all the left side of my face was swollen into a big puff. Such a looking object as I am! Whatever shall I do if it doesn't get better before Friday night when Commencement comes off in the Opera house and I have to read my essay?

I went to college, astonishing everybody by my vast amount of *cheek*. The doctor gave us our license exam numbers. I am no. 8. We also got our license time-tables. Three exams on Monday—English, History and Agriculture.

I came home and plunged into algebra. In the middle of it Jim came up again about that wretched valedictory. So I had to toss my problems aside and help Jim with it—or rather write it and compel Jim to give an opinion on the most important points. I·finally got it done in some fashion. Jim will have the *kudos* of it and I the grind. Well, what's the odds! It doesn't hurt to be obliging.

Just think, this night fortnight I will be in Cavendish! I cannot realize it. It does not seem to enter into my calculations at all. My vision cannot pierce beyond the darkness of next week. It is completely bounded by the gloomy shade of "License Exam."

Thursday, June 7, 1894
Got up at five this morning to study. My face is better but is far from being presentable yet. College closed to-day. I felt so sorry. My pleasant P.W.C. days are all over. Very sadly I gathered up my books and passed out—as hundreds have done and as hundreds more will do. But no one ever left or ever will leave that old college with deeper and more genuine regret in her heart than did I.

Friday, June 8, 1894
Ch'Town, P.E.I.
The curtain is down and the lights out—on my college year as well as on the stage of the Opera House where we spent such a delightful time to-night.

When I got up this morning my face was terribly swelled—worse than ever—and I was in despair. I determined just to let it alone—and then the contrary thing, seeing I wasn't going to coddle it, began to get better of its own accord and did so so rapidly that it was quite presentable after all by night time.

Mabel Fielding and Nellie McGrath came down in the afternoon to hold a Council of War about the License Exam. About four the dailies came out with the honor lists. I have five firsts and three seconds. We also got our Commencement programmes and they are very cute.

After tea we dressed in a flutter of excitement. I wore my cream challie with a bunch of pansies. Ida came along and we set out in great state for the Opera House. We got there, went on the stage—where there was a formidable array of vacant chairs—and by various dark windings found our way down to the dressing rooms where everybody was prinking. Then we came up and took our seats. The house was well filled and John S. was in the gallery smiling as a basket of chips.

My essay came after the first chorus and somehow or other I got out in front. I felt awfully scared, but didn't show it and got through all right. Louise Laird also read an essay and songs, speeches, and presentations of diplomas filled up the programme.

But the most delightful time must end. We sang "God Save The Queen" and it was over. In a few minutes the stage was empty and the lights out. As they vanished, leaving us in semi-darkness, I mentally said good-bye to my happy college life and turned with a sigh to the unknown future.

Jack S. came down with me and said all manner of nice things to me.

Saturday, June 9, 1894
Jim went out before breakfast this morning and got a *Guardian*. He passed it over the table to me with the remark that there was a very high compliment in it for me. There was a "puff" of about half a column over my essay and I felt pleasantly tickled. This afternoon the editor of the *Guardian* called to get the essay to print.

Monday, June 11, 1894
Ch'Town, P.E. Island

Well, this much dreaded day has come at last, and moreover has passed and left me in a tolerably satisfied frame of mind, for everything so far has gone pretty well. Mary and I got up at five and studied until 7.30. At 8 we went down to the college. We larked around, laughing at everything, and were hysterically gay with the recklessness born of nervousness.

Nine o'clock found us all in Dr. A's room waiting our doom breathlessly. We first class girls and a number of the Second were left in the room. Our English paper was a snap. Roman History was pretty stiff but I did it all. Then we had Agriculture and I think I got along all right in it, too. But that *awful* geometry comes tomorrow and I *know* it will be the death of me!

It was a real pleasure to come home to-day and stack away a big pile of books as *done with*. That dear old English class will always have a warm spot in my memory. Roman History, too, was always pleasant and interesting. As for Agriculture, I never liked it or the Professor who taught it. I have too many dismal recollections of getting out of bed in the dark and cold to go down at 8 the first term.

Just imagine. This night week I'll be in Cavendish—delightful thought! But— just imagine, this night week I'll be away from Charlottetown! Horrible thought!

Friday, June 15, 1894
Ch'Town, P.E.I.

I am F—R—E—E !

What a delicious sensation! We had English this morning and it was pretty hard but my foot is on my native heath with English.

After it was over Dr. A. came in to say good-bye to us all. Everyone was crying and for awhile I felt as if life would not be worth living away from the dear old college. Finally it was over and we all scattered as sheep without a shepherd. I cannot realize that it is all over.

Mary and I cleaned up our room this afternoon and had an enormous pile of rubbish to burn—all the notes, scribbles etc. which have seen so much honorable service during the term.

Saturday Morning, 8.30
June 16, 1894

It's a wonder that I'm alive to tell the tale for I've been having an exciting time. Last night, Annie Moore came down and proposed that, since we hadn't seen Professor Caven to bid him good-bye, she and Fannie Wise and Mary and I go to his house to see him. We went and he was so pleased to see us. We had a very jolly call but oh, my goodness, when we were leaving didn't the old fiend kiss us all round! I am sure I shall never be the same girl again—he was so whiskery and tobacco-y! I was sorry to leave him, though, for he has been a good friend to me during my college year.

Then we decided to celebrate the evening. We all met at nine and went to Carter's where we invested all our spare cash in caramels. Then we roamed about town until we were tired. Annie and Fan came down to stay all night with us, so we took off our boots on the doorstep, sneaked in, and tiptoed in single file to our sky-roost. We lighted a lamp, divided our caramels, and got on the bed to eat them. Such fun as we had! And we laughed until it was a wonder the caramels didn't choke us!

Then came the problem of how to stow ourselves for the night. It was finally agreed that Fan and I should have the bedstead and the chaff tick, while Annie and Mary were to have the feather bed on the floor. Fan and I took the sheet—there was only one—and a blanket and the bolster and let them have the quilt, the other blanket and the pillows. We had no end of fun and carried on half the night. We wanted to go down to the train at 7 to see some of the crowd off and resolved to get up at 5.30 but the first thing I knew was Annie's voice saying, "Girls, it's 6 o'clock." We all made one frantic leap out of bed and then such a scrimmage for clothes and brushes and combs! In a brief time we were ready and, scorning to wait for anything so commonplace as breakfast, we rushed to the station.

It was a delicious morning—clean, fresh and cool—and for the first time this spring I felt at liberty to enjoy the beauty of the world. The glorious arch of blue sky above us was no longer one vast concave on which to work geometrical problems, and the rustle of the leaf-laden trees no longer suggested only books and foolscap.

Later On.
I've had a very busy day of it. For one thing I went and had my tooth extracted and took ether. It was quite a funny experience and not at all unpleasant.

Norman came in for Mary this evening. I felt very blue to see her go and when they left I was just on the point of tears. I *didn't* cry however, for Jim had told me that John S. was coming down to say good-bye and I wanted to save my complexion for that. So I ran upstairs to dress and togged myself up just as nicely as possible. But Jack has never come yet and I don't believe he will now. I could just cry! The mean thing! I don't suppose I'll see him at all now to say good-bye and I don't care! If he thinks no more of me than that he can just stay away. I'm going straight to bed for I'm too cross to do anything else!

Sunday, June 17, 1894
But I was crosser still this morning when I found that Jack *was* here last night after all. While I was dressing I had heard the bell ring but hadn't my blouse hooked, so it was a couple of minutes before I could run down. When I got there I found only the milkman and supposed it was he who had rung. I cried myself to sleep last night, thinking all sorts of hard things about poor Jack and when Jim said this morning, "You went out after all last night," I said rather snappily, "No, I didn't!"

"Well," said Jim, "John came down and Mrs. McLeod next door told him everybody was out."

Just fancy how provoked I felt! I could have clawed Mrs. McLeod. Why couldn't she have minded her own business? I went to church in a very unchristian frame of mind but John was there and I contrived to explain the matter to him.

And this is really my last night in Ch'Town! I am not sorry to leave MacMillans but Ch'Town and Charlottetonian friends and days will always have a warm spot in my heart.

Monday, June 18, 1894
Cavendish, P.E.I.
Here I am in green old C. again. Grandma came in for me this morning. We had a charming drive home and got here about eight.

Wednesday, June 20, 1894
There are meetings every night in the church now and I went to-night with Pensie.

The result of the exams came out to-day. I am 6th on the list. Not too bad for one year! But dear me, they must have poured fire into them for out of 120 only *49* passed.

I had a letter from Mary. She is going to teach in her own school. Dear knows where I shall be teaching—if I can get a school at all. I fear it is not going to be easy.

Friday, June 22, 1894
Cavendish, P.E.I.
The school exam came off this afternoon and Mollie and I went because they are going to rebuild the school and it will never be "our old school" again. Ches, Austin, Nellie and Lu were the sole remaining four of the old classes. The rest were simply "kids". Sitting there, there came to me a sudden chill realization that I was "grown up" and the knowledge was not half so sweet as I had once dreamed it would be. And yet it seemed so *very* short a time since Mollie and I had been there in those seats ourselves, thinking school examinations occasions of state. Every old memory of school days came back to me.

But once my musings got an unexpected shock. Into the schoolroom popped *Nate*! Do my best, I can never suppress a start of surprise when I see him. He has such a faculty for appearing unexpectedly.

He is not as nice looking as he used to be—he has got thin and scrawny. I wonder if he is to be home long.

Thursday, July 5, 1894
Cavendish, P.E.I.
....I was re-reading "Last Days of Pompeii" to-day. Its charm never fails. I wish I could have lots of books. I teach myself to hope that such good fortune may be mine some day, but at times I weary of saying "Patience and Perseverance". It is so hard not to see all at once the results of those estimable virtues.

Saturday, July 14, 1894
Nellie McGrath is teaching at the Western Road, Nellie Rodgerson at Marie. Everyone but poor me can get a school, it seems. Dear knows, I've tried hard enough. I have sent applications for a score of schools, but so far the result has been discouraging silence. I cannot get to apply to the trustees in person and so I

have a poor chance. Other girls' fathers or friends drive them about to apply for schools but grandfather will not do this for me, or let me have a horse to go myself, so there is nothing for it but letters, which are generally not even answered.

I was reading "Vanity Fair" to-day. I didn't like it. The good characters are inane, sickly-sweet things and the bad ones are so clever and interesting that it is vexing to see their downfall.

Thursday, July 26, 1894

Well, I have got a school at last and it is away up at Bideford. I got the word to-day, and will have to go Saturday. I feel immensely elated, for I had almost given up hope of getting a school.

I had a letter from Laura to-day and I believe she will soon be engaged to Andrew Agnew. He keeps on going there and I begin to think that his perseverance will be crowned with success.

Friday, July 27, 1894
Cavendish, P.E.I.

I am all packed up and ready to start in the morning. Lu and Pen are going to drive me to the station. And so this is my last night in dear Cavendish for awhile and I go forth to-morrow to a new life among new people. I don't know how I will succeed but if hard and persevering work can bring me good-fortune I am resolved that I shall attain to it.

Saturday, July 28, 1894
Bideford, P.E.I.

"Here I be!" Amen!

Lu, Pen and I started gaily off at five o'clock this morning. It was blowing a hurricane but nevertheless we contrived to have a very jolly drive. We got to Hunter River in lots of time and when the train came I said good-bye to the girls and took my departure. Had a very pleasant ride and reached Ellerslie station—which is about two miles from Bideford—at 10.30. I was met by Bayfield Williams, a young law student and his fiancee, Miss Edith England, a fair, rather pretty girl. They told me I was to go to Mr. Millar's, one of the trustees, who would accommodate me until I found a boarding-house. We passed the school on our way down. It is large, about as artistic as a barn, and bleakly situated on a very bare-looking hill.

Mr. Millar's place, where I am at present domiciled, is rather pretty. There is a large family, among whom are no less than five of my future pupils. There is also a Miss Schurman visiting here. After dinner Miss S., Nettie Millar and I went for a walk to the river shore which is quite handy here. The Sewing Circle met here this afternoon—Miss England, Daisy Williams, Emma Ellis, and Maud Hayes—the latter a girl nearly twice as tall as myself who yet is to be one of my pupils. She is really the tallest girl I have ever seen.

Sunday, July 29, 1894

To-day was breathlessly hot. We did not go to church. There is a very nice Methodist church in Bideford. The nearest Presbyterian church is at Tyne Valley, about three miles away. I passed most of the day reading and eating the cherries which the Millar children bring to "teacher". What a comical sensation it gives me to hear that name applied to me! I suppose I shall be an object of curiosity around here for awhile. To-morrow I must take the plunge into "schoolmarming". Will I come bravely to the surface and strike out for the fair shores of success, or sink helplessly beneath the billows of failure?

Monday, July 30, 1894
Bideford, P.E.I.

This morning Mr. Millar drove me up to the school and I went in, feeling forty different ways at once and rather frightened into the bargain. The school is rather big and bare and dirty. There were about twenty children there, from six to thirteen years, and I called them in, said a few words to them and took down their names, feeling as idiotic and out of place as I ever did in my life. I have plenty of namesakes for there are three Mauds in the school.

I had a rather hard time all day. It was so fearfully hot and there seemed so much to be done. The children seem quite bright but are shockingly behind hand in their lessons and apparently have no idea how to learn. Looking back now, I really think I got on pretty well for the first day, but it was very trying, and when four o'clock came I was so tired I could have sat down and cried. I just felt discouraged.

It is over two miles from the school to Mr. Millar's and when I got here I was nearly at my last gasp. But after I had had my tea and got bathed and rested I plucked up fresh courage.

After tea Josh Millar drove me up to Mr. Estey's, to see if they would take me to board. He is the Methodist minister and his family consists of himself, Mrs. E. and one little girl, Maud, a sweetly pretty little maid of seven, who is one of my pupils. The parsonage is a nice house with pretty grounds, about half a mile from the school. Mrs. Estey seems like a very nice woman and was not at all averse to taking me but said she must first consult Mr. Estey who was away. She promised to let me know to-morrow. I do hope she will take me for there is no other nice place near the school where I have any chance of getting. I feel so unsettled in this homeless condition that I am perfectly muddled.

Tuesday, July 31, 1894
Bideford, P.E.I.

Had another very hot, hard day but a shade more satisfactory than yesterday. On my way home from school I called to see Mrs. Estey and was delighted to find that she would take me. But I cannot go until Friday, as she is to be away.

Friday, Aug. 3, 1894

I really believe I am learning to like teaching. But this week has seemed as long as a year.

After tea I came up to the Parsonage. I have a great big room—too big—

commanding a lovely view of the bay. Mrs. Estey seems very nice, but I am not greatly taken with Mr. E. Still, I am sure I shall like it here. But the night was close and rainy and oppressive and I took the worst spasm of homesickness and loneliness and discouragement I've had yet. Down came the tears in a shower. In the midst of my blues Gertie Moore called to see me. She is Annie Moore's sister and is teaching over at East Bideford across the river. Her call was not much of a consolation. She is the fastest, most unceasing talker I have ever listened to.

Saturday, Aug. 4, 1894
I have had no time for lonesomeness to-day at all for I have been on a jamboree. A big crowd, including the Millars went on a blueberry excursion up to "Lot 11" and I went, too. We left at ten, all in a big truck wagon, and had the roughest and jolliest drive imaginable. We made a day of it and had dinner and tea in the barrens, and laughed and talked and had a fine time. We had a merry drive home and were a rather tough-looking sunburned lot.

Sunday, Aug. 5, 1894
Bideford, P.E.I.
I have heard enough preaching to-day to last a month with care and economy. This morning I went to the Methodist church. It is small but very pretty. I went down with Nettie Millar and went with them to Presbyterian service in Tyne Valley in the afternoon. We heard Rev. William MacLeod preach—or rather jump and rant and howl. I was heartily glad when he finished. Shrieve Millar and I drove up to Lot 11 in the evening and heard him again. It is a nice drive but Shrieve is a nincompoop.

Wednesday, Aug. 8, 1894
Bideford, P.E.I.
I am really getting on splendidly now and enjoy my work—so different from last week when I was so tired and discouraged and hopeless. To-day I had a lovely time. Mr. Williams' folks, who live just across the road from here, invited me to a picnic to Indian Island, which they had in honor of the boys, Arthur and Bayfield, who are home on their vacation. Quite a crowd went with us. We got on board a big scow at Richards' wharf and had a delightful sail to the Island. We had a jolly time all through and after tea we had a dance in a house with an Indian playing the fiddle. We had a most delicious sail home but when I got back to the Parsonage I found the house locked up and deserted. I was sitting gloomily on the veranda when Shrieve Millar came along and took me for a drive. So I have had a pretty gay day and am tired enough to sleep soundly.

Monday, Aug. 13, 1894
Bideford, P.E.I.
....School goes on well. I have 38 on the roll now and am getting fond of them all. They are a nice little crowd and very obliging. Some of them bring me a bouquet every day, so that my desk is a veritable flower garden. I think they like me, too, from some encouraging reports I have heard. My favorite pupils are Jack Millar and Maud Estey.

Wednesday, Aug. 22, 1894

Who should pounce down on me to-day but Inspector Campbell! Of course the exam was necessarily mainly in the last teacher's work and so was not very satisfactory. I am resolved it shall not be so next time.

John Dystant, a young Methodist minister, was here to tea to-night and I had to entertain him while Mrs. E. was at work. He is quite nice.

I have a most wretched cold. What a horrid thing a cold is! Whatever induced that poor, unlucky Pandora to open that fatal box and thereby let loose so many ills on our ill-fated race?

Will Montgomery, a second cousin of mine, who lives over at Port Hill, came to see me this evening. He is real nice and is coming over for me some Friday night soon.

Sunday, Sept. 2, 1894

Will Montgomery came over Friday evening and took me back to Port Hill. It is a very pretty drive over there. Will lives with his mother and two sisters, Maggie and Louisa, both of whom are rather staid spinsters. Saturday morning we all went over to Bird Island to pick cranberries. We left at nine and drove to the shore where we all embarked in a leaky flat which wobbled painfully and alarmingly. Nevertheless, we all got over in safety and tumbled out on the Bird Island cranberry beds. I had never seen cranberries growing before and didn't exactly feel as if I were pining to see them now, but I couldn't stand around all day doing nothing, so I went to work rather half-heartedly. It might have been good fun if I had been dressed for the part but of course I had my good clothes on and they don't agree with cranberry beds. I kept up a pretence of picking until after dinner and then I sat down in a little hollow and talked to Will about books and Russia's foreign policy and education for the masses!! Will is interested in world doings and it was good to have a real conversation again with a man of some brains.

At about three we concluded to go home and started for our boat. Imagine our dismay at finding that someone—probably a prowling Indian—had stolen one of our oars. A nice pickle! Stay on Bird Island all night—cold, tired, and hungry! I mentally vowed that, let me be but safe on the mainland once more, neither sail nor picnic should tempt me off terra firma again in a hurry. Finally the men got a pole and after an awfully long time poled us over to Indian Island. Will went on shore and after another long dreary wait, he reappeared with a doubtful looking oar he had made himself. We started again and *did* get home finally....

We went to the English church in the morning and after dinner drove to the Presbyterian church at Lot 14. Will brought me home this evening.

It is very like the fall now—chill, high colored skies, mournfully-sighing winds, coldly purple seas, shorn harvest fields, all speak of vanished summer.

Tuesday, Sept. 4, 1894

....I was busy writing letters all the evening. I love letter-writing. To be sure, all my correspondents are not equally interesting. Some are dull and it is rather tedious to write to them. I have never heard from Edie Skelton since last November. I am sorry, for, although her letters were not of much account, I had a warm love for the girl herself and did not wish her to slip out of my ken. Alexina is rather dry, but Laura and Will are O.K. Mustard is a by-gone. I stopped writing to him last winter for I simply could not be bothered any longer with him. I suppose he is a full-fledged Reverend now. Hattie Gordon's letters are always capital and so are Selena's. The absence of Lem's letters wouldn't worry me at all. Mary C's letters are interesting but may cease to be so as our interests slowly cease to be mutual. Amanda's and Lucy's letters are generally interesting because they give so many details of home gossip. Pensie and Clara cannot write worth-while letters. Clara C. by the way, is in Boston now, working out as a domestic servant. It is absurd. Clara herself never had any lofty ideals or ambitions but I simply cannot understand her parents, especially Aunt Annie, permitting such a thing. If she wanted to earn her living they were quite able to afford to educate or train her to some occupation which would not have involved a loss of social caste. The idea of Clara Campbell "working out"! It would be laughable if it were not so tragic.

Thursday, Sept. 6, 1894

I gave the fourth class a written exam in grammar to-day—the first of the kind they ever had. Really, it was tough. I feel quite worn out. I suppose they thought they had a hard time but it wasn't as hard for them as for me! I remember when *I* used to grumble at exams and think the teachers imposed them on us out of pure malice. But I have a clearer insight into my former teachers' trials now. I may be teaching my pupils something but *they* are teaching me more—whole tomes of wisdom.

Friday, Sept. 14, 1894

Really, when September feels in a gracious mood and smiles on her eager lover, Autumn, she can be royally beautiful. To-day was a symphony in azure, pearl-veiled skies, peaceful fields, opal waters and cricket songs. However, the symphony was all *outside* the schoolroom.

Mrs. Estey and Mrs. Scott came up to the school at three to hear the recitations. The kiddies did well, and really we had quite an amateur concert, very like those we used to have "lang syne" in the old Cavendish school. How short a time it seems since I was a little schoolgirl, trotting to school o' mornings and finding a world of wonders all around me. And now here I am, a genuine live school teacher myself! I can never get used to that fact and wouldn't be a bit surprised if the kiddies were to rise in open rebellion and refuse to obey me. I wonder if the teachers I used to think such marvels of learning and dignity really felt as I do. I daresay they did.

Sunday, Sept. 16, 1894
Bideford, P.E.I.

The outside world was so beautiful to-day that after dinner I set out for a walk to a grove of spruce and maple in Mr. Williams' field. I was so warm and tired when I got there that I lay down in a mossy hollow among the ferns under the maples and fell asleep before I knew it. I slept for a couple of hours. I should have had fairy-like and sylvan dreams but as a matter of fact I did not dream at all.

Tuesday, Sept. 18, 1894
Bideford, P.E.I.

Ugh! Autumn must have played September false and she is weeping the tears of her widowhood.

Mr. & Mrs. E., Mrs. Scott, Maudie and myself went down to the shore at dusk. A thick pall of mist hung over the waters through which the opposite shores and the little points loomed phantom-like and unreal. A good natured oysterman took us for a row. The water was glassy-still and the lights along shore twinkled through the mist.

To-day, while I was hearing the primer class, I was rather appalled by seeing two lank, freckled, rough-looking lads stride in and sit down. They seemed rather formidable, but I hid my trepidation, recognizing the need of firmness from the start, for one was George Howells, the traditional "bad boy" of the district. He is the grandson of a man who served a life sentence in prison for shooting another man. It happened in Malpeque when I was a small child and as it was a *"cause celebre"* in those days I heard it much talked about. Let us hope George will not prove to be a case of atavism. His principal adornment is freckles.

His companion was George Murphy. They swell the roll to 48.

I dismissed school at recess, as I wanted to be home in time to see a wedding which was to come off in the parsonage at three o'clock. The party were up to time and for dress and behavior were the funniest I've ever imagined outside of a comic recitation book. The whole performance was as good as a play. The groom was badly scared and his attendants were drunk. Mr. Estey received the huge sum of one dollar for tying the knot and the whole party drove off, singing "Nearer, My God, To Thee",—which I suppose they thought appropriate. I had to sign their name to the marriage certificate as neither of them could read or write.

It is a regular fall rain now—a night wild enough to suit any novelist in search of suitable weather for a murder or elopement. Tried to play "logomachy"— "Methodist casino"—this evening but as Mrs. E. was tired, Mr. E. more than usually satirical, Maudie peevish, and Mrs. Scott and myself rather indifferent the game was not a notable success.

Saturday, Sept. 29, 1894
Bideford, P.E.I.

I spent most of to-day reading Macaulay's essays. His sparkling pages are never dull and he can invest the dryest details with interest and charm.

This evening I went to the P.O. for a walk. It was cold and chill; the sky was overcast with wrinkled gray clouds, save along the north where a strip of yellow sky gleamed palely. No living creature but myself seemed abroad and the cold gray shadows settling down over the withered fields lent to the landscape an aspect inexpressibly dreary and mournful. It made me feel hopeless, and as if the best of my life lay in the past. Externals have a great influence on me—too great, perhaps.

I have been reading this evening and petting "Coco", who is shamefully spoiled by everybody in the Parsonage. It made me think of poor old "Topsy". She is still alive at home and I have a warm corner of my heart for that old gray-and-white cat down in the old barns surrounded by the dark spruces where I used to play and dream, and romp with my pussies, regarding them as very important denizens of my small world.

And those old autumns when we picked apples among the fallen leaves on frosty mornings while the cats made mad rushes around us and the hens clucked slyly under the big sweet-apple trees.

Is it really the same world I saw then that I see now? It seems so very different. The "coloring of romance" is gone. *Then*, everything was invested with a fairy grace emanating from my own imagination—the trees that whispered nightly around the old house where I slept, the paths and lanes where I loved to stray, the fields, each individualized by some oddity of fence or shape, the sea whose murmur was never out of my ears—all were radiant with "the glory and the dream".

Tuesday, Oct. 16, 1894
Oh, why can't—but no, I won't! I closed with a silly question last time and I won't begin again with one—otherwise I intended to ask why couldn't pleasures last forever. I suppose it is better that they can't, or what would we accomplish in life? But I've been having such a perfectly jolly time—I've been to town and Mary C. was in, too. I went in on the train Saturday evening and was met at the station by Bertie and Lew and Mary C. Mary and I had a most rapturous reunion and I expect we made perfect geese of ourselves. Nettie Montgomery is boarding at Aunt Mary's and going to college. She is rather affected but very nice and full of fun.

After tea Mary and I went down to see Norman—who is going to college again—and then went for a walk around town. How delightful it was to be in town again!

It was late when we got back so we went straight to bed and talked all night. Sunday morning we went to dear old Zion. Really, it was delightful to be there once more. John and Will S. were there, too, and looked as natural as life.

After dinner Mary and I went down and made a brief—a very brief—call on MacMillans'. They don't seem to have improved any. In the evening after church John S. and Jack Gordon—a second cousin of mine who is in the bank here—came down and we had a jolly evening.

Monday Mary and I visited the dear old college. It was so lovely to be there again. We saw all the professors. Dr. A. and Caven are as nice as ever. I saw many familiar faces but alas, more unfamiliar ones. Monday evening John was down again and we had so much fun.

To-day I spent shopping. Grandma drove in for me and we came home in the evening.

Monday, Oct. 22, 1894
It is appalling how events pile themselves up when they once begin! Here I have whole oceans of news—some of it quite graphic, too. To begin with, I was at a party at Charley McKenzie's Friday night and had a splendid time—nearly danced my feet off. Ches drove us home and I danced the rest of the night in my dreams.

Saturday morning Pen, Lu, and I started off for a cruise to Park Corner and Malpeque, and you may be sure our drive was a merry one. We got to Aunt Annie's at eleven-thirty and had dinner. But oh dear, how lonesome it was there! The girls are both away—Clara in Boston and Stella at P.W. College. I had never before been there without them and I felt like crying all the time I missed them so. After tea we went up to Malpeque where we remained until church time the next day. We had a very nice time. From church we drove back to Aunt Annie's and after dinner Lu and Pen went to visit their respective relatives and I went to see Aunt Mary Cuthbert with whom I stayed till dark. I had just got back to Uncle John's when Lu came back and with her *Lem*. The instant I saw *him* I took a creepy fit. I don't know how or why it was but I felt instinctively that Lem's visit would not be as harmless as usual.

We spent a pleasant evening, but finally the others all drifted away and left me to my fate. I was desperately resolved to do my utmost to prevent Lem from speaking out. And until the very last moment I flattered myself that I would succeed. I laughed and joked and teased poor Lem. I was quite nice and chatty but if he became sober—which he did with alarming frequency—I would invariably give the conversation a frivolous turn which would quite rattle poor Lem and leave him precisely where he was when he began. It began to get very late and Lem kept saying he must go, but, like Harry in the song "he didn't". Finally, however he did get up to go and I rose, too, rejoicing, for I thought all danger was past.

But Lem was not out of the house yet. He followed me over to the table and put his arm around me.

"I suppose you'll go away up there to Bideford and forget all about me", he said.

"Oh, no, I won't—I never forget anyone—I have a remarkable memory", I answered flippantly.

I have this advantage over Lem—he can never tell when I'm in earnest or when I'm not. It was the case now. He tried several more baits but as I only laughed at each and wheedled him a little nearer to the door each time he did finally get there. I stepped to it with alacrity—a moment and he would be gone!

Then suddenly Lem stepped back, took me in his arms again and said seriously,

"Maud, I came up here to-night to say something. I haven't said it yet but I will now. I've been thinking about this—I've been going with you for a long while now and I've been thinking that perhaps I'm keeping you from going with somebody else you'd like better. But I love you and won't it be all right?"

I stammered, blushed and finally gasped in confusion, "Oh Lem, don't be foolish."

But Lem wouldn't take this sensible advice at all and went persistently on being foolish.

"I thought I'd speak now, for fear there *was* somebody else you liked better and..."

"No", I broke in desperately, "there is no one else..." and then I stopped, conscious that *that* wasn't exactly the wisest thing to say. I tried to be cool, but I am bound to say the attempt was a miserable failure for I wasn't in the least prepared for such a scene.

"Then, Maud, if you'll just say yes..."

But this was just what "Maud" couldn't say, so she broke in desperately,

"Oh, Lem, don't! I like you ever so much but I'm not thinking of anything of *that* kind, Lem. All I *am* thinking of is getting an education and..."

"Yes, and when you have got it will it be *all right*?" he asked again.

"I can't make any promises, Lem," I said more composedly, beginning to get my wits back again, "I'm too young and..."

"Yes, and I'm young, too," he said. "But I'm in earnest, Maud, indeed I am. And I hope you'll consent some day. Anyhow, I wish you may win success in everything. I wish you well ...indeed, I do."

We went out then and I stood dumbly and rather unhappily and held the lamp while he got his coat and hat. When he was ready to go I held out my hand.

"If you'll just say *one word*, Maud", he said.

"Good-bye, Lem", I said hastily, drawing away. There were a dozen soothing things I wanted to say but somehow I could get nothing out but that ungracious farewell.

"Good-night, dear", said Lem. "Perhaps we'll see it in the same light some other time."

And then he went away...to my huge relief. It is an abominable business...this telling a man you can't marry him. I went to the room, where the girls were asleep and quickly got into bed. Perhaps you think I did not soon go to sleep after my exciting interview, but I did, for I was tired out.

Poor Lem, I'm sorry things have turned out so. He is a good, manly fellow and I've always liked him. But I can't give him anything more than friendship. I don't know much about love but I *do* know I'm not a bit in love with Lem and never could be. I don't mean to feel badly over this, either. Lem will not be broken-hearted. He is not of the type that cares deeply or takes things hardly. He will be a good deal disappointed, but he will soon be looking for another "girl". "Love" with him means that he is quite fond of a tolerably good-looking girl whom he could feel proud of as a wife. He has an aptitude of a certain sort of business but he has no brains, culture, or breeding. So he is out of the running on every count. I've always been frank and friendly with him but I've certainly never pretended to be anything else. He cannot accuse me of having deceived him in anyway.

Wednesday, Oct. 31, 1894
Bideford, P.E.I.

A new kiddy started to go to school to-day and such an oddity as he is! His name is Amos MacKay and he disturbed the school work not a little by his naive goings-on.

Edith E., Daisy W. and I were invited down to Capt. Richards' this evening to meet their cousin, Miss Richards from Wales, and we enjoyed ourselves very much. Miss R. is very nice but she talks with such a decided accent that it is difficult to understand her.

I am getting on beautifully in school now and am even feeling encouraged about the fourth class. Ever since I came here that class has been the problem of my existence. I never imagined such a set of stupids. But they actually seem to be wakening up.

Monday, Nov. 5, 1894

"Guy Fawkes"' night—and I've been having a very pleasant time. The Orange Lodge at Ellerslie had a supper in the hall to-night and Lewis Dystant came out and took me. He is an Ellerslie youth who sings in the choir here; he seems nice and is quite nice-looking.

We had a fine time at the supper. There were about 50 there and as I'm getting pretty well acquainted with the people around here now I enjoyed every minute of the time. We came home at 12 and I promised to go with Lew D. to a week-night preaching service at Tyne Valley tomorrow night.

Tuesday, Nov. 13, 1894
Bideford, P.E. Island

Rev. Mr. Corbett preached at the Valley tonight and Lou D. came out to take me. It was a perfect night, clear, crisp and moonlight, and the drive seemed all too short. After the service we went for a drive through to the station. Lou is a nice fellow. That is, he does very well for somebody to drive me about.

Tuesday, Nov. 20, 1894

A wretched sort of day—bitterly cold and blowing a hurricane. I really thought I'd freeze going to school.

This evening Daisy W. and I went to a practice at Mr. England's. We are going to get up a concert for Xmas. We are to have three dialogues and I am in two—"Cinderella" and "The Irish Love Letter". "Cinderella" is quite a pretentious dialogue, as there are several scenes in it, with costumes, music, and dancing.

Sunday, Nov. 25, 1894

I went down to dinner at Mr. Millar's this morning as per invitation, but was in misery all the time because just before I left home Mrs. Estey unexpectedly asked me to take the organist's place at church to-night, Mrs. Currie, the regular organist being away. I felt dreadfully nervous but consented. When I went to church this evening I felt as if I were going to immediate execution, but I got on all right in spite of my dismal fears.

Thursday, Dec. 6, 1894

Last night about six Lou Dystant's sleigh-bells jingled through the frosty air as he came to take me to a lecture on "Prohibition" up at Lot 11, the lecturer being no other than my dear old teacher Mr.—now Rev.—Fraser. We were soon flying up the road in a dazzle of frost and moonlight. I never enjoyed a drive more. The night was bewitching, the roads were like gleaming stretches of satin ribbon, there was a white frost that softened the distant hills and woods to a fairy dream, and the moonshine fell white and silvery over all. Earth looked like a cold, chaste bride in her silver veil, waiting to be waked by her lover's kiss to warmth and love and passion. I was sorry when we got up and had to go out of the moonlit dazzle to the stuffy little church with its rows of commonplace, hum-drum people.

But the lecture was neither commonplace nor hum-drum. It was splendid.

To-day was hard. The attendance at school is large now and it makes the work much more difficult, for there are not half enough seats and the children are so crowded. I like teaching but I do get dreadfully tired some days.

Dear me, this time last year I was a gay college girl discussing approaching exams with my chums—and now here I am, a sedate Bideford "schoolmarm" well versed in the mysteries of rod and rule!

The dialogue practice was at Mr. Millar's to-night and Lou D. came out and drove me down. He is really a very *handy* person.

Monday, Dec. 17, 1894

After all, work isn't a bad thing to go back to when you've had a good sleep and feel in excellent trim. After school I went to Robert Hayes—a place I've never been yet. Had a poky time. Lou came in the evening and drove me home in mud to our eyes.

I heard today that Uncle John Montgomery has had a stroke of apoplexy and is very ill. I am very sorry.

I made my basket for the concert tonight—it is of apricot crepe paper and is very pretty. The affair is to come off Xmas night and I sincerely hope it will be a success.

Tuesday, Dec. 25, 1894

Well, my goodness!—or somebody else's goodness if mine isn't substantial enough! This morning was dull and gray. It was blowing a hurricane and spitting snow. I went down to Mr. Millar's and had a very dull time—which was just what I had expected—and at noon it began to rain and poured down in bucketsful. Of course I knew Lou wouldn't come out for me and at three Jack Millar drove me home. Night closed in with a downpour. No concert of course. Isn't it aggravating?

Friday, Dec. 28, 1894

My, I'm tired! Last night I went over to a Masonic supper at Port Hill with Edith E., James Richards, and Bayfield Williams. It was a simply fearful night of wind and rain and darkness. There were not many there and the whole affair was terribly flat and dull. It was three when we got home and after nine when we woke. They drove me to the school. It was a wet, unpleasant day but the kiddies all came and in the afternoon my dreaded first school exam came off. Twenty three visitors came and I was delighted. The children acquitted themselves very well in both lessons and programme. Then, of course, came the usual "speechifying" which was very gratifying as all present concurred in expressing thorough satisfaction. Mr. Millar moved a vote of thanks to the teacher "for her trouble" and I had my first experience in receiving a vote of thanks and making a little speech in reply. Then we sang "God Save the Queen" and dispersed. I came home very happy and most fearfully tired.

Sunday, Dec. 30, 1894

Our wonderful concert is over at last and that is much to be thankful for. It didn't look much like it all day yesterday for it blew and poured and froze but it cleared up at dark and there was an excellent audience and everything went off finely. Our programme was a big success. Then came the sale of baskets. Mine went the highest—Lou bought it. I stayed at Mr. Millar's all night and John drove me home this morning. The world was fairly lovely with a white frost.

37. First-class students at P.W.C., 1893–4
1. My cousin, Will Sutherland. 2. Annie Moore. 3. Myself [2nd row, in white. seated].
4. Fannie Wise. 5. Mabel Fielding. 6. Alberta Huestis. 7. David Shaw.

38. Fannie Wise

39. Jim Stevenson

40. John Riley

41. "The cream challie"
[LMM c.1894]

42. *Ellerslie Station*

43. *The Bideford parsonage*

44. Mrs Estey
[Bideford]

45. Maud Estey

46. *Where we picked apples*
[*Cavendish*]

47. *Lewis Dystant*

48. *Lem McLeod*

49. *The parlor at Park Corner*

1895

Sunday, Jan. 6, 1895

I felt lazy to-day so when the rest were all off to Sunday School I settled down by the fire with Tennyson and some doughnuts and was all ready for a cosy quiet time when I heard a knock at the door. I knew it was Lou and would just as soon it hadn't been; but we had a nice jolly chat—although it wasn't as good as Tennyson and doughnuts!

Thursday, Jan. 17, 1895

Lou came here after prayer meeting—for the meetings are still going merrily on—and brought me a novel to read. He brings me a new one every time he comes, which is a blessing, as of course novels are not among the plentiful furnishings of a Methodist parsonage. To be sure, the poor chappie is not the best judge in the world of an interesting story—sometimes he hits it, sometimes he doesn't; but anything does to fill up a tired or idle hour. I have a very pernicious habit of going to my room after Lou departs and reading for all hours. I am so crazy about reading that I *can't* let a book drop until I see its end, even if it is as dull as a cookery recipe. I am always making good resolutions about this—and breaking the same just as soon as I get a novel in my clutches.

Sunday, Jan. 27, 1895

I had a delicious time this afternoon reading. Reading is a luxury I don't have a great deal of time for now so that when I do get a quiet uninterrupted hour to sit down to a book I duly appreciate it. The first half hour I gave to Longfellow's poems—poems which never lose their witchery for me. There are undoubtedly many greater poets than Longfellow—many stronger, grander, deeper; but he is full of sweetness and tenderness and grace.

Then I read Hawthorne's wonderful "Scarlet Letter" over again. It is a marvelously powerful book, both in style and analysis. What a power of character-painting—and *such* character—such deep, stormy, passion-wrung character. The hero is a *man*, the heroine a *woman*, and the true portrayal of such must ever appeal forcibly to the great heart of humanity, throbbing through all its varied phases of passion and pain.

Tuesday, Jan. 29, 1895

Will Montgomery came Saturday afternoon to take me down to Malpeque to see Uncle John Montgomery who is very near his last. We crossed the bay that evening in a big snowstorm and found a houseful there. It was a sadly changed house. The life and soul of it was gone. I went up to see poor Uncle John. Could that haggard wasted creature be the big, hearty uncle of yore, with the ringing voice and the laugh that shook the house? The mental change was as great and pitiful as the physical change—the blurred eye, the indistinct speech, the clouded intellect.

We came back to Port Hill last evening and Will brought me home this morning. We nearly froze in school to-day as the supply of wood ran out so at two I dismissed school and came home, vowing deadly vengeance on the trustees.

Monday, Feb. 18, 1895
On Friday Edith E. sent down word for me to go up and when school was out I waded up over the banks. I had a lovely time there as usual. Saturday evening Lou came out and took me through to his place where I stayed till Sunday night. The drives over and back were very pleasant but I can't say I enjoyed myself very much while there. Sadie is very insipid—one of those jelly-fish sort of girls—and Mrs. D. worries you to death with fussy kindness—or what she means for kindness.

Sunday evening, as we drove out, was perfection—clear and sparkling, with lemon lights in the west and one great lucent evening star gleaming like a liquid jewel on the hectic cheek of dying day. It grew darker as we drove along over the white fields—the velvet sky was powdered with stars, and the spruces took on their mystic gloom!

Poor Uncle John M. is dead. They telephoned it over to me from Port Hill. It gave me such a shock although I had been expecting to hear it.

Sunday, Mar. 10, 1895
Friday night after school I went up to Edith's and stayed all night. I always enjoy myself there. I almost envy Edith E. her lovely home. It seems to me she has everything heart can wish for.

And yet, after all, I would not change places with her. In fact, with all my little trials and tribulations—of which I have always had my share—I have never yet met with anyone with whom I *would* exchange places—that is, if a change of personality were included, too.

Thursday, Mar. 14, 1895
There was a social in aid of the Valley church at Mr. Millar's last night and Lou and I were invited. I bade adieu to my books and fancy-work somewhat regretfully—for I knew we'd have a dry old time—and went.

Arriving there, I made my way through rooms already lined with blank faces and escaped upstairs to the spare room, where half a dozen girls were prinking and, without waiting to remove my wraps, sat down to inspect some letters Lou had brought me out. One was quite a delightful surprise for it was from the editor of the Toronto *Ladies Journal*, accepting a poem I had sent it, "On The Gulf Shore", and adding a few complimentary words. They don't pay for poetry, however, so that the "honor" is all the recompense.

After reading my other letters I took off my hat, fluffed out my bangs, and went downstairs. As music was being called for I filled the gap until I got tired, and then I settled myself between Maud Hayes and Lily Dalton. Everyone was evidently on his and her good behavior—at least, it seemed a penitentiary offence to speak and a capital crime to smile. As we knew we'd have no fun unless we made it ourselves Maud and I began making all the reckless speeches we could to each other and we laughed at our own wit until the old dames looked askance at us. For downright stupidity these church socials "take the cake". People look primmer and more hopelessly uninteresting then than at any other time, rooms are hot and stuffy, and everyone seems in everyone else's way. The main things to do seem to be,

1. Sit prim.
2. Look demure or disapproving according to your age.
3. Hang back and act cranky in any game other people try to get up.
4. Cram yourself with a lot of indigestible stuff, the effects of which will be ever present with you for a week.

I escaped the last number of this programme at least by becomimg a waiter. Of course I tired myself out carrying cakes around with a fixed, sickly, won't-you-have-some smile, but that was infinitely preferable to loading my protesting stomach with a lot of sweet stuff and going home with a violent headache and a malevolent temper.

After supper kissing games were started and flourished where all others had failed. As I do not play them I carried Lou off promptly and we left. If I thought I would have the moral strength to keep it I'd make a vow never to go to a church social again!

Thursday, Mar. 28, 1895
Bideford, P.E.I.
We have been having a delicious spring weather. The roads are getting sunken and slushy, the brows of the slopes are peering out barely from their crown of snows, little pools of water are lapping the feet of cold white banks which are gradually assuming a pitifully violated appearance; the hot kisses of that old libertine, the sun, have desecrated their virgin purity.

All this is poetry—but it is really very prosy prose to slush around ankle deep whenever you set foot outside the door.

I spent this evening at Mr. England's. One reason why I like to go there is that you can make yourself so thoroughly at home. They don't persecute you to distraction trying to "entertain" you. You are allowed to enjoy yourself in your own way.

Saturday, April 6, 1895
This week has been a hard one, owing to the mud and slush. Thursday evening Mrs. E. and I drove over to Mr. McKays at East Bideford and met there— Inspector Campbell. As he would visit my school the next day I felt pretty nervous. I went early to school yesterday morning, had it swept and garnished, and drilled up the kiddies. In due time he came and things were not too bad. The children did well and the order was excellent. He professed himself satisfied and gave us a half-holiday.

Friday, April 12, 1895
Bideford
The Grand Division met at Ellerslie to-day and I had promised to recite at the public meeting to-night, so Lou came out after me. The hall was crowded. I recited "Caleb's Daughter" and for an encore "The Schoolmaster's Guests".

Edwin Simpson was there from Bedeque, where he is teaching, and we had a short chat.

Monday, April 15, 1895
Last night we had our Easter Missionary service in the church. I recited and read a selection. Lou came down with us, and as the walking was vile Mrs. Estey made him stay all night. Rev. E. was away or she would not have dared to extend the courtesy. When Mrs. Estey got up this morning she found every door piled high with logs of wood! I discovered to-day, that it was done by Fred Ellis, Jos Miller and Cliff Williams, thinking, I suppose that when Lou went home he would have a picnic getting out. But as he did not go at all that little scheme fell flat and it was poor Mrs. Estey who had to open the doors when she got up this morning.

Saturday, April 20, 1895
This has been an uneventful week—one day just like another. Lou was out Thursday evening and again to-night and brought me my letters. One was from the Rev. Mr. Lacing of the Halifax Ladies' College, to whom I had written concerning going there. He wrote that I was so far advanced that he thought I had better take a selected course at Dalhousie if I did not care to enter as an under-graduate. "Care to enter." There is nothing on earth I would like so much but there is no use in thinking of it, for I could not afford to complete the B.A. course. I shall likely take the selected course if I decide to go at all. I am anxious to spend a year at a real college as I think it would help me along in my ambition to be a writer.

I shall be heartily glad when vacation comes for I need it. I get wet every day and naturally seep up the worst sort of a cold. I do not feel well at all.

Monday, May 6, 1895
Bideford, P.E.I.
Earth has not forgotten how to be lovely nor spring how to charm. It was delicious to-day. After tea Mrs. Estey and I walked over to the station and called at the P.O. on our way back. I am going to board there after vacation. Mr. and Mrs. Estey leave for another circuit early in June, so it is necessary for me to look for a new abiding place.

Lou came along as we left the P.O. and we all sauntered home in the cool, lovely twilight. Getting here, Lou and I did not go in but went around to the corner of the veranda where we perched ourselves on the railing and chatted for an hour. It was a simply delicious night. The moonlight fell in a misty golden shower over trees and grass, and the bay before us shimmered in glory. The wind was as soft as a wind of June and the frogs were singing. All my cares and worries melted away in sheer happiness and joy of living. I felt as light-hearted and care-free as a child.

Thursday, May 23, 1895
Cavendish

This week has been very quiet and pleasant. This evening Lu and I went to prayer-meeting and as we were too early we went for a walk in along the road. It was lovely. The trees and fields are a delicate fairy green, purple violets are peeping out of the grass under the spruces, and at evening the setting sun tints pond and bay and ocean until they are "a sea of glass mingled with fire."

Pensie was up at prayer meeting and asked us down tomorrow.

Tuesday, May 28, 1895
Cavendish, P.E.I.

I am just back from a visit to town and feel pretty tired after all my junketting about. I went up to the station on Saturday with the mailman and had a very wearisome drive. I got to town about six and went at once to Aunt Mary's. After tea Mary Campbell appeared, much to my surprise and delight, for she had written me that she was much afraid that she would not be able to get in. We went to Norman's boarding house, got him to escort us around town and had a jolly walk. Sunday morning we went to Zion. I certainly do love that church. We had hoped to hear Mr. Sutherland preach but he had been suddenly taken ill and his place was supplied by an imposing youth from Kensington Hall. He was so short that we could barely see his thin pompadour above the pulpit and his grammar was barbarous. His text, as he announced it, was "the 16th chapter of the 11th Psalm"—Echo answers "Where"?—and his treatment of this problematical text was quite in keeping with its undiscoverable nature.

After dinner Jack S. came down to see me. In the evening Norman and I went to church together and afterwards had a nice walk up Prince St. Monday morning Mary and I spent shopping and at noon went down to the college. We found the dear old doctor superintending an Academic exam in his room and he was delighted to see us. We sat and chatted with him for nearly an hour. I told him I was going to take a selected course at Dalhousie next year and then he told me I had "great literary talent" and ought to cultivate it, and went on to give me some good advice how to do it and said he had no doubt of my ultimate success. Words like those from such a man as Dr. Anderson are indeed encouraging. Then we went to see Mr. Caven—who is as rubicund and jolly as ever—Mr. Robertson and Mr. Shaw, and then we left. Mary had to go home on the afternoon train.

After tea Selena Robinson called and we had a jolly chat. Jack and Will S. and Jack Gordon came down and spent the evening and we had a most hilarious time.

This morning I had to rise with the lark to catch the early train. The ride out to Hunter River was charming. The country is a veritable "garden of Eden" now, with all the blossoms out. This evening Lu and I went for a walk up Lover's Lane, which is bewilderingly sweet now with wild cherry bloom.

Wednesday, June 5, 1895

Monday I began work again, with a turnout of 33 pupils, half of whom were in the primer class, so the amount of work was considerable. After school I went down to the Parsonage for tea. It seemed like home again. After tea Mrs. E. and I went to the Valley and had a pleasant drive. Tuesday evening I spent at the Millars'.

Thursday, June 6, 1895
Ellerslie

I have *the* experience of my life to chronicle—at least, I am very sure that one such experience is enough for a lifetime. Every tale must have a beginning, no matter how it is spelled, and I'll have to go back to my first arrival here to come to the root of mine. Soon after I came to Bideford I noticed on a hill not far from the P.O. a large, old-fashioned house of a very "shabby genteel" appearance, situated in once beautiful but now sadly neglected and overrun grounds. On inquiry I found out that said house had once belonged to a well-to-do family; but reverses came to them and after several changes, all tending downward, the property had passed into the hands of the present possessors, who, I was told, were a by-word for oddity and dirt. When Amos MacKay came to school I found that he lived at this place, old Mr. and Mrs. MacKay having adopted him. Well, last Tuesday morning Amos appeared with a letter addressed to me. I took it with inward misgiving, expecting to get a going-over for some sin of commission or omission in regard to Amos; but this is what I read.

"Miss Montgomery:—

As you have never been to see us since you came here I wish you to come and visit us and let us know by the bearer of this note when you will come.

Yours truly,

Archibald MacKay."

Well, of course I had to go, so I sent word that I would go Thursday evening. To make things pleasanter Maud Hayes and all the rest immediately began to prophesy what I would get to eat etc. etc. etc., and really among them all they succeeded in nearly driving me wild.

After I came home from school this evening I dressed and went over, wishing myself a thousand miles away. When I knocked at the front door there was a great hurrying and scurrying and whispering! The door was opened and I stepped into a large dim, *dusty* hall where I was met *en masse* by the whole family, down to Amos, who came sliding along the wall, looking like a small goblin in the extraordinary garments he wears. The first to greet me was the mistress of the mansion herself—a withered old dame with her hair twisted around her ears in the fashion of 50 years ago. I was really frightened that she was going to kiss me but I escaped this by hastily dropping her hand and extending mine to her lord and master, who was literally a hideous old creature, all whiskers and rags. Bringing up the rear were son and daughter who did not greet me at all effusively— probably for the excellent reason that they are deaf mutes!

I was pushed, pulled and cornered into the dining room where Mrs. MacKay took my hat and left me to talk to old Archie while she got the tea. He kept up a steady stream of questions in a mumbling indistinct voice and while I floundered through my answers I kept my eyes on the table, mindful of Maud's dismal prophecies, and saw to my dismay that "the half was never told".

Words fail to describe my feelings as I sat down to that meal! *Did* they really expect me to eat such stuff? I wished the floor would open and swallow me up but as it didn't, I grimly threw myself into the fray, determined to eat something or perish in the attempt—and I rather believed I would do the latter.

The old lady poured out tea in cups which looked as if they had never been washed since the day they were bought. Inside and out they were liberally daubed with ancient tea-stains. I tried vainly to find a clean spot to drink from and, failing, shut my eyes and took a wild gulp, the taste nearly finishing what the sight had begun, for it was an atrocious brew with huge lumps of *sour* cream floating round like ice-bergs in a muddy sea. As soon as I had partially recovered from this dose I opened my eyes and examined the contents of my plate to see what I could dare eat. It was nearly filled with a huge lump of—well, I suppose it was intended for pie. Peering out timidly was a leathery edge of thick brown crust. Inside this was a slimy mass of pale green stuff—presumably stewed rhubarb, although Maud insists that it was burdock!!—and a huge spoonful of coarse brown sugar, mingled with *sour*, *lumpy* cream was spread over this. This inviting mixture was furthermore crowned by a huge splurge of "cranberry sarse".

Well, *that* was hopeless! I did take one spoonful but had death been the penalty I could not have swallowed another. So I took a huge slice of bread fully an inch thick, plastered on some butter—*such* butter! I found three hairs in it:—and washed down each mouthful by a gulp of tea. I actually ate a whole slice and then, choked down a "patty pan". Honestly, I was afraid I would vomit at every bite. I shall *never* forget that awful meal. I would not have minded the food being poor and badly cooked if it had only been *clean*!

When all was over we went into the parlor where I had to sit for the rest of the evening and talk to my host and hostess. The floor was covered with hideous red mats and the chairs with equally hideous crocheted tidies—all of which, the old gentleman proudly informed me were "Maggie's work". Dirty lace curtains hung in the windows and the walls were adorned with a marvellous assortment of newspaper prints, cards, almanacs, prize pig cuts, etc.

Would that I could depict our conversation! But one example must suffice.

"D'ye understand *Lating* and all that?" demanded the old gentleman.

"Oh, yes," I responded, glibly and rashly.

"What's that?" he asked, darting a very dirty finger at the newspaper I held. "What's that in *Lating*?"

"This?" I gasped feebly, wondering if he expected me to translate the whole sheet off into "Lating" *extempore*.

"Yes. What's 'newspaper' in Lating?"

Now, considering that newspapers are rather more modern than the empire of the Caesars' I might be pardoned for not knowing but old Archie could not be made to understand this and my reputation for classical learning was at stake. But I solemnly aver that every word of Latin I ever knew fled from my memory except "papyrus" and I blurted it out as a drowning man might clutch at the proverbial straw.

But it answered the purpose for poor old Archie thought it was simply wonderful and remarked "De-e-arr, de-e-arr", in a tone of profound marvel at my erudition!

But everything comes to an end sometime, if you only live to see it, and at last I got away and crawled home. Verily, we schoolmarms have troubles of our own. And I have acutely realized the truth of Pope's line, "A little learning is a dangerous thing."

Monday, June 17, 1895

Went to preaching yesterday morning—and that is the last sermon I shall hear in Bideford church for Mr. Estey goes to conference tomorrow. It gave me a start to hear the announcement for it made me realize how brief my time here is getting. I have been too busy to think much about it but it came home to me very suddenly just then and with a sharp pang, too. I shall be so sorry to leave. I have had such a nice time here and have so many friends.

This evening Lou and I, George Walsh and Bertie Williams, Charlie and Maud Hayes all drove up to Lot 11 to preaching and had a merry drive. They are an odd-looking crowd up there. The most extraordinary people put on the most extraordinary clothes in the most extraordinary way, and the result is super-extraordinary.

I had 40 kiddies in school to-day—I have over 60 on the roll now—a pretty heavy school.

Mr. and Mrs. Estey went away to-day. How sorry I felt to bid Mrs. Estey good-bye! She has been so kind to me.

I have had a story accepted by the Toronto *Ladies Journal*. No pay yet—but that may come some day.

Monday, June 24, 1895

So it has come—my last Monday in Bideford school. Shall I ever forget the *first* Monday? One chapter of my life is nearly closed. Time's unseen fingers are already turning the last page. And it has been a varied chapter of pleasure and toil, hardships and joys. I shall be sorry to part with the children. Most of them have crept into my heart.

John Millar has been my favorite pupil—a fine manly little fellow he is. Arthur Millar is also nice but dreadfully mischievous and Gordon was an urchin I never liked and who has given me a good deal of trouble. Alice Millar is only a "kid", thin, sunburned, a thorough tomboy, always running with the boys, not particularly lovable at all. Little freckled Maud McKenzie with her elfin head of short silky red curls and "cute" face is a nice little thing. Fred and Lottie Ellis were two pupils I never liked although they gave me no trouble. I never felt at ease with them. Emma Ellis was the worst pupil I had and gave me more trouble than all the others put together. Claud and Rebie Williams, Reagh Gorrill and Maud Estey were all dear pupils. Then there are the "yard" children, poor and ill-bred for the most part; yet some have a promise—never, alas, likely to be developed—of better things. The two little McArthur boys, Arthur and Cornelius, are two perfect imps and shame dulness personified. They simply could *not* learn. Belle and Garfield MacArthur were slightly brighter, however. Belle and Lizzie McFadyen were very pretty girls and nice pupils. Maud and Annie MacDougall were quiet and commonplace. Then, coming over to Ellerslie, Maud, Bertie, Clifford, Irene and Ella Hayes were as nice pupils as a teacher could wish. Willie Cannon and Aldred England were two nice smart lads, while Frank Grant was a clever, conceited, restless, bullying boy—an extremely *wearing* pupil. A whole drove of Murphys, Sudsburys and Howells may be catalogued *en masse* as "fair to poor", and there are a few others who are a compound of faults and virtues—as indeed, when it comes to the last analysis, most of us are.

Friday, June 28, 1895
Bideford, P.E.I.
"The sceptre is departed from Judah"—I am no longer teacher of Bideford school. But I feel so badly that I half wish I had never resigned. This morning I went early to school. Every child brought a bouquet for decoration and the boys got huge armsful of ferns with which we adorned every adornable place, and the old school blossomed out into unusual splendor. Seventeen visitors came and the exam went off splendidly. At its close my pupils presented me with an address and a very pretty little jewel box of celluloid mounted in silver. The girls were all crying and so was I, and so were most of the women present. Then we sang "God Save The Queen" and I went down to Mr. Williams to tea. On my way home I called into the deserted school to say good-bye to it alone. As I stood there I thought of the first day I had crossed its threshold—a trembling confused young thing feeling scarcely less childish than the children I was to govern. This has been a very happy year for me and I shall never think of that old school without a very kindly feeling.

Tuesday, July 2, 1895
Cavendish, P.E.I.
It is all over—and I am glad for I have been having a rather miserable time of it these last few days.

Saturday I spent making farewell calls and went to Mr. Dystant's for the night. After dinner on Sunday Lou and I went for a drive up the Fourteen Road, which is a very pretty one, and then we went to Mr. Millar's for tea.

After tea I bade them good-bye and we came up to class-meeting. At its close came a shower of good-byes, some of them very hard to say, and then we went down to Mr. England's for a brief call.

When we got back to Mr. Hayes' everyone was in bed, so we sat down in the front hall. I felt decidedly uncomfortable and didn't know just what to expect. I have driven about with Lou for a year, but I certainly, most certainly never gave him any encouragement whatsoever to think that I cared anything for him except as a friend. On the contrary I have put myself to considerable pains, in all the indirect ways permissible, to *dis*courage him. Still, I could not tell how he might have deceived himself and he has been terribly blue and depressed for these past few days.

I was sitting on the lounge when he came over to me and one look in his face was enough!

We had a very dreadful talk about which I do not care to go into details. Lou said he loved me but admitted that I had never encouraged him and that he never supposed I cared for him, although he could not help coming to see me. I felt very much cut up. I never thought Lou would care half so much but he seemed simply distracted. I told him he would forget me in time and find somebody else better suited to him—but in common with all lovelorn suitors he couldn't seem to take that view of it at all. He did finally go, I felt very sorry for him—but really I think he might have displayed a little more dignity. His abandon of feeling was rather disgusting, to speak the plain truth.

I got up at five the next morning to finish packing. I felt tired out, and my head ached. Maud Hayes was going into S'Side to take her entrance exam and we left Ellerslie at 8.15. Lou was also going down on business and came with us. I watched the old school until it disappeared and then turned around with a sigh. Lou was sitting opposite to me, looking haggard and dreadful. *I* wasn't at all hilarious, so that Maud was the only cheerful one of the trio.

Everything was deserted at Kensington, as it was Dominion Day. As grandpa met me in a truck wagon I had a most wearisome, hot and dusty drive home, and arrived here almost worn out. I have been most wretchedly lonesome ever since— as homesick for Bideford as I was homesick for Cavendish my first week there.

Sunday, July 21, 1895

I am just beginning to get over my lonesomeness—I have been really half frantic. This afternoon Pensie, Alec, and I went to church at New Glasgow. We had no end of fun laughing—of course, after we came out—at poor Mrs. Albert Laird who came sailing down the aisle and plumped herself down in front of us with a sewing needle and a yard of white thread hanging from the crown of her bonnet down over her back. Every time she twitched her head—and she is noted for her twitches—the needle would fly. It did look perfectly ridiculous and the comments of a pewful of boys behind us on "the latest style in millinery" were hard to bear.

We went to Mamie Moffat's for tea and in the evening went over to the Baptist church at New Glasgow. It was a delicious evening for driving and I enjoyed that part of it quite well.

Friday, Aug. 16, 1895
Cavendish

Selena and I have been having a pleasant time. On Wednesday Uncle Leander came, bringing with him his new bride—his *third*, no less. She is not ill-looking, but has a rather *common* face. Her best point is her fine complexion and bright golden hair. She seems kind and pleasant but not at all intellectual—quite the reverse in fact. She appears to be quite uneducated and makes bad breaks in ordinary grammar—on the whole rather an odd bride for clever, fastidious Uncle Leander. But then I suppose a double widower with a large family of none-too- "easy" boys cannot pick and choose—if marry he must!

Selena goes tomorrow and I shall miss her horribly.

Saturday, Aug. 17, 1895
Cavendish

This is a lonely house to-night. There was a wholesale exodus this morning. All Uncle L's went and Pen and I drove Selena to New Glasgow. I miss her so much—our jolly rackets, our confidential talks, our little plots and designs. I think I'll go to bed and have a good cry.

Sunday, Aug. 25, 1895
I have had a very busy week. Last Monday Vinnie MacLure came to do my sewing for me and we have been at it steadily ever since. Vinnie is a very jolly girl and we have any amount of fun, skylarking round a bit in the evening when our work is over.

Thursday, Sept. 5, 1895
....I had a letter from Perle Taylor of Ch'Town this week. She was at Halifax Ladies' college last year and wants me to room with her next year. I presume I shall although I don't know her at all. But then I know nobody else there and one stranger is as good as another. Perle is the daughter of Dr. Taylor of Charlottetown.

Sunday, September 15, 1895
Cavendish, P.E.I.
This is my last night at home for another while—I start for Halifax tomorrow and have been very busy all the week getting ready. I feel tired and worried and discouraged—not a bit hopeful or expectant. Nobody seems really to symphathize with my going to Halifax. Grandmother is willing for me to go because I wish it so much but not because she has any understanding of my reasons for wishing to go. She is going to help me a little financially too as the hundred dollars I saved while teaching out of a salary of $180 is not quite enough for board at H.L.C. and tuition at Dalhousie. Grandfather has shown no interest of any kind in my going. Cavendish people generally show a somewhat contemptuous disapproval. Not a great many of them voice it but Mrs. Albert Macneill—who never cares what she says or how she says it—expressed their opinion in her own vulgar fashion when she remarked to me the other day, "I don't see what in the world you need with any more education. Do you want to be a preacher?"

Now, I don't care a snap for the opinion of Mrs. Albert or any of her ilk—with my mind, that is. But I like Mrs. A. with all her shortcomings, and there is something in me that feels hurt and bruised by this attitude of old friends and acquaintances. Others are jealous and sneering. A thousand pin-pricks can cause a good deal of suffering. If I had just *one* friend, whose opinion I valued—to say to me "You are right. You have it in you to achieve something if you get the proper intellectual training. Go ahead!" what a comfort it could be!

HALIFAX SEPT. 17, 1895
The date is surely worthy of capital letters! For the past four years the day when I should write that heading in my diary has danced before my eyes, an alluring will-o'-the-wisp of ambition and hope. It is come at last and I truly do not know if after all it is really worth all the toil and self-sacrifice and struggle that I have expended in bringing it about. I suppose there is a good deal of truth in that old proverb about anticipation and realization.

Anyway, I am here—at least, as much of me as has survived my tossings to and fro and my journeyings hither and thither upon the earth this day. This morning I was up early and Lou Dystant and Lou McIntyre went to the boat with me. I crossed in the St. Lawrence, a wobbling old tub of a boat. It was quite rough but at first it was pleasant enough. The sun, pouring through ragged, sullen clouds changed the water to burnished copper and the land came out from between its misty curtains. Later on, I was a little seasick and had to lie down until we got to Pictou Harbor. We changed cars at Stellarton and again at Truro. We arrived in Halifax about 7.30. Miss Clark, the L.C. housekeeper met me. She seems very nice and is engaged to Arthur Williams. When we got to the college she took me to Perle Taylor's room. Perle seems friendly and rather nice but it did not take me ten minutes to perceive that her brains are *nil*.

After I had my dinner I felt less tired, so went up with Perle to the Assembly room to watch the calisthenics exercises. Then we came back to our room with a troop of girls to be treated by Perle to a "feed" which I need not say is decidedly illicit. They are gone now and the room is quiet. I am too dazed and weary to know what I really think but I imagine I shall like it here. I daresay it would be pleasanter to room on "the third-and-a-half", as the floor where the other Dalhousie girls boarding here room is known. But I am too tired to speculate so here goes for the narrow little iron cot, two of which the room contains.

My old acquaintances, Edith and Marian MacLeod, are here and I am very glad.

Wednesday, Sept. 18, 1895
Ladies' College, Halifax
This morning Perle's alarm clock awoke me early and I got up and dressed, meanwhile absorbing information from Perle as to H.L.C. etiquette. Then we went down to breakfast. The dining room is a long, plain, bare room, lighted by 16 huge windows, and with the walls wainscotted in yellow. It is really a hideous and depressing apartment.

After dinner I interviewed the principal, Miss Ker, an elderly Englishwoman, unpacked, and then went up for my shorthand lesson. Miss Corbin is the teacher. There are three others in the class. I think I shall like shorthand very much.

I must now stop scribbling and get ready for bed as the rule is "Lights Out" at ten. If I roomed on the Third-and-a-half I would not have to fall in with this, but with Perle I must. Dalhousie opens tomorrow and I must gird up the loins of my mind and pitch in. Excuse my mixed metaphors.

Thursday, Sept. 19, 1895
H.L. College
It seems like a year since last Thursday. This morning I went up to Dalhousie. My companions were Bessie Cumming and Elma Baker—Seniors—and Rita Perry, a Sophomore. I did not take a violent fancy to any of them and they certainly did not try to help the stranger within her gates very much in her new departure.

It is about half a mile to the college which is a large ugly brick building in bare ugly grounds. When we went in we were greeted with terrific cheers from a crowd of freshmen who were singing glees on the staircase. As soon as possible we went to Dr. Forrest's room and were registered. Then we came home. By this time I was tired, bewildered and lonely and could hardly keep the tears back. In fact, I was just going to curl up on my bed and have a good comfortable *howl* when Miss Clark came in and asked me to go for a walk. We went out to the Park. It was beautiful—so quiet and natural. Miss C. is very nice and jolly and we found plenty to talk about. I felt like a new person when we came back at six. We were late for dinner so Miss C. asked me to wait and have dinner with her; we went into the parlor and finished out our chat. I am getting more settled here now and I think by next week I'll feel quite contented.

That eternal piano practice is going on as usual. It rings in my ears day and night. They tell me that after you are here awhile you get so used to it you never notice it. The gods grant this be true!

This is prayer meeting night at home. They are probably gathered in the church now. It is only a week since I was there but it seems like a year. I *am* homesick, that can't be denied, and I feel pretty blue by spells.

Tuesday, Sept. 24, 1895
To-day has been a pleasant one—or would have been if I had not been troubled with an intermittent headache. I got some letters in the morning that cheered me up. I had only one class in college to-day—French at two.

I have got acquainted with a Miss Shatford who lives in the city and who seems to be a nice girl. She is taking a special course like myself. So far I do *not* like the Dalhousie girls.

I had to come home in company with Reta Perry whom I cordially detest. This morning I studied Cicero—"Kikero", they pronounce it here. They use the Roman Method and I don't like it at all. It seems like a new language and actually gives me a curious homesick sort of feeling for old P.W.C. days and dear old Dr. A's careful watch over our pronunciation.

I'm homesick to-night—there is no denying that. It is a *horrible* feeling.

Wednesday, Sept. 25, 1895
H.L. College
Latin class to-day was splendid and so was Second English. We had to write a theme in the latter and the subject was "My Autobiography". Our English professor, Dr. McMechan, seems very nice, but is, I think, rather a weak man.

Miss Amy Hill, a Dalhousie girl, called on me to-day and I am invited there to a party tomorrow evening. I smiled a little in my sleeve over her call and her invitation. I think I know the motive. She is reputed to have quite a fancy for Murray Macneill and I suppose she has an idea that she can curry favor in his sight by showing a little attention to his cousin. This is amusing, in view of the cordial dislike Murray and I really feel for each other. He, by the way, is attending Dalhousie in the Senior year, but he has never even called on me since I came here. This of course does not matter to me at all. But considering the fact that he has been a guest almost every summer at my home one would imagine he would at least show the outward forms of politeness for his own self-respect. But Murray cannot forgive me for not bowing down to him and worshipping him—something which he demands from all feminine creatures. That is the plain truth. So I fear poor Miss Hill will not advance her hopes much by her attention to me.

I had a long letter from Edith England to-day. She is at Sackville college, taking music and painting—likes her work but hates the place. That, however, is probably mere homesickness and will soon wear off. Edith has been a petted only child, surrounded by luxury all her life, and the contrast must be rather hard for her.

Thursday, Oct. 3, 1895
It is a very pretty walk up to the college. The grounds about the hospital and poorhouse are lovely. The trees are turning golden brown and the fresh morning air is odorous with the woodsy smell of frosted leaves. I am beginning to feel at home in the big rooms and long halls of the college and to recognize a face here and there in the groups and clusters. Our English classes are very nice.

Wednesday, Oct. 9, 1895
Lottie Shatford asked me to go down with her last night. She is living with her married sister here and the latter is away at present so that Lottie is alone. They live in a very pretty cottage on the Park road and Lottie and I had a lovely time.

In Second English to-day Prof. McMechan gave us back our "autobiographies" with criticisms. He told me mine was particularly good and interesting. Then we had to write an account of "My Earliest Recollection". Mine happens to be that of seeing my mother in her coffin and of putting my tiny baby hand on her cold face.

Saturday, Oct. 12, 1895
How fast "the moon of falling leaves" is slipping away! This morning Miss Chase and I went down to the Greenmarket, partly because it is considered one of the "sights" of Halifax, partly because we have to write a theme on it in class next Wednesday. It was worth seeing. In the afternoon Chase and I went to see the football match between Dalhousie and the United Service. I never saw a football game before and as I didn't understand it at all I didn't find it particularly interesting.

Tuesday, Oct. 22, 1895
H.L.C.
I am getting shockingly dissipated. It is nearly midnight and I am not yet in bed. But then one *can* go to bed every night and one *cannot* go to the opera every night, and that is where I have been again.

After Senior English to-day Lottie and I went for a walk in the public gardens because we have to write a theme on them tomorrow. It was a delightful evening, clear and crisp. The gardens seem lonely and deserted now but are sadly beautiful even in their desolation. The gray paths were littered with whirls of crinkled leaves. The horse chestnuts were splendid amber-gold, and the lakes and ponds were calmly silver in the dusky light.

The opera tonight was "Iolanthe" and was very pretty. Coming home I happened to fall in with Miss Clark at the door and we came in and had a feed of crackers and gooseberry jam in the kitchen. That's what it is to be on the good side of the housekeeper.

Sunday, Oct. 27, 1895

I really don't know what has got into me. I am never well now for two days at a time. I have had a fearful headache and *eye*-ache all day.

Reid and Perry and I went to a missionary lecture at Dalhousie this afternoon and to Fort Massey church at night. They are to have a social at the latter place Wednesday evening and I intend to take it in.

Monday, Nov. 17, 1895

Truly, "there's many a slip 'twixt the cup and the lip". Who would have guessed when I laid down my pen that Sunday evening when I would take it up again, or what that "headache and eye-ache" of which I complained portended?

I have had *Measles*—and thereby hangs a tale! Several of them, in fact.

On the Monday and Tuesday succeeding the 27th I suffered everything from "a cold in the head"—as I supposed—but I went out as usual. I felt miserable enough, but I never thought of measles, which was odd, because they were in Dalhousie and I might have been suspicious. On Wednesday I felt worse than ever but went to college. Perry had also developed "a cold" and she felt so ill she stayed in bed.

When I came up from lunch I felt so badly that I went to bed, hoping that a good sleep if I got it might make me feel well enough to go to the Fort Massey social. I dozed fitfully all the afternoon and was dressing for dinner when Miss Claxton came in with a mysterious expression on her thin, inquisitive little face. Miss Claxton—commonly known as Clack—is the matron, an Englishwoman, and a fussy meddlesome Englishwoman at that. I must confess I dislike her heartily and so I did not hail her entrance with frantic delight. Nothing daunted by my cool reception, however, Miss Claxton spoke. "Few and short were the words she said", but alas, how crushing to my hopes! They all tumbled down like a castle of cards.

"Miss Perry has the measles and I am afraid you have them, too."

If she had informed me that Miss Perry had attempted to blow up the college with dynamite and accused me of being an accomplice I could not have been more thunderstruck. By the time I had rallied my scattered wits Miss C. had scrutinized my neck, found rash and decreed my doom. I was ordered at once to Perry's room and went, with no very pleasant emotions over the prospect of being shut up for an indefinite period—and with Rita Perry at that—a girl whom I dislike extremely.

"Clack" had sent for Dr. Lindsay who came, looked wise, pronounced it measles, and assured me I couldn't possibly be hungry when I was simply ravenous. The unkindest cut of all was that I had been caught before dinner—and it was roast beef night, too. Not a thing would that hard-hearted being let me have to eat but ordered us to be at once removed to the college hospital and quarantined there for three weeks.

The next thing was a nurse—a Mrs. Fraser, who was quite a dear old soul but earned her six dollars a week very easily I think. Speaking of money, the measles have made quite a sad hole in my scanty funds, alas!

We were whisked off to "the hospital"—a bare, barn-like set of apartments in a remote part of the college. Here we were put to bed. I was by now pretty sick and all that night and the next day I was quite ill and my eyes were very bad. But on Friday I was much better and from that out I improved rapidly.

But oh, how terribly dull and wearisome it was! The Dal. girls sent us amusing letters every day and Mrs. Fraser read us immaculate stories out of "Leisure Hours" and kindred publications but in spite of this the time dragged fearfully. I dislike Perry and she *must* dislike me quite as bitterly, for there is something in our very natures that is antagonistic to each other. She is one of the people on whom my soul declares war at sight. But we have always been civil to each other on the surface and now as we were companions in misfortune, we made the best of things, buried the undeclared hatchet and got on excellently well, talking freely of cabbages and kings—and men! *And* things to eat!

We were simply half starved most of the time for they would give us nothing but abominable "invalids' diet"—weak tea, toast, and various "slushes" were all we got for the first two weeks. I soothed my hunger pangs and whiled away some of the time composing a serial "pome" on our experiences, entitled "When Perry and Mont had the measles."

On the next Friday they let us get up and I never was so glad to get out of bed in my life before. As soon as our eyes could stand it we got books and papers, but still the time was long. Of course we had some fun. Plenty of funny things happened and we invented two or three brand new jokes every day. Then the girls would come to the bathroom window of Corridor 3—which was just across the court from us—and talk to us from there in the dumb alphabet, giving us news of the outside world. On Tuesday they let us go out for a walk and you may be sure we enjoyed it. After that we went out every day but were not allowed to meet any of our friends. Mrs. Fraser left on Wednesday and then it was duller than ever. How we counted the days until we would be free!

At last Monday came. This morning we were disinfected from head to heels and came down, reeking with cinnamon, but happy beyond words. And I assure you I've had a busy day. I am to room on the Third-and-a-Half until the week is out. How delightful it is to be back in civilization once more! But I'll have to study hard now, for of course I'm fearfully behind hand in everything.

My letters have piled up since I was ill. Letters from home tell me that Mr. Archibald has accepted a call to Sunny Brae, N.S. and leaves C. this week. I am very sorry. It will be a great change and it will seem very strange to have another minister in C. He has been there for eighteen years.

Sunday Morning, Dec. 1, 1895

I was glad enough to get back to college last Monday. In the morning Rob MacGregor asked me to write a paper on Ian MacLaren for the Philomathic Society on Friday night. I didn't want to, for I've so much back study to catch up with, but he urged me so hard that I consented and was promptly stuck up on the bulletin board—at least my name was—between "Crockett on Crockett" and "Simpson on Barrie".

I've "set up housekeeping" on my own account now. Miss Ker told me on Monday that she thought I'd find it nicer to room up here on the Dalhousie flat for good. I do not always agree with Miss Ker but in this instance I emphatically did and moved joyfully up. I have a cosy little room all to myself and feel as independent "as a pig on ice". I never liked rooming on Corridor Three. Perle is a nice soul enough but we have absolutely no interests in common. She is very deaf and this makes her rather tiresome. She has only three ideas in her head—to get something good to eat, something fine to wear, *and* a beau! I like all these in due proportion myself but I don't allow them to crowd everything else out. No doubt I bored Perle as much as she bored me so we are much better apart. Here I am as happy as a queen and can stew and putter round as I like without interfering with anyone or being interfered with.

I wrote my paper on Thursday and last Friday night Lottie called for me and we went up to Dalhousie together. There was a big turnout of students and I was a little nervous, but I think I got on all right—at least, folks appear to think I did.

To-night we went up again to the Missionary meeting of the Y.M.C.A. as Reid had to read a paper before it....

Thursday, Dec. 12, 1895
H.L. College
I spent most of to-day writing a thesis on "Character in Paradise Lost". I hated the subject and put off the evil day as long as I could but had to settle down to it to-day. I did not make a brilliant success of it at all. The subject is too big for me to tackle.

To-night I was invited to a social at Mr. Gandier's—Mr. G. is the "eloquent and popular" minister of Fort Massey church. I wore my cream crepon dress with a pink silk crush collar and a fillet of pale pink silk ribbon around my hair. The girls assured me that I looked "out of sight", whatever that may mean. I had a fairly pleasant evening—not dangerously exciting at all. Manse socials, where the guests are invited according to their position in the alphabet and are mainly unknown to each other, are not apt to be.

Monday Morning, Dec. 23, 1895
Exams began last Monday. We had Latin and French. The Latin was easy but the French very hard. Tuesday I had no exams, so studied hard all day for the three that came on Wednesday—Roman History and Second and Senior English. I did pretty well in the first two, I think, but am afraid I didn't do much in the last. The exam seemed to be mainly in work I missed when I was ill with measles. It is something new for me to go down to defeat in English!

Thursday afternoon John Dystant, who is spending his holidays at Lem's, called. I was glad to see John, who is a nice fellow, but I was *not* glad to hear him say that Mrs. Lem had sent him in to take me out there for the afternoon. There was no decent way of getting out of it so I had to go. They wanted me to stay all the evening, too, but I had to go to the "Break-up Concert" at Dalhousie. There was an enormous crowd there and it was rather amusing but not very enjoyable. Perhaps I was too tired. The torchlight procession was rather good fun however.

On Friday morning the general exodus took place. All the girls went home and I confess I felt rather blue to see everyone going home and poor me left behind. My fare home would not cost any more than my board here but grandma wrote that she thought I had better not go home for fear the roads might be bad for getting to the station etc. I know what that means. Grandfather doesn't want to be bothered meeting me or taking me back.

Miss Clark did not go until this morning. I shall miss her more than all the rest put together.

Evening
This afternoon about four I resolved to go for a walk, so I betook myself out to the Park and sat down on "Greenbank" to look over the harbor. It was very lovely. On my left lay the city, its roofs and spires dim in their shroud of violet smoke that drifted across the harbor and stained the fair blue of the sky darkly, as if some fell angel had spread his murky pinion across the calm beauty of heaven. George's Island loomed out of the mist and the water lay before me satin smooth in sheen and silver gray, while the gentlest of wavelets lapped against the granite crags. Far to my right stretched the harbor, taking on tints of rose and coppery gold as it reached out into the sunset until it lost itself in banks of dull, fire-fringed clouds. The sails of several pleasure boats gleamed whitely afar off and their long reflections wavered in the gray water. The tiny dark headlands cut the creamy expanse and the opposite shores, softened by the mist, folded into each other in hill and valley of dark and light. A mingling of sounds came through the ripe air. On George's Island the lighthouse beacon flared through the smoke like a baleful star and was answered by another on the far horizon. And far above all, in a concave of stainless blue, where no soil of earth could reach, shone a silver-white half moon with a maiden veil of pearly vapor drawn chastely over her pure face.

Tuesday, Dec. 24, 1895
Really, this is a somewhat monotonous existence. An account of one day's programme will furnish a pattern for all the holidays here. Holidays? Bah!!

Eight o'clock found me sleepily dressing—for early rising rules are in abeyance during vacation—and 8.30 found me sitting at the breakfast table with as prim and proper expression as my somewhat vivacious physiognomy can assume, hardly daring to smile. We have our meals in the library now, as the heat is shut off the dining room. In severe state at the head of the table sits Miss Ker. Nature must have meant Miss Ker for a man and got the labels mixed. She might have made a fairly good one, but as a woman I consider her a woeful failure. She is guiltless of corsets and her dress is in strict conformity with the rules of hygiene and ugliness. Her iron-gray hair is always worn in a lop-sided coronet and she posseses a decided moustache. She is a "Girton" product and no doubt very clever. But she has not one atom of charm or magnetism.

Opposite Miss Ker sits Miss Claxton who is her very anti-type. Miss C. is a fussy, nervous little old maid, with a hooked nose, an inquisitive expression and a thin rattling little laugh that sets my nerves on edge.

Miss Tilsley is another English lady of uncertain age, but rather more like other people. She is dark, black-eyed, and *very* "English". Miss O'Ellers (pronounced Erlers) the German teacher, is really the best-hearted and most nearly human of the lot, though she is very ridiculous in some ways. Miss Ker dislikes her and is always snubbing her most undeservedly, whereupon I feel that I would like to take

Miss Ker by her lop-sided braid and shake her violently. Miss Notting is a kindergarten teacher and is an aggravated specimen of old maidism. She could never have been very likeable even when a young maid. Miss Whiteside, the elocution teacher, is a Canadian, however, and besides is young and very pretty and I am not so much afraid of her as of the other grim cats. I am really frightened to speak for both Miss Ker and "Clack" seem to be lying in wait to pounce on any unguarded word or expression—and a snub from either of them is a rankling thing. They seem able to instil such cold venom into it. If I were a Ladies' College girl they would be within their rights, however ungracefully exercised, but as I am of Dalhousie and merely a boarder here, I rather resent their "bossing". I *did* get square with Miss Claxton the other day, though—beautifully square. I went into the teacher's parlor and seeing Miss Whiteside and Miss Tilsley there alone, as I supposed, I said, "Isn't this a lovely morning, girls?" Up popped Miss Claxton from a low chair where she had been squatted unseen. "You should not call us girls," she piped frigidly. "It is not respectful." "Oh, I beg your pardon, Miss Claxton," I said politely. "I did not see you there. Of course I would never refer to *you* as a girl." Miss Claxton liked it very little, for she does not relish an allusion to her age anymore than ordinary people, but she had to take it, for my apology was perfectly courteous in tone and matter and she had no excuse for resenting anything in it.

Breakfast over, we wait for the mail which is the chief event for the day here. After that, I read, write, study, crochet, or prowl forlornly around until late in the afternoon when I go out for a walk. Dinner at six is another formal affair and the evening is a repetition of the afternoon.

Wednesday, Dec. 25, 1895
H.L. College
This Christmas, which I expected would be very dull, has been a rather pleasant one after all. I got a number of pretty gifts and some delightful letters. We had a goose repast at night and a pleasant evening in the parlor afterwards.

50. *Uncle John Montgomery's house from the bay*
[Malpeque]

51. *Kensington Station*

52. *Ladies' College, Halifax*

53. *Lottie Shatford*   54. *Perle Taylor as a gypsy, at a masquerade*

1896

Tuesday, Jan. 7, 1896

All yesterday and to-day there has been nothing but arrivals, and the climax was reached to-night when the Dalhousie girls returned, all that could be heard was racing and chasing and kisses and yells of welcome on corridors and stairs. College opens tomorrow and I am not a bit glad. I've got lazy and contented in vacation and don't like the idea of starting in to struggle again. It must be, however, so I have religiously set my alarm clock for seven and intend to "buckle to" with all due "grit".

It has been gruesomely cold these last three days. I believe winter is really upon us at last and the next two months are likely to prove mortifying to the flesh. Well, well, I suppose I must give up my novels and my morning naps and all the other vacation indulgences and return to hard, systematic work.

Wednesday, Jan. 8, 1896
H.L. College

A cold bath may be unpleasant to get into but after the first plunge you don't mind it. So it is with a return to work after holidays. You shut your eyes, take a resolute header, and find yourself quite reconciled to it.

The results of our Latin exam were announced in class this morning. They follow quite a different method here from that which they use at P.W.C. Here no professor stalks in with a huge bundle of papers under his arm which he proceeds with malicious deliberation to dispose of according to value. The malicious deliberation is here to be sure, but for the rest, the Professor simply reads out the list in each "class"—viz. "First", "Second" and "Pass". Those whose name is not called read their fate in silence. I got a "First" both in Roman History and Latin and led the class in the latter. It was a pretty good showing and as I've worked hard for it I enjoy it.

Friday, Jan. 10, 1896

I got a "Second" in French—much to my surprise—and a first in English. Was down to a turkey-feed in Perle's room tonight and if noise and racket consitute a good time we must have had one.

It snowed heavily to-day and I suppose we must make up our minds to face winter in earnest now. I hope I won't have to wade through snow as I did last year. But then I'll not have the sleigh drives either. Poor Lou, he certainly did give me some lovely ones.

154

Saturday, Jan. 11, 1896
H.L. College
I went to see Mrs. McKenzie and Maudie this afternoon. They live on Maynard St. away on the other side of citadel Hill. She wants me to give Maudie music lessons. I hesitated at first for it is a long way out and I detest giving music lessons. But in the end I consented for it will mean five dollars and every cent has to count with me. I am to go Wednesdays and Saturdays.

We have a new Dalhousie boarder—Nina Church. She is a thin, nervous-looking girl and I know nothing about her either to like or dislike yet. Perry and Reid cordially detest her—to be sure, that is no guide. But Miss Clark does also, so there must be some good reason.

I have been fooling away my time to-night—first with the MacLeod girls, then with Miss Clark; and then all we Dal. girls sat in Reid's room and discussed love-letters and similar weighty and grave subjects. We are a happy-go-lucky crowd, I must say, and have a gay little world of our own up here on this flat. I am not very intimate with any of the girls but I like them all well enough except Perry. Miss Chase is my favorite, Reid next. Bessie Cumming and Elma Baker I do not quite fancy. But we all get on very well together and have lots of fun.

Monday, Jan. 20, 1896
H.L. College
The "itch for writing"—I forget how it is spelled or I would write it in Latin—is upon me to-night, so I must e'en get out this long-suffering old journal and scribble in it.

This morning Latin class came first. We have a very nice one. Professor Murray is charming, although I thought him a bit stodgy at first. I have got used to the "k" way of pronouncing Latin and once in a while prevail on my tongue to say "Kikero" when I mean Cicero. We are at Virgil now and are in Book V of the Aeneid—we studied the VI at P.W.C. with Dr. Anderson keeping us in the straight and narrow path of good Latinity. Latin is one of my favorite studies now. Little did I think it would ever become so when I first began to learn it in that old white schoolhouse under Miss Gordon's watchful eye. What fearful messes I used to make of my declensions and conjugations! I was quite sure I could *never* learn Latin; but time works wonders and there are harder things than Latin to be conquered after all.

The hour between Latin and English I spend in the library, browsing among books—and getting more real good than I do in classes. 'Tis a nice old place that library, with several tables where students read, a cosy corner here and there, and a bust of Cicero surveying the scene from his exalted position over the classics department. I wonder if it really looks one bit like Cicero.

It is a spot for chance gossips and the only place where a boy and girl dare chat together—always in a cautious undertone of course, for it is one of the rules of the domain that no loud talking is permitted, so that sounds there are none, save subdued whispers, rustling of leaves, tip-toeing footsteps and echoes from the outer halls.

English hour is generally an interesting one. Lottie and I sit on a front seat next the wall, beneath a picture of Titania and her fairy court, with a long row of Shakespeare's heroines staring us in the face. We are reading *Romeo and Juliet* now and as sentimental scenes are Prof. McMechan's forte it suits him admirably.

It is always a nuisance to go back to Dalhousie after lunch for German, because I feel that I am not getting one spark of benefit out of that class. Go I did, however, and put in the hour reading "Old Mortality". Very dreadful, do you say? But not so. It is part of our Senior English work.

Midnight

We had a "picnic" up on "Pandemonium Flat" tonight. It is one of the new rules that they have sprung on us Dals. this year that we must put out our lights at eleven, ostensibly to protect our health but in reality to save "Daddy Laing's" precious gas. Well, I needn't say that this rule isn't always strictly observed and less so than ever since the holidays. So that it was five minutes on the wrong side of eleven when I, standing before the mirror in a classic undress and brushing my hair, heard a faint tap at my door.

"Come," I called out, as unconcerned "as a pig on ice", for I supposed it was one of the girls. But you could have demolished me with the traditional feather when our austere principal herself poked her head in at the door.

"Aren't you going to bed?" she asked in a tone that conveyed her impression that I had some deeply rooted design of staying up all night.

"Yes," I gurgled faintly—"I—I—didn't notice that it was after eleven"—which was strictly true, for I hadn't troubled myself about the matter at all!

"Well, you *must* notice," said Mother Ker acridly, as she rustled away.

As soon as I dared I slipped out to see if anyone else had been lagged. Chase, Baker and Cumming had all been caught but, as the devil looks after his own, Perry and Reid had just turned theirs out before she passed.

Well, Chase and I resolved to stay up as long as we pleased, even if we had to do it in the dark, so I turned out my gas and went into Chase's room where we larked and laughed till nearly twelve.

Sunday, Jan. 26, 1896

This evening Reid and I stayed home from church as it was wet and we had colds and as we were passing along the corridor we happened to glance into Chase's room, her door being open. Now, Chase is notoriously untidy and had left her room as usual in a state resembling original Chaos. Reid and I were ripe for mischief, so we waded in—not to make things worse for that was impossible but to give a piquant arrangement to them. We succeeded admirably—you should have seen that room when we had finished. Then we dressed a broom and pillow in Chase's clothes and stood it up by the window. It was "flee for your life" when Chase got home.

Midnight

I suppose Miss Ker would have a kitten fit if she knew I was out of bed at this hour. About nine one of the maids came up to say that Miss Clark wished to see me. I hurried down, suspecting why I was wanted. Miss C. had confided her story to me before and I knew that the relations between her and Mr. Williams were strained almost to the yielding point. When I went in she was crying and simply held out her ringless finger to me. She has broken her engagement at last. She was driven to it. Williams has treated her shamefully and the poor girl is almost heart-broken. I am sorry for her but I think she is well rid of him. I don't think there is a spark of principle in him and I feel sure he would never make her happy.

Saturday, Feb. 15, 1896
My head is quite giddy—I've had an extra streak of luck to-day. In January the *Evening Mail* offered a prize of five dollars for the best letter on the question "Which has the more patience under the ordinary cares and trials of life—man or woman?" The letters poured in and the best of them were printed in the *Mail* every evening. At first I took small interest in the contest, but Lottie—whose brother-in-law is on the paper—urged me to send in a letter and finally I did. I was tired of the usual strain so I tried to produce something more original and wrote a short allegory....

Mr. Weir showed this letter to Lottie—of course he didn't know it was mine as all the letters were signed with a nom-de-plume—and said it was the prettiest thing sent in but that it wouldn't take the prize because it wasn't an argument. I ruminated another while and one night I arose in the middle of the night to write down the following verses:—

> "As my letter must be brief
> I'll at once state my belief
> And this it is, that, since the world began,
> Since Adam first did say
> 'Twas Eve led me astray
> A woman hath more patience than a man.
>
> If a man's obliged to wait
> For someone who's rather late
> No mortal ever got in such a stew,
> And if something can't be found
> That he's sure should be around
> The listening air sometimes grows fairly blue.
>
> Just watch a man who tries
> To soothe a baby's cries,
> Or put a stovepipe up in weather cold,
> Into what a state he'll get,
> How he'll fuss and fume and fret
> And stamp and bluster round and storm and scold.
>
> Some point to Job with pride
> As an argument for their side!
> Why, it was so rare a patient man to see
> That when one was really found
> His discoverers were bound
> To preserve for him a place in history.

And while I admit it's true
That man has *some* patience, too,
And that woman isn't *always* sweetly calm,
Still, I think all must agree
On this central fact—that she
For general, all-round patience bears the palm."

I signed this effusion "Belinda Bluegrass" and sent them in.

The competition closed on the 7th and the letters were handed to Professor McMechan who was to be the judge. This morning Lottie suddenly appeared on the Third-and-a-Half and exclaimed breathlessly,

"Oh, Maud, I believe you've won the prize! Dr. McMechan has sent the best and second-best in. Both are verse and one of them is by "Belinda Bluegrass" but I'm not sure which is first."

So I was in suspense all day. To-night when I was coming home from Maudie's lesson I bought a *Mail* from a newsboy. But I did not open it then. No, I scuttled home, flew upstairs, and dressed for dinner. Then I opened the paper and the first thing I saw was "Prize won by Belinda Bluegrass". Of course I was pleased! Moreover, my first letter won honorable mention on account of its literary merit.

Thursday, Feb. 20, 1896
I had another very pleasant surprise this morning. Sometime ago, I sent a short story called "Our Charivari" to a Philadelphia magazine— *"Golden Days"* and to-day I got a check for $5 for it. Isn't that lucky! And so encouraging, too. I feel so happy over it.

I went uptown to invest my *Mail* prize money to-day. I wanted to get something I could keep always and not get tired of, so I got Tennyson, Longfellow, Whittier and Byron. They are nicely bound and I've always longed to have them of my own.

Dear me, how quickly the winter is slipping away! It has not seemed like winter for it has been very mild and fine for the most part. How different from last winter in Bideford where we were surrounded by such huge drifts in the dear old Parsonage. I wonder who has my old room this winter.

Happening to glance up just here my eyes fell on a card on the wall in front of me with several views of P.A. on it—nearly all well-known spots to me. There is the "River Road" where Will and Laura and I went walking in those wonderful western twilights when the sky was rose and gold and crimson over far dim prairie slopes and the river waters mirrored back the colors in fairy-like shadings save where they were deep and dark beneath the thick poplars on the banks. What a witchery there was in a prairie twilight! And we three would loiter along the dim path, laughing and chatting in careless mirth. Then there is a view of the station and the long platform where we used to promenade when waiting for the train; and the thick poplar bluffs and purple-misted hills behind it, with beyond them winding trails and sheets of prairie sunflowers and blue-bells, and gleaming, gem-like lakes.

I wonder where all the High School Scholars of that year are now. I have half forgotten their very names. Poor Frank Robertson is dead. Then there were the Jardine boys and "Nitchie" Tom Clark and Harry Oram, whose face was never clean, and John McLeod and the McKay boys and that peculiar youth, Douglas Maveety, and Willy McBeath. I forget the others—except Will P. of course. How well I remember that first morning he came to school and sat behind me! I don't think we were ever introduced—just scraped up an acquaintance. The first remark I remember his making to me was a droll statement that he "couldn't study with such beautiful hair in front of him." In any other boy it might have sounded silly or impertinent but in Will P. with his ingratiating smile it seemed just the thing to say! Then followed pleasant days in the old "council room" where we wrote notes and exchanged our books and laughed over our jokes and afterwards walked home from school together. How like a dream it all seems now!

Saturday, March 14, 1896
H.L. College
….I have been pegging away at my thesis all the week. It is tedious, uninteresting work, and I cannot see what possible good there is in it for anybody. Tuesday, I had a letter from Mr. Dennis, the editor of the *Herald*. He is going to get out a special Dalhousie edition and wants me to contribute an article on "The Experiences of a Girl Student at Dalhousie". I want to do it but the request couldn't have come at a more inconvenient time.

Saturday, Mar. 21, 1896
H.L. College
I have had grippe most of this week and haven't been able to do anything worth while. I can't realize that the term is so near its end. The way time flies at college is appalling. Last Monday morning I got a check for twelve dollars from *The Youth's Companion* for a poem I sent them, called "Fisher Lassies". The editor also wrote some pretty nice things about it. It is such an encouragement because *The Companion* uses only the best things.

Thursday, April 2, 1896
H.L. College
I can't study to-night. A restless mood is on me and I *cannot* settle down to my books. May Taylor has just been up here for a chat. She is a Ladies' College girl, very nice and clever—a great contrast to the usual run of H.L.C. girls who, like Perle, seem to live only for dress, beaux and eatables.

To-day I had another pleasant windfall—a check for three dollars from *Golden Days* for a poem "The Apple Picking Time".

Last Sunday night Edith McLeod came up and slept with me. We both slept in the one bed and as the H.L.C. cots are rather narrow it was a work of art to keep in. Nevertheless, we had a "scrumptious" time and a real good old-fashioned talk. Monday night I went down and slept with her. I am going to sleep with Isobel Morrison tonight—it is Easter Holidays here now, hence all this sleeping around, which of course is not permissible at other times. Isobel is up here now, sewing buttons on her garters. She is a Cape Breton girl and very jolly.

Tuesday we had our last French lecture and our last in Senior English. I was very sorry to be done with English. I have enjoyed that class so much and got so much benefit from it. We had our last Latin lecture yesterday and I regret that, too. There is only one more lecture for me at Dalhousie—Second English on Monday.

Wednesday, April 8, 1896
Last night Mr. Dennis sent me tickets for the opera. Miss Clark and I went. The opera was "The Beggar Student" and was very pretty. I enjoyed myself immensely. I always do. I think opera is delightful. It has no bad after effects on me—never disgusts me with homely, workaday life; on the contrary, it sends me back to it with renewed zest and spice.

Saturday, April 11, 1896
This morning Isobel M. and I went for a long walk through the park. It was beautiful. We just rambled on past mossy-floored pine aisles and watched the pearly waters of the harbor cream and shiver beneath the silvery mists floating over them.

When I came back I had to begin packing up because I am going out to spend a fortnight with the Lem Dystants and my room is wanted for another girl. My poor room—it looks sadly dismantled and forlorn now—pictures, books, nic-nacs all gone and only a few stray garments and necessaries scattered around. My poor little room where I have been so happy! I wonder if old dreams can haunt rooms—if, when one leaves forever the room where she has dreamed and thought and joyed and suffered and laughed and wept, something of her, intangible and invisible, yet none the less real, does not remain behind like a voiceful memory.

Friday, April 17, 1896
Halifax
I have been domiciled at No 5, Chestnut Terrace this week. Monday morning I had two English exams, and I think I did all right in them. Yesterday afternoon I went in and took the extra French. Then this afternoon I went up and took the extra English exam—and it is not only the last exam I shall have at Dalhousie but probably the last exam I shall ever take! I remember the first one I ever had—it was in history, when Mr. Fraser was teaching in Cavendish. And between that time and this stretch twelve long years each of which has flourished its separate quota of exam papers before my weary eyes. First in that dear old schoolhouse of vanished childhood. What a fuss we used to make over our exams! At home in a tiny drawer of my upstairs room I keep a big bundle of those old exam papers. How anxious we were to do well—how gravely we discussed the questions afterwards—how proud or otherwise we felt when the teacher announced the results! Then there were the exams at P.W.C. before which Mary and I used to sit up half the night and cram. And oh, that dreadful, never-to-be forgotten "week of horrors"—the week of the License Exams! I don't believe anything could induce me to live that week over again.

Prof. McMechan told me to-day that I had handed in a splendid Senior English paper....

Saturday, Apr. 25, 1896
5 Chestnut Terrace, Halifax
I was at a rather nice little party at Amy Hill's Thursday night. Yesterday and to-day I have been very busy. I am going home Wednesday, as are most of the Island students. Convocation is going to be something of a fizzle. George Munro, the great benefactor of Dalhousie has just died and out of respect to his blessed memory they are not going to have a public convocation. It is too vexing, after I've waited over a whole week on purpose.

Wednesday, Apr. 29, 1896
Ch'Town, P.E.I.
"Back to my native land again"—it seems as if it must have taken more than a day to bring me here. This morning my alarm clock wakened me at 6. I hopped out, dressed, and got my breakfast in solitary majesty. At 7.45 my cab came, so I said my farewells and left, taking a last look at H.L.C. as I drove out of the gates through the misty gray morning.

A few minutes after I got on my train Mr. Rodgerson appeared and stuck to me all the morning. I wished him anywhere else because I simply cannot endure him and that is all there is about it!

At Pictou we took the *Stanley*; it was cold and rough crossing over but I was not seasick and we reached Ch'Town at five. Laura and Harry met me and I came up to Aunt Mary's. This evening Jack S. and Jack Gordon came down to see me and we had one of our merry old times.

Tuesday, May 5, 1896
Cavendish, P.E.I.
Have been busy seeing old friends. Was in church Sunday. It seemed very strange not to see Mr. Archibald there. His substitute, Mr. George, preached fairly well. He is only here for a time.

To-night, having nothing better to do, I went upstairs and read a lot of old letters—Nate's among the number. How vividly they brought back those dear old schooldays. I almost fancied myself a schoolgirl once more, going to the old school with my classmates, now so widely scattered; and a strong longing swept over me to go to those dear old merry days when life was seen through a rosy mist of hope and illusion and possessed an indefinable something that has passed away forever.

"Where is it now, the glory and the dream?"

Gone—gone with the lights and shadows of those olden years —gone never to return. The freshness of early dawn comes but once and nothing can ever recall its vanished splendors.

Tuesday, June 30, 1896
Grandpa and grandma went to town to-day and so "Monty" kept house alone in great state and glory. When they came home I got a few trifles I had sent for—among others, a dotted cream veil with a distracting border. I have a decided weakness for dainty veils. A woman who has the right sort of a veil and knows the

right way to wear it can always appear well-dressed. But the veils some women wear! *And* the way they put them on!! When I see a woman with a limp, skimpy, dragged-out veil barely reaching to the tip of her nose and clinging there for dear life I long to reach over and claw it off and hold it up to derision and contempt. A woman who dons such a veil really commits a social crime and I contend that it would be justifiable *veilicide*.

Wednesday, July 8, 1896
Cavendish
This afternoon Kate and I went back to the woods to look for berries and visited "Kentucky" and Wyand's stumps. We got our bowls full but we worked for it, scrambling through brush, climbing dreadful fences, and getting roasted in the hot sun.

Nate is home now and was down to-day on his bike. We had a pleasant chat. He looks very thin and has a genuine *moustache*. It gives him a grown-up look but I don't think it becomes him at all.

I got a five dollar check from *Golden Days* to-day for a short story. People envy me these bits of success and say "It's well to be you," and so on. I smile cynically when I hear them. They do not realize how many disappointments come to one success. They see only the successes and think all must be smooth travelling.

Saturday, July 20, 1896
Cavendish, P.E.I.
This afternoon who should come in but Alma Macneill—dear old Alma not a whit changed from the days of yore but still the same golden-haired Alma with the dimpled cheeks and the sweet smile. She went to Boston three years ago and this is her first visit home.

In April I sent a story to the McClure Syndicate and it has just been accepted and printed in the Chicago *Inter-Ocean*. The check ought to come soon—hope it will be a good fat one.

Sunday, July 26, 1896
I suppose I must go and get ready for evening service—somewhat against my inclination for I was out this morning and I honestly think once is enough to go to church on any Sunday.

Sunday is supposed to be a day of rest but in reality it is as hard worked a day as any in the week. We cook, eat, and wash dishes galore. We dress with weariness to the flesh and tramp to church in the heat, sit a long and mostly very dull sermon out in a stuffy pew and come home again not a whit better than we went—not as good indeed for we have got a headache and feel very vicious for our pains.

I have an ideal Sunday in my mind. Only, I am such a coward that I cannot translate it into the real, but must drift on with the current of conventionality.

But I would *like* to go away on Sunday morning to the heart of some great solemn wood and sit down among the ferns with only the companionship of the trees and the wood-winds echoing through the dim, moss-hung aisles like the strains of some vast cathedral anthem. And I would stay there for hours alone with nature and my own soul.

I think that would really do me great good. But how dreadfully unorthodox and *odd* it would be. The local spinsters would die of horror.

Tuesday, Aug. 18, 1896
Park Corner, P.E. Island
I came up here Saturday afternoon. Saturday morning Edwin and Alf Simpson called at our place. Ed has been teaching in his own school at Belmont this summer but is going to college in October. I had applied for the school and he called to tell me I had got it. I was very glad for I have been feeling fearfully discouraged over my chances of getting any kind of a school.

Yesterday morning I went with Stella to her school, stayed there until noon and then went on to Uncle Robert Sutherland's. Jack was home for a flying visit and we had a jolly time. He expects to go to Ottawa soon to take a position there.

I stayed there until this afternoon and was sorry to leave. It is such a lovely place—an ideal country house, big, roomy and delightful; and they are all so nice.

Thursday, Aug. 20, 1896
Park Corner
I have just been having a siesta on the sofa and have wakened up feeling rather stupid. So I think I'll try to work it off by writing—sitting by the kitchen table on the old blue chest. How very much like old times it seems!...

Belmont, P.E.I.
Wednesday, Oct. 21, 1896
Friday afternoon Lu and I left for Kensington. It was showery and we had a rather chilly and disagreeable drive, but got up about four and stayed all night at Mrs. Pidgeon's. Saturday morning I took the train to Miscouche where Mr. Simpson, Ed's father—known among the clan as "Sam" Simpson—met us.

Belmont is five miles from Miscouche and it is a rather pretty drive but the roads were mud to the axle. Belmont is a rather pretty place, owing to the bay scenery but I have a creepy, crawly presentiment that the natives as a general thing are not so pleasing.

I am stopping at Mr. Simpson's until I find a boarding place. They live too far from the school for me to board here. Mrs. Simpson—who was also a Cavendish Simpson and married her cousin as a matter of course—seems like a kind, mild woman but of a somewhat melancholy disposition.

Aunt Mary Lawson is here on a visit, which makes me feel quite at home.

There are three boys home now—Fulton, Alfred, and Burton. None of them is very good-looking—Ed would seem to have absorbed the good looks of the family. Fulton is a perfect giant, with the most enormous hands I ever saw on a man. He is a Simpson to the back-bone—the concentrated essence of Simpsonism. Alf seems to be the nicest of the three. He is jolly and not so "Simpsony" as the others.

I can't make much of Burt. He is another all-over Simpson but possesses one characteristic that is *not* of the Simpsons—he is very quiet.

There is one girl Sophy, aged 15. She is the most lifeless mortal I ever came across and I can make absolutely nothing of her. I really don't think she is quite normal. Aunt Mary says it is "too much of the one breed" and I fancy she is right.

On Sunday it poured rain all the morning. After dinner it did hold up a little and Fulton proposed that we go up to the Presbyterian church at Central Sixteen, about three miles away. We started and as soon as we did down came the rain again viciously. You can imagine what a nice agreeable drive we had!

Monday morning it was still pouring rain and Fulton drove me to the school. On the way we called in at a certain Simon Fraser's to see if I could board there.

It is a fairly decent-looking place about a quarter of a mile from the school. I can't say that I was greatly taken with the people though. All that I could extract from them was that they would consider the matter and let me know by the end of the week.

The school is situated on the bleakest hill that could be picked out. The view from it is magnificent, looking out over the head-waters of Richmond Bay. The building is very small and only fairly well furnished.

A forlorn sight greeted me on my entrance. The trustees were putting up the pipe and the children were huddled around. I waited dismally and damply for what seemed an endless time; finally the pipe was up, a fire built, my papers signed and the trustees gone. I drew a long breath, and "hoed in".

I have taught three days now. Owing to the abominable weather the attendance has been small, not exceeding sixteen. In spite of the fact that the last teacher, Mr. Fraser, was considered a great gun I find the children terribly backward. They are a scrubby lot of urchins, too, and I don't believe I shall ever like them very well. Most of them come from rather poor homes.

There are a good many large girls going. One of them is Marie Monro, who is a new scholar, having only recently come to the settlement. She lives with her uncle, Dan Campbell, *the* trustee of the school, according to all accounts. Marie has passed the P.W.C. entrance and now intends taking up the Second Class work. This doesn't suit me at all. There is more than enough work to be done in an ungraded school without doing work that is supposed to be done in P.W.C. However, there is no help for it. Marie impresses me as an odd girl—clever but eccentric. Her first greeting of me was, "I shall expect a great deal of you for ever since I can remember you have been held up to me as a paragon."

I must confess I found no reply to make to this—I was really too much amazed. I had never heard of her in my life and none of her connections that I can guess at ever knew me. So why or how or in what fashion they have held me up as a "paragon" to her is something I do not know and not likely ever shall know—for I certainly won't ask Marie.

This morning I enjoyed the pleasant sensation of being locked out of my own school. After my weary tramp of two miles I arrived there to find that the school was not open and after much investigation into the mysteries of cause and effect I found that the boy who was to make the fire had gone to Summerside and taken the key with him. The result was that we had to wait until nearly eleven while Willy Campbell went home for a duplicate key. We were nearly chilled stiff.

Thursday, Oct. 22, 1896
Belmont, P.E. Island

This morning I called at Mr. Fraser's, determined to extract a decided answer from them one way or another. They have finally agreed to board me. I don't know how I shall like them but it is simply "Hobson's Choice" for there is nowhere else to go. They keep the post-office, which will be a convenience at least.

There are only two mails a week in this forsaken place. How letters cheer one up when one is a stranger in a strange land, grubbing away for a living in a dead-and-alive country district like this! I loved teaching in Bideford but I do not believe I shall *ever* like it here!

Sunday, Oct. 25, 1896
Belmont

This has been another terrible day of wind and rain. But it cleared up at night and Fulton, Sophy and I drove up to the Methodist church at Central. No minister turned up however, so we left and went to a house where three maidens of the name of Campbell live. The youngest of them will probably never see forty five again but they are very nice and kind, if a little odd.

I am to move to Fraser's tomorrow. I know I shall be lonesome. I only hope the people will turn out better than I expect.

Tuesday, Oct. 27, 1896

....I came here from school last night, and as I am now a member of this family circle a word or two of description will not be out of place.

Imprimis, then, the oldest of "us" is an aged crone, well down the treacherous slope of the eighties, deaf, almost blind, wrinkled and tottering, who nevertheless, poor old soul, thinks herself in duty bound to entertain me by quavering remarks about the weather and "the bad cold going round". I wouldn't mind her if she would only leave me alone but when she persists in talking to me it makes me woefully nervous.

Then come mine host and hostess—Simon Fraser and wife. Simon and his fair bride, although only a few years married, are long past their first youth and, never very comely, have grown markedly less so with advancing years. Of Simon I have as yet seen little but I believe he is rather intelligent and has a leaning to skepticism which even good Mrs. Simon's rigid Presbyterian proclivities cannot straighten out. Mrs. Simon herself is "fair, fat and forty-odd". Her grammar is excruciating and her manners not at all highly polished. She acts as if she were dreadfully in awe of me, but she is very kind.

This promising couple have one daughter, Laura, a spoiled, blue-eyed little monkey of four.

Then there is Dan, Simon's brother, a confirmed old bachelor whose state *I* assuredly shall not attempt to change. Simon himself could never pose as an Apollo but compared to Dan he is "Hyperion to a Satyr." Poor Dan's lack of manly beauty is, I understand, attributable to the fact that when he was a child his father threw a stump at him. Dan never recovered from the effects of this gentle missile. He is post-master and evidently considers the position one of great responsibility.

Then there is a Miss Fraser, yclept Jessie, whose state of single blessedness has not prevented her from becoming a mother. She gravitates equally between here and the home of her daughter, Mrs. McLaurin.

At present I have for a room one of those detestable little "off-the-parlor" places hardly big enough for a closet. There is no table in the room—nothing save a tiny washstand above which is suspended a looking glass in which I see myself as I devoutly hope others do *not*. My trunk swallows up all the space left vacant by the bed and there is only one nail in the whole apartment on which I can hang anything.

I have my meals in solitary state in the sitting room. So far the table has been fair and, greatest of all boons, *clean*. Mrs. Simpson is a most estimable woman but she hasn't the faintest idea how to cook or serve.

My "den" has one redeeming feature. The view from the windows is exquisite. We are only about twenty yards from the bay shore and I can look out on a sheet of pearly shimmering water over to the misty purple coasts in the distance.

All this, however, did not prevent me from nearly freezing to death last night in bed. Just in time to save my life I remembered a fur coat—presumably Simon's—which I had noticed hanging on the parlor wall. I crawled out, got it, and spread it on the bed, and finally went to sleep under it.

Wednesday, Nov. 4, 1896
I feel tired out tonight. Marie Monro makes the school work so heavy for me. She has so many sums she can't do and as I have absolutely not a scrap of time to do them in school I have to do them at home and I worked three hours over them this evening. But on the whole I rather like Marie in spite of her oddities. There is a clever streak in her. I don't object to *her* but to the extra work she makes—and goodness knows there is no need of extra work in an ungraded country school.

I am trying to do a little literary work now but it is under such difficulties that I am half discouraged. I am "cabined, cribbed, confined,"—and can never lay my hand conveniently on a thing. Moreover, I have to keep everything locked up as this family, so I have discovered, are given to ransacking my room and possessions when I am away. Blessed be he who invented locks and keys!

Saturday, November 7, 1896
....I had a letter from Ed Simpson today asking me to correspond with him. He wrote quite a clever letter and I think I will agree to an occasional correspondence as it will keep me in touch with college life and lend a little spice to this dead-and-alive sort of existence.

The *American Agriculturist* has accepted a poem of mine.

Saturday, Nov. 14, 1896
I really have to come to you, old journal, for a little comfort. I am badly in need of some. By the way, would it not be a pat idea to call this my "grumble book" instead of my journal?

Never mind! I do all my grumbling here and it never gets outside your covers.

My especial cause of complaint to-night is that I'm half frozen and haven't been really warm for one minute to-day. It has been bitter cold, with a piercing wind that goes through this crazy old house as if it were made of paper, for not one of the doors or windows will shut squarely or tight. Cold seems to shrivel me right up. I can endure nearly everything else but if I get cold I am no good for anything, physically or mentally.

Friday, November 20, 1896
Belmont, P.E.I.
Another week put in, thanks be! I *did* manage to exist through last Saturday night. Sunday afternoon I fled up to Mr. Simpson's where I got thoroughly warm for the first time in 48 hours. Yesterday evening I went up to Mr. Campbell's and stayed all night—*getting warm* again! That comprises my highest ideal of earthly bliss at present!

When I went to school this morning there was no fire on and when we did light it, it sulked the whole morning. It was bitterly cold. I am half frozen this very minute and I shrink from the thought of the coming night.

I cannot say that this family have improved very much from closer acquaintance. They do not seem to be in such awe of me now and in some ways this is all right but in others not. For one thing, we often have our meals together now and I do *not* like that. No, I am *not* overly fastidious. If you only knew how rough and uncouth and *dirty* the men are you would wonder how I could eat at all.

The food still continues to be fair, however, and if I could only be warm I would not grumble over the other unavoidable ills of my existence. Why, last Sunday night it snowed and my pillow was actually *covered with snow* that drifted through the window!

Thanksgiving. Nov. 26, 1896
Belmont, P.E.I.
Hum! I rather think I've put my foot in it; someway or other. At any rate, I feel rather uncomfortable—partly, it may be, from the effects of too much Thanksgiving goose and partly from the events of last night—although I am sure I am not to be blamed for them.

To go back a bit—on the Sunday night that Sophy and Fulton and I were up at the Miss Campbell's they asked him to bring me up some evening and he said he would and I said "all right". He took sick almost immediately afterwards and I never thought anything more of the matter.

The night Alf and I went up to the Methodist church we called in there and they asked *us* to go up some evening; and on Sunday night as we came home Alf said, "If the snow lasts suppose we pay that visit up to Campbell's on Wednesday night."

Of course I assented. I knew that Fulton was too ill to go out for weeks yet and it seemed to me a very unimportant thing who took me up. And besides, Alf and I had been invited on our own account, quite independent of anybody else.

Last night Alf called for me on his way home from Summerside and I went on down to his place with him. Fulton was all right when I went in, but when he found out where I was going—for of course I told his mother when she asked me to take my wraps off—he went into the room and shut the door. Aunt Mary came out and told me he had gone in, mad as a hatter, and made quite a scene, saying very nasty things to Alf.

Naturally, I felt horribly uncomfortable and was glad to get away. We drove up to the Campbells' and found they were not at home. So we drove back. Alf wanted me to go home with him for Thanksgiving but of course I didn't feel like it after Fulton's behavior, so I came home. Thanksgiving has been a dull, gloomy day and I've been dreadfully lonesome. What a wretched old hole Belmont is! What a difference between it and Bideford!

Saturday Morning, Dec. 5, 1896
Belmont, P.E.I.
Well, I have managed to exist so far and as the cold snap is about over for this time I have hopes of surviving after all. But I assure you I've had a rare week of it.

This has been my daily programme.

Get up at seven and contrive to dress and do my hair by dint of running out every few minutes to thaw my numbed fingers at the fire. Then eat my breakfast, shivering all the time, and next, arrayed in jacket and gloves—for my room is too cold to endure it otherwise—make my bed and snug up my den.

This done and once more thawed out, I sit down and write till school time, when I muffle up and scud to school in the teeth of a biting wind.

After school I come home, get warm, and have a *comparatively* comfortable time until nine, when I begin to shiver again in anticipation of going into my ice-box of a bedroom and crawling into a cold bed.

However, after innumerable shrinkings of the flesh I do get in, get warm, and finally sleep, thus ending the day.

Yesterday evening May Campbell and I went up to Allan Fraser's. They are rather nice—as people go in Belmont anyhow.

Monday, Dec. 7, 1896
Belmont, P.E.I.
Saturday afternoon I sat off reluctantly enough to make another promised visit. I had asked Sophy Simpson to go to Mr. Lyle's with me. To go anywhere with Sophy is bad enough but to go alone to Lyle's was worse, so of two evils I chose the least.

We got there in due time. It was a lovely day—a stray bit from our lost Indian summer—but the walk was so long that I was tired out. And as for the afternoon I never put in a more doleful time. Mrs. Lyle is one of those women who speak in a wailing dolorous voice—you are nervously expecting her to burst into tears every moment. She gives you the impression that life is indeed to her a vale of tears, and that a smile, never to speak of a laugh, is a waste of muscle and time truly reprehensible.

Her daughters are all painfully quiet. Sophy is the reverse of vivacious, and although it is very seldom I cannot make some kind of small talk, yet to-day I was undeniably stuck and you can imagine what a lively time we had.

Burt and Alf came for us in the evening and I went to Mr. Simpson's to spend Sunday.

As I slept with Aunt Mary I found out a few amusing things. Among others, Fulton has taken a terrible spite against Alf—we will not inquire the reason?—and moreover is terribly cranky and childish. He does not seem to be getting much better and I suppose his slow recovery is trying to him. Anyhow, I'm completely disgusted with him of late. No gentleman would act as he has done.

Sunday was a dull, quiet day. There was preaching at the Methodist church in the evening and Alf asked me to go. As I was honestly afraid Fulton would make a public scene if I went alone with Alf I got Sophy to go too, though Alf was anything but pleased at the idea. When Alf drove me home after service he told me he was coming over, weather permitting, to take me to a concert at St. Eleanor's next Tuesday evening. I was delighted for it seems to me that I have been buried alive for the past seven weeks. I simply hate Belmont and all that pertains to it.

Monday, Dec. 14, 1896
Belmont, P.E.I.
Yesterday morning I went up to Mr. Simpson's—per invitation, I may say, as I don't go there unless I *am* invited. Fulton is ill again with pleurisy and he is simply an awful crank. His mother has a dreadful time with him, and indeed the whole household comes in for a share. Aunt Mary generally lets me into the sidelights of the subject.

Hitherto, Fulton has kept his crankiness pretty well out of sight when I am there but this time he didn't. I can make a good deal of allowance for the effect his tedious illness and long confinement indoors has had on him, but still he need not be so absurdly unreasonable and sore.

He is simply furious with Alf and suspicious of everybody and everything. Poor Alf cannot drive away on the most innocent errand without Fulton rushing up to the garret window to see where he is going; and if Alf drives in the general direction of Fraser's—Fraser's house itself cannot be seen—then the Simpson household pays the penalty for the rest of the day. I suppose if Fulton were well he would not behave in such an idiotic manner. I am sorry for his mother. Aunt Mary said Fulton told her (Aunt M.) that he "didn't care whether he got well now or not, he had been so wounded and disappointed." Pray, does Fulton imagine that because I talked pleasantly to him, drove to church once with him and his sister, and promised to visit a couple of harmless old maids with him, that I was bound to him for the rest of my life, to the exclusion of all other men, brothers or non-brothers? He surely can't be so ridiculous—and yet what else has he to complain of?

But I know this—I am out of all manner of patience with him and henceforth when I am there I shall simply ignore him unless he behaves with some decency.

Monday, Dec. 21, 1896
Belmont, P.E.I.

….Poor Fulton is in a pitiable condition. He is again laid up—this time with an abscess in his side; the doctor says it will be two months before he can stir out. He wasn't quite so cranky with me this time—indeed, he was very nice but seemed extremely dispirited. This softened my heart towards him of course and I was also as nice as Nature permits me to be. I really want to be friends with him, for it is not pleasant to be "out" with a member of any family where one visits often. On the other hand, I am afraid to be as friendly with him as I'd like to be lest it again inspire him with hopes or wishes that are quite impossible of fulfillment. I think it was really a special mercy of Providence for me that Fulton fell ill so soon after I came here. If he had not and if I had gone driving about with him as I would most likely have done his mad infatuation might have deepened into an intense passion, and I tremble to think what might have happened when he found that I could never care for him. William Clark of Cavendish went insane and hanged himself—it was said because my mother would have nothing to do with him. And Fulton Simpson with his intensity of feeling and lack of ordinary self-control impresses me as a man who might do anything in some overwhelming spasm of disappointment or thwarted passion.

It was bitterly cold in school to-day. I dread the night inexpressibly. I do not sleep at all well at nights now and I think it is because the room is so cold.

Monday, Dec. 28, 1896
Belmont, P.E.I.

Well, I've been having a lovely time—the old schoolday adjective of "scrumptious" is the only one which will fully express it. Of course I've been out of Belmont to have it!

Edith England invited me to spend Christmas with her and I accepted if she could send anyone for me. I knew there was no one she could get except Lou D. so I told her she might send him and he arrived along at 11.30 on Wednesday. We started for Bideford at two. It was cold but the roads were good, so we got on finely. Lou was nice but very quiet. When we reached Tyne Valley the road began to get interesting. The old Valley and the road up to Mr. Millar's all seemed so natural and it was real nice to be on it again. We reached Mr. England's about four and Edith and I had an ecstatic reunion.

They were going to have a concert at Ellerslie that night and I was to recite. The concert was merely a Sunday School affair and was rather flat but I had an exciting time meeting old friends and pupils. Then Edith and I went home and talked all night.

The next afternoon Lou took us for a drive on the ice. We had a splendid spin and called at Mr. Williams' on our way home. Christmas night there was a service in the church. Lou came home with us and came in. The poor boy hasn't got over his folly yet. He was very quiet all the evening and seemed dispirited. I was very sorry for him but I could do nothing better for him than treat him with merely courteous friendliness.

In the morning I went down to see Mr. Millars' and in the afternoon Lou came out and took Edith and me in to see his mother. As we passed the school I ran in to see the old room. It was the only thing in Bideford that seemed strange to me for I have grown used to the much smaller Belmont room.

In the evening Clifford and Luther Williams and Wesley McKinnon came in and we had a very jolly time. Wesley is an East Bidefordian who is home from the States on a visit. He was not around in my time. Edith seems to be carrying on a very marked flirtation with him, in spite of her engagement to Bayfield Williams. She told me all about it. She is really quite infatuated with Wes—who is not at all her social equal—but realizes that he is impossible for anything serious. He is crazy about her; so, in Bayfield's absence, they are snatching what they dare of the sweets of love-making. It would be a dangerous game for some types but Edith will not go too far. She will give Wesley a kiss or two and some walks and drives together and they will have a rather tragic parting scene when he goes back to the U.S. Both will forget and Bayfield will never know. That seems to be Edith's way of looking at it. Not that Bayfield deserves anything better. He is a notorious flirt himself. What I cannot understand is how Edith can care at all for a man like Wes MacKinnon.

Sunday was a bitterly cold day with the air full of flying frost. Lou and I started for Belmont in the evening. It was just sunset, clear, calm and crisp, delightful for driving; but as poor Lou seemed very low-spirited and I was dull over going back to Belmont we did not have a very exhilarating drive.

Edith had told me that Lou had been drinking hard—something he never used to do. So I twisted up my courage to speak of it. He denied it but in an evasive way that rather increased than banished my suspicions.

He said also that his love for me had ruined his life. I cried, foolishly enough, and told him he would think differently by and by.

"I might if you were any ordinary girl," he said, "but I shall never meet anyone like you again".

"You will meet someone far better suited to you", I said, a little impatiently— for there is a certain something about Lou when he begins to bewail his fate that disgusts me. His lack of birth and breeding betrays itself then.

We reached Belmont about 7.30. Lou stayed all night and went home this morning, while I betook myself to my school. I must say it ground hard to return to drudgery. Visiting is all very well while it lasts but the day of reckoning is sure to come.

Wednesday, Dec. 30, 1896

What can be going to happen? Yesterday and to-day have been deliciously mild and April-like. I have been working slavishly in school of late for I am going to have the semi-annual examination tomorrow. It won't be much of an affair, I suppose, for I have no programme. I simply had not the time or strength to prepare one. I don't expect many will come as I believe they never turn out well here.

I was up to Mr. Simpson's this evening. Fulton has had his side lanced and seems much better in some ways.

In the evening Alf, Milton, Charlotte, Sophy and I all went up to Mr. Campbell's. Sadie and Olive Fraser were there and we had the merriest evening imaginable playing "Apes and Angels".

It was eleven when we got back to Mr. S!—a highly respectable hour, I should say. But Fulton seemed to regard it as a terribly improper one and this morning aired his views on it, asserting that every house should be locked up for the night at ten. I rather pity his future family.

55. Miss Clark

56. *Uncle Robert Sutherland's*
[Sea View]

57. *Aunt Mary Lawson*

1897

Saturday, Jan. 2, 1897

Can it really be '97? The century is growing old—only three more years for it to live.

Thursday afternoon I had my exam and got it well over. After school I made up my report—a tedious piece of business—and then I went to a party at Caleb Lee's. We had a rather nice time, although of course in that strictly Baptist household there was no dancing.

We broke up about one and of course as soon as I got home my troubles began. I was chilled to the bone when I went to bed; I remained so all night and didn't get a wink of sound sleep the whole time.

New Year's Day was glorious—clear, sparkling, sunny. I was invited up to Mr. Campbell's for dinner and had an enjoyable time.

After dinner I went down to Mr. Simpson's for we had planned a drive over the ice to Hamilton. Alf, Milton, Charlotte and I were going. When I turned in at the gate Aunt Mary suddenly appeared at the front door and beckoned me in that way with a mysterious expression. She towed me into the parlor and shut the door as softly as if I had been dynamite. Then she told me in a conspirator's whisper that they didn't want Fulton to know I was going with the crowd. He is sick again and worse than ever, and she and Mrs. Simpson had decided to intercept me at the gate and smuggle me out again by the front way when the pung had driven around out of view of the kitchen windows. This proceeding was carried out and I suppose it saved Fulton an afternoon of jealous agony.

We had a nice drive over the bay. The ice was in splendid condition, all sparklingly blue and white, and the fair, cold expanse of the bay was gemmed with dusky purple islets, like jewels on the breast of a fair woman, and rimmed in by misty violet coasts. We enjoyed every minute of the time and reached our destination—Mr. William Simpson's—about 4.30. Charlotte stayed over but the boys and I came home at dark.

I slept with Aunt Mary and we had a good talk. They are almost worn out with Fulton. He is simply intolerable—sulky, jealous, meddlesome, querulous. In fact, I really believe his illness and sufferings have affected his mind or he would never say the things he does. He has the wildest, most unearthly look about him and keeps tormenting his mother by telling her that he doesn't want to get better and won't try to. He never speaks to Alf except to quarrel with or insult him. He was very nasty to me this time, too—this morning I mean, when he discovered I had been to Hamilton. But I took his nastiness very coolly. He must learn that that sort of thing does not worry me, when I have done no wrong to him.

Monday, Jan. 4, 1897
Belmont, P.E.I.

Well, this *is* a "spell of weather!" I have been grumbling so long at the cold that for very shame's sake I dare not turn around now and grumble at the rain, mist and mud! Otherwise—but I will heroically refrain!

Saturday was perfect *overhead*—mild as May, with misty horizons and the bay ice as glare as glass. But *underfoot*—well, the less said about that the better for my resolution!

There was preaching in the Baptist church yesterday morning for the first time since I came. Mr. Baker, an evangelist, has come to hold meetings here. On principle, I do not approve of "revivals", but anything is welcome to vary the deadly monotony of life here. He preached twice yesterday. I have to be organist— much against my will. But I wanted to oblige Mr. and Mrs. Simpson—or rather, the latter, for I do not care very much for "Sam". The Simpson flavor is so woefully strong in him. But I do really like Mrs. Simpson and she has been very kind to me.

I was up there to dinner yesterday. It is an understood thing that I spend Sunday there, and I should really die of loneliness here if I didn't. Besides, as long as Aunt Mary is there it is a great pleasure to go, although the fact that two of the boys are on bad terms because of me always makes me feel uncomfortable. And I never know what outburst may come from Fulton. He continues poorly and cranky, but seems to be slowly gaining.

To-day was rainy and muggy and horrible. I nearly got swamped going to school.

Went to "meeting" tonight. Simon hitched up a cart and took us all—not a fashionable conveyance at all but a perfect boon to a weary "schoolma'am" who comes home from school tired to death, with small taste for turning out again in the dark to walk half a mile through mud and water ankle deep.

Monday, Jan. 18, 1897
Belmont, P.E.I.

Yesterday was a dream—a poem—a symphony—a what you will so that your definition expresses the ethereal revel of color, the thrilling glory and splendor of the wonderful day that came in roseate and golden across frost-rimed hills and crept away at night in an elf-land of moonlight.

I went down to Mr. Simpson's after morning service. After I came down from taking off my wraps Fulton was glaring out of the room window.

I said amiably, "How are you getting on, Fulton?"

He threw a black glance over his shoulder and grunted surlily, "I'm improving".

I shrugged my shoulders, exchanged a smile with Aunt Mary, and betook myself to more congenial company in the parlor. I did not speak to Fulton again, nor did he speak to me, although he watched me with such cat-like and stealthy vigilance that it made me nervous. As far as health goes he does seem to be "improving", but the same can't be said regarding his manners!

We went to afternoon service and there was quite a number to tea at Mr. Simpson's afterward. Then we went to service in the evening. Alf drove me with his wild gray mare "Maud" (*not* a namesake!). Fulton did not speak when I said a general "good-night" but as we drove out of the yard I saw him silhouetted in the lighted kitchen window peering out—no doubt trying to discover whether Alf and I were alone or were properly chaperoned by Sophy. Evidently he could not make it out, for when we drove down the lane in front of the house he was pasted up against the parlor window and must have sprinted through the hall with considerable celerity to get there so quickly.

The church was so packed tonight that I had to sit on the organ stool the whole time and it nearly broke my unfortunate back.

Today it poured rain all day and things were on a rampage of disagreeableness.

Wednesday, Jan. 27, 1897
Belmont, P.E.I.
I have been through all sorts of adventures of late. "Listen to my tale of woe".

Tuesday evening Alf and I started over the bay to attend a meeting of the Grand Division at Port Hill. It was rather frosty and windy, but we got over to Will Montgomery's all right. There we found Fulton, William Simpson of Hamilton, and my especial pet among the Simpsons, Arthur Simpson of Cavendish, who had all gone over in the morning. No Grand Division, you understand, could possibly get along without the Simpsons.

Speaking of Fulton—he really seems to be getting quite well. Monday afternoon he came to the school after Sophy—just poked his head inside the door and called "Sophy"—didn't deign to notice my existence at all. So I was expecting to find him more grumpy even than usual if that was possible; but—perhaps owing to the genial effect of company, or it may be not wishing to make an exhibition of himself before my relatives and his own—he was positively amiable and even seemed able to endure Alf's presence calmly. I do hope he has come to his senses at last.

At the hall I fell in with Edith England and Lou Dystant, besides several other Bideford people, and I had lots of fun.

After the concert we all went up to Will's for supper—and a good satisfying Montgomery meal it was! We left about eleven—three sleighs of us. Fulton stayed over. It was fine and calm all the way down to the ice but we had hardly driven a mile on the latter when suddenly there came up a blinding snow-squall. In the twinkling of an eye we were enveloped in a white whirl so thick that we could not see from one bush to another.

We couldn't keep the road, though we hunted for the bushes for nearly half an hour. We got completely bewildered and at last, having driven long enough to get to Belmont twice over we pulled up to hold a council of war.

How those three men did howl and yell through the storm, all talking at once! Each one had a different opinion and plan, and each was positive he was right. When Simpsons disagree who shall decide? As they couldn't agree on any plan of action we just stayed where we were for half an hour to see if it would clear off. Alf held the buffalo around me so that I did not feel the cold so badly.

Finally, as the squall continued as thick as ever, we decided to take the wind in our faces and start. *If* the wind had not changed—a rather momentous "if"—this would take us across to Cape Malpeque. *If* it had—well, we might drive straight into the channel.

In no very long time, however, we reached land. At first the men thought it was Cape Malpeque but after driving along it for sometime they found it wasn't, but couldn't make out where we were.

At last we caught a faint glimpse of a light away over the fields and decided to steer for it. There was no use in looking for a road—we just had to make one. We turned slap up the bank, tore a gap in a fence and drove across two fields. The going here was fair, but the next field was a swampy one where the sod had been heaved up into huge hummocks by the frost and however we got through that *awful* place without smashing everything up is more than I can tell. I expected every moment to hear the runners go smash. I was half frozen and wholly frightened but I shook with laughter to hear Arthur Simpson shouting without any cessation, "Where are you taking us, Alfy? Where are you taking us, Alfy?" As he was well in advance of us and tearing madly onward it didn't look as if "Alfy" was taking him anywhere! The horses were terrified by the bumping of the sleighs and were neither to hold nor bind.

But in the end we did get through and the next thing we struck was a dyke. The other two horses went over all right but "Maud" balked and jumped and finally kicked. Our traces broke and I had to scramble out and wait while Alf fixed them and lifted the sleigh over the dyke—still in a blinding whirl of snow. I got chilled to the marrow but eventually we got underway again and reached that blessed house in ten more minutes.

Where do you think we were? At John McArthur's at Fourteen, not half a mile from where we started. The wind had changed with a vengeance! And all the time we had thought we were going straight for Belmont!

We had to stay there all night. I didn't sleep a wink—I was too tired and cold, and besides the accommodations were very poor. We started early in the morning and soon got home not much the worse of our adventure.

I almost wish these meetings would come to an end, for I have got fearfully behindhand with my work. Still, they enliven up the place a bit. Two or three a week would be all right. Baker did not speak tonight. A Mr. McLeod did and he is a narrow, uncultured fanatic of an intensely disagreeable type.

Saturday, Jan. 30, 1897
Well, this morning something happened. Mrs. Simon, with an important air said that the upstairs room—that long-promised, almost despaired-of room—was ready for me and I might move up at once if I liked.

You may be sure I *did* like. If there is one particular spot on this planet I detest it is that ice-box where I have been sleeping ever since I came here.

The upstairs room is a fairly nice one as rooms go in Belmont. It is a good size, warmed by a pipe, has a table, a clothes-closet and a mantel piece. I spent this morning "flitting" and by noon I had everything as neat and cosy as possible. I feel like a new creature.

Tuesday, Feb. 2, 1897
Belmont, P.E.I.

Yesterday I received a letter which surprised me more than any I ever received in my life—a letter from Edwin Simpson. I have written him two or three times since he asked me to correspond with him and have received three letters from him—quite interesting and clever ones, somewhat tediously involved in style.

Yesterday's letter was a long one of several closely written pages. It began innocently enough with comments on my last letter, college news, and an account of his visit to Halifax during the holidays etc., etc., down to the middle of the 5th page. Then he suddenly broke off abruptly with the statement that he felt impelled to tell me why he had asked me to correspond with him—that he had intended to tell me at Xmas had not eye-trouble compelled him to go to Halifax instead.

"Then", he wrote, "I could have told you personally what I now feel I must tell you. It is that I love you."

I was so amazed that I nearly dropped the letter. Ed went on to say that he had thought of me ever since our first meeting and that our old friendship of five years ago in Park Corner was still fresh in his memory—that he never forgot the impression although circumstances threw us apart so widely; and although he made no effort to meet me it was because he felt that it would be absurd for a person situated as he was to make any such advances. But now he "sees his way clear into 'life's field of action'," and his "former fancy has deepened into an uncontrollable passion."

I don't seen able to believe that this has really happened. Other men have loved me and I have always guessed it long before they told me but it never entered my mind that Edwin Simpson cared anything for me. We have been almost strangers for the past four years. In the old Park Corner days our little "affair" meant nothing to me—I did not like him as well as Lem then. Even when he asked me last fall to correspond with him I thought it was merely because he knew I could write pleasant amusing letters and give him all the home news. His mother is his only other correspondent here and *her* letters certainly can't be amusing or gossipy!

I must answer his letter tomorrow although I don't fancy the task at all. I can only make the one answer for I don't love him. I've had no opportunity to learn to care for him.

When he was at our place this summer I found him interesting and thought he had very much improved. But I never thought of anything more. I *might* learn to care for him. He is a handsome fellow, clever and educated; our tastes in many respects are very similar, and *if* I cared for him it would be a very suitable arrangement.

I know my family would not approve—at least, grandfather and grandmother. They hate all the Simpsons; grandfather is rabid against second cousins marrying; and Ed is a Baptist. For my own part, neither of these considerations would weigh against a real affection. But there is no use flying in the face of your family for anything less.

Wednesday, Feb. 3, 1897
Belmont, P.E.I.
I determined to stay home from the meeting tonight in order to get time to answer Ed's letter. I wonder if Mr. Baker would consider it a valid excuse!

I told Ed frankly that his letter had surprised me greatly and that I certainly did not love him, never having thought about him in that way at all. I said I *might* learn to care for him if he were willing to wait awhile and take the chances but if he wanted a final answer at once it would have to be "no".

I'm very glad the letter is written for it wasn't an agreeable task at all.

Sunday, Feb. 7, 1897
The meetings are still going on. Baker is evidently determined not to leave a sinner in Belmont. Everybody will have to "get good"—to quote Mrs. Simon's cultured phrase!

I have no use for Mr. Baker after last night. In the "after meeting" he came out with a narrow, bigoted preachment on immersion. I was secretly furious. Week after week I've gone up there and played the organ for him and I consider it an insult that he should say such things in my presence. Evidently he *did* feel some small pin-prick of shame for when he concluded he cast a rather deprecating smile at me and said, "Of course I suppose you are all Baptists here. If you are not, you ought to be."

I gave no answering smile. I looked as dour as my Scottish Presbyterian great-grandfather himself could have done. If Baker thought he was addressing only Baptists, why speak on immersion at all? *They* did not need to be convinced of that.

I went to the meeting again tonight, however, for reasons of my own quite unconnected with Baker or Baptism, and Alf and I got a fearful upset coming home. Just where the road turns in at Gamble's gate there is a bad slew and then a snowdrift. We were going at a terrific rate and when we slewed against the drift the sleigh tipped neatly over and spilled Alf and me and the furs in a heap. It was a fortunate thing that sedate old "Lady" was in the shafts and not that harum-scarum "Maud", or dear knows what would have happened. Alf and I scrambled to our feet to the tune of derisive yells from a crowd of "kids" behind us, righted the cutter, got in, and drove off, the whole affair having passed in ten seconds.

Wednesday, Feb. 17, 1897
Monday night there was no service here so Bert, Alf and I went up to Central. Mr. McLeod had a magic lantern—the latest dodge for revival meetings!—and the place was packed. His pictures were quite wonderful—especially one showing the heart of the unconverted man—a large red affair sliced open down the middle and filled with a lively assortment of snakes, hyenas, wolves and other unpleasant creatures. If the austere Teacher of Galilee had seen it and heard McLeod's hysterical yelps about it, I wonder what He would have thought.

Tuesday night Alf and I went to a "Birthday Social" in S'Side. We had a delightful drive and the social was rather enjoyable. We had a wild drive home for Alf and Woodland Simmons raced all the way. Woodland and Alf have both been "converted" through Baker's ministrations, and the former testifies vociferously every night. But neither seems reconciled to be beaten in the matter of horse-flesh because of this. "In honor preferring one another" doesn't hold good when your favorite trotter is in question. For my part I expected every moment to be tipped out, skimming over those fields of glare ice and missing the other sleigh by a hairsbreadth in the narrow gaps.

This evening Mr. Baker held his farewell service. He goes from here to Cavendish—where he will find a far less impressionable crowd, if I mistake not.

Alf and I had a glorious spin afterwards.

Tuesday, Feb. 23, 1897

To-day was very stormy. There were only 16 pupils in school and it seemed like play. But I simply detest teaching here. It is such hard work and most of the children are stupid, ignorant and rough. This is not surprising, considering the kind of homes they come from. It is all so different from Bideford where I had such pleasure in my work.

To-night I wrote a long letter to Mollie. I haven't any chum in Belmont and I miss that more than all else. How far away now seem those dear old days of our early teens—half childhood half girlhood. And yet, I do not really think if the choice were offered me that I would go back to them. I believe I am happier now than I was then, despite my hardships. Every age has its own troubles. My childhood and early girlhood had them and they were just as real and worrisome to me then as those of today are now. So after all I do not really want to go back, though at times I do grow desperately weary of struggling and striving, with not much prospect of anything better ahead.

Monday Morning, Mar. 1, 1897

I am sitting here half frozen for another cold snap is on and the mercury is down to 20 degrees below zero. I have just finished my hour's writing at my new story and my fingers are so cold and cramped I can hardly hold the pen. Verily, I have to pursue literature under difficulties. I dread going to school to-day for I know the room will be frightfully cold.

Friday evening they had choir practice at Mr. Simpson's and I had to go as organist. Nobody knows how I hate it. I stayed all night. Fulton started off to Cavendish on Saturday for a cruise. I hope he will take a good long one. He and I have been carrying out a policy of "masterly inactivity" of late and "never speak as we pass by". I grew tired of being insulted undeservedly, so I just ceased to take any notice of him, the ill-bred boor.

Well, I must be off to school. I only hope I won't freeze stiff before night.

Night.

No, I haven't frozen stiff, but I've come so near it there was no fun in it. However, school is over for to-day and I am sitting here trying to get warm before going on with my work.

I had a letter from Ed tonight. He said he would *not* accept my answer as final but would wait and hope for a more favorable one in the future. He begs me to continue the correspondence and not let this incident have any effect on our friendship.

Monday Morning, Mar. 8, 1897
Last evening Alf and Bert and I went up to Central to hear "Roaring Billy" hold forth. He *did* hold forth for something over an hour and a half on the absorbing analogy between a railway train and a Christian—according to *his* definition.

Yesterday morning Mrs. Simon and I drove ourselves up to hear Mr. Higgins preach in the Baptist church. Mr. H. is a marvellous creature from a physical standpoint. He seems to be made out of remnants all put together wrong end foremost! But he is not such a bad preacher.

After dinner I went down to Mr. S', per invitation, driving with Alf, Burt and Sophy in the box sleigh. Sophy was in one of her very frequent "moods" and wouldn't even speak. She is the weirdest bit of humanity I ever came across. I am never comfortable when she is around, even when she is in good humor. However, I chattered away to the boys, who are never afflicted with spasms of silence.

In the afternoon Alf and I went to S'Side. The day was delightful and we had a lovely drive. We had tea with some friends and went to the Presbyterian church in the evening. We got home at ten after a lovely moonlit drive.

But the fires were out and I was compelled to go to bed in a chilled condition. As a consequence I was cold all night, slept wretchedly, and felt seedy this morning. I suppose, though, one must always pay some penalty for her pleasures. *I* always have to anyhow—sometimes double.

Alf and I are planning a trip to Cavendish next Friday if weather and roads permit. Lu is going to have a party that night and I want to take it in.

Tuesday Night. Mar. 9, 1897
I am *fearfully* tired. Tuesdays and Thursday are always hard days in school but this particular Tuesday has seemed possessed of seven devils, if a day *can* be possessed.

I had two acceptances of stories to-day, however, and that has heartened me up a bit. One was from *Arthur's Home Magazine* and the other from the *Philadelphia Times*.

Oh dear me, *is* life worth living? Not when one is as tired as I am at present.

Monday, Mar. 15, 1897
Friday afternoon Alf and I started for Cavendish, although recent rains and thaws had left the roads in a very problematical condition. However, we got on very well and reached Clifton at three, where we had tea at William Montgomery's. It was just dark when we got home. Our arrival was a great surprise as I had not sent word I was coming.

Then we went over to the party but I can't say I really enjoyed it. Alf doesn't dance—thinks it the unpardonable sin, I believe—and I didn't like to leave him alone among strangers with nothing to amuse him. So I didn't dance much either but played croquinole most of the evening and was bored to the point of tears. I *love* dancing and I loathe croquinole.

We left Cavendish on Sunday afternoon and went to Park Ccrner where we stayed all night at Uncle John C's. This morning we had to make an early start. It was fine but very cold and as it snowed a good deal last night the roads were very heavy. By the time we got to Malpeque it began to blow and we had to drive over the bay in the teeth of a biting northwester and a drift that was as bad as a snowstorm. I was half frozen when I got here but no rest for the weary in Belmont. Had to hurry right off to school and put in the day feeling like something the cats had brought in.

Wednesday, Mar. 17, 1897
Belmont, P.E.I.
I have felt very lonesome and homesick since coming back this time. This household seems coarser and more vulgar than ever after my sojourn in Cavendish. I often wonder what these people I board with have to exist for. They seem to get no pleasure out of life—yet they seem contented enough. I suppose a man born blind never misses his sight.

There is Simon himself—the man seems to have no enjoyment or variety whatever—not even as much as falls to the lot of his neighbors. He works like a slave but he is poor. He never goes anywhere, not even to church. They never have company here and never visit elsewhere. His days are spent in an unceasing round of drudgery.

Mrs. Simon is the feminine counterpart of her liege lord. As for Dan, I hardly believe he is a human being. If he ever had any soul it must long sure have atrophied away.

With such people I naturally can have nothing in common. I live among them— eat, sleep, and talk—but I am not of them at any point of contact.

Monday, April 9, 1897
Belmont
I am heartily glad this school week is ended for it has been such beastly walking— or rather *wading*—that I feel fagged out. I suppose there is a long spell of it before me yet and I am ready to groan in agony of spirit, as I am sure I shall be intolerably lonesome. So no more sleigh drives for me, that is evident.

I have made up my mind that I will not teach in Belmont another year. The work is too hard and I simply cannot exist another year here at Frasers. I hate Belmont. The people, with the exception of three families are perfect barbarians. I suppose I shall have a dreadful time to secure another school but there is no sense in wrecking my health here. I have been very nervous lately, I sleep badly and I seem to have constant colds—the result of doing two teachers' work all winter and being half frozen most of the time.

I am still pegging away at my writing. The road of literature is at first a very slow one, but I have made a good deal of progress since this time last year and I mean to work patiently on until I win—as I believe I shall, sooner or later —recognition and success.

I am up in my room now and I think I'll jot down a description of it—just to help preserve its appearance in memory.

184

On the door—a dark brown with lighter trimmings—are tacked a pink duster bag, a beaded clothes brush pocket, and a medley of pictures clipped from magazines. On the wall above the mantel hangs a small photo of Jack Sutherland and a calendar of Uncle Leander's church. The mantel itself is decorated with an odd assortment—"sunbeam photos", a China dog given me by Well Nelson years ago, a vase, boxes, bottles, crimpers, thimbles etc. On the next wall hang three fancy calendars, a needle book, a curling tongs holder and some photographs. On my little table below are a few books, a stand mirror, a Madonna and my jewel box.

In the corner is a curtained shelf behind whose draperies of startling red calico hang my dresses. The top shelf is filled with hats and the lower is crowded with magazines and schoolbooks. The window is curtained by a lambrequin, also of Turkey red, and in front of it is my washstand with the appurtenances thereof. The window looks out directly on the roof of Simon's kitchen but beyond it is a beautiful glimpse of harbor. A 12 x 6 mirror hangs at one side and on the other above my bed hang a watch pocket and another calendar—my friends run much to calendars at Xmas times. At the foot of my bed is my trunk.

Thursday, April 15, 1897
Belmont, P.E.I.
I have been much shocked and grieved to-day. I have been wondering for the last three months why Will P. hadn't answered my last letter. To-day I received a letter from Laura telling me that Will had died on the second of April!

It was a great shock to me. Of course in these past busy years Will and I have grown away from each other but we have corresponded right along and I have always felt a comrade's affection for him. I cannot realize that *he* can be *dead*— he, so full of life and fun. He died of long and painful complications resulting from an attack of influenza some time ago. Laura says his sufferings were terrible and he was quite resigned to die although he wanted so much to get better and fought hard for his life. Poor Laura is heart-broken and his parents are crushed by the blow. Will was a model son and brother and his family fairly worshipped him.

When I had my cry out I went to my trunk and took out that old ten year letter of Will's. It is only six years since it was written but the understanding was that in any such event as this —but how little we dreamed it would happen—the letters were to be read.

I cannot describe my feelings as I opened the envelope. The letter seemed like a message from the dead—from the world of spirits. It was a letter of love, speaking more plainly than he had ever ventured to do in ordinary letters, and oh, how it hurt poor lonely me to read it!

Willie dead! And buried in his grave on that faraway prairie! It *can't* be! Wasn't it only yesterday that we sat in the old High School and wrote our notes and laughed over mutual jokes and walked home from school together in the winter evenings? Wasn't it only yesterday that we sauntered by the river in the purple June twilights or roamed over the prairies gemmed with bluebells? And wasn't it only yesterday we spent at the Maiden Lake picnic and cut our names together on the old poplar by the lake?

Alas, no, it is six long years ago! And Will is *dead*! How Laura will miss him! They were so devoted to each other.

Monday, April 19, 1897
Belmont, P.E.I.
I wrote a long letter to dear Laura Friday and the writing of it comforted me so much. To-day was spring-warm and sunny, with a mellow south-west wind blowing. The ice has all gone, leaving the bay blue and sparkling, and tiny green things are poking their heads up in garden nooks.   [END OF VOLUME 1]

Sunday, April 25, 1897
Belmont, P.E.I.
This is Sunday afternoon and I am curled up in bed, writing—a drowsy, sleep-flushed specimen of humanity, for I have just wakened out of a post-prandial nap and feel rather stupid. I have nothing to do so I purpose scribbling some nonsense in my journal to keep myself out of that mischief which his Satanic Majesty is popularly supposed to find for all idle hands.

This morning was one of April's darling days—warm south wind, hazy horizon mists, general summery feeling in the air. If the ground were only a wee bit drier I would start off for a walk—although Belmont is not a good place for solitary rambles at any time. There are no leafy lanes or secluded fields here as in Cavendish or Bideford. The only place is the bay shore and that is rather damp and boggy just now for promenading. One must be content to drink in from a distance its new beauty of sparkling blue waters and violet-shrouded coasts....

In a little vase on my table I have a couple of willow sprays thickset with silvery catkins. They remind me of the old willow-tree in the "Haunted Wood" that used to bud out so bravely every year, and the poplar in the front orchard with its wealth of pussy willows. How I love trees! Often and often, when I am alone in the woods I will put my arms tenderly about some old, gray-lichened trunk and press my face to it, feeling its life and balm flowing through every vein in my body as if it and I were one. There are some trees down home that I love so well that I would almost as soon have one of my fingers cut off as see one of them cut down—the old birches around the garden, the tall balsam poplars behind the house, the old spruces back of the well and the cherry trees down the lane.

I remember while in P.A. what an unspeakable comfort in my lonely moments was the one tree our lawn could boast—the leafy western maple at the gate. And out on the prairies I always had a wild feeling of kinship with the white-stemmed poplars—as if some of their sap were mingled with my life-blood. Perhaps—who knows?—it was. Perhaps I *was* a tree in some other state of existence and that may be why I love trees so and feel so utterly and *satisfyingly* at home in the woods. I have always had a sort of leaning to that old doctrine of transmigration. It is hard *not* to believe that I have lived somewhere before.

It is almost time for the mayflowers. I long for the sight of them—little pale pilgrims from summerland, with *their* memories of olden springs when we went rambling through "the barrens" for mayflowers, coming upon plots of them, sweet and fragrant and shy, hidden away in the spruce nooks and hollows.

186

Cavendish, P.E.I.
Wednesday, May 12, 1897
I came home last Saturday. The train was "full of schoolmarms and politicians",
as I overheard someone say. Grandfather met me at Kensington and we had a cold
drive home. Sunday I went to church. I find that I am beginning to feel a good deal
like a stranger in Cavendish church now. Sunday evening I went in to the Baptist
Church to hear Mr. Baker. He has been holding meetings here for some time now
but, as predicted, is not finding the C. people as impressionable as the "Sixteeners".
Monday night I went again and Jack L. came home with me. We had a very jolly
walk.

Thursday, June 3, 1897
Belmont, P.E.I.
Saturday morning I left home and reached here about five. I was fearfully tired—
so tired that I could not sleep but tossed restlessly about all night. In the morning I
went to church and down to Mr. Simpson's afterwards.

Monday morning I went back to school. As the key had been lost in the winter
the doors and windows had been nailed up and as nobody was there to open them
we could not get in. We had to wait for nearly an hour in a pouring rain before we
could get in. I was disgusted and am devoutly thankful that it is my last term here!
Finally we got a window pried open, got in and got to work.

When school came out I started for Miscouche. I had a letter I was very anxious
to mail as soon as possible and as there is no mail here before Thursday I resolved
to walk over to Miscouche and mail it there. As Miscouche is five miles away this
involved a ten-mile walk but I set off briskly. It was a fine evening and I walked so
smartly that I was back here at 7.30 having covered the whole distance in a little
over two and a half hours. But of course I was very tired—too tired to sleep and I
thought the night would never end. Wednesday evening I went to the shore with a
crowd of young folks, expecting to have a sail but it proved too rough. Last night I
did get a good sleep and felt more like myself today. This evening I had a
delightful ramble over the fields and enjoyed it to the core of my heart.

Wednesday Night, June 30, 1897
Belmont, P. E. Island
It seems years since I laid down my pen at the close of that last entry. Between
then and now stretches a century of suffering and horror, "counting time by
heartthrobs." The girl who wrote on June 3rd is as dead as if the sod were heaped
over her—dead past the possibility of any resurrection. I cannot realize that I was
ever she. And indeed, I was not. What or who I am now I do not know. I only
know that I have made a terrible mess of things and am the most miserable
creature on the face of the earth. It is all my own fault—and I wish I were dead!

I seem to have been in a horrid dream and to have lost my own individuality
completely. I feel as if I were in an unknown world where everything, outward
and inward, seems hopelessly changed. I am not Maud Montgomery at all. I feel
as if I must have sprung suddenly into existence and she were an altogether
different person who lived long ago and had nothing at all in common with this

new *me*. I have been an utter, complete, wretched little fool. I see it all now plainly, when it is too late.

I do not know if I can write down a lucid account of the events and motives that have led me to this, but I shall try. Perhaps it will help me if I write it all out.

To go back, then, to that letter which I received from Edwin Simpson last winter asking me to marry him and which I answered with a conditional "no". During the winter I thought a good deal about it off and on for I knew the matter would probably come up again when we met in the spring. The more I thought of it the more I was inclined to think that I might as well accept him.

I knew I did not love him but I thought I *could*. I had never *really* loved anyone although I have had several violent fancies that did not last very long. And having come so far in life without experiencing anything except these passing fancies I had almost concluded that it was not in me to love as *some* people seem to do in real life and *all* in novels. I had thought so much about Ed that I had come to feel a queer impersonal affection for him, as for some imaginary lover of dreams. Intellectually, he was more congenial than most men I have met and than any who have ever made love to me. In short, I thought life with him would be a very satisfactory existence. Ed was clever; he was studying for one of the learned professions and consequently his wife would have a good social position and a life in accordance with my tastes. He had no bad habits or traits of character. Above all—and in my lonely life this carried great weight—*he* loved *me*. I wanted love and protection. Life at times lately had worn a somewhat sombre aspect to my forward-looking eyes. The thought of a settled home and position was very alluring. My health had not been at all good all this spring and I felt tired and discouraged. I had had to work far too hard in school all winter and I was run-down and inclined to take a rather morbid view of my prospects. Hence, I was all the more tempted to grasp at what promised to lift me out of my Slough of Despond.

Of course, I knew that in deciding to marry Edwin Simpson I was probably making considerable trouble for myself. I knew my people would not favor the match for two reasons—Ed is a Baptist and is also my second cousin. These things were not a serious objection to me although I would have preferred them otherwise. But I knew that grandfather and grandmother would consider them almost as serious as if he had been a Mohammedan—especially grandfather who has an almost morbid hatred of relations marrying.

However, the upshot of it all was that I decided if, when he came home, I thought I could care enough for him I would accept him.

The Saturday night after my last entry—the fifth of June—I heard Simon Fraser say that Ed had arrived home. I went to church the next morning feeling somewhat excited for I knew he would be there too. He was on the platform addressing the Sunday school when I went in. He looked well—spoke well. "Certainly" I thought "it will not be hard to care for *him*".

When church was out he came over and shook hands. Mrs. S. asked me to go down to dinner and Alf, Ed, and I walked down together. Ed and I talked of college and Browning and a score of similar non-combustible subjects during the walk and afternoon. In the evening we all walked up to the Methodist church and I spent the night at Mr. S'. Ed was very attentive—I was pleased —flattered—God knows what—anyhow I felt quite sure I could care for him.

Tuesday night came—June 8th—a date that marks the boundary line between two lives for me. I went up to prayer meeting and Ed walked home with me. It was a lovely moonlight night. We talked as usual of books and studies. I did not expect him to say anything that night and I was flatly taken by surprise when, as we turned into Fraser's lane, Ed said abruptly, "I suppose you were surprised to receive that letter of mine last winter?"

Then I knew what was coming—and I felt dizzy. If Ed had only *not* spoken then—if he had left it for a fortnight or even a week I believe I would by that time have realized that I could never care for him and all that has come upon me would have been averted. But he *did* speak—and I sealed my folly.

I don't remember with any degree of clearness just what we did say. We walked up and down the lane and talked confusedly enough; finally I managed to stammer out that I thought I cared for him and that I would be his wife.

He kissed me and said "Thank You". We came in then. I took off my hat and cape in a daze giving Ed, at his request, the flowers I wore. It all seemed like a dream. I was conscious of no emotion whatever, either pleasurable or painful. We sat down by the window, with the June moonlight shimmering on the bay below and talked of the future and the past. When he went away I went upstairs and sat for a long time in thought. I did not feel at all unhappy—but neither did I feel happy—certainly not as a girl should feel who had just parted from the man she had promised to marry.

The next evening was Wednesday. A number of us met at the lobster cannery and went out boat sailing—Olive Fraser, May Campbell, Marie, Miss Compton, Alf, Burt, Sophy, Edmund, and others were in the party. Ed, of course, was there. I could not help seeing some faults in him that night; they were very glaring—and unfortunately they were the very ones I dislike most in a man—the faults common to so many of the Simpson clan. I thought he was far too self-conscious, too fond of saying and doing things for effect, and—in plain English—far too *conceited*. However, I reminded myself that I could not expect to find him perfect when I was a very imperfect creature myself. I told myself that character counted—not little flaws like that—a very proper and common-sensible view of the matter, as anyone would say. But I was yet to realize that there is a higher law than common-sense after all—the law of natural instinct which I had utterly disregarded in my practical arrangement of matters.

We walked home together across the fields. Ed came in and stayed late. I continued to feel emotionless and matter-of-fact. Of course he kissed me often. Those kisses roused absolutely no more feeling in me than if another girl had been kissing me. When he went away I went sleepily to bed, dully reflecting that this sitting up with one, even if he were my lover, was a very stupid performance, which left me feeling drowsy and incapable the next day at work.

I did not see him again for a couple of days. Then I went up to a choir practice at Mr. Simpson's and he walked home with me. That night it struck me what a restless, nervous mortal he was; it seemed impossible for him to sit still for a moment. Hands, fingers, and feet must be perpetually moving, tapping, twitching. I was tired and fagged and this habit of his had an absurdly exaggerated effect on me. I felt as if I must *scream* if he didn't sit still. When he went away I actually felt as worn out as if I had passed through some tremendous physical strain.

Of course, we had discussed several details in the course of our conversations. We decided that as our engagement must be a long one it would be best to keep it a secret for a time at least from all save a few intimate friends. On this account I declined to wear an engagement ring for awhile.

I felt decidedly ruffled when I learned what Ed's plans really were. I had supposed and he had in his letters certainly led me to believe that he intended to go in for law or else a college professorship. Now I found that he meant to enter the ministry. I would not have minded this so much—though I certainly think the life of a minister's wife is a rather hard one in many ways—if he had been a Presbyterian or indeed any denomination but a Baptist. But to marry a Baptist minister would necessarily involve my re-baptism by immersion—a thing utterly repugnant to my feelings and traditions. Of course, Ed said that, if I had any *insuperable* objections to his choice of a profession, he would give it up. But he did not try to conceal the fact that such a giving-up would seriously "inconvenience" him, and I, on my part, felt that I had no right to impose arbitrary restrictions to his choice in so serious a matter and that such a course on my part would be very selfish indeed. So I finally resigned myself to it and told Ed so as cordially as possible.

By the middle of June I was beginning to recover from my strange feeling of unreality. My numbed sensibilities were, alas, reviving. Vague doubts and fears and perplexities began to disturb me. I remember the night of the 17th of June with especial distinctness because it was the first night I became conscious of feeling a *dislike* of Ed's caresses. Hitherto I had accepted them unemotionally. Now they seemed to irritate me—my former torpor was replaced by a distinct sense of *physical repulsion*. I reproached myself for this and carefully concealed it; but my feelings were beginning to alarm as well as puzzle me.

On Thursday evening, June 17th, I went up to Allan Fraser's after school. I felt tired and bored with things in general. After tea Olive and I went botanizing in their swamp. Olive, in common with the rest of Belmont, was devoured by an unholy curiosity regarding Ed and myself and threw out numberless hints which I parried mechanically. I was amazed to discover that it *annoyed* me to be teased about Ed!

He had promised to meet me there and at sunset he came. We spent the evening there. I was dull and languid—Ed as voluble as usual. He has the Simpson habit of talking too much. When we left and walked together down the dark road he kept on talking until I felt tired of the sound of his voice. When we reached home he came in. As for me, I was suddenly in the clutches of an icy horror. I shrank from his embrace and kiss. I was literally terrified at the repulsion which quivered in every nerve of me at his touch. It seemed as if something that had been dormant in me all my life had suddenly wakened and shook me with a passion of revolt against my shackles. When Ed went away I rushed upstairs and flung myself on my bed. My God, what had I done? Was it possible I had made an awful mistake? I shiver yet at the remembrance of that terrible night. The veil seemed to be torn at once and completely from my eyes. I looked—and saw that I could not *bear* the mere touch of the man I had promised to marry!

This awful visitation seemed to me utterly inexplicable then. Looking back now, I can clearly see that my feelings that terrible night were merely the climax to an unconscious process that had been going on from the very first night of our engagement. It was the sudden revolt of my whole nature from the false bonds which I, ignorant of their real nature, had imposed on it.

My martyrdom had begun. Since then what have I not suffered?

How I got through the next day I don't know. I worked slavishly in and out of school—it was my only relief for it kept me from thinking, thinking, thinking!

There was a choir practice up at Major MacKinnon's at Central in the evening and I had to go. Ed and Fulton—who by the way is remarkably civil to me now—called for me. I grimly reflected as I pinned on my hat before the glass that Ed would not feel particularly proud of his fiancee's appearance that night. A more wretched-looking creature it would have been hard to find. I was as pale as a corpse, with black circles under my dull tired eyes. My head throbbed painfully. We called for Olive. The laughter and conversation of our little crowd gave me a certain stimulus and so helped me to keep up appearances at least. But when I found myself walking home alone with Ed, under the glistening stars, down the dusky, sibilant spruce road, all my depression returned. I wondered that he didn't notice it but he did not—he simply talked on and on.

When we reached home we sat down by the window. Ed put his arm about me and kissed me. Suddenly I felt as if that kiss scorched me with an intolerable shame. When he bent his head again I sat up abruptly and pushed his arms away; if he had kissed me again at that moment not all the resolution in the world could have prevented me from betraying my repugnance.

I moved away from him; he took this to be simply a bit of coquetry on my part and leaned back, looking at me with a quizzical smile. In a few moments I had recovered my self-command. Ed was perfectly unsuspicious. I was thankful for this. If he *should* suspect it seemed to me that it would be an unbearable humiliation for me. He thought me very quiet that night and said so but ascribed it to fatigue after our long walk. His belief in my weariness did not lead him to curtail his stay however. I thought he would *never* go. He lingered on—and kept talking of our future *together*. If he had been trying he could not have invented a greater torture for me. I writhed in soul at every word but I kept myself rigidly in hand. I did not again turn my cold, unresponsive face from his kiss; but when he had gone I went up to my room saying under my breath "God help me".

Somehow I got through Saturday and Sunday without breaking down. I went to Mr. Simpson's because I had no excuse for not going and was rained in for the night. That day brought to me a final conviction that not only I did *not* love Edwin Simpson but that I *never* could.

Monday morning was rainy and Ed drove me to school. He little dreamed what thoughts were seething through the brain of the pale girl at his side. Ed, like all the rest of the Simpsons, has not a great deal of perception. He is one of the men who are generally so busy talking about themselves that they fail to notice moods and tenses on the part of others. I was thankful for this just then—it necessitated less forced animation on my part. I had then no thought of trying to break the engagement—I was *afraid* to do it. Remembering Fulton's all but insane behavior I did not dare to speculate what Ed's might be, or what effect such a thing would have on him. I clung to the hope that in time I could conquer my physical loathing of him and be at least content. Happiness I no longer hoped for.

Engaged only a fortnight and in such a state of mind! There is, no doubt, a ludicrous and absurd aspect of the case but I am unfortunately incapable of seeing it. I see—and feel—only the tragedy of it.

The Tuesday after that rainy Monday was a holiday, being the Queen's birthday. May Campbell had arranged a picnic to Curtain Island. The picnickers were the Lyles, the Simpsons, the Campbells, Frasers and myself. We set sail at nine. It was a fine day but blowing hard and we had a distinctly exciting sail over. The exhilaration of the motion and the physical delight of skimming over the waves and through the spray lent me a sort of spurious animation. After all—perhaps I had been morbid—perhaps things were not so bad after all.

Arriving on Curtain Island we started on a tramp through the woods to the other side, from which we emerged tattered and torn to an alarming degree. After dinner Ed took me off to a grassy headland where we sat and had a long talk which I desperately anchored to books, studies etc., for I could not have endured a personal element. If marriage meant only a series of conversations on intellectual subjects I could marry Ed very well. I enjoy talking with him on such subjects. But just as our chat was veering towards personalities, in spite of me, a timely thunder storm came up which compelled us all to take refuge in a tiny lobsterman's hut. It rained almost continuously for the next two hours and we all got into a state of muddiness and dampness and general stickiness. The wind had died away when we started for home and the bay was like glass. The sail back seemed to me interminable. I was in the deeps of depression and my condition was almost one of collapse. My appearance must have been ghastly for everyone commented on it and asked me if I were ill. I could only reply that I was tired to death. Ed knew this perfectly well but it did not prevent him from asking me to go to prayer-meeting with him. I assented as I would have assented if he had asked me to walk to Summerside with him. It seemed to me that I must do everything he wished me to do in order to atone in some small measure for the wrong I was doing him with every breath I drew.

I do not want to do Ed any injustice. I admit that he is good, fine-looking and clever. *If* I loved him I suppose I would not notice his faults and imperfections—at least they would not jar on me so harshly. But I do *not* love him and sometimes I fear I will soon find myself *hating* him! What wonder that I hate and despise myself?

I wonder if I shall ever get *rested* again. I feel *so tired* all the time. It is such a hard task now to keep up with all my old-time everyday duties. I seem to loathe them. I cannot get up any interest in them and merely drag myself through them in a mechanical way.

The outer world about me is fair—very fair. Yet I care nothing for its beauty. A veil seems to have dropped between my soul and nature. This is hardest of all to bear.

Wednesday and Thursday passed in much the same way. In the evening Ed came. What a nightmare it seemed! There was only one thing that nerved me to endure it—and that was the fact that it would be the *last*, for a time at *least*, for Ed was going away on a visit to Nova Scotia on Saturday and I would be gone from Belmont before he returned. This was my one ray of comfort. If he had but known, as he lamented our approaching separation how *I* longed for it! But he did not know. He judged my feelings by his own and took them for granted.

I am and always have been a proud woman. It would have killed me if any outsider had guessed my state of mind, to sneer or pity. I know that no one has done so. To all in this household I have appeared my usual self, though quieter and graver. In society I have been my usual self also. I have laughed and jested and talked small nothings, wrapping the cloak of my pride over my gnawing fox as gaily and smilingly as did ever Spartan boy.

The day following that night I had my school examination. I took little trouble with it for I felt no interest in it and I dismissed the scholars apathetically, not caring in the least that it was the last time. I have never liked the scholars here, but even if I had I would not have felt the parting just then. One does not mind a pin-prick when a limb is being wrenched away.

Of course, there were a few of the children whom I liked, but the majority were very unlovable—rough, ignorant, lazy. A long and unregretful farewell to them! That night we were invited to a small party at Mr. Campbell's. We had a stupid time for most of the guests seemed dull and tired. As for myself, I had reacted into a wild, feverish fit of gayety. My eyes were burningly bright, my cheeks hot and crimson. Ed bent over me on our walk home—I spent the night at Mr. Simpson's as Sophy asked me and it was really too far to walk home so late—and whispered that he had never seen me look so beautiful and that he would carry with him forever the remembrance of my face that night. Such lover-like flattery ought to have seemed delightful to me; but instead I grew chill and cold and shuddered away from his arm in agonized repulsion.

Saturday morning I got up, listless and distrait, with the hot, defiant passion of the previous night burned out to dull white ashes. When I left, Ed, who was going to the shore, walked with me as far as the cannery road, and there we stopped to say good-bye. I gave him my hand passively and coldly lifted my face for his farewell kiss. "Good-bye, my darling," he said as he turned down the shore road. I drew a long breath of *relief* and walked on. *What* a relief it was! And how horrible that it should be so!

That evening I went to Miscouche and took the train to Alberton where I was going to attend a Teacher's convention and visit Nettie Montgomery. I had no pleasurable anticipations of the visit—I seem to have lost the power of feeling pleasure in anything.

Before me on the train two teachers were sitting—McIntyre and Trowsdale. They had both taught in Park Corner when Ed was attending school there and by a curious coincidence they were discussing him. They did not notice me behind them or if they did, would not have supposed that I had any special interest in their conversation. They did not like Ed, it was evident, and they said such things of him that even I grew angry and could hardly help flying out at them in his defence. Then I laughed miserably to myself at my mental picture of their amazement and consternation if I were to do any such thing. But, for all my anger, the things they said of Ed were *true*; "he was clever—*but*"—seemed to be the essence of their comments. He seems to affect most people precisely as he does me.

Nettie met me at the train and I remained there until this afternoon. I felt very tired and ill all the time but my depression lifted somewhat in such cheerful society. Monday evening Nettie and her father and I went out for a drive. The horse became frightened, ran away, and threw us all out. Fortunately none of us were much injured—Nettie had a slight cut on her cheek—but I felt the shock severely and have not yet fully recovered from it.

I left Alberton to-day at 3.30. I had a tiresome ride down to Miscouche and my head ached continually. When I finally got off at Miscouche I declare I just felt like sitting down and crying childishly. But that would not do, so I left my valise at the office for the mailman and started spiritlessly on my five-mile walk to Belmont. It soon began to rain and I plodded doggedly on through it, until about half way here John and Nettie Lyle overtook me and drove me to Fraser's gate. When I got here all my old gloom and depression settled back. I think this place has a wretched influence over me—I feel worse the minute I step inside the door. The people are so queer, the surroundings so coarse and rough that they jar on every fibre of my nature which is just at present strung-up to a peculiarly sensitive pitch of nervousness.

I got upstairs to my room, flung myself on the bed and cried my heart out. The tears were a distinct relief—the very first I have shed in all this dreadful time. I cried and cried until I felt utterly exhausted but the mental relief was unutterable. I felt as if something had been cleared away from my brain and for the first time I felt able to take up my pen again and write in this journal.

I am going home Saturday. I am sitting here in my poor old room. I shall be sorry to leave it—it is the only place in Belmont I *will* be sorry to leave—as I always am to leave an old room. A room where one sleeps and dreams and grieves and rejoices becomes inseparably connected with those processes and acquires a personality of its own. This room is not a pretty or dainty one but it has always been a retreat for me, the one spot in Belmont where I might be alone and possess my soul in quietness, the world forgetting. And now I must leave it and go out elsewhere. How many rooms I have left so and how many more am I fated to leave yet in my wanderings!

I wish I were home. I want to rest—rest—rest! At present I am utterly incapable of thinking calmly and dispassionately on any subject or coming to any abiding or rational decision. My mental balance has been too rudely shaken to recover its normal poise very readily.

I cannot express the self-contempt I feel when I think of my folly. I am in a gulf of self-abasement and humiliation and remorse, mingled with an unsubduable rebellion against the fate I have brought on myself. I see clearly now where I made my primary mistake. It was in ignoring the law which ordains that without real love any intimate bond becomes a galling and hated fetter and engenders hate and bitterness of soul. That I sinned in ignorance is small comfort and no aid.

Looking back over the past three weeks I wonder how I have lived through them without going mad. The physical effects are plainly visible. I am thin and pale, hollow-eyed and nervous. As for the mental and emotional detriment who can judge or measure it?

Oh, what shall I do? And there is no living mortal to whom I can go for advice or help. I must dree this weird alone. If only my mother had lived!

It is strange to think that Ed never suspected anything—never noticed my altered manner. Verily, "those whom the gods wish to destroy they first make blind"—as in my own case. But as for me, my days of blindness are over. Too clearly and plainly I see now and the sight is one which might well blast my soul's vision forever.

Up to this spring I have had a *fairly* happy life and what cares and worries I have had—and I have never even in childhood been free from them—did not weigh me down unbearably. Life looked to me fair and promising; I was young and ambitious. Now everything is changed and darkened.

To-night Ed is far away and I suppose he is thinking lovingly of me—wretched, wretched me! And I? I could strike my reflected face there in the mirror—I could lash my bare shoulders with unsparing hand to punish myself for my folly. It would be a relief to inflict physical pain and thereby dull my mental agony. Sometimes I drop my pen and walk wildly up and down my room with clenched hands. Outside the rain of a moist odorous June evening is falling on the roof. I hear men's voices calling to each other in the gloom of the barnyard. Afar off, the bay looms grayly through the curtain of rain and twilight.

In the morning I will dress and do my hair and go down with a smile to exchange greetings and tell about my visit and make business-like arrangements for my departure. But in this one precious little hour of solitude I can throw aside the mask and look on my naked soul, knowing that no prying human eye gloats over the revelation.

I know I am writing wildly and distractedly. But it is such a relief to pour out my misery in words. I am so tired. It seems a century since I was light-hearted and gay and ambitious.

Ambitious! I could laugh! Where is my ambition now? What does the word mean? What is it like to be ambitious? To feel that life is before you, a fair, unwritten white page where you may inscribe your name in letters of success? To feel that you have the wish and power to win your crown? To feel that the coming years are crowding to meet you and lay their largess at your feet? I *once* knew what it was to feel so!

I have been pacing the floor again—I can't sit still for any length of time. It is dark outside now and the rain is beating on the pane like ghostly finger-tips playing a weird threnody. Oh, *do* other people suffer like this? If they do, how can they live?

Perhaps when I am once home in my dear old room I will find something of peace and calm again. Perhaps when I lay my head once more on the pillow of my girlhood its spell may charm me back to paths of tranquillity and murmur "Peace be still" over the stormy waters of my troubled soul. Here to-night no such sleep will visit me. I will lie in the darkness and gaze out into it for hours—and then when the gray dawn comes up over the bay I will fall into the dull heavy slumber of absolute exhaustion of thought and feeling, to wake again in the golden morning sunshine and feel that in a world of beauty and gladness I am only a black unsightly blot of misery.

I am cold and tired and worn-out!

October 7th, 1897
Cavendish, P.E.I.

"Harvest is ended and summer is gone."

I have got out this journal at last—I have neglected it for months, for I *could not* write. The summer is over now. It is October and autumn. We are having delightful fall days, misty and purple, with a pungent, mellow air and magnificent sunsets, followed by the rarest of golden twilights and moonlit nights floating in silver. Maple and birch are crimson and gold and the fields sun themselves in aftermaths. But it is autumn and beautiful as everything is it is the beauty of decay—the sorrowful beauty of the end.

In one way this summer has seemed long—in another short. I have not been happy or at peace. I have suffered continually—and it has done me good. I have *grown* much in some respects and I think I have gotten a great deal nearer to the *heart* of all things. I was a *girl* up to last spring—now I am a woman and I feel acutely that girlhood is gone forever. I have learned to look below the surface comedy of life into the tragedy underlying it. I have become *humanized*—no longer an isolated, selfish unit, I have begun to feel myself *one with my kind*—to see deeper into my own life and the lives of others. I have begun to *realize* life—to realize what someone has called "the infinite sadness of living", and to realize how much each of us has it in our power to increase or alleviate that sadness. I understand at last that "no man liveth to himself".

I came home the first of July, leaving Belmont with no regrets. I did hate that place bitterly. I have been home all summer as I did not succeed in getting a school. It is always hard for me to get a school as I have only my own unaided efforts to rely on. Grandfather has always been opposed to my teaching—not for *my* sake, indeed, but simply because he has an absurd prejudice against teachers as a class, dating back to the time one who boarded here quarrelled with him and left. She *was* a detestable creature but he was quite as much to blame for the quarrel as she was and put himself very much in the wrong. He suggested once this summer that I go into a store at the Creek but I simply would not do that. He will not let me have a horse to take me to interview trustees personally so I have to depend on letters, a very poor plan when teachers are so over-plenty and the personal applicant stands the best chance. But at last I have obtained the Lower Bedeque school and I go in two weeks time to take charge of it.

Cavendish has been very quiet this summer. Uncle Leander and family were over for a month. Chesley Clark and Jack Laird have both gone out west and I miss them considerably.

I have heard from Laura only once this summer. When I opened the letter I found in it a tiny packet enclosing a little gold ring worn almost to a thread—the ring I gave Will six years ago and which he had always worn to the day of his death. I slipped it once more on my finger and thought of all the changes that have been, of all that has come and gone since last I wore it. It seemed like a golden link between me and my lost self, between the present and the past. Poor little ring! I shall always wear it in remembrance of those dear old days. Its circle is the symbol of eternity and eternal friendship. Surely, surely, those who knew each other so well and dearly here will meet again in some fair Hereafter.

Aunt Annie, Uncle Leander's second wife, gave me that ring long ago when I was twelve years old. It was never off my finger till I gave it to Will and it never will be again until it is worn out. Aunt Annie wore it when she was a girl, so it is very old.

The only *social function* we have had this summer was prayer-meeting, that faithful old stand-by. The prayer-meeting of today however is very different from its predecessor. It has evolved into a "Christian Endeavor Society". I can't say I approve of the change.

Looking back on my past life I think I have had a rather peculiar spiritual experience. I am not "religiously inclined", as the phrase goes, but I have always possessed a deep *curiosity* about "things spiritual and eternal". I want to *find out*—to *know*—and hence I am always poking and probing into creeds and religions, dead and alive, wanting to know for knowledge' sake what vital spark of immortal truth might be buried among all the verbiage of theologies and systems.

When I was very young—about eight or nine—I began to think of these things very deeply and passed through a great many bitter spiritual struggles, of which I could not have said a word to those about me. My theology was very primitive and I took everything very literally. I supposed heaven was a city of golden houses and streets, where we would always walk around with harps and crowns and sing hymns all the time and where it would be "one endless Sabbath day". I could not help thinking it would be dreadfully dull. *One* Sunday on earth *seemed* endless— how then would it be with one that really *was* endless? But I also thought that this was very wicked of me—that there was something in me radically wrong when heaven had no attraction for me. But anyway, it would be better than hell which I also implicitly believed to be a lake of fire and brimstone, haunted by the devil and all his angels. While I had a vague impression that heaven was spread all over the other side of the blue sky above us hell seemed to me to be situated away off to the southeast!! I was terribly frightened of hell and my fear frequently drove me into trying desperately "to be a Christian".

I had some bitter seasons. I remember that when I was about ten I got it into my head that the Catholic church was the only right one and that outside its pale all were heretics doomed to penal fires! I got these ideas out of a sample copy of a newspaper called "The Catholic World" which had been sent to the post-master. Its statements were so dogmatic that they impressed me as authoritative. How I suffered because of this! It seems both funny and pitiful to me now. But it was very real and inexorable then. And I was so miserably *alone*—there was no one to whom I could go for help. I would only have been laughed at, or, at best, met with some dogmatic statement which would have been of no help to me at all. In silence and secrecy I had to fight out my own battles and flounder through my quagmires.

Somehow or other I gradually got over or outgrew my difficulty about Mother Church only to stumble helplessly into another. The Baptist and Presbyterian girls in school—the "big girls"—were always disputing on doctrinal points, especially on Baptism, and I began to fear that the Baptists, and they only, were right and that I would certainly be "lost" if I were not immersed. I worried over this on many a sleepless pillow and argued fiercely with myself over it for weeks. Finally, however, I passed out from this shadow also.

At intervals—always in winter; I was never troubled with conscience spasms in summer—I "fell under conviction of sin"—that is I remembered about hell and got frightened!—cried, prayed, and determined desperately to be "good"—to like reading the Bible better than story books, not to get tired—that is to say "bored", only I wasn't acquainted with that word then—in church, and *not* to dislike Sunday. Besides, I would rigidly practise a hundred repressions and denials of my childish instincts. For instance, I would, when setting the table, conscientiously put for myself a certain knife which I hated and therefore thought everyone else must also hate. Last winter I read for the first time "The Story of An African Farm". The writer was describing just such experiences of childhood. When I came to the sentence, "We conscientiously put the cracked coffee cup for ourselves at breakfast" I leaned back and laughed. It was as if I had unexpectedly seen my own face peering out at me from a mirror. So this Boer girl, living thousands of miles away in South Africa, had had exactly the same experience as mine! Truly, we are not so different from each other as we like to imagine.

To resume:—the fit would pass in a few weeks and I would lapse back into "wickedness" and indifference again until the next attack.

As I grew up all this ceased. Then came that time in town when B. Faye Mills—who has since gone over to the Unitarians, by the way—turned it upside down. I hardly know what induced me to "join the church" then. The whole air seemed to be thrilling with a kind of magnetism and it was hard for anyone to resist the influence, especially one so extremely sensitive and impressionable as I am. Then there was Mary C. who really wanted to "come out" and wouldn't unless I would; and so, partly for her sake, partly because I was tired of being urged and pestered and harangued every time a revivalist came around, I surrendered and "came out", too. I think it was a mistake, for I put myself in a false position. To "join the church" meant assenting to certain teachings which I did *not* and *could* not accept.

I cannot recall just when I ceased to believe implicitly in those teachings—the process was so gradual. My belief in the fine old hell of literal fire and brimstone went first—it and others seemed to drop away like an outgrown husk, so easily that I knew it not until one day it dawned upon me that they had been gone a long time. I have not yet formulated any working belief to replace that which I have outgrown. Perhaps it will come in time. These things must *grow*, like everything else.

I have written a good deal this summer and had a few acceptances. Had a poem taken by *Munsey*. The latter is quite an encouragement as it is a good magazine.

Yesterday I was reading over Hattie Gordon's old letters. How much I would like to see her! What jolly times we did have when she taught school here! The old school is much changed now and nearly all the old scholars are gone. I am sure the children who go there now do not have half the fun we used to have; but then I have no doubt they learn a great deal more.

I have read several new books lately. "The Gates Ajar" interested me considerably. The author's conception of Heaven seems a helpful and reasonable one. In her idea, we shall keep on being just what we are here, along the lines of higher development and freed from all the clogs and trammels of earth. She does not think that we shall all at once expand into perfect holiness but that our aspirations and wishes will all tend to that, will develop towards it more and more, with every help and hindrance. It is a pleasing conception and I wish I could believe it firmly—for the mere inclination to believe is not enough.

"The Love Letters of a Worldly Woman" was another new book—new to me, I mean. It is a "far cry" from "The Gates". It is of the earth, earthy, dealing with earthly passions and appeals strongly to one side of our many-faceted nature. It is true to life, and therefore sad and tragical, as all life and all lives are, more or less. But some lives seem to be more essentially tragic than others and I fear mine is one of such. My outlook is indeed gloomy at present, bounded and narrowed in. To quote from the letters, "I feel like a prisoner who has shut the door on all possibilities".

I went in to the Exhibition in September. I stayed at Aunt Mary's of course and in the jolly, *human* society of my girl friends I forgot my cares for the time being, and my unwholesome broodings and speculations.

For my life this summer *has* been unwholesome. It has been spent too much among books and visions and dreams—there has not been enough electrical human interest permeating it to keep me in good mental counterpoise. It has been far too self-centred and analytical.

Mary C. was also in and we had a good time together. We went to the Opera House one evening to see "The Curse of Cain"—a very poor amateur performance. However, the "Rainbow Dance" at the end was really beautiful—to my eyes at least, for I have such a passionate love of *color*. It seems to me that color means to me what music means to its devotees.

One day Mary and I called to see Mrs. McLeod who occupies the other half of "Hotel De MacMillan". The "hotel" is vacant now, so Mary and I borrowed Mrs. McLeod's key and went all through it. Bare and vacant it is now, but peopled for us by many comic memories. We had our troubles and tribulations in that old house certainly, but they have assumed a merely amusing aspect through the mellowing mists of time. And we *had* fun there, too. We explored the old parlor which Jack Whear and Florrie used to haunt, the old sitting room where we studied, the stairs up which we used to race so wildly, regardless of Mother MacMillan's wrath, and, last but *not* least, our old room whose walls had so often re-echoed to our shrieks of mirth, where we wrote and read and entertained our chums and discussed our grievances. But it is all past now and the little colony of roof-mates is scattered far and wide. Florrie is married to her Jack and lives in town. Poor "Aileck" is in the States somewhere and so is Mary MacMillan—it is to be hoped for peace' sake that they aren't within a hundred miles of each other. Bertie Bell is out west, Stewart Simpson is at McGill, Jim Stevenson is in Ch'Town, Mrs. MacMillan is at Stanley—and dear knows where old "McMahon" and his fair spouse are. Norman and Mary are teaching and I—well, I am drifting about, tempest-tossed and mocked by fate.

58. *Edwin Simpson*

59. *Myself and the pupils at Belmont School*

60. *Interior of new Presbyterian Church*
[*Cavendish*]

61. *Aunt Mary McIntyre's house, Charlottetown*

1898

Lower Bedeque, P.E. Island
Jan. 22, 1898

I have been intending ever since New Year's to write up this journal, but alas for good intentions! The road to hell is said to be paved with them and I fear I have contributed not a little to the paving of late. However, I am going to devote this evening solely and exclusively to "journalizing".

When I last wrote I was home, dreaming, analyzing, brooding unwholesomely. Then I came to Bedeque and at once found myself whirled into a life the very antipodes of that which I had been living. The reaction was needed and proved wholesome. And yet—were the life I am living at present carried on too long the effect, I feel sure, would be even more disastrous than that of the former.

I am going to take a good dose of confession regarding my miserable affair with Edwin Simpson. I *could not* say anything about it in my last entry because I was in the worst possible state of mind over it and even to allude to the subject would have hurt me like a rude touch on a raw wound. But I am somewhat calmer now, so I may as well see how my wretched feelings look when written out in cold blood.

It would be useless to try to describe how I suffered over it all summer. I knew perfectly well I could never bring myself to marry Edwin Simpson and yet I shrank from telling him so. I hated and despised myself for my cowardice but I could not overcome it.

Ed wrote regularly and every letter reminded me more hatefully of my bondage. I dreaded the day I expected one, I breathed with a passionate sense of relief when the reading of it was over. Writing to him in return was another exquisite agony. Well, I did not write "love letters". But I tried to write as a friend and Ed did not notice any lack—or did not comment on it if he did. I hate to say anything uncharitable when I am doing him such a wrong, but nevertheless it is the literal truth, which no one who knows him will deny, that Ed is serenely sure that any girl he has honored with his affection *must* be superlatively happy and enraptured. He betrayed this conviction unconsciously a dozen times during our evening conversations in Belmont.

Ed was in Cavendish for a visit soon after I got home and he and Alf came down to our place Sunday afternoon and had tea. Again that horrible repulsion seized me. I remember excusing myself half an hour after they came and running up to my room where I simply flung myself on the floor and muttered over and over again, "I can never marry him—*never*, NEVER, *NEVER*!" That outburst helped me. I was able then to go calmly down, get tea, dress and go to church. I did not see Ed again until Christian Endeavor on Thursday night. He came down and after the meeting we went for a drive. It was horrible!

Ed left the next day for a trip to Miramachi, but when he came back it was worse than ever. His attentions to me soon set Cavendish gossip by the ears, he has a host of cousins there, most of whom do not like me, although I have never had anything to do with them—perhaps *that* is the reason—and I'm sure they were ready to tear me in pieces. At last, however, he went back to Belmont and I was comparatively free again.

When I came to Bedeque, after his return to college I had made up my mind that before his return next spring I would tell him the truth. His letters come regularly, as affectionate as ever and consequently as galling. As for mine they have grown colder and colder. It is a wonder to me that he has not noticed this. I have hoped that he would and by asking me the reason open an avenue for me to confess the whole humiliating truth. It would, somehow, be easier for me to open up the subject if he were not quite so complacently sure of his position.

As the Christmas holidays drew near I began to dread them for Ed talked of coming home and of course that would mean a visit to Bedeque. Finally however he wrote that he was not coming and I felt a great relief. The following Thursday Helen Leard and I drove up to Centreville to visit her sister after school and got back at dark. I went upstairs at once. Soon after Helen came up and said, "Who do you think is in the sitting room?"

The most horrible sort of presentiment swept over me.

"Why, who?" I said, but I knew the answer would be "Ed Simpson". Fortunately Helen could not see my face in the dusk or I think it would have startled her. Quite unsuspiciously, however, she went on to say that he had come to S'Side and found no one to meet him, so he concluded to come over and spend the night with them—he used to teach in Bedeque and was a chum of Al Leard's son so that this story sounded quite plausible and Leards had no suspicion of the real state of affairs.

After she had gone down I tried to rally my paralyzed wits. I felt sick at heart. But after a time I regained enough self-control to go down and meet him. Somehow the evening passed. The Leard family, not dreaming that there was anything between us, made no opportunities for leaving us alone and I was unutterably thankful that they did not. I had received a Christmas gift from him a few days before, a pretty silver paper knife with my initials on it. With his accustomed good taste he had written that it had "cost him some self-sacrifice"! Just imagine how it burned my fingers! However, I wrote a brief note of thanks for it and passed it to Ed as I bade him good night.

I hope I shall never have to live through another such night. I lay there, my hands clenched, biting my lips to keep from screaming aloud. I was denied the relief of tears for Helen slept in the same room. I thought morning would never come; but at last it did and with it my deliverance, for Ed had to leave to catch the morning boat.

But that fearful night confirmed me in the realization that I *must* break my engagement before I saw Ed again. I cannot live this lie any longer. I fear he will take it terribly hard and the thought tortures me. But bad as things are they cannot be bettered by living a lie and I must tell him the truth at all costs. I would make almost any sacrifice if I could blot out '97 from my book of life. It will ever be a nightmare of remembrance to me. Oh, I feel so bitterly ashamed!

Somehow or other, during all this unhappy time I have worn a mask of outward gayety and kept up with my usual pursuits. I have written a good deal and met with some success, having had several acceptances—and of course plenty of rejections.

Whom do you think was married in September? Why, Jessie Fraser, that ancient spinster of the household in Belmont. She married an elderly widower of New Brunswick and as both of them are verging on the sere and yellow leaf it is to be presumed that there is not a great deal of sentiment in the affair. I wonder if the widower in question knew all of Jessie's past—or if he cared. I wonder what a woman *does* feel like who has such a past as hers. Is there any sweetness in the memory of her sin—or is it all bitterness? And what a curious thing marriage is! I never really thought about it before this summer, save in an aloof, abstract way, as of something more or less inevitable some day in the future—always in the future. But during these past six months I have been compelled to look at it in every light, grappling with the perplexing questions of its relationships in an effort to understand them. Marriage is a different thing to me now. I have at least realized what a *hell* it would be with a man I did not love—and yes, what a *heaven* with one I did! Where and how have I learned this last, question you? Ah, I can't tell you that yet!

Since coming to Bedeque I have been having, *on the surface*, the best time I ever had in my life—and *really* enjoying myself when I could succeed momentarily in forgetting my worries and heartaches. The teacher here before me was Al Leard. He wished to get a substitute for six months during his absence at college and my application was accepted. I board at his father's—Mr. Cornelius Leard's. They are a very nice family. Both Mr. and Mrs. Leard are as kind as they can be. Helen Leard, a girl of my own age, is very nice and jolly. We get along together splendidly and have no end of fun. There are two other little girls, May, aged thirteen, and Feddie, ten, and two boys. The youngest, Calvin, is about eighteen and is staying up at Central Bedeque with his brother-in-law for the winter but comes home often. He is a pretty little chap with big blue eyes and a skin as pink-and-white as a girl's, and he is as nice as he can be. He and I are excellent friends and I pet and mother him at all times.

The elder boy, Herman, is about 26, slight, rather dark, with magnetic blue eyes. He does not impress one as handsome at first—when I met him I thought he was what might be called insignificant looking—but in the end one thinks him so.

All in all I am very happily situated. The lines of my professional career have been cast in pleasant places this time at least.

As for my school, I am not overburdened with work as there are only *fourteen* children in the district. Imagine the contrast to the large schools I have had! But a couple of advanced pupils give me comfortably enough to do and I simply *love* teaching here. The children are all so nice and intelligent. The school is about 200 yards from here and is a very comfortable one in a grove of spruces. I feel as if I had lived in Bedeque all my life. The people are so nice, friendly, and sociable. It is a lively place with lots of young people and I have had a lively time.

And so '97 is gone! Never before was I glad to see a year go but when '97 went out I was glad with a fearful joy. It was *gone*, that dreadful year, with all its mistakes and suffering. I turned my back on it with a pitiful delight.

Well, this is all—and yet it is "the play of Hamlet with Hamlet left out". Perhaps some day I may write it once again with Hamlet in—and perhaps I shall never feel that I can!

Friday, April 8, 1898
Cavendish, P.E.I.

It is just after dark; the shadows have gathered thickly over the old white hills and around the old quiet trees. The last red stains of the lingering sunset have faded out of the west and the dull gray clouds have settled down over the horizon again. All is very still and quiet here in the old kitchen and so, with much shrinking and reluctance—for a faithful record of my life during this past half year will be, I fear me, but sorry writing—I have brought out this book and set myself down this dull, chilly spring evening to write out the life—the stormy, passion-wrung life—that has been mine these past months. I am going to write it out fully and completely, even if every word cuts me to the heart. I have always found that the writing out of a pain makes it at least bearable.

I have grown years older in this past month. Grief and worry and heartbreak have done their work thoroughly. Sometimes I ask myself if the pale, sad-eyed woman I see in my glass can really be the merry girl of olden days or if she be some altogether new creature, born of sorrow and baptized of suffering, who is the sister and companion of regret and hopeless longing.

On March 6th, while in Bedeque, I received a telegram stating that Grandfather Macneill had dropped dead the preceding afternoon!

The shock was terrible. In all truthfulness, I cannot say that I have ever had a very *deep* affection for Grandfather Macneill. I have always been afraid of him; and in his recent years he has been very difficult to live with. Nevertheless, one cannot live all one's life with people and not have a certain love for them—the bond of kin and long association. When death comes this bond is revealed by its being wrenched asunder and we suffer keenly for the time being. Consequently, as I have said, I was shocked and stunned and felt as if everything in life had fallen blackly together. It seemed *impossible* that the news could be true. They had all been in good health at home the last letter I had had from Grandma.

It was Sunday when I got the telegram and I had to wait until Monday morning when Mr. Leard drove me over the ice to S'Side. There I took the train and reached Kensington at 1.30. John C. Clark came to meet me and it was eight o'clock when I finally reached home. Aunt Annie, Aunt Emily and Aunt Mary Lawson were here. It was such a relief to be with them all.

Grandmother was naturally sadly prostrated. Poor grandfather's death had been so terribly sudden. It was presumably caused by heart failure. He had been in good health up to noon on Saturday, then complained of a pain, and in a few minutes dropped from his chair and in a moment passed away.

I went into the parlor with Aunt Annie to look at him. His face was quite unchanged and looked more gentle and tender than in life. I have never, since I learned to *feel*, stood thus by the coffin of one akin to me and it was a new and bitter experience. But *once* before I had looked down on a coffined face in that very room—and that face was the face of my mother.

I was very young at the time—barely twenty months old—but I remember it perfectly. It is *almost* my earliest recollection, clear cut and distinct. My mother was lying there in her coffin. My father was standing by her and holding me in his arms. I remember that I wore a little white dress of embroidered muslin and that father was crying. Women were seated around the room and I recall two in front of me on the sofa who were whispering to each other and looking pityingly at father and me. Behind them, the window was open and green hop vines were trailing across it, while their shadows danced over the floor in a square of sunshine.

I looked down at the dead face of the mother whose love I was to miss so sorely and so often in after years. It was a sweet face, albeit worn and wasted by months of suffering. My mother had been beautiful and Death, so cruel in all else, had spared the delicate outline of feature, the long silken lashes brushing the hollow cheek, and the smooth masses of golden-brown hair.

I did not feel any sorrow for I realized nothing of what it all meant. I was only vaguely troubled. Why was mother so still? And why was father crying? I reached down and laid my baby hand against mother's cheek. Even yet I can feel the peculiar coldness of that touch. The memory of it seems to link me with mother, somehow—the only remembrance I have of actual contact with my mother.

Somebody in the room sobbed and said "Poor child!" I wondered if they meant me—and why? I put my arms about father's neck. He kissed me—I recall one more glance at the calm, unchanging face—and that is all. I remember no more of the girlish mother who has slept for twenty two years over in the old graveyard, lulled by the murmur of the sea.

Grandfather's funeral was very large. I had to return to Bedeque the next day, and there the old heartaches which had been deadened for a time by the newer pain, awoke to gnaw and sting and burn once more.

Of course my miserable affair with Edwin Simpson was one of these. Oh, I know I was guilty of wretched folly in this but have I not expiated it in suffering. For I *have* suffered—what no mortal can know. What a curse feeling is! I never really learned to *feel* before. It takes suffering to teach that and the knowledge is named Marah.

....I kept up my correspondence with Ed all winter after a fashion, writing stiff, constrained *soulless* letters. He *must* have noticed this—but if he did he gave no sign. The days I expected a letter from him were days of misery. I hated to read it. His letters were really tedious, pedantic, involved affairs —but oh, worst of all, so *loving*. His reiterated expressions of affection made me heart-sick. When I had finished the letter I flung it into my trunk and locked it up out of sight, never to be read again.

Matters dragged on thus until they reached a climax. I had intended to wait until I left Bedeque before confessing to him. But there came a day when I felt that I could not endure such a life any longer—it was killing me. So one day early in March I sat down and in a fit of desperation wrote him a letter—a wild, frantic epistle it was, but it made my meaning clear. I told him I had ceased to care for him and could not marry him. I did not mince matters. Neither did I try to excuse myself. I admitted in full my weakness and asked him to give me back my freedom in terms that could leave no possible doubt of my feelings.

I did not know and could not picture what effect it would have on Ed. I knew he was very proud—conceited, if you like—and this gave me a feeble hope that he would release me quickly—that he would not stoop to plead or strive to hold but would simply set me free with the scorn I deserved.

I mailed the letter just before I got the news of grandfather's death and for a few days it was almost driven out of my mind. I knew Ed would get the letter the following Thursday, would probably answer it on Sunday and I would get it the next Thursday. That Thursday came. When we went up to the Y.P. Union that night we called at the P.O. and I got it. But I did not open it that night—I was too frightened of its contents. I knew they would upset me, no matter what they were, so I decided not to read it until I came from school the next evening.

The dread of it hung over me all day Friday like a nightmare and even when I did go home I put off reading it on one pretext or another as long as I could. But read it had to be and so at last, at sunset, I summoned up all my resolution and read it.

It was twenty pages long—and a most frantic epistle. But it was not at all the kind I expected and would have infinitely preferred. I had expected accusation and reproach, contemptuous upbraidings—and if the letter had contained such it would not have cut me to the heart half as deeply as it did. For it was a heart-broken letter and I felt that the mere reading of it was punishment enough.

He declared he could *never* forget—that love with him was eternal. And then he seemed to have taken some very foolish ideas into his head as to the *cause* of my ceasing to love him. Had anyone told me anything about him? Were his letters *too tedious* and so on? As if love would be ended by such things, if it had ever had any real existence!

Now that I have had time to think the matter over a little more calmly some of these queries of his strike me as rather curious. Why should he think anyone had told me things about him? *Is there anything to tell?* And why should he have supposed I found his letters tedious? Tedious they certainly were. But I as certainly never wrote him anything that could imply I found them so—unless any avoidance of any reference to the abstruse subjects he discussed might have suggested it to him. But these speculations are idle.

He went on to say that he *could not* set me free in that letter —he must ask for more information regarding my alleged change. He *could not*, he declared, give up the hope that all might yet be right.

Of course, I had not told him that I had ceased to care—or rather, ceased to *fancy* I cared—for him in the first week of our engagement; I had not said *when* I ceased to care at all; and neither had I told him of the physical repulsion with which he inspired me whenever we came into intimate contact. *That* was something I *could not* tell him.

He did not in this letter ask the one question I dreaded—"Was there *another man*?" It was a question I could not have answered. Because by this time there *was* another man—in one sense, but not, after all, in the sense such a question or admission would have inferred. I knew I would never marry this other man. I did not, with the part of me that *rules*, *want* to marry him. If I had never met him it would have been just the same about Ed. I had turned against him before I ever met or saw the "other man". If I had not, I would have been true to him in spite of everything.

When I had finished that terrible letter I curled myself up on the lounge with my misery and wished again as I had wished a score of times during that awful winter that I had never been born.

I knew he loved me truly—and what a perverse fate it was that I could not return his love! How unutterably happy we might have been if I had only loved him as he loved me—or as I loved—the other man!

But there was only one thing to do and I did it. I wrote again, re-iterating all I had said before in even plainer terms, asking for a little pity and consideration although I deserved none and ended by imploring him to set me free from what had become a hateful fetter.

His answer came on the Friday evening before I left Bedeque but I did not read it then. I did not want to be made miserable my last night there—not with *that* kind of misery anyhow—so I decided I would not read it until I was on the train next day. I took the train at Freetown station about two o'clock Saturday afternoon and as soon as I was seated I grimly opened the letter and read it.

His first letter had made me wretched and remorseful and altogether subdued and humble. But this one made me angry. I had suffered so keenly—I had been so long in the depths of bitter humiliation, that the reaction came with unreasonable force. If I could have thrown his letter to the floor and set my foot on it—if I could have torn it to shreds and scattered it to the winds—if I could have walked savagely through the car—if I could have shrieked aloud—if I could have done any or all of these things it would have been an unutterable relief. But I could not—I had to sit there, outwardly calm, trembling from head to foot with the violence of repressed emotion while the train swayed on over bare bleak fields and through leafless woods.

The letter was long and for the first six pages was pretty much what he had written before. The first sentence that struck me like a blow was "Oh, Maud, I cannot, *cannot* set you free without sufficient reason!"

"Sufficient reason!" When I had told him that I did not and could not love him and that consequently life with him would be "an unbearable martyrdom"—my very words! Was not that "sufficient reason"?

He went on:

"Will this do? I set you free for the next three years—free to do as you please, keep company with anyone you please—yes, and marry anyone you please. If then you belong to another or are of the same mind as at present and the same attitude to me you shall be wholly free."

Then he proceeded to say that we must still be friends and keep up our correspondence.

No, I could not agree to this. My haunting humiliation and sense of bondage would never be lessened and would wear my life out. Besides, it would be foolish. I *knew* beyond any doubt that I would never change—that I would be of "the same attitude" to the end of my life.

I wrote to him as soon as I arrived home and sent the letter off before I had time to grow calm. It was not such a letter as I should have written. It was harsh and unjust and I am now bitterly sorry for sending it. But I felt like a wild creature, caught in a trap and biting savagely at its captor's hand. All things considered, I daresay it is just as well. It will probably do more than a dozen imploring, self-reproachful letters to convince Ed that I am desperately, dangerously in earnest, and more than all I hope it will go far towards curing his love for me and opening his eyes to the fact that he is well rid of me. I have not received his reply yet. I suppose it will come soon. That is how the affair stands at present. I am sick of writing about it and am glad to drop the subject, even though the next I must take up will be still more racking.

And it *is*! Yet I am going to write it all down from beginning to end. I suppose this is foolish—but I think it will help me to "write it out". It always does.

If I had known, that evening last fall when I crossed the bay to Bedeque and idly watched the great burnished disk of the sun sink below the violet rim of the water, and the purple shadows clustering over distant shores what was before me I think I would have turned then and there and gone no further—and thus I would have saved myself many a burning tear and bitter heartache, many a sleepless night and wild regret. But oh! Then, too, I would never have known the few hours of intense rapture, of unutterably sweet and subtle happiness that were mine also. While they lasted I thought they more than paid for all—and even yet I sometimes think that it was well to have suffered all I have to have known them. But I knew and feared nothing that October evening and went blindly to my fate.

Now for "Hamlet" with Hamlet in!

Up to the time of my going to Bedeque I had never *loved*. I had never known what it was to love, intensely and passionately and completely. Of course, I have had some attacks, more or less severe, of "calf love", and flirting, violent fancies for some men, bringing with them sometimes a few romantic daydreams. But *love*—no, it had never come to me!

Although I had never really loved, still, like every other girl in the world, I suppose, I had an ideal—a visionary dream of the man I thought I *could* love—handsome, of course—did ever girl dream of a plain lover?—educated, my equal in birth and social position and—most important of all—in intellect. On that last I laid particular stress. Never, so I fancied, could I care for a man who could not meet me on equal ground at least in the matter of mental power!

Well, I have learned the truth of the old proverb—"kissing goes by favor"—and not by rule!

Soon after I arrived at Mr. Leard's that evening tea was announced and the boys came in. Their mother introduced them and I looked them over with tepid interest. Herman came first. At first sight I did not greatly admire his appearance. He was under medium height, slight, and—I thought then—rather insignificant. Calvin impressed me far more favorably. I thought him much better looking than Herman—nevertheless, all through supper I found myself looking again and again at the latter. He was dark-haired and blue-eyed, with lashes as long and silken as a girl's. He was about 27 but looked younger and more boyish. I was not long in concluding that there was something wonderfully fascinating about his face. What it was I could not define. It was elusive, magnetic, haunting; whether it lay in expression or feature could not be told.

It did not take me long to get acquainted with the boys. I found Herman jolly and full of fun. I soon made up my mind concerning him—and I never changed it! He had no trace of intellect, culture, or education—no interest in anything beyond his farm and the circle of young people who composed the society he frequented. In plain, sober truth, he was only a very nice, attractive young animal! And yet!!!

The first three weeks glided by uneventfully. I was too busy with my new duties to have any thought to spare for anything else. Herman and I talked and jested and teased each other continually and kept the house ringing with mirth and laughter.

On Thursday nights we always went up to the Baptist Young People's Union meetings at Central Bedeque. We had no end of fun and jolly chatter on our way there and back, to say nothing of a pleasant drive.

The third evening of Union came the eleventh of November. I am not likely to forget the date—it marked the *first step* on a pathway of passion and pain. When we started home after Union it was a calm moonlit night. I remember every turn of that road—we drove down to Colin Wright's corner at Central Bedeque, thence down the long shadowy Bradshaw hill, over the creek shimmering with the reflections of the stars, up another long hill to Centreville and "Howatt's turn". I was tired and sleepy that night and did not feel like talking so I was very silent. Suddenly Herman leaned over, passed his arm about me and, with a subtly caressing movement, drew my head down on his shoulder.

I was about to straighten up indignantly and say something rather tart but before I could do so there came over me like a *spell* the mysterious, irresistible *influence* which Herman Leard exercised over me from that date—an attraction I could neither escape nor overcome and against which all the resolution and will power in the world didn't weigh a feather's weight. It was indescribable and overwhelming.

So I did not move—I left my head on his shoulder, voiceless, motionless, as we drove home in silence.

When we reached home I sprang from the buggy without a word and ran upstairs. I was overwhelmed by a flood of wholly new and strange emotions which I could neither understand or control. I was aware, in a dim, vague way, that danger of some sort was surely ahead and I resolved that never again would I allow anything of the kind. But the very next night when we were driving home from a party at Centreville it happened again. He drew my head down on his shoulder and pressed his cheek against mine; and as he did so a thrill of delight and rapture rushed over me—I could *not* speak—I could *not* forbid him.

The next Union night Herman went a step further. It was just below James Montgomery's—I recollect the moonlight gleaming on his white house, for every trifling thing seemed to stamp itself indelibly on my memory—Herman suddenly bent his head and his lips touched my face. I cannot tell what possessed me—I seemed swayed by a power utterly beyond my control—I turned my head—our lips met in one long passionate pressure—a kiss of fire and rapture such as I had never in all my life experienced or imagined. *Ed's* kisses at the best left me cold as ice—*Herman's* sent flame through every vein and fibre of my being.

It might have warned me—and it *did*. When I got home and found myself alone

I tried to look matters squarely in the face. *This must not go on!* I was engaged. True, it was to a man I did not love and whom I knew I would never marry; true, too, that before I ever saw Herman Leard I had known this. But that made no vital difference. For the sake of my self respect I *must not* stoop to any sort of an affair with another man.

If I had—or rather if I *could* have—kept this resolve I would have saved myself incalculable suffering. For it was but a few days later that I found myself face to face with the burning consciousness that I *loved* Herman Leard with a wild, passionate, unreasoning love that dominated my entire being and possessed me like a flame—a love I could neither quell nor control—a love that in its intensity seemed little short of absolute madness. Madness! Yes! Even if I had been free Herman Leard was impossible, viewed as a husband. It would be the rankest folly to dream of marrying such a man. If I were mad enough to do so—well, I would be deliriously happy for a year or so—and wretched, discontented and unhappy all the rest of my life. I saw this plainly enough—passion, while it mastered my heart, left my brain unclouded. I never for a moment deceived myself into thinking or hoping that any good could come out of this love of mine.

Oh, I *did* try hard to conquer it! But I might as well have tried to stem the rush of a mountain torrent. The very next evening after that fatal kiss we were alone. Mr. and Mrs. Leard were away and Helen was entertaining her own fiance, Howard McFarlane, in the parlor; the little girls had gone to bed. Herman who had been out goose-shooting came in about 8 and sat down on the sofa to read a novel.

I was sitting by the table, writing; we did not talk but it seemed to me that the whole air was thrilling electrically. After about half an hour Herman threw down his book impatiently and said that his eyes were bothering him too much to read. Whereupon I, having finished my writing and having nothing else to do, offered to read aloud to him. He assented and I took the book.

I don't think I read very well that night—for I had not been reading long before Herman reached out and took my hand in his, holding it in a warm close pressure. I was furious with myself because I could not help trembling like a leaf—he *must* have noticed it. Half a dozen times my voice faltered, my head reeled, the letters danced before my eyes. Finally Herman whispered, "never mind reading any more", and took the book away. Then he drew me over beside him and held me there, his arms about me, his face pressed against mine. For half an hour we sat there, without word or motion—save that now and then he kissed me. And for me all heaven seemed to open in his kisses. Disgraceful? Oh, yes, I suppose it was! But my love was so intense, so overmastering that it seemed to me at the time to justify my yielding to his caresses.

But regret came—afterwards—oh, how poignantly! When I went upstairs to my room I lay awake for hours to fight over and over again the old unavailing battle with myself.

I knew I was foolish and wicked—and what, too, must Herman think? Of course, he had heard the report that I was engaged to Edwin Simpson. I felt quite sure of that although he never spoke of it. But Helen had, so there was no doubt he had also. So I supposed he was merely flirting for pastime. Yet I certainly had as much power over him as he had over me. Herman burned his fingers at the game of fire as well as myself. Yet there were many things about his attitude I never could understand. Perhaps if I had encouraged him to talk the matter over I should have understood. But I dared not risk *that*. He must have thought me a wild, perplexing creature in very truth, so ready to meet his caresses half way, yet always ruthlessly cutting short any attempt at uttered sentiment. If I never fully understood him I have the sorry satisfaction of feeling that I, too, puzzled him.

When I was alone I suffered everything but when I was with him I forgot all else and was deliriously happy.

The next night—Saturday—we were alone in the evening and it was the same thing over again. Sunday afternoon, too, I was alone in the sitting room, reading on the sofa, when Herman came in and sat down beside me, putting his arms about me and drawing my face close to his. There seemed no need of speech—we hardly ever talked much when alone together—it was enough to sit there in dreamy, rapturous silence. Oh, it all comes back to me as I write—and I long with a wild, sick, *horrible* longing to be back in his arms again—to feel the warm, magnetic pressure of his cheek against mine—to ruffle his brown curls with my fingers—Oh, God!!!

It is a horrible thing to live in the same house with a man you love and ought not to love. There is no respite of temptation and what chance have you to conquer in the struggle?

Things went on thus, with our Union drives and stolen moments of lingering until the 28th of November came. It was Sunday night and Herman drove Helen and me up to the Methodist church at Centreville. I was feeling wretched that evening for I could not help brooding over my troubles—troubles about which I could not speak a word to any living creature but must mask under a smiling face and an assumed gayety—and over my unhappy love which was growing stronger every day.

We drove home in silence for Helen was in no mood to talk, I was too miserable, and Herman was a quiet mortal as a general thing. But when he lifted me out of the buggy he whispered in my ear,

"Will you stay down a little while with me tonight?"

I should have refused—oh, of course I should! We should always do exactly what is right at all times! But unfortunately some of us don't seem able to. The temptation was too strong—I went helplessly down before it and murmured a faint assent.

I went in like a girl in a dream. Helen hurried off to bed—she was in a pretty bad temper just then over Howard's failing to show up—and I sat down in the soft semi-gloom of the firelight to wait for Herman. For the moment I was happy beyond the power of words to express—and yet I was frightened, too—I almost dreaded to hear Herman's step at the door even while I longed for it!

At last he came in, threw off his cap and coat and came to me, pressing his cold face against my burning one. We nestled there together in the gloom and silence. Dangerous? That is too weak a word! I knew that I was tiptoeing on the brink of utter destruction—yet I could not turn back. I could realize nothing except that I was in the arms of the man I loved as I had never dreamed I could love. When we parted and I had gone to my room—then—*then* regret and shame overwhelmed me indeed and I paid the bitter price of my weakness!

The days seemed to me to come and go as in a dream. The only hours I *lived* were when I was with Herman. The rest of the time I was torn by conflicting passions until my life was one long agony and my sleepless nights began to tell on my health. But once let Herman's hands or lips touch mine and every other feeling was fused into one of unquestioning happiness.

So the time passed on and I lived my double life—the outward one in which I taught school and wrote and read and went to social functions and talked and laughed and jested, passing the hours in a seemingly pleasant routine—and the unseen, unsuspected inner one, wrung with passion and suffering, whose current flowed on side by side with the other.

Herman and I constantly found or made opportunities to be together. Naturally this new and unforeseen development was an added source of agony as regards Edwin Simpson. My engagement was more nightmare like and unbearable than ever, coupled with my miserable feeling of disloyalty. When, about this time, Ed began writing of his holiday plans, I suffered everything, for in my then state of mind I could not face the thought of meeting him. It is, by the way, a curious twist of the irony of that old jade Fate, that it was Ed's doings that I ever went to Bedeque. He knew Alf Leard and when I applied for the school he asked Alf to use his influence in my behalf, with the result that I got it—which it is not in the least likely I would otherwise have done.

At last, on Saturday the 11th of December, I received a letter from him saying that he had decided not to come. I fairly cried with relief.

That night was gloomy and rainy. I was writing in the sitting room when Herman came in. Helen was at the organ and under cover of the music Herman bent over me and whispered, "Will you stay awhile with me to-night?"

I nodded, and he went out. I went on writing, not knowing a word I was putting down. When all the others had gone to bed I slipped out to the kitchen where Herman was waiting for me. He flung down the book he was reading and came forward to meet me!

When, as I described before, Ed came so unexpectedly to Bedeque my state of mind cannot be described. There was I under the same roof with two men, one of whom I loved and could never marry, the other whom I had promised to marry but could never love! What I suffered that night between horror, shame and dread can never be told. Every dark passion in my nature seemed to have broken loose and run wild riot. I wonder the strife of them all did not kill me.

As to what Herman thought of it I do not know, for he never alluded to Ed's visit—a circumstance suspicious in itself. Yet I can surmise his thoughts for after that Herman was never the same again, save now and then when some passionate impulse seemed to get the better of him. I believe he thought I was engaged to Ed and was merely amusing myself with him. I cannot complain if he thought so. My behavior certainly gave him the right to think so. Doubtless he regarded me as a girl who was engaged to one man, yet was untrue to him—who could stoop to flirt with another man, yet never commit herself in words. It is a hard thing enough to have to believe that Herman thought this of me, yet it was better than that he should know the truth. Yes in all cold-blooded preference I would rather he believed me an unprincipled flirt, going recklessly as far as she dared, than that he should know how madly I loved him, even while I regarded him as my inferior. Anything, says stubborn pride, would be better than *that*!

The Wednesday night before Christmas Herman went to S'Side and was gone all day. I had just gone up to my room when I heard the carriage and when he came into the hall below I ran out to ask him if he had got a magazine I had sent for. He said he had not been able to do so, as the copies were all sold out, so I went back to my room and flung myself moodily down on my sofa. Helen was away and I was in the deeps of the blues. Presently Herman came upstairs and to my door, with a couple of books in his hand. He tossed them down to me, along with a box of chocolates—"Those are for you, Maud," he said, as he turned away before I could thank him.

Christmas Eve came. Helen was still away and during the evening Herman waylaid me in the hall as I came downstairs to ask me to stay awhile with him that night again. I had been tingling with pain over the subtle alteration in his manner since Ed's visit and my heart beat with joy at this return to our old footing, even though clear brain and unrelenting conscience both told me it would have been far better not to.

I have a very uncomfortable blend in my make-up—the passionate Montgomery blood and the Puritan Macneill conscience. Neither is strong enough wholly to control the other. The Puritan conscience can't prevent the hot blood from having its way—in part at least—but it *can* poison all the pleasure and it does. Passion says, "Go on. Take what crumbs of happiness fall in your way." Conscience says, "Do so if you will. Feed your soul on those blood-red husks; but I'll scourge you well for it afterwards."

I listened only to the former voice that night again and had a couple of hours happiness that were worth—yes, that were *well worth*—the afterlash of conscience. I *will* say it, for I think it!

The next day was Sunday. Cal and a cousin of his came down to spend the day and in the evening Herman drove them up to Central Bedeque. It was eleven when he returned. I had been reading in my room but was now sitting moodily on the lounge. When Herman came upstairs he came in. He had for his excuse another book and a box of chocolates. He gave them to me and sat down on a chair at the foot of the sofa.

I was tired and lonely—I dreaded the hours of darkness—and I could not find it in my heart to send him away. He sat there and talked to me while I nibbled candy. Finally he rose and went to the bureau for his lamp; then suddenly he changed his mind, came right over to the chair by my head, sat down, bent over, and laid his head on the cushion beside mine, his cheek against my forehead. I realized that this was going too far and I said—in as careless a tone as I could assume, for I did not wish to give the situation any added seriousness—"You run away. You'll be nice and sleepy tomorrow if you stay up any longer."

Herman seldom disputed or disregarded my expressed wishes; and he knew quite as well as I did that he had no business to be in my room at that hour of the night. He hesitated a moment, said, "I suppose I will," and bent down with a whispered good-night to kiss me. I had exhausted my powers of resistance in sending him away and I could not refuse him that. I flung my arms impulsively about his neck and kissed him. Then, when he had gone, the Macneill conscience said a few things to me!

When '97 went out and '98 came in I roused myself with an effort to look matters squarely in the face. I knew if I let matters drift on as they were drifting one of two things must inevitably happen. My health and it might be my very reason would give way—or I would fall over the brink of the precipice upon which I stood into an abyss of ruin. And I made a desperate vow to break the chain that bound me at any cost—at any suffering.

This resolution was hardly made before it was broken. I was alone in the parlor New Year's night at dusk when Herman came in and began making love to me again—and in the fatal rapture of the hour my resolution was forgotten. Nevertheless in calmer moments it came back to me and I struggled like a drowning man. I tried to keep out of Herman's way—to avoid him whenever possible. But I fear I couldn't have resisted actual temptation had it presented itself. However, it did not; for three weeks Herman left me alone. Possibly he felt and resented my avoidance, possibly it was the influence of Ed's visit. At all events we had no more "scenes", and *brain* said a cold "Thank God", conscience gave approval,— but *heart*—oh!!!

Suddenly another experience broke the bounds again.

It was a stormy Friday night near the last of January. In the evening Helen was writing a letter in the kitchen and I was sitting by the fire waiting till she should be through and ready to go to bed. Herman was lying on the lounge, fooling with Jink, the dog, and we all kept up a triangular chatter of jokes and nonsense. Finally Helen and I began making mysterious remarks to each other about a mutual joke we had and Herman, scenting a mystery, demanded to know what it was. Upon our refusing to tell him he sprang up, came over and sat down beside me, trying to tease me into telling him. But I would not and while we were fooling about the matter Helen in a spirit of mischief sprang up, snatched the lamp, shut the door and ran. I am sure Herman had no intention of asking me to stay down that night and I had as little thought of it. But we were neither of us strong enough to resist the temptation thus thrust upon us. As a result, the hard three week's struggle went for nothing and we were back on our old footing again.

Sunday evening I was feeling blue and headachy, so curled myself up on the sitting room sofa. Herman came in, sat down on the sofa at my feet and pretended to read. May was in the room and while she was in he read religiously holding my hand in his all the while under my shawl. His clasp, the little caressing pats of his fingers, all thrilled me with a delight that flushed my tell-tale face. To meet Herman's eyes was something I could never do. I remember that day, as I was furtively watching *his* flushed cheek, his long dark lashes, and dusky curls, he suddenly looked around and our eyes met—met and locked. What flashed from one to the other I do not know but when I dragged mine from that fascinated gaze he still looked down at me and finding that I would not look up again he shook my wrist until I did; and then —for May had gone out—he flung away his book and with one of his quick, lithe movements snuggled down beside me, his arm thrown around me, his dark head pillowed on my shoulder. I could not move or speak—I was too happy to wish to do either.

Monday and Tuesday were snow-blockaded and we got no mail. Herman went up after it on Tuesday evening. Howard MacFarlane also appeared and he and Helen betook themselves to the parlor. This left me companionless so I went bluely upstairs to my room. Herman came home at eleven. When he came upstairs he brought me in my letters. I was on the lounge, reading. He sat down on the chair beside me, gave me my mail, and a box of chocolates. I was too lonely to send him away. I read my letters, nibbled my creams and chatted to him. But it was not long until we heard Howard going and of course this was the signal for Herman to leave the room before Helen came up.

Friday night Helen and Herman went to a concert practice up at Central Bedeque, where Helen intended to stay for the night. When Herman came home he again came to my room with the mail. He sat down as usual and the first half hour passed harmlessly, looking over the mail and gossiping about Centreville doings. I made a desperate effort to keep the conversation going *all* the time for I had learned to dread nothing so much as those electrical *silences* of ours. But at last I suddenly found that I had nothing more to say. Herman grew silent at the same time. I was trying to summon up enough resolution to tell him to go when he suddenly slipped down beside me and buried his face on my shoulder. Voice almost failed me but I managed to say,

"You must go now."

He made no reply in words—merely raised his head for an instant and looked straight into my eyes. I suppose he saw there the miserable confession of strong wishes struggling with fainting will for he nestled down again, slipping his arms around me and pressing his face against mine.

Madness? I know it was! And I knew it *then* every whit as vividly as I know it now but *that* knowledge didn't help matters any. I knew I was running a fearful risk but I was under the old fatal, paralyzing spell, which only those who have experienced it can understand or condone, and I could not send him away. It was *heaven* to be there in his arms and I gave myself up to the delight of it, forgetting all else for the moment. The candle burned low, so as to leave the room in semi-gloom. We did not talk or try to. If he would only go! I could not *tell* him to go—I could *not* send him away—but oh, if he would only *go*!

Then—at last Herman whispered a single sentence in my ear—a request whose veiled meaning it was impossible to misunderstand!

I was not angry—how could I be? I had no right to be for I was as much to blame as he. And besides, I loved him too much to be angry with him for *anything* he might say or do. But his *spoken* words gave me a saving shock of recoil, which was lacking in the more insidious temptation of silent caresses.

"No—no", I gasped bluntly. "Go away to your own room at once. Herman—you ought to have gone long ago. Oh, *go*!"

I fairly sobbed out the last word. Herman did not go at once—he said nothing more for a minute or two. Then he slipped on his knees to the floor, drew my face to his for one long, clinging kiss—and then went.

I cowered down among my cushions in an agony of shame. Oh, what had I done? What had he said? Was it possible that things had come to such a pass with *me* that only a faintly uttered, hysterical "no" had stood between me and dishonor?

I never slept that night. What I suffered makes me shudder even now! When morning dawned my worst punishment came—to go down and face him. I lingered until I thought he would have gone out but when I went down all the family were at breakfast. I had to take my place opposite Herman and never dared to lift my eyes. Neither, I think, did he. Thereafter we ignored the incident and took no open account of it.

For the next week he was away most of the time and I was horribly lonely. The way in which I missed him frightened me. I shut my eyes in shuddering misery when I thought of our final separation.

But that interminable week passed and he came home Saturday. Sunday night he went over to S'Side to church and returned about eleven. I had no fear of him coming to my room that night for there would be no mail and consequently he would have no excuse for coming. So I was startled when he came to my door and asked if he might have Helen's lamp as he could not find one downstairs. I said "Certainly" and he came in and lighted it. But he did not go out. He loitered around the bureau on one excuse or another, trying on my rings, etc. Evidently he did not want to go but realized that he had no plausible excuse for staying. As for me, I had hardly seen him for a week and I was longing madly for his presence, his smile, his caress. After awhile he came and sat down by me and talked aimlessly for a few minutes about his drive to S'Side. I leaned back like one in a dream, my face burning, my heart beating so wildly as almost to choke my breath. I knew it was wrong and foolish enough to let him stay there but it was not so dangerous as before, since Helen might be up at any moment and Herman, knowing this, would not make another "scene".

I am not defending myself at all—I am only just telling what happened. I loved Herman Leard madly and, though I knew perfectly well I should be bitterly sorry the next day, his mere presence there brought me such unutterable happiness, so intense and passionate and all-pervading, that I could not thrust it from me at the command of conscience. So Herman stayed—leaned nearer and nearer—took me in his arms—kissed my lips! I gave myself over once again to the rapture of it and harbored only the delight of being in the arms of the man I loved, of pressing my cheek to his, of smoothing his curly hair with a hand that he would snatch and kiss as if every kiss were his last. I feel those kisses now, burning on wrist and fingers.

When twelve o'clock struck I said, "Lad, it's time for you to go." He obeyed me at once, kissing me good-night with that dangerous tenderness of his against which it was so hard to still my heart.

Thursday night of that week came. Helen was again away. Herman went up to a lecture at Centreville, intending to bring Cal home with him. He returned about eleven, came to my room with the mail, and said that Cal had not come home after all.

Of course it was the same thing over again. I was frightened—and yet happy. Yes, I *was* happy. That little room was heaven to me and Herman all the world. He held me in his arms—he kissed me again and again—he pushed the hair away from my forehead and laid his cheek against it. Oh, even as I write I can feel his arms tighten around me, the warm pressure of his dear curly head on my breast. I cannot subdue or endure the sick longing that comes over me for it to be again a reality! Twelve o'clock came. As the clock struck I said, "Did you hear that?"

"What."

"The clock striking twelve. It's time for you to go."

He did not reply except by an inarticulate murmur and a closer pressure. As unwilling to send him as he was to go I remained silent for a few minutes. Then I tried to push him away.

"Herman," I whispered, "didn't you hear what I said?"

He lifted his head and looked down into my eyes.

"Are you sleepy?" he said.

"Yes, I am," I forced myself to say, thinking it might induce him to go. It was a lie—and I suppose he knew it. He hesitated for a moment, looked at my clock, and then back again at me. Then, with a long drawn sigh, he slipped down beside me once more.

I gave up trying to send him away then. I sat there in silence—oh God, such a silence. It was eloquent with a thousand tongues. All the women of my race who have loved in the past spoke in me. I felt Herman's burning breath on my face, his burning kisses on my lips. And then I heard him making the same request he had made before, veiled, half inaudible, but unmistakable. For a moment that seemed like a year my whole life reeled in the balance. The most horrible temptation swept over me—I remember to this minute its awful power—to *yield*—to let him stay where he was—to be his body and soul if that one night at least!

What saved me? What held me back. No consideration of right and wrong. I was past caring for *that*. No tradition or training—that had all gone down before the mad sweep of instinctive passion. Not even fear of the price the woman pays. No, that which saved me from Herman Leard's dishonoring love was *the fear of Herman Leard's contempt*. If I yielded—he might despise me! His hatred, his indifference I could bear. But I could not bear his contempt. If it had not been for that I realize that I would have plunged recklessly into that abyss of passion, even if my whole after life were to be one of agonized repentance.

I pushed his clinging arms from me.

"Herman, *go*," I cried. "go—at once—*at once*, I say!"

"Oh, *no*," he murmured—and there is no power in pen to express all the pleading he infused into that one word.

Again—that dizzy shock of temptation. I had just enough fear, or resolution, or desperation—ay, that's the right word!—to gasp out imploringly,

"Yes, yes, you *must* go. You ought not to be here at all. Nobody ever was before. Now, Herman, *go*!"

For one breathless moment he was silent, with his lips pressed against my bare arm. If he had refused to go—if he had pleaded but once again—but thank God, he did not. At last he murmured in a low voice, "All right, dear. I'll go—"and the next minute he was gone.

From that night Herman was changed. Was it anger—or baffled passion—or what? I thought then and think still that it was partly his distrust of me in regard to Ed, partly that his eyes were opened to the precipice upon which we stood. And he knew, as I did, that safety lay only in putting an end then and there to the mad game of fire at which we had been playing. He never came to my room again—possibly because Cal came home for good and so he could not—and once more we became almost strangers.

What I suffered in the month that followed cannot be told. In a way I was thankful for the change in Herman—I knew it was my only chance of ever regaining self-control. But that did not make the pain any the less bitter. Oh, that nightmare month. Sometimes, even, a fierce brief temptation would sweep over me to yield to the love that possessed me—encourage Herman—marry him. But I never, even in my worst hours, *seriously* contemplated that. Love was a strong passion with me—but pride—and perhaps rationality—was equally strong. I could not stoop to marry a man so much my inferior in all the essentials necessary, not to a few hectic months, but to a long lifetime together.

I had never dreamed that I was capable of such love as possessed me—ay, *possessed* is the right word. Simply to be under the same roof with him brought a strange torturing sweetness that nothing could wholly embitter—a blow from him would have been sweeter than any other man's fondest caress. Oh, Herman, Herman, you will *never, never, never* know how I have loved you!

Of course, all this mental misery, these passion-wrung days and sleepless, tearful nights could not fail of having a destructive effect on my health. I grew thin and pale. Everyone noticed it but attributed it to fretting over Grandfather's death. I was thankful that they did for I could not have borne that anyone should have suspected the real cause. The time dragged away and the last of March drew near when Al—who came home about the middle of the month—would take the school again and I would return home. The thought of leaving Herman, of seeing him no more, was agony; and yet I looked forward with relief to my final departure for I hoped that when I was once really away from him and from all things connected with him, I might succeed in forgetting him, might regain—not my old, unquestioning, care-free happiness for I knew too well and truly that had gone forever—but peace and tranquillity, cessation of longing and pain. I might find *rest*.

But the thought that Herman might preserve the same coldness towards me until the last—that I might have to go away and leave him so, after all that had passed between us was the bitterest drop in an exceeding bitter cup.

But he *did* break through the coldness—thank God for that!

One evening—March 21st—there was a party at Central Bedeque and Herman drove me up. He was as silent as usual and so was I. Suddenly he said,

"How much longer have you to teach here?"

I was surprised for it was the very first time he had made any allusion to my approaching departure although it was frequently discussed by the rest of the family in his presence. But I answered, with the careless unconcern I always simulated before him when it came to spoken words.

"Just another week and a half, that is all."

He made no other remark for several minutes. Then he said slowly, "Have you any photos of your own?"

"No, I haven't any just now," I said. He said nothing more, as we were at our destination. But, foolish as it was of me, his question gave me an exaggerated sense of happiness—sufficient to brighten the whole evening for me. And going home that night, under the star-sprinkled violet sky, he once again as of old drew my head down on his shoulder and pressed his face to mine, and for a little space I forgot pain and heartbreak in the shelter of his arms.

It seemed as if that little indulgence brought down all the barriers again and brought us closer together than ever. The next Friday evening we were invited over to Millie Leard's. Coming home under the spruces—the crowd of us were in the big box sleigh and Cal was driving—Herman slipped his arm about me and drew me close to him. With a little sigh of happiness I nestled there during our drive over the gleaming marsh and through the snowy woods. He held me so closely and tenderly—he had such a dear gentle way of doing everything—and so often his lips met mine in those never-to-be-forgotten kisses that thrilled me "with all the flame of heaven and all the fire of hell."

Sunday Al and Cal were both away. After dinner Mr. Leard and Helen went to church but I had a headache and did not go. Herman and I found ourselves in the room alone all the afternoon. I was curled up on the sofa and he came over, nestling down beside me, his arms around me, his boyish head pillowed on my shoulder.

That last week went by. Friday night came—my last night in Bedeque. Helen, expecting Howard over, had lighted a fire in the parlor and was waiting there in the moonlit dusk for him. She called me in and, nothing loth to leave the kitchen, where the sight of Herman reading by the table, was alternately fascinating me and torturing me, I went and sat down on the sofa by the window. We chatted away until half past eight and Howard had not put in an appearance. We had just concluded he was not coming when Herman came in. Helen did not welcome his advent with a very good grace and gave him some rather plain hints to be off but he would not take them and presently Helen bounced out of the room in a pet. I rose to follow but Herman was at my side in a flash, his arms about me, his head on my shoulder. I was voiceless and motionless for a moment—and then, overcome by a rush of impulsive tenderness I bent and brushed my lips across his hair. Then he drew me down beside him. We stayed there until ten. I was divinely happy. Herman had the power—for me, at least, of blotting out temporarily everything but himself. I feared nothing, cared for nothing, grieved for nothing.

> "Life held for me then no enchantment, no charms,
> No vision of happiness outside his arms."

He asked me to send him a photo when I had some taken and when I promised I would he said,

"You'll be taking the school again after Al is done of it, won't you?"

"I'm afraid not," I said.

"Why not?" he demanded in such a surprised, startled tone.

"I don't suppose I'll be able to teach any more," I said wearily. "I'll probably have to stay home with grandma after this."

He was silent for a moment, then he said in a dismayed way, "But you'll be up for a visit this summer, won't you?"

"I'd like to if I can arrange it." I said.

Then there was a long silence. Once I said teasingly, "Have you fallen asleep?"

"No!" he said, "I could sit here forever without talking."

Well, so could I. But when the clock struck ten I said that I must go.

"You won't forget the photograph?" he said.

"No, I'll be sure to send you one," I promised.

He bent over me, and we exchanged some long, passionate kisses. Then he slipped back to his old place but I said quickly,

"Oh. I *must* go."

"When will we have a chance for a chat again," he whispered.

"I don't know," I said chokingly.

He held me to him with my hands crushed in his. I was in a daze of despair and pain. Then somehow we found our way to the door. We paused there in the glimmering radiance of the moonlight for what was our real good-bye. I thought my heart would break.

> "Who can conceive who has not proved
> The anguish of a last embrace?"

Who indeed? He held me close—our lips met in that last kiss.

"Good-night," we breathed—and so I left him standing there in the moonlight and went up to my room—alone—*alone*—as I must henceforth be!

In the morning I bade him good-bye on the doorstep and shook hands with him as with the others. He stood on the platform and watched me off. It was all over—and I only longed and wished that life was over too!

Since coming home I have spent a wretched week. I miss Herman heartbreakingly—I long for him—I *cannot*, strive as I will, keep him out of my thoughts day or night. He is dearer to me than ever. There are hours when I am frantic with longing for a glimpse of his face—the sound of his voice—a kiss—a handclasp. But I *will* conquer—I *will* live it down even if my heart is forever crushed in the struggle.

It has been a great relief to write this all out. A great pain, too, for it has brought everything back so vividly!

It seems very much of an anti-climax after all these confessions to write of other and lesser matters. But all things are mingled in this life—the most insignificant follow on the heels of the most tragic. All through this terrible winter, when my soul was being wrung with every passion that blesses or curses humanity, I have done all my little duties painstakingly—I have smiled and chattered at home and abroad and done proper homage to all the conventionalities. And so it is only in keeping with this that I turn from these passionate memories to other and lesser things.

I have had some successes in literature—several acceptances, some of them in new places. My work is a great comfort to me in these sad days. I forget all my griefs and perplexities while I am absorbed in it. I am very ambitious—perhaps too ambitious. Herman told me that once—he seemed to hate my ambition—perhaps he felt the truth that it was the real barrier between us. But at least it is all I have to live for now and I may as well hunt it down.

Novels—I have read some—mostly with a new realization of how far short they fall of actual life and what pale reflections even the best of them are. Only two were worth mentioning. "The Quick or the Dead" was striking. It is powerfully written but too morbid and lacks proportion. Moreover, it ends in an exasperating way that makes one conscious of a desire to take the heroine and shake a little common sense into her.

"Night and Morning" by Lord Lytton disappointed me. Lyttor. used to be my favorite author in old schooldays when Nate—who was also a frenzied admirer of his—and I used to have no end of animated discussions over his books and heroes. But my allegiance has sadly wavered of late years.

Apart from Herman, I was sorry to leave Bedeque and my school. I liked both and I was very successful in the school.

I shall have to give up teaching and remain home for grandma cannot live alone. I confess that my heart sinks at the prospect but it must be faced. Grandfather's exceedingly foolish will has placed Grandma—and consequently myself since I must stay at home—in a very anomalous position—a position which will I am sure, be extremely awkward and unpleasant, becoming more and more so as time passes.

Then, again, I feel virtually a stranger in Cavendish. I am entirely out of touch with its interests. But of course *this*, at least, is temporary and after a few months all will be as of yore in this respect. But *other* things can *never* be the same, and the knowledge of this confronts me like an unquiet ghost at every turn.

In my many long lonely moments I have been passing the time by reading over old letters and the part of my journal written when I was attending P.W.C. How light-hearted and merry and nonsensical it was! I have also been weeding out my letters—a process that is always gone through every time I come home, for I generally conclude that some have lost their interest and so I burn them. But there are some I shall never burn—at least it does not seem to me now that I ever will.

I have finished at last and I am glad for I am very tired. It is late and the house is still. I am worn out, for in writing all this down I have seemed to live it over again and that has been hard on me. I must close this book and go away to sleep in my little room upstairs. Oh, I am very tired—so tired of suffering and vain struggle. Perhaps—dare I hope it?—the future will bring balm and healing and nepenthe.

Sunday, July 10, 1898
Cavendish, P.E.I.
These three months seem to have gone quickly—yet it also seems as if a long time had passed since I last wrote in this old book. I have lived through so many phases of feeling that it seems impossible a short three months could embrace them all.

It is Sunday morning—a dull, sultry July morning with a creamy air full of bird trills and sibilant rustlings of poplar and the savor of red clover fields and balsamic fir woods. The house is still, the atmosphere one of dreams.

When I last wrote here I was miserably unhappy. Well, I am unhappy still. Yet life is more placid for me now. The active storm and stress of passion is past—a certain tranquillity is mine—and the surcease of pain is so blessed that it almost seems—by force of contrast—happiness. I have attained to a calm—but I have not attained to it without a bitter struggle.

Which thread shall I take up first? The one interwoven with Ed's life and mine I suppose. Well, thank God, I am free now—utterly and entirely free.

My last entry in this journal was just after I had written that bitter letter to Ed and I had not had a reply. I expected it on Thursday but none came. Saturday—none came—Tuesday and still no letter! But the next day it arrived. The moment I took it I knew that my photograph was inside of it—and *that* meant freedom. I hastened upstairs to my room. Yet I was half afraid to open the letter—for if he still refused to give me unconditional freedom I believe I should have gone distracted. I had endured and suffered until I could endure and suffer no more.

I sat down by the window and opened the letter. The photo fell out and with it a faded spray of apple blossom. That fatal June night last summer I had worn a spray of apple blossom and Ed had taken it as a souvenir.

The first three pages of his letter were very bitter. My last letter had incensed him but it also won me my freedom. He told me I was free—and I dropped the letter in a surge of passionate relief. For a minute every other pain was forgotten and I was happy.

Towards the last of the letter Ed softened and wrote in a more subdued and heart-broken strain. My anger had all gone and I felt bitterly sorry for him. So I wrote a short letter in reply—I thanked him for releasing me from my engagement and asked him to forgive me for all—and for that unkind letter I had written and regretted—and then I bade him good-bye. I hardly expected to hear from him again but on May 7th another letter came.

When Mollie was over here one evening after I came home and we were up here talking in the twilight she told me some queer ins and outs of a visit she had in Belmont last winter; among others that Sophy Simpson had told her that she—Sophy—had read one of my letters to Ed last summer.

I was bitterly annoyed. I had warned Ed so often not to leave my letters where anyone could possibly see them and it made me angry that he *had* been so careless after all. And Sophy, of all people! When he wrote, giving me my freedom, he said that he would burn all my letters except the *first* which he wanted to keep if I would permit him. I did not like the idea but I felt that I ought to give him all the consideration in my power. So when I wrote back I told him he might but added that he must be careful of it because one of my letters to him had been read by a certain person. This it was that caused Ed to write again. He was determined to know who that "person" was and insisted as his right that I should tell him who had done "such a contemptible thing". He wrote another long passionate epistle—and he would "always love me"—that I would always be his "ideal woman" etc. Ah, Ed, poor boy, if you only knew of what common, earthy clay your "ideal" is made!

I was just starting for town when his letter came so did not answer it until I came back. Then I wrote him a brief note and told him it was Sophy who had read his letter. What Sophy's fate has been I don't know—but if Ed came down on her about it it wouldn't be an enviable one.

Finally I burned his letters—they crumbled into ashes—and I was my own woman once more.

So ends it—and thank God, it does! It has been a bitter cup of humiliation and pain and I have drained it to the very dregs. It has leavened my whole life with its poison and blistered the fair page of my girlhood with despair and shame. Yes, shame. I truly feel it a far deeper shame to have been engaged to Edwin Simpson, feeling as I did towards him, than to have given my caresses to Herman Leard whom I loved. It is a memory from which I must always avert my eyes—but it *is* a memory *only* and not a present torment.

For a month or so after I came home my loneliness was almost unbearable. I had been away so long that I felt *outside* of everything. This has worn away; yet there is always a secret aching sense of blankness—nothing *satisfies*—but the worst has gone by. I have got back to my own place again and various duties and simple, unimpassioned pleasures have crept in to fill my life and bring its jangled chords into harmony once more.

Cavendish has been fairly pleasant this summer. I have got around a good deal—there are several boys who seem to enjoy driving me around. But they all bore me terribly. When one has been whirled as I have been into the most tragic passions it is unspeakably palling to be thrown back again on shams and pretences. I imagine that I feel very much as some classic student might who had drunk at the founts of undying genius and revelled in the masterpieces of the ages were he to be suddenly thrust back into the primer class of his childhood's school and forced to con over his A.B. C.'s from day to day again.

But I have a few pleasures which depend not on others and cannot be taken from me. I have books—those unfailing keys to a world of enchantment. I have re-read old favorites and a few new ones. Among the latter was "A Window in Thrums" by Barrie. It has a certain charm and simplicity which hold interest. Barrie touches common places and they blossom out into beauty and pathos. "Opening a Chestnut Burr" by Roe bored me horribly. I outgrew Roe long ago—to be sure, one need not be of a very stately mental height for *that*. He is too *preachy*. If a book can not point its own moral all the whittling of the best intentioned author in the world can't get it down sufficiently fine to strike home.

I sent for Ella Wheeler Wilcox's "Poems of Passion" this spring. They seem to be written for me. I have *lived* them every word.

Then I have read "Quo Vadis"—the novel of the year. It is immensely powerful—a perfect picture of the splendor and corruption of Imperial Rome and the court of Nero, out of which rises the pure and awful beauty of early Christianity; the which, could it but have retained its primitive simplicity, instead of becoming overgrown with dogma and verbiage would be as potent a force today as it was when the martyrs of the Colosseum sealed their faith with their blood.

I have written a good deal since coming home and am slowly but I think surely, climbing up the ladder. I think my recent work is much better than any I have yet done. I study hard and struggle to improve. I like writing verse best but when I get a good prose plot that runs smoothly I enjoy working it out, too.

I am writing here by the window of my dear old room. It is a veritable little haven of rest and dreams to me, and the window opens on a world of wonder and beauty. Winds drift by with clover scent in their breath; the rustle of leaves comes up from the poplars, and birds flit low in joyous vagrance. Below is a bosky old apple orchard and a row of cherry trees along the dyke where the old tamarack stands guard. Beyond it green meadows slope down to a star-dusted valley of buttercups and past that wide fields stretch up again to the purple rim of wooded hills in the background. There is a blue blue sky that at sunset will be curtained with wonderful splendors, and at night will be thick-sown with stars and at dawn will be washed with a silver sheen and radiance.

I have been skimming around these impersonal subjects and fighting shy of a real life issue. Concerning it, I hardly know what to say or how to say it. I only know and realize with each succeeding day the sense of *loss* in my life—the always existent hunger for what cannot be mine.

When I came home I made a certain wise and prudent and necessary resolution— namely, that since I *must* forget Herman Leard, I would proceed to do so by utterly refusing to think about him at all—that I would put him out of my mind "as a dream that is banished out of the mind when the dreamer awakes"—starve my wild love for him to death by refusing it "any food of glance or word or sigh"—or even of memory. I did not keep this laudable resolution intact—it was broken to fragments many a time and oft, but the failure was not due to any lack of effort or perseverance on my part. I fought with every scrap of determination and com- monsense *I* possessed to forget him. I struggled on through sleepless nights and weary days—and faced each lonely night and each unwelcome morning the con- sciousness of failure. But I believe I am slowly winning the victory—and I shall fight on till I conquer.

I sent him one of my photographs as I had promised. He wrote to acknowledge the receipt of it. If I had deluded myself into the belief that I was learning to forget him the moment when his letter was handed to me would have undeceived me. I turned icy cold, I shook from head to foot, a mist came before my eyes. I went dizzily upstairs with the letter pressed against my lips and sat down by my window to read it. I suppose it couldn't be called much of a letter. It was not very long, nor at all clever. There were some visible lapses of grammar in it; the writing and expression were rather crude. There was nothing in it that all the world might not have seen.

But never in all my life did I get a letter that was more welcome or that pleased and moved me so. I re-read it until I knew it by heart. I slept with it under my pillow for a week, waking often in the darkness to draw it out and press my lips to it as passionately as I would have done to Herman's had he been there!

Pensie is married and gone—was married last Wednesday evening. The whole affair was kept very close. Pen was up here a week before and never so much as mentioned the fact to me. Considering our old friendship I think this was very shabby treatment. Pen has seemed a bit queer of late years though. She has married Will Bulman and gone to live in New Glasgow so I suppose she has dropped out of my life forever.

I was over at Park Corner for a short visit about three weeks ago. Clara and Stella are both home and we had one of our old-time rackets with gales of laughter. Clara and I had a long talk one night. She has had an experience very like mine and our mutual suffering has brought us very close together. Cade had her cup of bitterness to drink while she was away and drained it to the dregs as I did mine—to find at the bottom wormwood and ashes.

Fannie Wise has also gone. She has taken a clerkship in a Ch'Town bookstore. I miss her very much but I am fast learning to take partings such as these very philosophically, as some of the inevitable ills of human existence. They cannot be avoided and it is both foolish and useless to fret over them. "Off with the old love and on with the new" is an excellent maxim—when it *can* be carried into practice. There are some instances where it cannot; these we have to bury and cherish their graves with what tenderness or bitterness we may. In the meanwhile, Time goes steadily and remorselessly on and we must go with him no matter what he bears us away from. By and by there will be an end and then we will be at rest forever—or at least long enough to forget the weariness and pain of our old life ere we are required to wake again to some other existence that awaits us—and in which we may perchance find all we miss in this.

Saturday, Oct. 8, 1898
The "moon of falling leaves" again! How swiftly it comes around from year to year, each year seeming swifter than the last. There is always something sorrowful in the fall despite its beauty and charm. I suppose it is because it is emblematical of life's autumn which must also come to us all. But then if we believe—and such a belief, in some shape or form, orthodox or unorthodox, is found in most of us—that after winter comes the spring of another life that ought not to sadden us. Life is a placid, uneventful thing for me just now. I have even learned to laugh again.

> "But yet I know where'er I go
> That there hath passed away a glory from the earth."

This has been a "lazy" day for me. I wasn't in a mood for work and couldn't even get up energy enough to go on with my new story. I have written a good deal this summer and have gotten into some new periodicals, as well as keeping up with the old. I really think I am improving a great deal. I seem to see more clearly into things somehow. I suppose it would be hard if all I have gone through didn't bring me some compensation. Sometimes I think it has taught me to see *too* clearly—I might be happier if my delusions and illusions were left to me. But yet—one would think blindness could never be considered a beatific state, and possibly when I get over the blinking and shrinking of new vision and accustomed to the fierce white light of reality I may feel as comfortable as of yore in my soothing twilight.

This latter part of the summer has been busy and—in spots—pleasant. Of *Ed*, I have seen nothing and heard little. He came home to Belmont in the spring. I was in dread that he would visit his friends here and that I'd meet him somewhere. He stayed away, I suppose, as long as he decently could, and when he finally did come on a flying visit, I had been warned in time and was far enough away, suddenly finding it convenient to pay a long promised visit to Bideford. He was gone before I came back.

I spent my Bideford week with Edith England. I had a nice time and enjoyed it all very much, although there was a sorrowful side to it, too. If any person wants to see clearly just how much she is changed—whether for better or worse—let her revisit after some lapse of time any place where she has once lived. She will meet her former self at every turn, with every familiar face, in every old recollection. She will see, in sharp contrast to the present, her old ideals, views, hopes, beliefs, as she would never see them in any other way. Such at least was my experience. I seemed to be *outside* of life, looking with cool, dispassionate eyes as might a disembodied spirit, on my old self, the Maud Montgomery who used to teach in Bideford school, and who, in some curious manner, seemed to be still living there. And I saw, as I had not before seen, the difference—in ideals and illusions, in estimate of people and things, in capacity for enjoyment and suffering. I saw how much I had gained in some respects, how much I had lost—irretrievably lost—in others. I had at times a curious sense of imposing on the good Bideford people who were so kind to me—because they thought they were welcoming the Maud Montgomery they had known of old, whereas I was not she at all, but a new creature altogether, who bears her name and inhabits her body but is only an impostor after all. That former Maud was so different—she was a happy, light-hearted girl with any amount of ideals and illusions and a comfortable belief in the stability of "things temporal". She had some strong ambitions and aspirations but her main object was to "have a good time" and she had a knack of succeeding with it. She believed in herself and other people, had a good conscience and a whole heart, and did not trouble herself greatly over the perplexities of life. But the girl of to-day—how different from all that is she! She has no illusions and few ideals; life is flat, stale, and unprofitable, viewed from her old standpoint and full of snares and pitfalls as viewed from her new. She has a "past" and its shadow falls ever across her path. She has looked below the surface and seen strange things. She could no more live that Bideford year over as she lived it then than she could gather up her old illusions and clothe herself in them as in a garment outgrown. And would she if she could? Do you know, that is a question I often ask myself— "If I could would I go back to my old self?"—and I can never answer it. I can never dare to say either "no" or "yes". The fruit of the tree of knowledge may leave a bitter taste in the eater's mouth, but there is something in its flavor that can never be forgotten or counterfeited.

At the end of my Bideford week I went to Bedeque!

Don't you wonder how I dared do it? I wondered not a little myself. But Helen had made me promise to go and I could hardly refuse, or put it off any longer. Besides, I had another reason which I did not proclaim from the housetops.

In the months that had gone by since I left Bedeque I had had a hard fight and, though often worsted, it would have been hard indeed if I had not gained some poor victory in the end. I had really succeeded in a measure in stifling my infatuation for Herman Leard—strangled it into unconsciousness. Was it really dead? That was what I wanted to know. That was why I went to Bedeque. If when I met him it could be without a tremor or a heartbeat then I would gladly realize that I *was* free from the thralldom of that tyrannical passion.

Helen met me at the boat in the evening and we walked up to the house. Herman was building a load of hay in the field by the road and came over to speak to me. The very moment I put my hand in his and looked into his eyes there surged over me the sickening conviction that I loved him as madly as ever. At that moment all the passion I had hoped was dead started with one agonizing throb into trebly convulsive life.

I went into the house as one in a dream. They had company that evening and, as of old, I was forced to mask my pain under smiles and vivacity. It was only when I got away to bed that I could find relief in a passionate fit of tears. When it was over the reactive calm enabled me to look the situation in the face with some degree of firmness. And I made the resolution that I would avoid Herman in every possible way during my visit.

You may not believe that I kept this resolution—but I did, although what it cost me cannot be expressed. The house was full of visitors most of the time and this made it easier. Then Helen and I were much away visiting and while we were home I kept out of Herman's way markedly. Oh, I was merry and unconcerned enough, but I cried myself to sleep every night I was there. On the last evening we were all out in the yard in the twilight. Herman came along, said he was going for the cows, that there was a very pretty lane on the way and "wouldn't I come and see it". I took one step forward—I *wanted* to go more than I have ever wanted anything in the world. Then I stopped. Something—I don't know what—held me back. It would be madness to go and undo the work of months—lose what I had so hardly gained. I said, "I'm afraid it is going to rain," and turned back. It was the wisest thing I ever did in my life—and the hardest.

I wonder what would have happened if I had gone. I shall never know—and to the end of my life I shall go on wondering.

I was so thankful that my visit was at an end. It seemed to me that if I had had to stay one day longer I would have died or gone crazy. I think Herman was angry because I had not gone with him for that walk—at anyrate, he disappeared Saturday morning and did not even come to say good-bye to me. And so it ends—yes, ends. For I will never go back to Bedeque and I expect and *hope* that I will never see Herman Leard again. I feel that no love can ever again be to me what mine for him was—that never again will I meet any man who will have the power to stir my heart and soul to their profoundest depths as did Herman Leard. And, all in all, I think it is best so for I believe that such love is hardly ever the forerunner of happiness—it is a "challenge to fate" and she punishes it surely and severely. I have had my love dream and it is dead—or murdered—and I have buried it very deeply—and now what I have to do is to forget it as utterly as may be.

When I had once left Bedeque I lapsed back into my state of mind before going—a sort of pangless resignation to my lot. I came home—I worked and studied and *thought* hard—and now I am at peace. I feel no active pain. Sometimes— for instance when I am writing like this—I feel a stab of the old agony and a sudden realization of *all I have missed* comes to me sickeningly. Then I close my eyes and pray to die. But it passes and I am calm once more. I am not unhappy now—at least not with a *positive* unhappiness. There is a certain *negative* unhappiness in my life—the unhappiness not of present pain but of absent joy. But I think there are very few *really* happy people in the world—I can count on my ten fingers all I know whom I believe are really perfectly happy—and I cannot expect to be more favored than the majority. And, after all, I frankly admit that my suffering was no more than my just punishment—although I don't know that a sense of having merited one's pain alleviates it any—rather aggravates it, I should say.

But I must stop turning myself inside out in this uncanny fashion. For after all, words, even the most felicitous, say either too much or too little. I have much to be thankful for—thankful that I did not wreck my life altogether in that mad passion of last winter. I came perilously near to it. Oh, thank God, it is *all over*!!!

I came home by way of Park Corner and Clara came down with me for a week. We had quite a gay time with picnics, drives, etc.

Cavendish is looking very beautiful now, with bloomy mists purpling over its dark spruce hills and all the splendor of crimson and gold among its maples and birches. Cavendish is really the prettiest country place I've ever been in. It is a long, narrow settlement, bordering on and following the outline of the north shore, whose wonderful waters, ever changing in hue and sheen, now silvery gray, now shimmering blue, now darkly azure, now misty with moonrise or purple with sunset, can be seen from any and every point....

Saturday, Dec. 31, 1898
Cavendish, P.E.I.

The last day of the old year—it has only five more hours to live—is surely the time of all times for "journalizing". People generally do a little raking over their inner consciousness at this time, as well as making more or less of good resolutions for the coming year. I am going to make just one—later on. At present, I am looking backward and in all truth I cannot say that the record of '98 is one on which it pleases me to look—far from it! I am taking one glance over its blistered pages before I turn my back on it forever.

It is mid-evening. Outside it is chill and frosty and starlit. The little snow that fell to-day has dusted the old sentinel spruces with white and flung a royal carpet over earth for the New Year's kingly feet to press. Everything is very quiet. Grandma is reading at one side of the table; I am sitting at its end; my cat "Coco" is curled up, a plump, silver-gray creature, at my feet. We are in the old kitchen where we always sit on these long winter evenings that are apt to be a little dull. If the first months of '98 were storm-tossed and passion wrung for me, these closing ones have been as placid and calm as months could be—*too* placid, to tell truth, and I sometimes dare to wish for a little stir and excitement. But then it might not be of an agreeable kind and heaven knows I have had enough excitement of a sort in the earlier months of the year to last me all my life.

I have been writing as steadily as possible, under rather uninspiring conditions and have had a good many acceptances, some of them in new places. How I love my work. I seem to grow more and more wrapped up in it as the days pass and other hopes and interests fail me. Nearly everything I think or do or say is subordinated to a desire to improve in my work. I study people and events for that, I think and speculate and read for that.

In some ways I have been having a rather nice time; and of course there are some worries as usual. I am seldom free from them now.

Cavendish is fairly lively at present. In October the Literary Society reopened and has a good programme prepared. I have enjoyed the meetings. In a quiet life such as mine even so insignificant an outing as a meeting of the Literary is a pleasure. The walk up is nice. We tramp briskly along over the dark fir-fringed road until we reach the hall. Then follows a half-hour's desultory chat with friends and an overhauling of books before we settle down to the particular delectation of the evening—lecture, debate, essay, as it may be. When it is over there is a walk or drive home with some convenient escort with whom you can lightly discuss the sayings and doings of the evening and poke fun at various Simpson idiosyncracies.

There have been several deaths in Cavendish this fall. One of them was "old Aunt Caroline" who was "old Aunt Caroline" ever since I can remember. In fact, I have my doubts whether she could ever have been young at all. Seriously, she was one of those people whom it is utterly impossible to picture as a dimpled baby or a pink-cheeked, bright-eyed young girl.

She lived at Wm. C's and was his unmarried sister and household drudge. Poor old lady. I don't suppose there is a soul in the world who really regretted her or will miss her in any way. She was not an exhilarating person, being one of those unfortunates who are constantly worrying, not only about their own affairs but everybody else's as well, and will not give themselves or others any rest at all. Nevertheless, she was a sort of landmark and one misses her in that respect. Wm. C's pew is in front of ours in church and old Aunt Caroline was unfailingly in her place—the corner by the window—year in and year out. I shall never forget her shirred black satin bonnets—or was it always the same bonnet? To my small eyes they were fearfully and wonderfully made. They fitted snugly around her head like a nightcap and framed her wrinkled face closely. (She had more wrinkles than any person I ever saw.) There never was anything like those bonnets, I am sure, or like the old black lace shawl that was always laid at precisely the same angle across her thin shoulders, and whose rusty patterns I generally amused myself by tracing out when we stood up to sing. In summer Aunt Caroline would generally carry a big pink "English rose" in her cotton-gloved fingers and hold it to her nose all through the service.

Very conservative indeed was old Aunt Caroline. Anything new her soul abhorred. *Hymns* were antichrist, and *bicycles*, heaven preserve us, were part of the direct equipment of the Prince of Darkness. I used to take an unholy delight in telling her I was going to get one, although I really hadn't any idea of so doing. I couldn't afford one, worse luck! It *was* such fun to see her horror. She couldn't have looked more aghast if I had told her I was going to appear out in trousers.

Well, poor old soul, she has gone, with all her peculiarities and prejudices. It gives me a lonely sensation to look at her old pew corner and find it empty, reflecting that the frail, bent, shrunken old figure in the faded shawl and preposterous bonnet is gone from it forever. It is to be hoped that in the grave poor old Aunt Caroline has found the rest that life denied her and has ceased to worry over the misfortunes and faults of poor humanity.

When I recall my state of mind this time last year and compare it with the present I see how much I have to be thankful for. I *could not* live that dreadful time over again—I do not know how I lived it once. But I did—and it is over—and buried deep! Yet not so deep but that its ghosts haunt me reproachfully, not so deep but that its bitterness is still potent to poison my cup, not so deep but that its cold loathly memory creeps like a snake across hours that might otherwise be happy.

I have been revelling in some new books of late. One of them was "The Christian", Hall Caine's much talked of new novel. I liked it fairly well although I confess I got heartily out of patience with the hero, *John Storm*, who, judged from a practical standpoint, is really a compound of fool and fanatic. But then I suppose neither the book nor its characters *are* to be judged from a practical standpoint. I have no doubt that there are many just such people in the world as *John* and *Glory*, and that the conflict of their emotions always works out to a tragic issue.

I have also read "The Manxman", an older book of Caine's. It is the only one of his books I really like. I am not easily "moved to tears" over a book, but I *did* cry over "The Manxman".

I got Kipling's "Ballads" for a Christmas present. They are capital—full of virile strength and life. They thrill and pulsate and burn, they carry you along in their rush and swing, till you forget your own petty interests and cares and burst out into a broader soul-world and gain a much clearer realization of all the myriad forms of life that are beating around your own little one. And that is always good for a person even if one does slip back afterwards into the narrow bounds of one's own life. We can never be *quite* so narrow again.

On November 8th I rather regretfully packed up a valise and started to make a long-promised visit to Aunt Emily. I say "regretfully", because Aunt Emily is not exactly a favorite of mine and Malpeque is a place I don't care for.

I went over to Park Corner and stayed there until Saturday. Ever since I can remember "going over to Aunt Annie's" has been a phrase that stood for a delightful jaunt. To begin with, it was such a pretty drive, those winding thirteen miles of hill and wood, river and shore. There are first the three miles through Cavendish and Bay View to the Bay View Bridge, spanning the pretty "Hope River". Three miles further on is Stanley, a pretty village on the banks of another river. There are two or three stores in Stanley and we have always gone there to buy household supplies. Stanley used to seem quite a town to my childish eyes. It was the hub of the universe then—or of our solar system at the very least. Beyond Stanley the road wound on to another little village—Clifton. And here, around a certain corner, is a certain small, yellowish-brown house, close to the road, that I always look at with a kind of fascination, for it is the house where my father and mother lived after their marriage, and where I was born and spent the first year of my life. The years have passed on and each succeeding one has left the little brown house something shabbier than before, but its enchantment has never faded in my eyes. I always look for it with the same eager interest when I turn the corner....

And so '98 ends! I am truly thankful. I turn to '99 with a chastened joy and a trembling hope that I may pass out from the old shadows into the sunshine of its dawning—may throw off the mantle of the past year as an outgrown garment. This night last year I was at the Gardiner's dance and danced the New Year in with *Herman*. We were dancing together as the clock struck twelve. I took it then as a good omen—but it was not. Oh '98, how much I have suffered in you! How much of good and evil you have taught me, stern, cruel, relentless teacher that you were! Yet after all, '98, your harsh discipline has borne good fruit—and bitter as it was, I thank you for it. Thank you and farewell!

62. *The old kitchen*
[*Cavendish*]

63. *The old parlor*
[*Cavendish*]

64. My mother
[Clara Woolner Macneill Montgomery]

65. Picture cut from magazine. As much like
Herman Leard as if it were his photograph.

66. Edith England

67. Edith England's home
[Bideford]

68. The house where I was born
[Clifton, now New London]

1899

Tuesday, April 4, 1899
Cavendish, P.E.I.

This is April—and ought to be spring but isn't! One expects spring in April—expects mud and slush and bare fields and warm sunny days. Cold winds, good sleighing, and as much snow as we have at present seem very unseasonable. However, spring will surely come even if it is late, and it will be doubly welcome for we have had a very severe winter. It has been woefully cold ever since New Year's and much shivering is a weariness to the flesh. The last three months have been busy and not unpleasant but they have not been at all eventful, so that any spice of interest this entry may contain will not arise from a recital of startling or unusual matters. However I'm going to write out the details of my quiet humdrum life this winter simply and solely for my own amusement. I enjoy this writing down my impressions of life and things as I go, even in my narrow orbit, and reading them over afterwards to compare them with newer ones.

It is just a year, almost to the day, since I came home from Bedeque, an unhappy, disillusioned, hopeless girl. Looking back now, I know that nothing in the world could induce me to go through that dreadful time again. Good God, how I suffered! I wonder how I lived through it! Things are changed for the better now. Pain, even the fiercest, wears itself out, even though its *effects* must endure to the end of time—and perhaps through all eternity, if such there be for us as sentient creatures. And so I, someway or other, have come up from the depths, and am not minded to go back to them.

In a way, I have been having quite a nice time this winter. I say "in a way" because in reality the gayety was all on the surface and away down underneath my new inner consciousness was coiled up, brooding like a snake in its den and every once in a while darting a pang into my soul's vitals. But I must not go into self-analysis yet awhile—we will stick to the outside of things if you please.

The Literary Society has been in a flourishing condition this winter and I owe to it the few books that have delighted my soul. I have no doubt that it is a wise ordinance of fate—or Providence?—that I cannot get all the books I want or I should certainly never accomplish much. I am simply a "book drunkard". *Books* have the same irresistible temptation for me that liquor has for its devotee. I *cannot* withstand them. For instance;—the first new story I read in '99 was "Phroso" by Anthony Hope. I brought the book home from the hall one wretchedly cold night and sat up in bed until two o'clock, shivering and freezing but quite indifferent to it, and finished the book before I could sleep. It was a glorious yarn—full of life and "go". It was romance pure and simple, without any alloy of realism or philosophy. I like realistic and philosophical novels in spells, but for pure, joyous, undiluted delight give me romance. I always revelled in fairy tales.

But I have read one book recently—heaven send I never have to wade through such another. I cannot imagine a worse "future punishment" than to be condemned to read such books for all eternity. It was an old tale—"The Children of The Abbey" and was the mushiest, slumpiest book I ever read, possessing a most lachrymose heroine who fainted in every chapter and cried quarts of tears if anyone looked sidewise at her. But as for the trials and persecutions which she underwent, their name was Legion and no fair maiden of these degenerate days could endure one-tenth of them—not even the newest of "new" women!

I have been to several concerts and "socials" this winter. I had to recite at most of them and as a rule enjoyed them. But preserve me from "pie socials". They are the abomination of desolation. The programme is only a pretence—the real business of the evening is selling the pies, attended by fearful excitement in the pit. An auctioneer, chosen for strength of lung and ability to crack dollar-coaxing jokes is selected, and the pies are auctioned off to the highest bidder, who shells out his cash, get his pie, and is whisked upstairs by the powers that be to find the fair builder thereof and eat it with her. Those who don't or can't buy pies raise all the disturbance they possibly can and settle old scores by several hand to hand encounters. The Babel is so great that you can't hear yourself think and the scene more nearly resembles the proverbial "bear-garden" than anything you have ever seen.

However, the pies are all sold at last and your escort comes along clinging to a pie with one hand and to the shy little schoolgirl who brought it with the other. He whisks you off to the higher regions where the matrons are dispensing hot coffee. You capture a vacant corner, grasp a knife and attack that pie, cased in sheet armour of frosting. It makes a valiant resistance but is finally overcome and proves, alas, to be but a whited sepulchre. However, by this time you are so hungry you can eat anything, so down goes a generous section of the pie, helped along by gulps of scalding coffee. The whole room is in a buzz, with laughter, conversation and crunching. When you are done, leaving the remnants of the pie behind you on the principle that to the victors belong the spoils, you get on your wraps and start homewards, wondering who first invented a pie social and what was done to him for it.

This winter we organized a "sewing circle" in aid for a new church building fund. It has taken a good deal of time I could ill spare and has been no end of a bother. But that is the seamy side. There is another side in our pleasant afternoons of work and gossip—strictly harmless and clarified gossip, of course, patented for the use of church sewing societies!—and our evenings of fun when the boys came in and we play games of the same brand as the gossip. Of course there are some "cranks" in the crowd—is there ever anything free from them?—who try to make things as difficult as possible for all concerned.

We are losing our minister. He has accepted a call to Tryon and Hampton, and is "flitting" today. I do not think he will be much regretted. He was a fairly good preacher but no pastor and his wife and family were certainly fearful and wonderful creatures—whole reams of description could not do them justice. What Cavendish will find to talk about when Mrs. Robertson is gone I really do not know. Her sayings and doings quite usurped the place of the weather in current greetings. "Have you heard Mrs. Robertson's latest?" or "*What* will Mrs. R. do next?" being standard questions. She is really so eccentric as to be abnormal and her escapades have been many and startling, from going to church with boots on but no stockings, to tearing Mr. Robertson's harness to pieces and blaming it on the boys of the congregation. I think and have always thought that the woman is not really sane in some respects. If she *is* sane, there is no excuse for her actions.

May 1, 1899
Cavendish, P.E.I.
There is a magic about the spring—some power that revives half-dead hopes and faiths and thrills numbed souls with the elixir of new life. There is no age in spring—everybody seems young and joyful. Care is in abeyance for a little while and hearts throb with the instinct of immortality.

These days are so beautiful—mellow and breezy and sweet. There are no leaves yet but every little brown bud is swelling and in sunny, sheltered spots there is a hint of greenness. The days are long and the twilights full of a mellow graciousness—and all the snow is gone, gone, gone! There are such lovely blue skies and such faint purple mists over the bare hills; and last Friday night I got some tiny pink-and-white mayflowers—the initial lettering of spring. It is worth while to live through the winter just to have the spring.

April has been such a busy month that there has been time for nothing but work—and if there had been time there were no roads, so one stayed home perforce. Since going out was impossible I filled up my spare evenings reading. The first book I read this month was the "Tower of London", which is sugar-coated history. I read it once before, long ago when I was a kiddy of ten up at Grandpa Montgomery's. The chapter in which the burning of a martyr at the stake is described made an impression on me that haunted me for weeks. I never saw the book again until this spring and I was half afraid to re-read it, for I thought it wonderful when I first read it and so few of our childish opinions wear. I have in mature life re-read with bitter disappointment so many books that I loved in childhood. It is only a foolish fancy, I suppose, but to me the disillusionment is almost as painful as to meet some old loved childhood chum and find her nothing that your memory had painted. But "The Tower" stood the test fairly well. I found it interesting still and the "terrible chapter" still made my blood freeze with horror.

Among all the flotsam and jetsom of newspaper and magazine stories I have read one that made a powerful impression on my mind. It was a short one in the March *Atlantic*, and dealt with the first experiences of a disembodied spirit after death. It appealed to the curiosity that is in us all regarding the future —a curiosity that can never be satisfied until we are dead—and perhaps not even then. But if not—there will be no curiosity.

I have moved upstairs again to my own dear den and feel as if I had returned from exile. I do not like that downstairs room. Just as soon as it was warm enough I marched up here and began scrubbing and renovating. Then I moved all my Lares and Penates up—and here I am, a queen in my own little independent kingdom. Woe to the poor mortal who has not even one small room to call her own.

Our Literary closed on April 21st with a paper by Mr. Jackson—the new Baptist

Minister—on "Religion vs Morality". He *said* it wasn't an old sermon and I suppose we are bound to believe him; otherwise, I should think—but I *won't* think! It is a dangerous habit.

The paper was dry and quite hazy; it is my private belief that the Rev. Jackson was all befogged on the subject himself. But there, he is really a very nice little fellow and it was not his fault that "Religion vs Morality" was not a very enthralling subject.

It is evening while I am writing. The sun has got down behind the trees and their long, lazy shadows are falling over the lane and fields. Beyond, the brown hills are basking in an amber radiance underneath a pale aerial sky of rose and blue. The firs on the south hill are like burnished bronze and their long shadows are barring the hill meadows. Dear old world, you are very beautiful and I love you well.

May 28, 1899
Cavendish, P.E.I.
....May has been very busy, Uncle Leander has been here the greater part of it and will be here until July. He is on "sick leave", as his nervous system seems to be badly broken up.

When he came he brought a lot of new books with him and I went on one of my literary "sprees". For a week I simply revelled in books day and night and even read between bites at my meals. The first I plunged into was "The Soul of Lilith" by Marie Corelli. Judged from a literary standpoint Corelli doesn't amount to much but she can certainly write interesting yarns. "The House of the Wolf" by Weyman was capital. Then came "The Black Douglas" by Crockett. Viewed from a critical standpoint I am afraid Crockett has made a miscue in this instance. The plot lacks unity and is very sensational, but for an exciting and fascinating and blood-curdling yarn, warranted to be finished at one sitting, I can recommend "The Black Douglas". In childhood, when I wasn't afraid to say I liked a book, not caring whether the confession "gave me away" on taste and judgement or not, I would have said it was "simply scrumptious"....

July 24, 1899
My Den 3:30 P.M.
Cavendish, P.E.I.
Haying began to-day, which means that the best half of the summer is over. And now the field before my window is a sweep of silvery swaths gleaming in the hot afternoon sun and the wind that is rustling in the poplars is bringing up whiffs of the fragrance of ripening grasses.

I am lazy this afternoon—too lazy to carry out a planned photoing expedition. I was down this morning and took a photo of "Victoria Island"—that dear old spot down in the school brook, with the old firs on it, and the water laughing about it, just as it glimmered and rippled and laughed in those dear days gone by when we schoolgirls and boys played there. Nobody ever goes there now but myself—and I not often. Only once and again I stray down and listen to the duet of the brook and wind, and watch the sunbeams creeping through the dark boughs, the gossamers glimmering here and there, and the ferns growing up in the shadowy nooks.

We had a Tea here this summer in aid of a new church. It really deserves to be spelled with a capital for the amount of work and worry involved was immense. But it is all over now and everybody up to last reports has survived.

We Sewing Circle folks got it up and bore the burden and heat of the day. Mrs. Albert Macneill and I had to canvass Mayfield as our share of the preliminary operations. It is not a long road—which saving fact accounts for my keeping any semblance of sanity at all. I shall never, as long as I live, be inveigled into canvassing a road again on behalf of a tea! At every house we entered I shrank at least an inch—sometimes two or three—and at the end I really believe I must have been invisible to the naked eye. They tore the old church down in June. How badly I felt! I cried the day they began at it.

It was never a handsome church inside or out. It was very large and our pew was the second from the top on the left-hand side. It was right by the window and we could look out over the slope of the long western hill and the blue pond down to the curving rim of the sandhills and the sweep of the blue gulf. William C's pew was just ahead of ours. Mollie and Tillie always sat there; the choir used to sit up in the gallery long ago but of late years they have sat in the cross seats in the corner just ahead of us. This was for preaching. For prayer-meeting the highwater mark was lower down, in the middle pews, around the stove and in the seats under the gallery. The gallery itself was seldom used of late years save when Communion service filled even the big church to overflowing. Long ago it was always used and I always hankered to sit there—principally because I couldn't, no doubt—another example of forbidden fruit. Only when the annual Communion Sunday came was I allowed to go up there with the other girls and I considered it a great treat, especially if we were fortunate enough to get in the front seat. We could then look down over the whole congregation which always flowered out that day in full bloom of new hats and dresses. "Sacrament Sunday" then was, in that respect, what Easter is to the dwellers in cities and harassed dressmakers had worked overtime for weeks getting new frocks finished in readiness for it. So a front gallery seat was very convenient for we could take in all the new costumes and I fear we thought more about them than we did about the solemnity of the service and what it commemorated. It was always exceedingly long in those days for they adhered to the old custom of a double service with the Communion in between. How dreadfully tired we poor kiddies would get and how we envied the boys and irresponsible people who got up, and went home while the congregation sang, "Twas on that night when doomed to know". *We* dared not stir but we realized acutely that caste has its penalties. And then what a hush fell over the building while the bread and wine were being handed around, the elders tiptoeing reverentially from pew to pew. I used to believe that there was something peculiar about the bread—it could *not* be just ordinary, home-made bread, much as it looked like it. It was a real shock to me when I found out that it was and that the buxom wife of "Elder Jimmy" had made it! I could not understand either why the women always buried their faces in their white handkerchiefs when they had eaten it; but of course I supposed I would understand it all when I grew up. And how glad I was when it was all over and we got down and out under the blue sky

240

once more, where we could drink of the wine of God's sunshine in his eternal communion that knows no restrictions or creeds.

But the old church is gone now, with all its memories and associations. They will put up a modern one which will be merely a combination of wood and plaster and will not be mellowed and hallowed by the memories that permeated and beautified that unbeautiful old church. Churches, like all else, have to be ripened and seasoned before the most perfect beauty becomes theirs.

I have something else to write here yet before I conclude—no less than the "finish" to the most tragic chapter of my life. It is ended forever and the page is turned.

Herman Leard is—*dead*!

I had not heard from Helen since May. On July first when the mail came I was too busy to look at the Island papers for we were fixing up the tea grounds that day. When I came home and sat down to tea grandma said, "Wasn't there a Herman Leard where you boarded in Bedeque?"

I nodded, wonderingly. "Yes. What about him?"

"He is dead."

"Dead!" I stared at her stupidly. "How do you know?"

"It is in the *Pioneer*," she said.

I went and got the paper. There in the local column was the fatal item, coldly brief and concise. He had died the previous day after a seven weeks' illness brought about by complications of influenza—as I learned later. The funeral was to be Sunday afternoon. That was all.

When Herman Leard and I parted I knew that that chapter of my life was closed forever. So that this death could make no *real* difference to me. And yet when, with one swift pang, there came to me the realization that he was *dead*—gone from me forever into the dim and dread Unknown—and that never again, here, or, as it must seem, hereafter, should we two meet—oh, my God, how awful it was!

I did not shed many tears. I shed too many over Herman long ago to have any left now. There were once nights when I writhed on sleepless pillows until dawn and cried my passionate heart out because he was not worthy of my love. And so now, when he was dead, there was no need of tears for me. No agony could ever equal what I once endured. It is easier to think of him as dead, mine, *all* mine in death, as he never could be in life, mine when no other woman could ever lie on his heart or kiss his lips.

But that night, when all the house was still I knelt down by my window and, looking out into the dim, fragrant summer night, alight with calm stars, tried to realize that at that very moment Herman Leard was lying in his coffin, cold and silent, in the very room where I had kissed him farewell forever, and that if I stood by him and called to him not even my voice could reach him now. There would be no answering smile on his pale cold lips, no tender light in the dark blue eyes whose flash used to stir my heart into stinging life. Oh, kneeling there I thought it all over—that winter in Bedeque with its passion and suffering, all its hours of happiness and sorrow. I lived again in thought every incident of my acquaintance with Herman Leard from first to last—all those mad sweet hours and those sad bitter hours. I thought of that last night before I came home when our real parting was—a parting that was more bitter than death. I could stand by Herman's grave and hear the clods rattle on his coffin without half the agony that was my portion that night, when we stood in the moonlight and I felt his arms about me and his lips on mine for the last time, knowing that it *was* the last time.

Yes, I thought it all over unflinchingly—and then I bowed my head on the window sill and wished that I were lying in Herman's arms, as cold in death as he, with all pain and loneliness lost forever in an unending, dreamless sleep, clasped to his heart in one last eternal embrace.

Herman is *dead*. Is *he* dead, or is it only his outer shell and husk that is dead? Does *he* live somewhere yet; and if so does he remember or forget? It is a horrible thought to fancy that he *does* live yet and now *knows* how I loved him and so nearly sinned and so greatly suffered for his sake. I would go mad if I believed *that*. But I do not. And yet it is almost as dreadful to think of him as some chill, impersonal spirit who would pass me coldly by if we met in the shadows of the Hereafter with no warm lips to kiss and no strong hand to clasp in the love of earth. No, no, I prefer to believe that never, never, in any life shall we two meet again—for be the meeting as it would, it could be fraught with nothing save pain and shame on my part—and on his—what?

I cannot answer that question. Herman loved me—or pretended to—with a love passionate and sensual enough, of no very lofty or enduring type; but never, never as I loved him. Well, it is all ended—for this life at least, and as I believe and hope—or *fear*, I cannot tell which—for all and every life to come.

Sunday Morning, Oct. 8, 1899
Cavendish, P.E. Island
We have just been having a regular fall rain. It is over now and to-day is sunny and crisp and beautiful, as if earth were harking back to her lost summer. But it lasted two days, and what a gloomy world it was—sodden meadows, drenched, mangled leaves, valleys abrim with chill mists and a raw wind that came blowing over "the sea's long level, dim with rain." Night before last I could not sleep for the noise of rain streaming on the roof and the shriek of wind around the old eaves and in the trees outside. It seemed as if all the demon forces of night and storm were in conflict in mid-heaven.

Aunt Mary McIntyre and James called one day not long ago. It was such a surprise for I did not know James was home. How glad I was to see them! They couldn't stay long but our tongues went while they did.

I have always liked my cousins on the Montgomery's side much better than those on the Macneill side—except Aunt Annie's girls, and *they* are half Montgomery on their father's side. I have never cared for any of Uncle Leander's boys or Uncle John's. But the McIntyre and Sutherland boys almost seem to me like brothers, dear, jolly, companionable fellows that they are! I always feel thoroughly at home with them. There are dozens of people, near of kin and association, with whom I am more ill at ease and tongue-tied than with the veriest stranger. I can't explain it but I am painfully conscious that it is so and I cannot overcome it. I am, with them, an utterly different creature from what I am with others. It is the unwritten law of "like to like" I suppose. If two *souls* do not know each other all the accidents of birth and association will be of no avail to bring them together. They must forever remain strangers, even if one roof were to cover them for half a century.

I was over to Park Corner for a fortnight in August and had a pleasant time, as Stella and Fred were both home. Henry McLure drove me over. He has been driving me about this summer, although he clearly understands that he can have nothing, now or ever, but friendship. He is a crude young farmer of Rustico, whose best point is the possession of a dandy gee-gee and I neither like nor dislike him. He is nil—but convenient.

I took my camera over to Park Corner and got a number of pretty views. There is such a magnificent grove of maple and beech behind Uncle John Campbell's house. I could never tire of rambling through it. The winding paths are bordered thickly with ferns and the light comes softly down sifted through so many emerald screens that it is as flawless as the heart of a diamond. How the girls and I used to scamper through those trees when we were children and race down the long avenues among fallen leaves that rustled under our flying footsteps, while the tall old trees gave back a myriad of echoes to our joyous laughter.

I had a letter from *Ed* in September. What a chill of fear and repulsion went over me as I took it! When I read it I found it rather hard to decide why he had written it. Ed's style is not especially lucid at the best of times. But it seems that he has heard some rumors—though what they are he does not say—about our affair and seems to insinuate that he thinks they originated with me or with something I have told someone. I must say the implied accusation annoyed me. Does Ed imagine that I indulge in talking about him promiscuously—or desire to?

Other parts of the letter were painful. He said he had tried to obey my injunction to forget me, but had not succeeded—"loved me as much as ever"—etc.

I had to reply to the letter. I told him—what was the literal truth—that with the exception of a brief announcement concerning my broken engagement to the few who had known of it, his name had never crossed my lips since the termination of that unhappy affair, and that therefore any rumors that might be afloat could only be the product of surmise and gossip.

I have read only one new book lately—Mark Twain's "More Tramps Abroad". It was delightful. *How* I would love to travel and see all those old world lands and wonders. I wonder if I ever shall! England and Scotland first—then Italy and Greece—then Egypt and the Holy Land—but there, why not include the moon and have done with it? One is about as likely as the other. I expect the greater part of my travels will be on paper and I daresay that is much less trouble—and expense!

One cold, rainy, dismal day last week I had nothing to do, so I sat me down and read over Will's old letters. Reading them, it seemed impossible that he should be dead—that there was *no* Will now—on this plane, at least.

Looking back over all the men I've known I think there was not among them a better *comrade* than Will—no, not even Herman. I never *loved* Will, but I thought—and think him still—the *nicest* boy I ever knew. Our friendship was perfect. Those P.A. days seem very far away now—in fact, they *are* far away. But Will's letters carried me back to them once more—the rackets in the old High School where we teased poor Mr. Mustard so dreadfully, our walks home on the crisp winter evenings, our rambles in the summer twilights, the books we read and discussed, and all the thousand and one little incidents of our acquaintanceship. I think I regret the loss of his friendship even more now than when I first knew he was dead—because I see and appreciate its real value more clearly now. But I know, too, that if he were living, and we were to meet again, it would be no longer possible. It might be the friendship of man and woman with *love* as its finale. But the comradeship of yore would be impossible.

I went for a walk in Lover's Lane yesterday. It is the dearest spot in the world to me and has the greatest influence for good over me. No matter how dark my mood is, no matter how heavy my heart or how vexed my soul, an hour in that beautiful solitude will put me right with myself and the world. Perplexity and sorrow melt away and the balm of the woods falls on my troubled thoughts like a boon of infinite peace.

It is always the same old way I go—down the lane under the birches and across the old school playground worn bare, and hard by many restless feet. There in the October sunshine are the old woods where the wind sweeps through the swaying spruce tops with a sound as of surf breaking on a far distant shore. There is a fence to be climbed here and then a winding path to follow, sloping down into the heart of a peaceful hush where now and again a sudden gap in the boughs lets in a glimpse of faraway purple hills or a shining bay of blue sea.

The old spring, deep and clear and icy cold is on our path. The brook purls softly by and the old firs whisper over it as of yore. The ferns are drooping from the banks and the wild vines are running riot over stumps and roots. A maple adown the brook is gloriously gold and crimson and above through the boughs is a glimpse of blue autumn sky. Past the school woods come two autumnal fields rimmed in with golden-hued birches and frosted bracken fern. Beyond them is the dear lane itself, running on along the rim of the woodland, with the maple and birches and wild cherries and spruces meeting overhead and the low murmur of a hidden brook ever in our ears—every step a revelation and a benediction. The air under the firs is purple and the sunshine is as exhilarating as wine. Finally it ends in a bridge over the brook and a silvery field beyond that leads out to the red ribbon of the main road and so, over the crest of the hill home.

69. My own dear den
[Cavendish]

The funeral of the late Herman Leard Bedeque, took place yesterday to Central Bedeque. It was one of the largest funerals seen in that vicinity for years, there being over 100 carriages in the procession. Rev. W. H. Warren conducted the funeral services. The deceased was a son of Mr. Cornelius Leard, Lower Montague, and a brother of Dr. Alpheus Leard of S'side. He contracted a severe cold not long since and never recovered from its effects. Mr. Leard was 29 years old yesterday, the day of his funeral. It is a remarkable fact that within the last few weeks a funeral has taken place from three adjoining homes in Lower Bedeque. The bereaved parents, relatives and friends of the deceased have the sympathy of the whole community.

It is with deep regret that we record the death of Mr. Herman Leard, son of Mr. Cornelius Leard, of Lower Bedeque, who was probably the most popular young man in the district. He died on Friday morning, after an illness of seven weeks, during which he had the most skilled medical attendance and the most loving care. His death will be very seriously felt and is deeply mourned in the community. The funeral takes place on Sunday at 2 p.m. The deceased is a brother of Dr. Leard, of Summerside. To the bereaved parents and relatives the PIONEER tenders its deepest sympathy in their affliction.

70. Obituary notices

71. My window
[Cavendish]

72. Frederica Campbell

73. A magnificent grove of maple and beech
[at Uncle John Campbell's, Park Corner]

74. Lovers' Lane
[Cavendish]

1900

Sunday Evening
Jan. 14, 1900

How strange it seems to write that date! It really makes me feel homesick for the old 18's. It seems to me as if I belonged back in them.

I don't feel like writing to-night—I feel dull and stupid. I've been very busy of late and that is all there is to it. My life recently has certainly been uneventful. I haven't been anywhere since I last wrote except for a flying visit to town one day in October. I shall grow *mossy* in such an existence!

There, I feel better for that little outburst of discontent. After all, I'm passably contented. I suppose that into everybody's life there come days of depression and discouragement, when all things in life seem to lose savor. The sunniest day has its clouds; but one must not forget that the sun is there all the time.

(Item:—If you are out in a pouring rain does it do you much good, or keep you dry, to remember that the sun is there, just the same?)

Blessings be on the inventors of alphabet, pen and printing press! Life would be—to me at all events—a terrible thing without books. I cannot remember ever learning to read. I suppose there must have been a time when I took my first step into an enchanted world by learning that "A" was "A", but for any recollection of it, I might as well have been born with a capacity for reading just as for breathing or eating. It is fortunate, situated as I am, that I can read books over and over again with never failing interest and zest; otherwise I could never get enough reading matter to satisfy my voracious appetite.

This fall I read all Scott's poems over again. They were one of my childhood loves that have worn well. In the old "Sixth Royal Reader" was the whole of the "Lady of The Lake". How I always gloried in that poem—its spirited descriptions, its atmosphere of romance, the dramatic situations with which it abounded! What food it was for my eager young mind and fancy! I used to pore over it in the old schoolhouse when I should have been wrestling with fractions—or when the teacher thought I should. But, all the same, it did me more good than the fractions would ever have done. It was nourishment for heart and mind and soul—even for body, too, I verily believe—at least I never was conscious of hunger or thirst while poring over Scott's magic page.

In November I got "Rupert of Hentzau", by Anthony Hope. It came one day at two o'clock in the afternoon. I sat down and began it, never budging until sunset, when I finished it.

It made me *mentally drunk*. I was as thoroughly intoxicated in brain as the most confirmed drunkard ever was in body. For a week after I could read nothing else—nothing else seemed worth reading—everything was tasteless and savorless

247

after that pungent draught. In fact, I think I have hardly got over it yet. Certainly, books like that wouldn't be very healthy for a continuous diet. They would spoil one for everything else. But —once in a while—just for a spree!

At the outbreak of the Transvaal war I re-read "The Story of An African Farm". It is one of my favorites. It is speculative, analytical, rather pessimistic, iconoclastic, daring—and *very* unconventional. But it is powerful and original and fearless, and contains some exquisite ideas. It is like a tonic, bitter but bracing. Also, many people call it a dangerous book. Perhaps it is so, for an unformed mind—but there is more of truth than pleasantness in many of its incisive utterances.

I re-read *Vanity Fair* in December. I read it long ago—back in those enchanted years of early girlhood when one believes in everything. I did not like it then— probably because it hit some of my pet illusions too hard. I was too young. It takes a more mature mind than mine then was to appreciate Thackeray. When I read it this winter I wondered how I failed to see its charm before. Oh, that delightful *Becky*!

I had an unpleasant experience in November. One Sunday evening Mr. Millar preached in the hall. I was sitting on one of the side seats, watching the people come in. Presently the door opened and Edwin Simpson entered!

I was completely taken by surprise for I had not even known he was on the Island. He walked up the aisle and took a seat behind me. When the service was over I hurried out at once for fear I should meet him. But the platform was crowded and I could get no further than the door. And there we met face to face in the glare of the porch light. Well, people *can* meet horrible moments so calmly that no onlooker would dream of the passions let loose. I bowed coldly and said "Good-evening". Ed lifted his cap and said good-evening in a voice as emotion- less as my own. Then he passed on and it was over. Over—yes! But the effects were with me for days.

In October war broke out between England and the Transvaal Republic and has been raging ever since. Canada is in a state of red-hot excitement from shore to shore because several regiments of Canadian boys have volunteered for service in South Africa. Among those who went from the Island was Hedley McKinnon, my old P.W.C. friend and classmate. There is something stirring and exciting and tingling about it all even here in this quiet little Island thousands of miles from the seat of war. Everyone is intensely interested in the news.

May 1, 1900
Cavendish, P.E. Island
On the morning of January 17th I was awakened to receive this telegram:—

"Prince Albert, N.W.T.
Jan. 16.
Hugh J. Montgomery died to-day. Pneumonia. Peacefully happy and painless death."

I have no words to describe how I felt! For weeks I only wished to die.
The news was a thunderbolt from a clear sky. Only a short time before I had had

a letter from him written in the best of health and spirits. The next was that brutal telegram.

Oh, it meant so much to me! Others, losing a father, have still a mother or brothers or sisters left. I have nobody except poor old grandmother. And father and I have always been so much to each other. He was so good and kind and tender. Long, long ago, before he went west, when I was a tiny girl, we were much together, and how we loved each other! Even when he went so far away and for so many years we never grew apart, as some might have done. We always remained near and dear in spirit. Oh father, can it really be true that you are dead? Have you left your "little Maudie" all alone? That was not like you.

Oh, what a long, dreary, dismal winter followed! I have tried so hard to be brave and look out on life courageously but it is hard—hard. I grow tired thinking of it. This is the hour of the evening when I always think of father. The sun has set and the twilight shadows are creeping over the hills. I am all alone and I think of him—ah, I think of him as I used to know him.

Yes, it has been a sad dark winter, but a busy one, too. What a blessing work is! Truly,

"God, in cursing, gives us better gifts
Than men in benediction."

To be sure, in those first dark weeks after father's death I could not work. I had no heart for it. Even my ambition seemed dead within me. What good was it when there would be nobody to care whether I succeeded or not? Father was always so proud of me and of my little talent—and now he could never know or care.

But after a time I roused myself and went to work again. With the effort came strength and the old love, inborn and bred, for my pen came back to me. Oh, as long as we can work we can make life beautiful! And life *is* beautiful in spite of all its sorrow and care. I seem to realize the truth of this afresh every day and to see its beauty more clearly. There is so much in the world for us all, if we only have the eyes to see it and the heart to love it and the hand to gather it to ourselves—so much in men and women, so much in art and literature, so much everywhere in even the narrowest, most circumscribed life—so much to enjoy and delight in and be thankful for.

Well, I must henceforth face the world alone. Let me see what my equipment for such a struggle is. I am young; I have a scanty and superficial education, gained in a winter at an academy and another at Dalhousie college; I have three hundred dollars—father left me two hundred in his will and I saved another hundred these last two years. I have no training for anything save teaching, which I cannot at present do; I have no influence of any kind in any quarter. Is that all? It seems a meagre list. Yes, there is something else—my knack of scribbling. Is it a feather's weight—or is it a talent of gold that will eventually weigh down the balance in my favor? Last year I made exactly ninety six dollars and eighty eight cents by my pen! That does not promise extravagantly. But we shall see. I have forgotten to mention another asset and a very valuable one—a belief in my power to succeed. As long as I possess that I shall face the future with an unquailing heart.

The other day I re-read Racine's *Athalie* in the original. It served the double purpose of brushing up my French and recalling bygone days at Dalhousie when Lottie Shatford and I sat at our front desk in Professor Liechti's room and heard him read French with a German accent that might have made Racine turn over in his grave. Poor old professor—what a curiosity he was in the Professorial line! But he was such a perfect gentleman, of the fine, "old school" type you never see nowadays.

I also re-read "King Solomon's Mines" lately. I always liked it because it was so full of adventure and I *do* love that with a love that has outlived childhood. What care I if it be "wild and improbable" and "lacking in literary art"? I refuse to be any longer hampered in my likes and dislikes by such canons of criticism. The one essential thing I demand of a book is that it should interest me. If it does, I forgive it any every other fault.

In March I read "*The King's Mirror*" by Anthony Hope. It is in quite a different vein from his other books. It purports to be the autobiography of a king from his childhood to his marriage and I found it extremely interesting.

How hard our childish prepossessions die! I have never been quite able to divest myself of my original belief that kings were happy beings—bound by no rules, existing only for their own pleasure, in short, having everything gloriously their own way. When I grew older of course, I understood that this was not so, but the real deathblow to that old delusion was never given until I read *The King's Mirror*. Then I *realized*—a very different thing from believing—that kings were in no respect different from other people—unless it was in that they ran much greater risks of being miserable—and had less freedom in vital things than the veriest serf in their realms. So I don't think I shall ever again dream of being a queen—to be sure, it is long since I did!

Until very lately I have cared most for fiction—history and biography did not attract me. But of late my taste in this respect has changed very much. Fiction no longer satisfies me. I want to read what *real* men and women have done and thought and endured. Lately I have read McCarthy's "Four Georges" and Parkman's "Wolf and Montcalm" and found them all fascinating. In connection with the latter I re-read "The Last of the Mohicans", a novel which I first read long ago in schooldays, having borrowed it from Nate. We were both charmed with the story and used to discuss its characters and incidents enthusiastically.

The other night I took the "Ascent of Man" by Drummond out of the hall library, came home, and read it till long after midnight, so absorbing did I find it. It is a remarkably clear and convincing statement of the theory of evolution. Moreover, Drummond makes a good, but not, I think, wholly successful attempt to reconcile science with—so-called—revelation. His analogies seem good as far as they go, but if he followed them out to their logical completion he would be sometimes forced to a conclusion very different from the one he does draw. He stops when it suits him and that is generally the weakness of all such attempts.

At present I am reading "Farthest North" by Nansen. It reads like romance. Besides, it is so recent that one feels as if one had a share in it somehow. To me, it lends a reality to it to remember that during the years Mary and I were at P.W.C., when I was teaching in Bideford, and prowling about Dalhousie library, Nansen was exploring the fastnesses of the polar sea and getting nearer than any other man ever did to that mysterious bourne so many have tried to reach but never have reached. It would be rash to say that no one ever will. I certainly think someone will some day. There are few chances for immortality nowadays but this is one of them. Earthly remembrance is assured to the man who reaches the North Pole. It seems odd to think of it, too. It will do nobody any good. But it will satisfy human curiosity on that point and as it is human curiosity that has accomplished almost everything of value it deserves to be indulged in some of its whims.

Sunday Evening, May 20, 1900
Cavendish, P.E. Island
A pouring rain in a city is an undesirable thing, but in the country—when you don't want to go anywhere—it has charms of its own. We have had a regular rain to-day, coming down in torrents over hills that are faintly green and woods where the buds are just beginning to open, and valleys where in sunny spots blue violets are pushing up through faded grasses and looking out on the world from under their purple hoods.

But it has cleared up now and tomorrow when the sun comes out, warm and bright, things will grow and the hill meadows will be emerald in a day.

I have something to do this evening that I don't like to do—and that is, write to Edwin Simpson. A fortnight ago I had an unexpected letter from him. It frightened me, as his letters always do; but there was no cause for alarm. He wrote that he had heard I was ill in the winter—as I was for a few weeks after father's death, with influenza and neuralgia—and that it had troubled him; and he asked if I would not write to him and tell him how I was and what I was doing. He put the request in such a way that it would have seemed unkind and ungracious to refuse—and I surely owe him what kindness I can give him. So I will answer his letter this once but if he ever writes again I will not. I made a mistake and paid a heavy penalty for it; but I *did* pay it and have done with it and now I will not have the matter brought up again and again, like the periodical exhuming of a loathsome corpse. My dead past must bury its dead; for me there shall be no assisting at belated obsequies, even if the man I wronged has a fancy for officiating as High Priest. I have put it behind me....

Thursday, June 7, 1900
Cavendish, P.E.I.
...."Isabel Carnaby" helped me pass a pleasant hour or so yesterday. The book is clever but too "talky". The people in it seem to be so constantly occupied in saying "smart" things and perpetrating epigrams that they haven't time to *do* anything of consequence. Also, after several pages of unalloyed sparkle one feels a little dazzled and wants to look at something green and dull for a rest. However, I really enjoyed the book very much, so it is rather thankless of me to carp at it.

"Janice Meredith", another "best seller", was fairly good. To be sure, I'm getting very tired of the American Revolution as a background for stories, and *Janice* was spun out much longer than was necessary, but the book is after all a welcome addition to the rows in my plain little bookcase. I like to look up from my work occasionally and gloat my eyes on them. They are all my pets. I never buy a book unless I have read it before and know that it will wear well, unless it be by an author in whom I have sufficient confidence to buy "sight unseen". There are the poets I love and the Alcott and "Gypsy" stories I read in my teens—and have a liking for yet—and novels picked up here and there as opportunity offered, and which have been read and re-read, loaned and re-loaned until they are almost worn out....

Sunday, Aug. 5, 1900
Cavendish, P.E.I.
If, as is said, the way to hell is paved with good intentions, then I fear me I have contributed not a little of late to the paving. I have been "intending" for a month to write up this journal but when I had the time I wasn't in the mood and when the mood came there wasn't any time. But for a wonder the mood and the time have come together this lovely Sunday evening and here in "my own old spot" by my open window I sit me down to scribble a bit for my own amusement—something I very rarely do nowadays, for when I write I must write for the purpose of poking some dollars into my slim purse and there is not much fun in that, though there is some profit. Long ago, before my scribbling possessed marketable value I wrote for pure love of it....

In June Mary Campbell was married. I drove myself up to Darlington on Tuesday afternoon and arrived there at five o'clock to find the bride-elect churning and all the other girls—Donald E. has such a swarm of daughters—flying around doing a dozen things at once. Such fun as we had! And at dusk Mary and I got away in the spare room and had a long talk together—the last talk of mutual girlhood. And we had a bit of a cry, too.

Wednesday was a lovely day and a busy one. After dinner, Archie Beaton, the prospective groom arrived. I had never seen him before. He is a big, quiet, stolid-looking Highlander and seems very much older than Mary. I cannot say I found anything attractive in him, and I could not help wondering a little what Mary had seen in him. I have never thought she was very deeply in love with him. I wonder if his Klondike gold—of which he is said to have a store—invested him with any aureole in her eyes. It would doubtless weigh strongly with Donald E. but I can hardly believe that it would influence Mary to that extent.

After his arrival I helped Mary dress; then I went down to help receive guests and unwrap wedding presents. About eighty people came. Norman arrived from town at dusk, bringing Bertie and Laura with him. At eight o'clock Mary was married. The ceremony was performed out under the trees of the orchard. The pretty wedding group, the bright dresses of the guests, and the glow of the sunset softly fading in the western sky, all made quite a charming picture. Mary was the most composed and matter-of-fact bride I have ever seen. I stood under a cherry tree in the background and tried to feel solemn and romantic as befitted the occasion and scene, but couldn't quite manage it, somehow, because the Campbell dog was having a fit quite close behind me, and making the weirdest, most unearthly noises.

When it was over—the ceremony, not the fit—the girls and I flew in to light up. After supper the minister considerately went home and the rest of us betook ourselves to dancing. They had a splendid big dancing pavilion built out in the garden and roofed over with maple boughs. It made an ideal ballroom, for the night was dewless, and the air kept so cool and pure all the time. We had three fiddlers; there were lots of boys out from town who were dandy dancers, so we had a pretty good time. We danced the night out and the sun was just rising as we finished the last lancers.

Then we had breakfast and a rather fagged looking lot we were in the merciless daylight. But after breakfast I took a picture of all the survivors and then I drove the bridal pair to the station. A lot of the boys turned up with pounds of rice and as I was carrying Mary's parasol Paddy Clarken and I sneaked off behind a pile of lumber and filled it with rice. Mary went off with it, never suspecting, and I would have given a plum to have been around when she opened it.

I came home the same day, very tired and sleepy....

Sunday, Oct. 7, 1900
Cavendish, P.E.I.
....This afternoon I was re-reading "Undine"—that exquisite little idyll. I read it years ago in my early teens. Nate had it—a little volume given him by a literary uncle. He brought it to me one day in school and I read it all behind my desk in that delightful, roomy old "back seat" which was so splendidly convenient for such doings. No doubt I should have been studying English History or geography at the time—but then I would soon have forgotten the history and I have never forgotten *Undine*. When I finished it I registered a solemn vow that some day in the bright, beautiful future—I was so sure *then* that it would be bright and beautiful—I would get the book for myself. The other day in Ch'Town I was in Carter's bookstore— where the aroma of books and new magazines was as the savor of sweet incense in my nostrils—and I saw the dearest edition of *Undine* bound in white and gold. I paid the price without a murmur, brought it home in triumph and read it, finding to my delight that its charm was every whit as potent as when, years ago, behind that old brown desk in the little white schoolhouse, it lured me into By-path Meadow and opened a world of fancy to my delighted eyes. That is, after all is said, the true test of a classic. It must please every age, from childhood to gray hairs.

Last week I betook myself to Ch'Town to attend the Exhibition and get my gray matter stirred up a bit. We would get too mossy if we stayed always in the same place!

But there! I'm getting so horribly tired of my own style that I'm going to stop for to-night.

Thursday, Oct. 18, 1900
Cavendish, P.E. Island
Ten years ago, when I was a schoolgirl of fifteen, I had a mania for writing "ten year letters"—which being interpreted means a letter, "written, signed, and sealed," to be opened and read ten years from the date of writing. I don't know exactly where I got the idea—I think I'd read something like it in a "Pansy" book. At any rate I adopted it for my own, for it seemed so fine and romantic. And *then*

ten years seemed a veritable lifetime and twenty-five a very venerable age indeed.

Now, when the reading of these letters is falling due, it does not bring me the pleasure I once anticipated. Instead, I have an uncanny feeling, as if I were reading a letter from a ghost or across a grave. They give me far more pain than pleasure.

This evening, at eight o'clock, I had to open one of these epistles written ten years ago in old "Southview" in Prince Albert by Edith Skelton. I remember very clearly the night we wrote them. We had been having a gay time as usual, for Edith was such a jolly girl. And we wrote those letters very light heartedly, never doubting that our friendship would outlive the years. It has not done so—it has just dropped away. I haven't heard from or of Edith for six years. I wonder if she remembered to open my letter to-night.

I opened hers and read it. It was a merry letter, full of our old jokes, some of which I have so entirely forgotten that their significance is quite lost for me. It was not a brilliant epistle at all—Edith's talents did not lie in the direction of letter writing; and all things considered it was not worth keeping for ten years to read it.

Saturday, Nov. 10, 1900
Cavendish, P.E.I.

To-day the *November* issue of *Good Housekeeping* came, with some verses of mine in it entitled, "A Pair of Slippers". I consider the occasion worthy of mention because they were given a whole page to themselves and illustrated—the first time ever my verses were so honored. They are trashy enough little things in themselves I know, but they *did* look so dignified that a careless observer might fancy that there was really something in them. Blessings on the good editor who was inspired to have them illustrated! He has bolstered my self-respect very considerably.

Saturday, Dec. 22, 1900
Cavendish, P.E.I.

We are surely going to have a white Christmas to celebrate the end of the century—the first we have had for years. Winter is here to stay. I hate it because I can't prowl around by myself outside in the evenings. When the dim wintry twilight comes down there is nothing to do but drop my work with a little sigh of weariness and creep away into a dark corner to nurse a bit of a heartache. If it were summer I could get away outside under the trees and the stars and my soul would be so filled with their beauty that pain would have no place.

To be sure, I did start out to-night, grimly resolved to do a constitutional and walked around the square without seeing a soul. It was cold and clear and frosty-white—white, white everywhere, soulless and lifeless, except where a strip of orange ran along the west and far down over the lowlands the sea was black and sullen. I walked around the square and then my resolution gave out and I came in. It was too deadly still and lonesome outside—I wanted to scream out to break the awful silence.

It is not much better inside—just a different kind of loneliness. Grandma sits and sews or reads the papers all the evening. I sit and read—or write—and eat my heart out into the bargain. The monotony is dreadful. I never rebelled against it as

I do this winter. To be sure, I keep my rebellion to myself and nobody suspects it. But it is there for all, seething and fermenting.

I love bright, cheerful companionship, laughter, sparkling conversation. I get nothing of them. Grandma has always been a reserved, distant woman, caring less than anyone I ever knew for social intercourse with her kind, and possessed with an odd *resentment* against the liking or desire for it in anyone else. My inner life has, for the most part, been lived entirely alone and those with whom I have had to associate most have been in all times and in all crises the farthest removed from me. The friends who have been a real help and inspiration to me are seldom near me. Sometimes I am conscious of a great *soul loneliness*. Spiritually, and mentally I have always had to stand alone. I suppose it has made for strength and self-reliance—but it is hard.

Well, I'm going to stop growling. But I really do feel discontented by spells. I feel as if I were hemmed in on all sides by a hedge of petty, trivial, unceasing annoyances that prick and sting continually and so "get on the nerves" more than would a great pain.

Tonight, in reading over some old letters I tried to read one of *Herman's*—the only one I ever had from him. Well, I could not do it! I opened it, read the first page and then I had to fold it up and put it away. The pain was intolerable. What an influence that man had over me! His mark is branded on my soul forever. To think that now, two years after his death, I cannot bring myself to read a crude, impersonal letter of his, containing nothing but commonplaces, without feeling as if a brutal hand had twisted itself among my heartstrings and was wrenching them at will. Yet I do not often think of him now and that wild passion is dead and buried with him. It is only when, as to-night, I try to read his letter or the pages of this journal written about him that the old agony wakes and lifts its head and defies me to forget its former power.

After all, in spite of all discouragements and heart-burnings I am getting on pretty well in a way. That is to say, I'm beginning to make a livable income for myself by my pen. Oh, *outwardly* I'm getting on all right. It is *inwardly* that all the tumult is. Yes, I *am* getting on and I mean to get on, let come what will of rebuff and discouragement and failure. I have conquered this dismal trio so far and I mean to continue. "What man has done, man may do".

Now, I'm off. This grumble has done me good. I work off all my revolutionary tendencies in this journal. If it were not for this "went" I might fly into a thousand little pieces someday.

Wednesday, Jan. 23, 1901
To-day when the mail came I pounced on the *Daily Patriot*—published yesterday— and the first thing I saw, blazoned in great black letters across the page, was "The Queen died to-day".

The news was expected for she had been very ill and little hope was held of her recovery. Still, it was a very decided shock. One felt as if the foundations of all existing things were crumbling and every trustworthy landmark swept away. Who ever thought that Queen Victoria *could* die? "The queen" seemed a fact as enduring and unchangeable as the everlasting hills. The sense of loss seems almost personal.

75. *Mary and Archie Beaton*

1901

....This is certainly the greatest house in the world for fun. We have had so many jolly rackets here that the very walls seem to be permeated with the essence of "good times". From my earliest recollection a visit to Park Corner was the greatest treat in the world. Each room has its memories—the kitchen where we toasted our toes at the glowing old "Waterloo", the front rooms where we spent so many jolly evenings, the big bedrooms upstairs where we slept and talked; and best of all, that famous old pantry, stored with good things, into which it was our habit to crowd at bedtime and gnaw bones, crunch fruitcake and scream with laughter. That pantry is historical.

There is a certain old screw sticking out from the wall on the first stair landing which always makes me realize clearly that I am grown up. When I used to visit Park Corner in the dawn of memory that screw was just on a level with my nose. I used to measure myself by it every time I went over. *Now*, it comes to my knees!

I miss Clara very much. There is a sympathy between her and me that does not and cannot exist between Stella and me. Stella is the girl for fun and jollity and *surface* things but I could never confide in her as I can in Cade. The dear old days are gone and can never return. There are times when I would give much to be as care-free and *blind* as I was then. Only at times though. Generally I am sane enough to prefer clear-sightedness to a fool's paradise....

Wednesday, Mar. 6, 1901
To-day when I picked up the *Daily Patriot* the first thing I saw was a long editorial in which somebody had laid himself out to write up all the "poets" of this tight little island. Half way down this outburst I came upon my own name written out in cold-blooded fulness—"Lucy Maud Montgomery" which I detest! I was catalogued as "the foremost of the younger school of writers", and then followed several paragraphs of compliments and quotations.

I laid the paper down with a little smile and a little heartache. Long ago, in old schooldays, this would have seemed to me a very lofty height of ambition. Olive Schreiner says, "When all the sweetness is taken out of the things we long for—they come". Perhaps not *all* the sweetness was taken out of this little morsel of fame. It *did* please me, not because of its praise but because it was the visible testimony of a place won for myself by hard toil. But the pleasure was mingled with a pain still keener—for *who was there to care*? Since father died—no one. How proud and delighted he would have been. But now what does it matter? My success can please no one but myself. I am alone.

Life has never seemed the same to me since father died. Something is *gone* and in its place is a pain and loneliness and longing that is sometimes dulled but is always there. I do not mean to say I am unhappy. I am not. But my existence is a sort of *negative* affair. I enjoy life on the whole and have beautiful moments. I have success in a growing measure and a keen appreciation of all the world and the times offer for delight and interest. But underneath it all is the haunting sense of *emptiness*.

Friday, March 21, 1901
Cavendish, P.E.I.

"Munsey's" came to-day with my poem "Comparisons", in it, illustrated. It really *looked* nice. I've been quite in luck of late for several new magazines have taken my work.

I *know* that I am improving in regard to my verses. I suppose it would be odd if I did not, considering how hard I study and work. Moreover, I feel that I am developing. Every now and then I write a poem that serves as a sort of landmark to emphasize this fact. I know, looking back, that I could not have written it six months or a year ago, any more than I could have then worn a garment the material of which was then unwoven. I have written two poems this week. A year ago I *could not* have written them, but now they came easily and naturally. This encourages me. Perhaps in the future I can achieve something worth while. I never expect to be famous—I don't want to be, really, often as I've dreamed of it. But I *do* want to have a recognized place among good workers in my chosen profession. That, I honestly believe, is happiness and the harder to win the sweeter and more lasting when won.

I really think that I must possess the saving grace of perseverance. What failures and discouragements I used to meet at first when, in my teens, I sent out my wretched little manuscripts—for they *were* wretched, although I thought them quite fine—with an audacity that I actually wonder at now. I cannot remember the time when I did not mean to be a writer "when I grew up". It has always been my central purpose around which every hope and effort and ambition of my life has grouped itself.

I remember—who could ever forget it?—the very first commendation my writing ever received. I was about twelve years old and I had a stack of "poems" written out and hidden jealously from all eyes—for I was very sensitive about my scribblings and could not bear the thought of having them seen by those who would probably laugh at them. Even then I felt strongly, though inarticulately, that there was no one about me who understood or symphathized with my aspirations. I was not like the other children around and I imagine that the older people of my small world thought there was something uncanny about me. I would have died rather than show to them those foolish, precious little rhymes of mine.

Nevertheless, I wanted to know what others would think of them—not from vanity but from a strong desire to find out if an impartial judge could see any merit in them. So I employed a pardonable little ruse to find out. It all seems very funny and a little pitiful to me now; but then it seemed to me that I was at the bar of judgment for all time. It would be too much to say that, had the verdict been unfavorable, I would have forever surrendered my dreams. But they would certainly have been frosted for a time.

A school-teacher was boarding here then—Izzie Robinson. I liked her not and she liked not me. Had I shown her a "poem" and asked her opinion of it I would certainly have received no encouragement. But she was something of a singer and one evening I timidly asked her if she had ever heard a song called "*Evening Dreams*". She certainly had not, for the said *Evening Dreams* was a composition of my own which I then considered my finest effort. It is not now extant and I can remember the first two verses only. I suppose they were indelibly impressed on my memory by the fact that Miss R. asked me if I knew any words of the "song". Whereupon I, in a trembling voice, repeated the first two verses.

> "When the evening sun is setting
> Quietly in the west
> In a halo of rainbow glory,
> I sit me down to rest.
>
> I forget the present and future,
> I live over the past once more
> As I see before me crowding
> The beautiful days of yore."

Strikingly original! Also, a child of twelve would have a long "past" to live over! I finished up with a positive gasp, but Miss R. was busy sewing and did not notice my pallor and general shakiness. For I *was* pale—it was a moment of awful import to me. She placidly said that she had never heard the song but that *the words were very pretty*.

The fact that she was quite sincere must certainly detract from her reputation for literary discrimination. But to me it was the sweetest morsel of commendation that had ever fallen to my lot—or that *has* fallen since. Nothing has ever surpassed that delicious moment. I went out of the old kitchen as if I trod on the amber air of the summer evening and danced down the lane under the birches in a frenzy of delight, hugging to my heart the remembrance of those words.

It was a little bit ironical, was it not? that my first literary encouragement should have come from a person who was certainly not my friend and who would have bitten her tongue out before she would knowingly have praised me or my works.

Perhaps it was her dictum that encouraged me, sometime during the following winter, to essay my first step on the slippery path of literature. I wrote out my *Evening Dreams* very painstakingly—on both sides of the paper, alas—wrote them over many times before I got a copy to please me, and sent them to the editor of *The Household*, an American family magazine which grandmother took. The idea of being *paid* for them never entered my head. Indeed, I am not at all sure that I knew at that time that people ever were paid for writing. At least my early dreams of future fame were untarnished by any mercenary speculations!

Alas! The editor of *The Household* was less complimentary but more discriminating than Miss R. He—or she—sent the verses back, although I had *not* "enclosed a stamp" for the purpose, being in blissful ignorance of such a requirement.

By the way, I may state that the other day that same magazine took a poem of mine for the first time. But I don't think it has the same editor. There is quite a gap in time between that first rejection and this first acceptance—as wide a gap I daresay as that between the different poems—or between the writers thereof, for that matter.

My aspirations were nipped in the bud for a time. It was a year before I recovered from the blow. Then I essayed a more modest fligh*. I took my *Evening Dreams*, in which I still had some faith despite the cruel editor, copied them out afresh and sent them to the Charlottetown *Examiner* of weekly appearance. I felt quite sure *it* would print them for it often printed verses which I thought and, for that matter, still think, were no better than mine.

For a week I dreamed delicious dreams of seeing my verses in the Poet's Corner, with my name appended thereto. I saw myself the wonder of my schoolmates—a little local celebrity. When the *Examiner* came I opened it with tremulous eagerness. Alas, there was not a sign of an evening dream about it.

Still, I did not quite despair. I thought it might appear in the next issue. But it did not. Then I gave up and drained the cup of failure to the very dregs. It seems all very amusing to me now but it was horribly real and tragic to me then. I was crushed in the very dust of humiliation and I had no hope of ever rising again. I burned my *Evening Dreams* and though I continued to write because I couldn't help it I sent no more to the cold and cruel editors.

I may say that all these doings were conducted in profound secrecy—a secrecy made possible by the fact of our having the post office. I smuggled my editorial correspondence into the letter packet myself, and so not a soul but myself knew of my *Evening Dreams* peregrinations. Thus, if I suffered over the loss of anticipated success I was spared the mortification of having anyone else know of my failure. I shut my pitiful little hopes and my still more pitiful little despairs up in my own soul and dreed my weird alone.

After this mortifying experience three years passed. Then I went out west. I still perpetrated things I called poems. They were pretty bad but they really were an improvement on *Evening Dreams*. By this time my long paralyzed ambition was beginning to recover and lift its head again. I wrote up the old Cape Leforce legend in rhyme—most of it was written at my desk in the old High School under Mr. Mustard's suspicious eye and in agonies of homesickness—and sent it down home to the *Patriot*. No more of the *Examiner* for me!

Four weeks passed. One Sunday afternoon, just as I was starting for Sunday School, father came in with the Saturday night's mail—the *Patriot* among it. I snatched it up, tore off the wrapper and saw my verses!

The first thing I did, before I ever read them myself, was to thrust the paper into father's hand in a tumult of joy and pride and then I rushed off to Sunday School in a whirl of excitement. It was the first sweet bubble on the cup of success and of course it intoxicated me. When I got home from Sunday School I took the paper and stole off by myself to gloat over it. There were some fearful printer's errors in it which made the flesh creep on my bones, but it was *my* poem and in a real newspaper. The moment we see our first darling brain child arrayed in black type is never to be forgotten. It must have in it, I think, some of the wonderful awe and delight that comes to a mother when she looks for the first time on the face of her first born.

During that winter and the following summer I had other verses and some prose articles printed. My little *Marco Polo* story appeared in the Montreal *Witness* and my article on Saskatchewan came out in the *Times* and was copied and commented on favorably by several metropolitan papers. Also, several effusions on "June" and kindred subjects were published in that long-suffering *Patriot*. I was beginning to plume myself on being quite a literary person.

But the demon of filthy lucre was creeping into my heart. I wrote a story and sent it to the New York *Sun*. I didn't know one thing about said *Sun*; I had never even seen a copy of it; but I had been told it paid for articles. The New York *Sun* sent my story back to me. I flinched, as from a slap in the face—but I kept on writing. I had, even then, learned the first, last, and middle lesson "Never Give Up".

I may remark just here that one day last fall I took the plot of that identical story, wrote it up, sent it off, and took first prize in a story competition. But needless to say it was entirely unlike its former incarnation.

I went on sending things away and getting them back. But one day, during my P.W.C. year, I went to the Ch'Town post office and got a thin letter with the address of a third-rate magazine in the corner. In it was a brief note accepting a poem "Only a Violet", which I had sent to *The Ladies' World* and offering in payment two subscriptions to the magazine. I kept one myself and gave the other to grandma; and those magazines, with their vapid little stories, were the first tangible recompense my pen brought me. However, the price was as good as the verses. They were trash....

The year I taught in Bideford I wrote a good deal and learned a good deal—but still my stuff came back, except from two magazines whose editors evidently thought that literature was its own reward, and quite independent of monetary considerations. I often wonder that I did not give up in utter discouragement. At first I used to feel dreadfully bad when a poem or story over which I had agonized and labored came back with one of those icy little rejection slips. Tears of disappointment *would* come in spite of myself, as I crept away to hide the poor crumpled manuscript in the depths of my trunk. But after awhile I got hardened to it and did not mind. I only set my teeth and said "I *will* succeed". And never, at any time had I any *real* doubt that I would succeed at last. I cannot account for this abiding faith—this confidence in my star—but it was there. I believed in myself and I struggled on alone—always alone—in secrecy and silence. I never told my ambitions and efforts and failures to anyone. I listened unmoved to the sneers and ridicule of various relatives who thought my scribbling rank folly and waste of time. *That* never disturbed me at all. Down, deep down, under all discouragement and rebuff I knew I would "arrive" some day.

That day came at last in Halifax when I received a five dollar cheque from *Golden Days* for a story. It was the first money my pen had earned—it was not much in itself, but it stood for a vast deal to me. It was the first of the letters that spell success; and since that day I have gone on and on, meeting with failures in plenty still, but with enough successes to out balance them. To-day I have a foothold. I *have* succeeded.

August 23, 1901
Cavendish, P.E.I.
....I have been industrious and respectable all summer. Have written stories and letters, read novels, histories and encyclopedias, and gone to church painstakingly. I have picked berries, dabbled in fancy work and photography, made cakes, pies and puddings, called and received calls! I have piped and danced to other people's piping. I have laughed and wept, exulted and groaned, and I am tired, tired, tired, of it all. I wish I could go to sleep "for an eon or two". But, after all, that is extravagant. Eight hours sleep will do just as well and I will get up in the morning, rejoicing as a strong man to run a race.

Well, about these occupations of mine? Writing letters? Oh, I do it. I can't very well help it although, as regards a great many of them, I might prefer not to—for what is the use of writing letters when you can't put any soul into them? Or reading them, under the same disadvantage?

Some letters I love to write. I have plenty to say and my pen glides smoothly along the track of my thoughts until an epistle is produced to which I am not ashamed to sign my name. But there are other letters that I never sign for very shame of such silly inanities. These are the letters I hate to write and which I grind out mechanically to correspondents with whom I have ceased to have much in common, yet whose acquaintanceship I do not wish to lose altogether.

Then, church? I sometimes ask myself why, after all, I go to church so regularly. Well, I go for a jumble of reasons, some of which are very good, and others very flimsy and ashamed of themselves. It's the respectable thing to do—this is one of the flimsy ones—and I would be branded black sheep if I didn't go. Then, in this quiet, uneventful land, church is really a social function and the only regular one we have. We get out, see our friends and are seen of them, and air our best clothes which otherwise would be left for the most part to the tender mercies of moth and rust.

Oh, you miserable reasons! Now for a few better ones!

I go to church because I think it well to shut the world out from my soul now and then and look my spiritual self squarely in the face. I go because I think it well to search for truth everywhere, even if we never find it in its entirety; and finally I go because all the associations of the church and service make for good and bring the best that is in me to the surface—the memories of old days, old friends, and childish aspirations for the beautiful and sacred. All these come back, like the dew of some spiritual benediction—and so I go to church.

Then I have read—oh, my faithful old key to the gates of fairyland! Novels—some delightful ones, so delightful that I could not sleep until I had finished them but pulled my table to the bed, bolstered myself up with pillows, and read until the hero had reached the end of his adventures and I came back with a mental jolt to the real world, to discover that my oil had almost burned out, that my back and eyes were aching and that I was very sleepy.

However, I have not confined my reading exclusively or even mainly to fiction. History and biography I have revelled in, and in *encyclopedias*, too, having lugged two or three huge volumes home from the hall every month and browzed through them for miscellaneous information. When I get book hungry, even the whole of an encyclopedia is better than no loaf!

As for my pen-scratchings, I have toiled away industriously this summer and ground out stories and verses on days so hot that I feared my very marrow would melt and my gray matter be hopelessly sizzled up. But oh, I love my work! I love spinning stories and I love to sit by the window of my den and shape some airy fancy into verse. I have got on well this summer and added several new journals to my list. They are a varied assortment and their separate tastes all have to be catered to. I write a lot of juvenile yarns. I like doing these but would like it better if I didn't have to lug a moral into most of them. They won't sell without it. The kind of juvenile story I like to write—and read, too, for the matter of that—is a rattling good jolly one—"art for art's sake"—or rather "fun for fun's sake"— with no insidious moral hidden away in it like a spoonful of jam. But the editors who cater to the "young person" take themselves too seriously for that and so in the moral must go, broad or narrow, as suits the fibre of the particular journal in view.

I intend going down to Halifax next month to attend the Exhibition. I feel that I must have a short outing to brace me up for the winter.

Cavendish, P.E.I.
Aug. 28, 1901

There is nothing in the world so sweet as a real, "old-timey" garden. I have always known this but it came home to me with fresh force yesterday afternoon when I was down at "old Mrs. George Macneills" taking some photos for Bessie. The photo part was a bore but the garden more than made up for it.

There are certain essentials to an old-fashioned garden. Without them it would not be itself. Like the poet it must be born not made—the outgrowth and flowering of long years of dedication and care. The least flavor of newness or modernity spoils it.

For one thing, it *must* be secluded and shut away from the world—a "garden enclosed"—preferably by willows—or apple trees—or firs. It must have some trim walks bordered by clam-shells, or edged with "ribbon grass", and there must be in it the flowers that belong to old-fashioned gardens and are seldom found in the catalogues of to-day—perennials planted there by grandmotherly hands when the century was young. There should be poppies, like fine ladies in full-skirted silken gowns, "cabbage" roses, heavy and pink and luscious, tiger- lilies like gorgeously bedight sentinels, "Sweet-William" in striped attire, bleeding- heart, that favorite of my childhood, southernwood, feathery and pungent, butter- and-eggs—that is now known as "narcissus"—"bride's bouquet", as white as a bride's bouquet should be, holly hocks like flaunting overbold maiden's, purple spikes of "Adam and Eve", pink and white "musk", "Sweet Balm" and "Sweet May", "Bouncing Bess" in her ruffled, lilac-tinted skirts, pure white "June lilies", crimson peonies—"pinies"—velvety-eyed "Irish Primroses", which were neither primroses nor Irish, scarlet lightning and Prince's feather—all growing in orderly confusion.

Dear old gardens! The very breath of them is a benediction.

Wednesday, Nov. 13, 1901
The Echo Office
Halifax, N.S.

Yes, I think I can write it all up now. I have got over my first agony of loneliness and homesickness, I have become accustomed to my daily routine, and I have made a little niche for myself which is snug enough although somewhat narrow. So I think I have sufficient "sand" to take up the thread of this journal where I dropped it two months ago.

I am here alone in the office of "The Morning Chronicle" and "Daily Echo". The paper has gone to press and the extra proofs have not yet begun to come down. Overhead they are rolling machines and making a diabolical noise which jars the shades on the Auer lights wildly. Outside of my window the engine exhaust is puffing furiously. In the inner office the news-editor and the "Beach-Comber" are having a friendly wrangle. And here sit I—*Echo* proof-reader and general handy-man. Quite a "presto change" from last entry.

I am a newspaper woman!

Sounds nice? Yes, and the reality is very nice, too. Being of the earth, it is earthy and has its drawbacks. Life in a newspaper office isn't "all beer and skittles" any more than anywhere else. But on the whole it is not a bad life at all.

I left home on September 11. Just before I left I received a telegram from the *Echo* news-editor offering me the position of proof-reader for the winter. Lottie Shatford, who does a good deal of work for this concern, had recommended me to him.

I could not decide on the spot—I was dressed to go with the mailman to the train. However, I supposed that if I did take the place I'd have time to return home and pack my trunk at least. So I started gaily off—and haven't seen Cavendish since.

I stayed in Charlottetown from Wednesday to Friday and then came down to Halifax. Had a pleasant trip but reached Halifax at eight o'clock in a pouring rain. I took a cab and went to the W.C.A. where I understood Bertha Clark had, according to promise, engaged a room for me. When, however, I rang the bell and so brought the secretary to the door I was posed by her information that no such room had been reserved.

I was fagged out after my day of travel and I felt just like sitting down on my valise and crying, under the cabby's eye and all. However, I didn't. Perhaps it was out of consideration for the cabman's feelings. More likely it was because the secretary hastened to add that they would take me in for the night anyhow.

So I limply paid my cabby and tugged my valise upstairs to a big barn-like apartment which, with its three cot beds, looked as much like a hospital ward as anything you can imagine. I gave myself a bit of a grooming and then went down to supper. But I was too tired to eat. After supper I went to bed. My roommates were a Miss Brag, who was a business college girl, and a Miss Messenger, a

Dalhousie college student. Just then however, I didn't know who they were and didn't care. I slept poorly, owing to the unaccustomed clang and clatter of the cars, and next morning I felt stiff and grumpy. It was pouring rain still and I toddled down to the Echo office in no very jubilant mood.

Eventually I found my way to the lair of the news-editor, Mr. Taunton, and by him was referred to Mr. Dunn, the business manager, with whom I had a confab. At first I hardly knew whether to take the place or not. The salary was only five dollars a week. But it was not so much money I was after as experience and a *start* in journalism. So I finally agreed. I knew grandma could get Prescott to stay with her for the winter. He probably wouldn't like it, but he would be ashamed to refuse; and he and his have got enough—and *taken* enough, too—to pay him for it. Grandmother was willing for me to stay, also.

The worst of the business, however, was that I had to go right to work. There was no returning to Cavendish.

After leaving Mr. Dunn's sanctum with instructions to report myself for duty on Monday morning, I returned to the W.C.A. and went to bed, because, by this time, I felt really ill. That evening two more girls arrived and were deposited in our room. The secretary had agreed to keep me until I found a boarding house, if I "did not mind" sharing a room with as many others as could be stowed into it. I *did* mind; but as it seemed Hobson's choice I assented as cheerfully as possible.

As the next day was Sunday I spent the morning in bed and the afternoon in writing a letter home with instructions about the sending of my trunk. Then I resigned myself to spending a fortnight on the contents of a valise which had been packed with an eye single to visiting and carousing and not to working in an office. However, "needs must go when the devil drives".

After tea Sunday evening I went to see Bertha Clark. She is housekeeper at the Halifax hotel and is quite unchanged. What a comfort it is to find our friends unchanged. She is as jolly and friendly as in the days of yore when we were such chums at H.L.C.

At first I used to inflict myself on her every other night to exorcise my demon of nostalgia. Several times I have been down to dine with her—green oases in the desert of boarding house life. *I do like a good dinner!* I feel much more *Christianic* afterwards—just as good as gold and as if I could smile at anybody and any fate. I'm sure most of the crimes in the world must be committed by hungry people. I always feel "fit for treasons, stratagems and spoils" when I'm hungry. That is why I am cross and grumpy at the present moment. There is a fearful "goneness" in my inner girl.

Echo Office, Halifax, N.S.
Thursday, Nov. 14, 1901
I am still cross and hungry and grumpy—but fortunately haven't been so continually ever since my last entry. I was interrupted then and this is the first chance I've had to resume. It is now five o'clock and quite dark in the office. Must climb up and light the gas before I proceed.

There, thank goodness that is accomplished with safety to life and limb and— "what's more"—no male man coming in while I was up in mid-air.

Well, where was I at?

On Monday morning, September 16th I solemnly waddled down to the *Echo* office and was initiated into the mysteries of proof-reading. I encountered nothing very formidable and got on all right.

I come down at nine in the morning. My first duty is to skim through the *Chronicle*—the morning edition—clip out and mail such editorials as I think will make their recipients either beam or squirm. That done, I dive—on my own account—into the reading room and skim with an avid eye over the *Island* dailies. By the time I have finished with them the proof rolls are beginning to come down in a queer little box through a queer little slide from the composing room, so I go to my desk, dragging thereto the most comfortable chair I can find and "hoe into" proof reading. This is not hard but somewhat tedious. The headlines and editorials are my worst thorns in the flesh. Headlines have a natural tendency towards depravity, anyhow, and the editor-in-chief has a ghastly habit of making puns over which I am apt to come to grief. In spite of all my care "errors will creep in" and then there is the mischief to pay. When I have nightmares now they are of headlines wildly askew and editorials hopelessly hocussed which an infuriated chief is flourishing under my nose.

Proofs come down pretty steadily all the forenoon and between them I employ my spare time as I see fit. At noon I have an hour off when I go around to Woolnough's restaurant and get my dinner and then take a prowl around town. After dinner proofs come down fast and furious until about 2.30 when the paper goes to press and there is a sudden lull. But I have to stay until five and sometimes six to answer the telephone, sign for wires, read extra proofs of ads etc. This is always a rather poky time but release comes at last.

The foregoing is the regular daily routine. On Saturday the *Echo* has a lot of extra matter, a page of "society letters" among the rest. It mostly falls to my lot to edit these. Can't say I fancy the job very much, but the only thing I positively abhor is "faking" a society letter. This is one of the tricks of newspaperdom. When a society letter fails to turn up from a certain place—say Windsor—in due time, Mr. Taunton slaps a Windsor weekly down before me and says blandly, "Fake us up a society letter from that, Miss Montgomery".

So poor "Miss M." goes meekly to work and concocts an introductory paragraph or so about "autumn leaves" and "mellow days" and "October frosts", or any old stuff like that to suit the season. Then I go carefully over the columns of the weekly, clip out all the available personals and news items about weddings and engagements and teas etc., hash them up in epistolary style, forge the Windsor correspondent's nom-de-plume —and there's your society letter! I used to include funerals too, until I found that the news-editor invariably blue-pencilled them. Evidently funerals have no place in society.

Then I write a column or so of giddy stuff for Monday's *Echo*. I call it "Around The Tea-Table" and sign it *Cynthia*. I think it rather goes. Mr. Simpson, the staff artist, has made a heading for it in which four or five rather melancholy and spinsterish maidens sit around a table, presumably talking gossip. As for the stuff itself, everything is fish that comes to *Cynthia's* net—fun, fashions, fads, fancies.

The *Chronicle* Building is of red brick and is situated on Prince St. The editorial offices are on the second floor. My office is a back room looking out on a back yard in the middle of the block. I don't know if *all* the Haligonian washerwomen live around it or not but certainly a goodly percentage of them must, for the yard is a network of lines from which sundry and divers garments are always streaming gaily to the breezes. On the ground and over the roofs cats are prowling continually and when they fight the walls resound with their melancholy howls. Most of them are lank, starved-looking beasties enough but there is one lovely fellow who basks on a window sill across the corner and on whom I long to get my hands. He is so sleek and plump and gray that he makes me think of my old pussy "Bobs" at home. (Here I could really squeeze out a homesick tear if I were not afraid that it would wash a clean streak on my grimy face. This office is really the worst place for getting dusty I ever was in.)

I enjoy the distinction of being the only girl on the staff, but there are two below in the business office—Miss Hensley, with whom I have merely a speaking acquaintance—and Minnie Macdonald who is a chum of mine and a lovely girl. But there are men galore. I had a shocking time getting them all placed when I came first, for introductions seem to be unknown in newspaper offices. For the first two weeks, whenever anyone was rung up on the 'phone I had to rush wildly about the office demanding of all and sundry, "Your name or your life?" But I've got them all sorted out now.

Mr. Dunn is at the head of the procession—that is to say, he is business manager of both papers and seems to be cordially detested by all who are under his thumb. He has always been very civil to me but I have little to do with him or he would probably comb me down too. He is a fine-looking man of a certain type, with an aggressive chin and when anything goes wrong he is heard from in no uncertain tones.

Mr. Taunton, the news-editor, is a man for whom I have a "Doctor Fell" aversion. I ought not to dislike him for he has been very kind to me and always takes my part in a ruction over proof errors, but I do and I can't help it. I am uncomfortable in his atmosphere and never feel at ease.

Mr. Baxter, the marine editor, shares my office and is my favorite of the staff. He is really on the night staff but drops in frequently during the day to write out shipping notes and fire off puns, more or less ghastly, at the handiest victim, generally myself. He is tall and raw-boned and red-headed, very jolly and off-handed and kind.

"Jimmy" Gowan, the policeman, also inhabits this office. He is one of those people who believe silence to be golden. At first I thought him a grumpy old fossil but he is really a good soul and his silence is his misfortune not his fault.

There is an also an office boy who haunts the place.

Mr. McLellan is the editor in chief, a polished elderly gentlemen, very affable and courteous except when good editorials go wrong. I have no fault to find with him except his aforesaid propensity for punning, but punning seems to be in the air here. I must have swallowed a germ—probably Baxter gives them off by hundreds—for I found myself making a pun the other day—a thing I never did in my life before. I must try to discover an antidote before the disease makes headway.

Mr. Fraser runs the "Beach-comber" column and generally writes the *Echo* editorials. He has a shallow cleverness and thinks Tommy Fraser is about the only thing of any importance that ever happened. He is passably good-looking and very snobbish.

Mr. Simpson is the staff artist. I rather like him but he doesn't seem to be popular. I think he is a bit of a sap-head. Messrs. Hickey, Hamilton and MacDonald are all night folk who drop in occasionally and seem quite nice. Messrs. Jost and Kellaher are in the business offices; the latter is quite likeable.

I have been gluttonizing on papers ever since I came here. We get lots of exchanges and I browse among them in my spare moments—generally with an eye cocked for ideas that can be worked up by "Cynthia"—that young person having an amiable habit of taking her own wherever she finds it.

Saturday, Nov. 16, 1901
Echo Office
Halifax

I have to write up this journal as I do everything else nowadays—by fits and starts. I forget what interrupted my last entry. Probably I got so hungry I had to stop. Anyway, this is Saturday afternoon with the slave still chained to her oar. No nice, delightful "Saturdays off" in newspaperdom! Saturday is my busiest day here because the Sat. *Echo* is the biggest of the week. However, it has gone to press and I have nothing much to do. I am going to dine at the Halifax and spend the evening with Bertha, so I feel good-humored, and here goes to pick up the dropped threads.

Lottie Shatford ran in to the office one day in Exhibition week and I have seen her several times since. She has changed very little. One evening she and her brother called on me, the latter having been very anxious to meet me. No, don't imagine you scent a romance. He is not only married but twice married and his interest in me is purely intellectual. He admires my scribblings.

I was disappointed in him. He is not as I had pictured him from Lottie's letters—seems a rather common and opinionated sort of person, anxious to air his "liberal" views, especially on the matter of religion, in season and out of season.

Lottie's sister Edna was married from another brother's house here in Halifax last week. I was invited to the wedding, got half a day off, and took it in. Didn't enjoy it at all. Except Lottie and two or three members of her family circle I didn't know a soul and naturally they were too busy with their many duties to have any time for me. There is no loneliness like the loneliness of a crowd. I was bored to death and glad when I could decently get away.

But oh, oh, oh! Lonely? Homesick? Don't mention it! For the first ten days I was here I thought I should die and hoped I would. I can laugh at myself now but while it lasted it was no laughing matter. I have had such a bad attack only twice before —out west and when I first went to Bideford. I wasn't feeling very well physically and, not being settled down, had nothing to do out of office hours and this all helped things the wrong way.

It wasn't so bad all day; but when I left the office and, after walking through half a mile of streets without seeing a face I knew, found myself alone in a strange narrow little hall bedroom, with not one of my own household gods around me, loneliness seized on me body and soul, and I cast myself down on the bed and refused to be comforted. But it is all over now and I am acclimated. The only time I feel rather blue now is when I leave the office and walk home through the chill gray autumn dusk. Then I do long bitterly for my own dear "den" at home and the old red road over the hill.

It was just when my homesickness was at its very worst that I visited the Exhibition. I remember that as the nadir of my woes—I sounded the deeps of ghastly, soul-sickening loneliness that day and was never quite so bad again. Having got as low as possible I began to ascend.

To begin with it was a dull day. I got off at 3.30, rushed to the W.C.A., dressed, and got on a street car. It was crowded and everybody in it knew somebody else—everybody but me! When I got off at the grounds I left my raincoat on the car—didn't miss it until the car was gone and rain began to fall. I recovered the coat later on but just then it was the last straw. For one cent I would have turned then and there and gone back, not caring whether I ever saw that Exhibition or any other.

But nobody offered me the one cent so I wandered on, shelled out my quarter, and went in. I would not like to be called on to describe that Exhibition for much I fear me I should brand myself as one of those "who having eyes see not". I wandered forlornly around among throngs of people and looked idiotic. I know I looked it for I felt it.

If I had been just here for a visit, as I had expected to be when I came, I would not have cared if I had been alone in a million. But the thought that I had to *stay* here among all those strangers spoiled everything. I just felt out at the elbows and was glad when I could decide that I had stayed long enough for the money and might decamp.

I sallied out in a pouring rain, waited ten minutes until a crowded street car came along, scrambled recklessly on with a score of others, and stood on the outer edge all the way home, hanging to a strap and wedged in between two brutes of men—I'm sure they were brutes—in long wet rubber coats, one of whom smoked a bad cigar all the way.

So my trip to the Exhibition wasn't an emphatic success. Never mind, it's fun to look back on it now.

Monday, Nov. 18, 1901
Echo Office
Halifax, N.S.
This has been one of the days when things reveal their naked, natural *cussedness*. I didn't sleep well last night and felt grumpy all day, and so did everyone else apparently. Then one of those wretched editorial jokes got off its trolley again this afternoon; and altogether life has seemed like a howling wilderness.

However, the cloud is lifting now. The paper has gone to press and somebody below in the business office has just sent me up a big molasses "kiss" in the copy box. This delicate attention has smoothed my ruffled plumage.

Well, "to resoom and to proceed":—after a week at the W.C.A. I removed to my present domicile at 23 Church St. I like it only fairly well....

I have had a hard time trying to arrange for enough spare minutes to do some writing. As my salary only suffices for board and bed and as it is against the law, not to mention the climate, to go about naked, I have to make enough money to clothe myself in other ways.

My first idea was to write in the evenings. Well, I tried it. I couldn't string two marketable ideas together. Besides, I had to keep my stockings darned and my buttons sewed on!

Then I determined to get up at six every morning to write before going to work! I did that twice—or maybe it was three times. Then I concluded that was impossible. I could not do good work in a chilly room on an empty stomach, especially if, as was often the case, I had been up late the night before. So I said to myself, very solemnly,

"Now, Maud, what are you going to do? Leaving the tenets of the Plymouth Brethren out of the question, you have to choose between two courses. You must either decamp back to the tight little Island or you must hit upon some plan to make possible the production of pot-boilers."

So Maud thought hard.

Now, it used to be at home, that I thought undisturbed solitude was necessary that the fire of genius might burn. I must be alone and the room must be quiet. It would have been the last thing to enter into my imagination to suppose that I could ever write anything at all, much less anything of value, in a newspaper office, with rolls of proof shooting down every few minutes, people coming and going and conversing, telephones ringing and machines thumping and dragging over-head. I would have laughed at the idea—yea, I would have laughed it to scorn. But the impossible has happened. I am of one opinion with the Irishman who said you could get used to anything, even to being hanged!

Every morning here I write and not bad stuff either. I have grown accustomed to stopping in the midst of a paragraph to interview a prowling caller and to pausing in full career after an elusive rhyme to read a batch of proof and snarled-up copy. It's all in the day's work—but I don't like it over and above. It's trying. However, it has to be done and I won't grumble, no, not one little bit!

I have got into some first-class magazines lately, so you may pat me on the back. Among others, the *Delineator, Smart Set* and *Ainslee's* have opened their fold to this poor wandering sheepkin of thorny literary ways.

Saturday, Nov. 23, 1901
Echo Office
Halifax
....I have just received a check for $25 from the Delineator for a story. *Watch me smile*!

Another week has come to an end. Tomorrow is Sunday, glory be! I have been indulging in a sort of religious dissipation every since coming to Halifax—that is, I've been making the rounds of all the churches. Last Sunday evening I went up to the North End to the Universalist Church. I found it quite interesting but certainly would not care for it as a steady thing. It is much like a lecture and a concert combined. The pastor gave a very logical and painfully truthful talk on "What Do

Men Really Believe concerning Immortality?" The music was charming and I enjoyed the whole service but couldn't exactly see where the religion came in. I couldn't help smiling as I imagined what some of the dear orthodox bodies in Cavendish would think of the whole performance. To be sure, they wouldn't understand half of it and the other half would probably fill them with horror.

The service was very simple. I was at the other extreme the Sunday I went to St. Luke's. It is very "high" and religious observance there has become positive mummery without pith or meaning. The kernel of Christianity is so shrouded in the husks of ritual that it is almost lost altogether.

I don't know what they are doing overhead in the composing room but they seem to be celebrating a very carnival of thumping and rolling and dragging. I expect every minute to see the ceiling come crashing in.

That composing room is a curious place. I ventured up one day and found myself in a big grimy room, with a lot of grimy figures bending over grimy galleys of type, and a grimy row of linotype machines along one side. It looked like a dingy workshop of gnomes. As for the linotype, I believe it is magic! It seems fairly to possess a brain of its own, so wonderful are the things it can do.

My next visit was to the basement—"Hell's Kitchen" as it is poetically termed here—where the big press takes a huge roll of white paper in at one end and drops it out of the other, cut and folded *Echoes*. Truly the epic of human genius in this century is its colossal mechanical contrivances. Two and three thousand years ago men wrote immortal poems. To-day they create marvellous inventions and bend the erstwhile undreamed-of forces of nature to their will. Which is the better, oh, ye gods of the Golden Age? After all, have we not lost as much as we have gained? The beautiful childhood of the world is gone forever. I believe its happiest days were in the dead-and-gone centuries of its song-singing, love-making, war-waging youth!

Bless me, I have forgotten that I am in a newspaper office.

The great Haligonian event of the season was the Royal Visit in October. Halifax fairly stood on its head, tricked out in bunting which might be gay and gorgeous and patriotic enough but was certainly not beautiful. Our office was adorned with yellow-and-green and looked as if it had jaundice.

The Duke and Duchess arrived here on Saturday afternoon, Oct. 19. Everybody had a holiday except us newspaper fags. However, we rushed things to get off by two o'clock. About eleven I slipped out and ran over to the Provincial building where I stood freezing for half an hour before the gates while some corner stone was being laid. At last I had my reward and when the carriage containing the Duke and Duchess left the gates I had a good, unhindered look at them.

Our future king is an insignificant man with a red nose. The duchess looks to be the best man of the two. She was a big, rather fine-looking woman dressed rather dowdily in black.

I got off at 2 o'clock but I did not go to the review on the common although I suppose everybody else in Halifax went. I had nobody to go with and I knew I wouldn't be able to see anything if I did go so I just stayed home and celebrated my quarter-holiday by reading a new magazine and eating candy.

In the evening I went out with Minnie MacDonald and her sister Kate to see the illuminations. They were all good and the warships were magnificent—"like one's childish dreams of fairyland", as Cynthia took good care to remark in her next "copy". There were twelve warships in port and all, hulls, spars and funnels, were picked out with electric lights. The effect against the inky blackness of the harbor was magical.

In due time it began to rain and as I did not have my umbrella with me, I got well drenched and went home in a very disgruntled mood, vowing that I had had enough of royal visits. I caught a fearful cold and my best hat has had a cowed, apologetic appearance ever since.

Well, I have at last brought this journal up to date and written, I doubt not, a vast deal of nonsense. But then, one must have a little nonsense somewhere to give zest to existence and there certainly isn't much elsewhere in my life. It is so deadly serious that it is no wonder my account of it is frivolous. So let it be!

Saturday, Dec. 8, 1901
Echo Office, Halifax
Have been busy of late—as if that were news indeedy! But I have been Busy with a capital B. 'Tending to office-work, writing pot-boilers, making Xmas presents— or buying them, which is just as harrowing—etc., etc., etc....

One of the "etcs" is a job I heartily detest. It makes my soul cringe. It is bad enough to have your flesh cringe but when it strikes into your soul it gets on your spiritual nerves terribly. We are giving all the firms who advertise with us a free "write up" of their holiday goods, and I have to visit all the stores, interview the proprietors, and crystallize my information into "two sticks" of copy. From three to five every afternoon I potter around the business blocks until my nose is purple with the cold and my fingers numb from scribbling down notes. So "no more until next time". Perhaps I shall have got back my self-respect by then. It has quite wilted under the haughty patronage of the Halifax clerks.

Wednesday, Dec. 12, 1901
Echo Office, Halifax
If I have not got back my self-respect I *have* got a new hat! It's an ill wind that blows no good and my disagreeable assignment has brought me some. The other evening I went in to write up the *Bon Marche*, which sets up to be *the* millinery establishment of Halifax. I found the proprietor very genial. He said he was delighted that the *Echo* had sent a lady and by way of encouraging it not to weary in well-doing he would send me up one of the new walking hats if I gave them a good write-up. I rather thought he was joking—but sure enough when the write-up came out yesterday up came the hat and a very pretty one it is, too. Thanks, *Bon Marche*.

Thursday, Dec. 20, 1901
Echo Office, Halifax

All the odd jobs that go a-begging in this establishment are handed over to the present scribe. The very queerest one up to date came yesterday.

The compositors were setting up a story called "A Royal Betrothal", taken from an English paper, and when about half through they lost the copy. Whereupon Mr. Taunton requested me to write an "end" for the story. I gasped, not seeing how I could. I had never seen the story and what was set up was not enough to give me any insight into the final development. Moreover, my knowledge of royal love affairs is limited and I have not been accustomed to write with flippant levity of kings and queens.

However, I went home last night and fell to work. I got it done somehow or other. So to-day out came "The Royal Betrothal" bravely and as yet nobody has guessed where the "seam" comes in. If the original author ever sees it I wonder what he—or she—will think.

76. *The pantry, Park Corner*

77. Stella's room
[Stella Campbell in her house at Park Corner]

78. Myself at the date of my first venture
[c. 1886]

79. The old garden
[at Mrs. George Macneill's, Cavendish]

80. The Echo office
[Halifax]

81. Myself at the date of my going to Halifax
[*LMM inserted in her journal two studio portraits that were clearly taken at the same time. The one above appears in the entry for April 8, 1898, with the caption "Myself in 1898". A head-and-shoulders appears in the entry of November 13, 1901, with the caption used above.*]

1902

Monday, Jan. 20, 1902
Echo Office, Halifax
Last night Myrtie Clark inveigled me down into the Fort Massey school hall to teach a Chinaman. I went meekly, avid for "experience". They had about thirty of them, and—on the principle of "greens to the green" I suppose—they assigned one to me—or me to one—who was just out from China. He didn't know a word of English and I set to work to teach him to read it!!

He had a well-developed pig-tail and oh, how horribly he *did* smell! But some of the small Chinese boys are as cute-looking as they can be. Well, my pupil can't be much harder to teach than "Amos" of Bideford school, and I taught *him* to read.

Goodness! I've just thought of the time I had tea at old Archie's!

Saturday, Feb. 1, 1902
Echo Office
Halifax
The "cold snap" which has been snapping all the week is abating somewhat. I have been in such a state of "freezation" ever since it began that now when I find myself gradually thawing and revivifying, the sensation has all the charm of novelty.

I have just finished writing up weekly yard of "Cynthia" and in spare moments have been re-reading the "Scarlet Letter". I've read the book often since that first time years ago when I read it behind that old brown desk at school, where so many delicious "forbidden fruits" from green apples to novels were devoured.

Lottie Shatford was in to see me one day this week. Dear me, I *must* confess! There is really *nothing* in our so-called friendship!

There, *that's* a relief!

I always felt it—even years ago at Dalhousie. There was a certain intellectual comradeship between us but I never felt really at home in her company. Bright and clever as she is, I can never shake off a feeling of restraint. There is something in my nature that shuts up instinctively when she approaches, and refuses to expand again until she is gone. Lottie is up-to-date, vivacious and merry. I would not like to forfeit her good opinion. But the all-important element of mutual sympathy—that mysterious thing we call affinity—is wholly lacking and nothing can compensate for it. It may exist between two people who may seem to have very little in common. And, as in this case, it may be lacking between two whose opinions, tastes and pursuits are so very much alike that it seems almost weird that no real communion of spirit can exist.

One may as well be honest. I have tried for a long time to pretend to myself that the nebulous tie between Lottie and me was really that of a high-plane friendship. But it is not. She really counts for nothing at any facet of my life. There is nothing in either of us that belongs to the other and so neither of us can find and claim our own in that other. Lottie, admirable as she is in many ways, is not for me and henceforth I will accept our relationship for what it is worth and no longer try to find any greater value in it and, failing, taste the bitterness of repeated disappointment. Affection cannot be generated by any intellectual rule of thumb. I will give up the vain attempt.

Saturday, March 15, 1902
Echo Office, Halifax
I am *not* dead, as might perhaps be inferred from my somewhat long silence and the general tone of glumness that pervaded my last entry. On the contrary, I am well and flourishing. But I look back yet with a cringe to that terrible time.

I got well almost as suddenly as I got sick. And how jolly it was! I feel as if I'd been made over new and I've been enjoying life ever since—except when Golding's bad tobacco shrivels up my soul within me. Golding is a sub., doing duty in Mr. Taunton's absence and some day, just for curiosity's sake I'm going to ask him what brand of tobacco he uses and where he gets it!

Baxter has just made a joke. I must stop and laugh. Excuse me for a moment. There, that duty is done!

Yes, I'm all right again, glory be! But I've nothing to write. I've been doing and seeing nothing of late worth recording.

This is Saturday night. Tomorrow I am going to have a walk in the park—if the weather permits, that is, and the forecast *says* it is going to be fine.

Saturday, March 29, 1902
Echo Office, Halifax
This week has been miserable. It has rained and "fogged" continually—the damp has crept not only into my bones and marrow but into my soul as well and is smothering it.

However, I've lived on in spite of it. I've read proofs and dissected headlines and fought with compositors and bandied jokes with Baxter. I have ground out several Sunday-Schooly rhymes for a consideration of filthy lucre and I have written one *real* poem out of my heart.

I hate my "pot-boiling" stuff. But it gives me the keenest pleasure to write something that *is* good—a fit and proper incarnation of the art I worship. After all, the malevolent gods can't embitter everything. There is one thing at least they cannot touch.

Tuesday, April 8, 1902
Echo Office, Halifax
Last night I dreamed about Pensie. I dreamed we were children together again, wandering along the shore. It has brought the past back to me in the vivid fashion such dreams do—as no mere retrospection of waking hours can do....

Pensie and I grew apart as we grew up. It was the fault of neither. Childhood and its bond of fun once past we had no interests in common. But nothing can rob us of that sweet old past.

Pensie is a wife and mother now. And I am so different from the child of those old frolics that she seems to me a different creature altogether—poor little lass, so often misunderstood, with her wayward fancies and her strange, inner dream life that nobody guessed at. She was a quaint little Maud—that Maud of the old days, with plenty of faults and shortcomings but at heart very loving and warm. I *had* such a warm, loving, hungry, tempestuous little heart in those days! I wonder if the embers are all burned out. I think not. They flame sometimes still in a smouldering way and then my soul aches. Poor soul! And poor heart! You have always struggled together in an unequal companionship. But in those days I had *no* soul—very little, anyway—just in an embryo state perhaps—and so I was happy and didn't know it. When the process of soul evolution began then came suffering. Still, it must be good to have a soul and perhaps some day its growing pains will cease and all will be well and worth while.

Thursday, May 1, 1902
25 Morris St. Halifax

I have "flitted". The McDonalds gave up housekeeping this spring and went boarding for the summer, so I gave warning and moved, too. I am in a much nicer place now and my congealed soul is beginning to thaw out.

25 Morris is a big, gray, stone house and is kept by a Mrs. Andrews and her daughter. I was at first under the impression that Mrs. A. was a widow but I have since found out that Mr. A. is still in the flesh, although he appears to have been suppressed.

I have a little third-floor room looking out on a few acres of back yards. Back yards seem to be my fate.

Kate M. and Mrs. M. have a large room next to mine and Minnie has the front hall bedroom on the same floor. Needless to say, we have hilarious times. Three other boarders are on our "flat". One is a Mr. McAfee who is a clerk in a dry-goods store. He is short and bald but very good fun. Mr. Colborne is another dry-goods man. "Colly" is a good soul, with big "cowey" eyes. He would have made a nice girl but—well, "God made him and therefore let him pass for a man".

"Andy" his roommate is a druggist and no fun at all.

A Mrs. Pearson, with three children has the big room on the second floor. She is a nice, good, uninteresting soul. Then the last of our circle is Mr. Grant, a youthful bachelor of 84, who works in a wholesale liquor store all day and plays whist with Kate, McAfee and myself in the evening. Besides, he serves as a peg on which we girls hang any number of jokes, good, bad, and indifferent. One can be useful, you see, even at 84.

Sunday, May 4, 1902
25 Morris St. Halifax

I am writing this in my room. Everybody else, except Father Grant, is away to church. I stayed home to "expurgate" a novel for Mr. Taunton's use and behoof.

When Mr. T. was away Mr. Golding started to run a serial in the *Echo* called "Under the Shadow". Instead of getting some A.P.A. stuff as he should have done he simply bought a sensational novel at a bookstore and started it. It was very long and was only half done when Mr. T. returned. So, as it would run all summer in its present form I was bidden to take it and cut out mercilessly all unnecessary stuff. I have followed instructions, cutting out most of the kisses and embraces, two thirds of the love making and all the descriptions, with the happy result that I have reduced it to about a third of its normal length—and all I can say is "Lord have mercy on the soul of the compositor who has had to set it up in its mutilated condition."

I shall be going home the last of this month. I shall be sorry to leave the office but not to leave Halifax. I like the office extremely but I *don't* like Halifax.

Monday, May 12, 1902
Echo Office, Halifax
Today I've laughed more than I've done for a month together. I've been re-reading "A Bad Boy's Diry".

That book is responsible for *you*, my journal. 'Twas from it I first got the idea of keeping a "diry". When I was about nine years old Mr. Fraser, the Cavendish school teacher, who boarded at our place, had the book. I think I regarded it as a classic then. I read it and re-read it and promptly began a "diry". I folded and cut and sewed four sheets of foolscap into a book and covered it with red paper. On the cover I wrote "Maud Montgomery's Diry".

Years ago I burned it in one of my iconoclastic fits. It was a pity, for it really should have been preserved as one of the curiosities of literature.

The "bad boy" was, of course, my model. He spelled almost every word wrong; therefore so did I of malice prepense. He was always in mischief and wrote accounts of it in his diary. Although not very mischievous by nature, being bookish and dreamy, nevertheless I schemed and planned many naughty tricks for no other reason than that I might have them to write in my "dere diry."

But I had never seen the book since then and had forgotten it so completely that it was new to me. I just howled over it today for it was absurdly funny still—even funnier than I used to think it, I imagine, for I took it quite seriously in those days, when I made a hero and model out of "little Gorgie."

Friday, May 20, 1902
25 Morris St. Halifax
I had a good internal laugh today. Miss Russell, a Dartmouth girl, who was recently added to our staff and who is rather nice, said to me:—"That story *Under The Shadow* is the strangest one I ever read. It wandered on, chapter after chapter, for weeks and never seemed to get anywhere; and then it just finished up in eight chapters, *lickety split*. I can't understand it."

I could have solved the mystery for her but I didn't!

Saturday, May 31, 1902
Echo Office, Halifax
My last day in the office! Well, I'm sorry.

I am perched here at my desk. The day is fine and bright and everything is jogging on as usual. Pshaw! I believe I have a heart-ache.

Anyway, I have the comfort of knowing I have got along all right here. Even the redoubtable Mr. Dunn assured me of that. Mr. McLellan told me I could have the place back again in the fall if I'd like to come. I would like to; but I don't think I shall. I feel badly over giving up the chance, for I may never get another one. But I feel that I ought to stay home with grandmother. She is not happy or contented with Prescott. He has behaved very nastily to her. He always was a cad and a cad he will be to the end.

Monday Night. June 2, 1902
25 Morris St., Halifax, N.S.
I am tired and my ribs ache from laughing. I really didn't know there were so many different ways people could make fools of themselves. But as Josiah Allen's wife says, "I must not anticipate". *Is* it Josiah Allen's wife? Well, if not she some other celebrity.

Yesterday morning Kate McDonald and I "looped the loop". That is to say, we got on a street car at our door and rode on and on, until we came back to our door again. It was a five mile jaunt and we saw all of Halifax that is worth seeing. Even Halifax is pretty now. The trees are respectably leafy and every grass plot is gay with dandelions.

In the afternoon I went to tea with Mr. and Mrs. McLellan. Annie Fraser of Charlottetown was there and I had a very nice time. Annie and I went to Fort Massey in the evening. I was not sorry that it was my last Sunday at Fort Massey for as a church I have no use for it. Church, indeed! I should call it cold storage! I have been going to it regularly ever since last fall and not one living soul in it, not even the minister has ever once spoken to me. I have taught in the Chinese school every Sunday evening and not one of the teachers has ever spoken to me. When Myrtie Clark introduced me to the Superintendent and told him I would take a class he said he was very glad. When I went to him last Sunday and told him I would have to give up the work as I was going away he said he was sorry. He did not even thank me for what I had done. That was the extent of my intercourse with anyone in the school!

After the service Mr. Falconer read a telegram to the effect that at 12 o'clock that day Lord Kitchener had signed a treaty of peace with the Boer generals. This meant that the long dragged-out war was at an end at last. Everybody in church drew a long breath. The moment was quite dramatic.

I shall never forget the excitement of the first stages of that war. It was worth while to be alive then. But of late it has been a tedious bush-whacking affair.

Being Sunday night all they could do by way of celebration was to ring the bells. This they did with might and main. After I came home Miss Andrews and I went for a walk in the Park which was full of the servant girl and her soldier, as usual.

After I got home for keeps I read a perfectly harrowing ghost story. It was the most gruesome thing. I read it in bed and after I had finished it do you suppose I could get out of bed to put the light out? No!! And if Kate M. had not fortunately come in late that lamp would have burned good and bright until morning. When I heard Kate's airy footfall on the stairs I called her in, explained my predicament, and got her to put out the light. If I had got out myself to do it I was sure something would grab me by the feet when I was getting in again.

The story was Lytton's "The Haunters and the Haunted" and I can conscientiously recommend it.

Well, to-night Halifax turned to and stood on its head—raised Cain by way of celebrating the peace. Everybody who could stand on his legs was out, Min, Kate and I among the rest. It was all too funny for words. I fear I shall never get my face straightened out again. It will wear a spectacular grin for the rest of my days.

Sunday, Sept. 21, 1902
Cavendish

I have made a new friend recently. This, in Cavendish, has a flavor of the miraculous. The person in question is Nora Lefurgey, who is the school teacher here and boards at John Laird's. We "took" to each other from the start and have been enjoying our congeniality ever since. Nora suits me exactly. We never bore each other and we have no end of fun together. She is a positive God-send to me for I have no other close friend in Cavendish. Amanda and I have grown so far apart that our friendship is merely a hollow show. Lucy and I used to be intimate in a superficial way. But a year or so ago I discovered deceit and treachery in her, such as I had always known her to be guilty of in regard to other people but which I had been foolish enough to believe she did not practise towards me. This utterly destroyed my old affection for her. As I am situated I could not openly break with her; but I shut her out of my intimacy wholly ever since. So Nora fills a "long-felt want".

Sunday, Nov. 30, 1902
Cavendish, P.E.I.

I'm extremely sleepy. Instead of scribbling here I ought to be in bed—and thither shall I go, "immediately and to onct," as soon as this journal is brought up to date.

November has really been quite an exciting month. Early in it the Baptists started up a series of revival meetings. They got an "evangelist" to help them called MacDougall—Christian name, Sam.

Really, he *was* delicious! He was good-looking—if you happened to fancy his style—and had *such* melting dark eyes. The fifteen-year-olds went down before those eyes like ninepins. *And* he could groan so heart-rendingly! Also he could sing! For the rest, he was illiterate, sensational and so vulgar that he set the teeth of my spirit on edge. But I went—bless you, yes. It was fine fun. I was sorry when I had to miss a night!

This went on for about three weeks—and then came the *expose*. Cavendish hasn't enjoyed such a scandal for a decade. The Rev. Sam turned out to be, not only a fake—that might have been endured—but a *Presbyterian*—or, as he pronounced it, *Presbytarian*. The Baptist blood curdled with horror. Poor Sammy was hustled out of the place and since then peace and dullness have resumed their reign.

Nora was here all Friday night and we talked until the tiny hours. Then last night Frede Campbell and her cousin Jim Campbell arrived and Frede and I conferred on sundry subjects very near to our hearts. Hence I have two nights' lost sleep to make up—and I'm off to do it.

82. *Lottie Shatford*

83. *Nora Lefurgey*

1903

Tuesday, Apr. 12, 1903

And a snowstorm! But *that* is no novelty. We have had several the past fortnight, with cold rainstorms sandwiched in between. It has been a very disagreeable spring—cold and dull. The weather has had a bad effect on me and I have been dull and depressed—sick of life and of myself. My only guard against absolute misanthropy this past week has been the re-reading of four old favorite books. To-day I read "The House of Seven Gables"—a rather unfortunate choice for such a day in such a month, for it is a weird, melancholy creation, and every few paragraphs I would stumble over a sentence that brought stinging, painful tears to my eyes. Such tears always hurt me now. Once, tears over a book-woe were something sweetly, sadly pleasant—tears over imaginary pain always are. But now—oh, they are bitter—bitter! Still, I love the book and found pleasure in reading it. I have by this time become accustomed to taking my pleasure diluted with pain. Once I protested against it fiercely, but have grown reconciled to it of necessity and feel thankful that there *is* pleasure mixed with the pain. The "Seven Gables" has the indefinable charm of all Hawthorne's books—that airy, fantastic, elusive fancy of his permeates every line of it.

But one of my books did not hurt me—Irving's "Alhambra". It was a volume of pure delight and I burned the heart out of a dismal day with it. For a time I forgot everything and wandered happily in the deserted halls and courts of the old Moorish palace with Irving, seeing with his eyes, hearing with his ears, and drinking in with him the romance and charm of a civilization long dead and an empire long passed away. The book seemed to me the gateway of an enchanted world. I stepped in and lo, I walked with happiness and youth and pangless pleasure again. Washington Irving, take my thanks. Dead and in your grave, your charm is still potent enough to weave a tissue of sunshine over the darkness of the day. I thank you for your "Alhambra".

Then I read George Eliot's "Adam Bede"—another cup of mingled pain and pleasure, bitter and sweet. It is a powerful book, with an inartistic ending. Her delineation of character is a thing before which a poor scribbler might well throw down her pen in despair.

Last of the four came "The Rubaiyat"—a string of pearls threaded on the blood-red cord of an oriental fancy. How very modern was that old Persian poet who lived nearly a thousand years ago—modern in his skepticism, his epicurean-ism, his philosophy. He was probably an unhappy man in spite of his "Let us eat, drink, and be merry for tomorrow we die" dictum. People who have come to that stage always are unhappy. They have only a gloomy future to look forward to and so they give themselves over with a fierce intentness to getting all they can out of today. "To-morrow!" exclaims old Omar scornfully,

"Tomorrow I may be

Myself with yesterday's seven thousand years."

So he means to have a good time of it to-day, the frank old sinner. But does he have it? Do we, any of us, ever have a good time simply by flinging ourselves after it? Oh, no! Happiness is an elusive thing. We may not lay violent hands on it or cajole it into our hearts by "the cup of wine"—or whatever equivalent we may take to coax it to us.

I wish spring would come. I'm tired of existence. Life has been a sorry business for me these past five years. I don't think anybody suspects this. To those around me, even my most intimate friends, I am known as a "very jolly girl", seemingly always light-hearted "good company" and "always in good spirits". It makes me laugh rather bitterly to hear people say this. If they could only see below the mask! I am thankful they cannot. I don't want to be pitied. And pain would not be any the less because it were known—nay, it would be—for me, at least—far greater.

The worst of it is, I don't think things will ever be much better. Life will just go on getting a little harder for me every year. I am practically alone in the world. Soon youth will be gone and I shall have to face a drab, solitary, struggling middle age. It is not a pleasant prospect.

I think the weather is largely responsible for my blues. When the sunshine comes again I shall find life quite tolerable—yea even pleasant. Not an ecstatic, rapturous affair at all but something one can jog along very comfortably with. In sunlight the soul of me shines out and conquers the flesh.

What a comfort this old journal is to me! It is my one outlet for my dark moods. Into it I pour the bitterness which might otherwise overflow and poison other lives. My greatest fear is that eventually the bitterness will grow so deep that I will not be able to write it out. That will be my darkest day. It will probably come when I leave this old home. The mere thought of it makes me sick at heart. I am not very happy here but I should be wretchedly miserable, I fear, anywhere else. I consider it is a misfortune to love any place as I love this old homestead—the agony of parting from it is so intolerable. I shall never forget what I suffered in Halifax last fall. And when I must go, knowing that there will be no return, will it not be tenfold worse?

When Nora came here we started for sport's sake a sort of co-operative diary, she writing it one day and I the next. It was to be of the burlesque order, giving humorous sketches of all our larks, jokes, etc. and illustrated with cartoons of our own drawing. In short we set out to make it just as laughable as possible. I think we have succeeded. Nothing could be more ridiculous than its pages—yes there could be and is! And that one more ridiculous thing is that *I* should have helped to write them. If a stranger were to read that record he would be sure to think that it was written by a couple of harum-scarum girls in their frivolous teens who had not yet attained to the remotest conception of real life and had never felt or known a sorrow. Yet it was written—at least half of it—by *me*!

Tuesday, June 30, 1903
Cavendish, P.E.I.

I have decided that June has been a delightful month—a sheaf of happy days. I have enjoyed it. The world has been bright and beautiful. One cannot fall into gloomy moods in June. That must be left for the drear November days.

Nora went away a few days ago. She has given up the school. I miss her terribly; and yet her going was a real relief to me. For this reason:—grandmother, never at any time of her life, very tolerant of the tastes and ways of other women, has become so childish in this respect that she is not now fit to have any stranger in the house. The way she has acted towards Nora this winter would have been positively ludicrous if it had not been so bitterly unpleasant for all concerned—and especially for me, as I was between the hammer and the anvil. What with trying to make things decent for Nora and trying to screen grandmother's absurd behavior I was worried to distraction nearly all the time. I wouldn't live some of the days of last winter over again for the most congenial companionship in the world....

Sunday, Aug. 16, 1903
Cavendish, P.E. Island

Aunt May and I went up to the B. Church this morning. Lizzie Stewart showed me into a pew and when I sat down I discovered that Edwin Simpson was sitting right behind me teaching a Sunday School class! When he dismissed the Sunday School with prayer he was bending right over my head. I wonder if anyone would have supposed from the expression of my face that I was enjoying myself hugely!

Ed's sermon was very good, though it was nearly an hour long. I have always been willing to do perfect justice to his intellectual gifts. Just at the last he said,

"To some of us, standing here this morning and recalling memories of past happiness as contrasted with our present hopelessness"—then he looked straight at *me*. What application he went on to make I shall never know for I did not recover my power of attention until he was away on in something else.

We went again to the evening service. When we came out we met Ed on the platform and this time I managed to hold myself still and talk to him in platitudes for a few moments. It was *beastly*—with all John Clarks and Arthur Simpsons staring covertly at us.

Sunday, Aug. 23, 1903

Lu, Fannie and I have been "on a jag" of visiting this week and were out every afternoon. We had fun and are tired to death. And of course *I* had my own private and particular *pleasure* out of it. Take this as an example.

Scene:	Mrs. Alec Macneill's parlor. Mrs. A. Macneill, crocheting in foreground. Maud, in centre of stage, netting. Lu to right, Fannie to left, slightly in background, embroidering pillow shams.
Mrs. Alec:	Were you up to hear Mr. Simpson preach last Sunday evening, Maud?
Maud:	Oh, yes. (Misses a loop in her netting.)

Mrs. Alec:	Isn't he just a splendid preacher?
Maud:	Very good. (Feels Lu and Fannie exchanging significant smiles behind her back.)
Mrs. Alec:	And I think he's very fine looking, don't you?
Maud:	Oh yes. (Nets furiously and says "Darn" under her breath.)

That is just about the way it has been right along. I really don't know which were the worst—the people who knew that there was once something between Ed and me, or the people who have no such suspicion. Those who do know say mean things and watch me to see how I take them. That is bad enough, but there *is* a limit to the things they dare to say. On the other hand, those who don't know blunder into some speeches and questions that are positively dreadful to me.

Monday, Sept. 14, 1903
Last night Ed preached again in the B. church. Soon after I arrived there Sophy Simpson walked in. Oh, that dear Sophy! How I *do* love her!! When we went out I went and spoke to her. She at once asked me in a voice loud enough to be heard all over, "Have you seen Ed?"

I responded that I had but perhaps Sophy thought I was prevaricating, for, as Ed passed by at that moment, she clutched him and said loudly,

"Ed, here's Maud!"

If Ed were blessing Sophy as devoutly at that minute as I was she would be beatified forever!

This evening Sophy and Ed called. We all sat in the parlor and talked for about an hour. I don't know what *I* said, or much of what *he* said. Everything seemed very unreal. As for Sophy, she was as impossible as ever but her gaucheries served a good purpose since they gave me something to think about. I don't think I made a fool of myself outwardly. Ed did pretty well also. Goodness only knows, though, what we were all thinking about—for I suppose even Sophy does occasionally think. That girl makes the flesh creep on my bones. She seems to radiate a repulsive force. I never heard one living soul say they liked her, (Grammar? Grammar!) so the poor soul is to be pitied. And I *do* pity her—but I like to do it from a distance.

I was thankful when their call was over. As they rose to go Ed picked up my *Omar* which was lying on the little table under the mantel and said that he had admired the Rubaiyat—very much ever since he had heard a college professor quote a quatrain from it. Then *he* quoted it, looking straight into my eyes.

"A book of verses underneath the bough,
A loaf of bread—a flask of wine—and *thou*
Beside me singing in the wilderness,
O, wilderness were Paradise enow."

It was not in especial good taste to quote it under the circumstances. But then good taste is not Ed's long suit.

He leaves for Chicago next Thursday so there will be no further danger of meeting him everytime I stir abroad.

Wednesday, Dec. 3, 1903

Got a check for another serial to-day—the second I've sold. This has been a pretty good year for me in regard to literary work. I have attained a pretty firm foothold and have made $500 also. Editors often *ask* me for stories now; my name has been listed in several periodicals as one of the "well-known and popular" contributors for the coming year, and the Editor of the Pres. Board of Publication in Philadelphia wrote recently to ask for my autographed photo.

Yes, I *am* beginning to realize my dreams. And the dreams were sweeter than the realities. Yes, but the realities are quite decent, too. I enjoy my success for I've worked and thought hard for it. I have the satisfaction, too, of knowing that I've fought my own battles. I have never had any assistance and very little encouragement from anyone. My ambitions were laughed at or sneered at. The sneerers are very quiet now. The *dollars* have silenced them. But I have not forgotten their sneers. My own perseverance has won the fight for me in the face of all discouragements and I'm glad of it now.

84. In the parlor
[Cavendish]

1904

What a day! One huge snowstorm from end to end and the thermometer at zero. I feel smothered. Even the windows are so thickly covered with snow and frost that the sensation is of being literally imprisoned. This has seemed as long as three days.

The other day I came across this sentence in a magazine:—"It is the unhappy people who keep diaries. Happy people are too busy to keep diaries."

At the time it rather impressed me as clever, but after thinking it over I have decided that it may be epigrammatic but it is not true. To be sure, I am not exactly a happy person; but I kept a diary and enjoyed doing so when I was quite happy. Besides, if being busy made people happy I ought to be a very happy mortal. No, the epigram should have read, "It is the *lonely* people who keep diaries"—people who are living solitary lives and have no other outlets for their moods and tenses. When I have anybody to "talk it over with" I don't feel the need of a diary so strongly. When I haven't I *must* have a journal to overflow in. It is a companion— and a relief.

To-day I was reading over the Prince Albert part of my diary. It brought back those days and sensations with almost startling vividness. That is what I like best in diary keeping—its power to reproduce past scenes and feelings and emotions.

I certainly would not wish to live that P. A. year over again in all its entirety for my stepmother made it very unhappy for me as far as her power went. But if I could live the part of it segregated from her atmosphere again I would gladly do so. What "larks" Will and Laura and I had! My heart ached a bit when I was reading about them.

I don't know what to do with myself tonight. I feel like a caged creature. Sitting round all day with the storm howling outside, reading and reading *and* reading but with nothing new to read has induced a condition of brain-fag and restlessness which I seem to have no power to control. I honestly feel that it would be a relief to stand up and *swear hard* for ten minutes on end. That accurately expresses my state of mind.

However, I feel better for writing it out. It is almost as efficacious as swearing would be and much more respectable.

Monday, March 11, 1904
Cavendish, P.E. Island

....I am no longer a prisoner—I can get out to the dear comradeship of woods and field again. I went across the snowy fields to Lover's Lane. I love that place idolatrously—I am happier there than anywhere else. What is the power of that silent shadowy wood lane, even in its white winter solitude? Why can it always steal away the sting of life and pour the oil of gladness into my heart? I do not know why or how—but it always does and so I love it with an intensity that sometimes makes me ask miserably how I'm ever going to live without it, when the day comes for me to leave Cavendish; it certainly will come in near or far and the thought is always unspeakably bitter to me.

....Looking back through the mellowing mists of the years and contrasting their bright hues with my dull and subdued present I am often tempted to think that they were better than they really were—to overrate them. But in sober truth there were often, very often, times even then when I was very unhappy. And I do not think that if the choice were offered me I would go back. I am not so *happy* as I was then but, paradoxical as it may seem, I am more *contented*. Life is richer and I get more out of it in many ways. No, dear early girlhood, you were a good and beautiful thing, and I enjoyed you; but, in this present mood of calm clear-sightedness, I do not hold you as the best or most desirable. And I would not go back to you if I had to go back to your limitations also.

Wednesday, Mar. 16, 1904
Cavendish, P.E.I.
I did a crazy thing this evening—and now I'm suffering from it.

To-day was a furious snowstorm. I did not feel well all day —not well enough to be able to throw myself absorbingly enough into work to help me fight off "the blues". For oh, I *do* try to fight them off and not give way to morbid broodings. And I have pretty good success all things considered; but to-day I hadn't enough spirit to try. This evening I had nothing to read and wasn't well enough to work—my only safeguards against the "horrors". In an evil moment I unlocked my little trunk, saw there a packet of Will Pritchard's letters, took them out and read them. I knew it was a foolish thing to do—I knew they would make me blue and restless—but I did not anticipate the effect they did have! I don't know what has got into me. As I read on and on it seemed as if a cruel hand were tightening its clutch on my throat. Yet I dreaded to come to the end of them and stop reading. It was awful—horrible. When I had read the last I fled to my room and thought for a few minutes that I would surely go *mad* if I couldn't scream out loud until I had exhausted all the feelings that were in me. I couldn't do that so I cried madly instead—horrible crying it was and hurt me cruelly instead of relieving me.

I am sitting up in bed writing this and I am half frozen but I *must* write it out. Oh, how am I ever going to put out the light and lie down here alone in the dark? I *can't*!!

I don't know why Will's letters should have such an effect on me. He was never anything to me but a good comrade. And while his letters were pleasant and friendly they were not such as would be expected to stir up such a riot of feeling in me. But I've been lonely and sick at heart all day, and I just long wildly for his bright *friendliness* again. He *was* such a good friend—and we had such good times together. And he is *dead*!!

I cannot understand my mood at all. And I have no one to help me out of it. I am so horribly *alone*. Poor grandmother is old and deaf and in some respects very childish. She is no companion to me in any way. I have no *real* friend near me and when I am pent up here for a week at a time without even seeing an acquaintance to speak to I can't help my soul getting sick within me!

This old journal is a regular grumble book but that is all it is good for. I work it off here and don't let it flow in any other direction. In reality I am not discontented. I love this old home deeply, although grandfather's more than foolish will has made it no home to me—and I love Cavendish. I would be perfectly contented here if I had just a little companionship and the average freedom to come and go. And when I read those letters I wanted to get back to the days I received them and answered them with jest and chat and delightful foolishness.

I'll be all right again when the sunshine comes back and I'm able to work. But that doesn't make it any easier now. Oh, I'm so alone—alone—and just now I can't endure it—I can't indeed. I feel like a sick, frightened baby with no hope or strength or courage or—anything! I'm afraid of the dark and the wail of the wind. Oh, such feelings as are in my heart! If I could drag them out and put them into words it would help me. But I can't—I can't describe or define them.

I said in my last entry here that I would not change back to the old days and I thought I meant it. I felt so then—but now I would—I would! Those letters of Will's showed me what I was then—brought back the old life for just one maddening space. And then it went and the present by contrast seemed intolerable—the present with which I was almost satisfied the other night—and with which I will be almost satisfied again, I suppose, when this wears off.

But I know one thing—I won't read old letters again under such conditions as to-day's—no, no, no—I don't want the past made alive any more to show how dead the present is. The present may be dead—but so long as I don't realize it I can get along.

Oh, Will, Will, if you could only come back and be my friend again! I'm not thinking of *love* at all—that has nothing to do with *this* mood—indeed, I feel just now rather a distaste for the thought of love. But I just long bitterly for the old good comradeship—the sense that Will was *there* to turn to when I would. Oh, Will, where are you? Are you anywhere?

I just wish I could die! I hate the thought of living—of the miserable night before me—of getting up tomorrow to another dull lonely day. I know when I put out the light I'm going to cry wildly. That's why I'm writing on and on—all this foolish stuff. It reads like drivel but I don't care.

It's strange—but if I had my choice tonight of calling *Will* or *Herman* out of that black outer void I'd call *Will*. I never cared for him in the way I cared for Herman—but it is he I want tonight. I want to see him—to laugh with him—to look into his gray eyes and bring the smile to his crooked pleasant mouth—I want to talk nonsense to him—to have him talk nonsense to me—about dances and picnics and flirtations, just as he talked in his letters. I want to be saucy and frivolous with him. I want him to say nice things to me and pay me boyish compliments.

But he's dead—he's dead. And if he is living somewhere he doesn't care for these things now—nothing like that matters to him. Oh, I don't *want* to believe in another life just now. There is something oppressive in the thought. It can't be like *this* life—everything would be different! No, no, I don't want to believe in it.

This is getting crazier. I will stop writing. But I won't put my light out yet for awhile. Oh, I am so tired of living!

March 17, 1904
Cavendish, P.E.I.
Morning

I've been reading over what I wrote last night. It is pretty bad but no worse than I felt, so I'll let it stand. After I managed to put out the light I cried myself to sleep. This morning when I woke I didn't want to get up—it didn't seem worth while. But now that I am up things are better. It is a fine bright day and I'm well enough to work. If I could only get out for a run I'd be all right again. But we are worse drifted in than any morning all winter. It is dreadful. Here it is mid-March and ought to be spring-like. Instead we have a January landscape and temperature. Winter is jolly enough under some circumstances but under my present ones it is just dismal and I long madly for summer and freedom.

April 9, 1904

....If I could ask my friends here occasionally my life and my outlook on life would be much more normal and wholesome. But that I cannot do. My friends, even those of my own sex, have never been welcome here. Grandmother is in many respects a peculiar woman. She has never at any time, since I was old enough to remember at any rate, seemed to want *anyone* to come here, except her own children. My visitors have always been made to feel distinctly that they were unwelcome. Naturally they did not care to come again. This unfortunate failing or lack of hers has increased with age and finally I have ceased to ask anyone to come here. I have been compelled to do this. Of course it places me in a very embarrassing situation in regard to my acceptance of invitations elsewhere but it cannot be helped. I have tried at times to talk the matter over with grandma. But she has always been a very difficult woman to hold any such discussion with. She is up in arms at the slightest hint that there is anything I can be dissatisfied with in her conduct and takes refuge in blank denial of anything I may ask the reason of. "I never did this"—"I never did that." These incidents have been so unpleasant and futile that I have decided that it is wisest to submit and say nothing. She is old and has a good deal to contend with. Grandpa's absurd will placed her in a very disagreeable position and Uncle John and his boys treat her very badly. I make allowances for her in all this and for my own part have resolved to let all attempt at social life go.

....It is really beginning to look a little like spring. There have been some thaws and there are a few bare spots. I have been cheering myself up by planning out and ordering some new spring toggery and in getting ready to think of a garden by and by. Both are quite pleasant occupations for I am very fond of pretty clothes and I love flowers....*I* want to put on bright hues and pretty garments, just as the flowers do. God intended people for his human flowers but left their choice of raiment to themselves. And a very poor choice some of them do make, it must be confessed! One is almost tempted to think it would have been better if He had let them *grow* their clothes like the roses and the tulips.

Wednesday, July 6, 1904
Cavendish, P.E.I.

I think that Cavendish just now is really one of the prettiest spots on earth. I thought so this evening when I was out for a walk. Everything is so green and fresh, the ripe but not over-ripe luxuriance of midsummer without as yet a hint of decay. And beyond the green fields and slopes was the blue girdle of the gulf, forever moaning on its shining shore. Cavendish would suit me perfectly as a place to live in if I had a home here and a little social life. There are so few young people in Cavendish now and the most of them are shallow, commonplace souls.

Wednesday, Aug. 3, 1904

I've had a *good* fortnight. Nora has been down. She stayed at John Laird's for of course I could not have her, since Uncle L's were here. But we spent most of our spare time together and I just lived with all my might. Several afternoons we spent at the shore, going down with our cameras and lunch baskets, donning bathing suits as soon as we got down and living a sort of amphibious life, wading and diving and snap-shotting. One day we had a never-to-be-forgotten surf dip. It was glorious.

Nora went home to-day and I shall miss her terribly. But I'll live on the memory of those two weeks for many moons.

Monday, Nov. 14, 1904
Cavendish, P.E.I.

What a fit of bad temper the world has indulged in! Day before yesterday she was not unbeautiful—a dignified old dame in fitting garb of brown and ermine. Yesterday she tried to ape juvenility, putting on all the airs and graces of spring, with warm sunshine and blue hazes—and what a bedraggled, uncomely old hag she was, all tatters and wrinkles! She grew angry then at her own ugliness and has raged all night and all day. I wakened up in the wee hours and heard the wind shrieking in the trees and tears of rage and spite sleeting against the panes. I like to hear a storm at night. It is so cosy to snuggle down among the blankets and feel that it can't get at you.

To-day was outwardly wild and dismal and so is to-night. It is difficult to believe it is the same world it was a few weeks ago.

This evening I spent in my dark room developing some photos. One mild gray day last week I took my camera and went to the woods. I wanted some pictures of the year asleep and I got them —still, pasture corners, a brook under the spruces, birches all leafless and white limbed. They came out well and I already foresee them finished and mounted on some spandy new mounts I got in town. What a boon all my little hobbies are to me!

After I finished with my negatives I sat me down and wrote a letter or two to people whom I have never seen and hardly even expect to see. If they are the right sort of people such letters, both for writing and receiving, are among the greatest pleasures of my existence.

Four years ago a personage, styling himself a writer, yclept Frank Monroe Beverley of Virginia—his name was the best thing about him, poor soul—wrote to me, saying he had read a poem of mine—"Rain In The Woods"—in a magazine and asking me to correspond for mutual advantage in our literary career. I assented quite eagerly for I had no such friends or any chance of making any. But I soon found that although F.M.B. might call himself a writer nobody else would. He couldn't write *at all*, desperately as he tried. His letters were nonentities—neither helpful, interesting or amusing. This correspondence dragged on for three years and then I simply dropped it. Before this, however, Mr. B. had "introduced" me to another "literary" correspondent of his, a Miss Miriam Zieber of Philadelphia. The name seemed formidable but I entered into the correspondence with vim and interest. Alas! Again I was disappointed. Miss Zieber could certainly be of no help to me in any way. Still, *her* letters were hugely amusing and I enjoyed the correspondence after a fashion. Miriam Zieber was a curious character, as unconsciously depicted in her letters. As a *personal* friend I fear she would be a nerve racking failure, so unbalanced in temperament, so exacting in emotional phases, was she. As an *im*personal correspondent however, she lent considerable spice to life and I rather regret that our correspondence has ceased. Miriam got married last June. What effect it had on her I can only surmise for I have never heard from her since.

Before this, however, she had in her turn, introduced me to two of her correspondents, one, Ephraim Weber, of Didsbury, Alta. and the other Geo. B. MacMillan of Alloa, Scotland.

I began my correspondence with Mr. Weber with but little enthusiasm, for my experiences with Mr. Beverley and the eccentric Miriam had sobered my young dreams. Moreover, I did not expect much from anyone who was so congenial to Miriam as she affirmed Mr. Weber to be—although she had never met him personally. From this can-any-good-thing-come-out-of-Nazareth attitude I was pleasantly aroused. Mr. Weber turned out to be an ideal correspondent. His letters are capital. The man himself I rather think is a dreamy, impractical somewhat *shiftless* person, hampered also by delicacy of health. But his intellect is unquestionable. His letters are cultured, thoughtful, stimulating epistles to which I look eagerly forward. They are written from a lonely Alberta ranch but they sparkle from beginning to end.

My other correspondent, Mr. MacMillan, a Scottish journalist, is also a success. He is not so academically clever as Mr. Weber but he makes a good second, and I think that, as a man, he is superior to the former. His land, too, lends him an added interest.

If I lived where I could meet with intellectually congenial friends I suppose these correspondences would not mean so much to me. But under my present limitations these unseen friends are of vital interest to me. In my letters to them I "let myself go"—writing freely from my soul, with no fear of being misunderstood or condemned—or worst of all, meeting with a blank wall of noncomprehension. Between these letters and my journal I manage to keep my intellectual life tolerably wholesome. If I could not "write out" freely certain words, opinions and fancies they would remain bottled up in my soul and would probably ferment and sour and cause some acute disturbance.

85. Twilight of a stormy day
[*Cavendish*]

86. Nora Lefurgey
[*Picture-taking at the Cavendish shore*]

87. *Miss Zieber*

88. *E. Weber*
[*Ephraim Weber*]

A Yule-Tide Wish.

G reetings, friend, this festal day,
E very joy be thine for aye,
O ver hills and valleys wide
R ing the bells of Christmas-tide.
G oodwill to men their theme, and every chime
E choes the burden of that song sublime. •

B ethlehem's spell this day has come
O ver world-wide Christendom.
Y oung and old, with one accord
D eem Christ worthy, own Him Lord.

M ay we, then, with hearts aglow,
A t His cradle bending low,
C ome with gifts, as did of old
M agi from the Chaldean wold.
I n our hearts prepare His throne,
L earn from Him, and Him alone.
L ife will then become sublime.
A n eternal, bright and vernal,
N ever-ending Christmas time.

34 Castle Street,
Alloa.   Christmas, 1903.

89. *G.B. MacMillan*

1905

Monday, Jan. 2, 1905
Cavendish, P.E.I.
This evening, reading over a packet of old letters, I came across a very old one written to my mother in her girlhood by a girl friend. I found it a few years ago in a box of old letters and have kept it among my treasures ever since. It gives me such a delightful *realization* of my mother—that girlish letter full of old jests and allusions at whose meaning I can only guess.

It is a dreadful thing to lose one's mother in childhood! I know that from bitter experience. How often, when smarting under some injustice or writhing under some misunderstanding, have I sobbed to myself, "Oh, if mother had *only* lived!"

But quick on the heels of that wish always came the instinctive thought, "But oh, if she were like Aunt Emily, or even like Aunt Annie, that would only make it worse". Even in childhood I realized that *that* would have been for me a worse tragedy than her death.

Aunt Annie is a woman I have always loved. She is kind, jolly, and good-hearted. But she is otherwise merely a practical soul—grandmother without grandmother's narrowness of mind and intolerance. She is a capital *aunt*; but as my *mother* she would have been a failure.

As for Aunt Emily, I have never cared for her. She jars on me in every fibre; she has no intellectual qualities; she is unsympathetic, fault-finding, nagging and "touchy". I can never forgive her for the sneers and slurs she used to cast upon my childish ambitions and my childish faults.

This fall in town I spent an evening with a Mrs. Campbell *nee* Eliza Macneill, a second cousin and girlhood friend of my mother's. She told me that my mother did not resemble Aunt Annie or Aunt Emily in the slightest respect physically, mentally, or emotionally. She assured me that if mother had lived I would have found in her all that I could wish in a mother—she spoke of her as a beautiful, spiritual, poetical girl full of fine emotions and noble impulses. I cannot express how glad I was to hear this. It seemed to me that Mrs. Campbell had given me a talisman to make life beautiful. There was now no hindrance to the wish that went out from my heart for my mother. *She* would have understood—*she* would have sympathized.

The older I grow the more I realize what a starved childhood mine was *emotionally*. I was brought up by two old people, neither of whom at their best were ever very sympathetic and who had already grown into set, intolerant ways. They seemed to cherish and act upon the contradictory opinions that a child of ten or a girl of fifteen was as old as themselves and as young as a baby—that is, she should have no wish or taste that they did not have, and yet she should have no more right to an independent existence than an infant. Grandfather Macneill, in all the years I knew him, was a stern, domineering, irritable man. I was always afraid of him. He bruised my childish feelings in every possible way and inflicted on my girlish pride humiliations whose scars are branded into my very soul and which were not at all atoned for by his rare and spasmodic freaks of arbitrary and often embarrassing kindness—embarrassing because it nearly always conflicted with and overturned little arrangements which I, never expecting him to concern himself about me, had already made.

I seemed to myself in those years to be alone, with all the world—*my* world—against me. My childish faults and short comings—of which I had plenty—were all detailed to the Macneill uncles and aunts whenever they came to the house. I resented this more bitterly than anything else. Other children's faults were not exploited by their parents in family conclave. Why then should mine be? Again, these aforesaid uncles and aunts arrogated the right to reprove and scold me at their own will and pleasure, as they would never have dared to do had I had parents to resent it. I had a remarkably keen sense of justice even then. I acknowledged the right of grandfather and grandmother to correct me but I felt no such right in the others and my revolt against it did not heighten me in their good opinion at all. I thought then—and I think still, for that matter—that they would better have devoted their reforming energies to their own children. Judging by the way some of them have turned out they must have needed it quite as much as I did.

As for grandmother she was very kind to me in a material way. I was well-cared for, well-fed, and well-dressed—and I may also add that these benefits were unfailingly cast up to me whenever I showed any rebellion. But nature never made two people more dissimilar in every respect essential to mutual comfort. I was impulsive, warm-hearted, emotional; grandmother was cold and reserved, narrow in her affections and sensibilities. When two such people are compelled to live under one roof one of them must invariably be uncomfortable and that one is the dependent one. Grandmother was kind to me "in her own way". Her "way" was very often torture to me and I was constantly reproached with ingratitude and wickedness because in childhood, before I had learned any self-control or understanding of my position, I sometimes rebelled against "her" ways.

I would not, however, convey the impression that my childhood was actually unhappy. It was never as happy as childhood should be and as it easily might have been; and there *were* times when it was fiercely unhappy. But between these times I got on very well. It has always seemed to me, ever since I can remember, that, amid all the commonplaces of life, I was very near to a kingdom of ideal beauty. Between it and me hung only a thin veil. I could never draw it quite aside but sometimes a wind fluttered it and I seemed to catch a glimpse of the enchanting realm beyond—only a glimpse—but those glimpses have always made life worthwhile.

I had besides, then as now, two great refuges and consolations—the world of nature and the world of books. They kept life in my soul; they made me love my home because of my dreams and rambles and the deep joy and delight they gave me—because of the halo they threw over what was otherwise bare and savorless. To be sure, I never had an unhampered indulgence in them. I was always nagged about "reading too much" and scolded because I preferred stories to the "Peep of Day" series. Also, if I crept away for a solitary ramble in the woods or along a country lane, poor unwise grandmother, who never could understand in the slightest degree how anyone could find pleasure in what gave no pleasure to her, would conclude that I had sneaked off for some improper motive and would greet me on my return with remarks that made me hate living.

All this was not because she did not love me. She did and does; but her love has never had the slightest saving grace of understanding in it and so had no power to draw us together. Looking back now, calmly and reflectively, I unhesitatingly state that grandmother's method of dealing with my nature and temperament was the most unwise she could possibly have adopted.

Of late years I have learned, under the bitter compulsion of necessity, to be sufficient unto myself. I stay here with grandmother, because if I did not do so she could not remain in her old home and it would break her heart to leave it. I try to bear patiently with her in all things because I acknowledge the debt of care and shelter she bestowed upon me in childhood. But she makes my life hard in a score of petty ways and is quite incapable of understanding that she does so.

I well remember the *first* sorrow that came into my life. I could never forget its bitterness. I was nine years old. I had a little gray kitten, a playful, winsome little creature, which I loved with passionate intensity. It died one day of poison. I can never forget the agony I endured. At first I could *not* believe that my little pet was dead. When I realized it I almost went mad. I was beside myself with grief. It was my baptism of sorrow and I was submerged beneath the waters of Marah. I have never since laughed at my passionate sorrow over that little death. It was too real—and too symbolical. I had *learned what pain was*; my poor little heart was almost broken. If I had had a mother—a wise, tender mother—to take me in her arms and comfort me understandingly, not underrating the suffering through contempt of the cause, it would have been well for me. Instead, grandmother only said, sneeringly, "You'll have something to cry for some day", and left me to sob my soul out in loneliness over the poor gray body of my little pet. I grieved stormily all that day and more quietly for weeks afterwards. Sorrow found me a hard pupil, determinedly light-hearted and joyous, so she made her first lesson a severe one. It was the Alpha of life's pain and it was branded deep into my consciousness. I think I have spelled the alphabet nearly through since then. Oh, Sorrow, will I not soon have learned all your dreary primer? I have lost many dear things since that little gray kitten died; I have taken each successive loss a little more quietly, a little more restrainedly, until now the tears and cries are all inwardly at my heart. Will not the discipline soon be accomplished? Ah, perhaps sorrow knows that the self-control *is* only outward—that underneath it the capacity for passionate feeling is as strong and vivid and greedy as ever. And so the end is not yet.

Probably when grandfather and grandmother were young they were not as I have known them. But their children left them early in life and they remained alone together with no influence to prevent them from growing narrow and set and warped. Emotionally they grew old before their time, getting into a rut of feeling and living which suited them but was utterly unfitted to anyone who was yet growing in soul or body. It is a great misfortune for a child to be brought up by old people. The gap between youth and age is too wide to be bridged, save by those exceptional natures that do not grow old in heart.

Friday, Jan. 27, 1905
Cavendish, P.E.I.
We have had a terrible two days' storm—I would say the worst storm we ever had if I didn't know that every bad storm seems the worst by reason of the contrast its present badness offers to the badness of past ones grown dim. But I am quite within the mark in saying that the drifts *are* the worst we have ever had. They are as high as the house, hemming us in on all sides—"Alp on Alp". The rooms on the ground floor are as dark as twilight. The drifts are certainly very beautiful; but one does not care greatly for architectural beauty in a prison. We have had no mail for two days. When I look out on those huge white barriers I feel like screaming.

It is well I am used to dullness or the unutterable dreariness of these past two days would have mildewed my very soul. As it was I kept myself sane by working; a story was finished, a lot of typewriting done, a fancy collar made, and a book re-read that took me away from my snowy prison into a wonderful world.

Our front orchard is worth looking at—the very trees are coated with snow until it is like some fairy court of marble seen in a splendid dream. Tonight the weather cleared and there was a wonderful sunset of fiery rose and gold. When its light fell down through that orchard I forgave the storm. Nothing more lovely could be imagined.

Wednesday. (Is it Wednesday? Yes, it is)
Feb. 8, 1905
I did not have to sally out and shovel snow this morning after all—for the excellent reason that I could not get out. This morning the door and every window on the east side of the house was completely snowed over. I do not think the like of this storm has ever been seen on P.E. Island in the memory of living man. The storm has raged all day.

After breakfast I forced myself to finish writing an Easter story which a Sunday School paper lately ordered. (Item:—I *hate* writing stories to order!) Then I type-wrote until dinner time. After dinner more typewriting; then worked half an hour at a point lace centrepiece. Then, there being nothing more that had to be done I amused myself jotting down in a note book all the detachable epigrams in my books. They are easily discoverable as I have them all marked. I've always had the habit of marking my books. I do it now with a pencil. I was not so wise in my teens and used ink. Consequently, I cannot now erase the marks of passages and opinions I no longer agree with, and they stare me in the face as reminders of my sentimental "salad days".

After dark I wrote a letter, did fancy work and read. I am steeped in dullness. We can have no mail tomorrow. All this accumulation of ills beggars complaint. As the old Scotch emigrant said when he came home, found his house burned, and his entire family butchered by Indians, "This is perfectly ridiculous".

Thursday, Mar. 3, 1905
Cavendish, P.E.I.

It is no use—I *must* growl out my growl in this poor journal again tonight. I've just been having a bitter cry in the twilight and now I must work off the rest of my dark mood with my pen. This life is simply terrible!

The day after my last entry word came that George Campbell's baby had died of pneumonia. I went over to Park Corner the next day and remained for a fortnight. I am thankful I did for I think if I had been here I should have lost my reason. It was storm after storm. The trains were completely blocked. For *ten* days there was no mail. Then they began to *drive* the mail from the boats and from town and they are still doing this as no train can yet get through. Nothing like it has ever been known on the Island.

As I was at Park Corner I did not mind it so much. Stella and I kept ourselves amused. We got around and had a good time in spite of the storms. I came home last Sunday and have worried along so far in this dismal week without slumping. But all strength and courage seem to have gone out of me tonight. There has been no mail since Monday. I cannot even get out for a walk and the lack of all exercise and companionship makes me feel positively wretched, mentally and physically. I can't work *all* the time. I have nothing to read; and the long and short of it is I hate to wake up to another day every morning. I haven't the spirit for *anything*—even work is a drag.

I've been trying to get up a paper on Mrs. Browning to read before the Literary tomorrow night. My heart isn't in it—I don't care a hoot for Mrs. Browning—and it has dragged horribly. I hate the thought of going up there tomorrow night to read it. My whole being seems out of tune—nothing but jangling discords. This is only "nerves" of course; if ever this fearful blockade lifts I shall soon recover my normal poise. But just now I seem eaten up by an internal fire of restlessness and loneliness.

I have nothing to write about and yet I fear to stop. It seems to me I can only preserve an outward calm by writing, and that if I stop a choking fit of tears and sobs will come on. If I could only get away by myself and "cry it out" I would feel better but that I cannot do because the rooms are all too cold. I must not let grandma see me crying—it always seems to anger her. Grandmother is a curious woman. She always seems to resent bitterly anyone else not being perfectly happy in a life that suits her. Moreover, she also resents bitterly any independence in thought, taste, or wishes of those she lives with. In summer I can escape up to my own room and enjoy enough of freedom there to reconcile me to other evils but in winter I cannot do this.

I suppose grandmother cannot help it and I have resigned myself to it as to any other unavoidable ill. It is my duty to stay here and I do it willingly, but she makes it very hard for me in a hundred petty ways.

Just for example:—grandmother goes to bed at nine o'clock; everyone else must go at nine o'clock, too, whether they want to or not. Grandmother *never* takes a bath; it seems to drive her into a perfect frenzy of childish rage because, in winter when my room is too cold, I insist on staying up *once a fortnight* after she goes to bed, to take a bath in the warm kitchen. Grandmother is angry if I use any lamp but my own small and insufficient one to curl my hair and shows it in pitiful petulance. She will not permit me to have a fire in the room on the rare occasion when a friend comes to spend the afternoon—I must entertain her in the kitchen. Grandmother will not allow me to bake a cake if the smallest, stalest piece of an old one remains in the house. She resents it if I venture to sweep my bedroom oftener than she sweeps hers—and so on and so on in every detail of my life. I do try to bear this patiently but I am sick at heart.

Another thing, too, is grievous to me. I fear that this life I am living is unfitting me for any other life. I am being compelled to shape myself into habits that will—or may—hold me prisoner when the necessity for them is removed. I shall, I fear, be unable to adapt myself then to any other existence. I know, too, that although my present life is anything but a happy or satisfactory one, it is likely to be still less so when changes come. This thought often rebukes me when I feel discontented with my present conditions. Yet the fact that a pain is going to be worse in its later stages than in its earlier does not much help one to bear the earlier—rather makes it harder indeed. Even so, I could bear all the hard things in my life now if I could look for something better beyond. But it is all dark and uncertain.

Oh, you poor pessimist, writing in this strain because you can't write in any other just now and yet afraid to stop lest this pain that is gripping your soul break out in tears! Cheer up—do! Spring will come and then you will be cheery and hopeful again and life will seem pleasant enough to be quite worth while in spite of all its pin-pricks.

Saturday, Mar. 11, 1905
Cavendish, P.E.I.
No, I'm not going to grumble tonight—even though it is stormy and we have had no mail. In spite of this I feel quite contented and cheerful. The blue fit has passed and I am interested in things once more.

The next night after my dismal entry I went to the Literary and read my paper. The thought of it bored me all day; nevertheless when evening came I put on a cream silk blouse, did my hair elaborately, and betook myself to the hall. In the end I rather enjoyed the affair although the whole business was really time and gray matter wasted. That Literary is a very dull affair nowadays. I only hold to it for the sake of the new books we get. We have about thirty new ones coming if *ever* the ice blockade lifts in the Strait. When they do come I'm going on a jamboree.

Thursday, Mar. 23, 1905
Cavendish, P.E.I.
We have had a thaw—a really, truly thaw. Oh, the joy of it! I think even the hearts half a century dead over there in the graveyard must have throbbed in unison with the beating of the great heart of spring. There are bare spots in the fields—they are not so beautiful as the white drifts but oh, so dear to see for their promise. I feel like a prisoner released. There are mountains of snow yet—but spring is coming. I could clap my hands for joy—I *did* clap them tonight up on the hill and laughed

aloud for sheer gladness of heart. All at once life seemed beautiful again. I felt as if I could run, dance, sing with delight, like a child.

Sunday, Mar. 26, 1905
Cavendish, P.E.I.
This has certainly been a rather dreary day—rain and fog, and no service. But I did not really mind its dullness because it means spring. I could put up with anything that means that. I ventured out tonight in defiance of fog and slush for a walk around the square. The old mill-bridge hollow is a sight—the water is over the tops of the fences. This means no mail tomorrow—but never mind, it also means spring.

I've read all day. One story in a magazine brought vividly back an odd fancy of my early childhood. The story was of a lonely little girl who lived with two grim aunts; having no real companion she evolved one from fancy. This companion, whom she called *Elizabeth* "lived" in a grove on the hill, and the child shocked her unimaginative aunts by persistently retailing "lies" to them concerning her talks and adventures with *Elizabeth*.

In our sitting room there has always been a big bookcase used as a china cabinet. In each door is a large, oval glass, dimly reflecting the room. When I was very small each of my reflections in these glass doors were "real folks" to my imagination. The one in the left-hand door was *Katie Maurice*, the one in the right-hand *Lucy Gray*. Why I named them thus I cannot say. Wordsworth's ballad had no connection with the latter, because at that time I had never read it or heard of it. Indeed, I have no recollection of deliberately naming them at all. As far back as consciousness runs *Katie Maurice* and *Lucy Gray* lived in the fairy room behind the bookcase. *Katie* was a little girl like myself and I loved her dearly. I would stand before that door and prattle to her for hours, giving and receiving confidences. In especial, I liked to do this at twilight when the fire had been lighted for the evening, and the room and its reflections were a glamor of light and shadow.

Lucy Gray was grown-up—and a *widow*! I did not like her as well as Katie. She was always sad and always had dismal stories of her troubles to relate to me; nevertheless, I always visited her scrupulously in turn, lest her feelings should be hurt, because she was jealous of *Katie*, who also disliked her. All this sounds like the veriest nonsense, but I cannot describe how real it was to me. I never passed through the room without a wave of my hand to *Kate* in the glass door at the other end.

Monday, May 20, 1905
Cavendish, P.E.I.
....The long-delayed library books arrived about a fortnight ago, also a few I had sent for for myself. I broke all decent bounds and read day and night.

I bought Kipling's "Jungle Books" this spring. They are glorious. I'm sorry I couldn't have had them when I was a child. But the next best thing is to have them when grown up. I also bought and re-read "Pickwick Papers" and "David Copperfield". I first read the immortal "Papers" when a child—there was an old racked, coverless copy lying around the house and I revelled in it. I remember that it was a book that always made me *hungry*—there was so much "good eating" in it, and the folks were always celebrating with ham and eggs and "milk punch". I generally went on a cupboard rummage after I had been reading "Pickwick" for a little while.

I brought home a library book the other night—"Elizabeth and her German Garden"—taking it as Hobson's choice because I couldn't get anything else. I didn't know anything about it, didn't think it was worth much, and made no haste to read it. Finally last Thursday I began it. Before I had read a chapter I was ready to kick myself for not having found out what it was before.

It was delightful—the whole book. My "twin soul" must live in *Elizabeth*—at least, as far as gardening is concerned. She has said a hundred things that I always meant to say when I had thought them out sufficiently. I shan't have to say them now—*Elizabeth* has done it so well.

I escaped to Lover's Lane as soon as I could. I hadn't been able to get to it since December until May 5th. It was like a new birth to find myself in it once more—I don't know what I'm ever going to do without that lane in heaven!

I have moved upstairs again—which means that I have begun to *live* again. It seems odd that such a thing can be brought about by simply changing rooms! But it is so. To me it means the difference between happiness and unhappiness. I almost live up here—what time I don't live in my garden. It is such a pleasant life I thus shape for myself that I am almost contented in it.

July 30, 1905, Sunday Evening
Cavendish, P.E.I.
Over two months' silence! Not a grumble! Not a "blue"! What does this mean? Well, this has been a pretty good summer—I've been less worried than usual and I feel quite happy and cheerful. But it does seem a pity to fill this journal up all winter with moans and groans and not put in a single bit of the summer pleasantness.

For one thing we are alone this summer. Uncle Leander's family did not come over—and that means a great deal to me! I write and read and ramble and dream and revel in my garden—and life is so pleasant and peaceful that it actually frightens me. I feel that it *can't* last—that it is the calm before a storm.

My garden—oh, the delight it has been to me this summer! I am positively revelling in flowers. Roses—such roses! My big bush of blush doubles, which never did anything before, flung all its hoarded sweetness of three years into bloom—dozens of the most lovely blossoms. There is a big vaseful on my table before me now. And behind me are other vases full of the sweetest of sweet peas and yellow poppies, and nasturtiums like breaths of flame. It is the greatest pleasure my days bring me to go out to my garden every morning and see what new blossoms have opened overnight. At such moments my heart fairly bursts with its gladness. Oh, what a wise old myth it was that placed the creation of life in a garden. Oh, you dear pink rose, here is a kiss for you! I think that long ago in heaven you and I were sister spirits. You were born a rose and I a woman. You are the happier, perhaps. But yet I'm glad to be a woman with a garden and a work and a sorrow. Three blessings—ay, three blessings all!

I must try to write oftener in this journal this summer because I'm sure to be grumbling next winter again and I don't want this dear old journal, which I love as if it were a living friend, to be *all* grumbles.

This afternoon I was looking over an old scrapbook made years ago when I was going to school and college. I had many a laugh over it—and many a sigh! It seemed to hold the jests and merriment of those old days. Selena Robinson, who was teaching here when I began it, made one at the same time and we collected "screwveneers" for those scrapbooks with zeal and diligence. On the first page of mine is a tiny shoe-buckle which once adorned one of Selena's slippers and which she gave me for a mascot for my scrapbook because it was in the shape of a horse-shoe. Underneath it is a little fancy calendar which Will P. sent me the year I was at P.W.C.

Here's another calendar which "Aileck" of "Hotel de MacMillan" fame gave me one day. Poor "Aileck", I wonder what has become of him. What fun Mary C. and I used to have over him. But then, was there *anything* in those times that Mary C. and I did *not* have fun over!

A page or so is given to time-tables and pass lists of my entrance exam. What a lot of heart-throbs they stand for! I don't believe I could pass that exam now—but—well—I could pass some others.

There are any number of fancy "cards" in the book. These cards, where the name of the owner was concealed under a gorgeous cluster of flowers held in a slender hand cut off at the wrist, were a beloved fad of our schooldays. Anybody who at all aspired to be fashionable sent for a packet of these cards and exchanged them with her mates. Nowadays "picture postals" have usurped their place. "Other times, other fads".

Here is a programme of my first opera. Hedley Buntain's sharp, prim little face rises up before me, also that frantic *fiancee* of his who came to town in such hot haste because she heard I was "cutting her out" with Hedley. I was entirely innocent of the deed or wish. But I daresay Hedley needed looking after for he slipped through her fingers after all and married some other girl.

A piece of wood chipped from my desk in Dr. A's room—what a Vandal I was!—is cheek by jowl with a card of Mr. Mustard's—a *bona fide* visiting card, for Mr. M. was never guilty of anything so frivolous as a "fancy card" of course—and a piece of one of Laura P's ball-dresses. A burned-out match—relic of some frolic of Mary C's and mine—is next to the account of Florrie Murchison's wedding.

Here's a splinter from the famous old lamp-post on Prince St. and next to it a bit of the fringe of a cream-colored shawl I wore the very first night I ever had an escort home. No girl ever forgets *that* momentous occasion—at least no country girl. I stepped over the threshold of young ladyhood that night. Cream-colored shawls—or "squares" as they were called, were "all the rage" that fall. Every girl had one or wished she had. When new and soft and fluffy they were very pretty and becoming.

"Prince of Wales College Commencement Programme", with a scrap of red and blue college ribbon fastened thereto! I read an essay that night—which a kindly reporter, glory be to his memory, puffed fulsomely in the next morning's daily. Here is my name, and here are the faded flowers I wore that night. And then a "License" time-table! Up come all the faces of those "examinees"—Mary C. here—Ida over there—Nellie McGrath in front of me—Fannie Wise at the right—Nell Rodgerson yonder. Pshaw! Nell had her *fourth* baby christened the other day—named after me! That puts the license exam very far back!

Here are a squirrel's tail, a four-leaved clover and a piece of McGill ribbon. Surely there's no lack of variety. And "Firefly's" fur—*Firefly* of old Prince Albert days. Any more cats? Bless you, yes—"Coco's", "Carissima's", "Max's", "Mephistopheles"', "Tom's", "Lady Katherine's", "Topsy's"—a whole host of dead and gone pussies of whom only these scraps of fur remain.

What is this? A piece of ornamentation—a woollen rose, to be exact—taken from a sofa cushion. Yes, I was sitting on that cushion the night Lem McLeod proposed to me at Park Corner!! Lem is out west now—a spruce business man with the beginning of a bald spot. He was married last winter to Maggie Sellars of Ch'Town. Of course she knows nothing of that memento in my scrapbook—nor of another further on, a piece of poetry Lem once sent me in a letter. He didn't write it himself of course—Lem was never guilty of writing poetry or of reading it either, for that matter—but he clipped it out of a paper and sent it with a "them's-my-sentiments-too" letter. It's very sentimental.

....A time-table of Bideford School—did *I* ever make out such a fiercely tabulated document with every minute accounted for—and the address my Bideford pupils gave me when I left.

Ladies' College ribbon—Halifax looms up now. And oh, yes, more poetry! Lou Dystant eclipsed Lem in sending poetry in his letters. Lou's taste in verse was fearfully sentimental and he underlined like a school miss. Here is one gem:

> "She was so small—
> A wee, pure bud from God's own garden lent
> To fill my life with one bright dream of joy."

Did Lou really consider me "a wee, pure bud?" How Bertha Clark and I used to scream over those frantic clippings!

An old-time fashion plate with big sleeves! The big puffed sleeves are in again now. When I put on a new dress the other day with big sleeves it gave me the oddest sense of being a Dalhousie girl again—for that was the year they came to their fullest balloon-like inflation, stiffened out with "fibre-chamois" etc. "Stuff me in" was an inelegant phrase constantly heard when one girl wanted another to poke the huge sleeves of her dress into the sleeves of her coat.

Friday, Aug. 11, 1905
Cavendish, P.E.I.

I have been re-reading *Eugene Aram*. I read it for the first time when I was fifteen and never since. Nate read it at the same time and we were both enraptured with it—we were Lytton-crazy at that romantic period. I remember us both sitting down under the firs on the school hill discussing that book, and it is inseparably connected with those firs and Nate's memory ever since. One of Nate's letters the other night, in which he wrote about the book, aroused in me a wish to read it again.

I found that I still liked it—though not with the frantic adoration of fifteen. Much of what I admired then seems strained and florid now. But I think the book is written in a purer style than most of Lytton's and with all its faults there is something in it that holds the interest. It is very sad—perhaps that was why I liked it so well long ago; youth revels in sadness—and leaves a certain haunting impression like a cadence of dying minor music. Nate was fascinated with the character of Aram. I wonder if it is still his ideal. It is not in the least likely. Our ideals change as we grow older—change and, alas, *lower*! We are driven to compromise with the insistent *Real*.

October 1, 1905
Cavendish, P.E.I.
The summer is over! How I shrink from facing that fact! I look forward to the winter with inexpressible dread!

I am half sick now with anxiety and worry and have been so for the past two months. Uncle John and Prescott have been using grandmother shamefully all summer. In short, they have been trying to turn her out. Prescott, forsooth, wants to get married and get this house to live in! Grandmother is nearly broken-hearted and I have had a terrible time with her. Grandfather's absurd will put her completely in their power—the power of selfish, domineering men eaten up with greed. Grandmother told them she would *not* leave the home where she had lived and worked for sixty years and since then Uncle John has never spoken to her, or visited her, and all the mean, petty spite they have shown in a score of ways would be unbelievable.

What the outcome will be I do not know. For my own part I care little. It is on grandmother's account I worry. It will, of course, hurt me deeply to leave this old home which I have always loved so passionately even in years when I have been far from happy in it. But I have known, ever since grandfather's death, that the time would come when I would have to leave it, and the reality can scarcely be much worse than the long anticipation has been. Indeed, I believe that, were the final wrench over, it would be a relief not to have such a sword of Damocles hanging over my head any longer.

Uncle John and his brood detest me because I have been the stumbling block all along in their scheme of ousting grandmother from her home. If I had not been here she could not have stayed here alone and they know it and hate me because of it. I shall never forget and I feel I can never forgive the way they have used me ever since grandfather died. They have shown their petty spite and jealousy in a thousand ways. Uncle John is a man whom, from my earliest recollection, I have disliked. When I was a child I feared him unspeakably. He never spoke a kind word to me. He was a domineering, insulting, unjust, bad-tempered man, without one spark of consideration for the rights and feelings of other people. When I grew up he had to treat me civilly for, like all bullies, he only bullied those who were too weak to defend themselves. I ceased to fear him but I have never ceased to dislike him. My success in literature has further embittered him against me. His family are brainless—and he knows it and hates me because of it. However, I care nothing how they regard me. It is only on grandmother's account I am worried.

Oct. 15, 1905, Sunday Evening
Cavendish, P.E.I.
....Frede Campbell spent last Saturday and Sunday here and was an unspeakable comfort to me. I had been so lonely and sad-hearted but felt so much better for her visit. I am not naturally a blue or melancholy person but I do not think even *Mark Tapley* himself could keep his spirits up under my present circumstances....

Friday, Nov. 24, 1905
I'm sleepy. Last night there was a party at Wedlocks' in Stanley and I was invited. Jim Simpson took me up. It's no difference who Jim is or how he came to take me. He's *nil*. And I was bored to death.

I had a chat with Frede which made the evening worth while to me. I didn't know many of the guests and wished I knew fewer for I had to talk to those I did know and they were sinfully uninteresting. How *can* people live in such an interesting world and be such bores?

The Wedlocks evidently thought the supper they served would delight people. It was very lavish. If the table didn't "groan" it should have. There was so much piled on it that one couldn't decide what to eat before the time was up. My right-hand neighbor was a man who made "funny" speeches all through the meal and kept me wondering for what good purpose God had ever fashioned him. I would like to have a house of my own just to see if I couldn't set a table as it should be done and bring together some people who could talk and be interesting.

But then there isn't the least likelihood I ever shall have a house of my own. I suppose, when grandmother has gone, I shall migrate to Ch'Town or some similar burg, get a cheap boarding place, and write pot-boilers for a living. A pleasant outlook, truly! But I suppose it's better than charity or the poorhouse and so, thanks be!

Sunday, Dec. 10, 1905
A big snowstorm! Dear me, I suppose this is the beginning of sorrows. How I hate the winter! And yet how I might love it, the wonderful white thing under other conditions! I used to love the winter as I loved all the seasons. Will I ever love it again I wonder?

I've been quite busy these past three weeks. Bertha McKenzie is to be married on Christmas day and I am to be her bridesmaid. So I'm having a little pleasure for a change. But today I can only look at the dismal side of things. I'm not feeling well and all the world is one thick, blind whirl of snow.

My 'mums are still blooming but are beginning to fade. I shall miss them like human friends when they are done. But I have some hyacinth and narcissi poking their dear heads up in window boxes and I have great hopes of them by and by.

Later On.
I feel better. Fancy why? Because it is raining out now and it will stop the drift and I shall not have to turn out and shovel snow in the morning.

When I've nothing new to read I generally go prowling in an old trunkful of books upstairs. My best books I keep in a little bookcase in my room; but the

312

aforesaid old trunk is full of school and college books, paper covered novels etc. I came across a book tonight—*The Safe Compass*—and brought it down for old associations.

That book was a classic of my childhood. It had belonged to my mother and her name was written on the fly-leaf. It was very religious; but it was also interesting and consequently a great stand-by for Sundays. The frontispiece had a gruesome fascination for me. It was the picture of a boy lying under a tree, with the legend, "His neck was broken and there lay the young Sabbath breaker *dead*." The heinous crime which the defunct had committed was climbing a tree to eat some cherries on Sunday!

The book had the faults of its class but its virtues were its own. Probably it helped to form what good there is in my character—although I'm afraid I'd eat cherries on a Sunday even yet! I must keep that little red book forever. The child I was haunts every page and story of it. I remember what a fascination the chapter on "garden" had for me. The "garden" was the "heart" and I used to struggle desperately—by fits and starts, after I had been reading the book—to root up the "weeds" of temper, selfishness etc. and plant the "flowers" of all the virtues instead. I wonder if it really did me any good—any lasting good, at least.

Dec. 24, 1905, Sunday night
Cavendish, P.E. Island
To-morrow is Christmas and Bertha's wedding day. I am sitting here with my hair tortured up into a dozen or so braids and "kids" so that it may be properly fluffy and fashionable tomorrow. May my hair be naturally curly in my next incarnation!

My bridesmaid dress is lying in chilly state on the spare room bed; it is a sweet thing of flowered silk organdy, all frills and puffs and laces, looking somewhat unseasonable in a world of snow and frost; and my bouquet of white carnations and white hyacinth and asparagus fern—which latter, in spite of its kitchen-gardeny name looks like the soul of a fern—is in a vase on the sitting room table. It came yesterday and reconciles me to much I dislike in the fuss and details of this marrying and giving in marriage.

Weddings seem, for the most part, to be rather vulgar things, stifled in a dust of sweeping and scrubbing and baking and borrowing, with all the various harrassments thereof. The beauty they should stand for seems wholly lost sight of.

I know how I would like to be married—and never will be, for even supposing I should ever marry I should have to conform to the conventionalities. But that doesn't prevent me from having an ideal of what a wedding should be, and—if I lived in an ideal world—this would be mine.

In the morning—a June morning when a glorious sunrise should be blossoming over the silvery east and the roses in gardens and wilding lanes should be as sweet as roses could be—I would rise early and dress—dress *for* the one man in all the world and for the eyes of no other and make me as fair as might be for his delight; and then in the expectant hush of dawn I would go down to meet him, unknown of any others and together we would go to the heart of some great wood where the arches were as some vast cathedral aisle and the wind of the morning itself sang our bridal hymn; and there we should pledge to each other a love that should last for all time and all eternity. Then we would turn, hand in hand, back to the busy world that would forevermore be glorified because of our life together!

Well, there's my *ideal*. But the *Real* is quite another thing!

Only—I *swear* that *if* I ever do marry I will *not* be married under an "arch" of tortured spruce boughs, decorated with pink and white tissue paper "roses" and looking like nothing that God ever thought about! If I were to outrage my ideal as flagrantly as *that* I should be looking ahead to the divorce court while the minister was reading the marriage service!!!

Yesterday, Friday, and Wednesday I spent with Bertha, mixing and icing cakes, making candy, sweeping, dusting, decorating. These things made me physically tired; but what wearied me mentally and robbed life of all its "bouquet" was having to talk to Bertha's two brothers, Bob and Milton. Milton is a cub and a bore, and does more than anything I've ever read or seen to make me disbelieve in the existence of a soul. Bob is a decent enough fellow but he, too, is a hopeless bore. I can tolerate him along the lines of acquaintanceship but when he inflicts his unwelcome attentions on me—the nauseating attentions of a country *clod*—I feel as if I were being spiritually smothered. Yet I have to be civil to him on Bertha's account—and even on my own, since he is one of the few folks I can depend on to take me anywhere I have to go. I loathe these necessary makeshifts and the galling dependence they imply. But in this world of material facts such things have to be reckoned with.

Tuesday Evening
Dec. 26, 1905
Cavendish, P.E. Island

It is all over and I have just arrived home feeling that the greatest blessing life can offer is a warm bed and a good sleep!

Yesterday was quite the merriest Christmas I have ever spent. I went down to Bertha's in the morning and must say I enjoyed everything to the full. The ceremony was at twelve and then we had dinner and a very jolly afternoon. At three we—Bertha and Will, and Bob and I—left for *Ebenezer*. Ebenezer is the name of the place where Will lives, but that is his misfortune not his fault! As the day was fine and the roads good we enjoyed our drive very much. When we got there, however, the fun was over. There was a reception that night and as I didn't know the people—or want to know them—I was bored to death. The only fun of the evening was a drunken fiddler. It sounds rather awful; but he *was* drunk and he *was* funny. At two o'clock I went to bed, so tired that I couldn't sleep. Everybody seemed dragged out the next day. Bob and I came home this afternoon.

Well, it's been pleasant, getting all this up. I daresay I'll be lonely for awhile—and, what is worse, have time to worry again! Oh, how sick I am of worry. It is the hardest thing in the world to endure. I've had so much of it here since grandfather died that my strength to bear it seems getting frayed out.

90. *Aunt Annie Campbell*

91. *Aunt Emily Montgomery*

92. *Grandfather Macneill*
[*Alexander Marquis Macneill*]

93. *Grandmother Macneill*
[*Lucy Woolner Macneill*]

94. Sitting room with bookcase
[*Cavendish*]

1906

Monday, Jan. 1, 1906
Cavendish, P.E. Island

A lovely New Year's day. But I do feel so sad to-night. I was over to New Glasgow to-day with Russell Macneill to see Pensie. Poor Pensie is dying of consumption and I do not know when I have made a more sorrowful visit.

It is wonderful how old ties formed in childhood hold. They may grow so slack and be so overlaid with newer interests and affections that you forget their existence. But suddenly some wrench reveals it. Pensie and I have seen very little of each other since her marriage because she lived too far away for frequent meetings. But now when she is ill our old friendship revives. How we talked today of our childish games and schooldays. We were so often together then and had such jolly times.

We are on the threshold of the New Year. Oh, I wonder what it will bring me! I only ask release from worry—I would be content with that.

I feel tired and lonely and discouraged. Patience, sad heart. There is eternity. This life is only a cloudy day in what may be a succession of varied lives.

Thursday, Jan. 26, 1906

This past week has been a gayer one socially than often falls to my lot. Annie Stewart is home for a visit and last Saturday evening George R. and I were invited up for a game of whist. We had it and it was very enjoyable. Then we had a "seance" and made a table rap. Of course this was lots of fun. But it is a curious thing and a little uncanny, give it what scientific "explanation" you please.

Monday evening Mrs. J.R. Stewart gave a "goose supper" to the members of the Literary Programme Committee. Both the ministers, Messrs. Belyea and Macdonald, were there and we had another table rapping. We made the thing do various stunts, such as standing up on one leg, walking round the room etc.

Last night there was a dance at J.R. Stewart's and I took it in also. Had a very nice time. That is, as nice as I can ever have nowadays with my subconsciousness of worry grumbling away under everything else, like a partially disregarded aching tooth.

Saturday, Feb. 3, 1906
Cavendish, P.E.I.

Yesterday I spent the afternoon with the Belyeas in the Parsonage. Mr. and Mrs. Belyea are both very nice and particular friends of mine. I borrowed a much talked-of book from Mr. Belyea—"The Law of Psychic Phenomena"—I began it at ten o'clock last night upstairs in bed and found it so fascinating that I read until one and then only stopped because I was too cold to go on. Today I finished it. It is a wonderful book and I am intensely interested in some of its theories and conclusions....

Saturday, March 6, 1906

This evening was lovely and Wilbur Clark and I went up to Stanley to visit Wedlocks. I sometimes wonder what I would have done if Darnley Clark had not had a family of boys!!! They have all been so kind to me and they are nice brotherly chums, always ready to do a good turn, with no nonsense of sentiment in the matter.

I saw Frede and had a little confidential talk which did me more good than I can express. These little occasional outpourings to a trusty and understanding friend are veritable safety valves for my intense nature and keep my worries from moth-eating my soul. There is no one in Cavendish to whom I can turn for advice or assistance. I cannot bear to expose the seamy side of my life to the gaze of any outsider. To all here I preserve the same unbroken front of smile and jest and composure. But *some* outlet I must have and between Frede and my journal I continue to muddle along quite respectably. But oh, life is such a starved, ugly thing when, if I possessed even the average measure of freedom, I could make it a rich beautiful thing. I *know* I could; it is in me.

Thursday, April 5, 1906

I feel rather too seedy to amount to anything to-day after the party at Joe Stewart's last night. Wellington MacCoubrey was there. He has been living in Sydney for three years and he told me some news about Nate who was practising law down there during the same time.

Nate, as I saw by the papers some time ago, is *married*. Actually! He married a Miss Mabel Saunders of Wolfville and immediately thereafter left for Sydney to practice his profession there. His many friends etc. etc.

Wellington M. told me two things about Nate that amazed me. One is that he is *very gray*. Nate *gray*!!! What an idea! Why, wasn't it only the other day that he was a curly-headed schoolboy? What business has he to be getting gray? Nate! *Gray*? The other thing was still more surprising. Wellington said Nate had not done much in Sydney, that he seemed "such a dull fellow without a spark of life or ambition". This amazed me. Nate, who used to be simply full of life and ambition and energy! Is it possible he can have changed so? It does *not* seem possible. I know he had a long and hard struggle to get through college. Perhaps it was *too* long and hard and ate up all his supply of energy and pluck. I should certainly have thought Nate just the man to succeed in law.

Poor Nate, I hope he is happy and that he has a nice little wife. Wonder what he said when she asked him if he had ever loved anyone before her—for of course she *would* ask him. But I daresay he had loved a dozen—*I* was only the first; and I daresay he would assure her he had never *loved* anyone; and I daresay again that he would honestly think he was telling the truth—which is all as it should be! World without end! Amen!

But—Nate—is—gray! Verily, the next thing that I will hear about him will be that he is a grandfather!

Tuesday, April 18, 1906
Cavendish, P.E.I.

....I don't think Prescott will try to meddle with grandmother for awhile at any rate. He is very ill—has been ill all winter—and looks ghastly. I believe his doctor is afraid of some variety of tuberculosis. It is hard to feel sorry for him after the way he has acted. It is almost enough to make one believe that there *are* such things as "judgments".

Sunday Evening
May 13, 1906

Why am I writing in this diary tonight? This is not a conundrum. I really know of no reason why I should be, except that I am blue and lonely and worried. And *that* is too commom a state now with me to be worth writing about....

Sunday Evening
October 7, 1906
Cavendish, P.E.I.

Never a word since last May! Well, I've been too busy most of the time. Now, in the moon of falling leaves there are long evenings when I have some spare time. This evening it is too windy to go up to the Baptist church as I had planned so I'll pick up my dropped threads. Yet there really isn't a great deal to write.

The summer is over. It has been for the most part a pleasant one with fewer worries than last year. I look forward to the winter with no pleasurable anticipations. It promises to be a lonely one.

I have not roamed much abroad this summer. In June I had a brief but very enjoyable trip to town. I went in one day and out the next. As Bertie and I had only one night to talk we made the most of it. We never went to bed at all—just sat up and talked. How I wish it were possible to see her oftener.

A month ago I drove over to Park Corner one Sunday morning and back again in the evening. I had not been over for a year and a half and I was overjoyed to see the dear old spot again.

Uncle Leander, Aunt May and Kennedy spent five weeks here in July and August. Their sojourn was not as disagreeable as it was the last time. Uncle L. has found a drug which alleviates his trouble and consequently his temper. Aunt Mary and I had lots of fun bathing and visiting together. I was rather sorry to see them go. Uncle John and his family never dare to show their meannesses quite so blatantly when they are here.

One afternoon in August we had a picnic on the manse grounds. While I was crossing them on an errand I met Edwin Simpson!

Well, there is not much to say about it. All at once, I found it did not matter. I simply felt utter indifference. There was no pleasure in meeting him and as a mere matter of preference I would rather not. But all the old shame and humiliation and restraint were gone. The past was—at last—dead.

I stood and talked for an hour to him before all the crowd and didn't mind it in the least—that is, as far as onlookers were concerned. In one way I *did* mind it for, to confess the whole truth, I was *bored*. But I couldn't escape so I stood first on one foot and then on the other and listened perforce. I should not have said that *I* talked to *him*. It was entirely the other way round—*he* talked to *me*. He evidently was bent on showing me while he had a chance how vastly much he had crammed into his head during the past eight years. His whole personality seemed to exhale as a breath, "See what you've lost, young lady!" Meanwhile, in the back of my head I was saying "Thank God, I've escaped this man. Why, in a week he would have me talked to death."

He is as good-looking, as clever, as conceited, as superficial as ever. He is pastor of a city church in Illinois and from one standpoint he is a successful man. But nobody seems to like him and he talks entirely too much about himself—what *he* has said, thought, done, etc. He spent Monday afternoon here and took tea with us. He left Cavendish next day and that was the end of it. Poor Ed, what a pity he is so conceited! But I daresay it makes him very comfortable!

Friday, Oct. 12, 1906
Cavendish, P.E. Island
This afternoon Ewan Macdonald called to say good-bye before leaving for Scotland, where he intends studying for the winter at Glasgow University. And I am sitting here with his little diamond solitaire on my left hand!

Yes, it is a surprising thing. And I think nobody could be more surprised at it than I am myself. I wonder if I can analyze clearly the events and motives that have led up to it.

Three years ago, our congregation called Ewan Macdonald as its minister and he was inducted in September 1903. He had preached here in the preceding spring, just after his graduation from Pine Hill, and made a very favorable impression. He was an Island man and belonged down east near Valleyfield. His people were Highland Scotch and although he was Canadian born he had a pronounced but not unpleasing Scotch, or rather Gaelic, accent. He was considered a handsome man by many but I should rather call him fine-looking. He is of medium height, with a good but somewhat stiff figure which is erect and dignified now, but may become "paunchy" in later life. He has thick black hair, black, roguish eyes, a clean rosy wholesome face, a fine profile and a very pleasant smile which brings out engaging dimples in his cheeks—altogether a very personable young man of about 34.

His induction service was held in Cavendish church on Tuesday, Sept. 1, 1903. It was a social function quite as much as a religious one and the church was crowded. Rev. Edwin Smith of Cardigan preached the sermon *and* Rev. Edwin Simpson sat in the audience and thought, as he told me a few days later, that Mr. Macdonald struck him as "a good-looking boy whose mother had told him to put on his best suit for his ordination". I had no earthly interest then in Ewan Macdonald as a man; but I did not think the remark in very good taste, coming from an outsider to a member of the congregation which had just called him, and who therefore would not care to hear criticism or ridicule of her minister.

I "sensed" somehow that Edwin Simpson did not altogether relish the idea of a young unmarried minister being let loose in the community where *I* lived and thought that a timely bit of a sneer might prejudice me against him.

Mr. Macdonald could not get a boarding house in Cavendish so he boarded in Stanley until the spring of 1905. During those years I saw little of him socially but considerably of course in the church services and work. Gossip, always ready to buzz about an unmarried minister, used to link up his name with those of the only girls in the congregation, who, by reason of age, some modicum of cleverness, and aptitude for church affairs, seemed "suitable" for ministers' wives—Margaret Ross of Stanley, Mabel Woolner of Rustico, and "me, mineself" of Cavendish.

I do not know Margaret Ross, save by sight, but I doubt if she were in any sense a candidate for his favor. She was then, I believe, in the throes of an unhappy love affair of her own and had little thought to spare for other men. Mabel Woolner, however, looked upon him with favor and, as I have since discovered, made no scruple of letting him see it. But, according at least to the gentleman himself, when he first saw me he made up his mind that if I were not already "bespoke" he would try his luck. The poor fellow could not, however, find out very easily whether I was or whether I wasn't. Gossip was always engaging me to somebody and the Edwin Simpson tradition lingered, reinforced occasionally by Ed's appearance in C. and his calls on me.

As for me, I was most certainly not in the field to get me a husband. Neither had I the least hankering to be a minister's wife. The life of a country minister's wife has always appeared to me as a synonym for respectable slavery—a life in which a woman of any independence in belief or character, must either be a failure, from an "official" point of view, or must cloak her real self under an assumed orthodoxy and conventionalism that must prove very stifling at times.

Why, she wouldn't even be able to play whist!!

I did not want Mr. Macdonald for a lover; but I rather hoped at first that I might find a friend in him. But after meeting him a few times I decided I could not. He was likeable and pleasant but I did not discover any especial congeniality in him and was not in the least attracted to him. He was not an intellectual man and had no culture in spite of his college education. He preached good, solid sermons but out of the pulpit he possessed no fluency of speech; he was somewhat shy and awkward in society with a very narrow conversational range. He was very well liked by all—I liked him very well—but he was, and remained a practical outsider as far as my life was concerned until the spring of 1905, when he came to live in C., boarding at John Laird's. He came up for the mail very frequently and before long fell into the habit of lingering for an hour or so and talking to me. As I came to know him better I found more in him than I had expected—a certain depth of thought and feeling that was generally hidden and repressed, partly by his natural reserve, and partly I think by the poverty and stiffness of his vocabulary. I began to enjoy our chats on theology and philosophy—the only subjects he had a real grasp of—and moreover, I began to be attracted by the man himself—just why or how I could not say. I liked him—I was glad to see him—I felt the loneliness of my life more keenly when he went away. But, although gossip was by the ears over his calls, I did not think seriously about him until last spring. After all, he had never done anything but call in the afternoons to talk on impersonal subjects, and once or twice drive me home from Literary. I had no reason to suppose that he meant anything but simple friendliness. He had never made the slightest attempt at love-making—had never looked, or implied, or hinted at any such thing. In most men this would have indicated an utter absence of any wish to be more than friend. I was not quite sure that it indicated this in the case of Ewan Macdonald, however. There were times when I *felt*, without any valid reason at all for so feeling, that he cared for me and would, sooner or later, ask me to marry him. And, by this time, I was interested in him to the extent of asking myself very seriously what answer I would make if, and when, he did.

I found it an extremely difficult thing to decide and for months I could not make up my mind. Last spring was a troubled and rather unhappy time for me.

As aforesaid, I did not care for the idea of marrying a minister. On the other hand, viewing marriage in the abstract, *I* would be glad to marry *if* the right man asked me to marry him. I wanted a home and companionship; and more than all, to be perfectly candid, I wanted children. It has always seemed to me a terrible thing to go out of life leaving no life behind you to which you gave birth; and a childless old age is a bitter thing to contemplate.

But much as I wanted all these things I did *not* want them badly enough to marry anyone if I could not be reasonably happy in such a marriage—*reasonably* happy, I repeat. Perfect and rapturous happiness, such as marriage with a man I loved intensely would give me, I have ceased to hope for. I would be content with a workaday, bread-and-butter happiness—so humble has the unhappiness of these past eight narrow, starved years made me in my demands on life.

But suppose a marriage with Mr. Macdonald would not give me even this. I would make him unhappy, too, in that case. Or, worse still, suppose that, having married him, I met a man whom I could love as it is in me to love, with an overmastering passion and devotion. For a few years after I put Herman Leard out of my life I was so numb from the anguish of it all that I believed I could never love again. But now I know I could if I met a man of the type which attracts me strongly. The type is uncommon and the chances are a hundred to one against his ever coming into my life. Yet, if the thing should happen, the result, I am absolutely certain, would be tragedy of one kind or another to me and it might be to others. There were times when I said, "I will not risk it."

On the other hand, I dreaded unspeakably the *loneliness* of the future when I should be alone, absolutely alone in the world, and compelled to make a new home alone in some strange place among strangers. There were moments when I could not face *that* alternative either. Viewed in the abstract, without reference to any particular man it honestly seemed to me a choice of evils—and which was the least? I balanced them one against the other—but could come to no decision. In some moods—my morning moods —I inclined to think that I would be wiser to keep my freedom and trust life. In other moods—my evening and three-o'clock-at-night moods—I inclined to marriage. In one mood loneliness seemed the greater evil, in another a companionship from which I could never escape even if it should prove to be uncongenial.

Again, I was considerably worried over this problem:—I cannot in any case marry as long as grandmother lives. Would I then be acting fairly to bind a man down to wait for me for an indefinite time—perhaps till my youth and bloom were entirely gone. But, after all, this was for him to settle not me. If he cared enough to do it well and good. If he did not he was quite free to seek a wife elsewhere.

Again and again I asked myself did I care enough for Ewan Macdonald to justify my marrying him. There were moments when I was intrigued by his smile, and by a certain undeniable, though not overmastering or especially subtle, physical attraction which he had for me, into thinking I did. But generally it seemed to me that I did not. I liked him—I respected him—I saw all his good qualities of heart and character; to put it plainly, I was *very* fond of him. But I knew that was all.

Suddenly, during the summer, in the midst of my perplexed self-grilling, came the news that he had resigned and was going to Scotland. Somehow then, I felt that I could not let him go out of my life. He seemed to *belong in it*. I couldn't face the thought of the emptiness and blankness he would leave.

One evening he called for me and we drove down to Will Houston's. On the way home, through a dark, rainy night, he said suddenly,

"There is one thing that would make me perfectly happy but perhaps it is too much to hope for. It is that you should share my life—be my wife."

I told him that I would marry him if he could wait until I was free. He said he would willingly do that rather than give me up. So it was settled at last.

I think I have done the wisest thing in assenting. But the future alone can prove that. One takes a risk in any marriage—the very "for better or worse" of the ceremony shows that. I feel content.

Sunday, Nov. 4, 1906
Cavendish, P.E.I.
Such a horrible day! It has blown a most fearful hurricane from the north and is bitterly cold. It has also rained hard from Wednesday afternoon until last night. I can't help feeling blue for the weather has got on my nerves and it is so lonely here in this dreary time of year. I miss Ewan's cheery calls so much. I suppose he is in Scotland to-night. It will be a fortnight yet before I can hear from him, I suppose....

November 6, 1906
Cavendish, P.E.I.
One o'clock Tuesday Night
....I had a letter yesterday from Edwin Simpson!

Did I say the past was dead? Well, he has evidently a ghoulish propensity for digging it up. His letter has upset me completely.

When grandmother handed it over to me yesterday there came across me the same horrible old sensation I knew so well and experienced so often eight years ago. It was an hour before I could summon courage enough to open it.

Of course, I knew before I opened it that his motive in writing was simply to find out if there was anything between Mr. Macdonald and me. He naturally heard the gossip when he was home last summer and it seems to have affected him more than I could have supposed was likely or even possible.

....Much of Ed's letter annoyed and irritated me; but some of it also saddened me and barbed the sorrow with remorse. I feel that I have done him a great injury. I had surely thought that the oblivion he speaks of had come long ago. I regret that it has not. And I cannot understand how Ed *can* have any such feeling left for me. I would expect him to feel only resentment and contempt for me, if he retained any feeling whatever concerning me. Yet it is only too evident that he does not and I fear that he still hopes that the future will re-unite us—a hope utterly vain even if there were no question of Ewan Macdonald.

Well, Ed shall have his belated explanation. We shall hold a coroner's inquest over our dead past. It will be a gruesome proceeding but if it will lay the old ghosts forever it will be justified.

Well, it is two o'clock. I'm going to put out the light and try to get to sleep.

Tuesday, Nov. 20, 1906
Cavendish, P.E.I.
This has been a *good* day. Good every way! It was fine and sunny and mellow. I felt well physically and mentally; got a good day's work done; had a charming walk tonight.

But Sunday and yesterday were bad bad days. I did not get my expected letter from Ewan Saturday and that made me feel disappointed. Then Sunday night I wrote to Edwin Simpson. It was so unpleasant a task that it made me feel actually ill. I had to lie down for awhile after I had written it. It is certainly unfortunate that these things should have such power over me. But thank "whatever Gods there be" it *is* written. I would feel more thankful still if I did not fear that it will bring another letter from him which will be still harder to answer.

Still, it is quite possible that it may not do so. I have told Ed that what I have to say will not be pleasant reading for him. His colossal vanity will quite likely take alarm at this and he may not choose to run the risk of having it wounded. It will be a conflict between his vanity and his desire to know the truth and it is quite possible that the former will win. But even so I shall have robbed him of his weapon of offence. He will never again be able to reproach me with not having told him my real reasons if he refuses now to take advantage of my offer to do so.

Of course the writing of this letter upset me to such an extent that I had another white night—couldn't sleep at all, tossed miserably, and imagined vain things. As a result I had a headache all day yesterday. Wasn't fit to do anything. But Ewan's belated letter arrived and cheered me up somewhat. I went to bed, got a good sleep and so felt like something worth while to-day.

It was lovely out this evening. I went up over the hill in the clear pure November air and walked about until twilight had deepened into a moonlit autumn night. I was alone but not lonely. Thought was quick and vivid, imagination active and bright. I held a series of imaginary conversations with imaginary comrades, and thought out so many epigrams that I was agreeably surprised at myself. Then I came in, still tingling with the strange, wild, sweet life of the spirit, and wrote a chapter of my new serial—wrote it easily and pleasureably, with no flagging or halting. Oh, it is *good* to feel well and vivid and interesting and all alive!

Sunday Evening
Dec. 2, 1906
Cavendish, P.E.I.

We are having the first real snowstorm of the season. It has snowed and drifted all day and consequently has been very lonely and dull.

I've been jogging on of late in a rather uninteresting rut. But a nice thing happened last Tuesday. *Everybody's* accepted a short story of mine—"The Quarantine At Alexander Abraham's"—and sent me a hundred dollars for it. *Everybody's* is one of the big magazines and to appear in it is a sign that you are getting somewhere.

To-day I was reading a new book, "The Future Life". It was very interesting but after all did nothing to solve the problem. There has never been any authoritative answer to that old, old question, "If a man die shall he live again?" Yet man will keep on asking it from age to age.

To-day, too, I read in the earlier pages of this old journal wherein I had written concerning my love for Herman Leard. What a mad infatuation it was! And yet it taught me some lessons it was well to know. I am not sorry I felt it—nay, I'm glad. Every experience enriches our life and the deeper such an experience the greater the richness it brings. I am a deeper-natured, broader-minded woman than I would or could have been if it had not been for that old love, that old temptation, that old anguish. It stirred my soul to depths that I would never otherwise have sounded or been conscious of. I am glad I knew it. It would have been a sorry thing to go through life and never have known love, even though it was an unhappy and unsatisfied love. I shall never know the *fulness* of life—to love absolutely and give myself to the man I so loved, knowing he loved me as well. But I have not been cheated out of everything.

95. Uncle Leander, Murray, Edith, and Grandmother Macneill
(4 generations)

96. Chesley Clark

97. *The Rev. Ewan Macdonald*

1907

I wonder if, sometime in the future, I shall ever again find Sunday evenings pleasant. For the past six years they have for the most part—in winter at least—epitomized for me all that was dreary and lustreless in my existence. This is a typical one. There was no service to-day and it is raining heavily and blowing. Grandmother is reading hymns and crying over them. Her continual "sniffing", which has none of the dignity or pathos of real grief, keeps me rather nervous and "raw".

I have not written in this journal for a long time. Somehow I haven't had the heart. I have felt depressed and worried. For the past six weeks Ewan's letters have only made matters worse. He seems dreadfully blue and downhearted. He says he is troubled with headaches and insomnia but he tells me nothing else and I cannot find out what is the cause of this. I cannot help fearing that something serious is the matter with him, for otherwise why should he be so depressed and discouraged. His letters give me the dismal feeling that he is *compelling* himself to write them and has no real interest in writing them—as if his mind and thoughts were exclusively taken up with something else. I didn't know how much I had been counting on his letters to help me through the winter until they failed me. As it is, I really dread getting them, they worry and depress me so. I have asked him repeatedly if he has been to a doctor but he will only say doctors cannot help him—nothing more, to all my questions. It would not be so hard if I only *knew* but as it is I disquiet myself with all sorts of harrowing suppositions and fears. One thing is certain, he is not able to study and his time is being wholly wasted.

I have really only one thing to cheer me just now—a big box of golden daffodils out in luxuriant blow. It calms and heartens me just to look at them.

We are trying to get up a concert and "supper" for the church debt. It is a sickening piece of business, with this one getting "mad" and that one feeling slighted and half the choir at loggerheads with the other half. I am sick of trying to keep the peace and smoothe down ruffled plumage. I detest these petty affairs for raising money anyhow. Religion ought to be above such sordid things. If it doesn't mean enough to people to make them put their hands in their pockets and pay properly for their churches it doesn't mean much. But I suppose we must take people as we find them in this world and do the best we can under their and our limitations. *These* worries, at least, are only external and don't go very deep—unlike the others in my life. I wouldn't mind them—I'd merely laugh at them in a normal existence. But when one is miserable and harassed all the time even an added pin-prick seems unbearable. This journal of mine is certainly my "blue" book.

There are times when I hate life! Other times again when I love it fiercely with an agonized realization of how beautiful I *could* make it if I had only half a chance. It seems to me that every instinct of my nature is thwarted except that which urges me to literature and which is fortunately beyond the power of anybody or anything here to thwart. Everything else is denied me. I cannot garden, I cannot have any social life, I cannot have any friends visit me. I cannot travel.

But, thank God, the soul, the mind, is *free*—nothing can trammel it. At a bound it overleaps the prison of the material and soars among the stars.

Our Literary Society this winter has been a failure, as all but two of the nights were stormy. I don't care muchly. I only go to it now because it is easier to go than to explain a hundred times why I don't go—especially as I couldn't after all give a truthful explanation but would have to concoct some decent fib.

There is no pleasure in the Literary for me now—or so little that it is lost amid the annoyances. I have to walk up alone over a mile of bad roads through the dark. Yet I don't mind this half as much as the coming home with a crowd of giggling girls and gawkish boys among whom I feel wretchedly out of place. None of my old set are left to go to the Literary now.

I haven't been very well physically of late. So I'm blue and lonely and discouraged, except for a few rare hours when a young moon shining through darkling firs or the white hush of a winter twilight wrapping me around lifts me out of myself for a space. Or when I look at my daffodils! I have looked at them just now and they make me ashamed of my blues and my despondency. After all I've lots to be thankful for—I'm not hideous—I'm not stupid—I'm going to do something with my pen yet—I've got a lovely gray cat—and I wouldn't be anybody but myself for all the world—not even a better or nobler anybody. *I* want to grow better and nobler—to root out faults and prune off unsightly growths—but I want to be *I* and nobody else through all the ages of eternity, through all the lives that are to follow this. Sometimes I take a queer, whimsical comfort out of the thought, "Never mind! Next time I'm born I'll have what I've missed in this life."

I'm reading Gibbon's "Rome" just now. It is a massive work. What millions of men and women have lived and toiled and suffered and succeeded and failed!! What is *one* among such a multitude? Isn't it presumptuous even to hope for an individual immortality?

Tuesday night
Feb. 5, 1907
Cavendish, P.E.I.
It's very cold and there's a northeast storm on. But I don't feel as blue and lonely as usual tonight for I had a nice letter from Ewan to-day—the first cheerful letter he has written since November. It cheered me up at once. How different it used to be when I received Ed's letters! How I hated to read *them* and answer them! I never read one of them twice. How strange some things are in life....

Monday, Feb. 25, 1907
Cavendish, P.E.I.

I *must* have a good fierce grumble! I've been keeping it off as long as possible but it has got to come tonight or I shall *burst*. We have had "a dreadful cold spell"—five days away below zero. The house has got so cold that it is really not fit to live in, as grandmother will not have a fire anywhere but in the kitchen. I've been shivering for twenty four hours. When physical discomfort is added to mental and emotional discomfort the last stage is reached in my endurance. I *have* to succumb and growl it out in this journal.

This is the most utterly lonely winter I have ever put in. And Ewan's letters, after that one cheery one early in the month have been so gloomy. *What* can be the matter? And why won't he tell me? There *must* be something worse than headache and insomnia to account for his despondency. Day after day drags by, cold, lifeless, monotonous. Oh, if it were *only* spring!

One really nice thing happened a week ago, though. I had never seen Frede since the middle of October but last week I got a chance up one evening. It did me good, mentally and emotionally, yea, and spiritually and physically. Frede and I got in her room, wrapped shawls about us, squatted on the floor with a box of chocolate caramels between us, and talked ourselves out. Oh, it was jolly! I've been living on the memory and taste of it ever since....

Friday, Aug. 16, 1907
Cavendish, P.E.I.

Here is a gap with a vengeance! But there has not been much to write about and I've been very busy and contented. Since spring came I haven't been dismal and life has been endurable and—by spells—pleasant.

One really important thing *has* come my way since my last entry. On April 15th I received a letter from the L.C. Page Co. of Boston accepting the MS of a book I had sent them and offering to publish it on a royalty basis!

All my life it has been my aim to write a book—a "real live" book. Of late years I have been thinking of it seriously but somehow it seemed such a big task I hadn't the courage to begin it. I have always hated *beginning* a story. When I get the first paragraph written I feel as though it were half done. To begin a *book* therefore seemed a quite enormous undertaking. Besides, I did not see just how I could get time for it. I could not afford to take time from my regular work to write it.

I have always kept a notebook in which I jotted down, as they occurred to me, ideas for plots, incidents, characters and descriptions. Two years ago in the spring of 1905 I was looking over this notebook in search of some suitable idea for a short serial I wanted to write for a certain Sunday School paper and I found a faded entry, written ten years before:—"Elderly couple apply to orphan asylum for a boy. By mistake a girl is sent them." I thought this would do. I began to block out chapters, devise incidents and "brood up" my heroine. Somehow or other she seemed very real to me and took possession of me to an unusual extent. Her personality appealed to me and I thought it rather a shame to waste her on an ephemeral little serial. Then the thought came, "Write a book about her. You have the central idea and character. All you have to do is to spread it out over enough chapters to amount to a book."

The result of this was "Anne of Green Gables".

I began the actual writing of it one evening in May and wrote most of it in the evenings after my regular work was done, through that summer and autumn, finishing it, I think, sometime in January 1906. It was a labor of love. Nothing I have ever written gave me so much pleasure to write. I cast "moral" and "Sunday School" ideals to the winds and made my "Anne" a real human girl. Many of my own childhood experiences and dreams were worked up into its chapters. Cavendish scenery supplied the background and *Lover's Lane* figures very prominently. There is plenty of incident in it but after all it must stand or fall by "Anne". *She* is the book.

I typewrote it out on my old second-hand typewriter that never makes the capitals plain and won't print "w" at all. The next thing was to find a publisher. I sent it to the Bobbs-Merrill firm of Indianapolis. This was a new firm that had recently come to the front with several "best sellers". I thought I might stand a better chance with a new firm than with an old established one which had already a preferred list of writers. Bobbs-Merrill very promptly sent it back with a formal printed slip of rejection. I had a cry of disappointment. Then I went to the other extreme and sent it to the MacMillan Co. of New York, arguing that perhaps an "old established firm" might be more inclined to take a chance with a new writer. The MacMillan Co. likewise sent it back. I did not cry this time but sent it to Lothrop, Lee and Shepard of Boston, a sort of "betwixt and between" firm. They sent it back. Then I sent it to the Henry Holt Co. of New York. *They* rejected it, but not with the formal printed slip of the others. They sent a typewritten screed stating that their readers had found "some merit" in the story but "not enough to warrant its acceptance". This "damning with faint praise" flattened me out as not even the printed slips could do. I put "Anne" away in an old hat box in the clothes room, resolving that some day when I had time I would cut her down to the seven chapters of my original idea and send her to the aforesaid Sunday School paper.

The MS lay in the hat box until one day last winter when I came across it during a rummage. I began turning over the sheets, reading a page here and there. Somehow, I found it rather interesting. Why shouldn't other people find it so? "Ill try once more," I said and I sent it to the L.C. Page Co.

They took it and asked me to write a sequel to it. The book may or may not sell well. I wrote it for love, not money—but very often such books are the most successful—just as everything in life that is born of true love is better than something constructed for mercenary ends.

I don't know what kind of a publisher I've got. I know absolutely nothing of the Page Co. They have given me a royalty of ten percent on the *wholesale* price, which is not generous even for a new writer, and they have bound me to give them all my books on the same terms for five years. I didn't altogether like this but I was afraid to protest, lest they might not take the book, and I am so anxious to get it before the public. It will be a start, even if it is no great success.

Well, I've written my book. The dream dreamed years ago in that old brown desk in school has come true at last after years of toil and struggle. And the realization is sweet—almost as sweet as the dream!

Ewan came home in April. He seemed very well and quite recovered from his headaches and insomnia.

Wednesday, October 9, 1907
Cavendish, P.E.I.

....Yesterday I wrote the first six pages of my new book—the sequel to "Anne". I have been busy all summer collecting material for it, blocking out chapters, devising incidents and fitting them into each other, and "brooding up" the characters. This is the disagreeable part of the work but it is done now and the rest is pure joy. To breathe the breath of life into those dry bones and make them *live* imparts the joy of creation. *Anne* is as real to me as if I had given her birth—as real and as dear.

Monday, Nov. 18, 1907
Cavendish, P.E.I.

I had a walk through Lover's Lane at dark tonight—or just as the dark was coming down. I was never there so late before and while I enjoyed it I was really a little bit afraid, with a not unpleasant fear. The whole character of the lane seemed changed. It was mysterious, sibilant, remote, eerie. The trees, my old well-known friends, were strange and aloof. The sounds I heard were not the cheery, companionable chorus of daytime—they were creeping and whispering and weird, as if the life of the woods had suddenly developed something almost hostile—at least alien and unacquainted and furtive. I could have fancied that I heard stealthy footsteps all around me and I felt the old, primitive unreasoning fear that was known to the childhood of the race—the awe of the dark and the shadowy, the shrinking from some unseen danger lurking in the gloom. My twentieth-century reason quelled it into a rather piquant watchfulness—but it would not have taken much to deliver me over to a blind panic in which I would have turned and fled shamelessly. As it was, when I left the lane I walked more quickly than my wont and felt as if I had escaped from some fascinating but not altogether hallowed locality—a place still given over to paganism and the revels of fauns and satyrs. None of the wild places are ever wholly Christianized in the darkness, however much so they may seem by daylight. There is always a lurking life in them that dare not show itself to the sun but regains its own with the night.

Sunday, Dec. 14, 1907
Cavendish, P.E.I.

To-night I did something which twenty years ago I could never have imagined myself doing. What was this startling thing? Why, I walked *alone* through the "Cavendish Road woods" *after dark*.

When I was a child I had the greatest horror of those woods. A mile in along the road lived a family of "Jacks", who kept a small—a very small—shop where they sold tea, sugar etc. I was frequently sent in to buy some household supplies and I shall *never* forget the agony of terror I used to endure going along that wooded road. The distance through the woods was not more than a quarter of a mile but it seemed endless to me. I never dared tell anyone of my terror for I would have been laughed at and ridicule was even more dreadful to me than the nameless horrors that lay in wait for me in those woods. I cannot define just what I was afraid of—I could not have put my dread into words. It was just the old primitive fear handed down to us from ancestors in the dawn of time who were afraid of the woods with good reason. It was on my part just a blind, unreasoning terror. But this was all in the daylight. To go through those woods *after dark* was simply not to be contemplated. I could not understand how anyone *could* do it. I remember a young schoolteacher who boarded here and who used to go in there at night to transact school business with a trustee who lived on the other side. In my eyes he was the greatest hero the world has ever seen.

But tonight I came through them. I don't remember ever coming through them after dark *alone* before. They are out of the way of my twilight peregrinations and I've always had company on that road. But I was alone tonight and I liked it. I never even remembered that I used to be frightened of those woods long ago until I came home. I don't feel at all heroic.

I wonder if all the things we look forward to with dread in the future will not be like this. When we come to them we shall not mind them—we shall not be afraid.

Tuesday, December 17, 1907
Cavendish, P.E.I.
....The nights are *so* dreary now and so long, and there is such a brief space of gray, sunless day. I work and think all day; and when night comes early dour gloom settles down on my soul. I cannot describe the feeling. It is dreadful—worse than any actual pain. In so far as I can express it in words I feel a great and awful *weariness*—not of body or brain, but of *feeling*, coupled with a heavy dread of the future—*any* future, even a happy one—nay, a happy one most of all, for in this strange mood it seems to me that to be happy would require more effort, more buoyancy, than I shall possess. The fantastic shape my fear assumes is that it would be *too much trouble* to be happy—require too much energy. At such times the only future to which I could look forward with resignation would be a color-less existence making absolutely no demands on my emotional nature. At such hours I am bankrupt in hope or belief. I become convinced that I am a creature whom no one could love. Every hateful thought that ever came across my mind creeps out of its lurking place like some slimy hateful thing to which I had given birth. Every error and mistake of my life—and my accursedly good memory retains every one from the earliest dawn of consciousness—comes back to shame me.

I try to reason myself out of this. I say, "Now this is morbid nonsense, induced by certain abnormal conditions in my present environment. I have plenty of faults and shortcomings; but I am on the whole an average person with the average share of lovableness and the average number of friends." It is all no use. I might as well be reciting the alphabet. Another curious thing about these moods is that while I am in them I am thoroughly convinced that I will always feel like that. It is no use to tell myself that I have often felt so before and got over it. "Yes, *those* moods passed away but *this* will be permanent", is the unreasonable answer suffering consciousness makes. This condition lasts until some pleasant happening or out-ing, or even a sound sleep, restores me to my normal state. Then I am quite likely to re-act to the opposite extreme—to feel rapturously that the world is beautiful and mere existence something to thank God for.

I think I must be more sensitive to my environment than most people. I suppose it is the fatal shadow of the imaginative temperament. "The gods don't allow us to be in their debt". For all their so-called gifts they make us pay roundly.

1908

Sunday, Jan. 12, 1908
Cavendish, P.E.I.
....I am pegging away at my new book, but it is rather discouraging work in winter. I have to write in the kitchen, as none of the other rooms are warm enough, and there is so much coming and going in connection with the post office I am constantly interrupted. There are six unused rooms in this house and there is no good reason why I should not have one fitted up and warmed as a library—no reason except the all potent one that grandmother would not hear of such a plan for a moment....

Sunday, May 3, 1908
Cavendish, P.E.I.
....But now spring has come and I may be better when I can get out to the companionship of my dear nooks and woods, so well loved—*too* well-loved, since the thought of parting with them seems more than I can bear....
....Mr. Macdonald was down in March for a brief visit. He is settled up west at Bloomfield so I see him very seldom. I wonder if I am fit to be his or anybody's wife—so hopeless, so "played-out" do I feel. Perhaps this is only temporary. But if it should not be? There are moments when I feel that I can never undertake the responsibilities of marriage....

Sunday, May 24, 1908
Cavendish, P.E.I.
I am so much better now. Perhaps it is the tonic I've been taking—with many grimaces—that has helped me. But I believe it is rather my escape from the bondage of cold and wet and gloom to the beautiful—oh, so beautiful!—outdoor world—my darling lanes and woods and fields. Oh, *how* I love them—love them more every day of their dear companionship. It breaks my heart to think of ever leaving them.

To-night—this lovely May night—I walked to the shore. It was as beautiful as ever. I think the Cavendish shore is the most beautiful in the world. This is not merely my fond and foolish fancy. I once heard a man who had been all over the world say he had never seen a more beautiful beach than that of Cavendish sandshore, as far as natural advantages were concerned. As I sat there alone to-night—alone but not lonely—I felt keenly and clearly that I can never *love* any place as I have loved Cavendish. And I have never been really discontented here. At times, when ill or worried, I have had moods of discontent and written them out in this journal to get rid of them. But such moods were passing and comparatively few. And even then, they were with existing conditions, not with the place. If I could have a wish granted to me it would be to live here all my life but freed from the painful environment of the past few years. If Uncle John's family did not exist and if I had an independent home and existence here I should never in sincerity wish for any lasting change.

The day has gone by when I could make changes—even desirable ones—easily. I am thirty three; my tastes and habits are formed—or rather have been formed for me by the irresistible pressure of circumstances; I am bound to this spot by all the thousand ties of old associations and natural affections—bonds, not of the intellect, which sees and admits the flaw and drawback, but of the heart which cries, "Yes, I see them but I love in spite of them."

Saturday, June 20, 1908
Cavendish, P.E.I.

To-day has been, as *Anne* herself would say "an epoch in my life". My book came to-day, fresh from the publishers. I candidly confess that it was for me a proud, wonderful, thrilling moment! There in my hand lay the material realization of all the dreams and hopes and ambitions and struggles of my whole conscious existence—my first book! Not a great book at all—but *mine, mine, mine,*— something to which *I* had given birth—something which, but for me, would never have existed. As far as appearance goes the book is all I could desire—lovely cover design, well bound, well printed. *Anne* will not fail for lack of suitable garbing at all events.

On the dedication page was the inscription "To the Memory of my father and mother". Oh, if they were but living to be glad and proud. When I think of how father's eyes would have shone!

June 30, 1908
Cavendish, P.E.I.

I cannot recall such a beautiful June as this. It has been the sweetest month of sun and shower imaginable and the greenness of everything is something to steep your soul in. It is a benediction to walk past a clover field.

I am feeling much better. The depression and nervousness of last winter have passed and I feel hopeful and cheerful, once more. It would cure anybody to walk over the hill every morning as I do before sitting down to write, with the spruces on either hand and the green meadows beyond. I tramp along "thanking the Lord for a life so sweet."

Our old house is billowed about with caraway just now—great, lacy waves, swaying in the June winds and sprinkled with buttercups.

And I have been picking early strawberries. I went this evening down the shore lane and picked a cupful among those windy, sweet smelling grasses. I love picking strawberries. The occupation has something of perpetual youth in it. The gods might have picked strawberries in high Olympus without injuring their dignity.

These days are perennially interesting because of the reviews of my book. So far they have been very favorable. *Anne* is already in her second edition. My publishers are hurrying me now for the sequel. I'm working at it but it will not be as good as *Green Gables*. It doesn't *come* as easily. I have to force it.

July 16, 1908
Cavendish, P.E.I.

A busy fortnight has slipped away. Uncle Leander and Aunt Mary have been here since the first of the month. Aunt M. and I have had several delightful "dips" on the old, dear shore. Alma Macneill has been home for a month and we have had some jolly chats and walks and one glorious bathe. I am feeling quite well again and the change is unspeakably delightful. We are having such a beautiful summer that one could hardly help feeling better.

I had an encounter tonight which was at first disagreeable, then amusing, and finally rather upsetting.

Amanda called for the mail and I went to her gate with her for a walk. On my return I met—Edwin Simpson and *his bride*!

I heard last winter that Ed was to be married. I did not hear the name of the lady nor have I heard it since. Ed, I may say, never took advantage of my offer to tell him the real reason why I broke my engagement. I was not surprised at this. He was not sincere in asking for it—or rather *hinting* for it. He merely thought I never would tell and that he could always make use of it as a matter of reproach to me. I daresay he was very much taken aback at my offer to do so. Moreover, my utter disregard of his hints regarding Mr. Macdonald would lead him to believe that there was something after all in those "rumors" to which he "gave little credence".

The news of his prospective marriage in so far as it affected me at all, gave me a feeling of relief. I was glad for his sake. I do not flatter myself that Ed has remained unmarried all these years on my account. From my knowledge of his character I should be very much surprised if such were the case. But I certainly did do him a wrong and the sense of it has always been an uneasy one to me. I was also glad for my own sake. I would henceforth be free from any dread of meeting him or getting letters from him.

I thought no more of the matter until one day in June when I saw a newspaper notice of his arrival on the Island with his bride. This rather disturbed me. I knew he would visit his Cavendish friends and I should probably meet them somewhere. I would not at all mind meeting them in a strange place—nay, I should have liked to do so, for I was naturally curious regarding *her*. But I did *not* like the thought of meeting them before *their* friends and *my* friends, who knew or suspected our old relationship and would be watching to see "how I took it". Altogether, the meeting could not but be embarrassing to at least two out of the three of us, and so I wished to avoid it, while at the same time I *did* want to have a peep at Ed's bride.

They came to C. and Ed preached last Sunday evening in the Baptist church. We had service in our church that evening also, which neatly prevented my going to the B. church or his coming to ours. I had not heard anything of them since and supposed they had left Cavendish by this time.

After parting with Amanda at her gate I walked back briskly. As I came down David Macneill's hill I was aware of a buggy with two people in it coming down

Pierce's hill. But I did not suppose it was "anyone in particular", and I was so interested in trying to make out who was on the pond in a boat that I never looked around at the buggy until it was right by me, when I turned my head indifferently to see if it were anyone I ought to speak to I found myself looking at Ed and his bride.

I shall never forgive myself for not having turned my head sooner. Had I done so I could have had a good look at her and seen what she was like. As it was, I had just barely time to bow and smile to Ed, before they were past. I had not a moment to look at his wife. I simply got a fleeting impression of a woman in a gray suit, "merry widow" hat, and thick chiffon veil. For all I saw of her face she might just as well not have been there at all.

In spite of my surprise I had presence of mind enough to make my bow and smile very cordial. But there was no cordiality about Ed—not the shadow of it. I rather suspect the very fact that I *was* cordial would seem an insult to him as indicating an unflattering indifference to the fact that I had finally lost him through my own unreasonable stubbornness in refusing him. At anyrate he did not even smile. He merely raised his fingers very stiffly to his hat and gave an almost imperceptible bow. As for his expression—well, it really looked "plain mad", as the children say; but of course it was merely the result of his embarrassment at the sudden and unexpected encounter. I knew my own feelings and could guess with tolerable accuracy at his. What his wife's were is problematical. Likely she had none at all, never supposing that the woman who had just passed had any connection with her husband's "past". If I know Ed, he has never told her of his affair with me.

By the time I had reached the bridge my breathlessness of surprise had passed and amusement had set in. I laughed softly to myself. What an encounter! A little over a year ago Ed had written to me that "time had not brought oblivion and could not"—that "the skeleton in his closet was still very real to him" etc. "Oblivion" must have been nearer than he fancied. Well, well, he is not the first man to have been led by his love of fine phrases into saying much more than he meant. It is not fair to laugh at him for it.

After the amusement came the "unsettling" part. Edwin Simpson is not anything to me now, not even a disagreeable anything. But still, the sight of him always brings back the past so vividly, with all its hatefulness and anguish, that I seem to live it over again and I cannot endure doing so.

My curiosity regarding Mrs. Ed was not doomed to be wholly unslaked. When I was down at Alma's day before yesterday she, having seen her in the B. church, told me some things about her, not knowing at all how keen my interest was. She is "not pretty but is said to be very clever and to have money". I had to choke back a smile over this. It reminded me of one of Ed's felicitous speeches to me long ago. In speaking of his early "dreams" he said he always thought he would be "quite satisfied if he could marry a lady who was nice looking and *had money*". I might have claimed to be passable as far as "looks" were concerned but I certainly had no "money" or the prospect of any! Ed was really trying to pay me a Simpsonian compliment—to convey the idea that I was sufficiently charming to make him forego this requirement; but he only succeeded in making me feel that *he* thought *I* should be very grateful for his condescension in waiving this important qualification in my case. The vanity and sordidness revealed in his speech disgusted me.

Well, his shadow has at last gone out of my life. I wish him prosperity and happiness and that is all there is about it.

Friday, July 31, 1908
Cavendish, P.E.I.
We had a most exciting and unpleasant sensation here this morning. I feel so shaken over it that the mere recollection makes me tremble.

It was a very hot morning with a high wind. After I had finished the morning's work I went for my customary walk over the hill before sitting down to write. When I came back I mounted to my den and had just begun work on the last chapter of my new book when I heard Aunt Mary run through the sitting room screaming, "Maud, the house is on fire!"

I don't know how I got down and out—I don't remember that part at all. A space about two feet square was ablaze on the kitchen roof, evidently having caught from a spark. There was no decent ladder about the place, everything of that sort having been long since carried off by Uncle John's. But I recalled an old rotten ladder with half its rungs missing which had been lying in the woods behind the pighouse for three years. Somehow or other, Aunt Mary and I dragged it to the house and lifted it against the roof. There I seized a bucket of water and scrambled up it. Fortunately the rungs did not give way under me as I had feared they would. I could not get very near the fire but I stood on the top rung and flung the water at it. Luckily, my aim was good. The water struck the very centre of the flames and put them half out; another bucket passed up by Uncle Leander completely extinguished them, as the fire was only on the surface and had not had time to eat in. I feel sure that ten minutes later would have been too late.

When I realized that the danger was over my sustaining excitement left me and I went to pieces—burst into tears, trembled from head to foot and had to go to bed. In my present condition of nervous weakness such a shock is rather a serious thing. I don't seem to have the reserve strength to meet it.

I have such a horror of fire. And all my life I have been haunted by an ever recurring dream that the house in which I am living is on fire and that I have to stand and watch it burning, unable to make any effort to quench it. I wonder if this means that I am some day to be "burnt out".

Monday, Aug. 3, 1908
Cavendish, P.E.I.
To-day I finished my second book. I've been mulling over it so long that I'm not capable of judging it correctly but I know it is not nearly so good as *Green Gables*. I began to write it last October but was blocking it out and collecting and arranging materials for it all last summer. All this time I've been the prey of worry and nervous ills—not very favorable circumstances for the production of a good book. Anyhow, I am thankful it is done—though after all I enjoyed writing it. There still remains much of revision to do—and then the worst job of all, typewriting it. That is so tedious and slow.

Saturday, Aug. 29, 1908
Cavendish, P.E.I.

Uncle L's went away Tuesday. Thursday morning I went to town to meet two American ladies, friends of a literary friend of mine in Boston, who were touring the Island and wished to meet me because they had read my book. It was difficult for me to go to town just now. But I could not ask them to come to this tumble-down place. They would not understand why I, a successful writer, should be living in a house in such wretched repair, surrounded by outbuildings almost falling to pieces. And I could not explain to strangers why it was. So I vexed my tired soul making arrangements to go to town and meet them. I had a pleasant trip and enjoyed meeting them. They were boarding on a farm out at Brighton—the prettiest spot I ever saw in my life.

I came home Friday night to find Frede Campbell and Clara and Clara's husband, Fred Wilson, here. Fred is a fine looking fellow and seems nice and kind. Clara is fat and jolly. I was glad to see her; but the gulf between us now is too wide to be bridged. We have *nothing* in common now that girlhood is past—neither ideals nor opinions nor tastes nor hopes—I was going to write "ambitions" but it would be absurd to talk of Clara having ambitions. She seems very happy and satisfied with her life and her husband and I am sincerely glad that it is so; but I would soon weary of her society now. It is hard to believe she and Frede can be sisters—they are so utterly unlike in all vital respects.

Thursday, Oct. 15, 1908
Cavendish, P.E.I.

I had a delightful trip over to Park Corner on Tuesday, getting an unexpected chance over with Will Houston. It was two years since I had been over. It did me so much good to see the dear old place again and have a jolly afternoon with Stella. I have been feeling a good deal better this past fortnight—have a better appetite and more energy, and have lost much of my morbid aversion to seeing people. But I dread the winter. I feel that I have not strength to face it and the worries it is sure to bring. Grandmother is already suffering much from rheumatism and I fear she will have it badly this winter. I do hope it will not be a severe one.

I had a letter from Page to-day asking me for my photo and a personal sketch of how "Anne" came to be written to give "inquisitive editors". It seems that *Anne* is a big success. It is a "best seller" and is in its fifth edition—I cannot realize this. My strongest feeling seems to be incredulity. I *can't* believe that such a simple little tale, written in and of a simple P.E.I. farming settlement, with a juvenile audience in view, can really have scored out in the busy world. I have had so many nice letters about it—and no *end* of reviews. Most of them were very flattering. Three or four had a rather contemptuous tone and three were really nasty.

One of the reviews says "the book radiates happiness and optimism". When I think of the conditions of worry and gloom and care under which it was written I wonder at this. Thank God, I can keep the shadows of my life out of my work. I would not wish to darken any other life—I want instead to be a messenger of optimism and sunshine.

Pleasant? Yes, of course it is pleasant. It is a joy to feel that my long years of struggle and unaided effort have been crowned with success. But that success has also evoked much petty malice, spite and jealousy. It does not hurt me, because none of my *real* friends have been guilty of it. But at times it has given me a sort of nausea with human nature.

Friday, Oct. 23, 1908
Cavendish, P.E.I.
To-day I finished typewriting "Anne of Avonlea"; and heartily glad I am, for it has been a tedious and back-breaking job in very truth. These past few days have been hard ones. I've been feeling badly again—depressed, tired, broken, a prey to indescribable and unconquerable unrest. These attacks must have a physical cause. They seem to be growing worse and of longer duration. I ought to have medical advice; but I cannot consult any doctor here, for that would mean running the gauntlet of gossip and surmise; and it is difficult to consult one far away. But if I get much worse I shall have to try. Oh, the misery of these past few days and nights. Generally I can sleep but one night I could not and it seemed as long as a year. I could not even *think* to pass the time. My personality seemed turned wrong side out and I disliked everything I normally like and shrank from the thought of all I normally desire.

Wednesday, October 28, 1908
Feeling a little better to-day I went for a walk back to the woods, through the beautiful day. A friend I met on the road called out, "Just like spring, isn't it?" I nodded—but I did not think it in the least really like spring. It was as warm and sunny and blue-skied as spring—but the whole *spirit* of spring was lacking—that indefinite, keenly-felt spirit of growth and awakening. Instead, there was abroad in the world a spirit of rest and peace, of work accomplished and over, of a folding of the hands in slumber. It fitted in with my mood—I, too, would like to lie down and sleep. When the worst of these fits of gloom and unrest pass they leave me feeling "played out", as if I had just passed through some severe struggle—a wrestling with "principalities and powers" of evil and darkness.

I saw a pretty thing tonight as I looked from my room window in the twilight—a new moon just over the slender top of the big larch tree on the dyke. I am glad I happened to glance out of my window just then—and I'm glad I live in a world where there are new moons.

Saturday, Oct. 31, 1908
Cavendish, P.E.I.
Our beautiful October has not gone out beautifully. Yesterday and to-day have been days of storm—heavy rain, showers of snow, and high winds. The trees are lashed and ragged and the world looks unsightly. I haven't felt at all well either of these days. I seem to be haunted by a vague, teasing dread of impending evil—as if I were expecting a blow and shrinking from it. This feeling visits me very often now. It has no foundation in fact but reason has no effect on it. As a result, I cannot do anything—not even read—with pleasure or satisfaction. I compel myself to

work, read, sew, talk—and under it all I am nervous and tense with this absurd and reasonless dread which I cannot control or banish. It is harder to bear than anything else.

I suppose I am too much alone. My temperament has a natural bent toward introspection and self-analysis and it has become morbidly intense of late. Some of my present mental, or rather psychic, processes are as curious as they are disagreeable. For instance, as I have said before, when I was a child I received many harsh words and cruel "cuts" and not less cruel teasings from many of the members of my mother's family. At the time they hurt me; but the pain soon passed and I cannot recall ever feeling any resentment or sullenness towards those who had caused it after it had passed. I forgot it promptly. Well, of late all these incidents seem to have returned vividly to my memory, as if they had been churned up from some lower depths by some disturbance in my inner consciousness. And the curious part is, the intense, unforgiving, *bitter* resentment I *now* feel against those who inflicted those injustices and "harshnesses" upon me. I feel as if I could *never* forgive them or look upon them with any feeling but anger and hatred—emotions which I never felt at the time of the infliction with anything like the intensity I feel now. This is unnatural, whatever the cause.

Writing this out, or talking it out to an understanding friend, always helps me. It is like lancing a fester and letting out the pus which is causing the pain. I always feel a good deal of relief for the time.

But nothing seems to help this vague dread of evil much. I can't write *it* out because I cannot find words to express it with any nearness to truth. I shall be glad when it is bedtime so that I can go to sleep and be oblivious to this misery for a time. It is such a blessing that I can generally sleep well. Time was when I chafed somewhat over having always to go to bed promptly at nine o'clock simply because grandmother so decreed. But now I'm only too glad to go—ay, and earlier if I can. It is such a relief to get upstairs alone and *let myself go*—not to feel that I must be bright and smiling and cheery. It is a real relief to lie down on the bed and feel that I can be just as miserable as I want to be.

Poor grandmother, she has to endure a great deal in many ways. I try to do my best for her, but I am very helpless in many respects, partly owing to Uncle John's shameful behavior, partly to poor grandmother's own stubborn childishness in adhering to all her old ways and customs in defiance of changed circumstances. There are times when I feel a sort of savage despair over my helplessness. Grandmother has five living children and not one of them makes, or ever has made, any attempt to share the responsibility of her care. It never seems to occur to them that grandmother is not the capable woman she was twenty years ago, with a husband to protect her. Aunt Emily has had a houseful of grown-up girls for ten years and she has never once offered to send one of them to take my place for a week or two while I get away for a change. Her children are almost strangers to grandmother; she herself has visited her mother *once* in the past three years and written *twice*. Yet she lives only 26 miles away.

Tuesday, Nov. 10, 1908
Cavendish, P.E.I.

These two days have been hard ones for me. They have been cold, wet and dull; and though this is not the cause of my suffering it aggravates it. That horrible feeling of dread has returned. I have a morbid horror of seeing anyone and feel like *hiding* when anyone comes to the house. Besides, I have felt physically miserable. There was a strange feeling in my head as if something were grinding back and forth continually. I had neuralgia in my face and a nasty, irritating "cold sore" on my mouth. I wanted to walk fiercely all the time. I couldn't even read. Last night I couldn't sleep until nearly morning.

This lasted all this forenoon. But this afternoon I felt better again. I could think, read, and enjoy a twilight walk over the hill.

Ewan is much concerned over my condition and has insisted that I do no writing for a month. I have yielded to please him but I do not think it is a wise thing after all. When I am writing I am happy for I forget all worries and cares. If I do not write I have all the more time for morbid brooding.

I had a letter to-day from a Toronto journalist who had been detailed to write a special article about me for his paper—wants to know all about my birth, education, early life, when and how I began to write etc.

Well, I'll give him the bare facts he wants. He will not know any more about the real *me* or my real life for it all, nor will his readers. The only key to *that* is found in this old journal.

I've been reading *Waverley* this evening. Splendid old Scott! His magic never fails. After a surfeit of glittering, empty modern fiction I always come back to him as to some tired old friend who never fails to charm. What a delight the few novels of Scott which I could get to read in early life were to me! There was one around the house—an old paper-bound *Rob Roy*—over which I pored until I read it to pieces. Then I got hold of *The Talisman* and *Ivanhoe*, thanks to Nate, who got them out of the hall library and lent them to me—a very unlawful proceeding of course! I was not allowed to attend the Literary or become a member of the society, much as I yearned to do so. This was another mistake of grandfather and grandmother. It would not only have been a great and innocent pleasure to me but a real and lasting benefit if I had had access to that little library. But now and then I got a book of it to read and what a delight it was! To me, Scott's novels are blent with the brightest memories of those old days and so have the added charm of old associations.

Tuesday, Dec. 1, 1908
Cavendish, P.E.I.

I heartily wish I could see a competent doctor whom I could trust and discuss my condition with him. I cannot go to the nearest doctor here—Stuart Simpson of Stanley. He takes "sprees" now and again and at such times tells the first person he meets all about his patient's ailments, with smutty comments. And in any case he would not be competent to treat a nervous disorder. Yet some medical advice I believe I ought to have and that soon. Thursday, Friday, and Saturday of last week, were, in all calm decision, the most utterly wretched days I have ever passed in my life. Nothing I have ever before experienced at the worst of times could compare with them. During the earlier part of the week I felt quite well and cheerful—almost my normal self. Wednesday evening the change came again, suddenly and without warning. It was as if a black cloud settled down over my soul. I felt the most intolerable nervous unrest, coupled with an equally intolerable dread of coming disaster. I could not sleep at all that night. Thursday was worse. I could not do anything—read, work, or eat. Thursday night again no sleep. Friday, still worse—Friday night, no sleep. As for Saturday, it was indescribable. Every moment was an agony. I shut myself in a cold room and walked the floor for hours. By this time I was also physically ill from lack of sleep and utter inability to eat anything; but it was the hideous nervous distress that nearly killed me. Oh, I cannot describe how I felt and it is puerile to try. But in all candor I'd rather die than go through such a time again.

Then all at once, about dusk, the cloud lifted. The horrible feeling passed away and in a few minutes I was lying on my bed utterly exhausted but so blessedly at *peace, at rest*. No words can describe the relief of it. As soon as I had enough strength to move I undressed and went to bed. Oh, it was so blessed to sleep soundly,—nay, more, it was so blessed before going to sleep just to lie there at ease and think happy thoughts! Since then I've been improving steadily, although I still feel the weakening effects of that dreadful time and am not good for much yet.

Thursday, Dec. 3, 1908
Cavendish, P.E.I.
This has been another bad day, but this time the suffering was physical, the consequences of a very bad cold. I began to feel it coming on last evening and passed a very bad night. My head ached so severely that I could not sleep. Then it was very cold—several degrees below zero and a strong wind blowing. The air in my room was so cold that I could not endure my face over the clothes and consequently passed the seemingly endless hours alternately freezing and stifling. To-day I spent on the kitchen sofa, racked with cough and headache, with people coming in for the mail all the time. However, ill as I feel, it is as nothing to those dreadful days last week.

The mail, as usual, brought me a grist of letters about my book and a bunch of favorable reviews—hard, cold, glittering stones to a soul that is asking vainly for the homely bread of a little human companionship and tenderness in its hard hours.

Sunday, Dec. 13, 1908
Cavendish, P.E.I.
That terrible mood of a fortnight ago seemed to be the "crisis" of my moods. At anyrate, I have had no return of them since and the relief is indescribable. To be sure, I'm not really well for I'm tired all the time and have no energy: but that seems nothing compared to those horrible attacks of nervous unrest. Perhaps, if those moods do not return, I'll gradually get rested. I seem to expend all my strength wrestling with them and they leave me exhausted....

FICTION

L. M. Montgomery—a face of balance and refinement. The smooth high forehead shows love of stories and sympathetic perception, the height and squareness above the temples and the arched eyebrows suggest poetic feeling and artistic taste, while the full eyes show facility of expression.

98. "Me, mineself"

99. A view from my window
[*Cavendish*]

1909

Jan. 10, 1909
Cavendish, P.E.I.

The New Year is ten days old. It brought me a new sorrow for its guerdon. On the second of January I received a letter from Bertie McIntyre telling me that her mother had died New Year's morning.

To me it was a bolt from the blue. I had known Aunt Mary was not quite well, as she was suffering from a return of her chronic throat trouble; but I had no idea that she was seriously ill; and indeed, she did not die from that, although it would probably have been fatal in the end, but from heart failure induced by an attack of pleurisy.

It was a bitter grief to me. Of all her generation there was no one so dear to me. I never really knew Aunt Mary until the year I went to P.W.C. I had met her only once or twice in my whole life before; and I am sorry to say that I felt against her a prejudice and distrust which had been early instilled into my childish mind by the things I had heard grandmother and Aunt Annie say about her. I know now that most of those things were either untrue or so warped and distorted by the prejudice and narrow mindedness of those who uttered them as to be worse than falsehoods. But I did not know this then; I was still under the delusion that grandmother and Aunt Annie were quite infallible in all their judgments and that their opinion on every point was the last word.

But I had only to know Aunt Mary to realize what injustice they had done her. Never was there a braver, sweeter, pluckier, kinder, more loving and loyal soul ever pent in flesh—and the circumstances of her married life called for all the bravery and loyalty she possessed. Uncle Duncan was a very dissipated man and the care and upbringing of her large family fell wholly on her.

I loved her from the moment the scales of prejudiced ignorance fell from my eyes and in all the years that have followed every meeting has drawn us closer together.

I went into town on Thursday to the funeral, which was to have been Saturday but as James and Laura were delayed by washouts and did not arrive home until Saturday afternoon it had to be put off till Sunday and I could not stay having to come home Saturday evening. At such times I feel keenly being tied down as I am. I do not mind so much giving up pleasures but it is hard not to be able to stay by my friends in their time of trial.

Still, I saw dear Aunty in farewell. She was always a beautiful woman and she looked more beautiful than every lying among her flowers with a face of perfect peace and sweetness. Then there was a sorrowful pleasure in meeting my cousins and Aunt Maggie again. It was so long since I had seen them. Harry and Cuthbert are such dear boys.

When I came away I felt as if my heart would break. I had never before left there that Aunty did not come to the gate and wave her hand to me with her little characteristic gesture of farewell. I could almost hear her saying, as always, "Come back soon". But there was nobody there, only poor Harry, standing in the wintry sunshine and I felt as if I should never care to visit Ch'Town again.

Feb. 20, 1909
Cavendish, P.E.I.
This afternoon I read a very beautiful book—Bliss Carman's "Making of Personality", which Ewan sent me recently. It is one of the most helpful books I have ever read and has done me a vast amount of good—I feel better, braver, more hopeful, more encouraged, more determined to make the best of myself and life since I have read it. It is a series of lessons on "the oldest of all arts—the art of living"—a subject on which most of us require a good deal of instruction and which is never taught in the schools. The book is a mingling of glorified common-sense and starry aspiration. The first essay is on the "meaning" of personality. He tries to define it—I hardly think he succeeds. It is a very elusive thing—and the greatest force in the world. It is not to be commanded by wealth or education.

Carman insists on the tri-une cultivation of soul, mind, and body—and he is right. The great lack of Christianity—its cardinal mistake—lies in the fact that it has *over*-emphasized the spiritual—taught that the body must be mortified—or at best, disregarded as of no importance—a false and ugly—yea, and a blasphemous doctrine—blasphemous because it lowers the "image of the Creator" below the brutes. Mind and soul can express themselves only through the body and therefore we should try to make it and keep it as perfect an instrument for their expression as possible.

The essay on the value of Instinct is exquisitely true—as I too well know, having disregarded instinct many times to my cost and in my bitter punishment having learned what a safe guide it is. One sentence was peculiarly vital. "We often over-persuade ourselves, against the subtle intimations of instinctive preference, to enter into relationships that turn out disastrously for all concerned and *to attempt friendships that could never be worth while*."

How often I have done this and how I regret the wasted effort now. I have done it in childhood when I was *not* to blame for it. I had a child's natural craving for companionship. The right sort was not to be had so I took what I could find and formed schoolgirl intimacies which did me no good—nay, did me positive harm— and which cling around me now, hampering and valueless. I have done it in mature years when I *was* to blame for it, because I disregarded my instinct, trying to find friendship in someone who was pronounced by other people to be good, or clever, or nice, and I thought it must be of value to have companionship with such.

I am wiser now. I never try to cultivate *intimacy* with anyone in whose society I do not feel *thoroughly at ease*. I shall always try to be cordial to all but I shall never try to open the gates of my soul to anyone who, as my instinct warns me, is not in sympathy with me—who is not, in Frede's favorite phrase, "of the race that knows Joseph."

Tuesday, Mar. 16, 1909
Cavendish, P.E.I.

I'm good for nothing to-night, I am so tired. So, as usual, I'll seek a refuge from brooding and carking thoughts by writing in this journal. A fortnight ago the Page Co. wrote me asking for a later photo than the one I had sent them last summer as a prominent book magazine wishes to publish it as a frontispiece. I wrote back that I couldn't conveniently get to town before spring; but last week I had another letter urging me to have one taken at once if possible, as the matter was urgent and important. I hardly think it so very "urgent and important" that the great American public should see my face; but I wearily surrendered and set about putting the necessary machinery in motion.

When I was a child a trip to town and a trip to Park Corner were the only outings that ever entered my life and both were looked upon as great pleasures. A trip to Park Corner was of comparatively common occurrence—usually twice a year. A trip to town was a very rare treat—once in two or three years—and loomed up in about the same proportion of novelty, excitement and delight as a trip to Europe would now. It meant a brief sojourn in a delightful and fascinating place, where everybody seemed always dressed up and able to get all the nuts, candies and oranges they wanted, to say nothing of the exquisite delight of looking at all the wonderful things in the shop windows.

I remember the first trip to town of which I have any recollection. I could not have been more than six at most and I think I was only five. Grandfather, grandmother, father and I all went to town in a big double seated wagon. To go anywhere with father was sheer happiness for me. I had a glorious day of it but the most delightful part was a tiny adventure I had just before leaving for home. The others had met some friends at a street corner and stopped to talk. Finding that I wasn't being "looked after" I promptly shot down a nearby street in search of adventures. It was *so* jolly and independent to be walking down a street alone! It was a wonderful street. I've never seen it since—not with the same eyes anyhow. No other street has ever had the charm that had. The most amazing sight I saw in it was a woman shaking rugs *on the top of a house*. I felt dizzy with astonishment over such a topsy-turvey sight. *We* shook our rugs in the back yard. Who *ever* heard of shaking them on the top of a house?

Arriving at the bottom of the street I coolly ran down the steps of an open door I found there and discovered myself to be in a most charming dim spot full of barrels, with a floor ankle deep in beautiful, curly shavings. But just as I reached the foot of the steps I saw a man over in a corner and, overcome, not by fear but by bashfulness, I beat a prompt retreat. On my way back I met a little girl with a jug in her hand. We both stopped and, with the instinctive, unconventional *camaraderie* of childhood, plunged into an intimate confidential conversation. She was a jolly little soul with black eyes and two long braids of black hair. We told each other everything about ourselves, except our names which neither of us thought about. When we parted I felt as if I were leaving a lifelong friend. We "never met again".

When I rejoined my grown-ups they had not missed me at all and knew nothing of my rapturous voyage into wonderland.

But there is no such romance about a trip to town nowadays. I got up at five yesterday morning and by the time I was ready the team which I had engaged to come down for me from the station had arrived. This way of getting to the train is a vast improvement on going up with the mailman as I used to have to do when I was poorer. But it isn't pleasant. The driver is always some stupid French boy and the drive is long and tiresome. It was particularly so yesterday morning for the roads were so rough and full of slews. I was tired out when I reached Hunter River—tireder still when I got to town. There I was overcome by a sudden sense of desolation. Always before the first thing was to go to Aunt Mary's where a warm welcome waited for me. But there was no doing that now. Bertie would be at her school and the dear little aunt with her sweet face and voice, was out in the cemetery. Feeling curiously heartsick I went uptown and sat for a picture, hoping that I wouldn't look in it as tired and hopeless and out-at-elbows as I felt. Then I rushed feverishly about town getting some necessary shopping done. I seemed to be wandering in a species of nightmare with much the same feeling I occasionally have in dreams when I am roaming in some strange place unable to find my way out. I hated to meet people—to force animation of voice and manner, receive congratulations gracefully and talk small talk. At two I met Bertie in the library and we had a chat, the only pleasant spot in my visit. At three my train left. Reached Hunter River at four and drove again over the eleven miles of rough road.

When I got home I was more utterly tired out than I ever remember being in *all* my life before, and *so* wretchedly nervous. I was too tired even to lie down. I felt as if I must scream at the slightest noise—the ticking of the clock seemed unbearable. I went to bed and had a wild, passionate fit of nervous crying, the result of my intolerable weariness. But it calmed me so that I fell asleep as soon as it was over, but suffered from distressing dreams all night. Today I've been miserable enough. It is dreadful to feel so tired. Pain is really easier to bear. I shall not recover from the effects of yesterday for some time.

Sunday, April 11, 1909
Cavendish, P.E.I.
....If anyone wants to find out what has become of her submerged friends let her write a book. They will then "bob up serenely" from the deeps of the lost years in all quarters of the world. Yesterday I had a letter from Lottie Shatford—now Mrs. Handy of Vancouver. I had not heard from or of her for seven years. Now she has read *Anne* and writes to me. Her letter was, like all her epistles, a frank, kind, and generous one. I always enjoyed Lottie's letters—much more than her personal society indeed. Our *intellects* seemed to be perfectly in accord; it was something in our *personalities* that was out of tune. Lottie had a nature free from all envy or pettiness—a candid, sincere, and honorable one. I always recognized and admired her good qualities, even while I felt that there was not in her that subtle "fitness" which is the very essence of real friendship. I was pleased to receive her letter and shall write in return. But I do not think any real good or pleasure could accrue to either of us from a re-opening of our correspondence and I shall make no attempt to do so.

Yesterday also a copy of the London *Spectator* came with a two column review of *Anne*—the most favorable review of any yet. I *do* feel hugely flattered—I admit it frankly. The *Spectator* is the biggest of all the "big" literary reviews and praise or blame from it carries tremendous weight.

Friday, April 16, 1909
Cavendish

Two days of this week the weather was really heavenly. The rest—well, they were the place-opposite-to-heavenly!

Tuesday and Wednesday were the lovely days—sunny and warm as June. Whether it was the effect of the weather or if it just happened so I don't know but for those two days I felt perfectly well and like my "old self"—hopeful, peaceful, all the bitterness gone out of my memories of the past and my feelings of the present. I had some lovely evening walks—one of them to the graveyard! Not exactly a cheerful place for a walk one would suppose? But I always like to wander over that westward sloping hill of graves in the gentle melancholy of a spring evening. I like to read the names on the stones and note the ages, and think of all the loves and hates and hopes and fears that lie buried there. I would like to be buried there myself, when my time comes—by mother's side.

After my walk that evening I came in and studied a new book on astronomy—just plain, every night astronomy that anybody can understand. It was so fascinating that I carried the book to bed with me and sat up on my pillows half the night, poring over the charts of the constellations. Astronomy has always been a subject possessing a great charm for me. I would give much for a peep through a telescope.

On Thursday evening I received a telegram from my half sister Kate announcing her mother's death on the previous day—a very sudden and unexpected death.

I had no reason to love Mrs. Montgomery but I never wished her ill and I was very sorry to hear of her death for the sake of her children. They are now doubly orphaned at an age when they most require a parents' care and counsel. But at least they will have plenty to provide for them, as I understand Mrs. Montgomery has made a great deal of money these past few years in real estate business; and they have many near relatives near them to look after them.

To-day I received a letter from a Toronto journalist asking me to read a paper before the International Council of Women, meeting in Toronto in June. The honor is to my book, of course. I cannot go—and what is worse, I do not wish to go. All my old desire for travel seems to have died out completely. I shrink from any change, even a desirable one.

Tuesday, June 1, 1909
Cavendish, P.E.I.

This evening I had a good hour. I went in over the hill to call on a friend. *This* was not the hour referred to. My friend, so called, is merely an old acquaintance whom I like well enough. The good hour came as I was walking home alone. Before me arched the afterlight of a glorious sea-sunset. The tall slender firs along the moist red road came out against it in a grace and beauty that made me ache for joy; and behind me a full moon deepened until the white radiance mingled with the gold and flame of the west. I came down the hill and up the lane. The birches hung out young-leaved boughs over me. The apple trees crowded lovingly about the old house. The moonlight softened all until it looked as it used to look long ago—a bowery "haunt of ancient peace". It is at such moments that I realize how deeply rooted and strong is my love for this old place—a love of instinct and passion, blent with every fibre of my soul.

It is terrible to love things—and people—as I do!

Today I began work at my new book "The Story Girl". The germinal idea has been budding in my brain all winter and this evening I sat me down in my dear white room and began it. I think it is a good idea and I think I shall be able to make a good piece of work out of it. But I feel sad, too, for I cannot be sure that I shall be long enough in this old house to finish it and it seems to me that I could never write it as it should be written anywhere else—that some indefinable, elusive "bouquet" will be missing if it is written elsewhere. I suppose this is a foolish fancy. And perhaps I shall be able to finish it here. But I cannot banish these thoughts and they are very saddening.

Yet it is a joyous young world now and its beauty is as new wine to me. The improvement in my health continues and I feel again my old joy in mere existence—in the blue sky, the greenness of the southern slopes and the airy charm of pussywillows.

I am re-reading Andersen's Fairy Tales and find them as delightful as ever. I am glad I had the privilege of reading them in my childhood. The child who has not known them has missed much. Mr. Fraser, one of my early teachers, offered prizes in school for various things. The offer made great excitement. In the fourth class—mine—the prize was for the pupil who was "head" oftenest. I won that. Wellington Nelson won the prize in the arithmetic class and his was a volume of Andersen's Tales. I shall never forget the happiness the perusal of them gave me. After Wellington went away I never read them again until now, for I never could get a complete edition. At last I have succeeded in doing this by sending to England for it. It is the same edition Wellington had and the stories have lost none of their charm. I am glad I can find pleasure in fairy tales still.

My own prize was also a volume of fairy tales of which "The Honey Stew of the Countess Bertha" and "Gaffer Wind and Dame Rain" gave me no end of delightful "thrills". I have it yet. The "Honey Stew" abounded in ghosts and ghosts had a special fascination for me then. Indeed, to this very day I like nothing better than a well-told ghost story, warranted to send a cold chill down your spine.

Thursday, June 3, 1909
Cavendish, P.E.I.
This evening I went to the shore. As usual now, it was very quiet and lonely. When I was a child it was not so. Those were the days when the mackerel fishing was good and the shore was dotted with fishing houses. Grandfather and Uncle John fished together at the latter's shore. "Tony" Wyand, a peculiar local personage, also had a fishing house there, and Geo. R. had his close by. A few yards along the shore, at the end of the "Big Lane", where the rocks left off and the sand

hills began was quite a little colony of fishing houses. This was called "Cawnpore"—owing to the fact, I believe, that on the day the last nail was driven into the last house news arrived of the massacre of Cawnpore in the Indian Mutiny. There is not a house left there now and the name is forgotten, too.

When I was a child I spent much time at the shore. The men would get up at three or four and go out fishing. Then we children had to take their breakfast down at eight or nine—later on, their dinner and, if it were a good day for fish, then teas also. If they were not "in" when we went down we had to wait—sometimes for hours if the mackerel were biting. I soon, therefore, came to know every cove, headland and rock on that shore. We would take the spyglass and watch the boats, paddle in the water, gather shells and pebbles, or sit on the rocks and dream dreams. The pebbles were many and beautiful and some were curious.

The rocks at low tide were covered by millions of "snails" as we called them. I think periwinkles is the correct name. They had shells of all sizes, from those as big as a hazel nut down to shells as tiny as a pin head. I used to think—perhaps I was right—that these tiny ones were baby snails which would afterwards grow big. And I could not understand how the *shells* could grow, whatever their occupants might do. And I don't understand it yet, for that matter, if it be really the case. We often found great empty "snail shells", as big as our fists, which had washed ashore from some distant strand or deep sea haunt.

Then there were mussels, which were thought quite a delicacy by most people when brought home and baked. I never really liked them but used to eat them because it seemed rather the fashion. For the same reason I ate dulse, not caring a bit for it. I liked better to gather the long shirred ribbons of "kelp" or a queer little sea-weed with clusters of grape-like things that exploded with quite a noise when pinched.

The sea, constantly dashing against the soft, sandstone cliffs wore them away into many beautiful arches and caves. Somewhat to the east of our fishing houses was a rather bold headland. Through the "neck" of this headland a hole became worn—a hole so small that we could hardly thrust a hand through it. Every season it grew larger. One summer Pensie Macneill and I adventurously crawled through it. It was a tight squeeze and we used to exult with a fearful joy over having done it and speculate as to what would have happened if we had got stuck half way through!

In a few years we could walk upright through the opening. Still a few more years and a horse and cart could have been driven through it. Then the thin bridge of rock at the top gave way and the headland became a sort of island, as if a gateway had been cleft through its wall. It is a spot I have always loved.

There were many stories and legends connected with the shore which I heard older people tell and talk of. Grandfather liked a dramatic story, had a good memory for its fine points and could tell it well. There was the history of the terrible American Gale or "Yankee Storm" in the early '50's—so called because hundreds of American fishing vessels out in the gulf were wrecked along the north shore. One of the most striking and pathetic tales of this great storm was that of the *Franklin Dexter*. I never tired hearing it. The *Franklin Dexter* was a vessel which went ashore down at Cape Turner. All on board were lost, including four brothers, one of whom was captain and owner of the ship. They were the only sons of their father, a man in Portland, Me. After the storm their bodies came ashore and were buried, along with many others, in Cavendish churchyard. Their father, a broken-hearted old man, came on and insisted on having the bodies exhumed, saying that he had promised their mother that he would take her boys home to her. The coffins were put on board a trading vessel at New London, while the father returned home in a passenger vessel. The trading vessel was called the *Seth Hall*. She left New London harbor with the four bodies on board—*and was never heard of again*. It always seemed to me as if it were a thing foreordained— that the bodies of those boys were doomed to the sea. There was also a story that the captain of the *Seth Hall*, a profane man, had sailed out of the harbor at a time when the tide rendered it difficult to get out. He was told that he wouldn't be able to get out that night and he retorted that he would sail out of New London Harbor that night if he sailed straight to hell, and God Almighty shouldn't prevent him!

Then there was the Cape Leforce story—a bit of tragic, unwritten history, harking back to the days when the "Island of St. John" belonged to France. It was some time in 1760's (I can never remember dates). The only two dates that remain in my memory out of all those so painstakingly learned in schooldays, are—Julius Caesar landed in England 53 B.C. and the Battle of Waterloo was fought in 1815).

France and England were at war. French privateers infested the St. Lawrence gulf and plundered the commerce of the New England colonies. One of these was commanded by a Captain named Leforce. One night it anchored off what is now Cavendish shore—at that time, of course, a wooded solitude. For some reason the crew came ashore and spent the night, camped on a headland. The captain and his mate shared a tent and endeavored to come to a division of their booty. They quarrelled and it was arranged that they should fight a duel at sunrise. But in the morning, as the Captain was pacing off the distance, the mate treacherously raised his pistol and shot him in the back. I do not know whether the mate was ever punished for this in any way. Probably not. It was a mere sentence in a long page of bloodshed and piracy. But the captain was buried by his crew on the spot where he fell. I have often heard grandfather say that his father, old "Speaker" Macneill had seen the grave in his boyhood; but it had eventually crumbled off into the waves.

Nowadays the headland I have referred to as having the hole in it is called Cape Leforce, probably because it is the only striking looking headland on the shore. The real Cape Leforce is an insignificant little point further down.

Away to the westward six or seven miles the view was bounded by New London Point, a long, sharp tongue of land running far out to sea. In my childhood I never wearied of speculating what was on the other side of that point—a very realm of enchantment surely, I thought. Even when I gradually grew into the understanding that beyond it was merely another reach of shore like our own it still held a mystery and fascination for me. I longed to stand out on that remote, lonely, purple point, beyond which was the land of lost sunsets.

I have seen few more beautiful sights than a sea-sunset off that point. Of late years a new charm has been added to it—a revolving light which, as seen from here, flashes on the point in the dusk of summer nights like a beacon

"O'er the foam
Of perilous seas in fairylands forlorn."

The wreck of the *Marcopolo* occurred within my own remembrance. I was only seven years old but I have a very vivid recollection of the dramatic event, and of the exciting summer that followed it—a summer so different from the usual quiet, sleepy summer of Cavendish.

The *Marcopolo* was a very famous old ship—the fastest sailing vessel of her class ever built, her record never having been beaten. She had a strange, romantic history and was the nucleus of many traditions, some reliable, others mere flights of fancy, or pertaining to other ships. She had finally been condemned in England, under the Plimsoll Bill. Her owners evaded the bill by selling her to a Norwegian firm and then chartering her to carry a cargo of deal planks from Canada. On her return she was caught in a furious storm out in the gulf; she sprang a leak and soon became so waterlogged that the captain—Mr. *Bull* of Christiana—determined to run her on shore to save crew and cargo.

That day, the 25th of July, 1883, was a terrible windstorm here. We were in school; suddenly through the noise of the wind came the sound of a crash. The boys said it was a tree blown down in the woods. But to me the sound seemed to have a certain quality of *distance*—as if it had happened so far away that no crash of a fallen tree could reach our ears.

Meanwhile, although we did not know it, a crowd of people were already gathered on the sandshore, watching a magnificent sight—a sight I shall always regret not having seen—the sight of a large vessel coming straight on before the north gale with every stitch of canvas set. She grounded about 300 yards from the shore and as she struck the crew cut the rigging and the huge masts, one of them of iron, went over with the crash that we heard in the schoolroom a mile away.

The next morning the crew of 20 men got ashore. They found boarding places about the settlement and being typical tars, painted our quiet village a glowing scarlet for the remainder of the summer. It was their especial delight to crowd into a truck wagon and go galloping up and down the roads yelling at the tops of their voices. They were of many nationalities—Norwegians, Swedes, Dutchmen, Germans, Irishmen, Englishmen, Scotchmen, Spaniards and—most curious of all—two Tahitians, whose woolly heads, thick lips, and gold earrings were a never failing joy to myself and the little Nelson boys who were here then.

Captain Bull boarded here. He was a Norwegian, a delightful, gentlemanly old fellow who was idolized by his crew. He spoke English well but was apt to get mixed up in his prepositions and was as likely to thank you for your "kindness against" him as "to" him. The three mates boarded down at "Uncle Jimmie's". Owing to the captain being here, the crew haunted the place also. I remember on the night they were paid off, seeing them all sitting out on the grass under the parlor window, feeding our old dog "Gyp" with biscuits and trying to pronounce his name—"Yip", "Ship" and "Schnipp". Well and Dave and I saw, with eyes as big as owls', the round mahogany table in the parlor literally covered with gold sovereigns, which the captain paid out to them. Never had we imagined there was so much wealth in the world. The whole summer was a series of "pictures" to me.

Finally, after an immense amount of "red tape" the business was concluded.

The ship and cargo were sold to a St. John firm and Captain Bull and his motley crew took their departure.

A company of men were hired to take out the cargo, most of them being people belonging around here. Eighteen schooner loads of plank were taken out of her. The planks had so swelled from the wet that it was found necessary to cut through her beams to get them out. Consequently she was soon a mere shell, with half her cargo still in her.

Meanwhile, I was having a delightful time of it. The huge cables, as thick as a man's body, were coiled in our barnyard and made the most delightful playhouses imaginable. Then came a big auction which was held at our barns. That was quite a tremendous day for us small fry. The thing I most clearly remember was that a big sail was spread on the ground in the barnyard and piled with "hard tack", to which all and sundry might help themselves. It was about as easy to chew as a board but it was all gone by night. If you could succeed in gnawing some of it off it had a very sweet taste and Well, Dave and I chewed away at hard tack all day.

One fine evening the wreckers decided to stay on board all night—a very risky proceeding. By dawn another furious storm was raging and soon the shore was lined with a horrified crowd. You may be sure that "Well, Dave and I" were on hand. It was a never-to-be-forgotten scene.

Almost everyone there had a friend or relative on the vessel but nothing could be done. It was realized that the ship must soon break up. Three of the men on her, mad with fear, got into their boat, despite the fact that it had been "stove in" by the waves, and tried to reach shore. Of course the boat was instantly swamped. Two of the men managed to regain the wreck. The third was drowned before our eyes.

Suddenly the ship parted in two at the forecastle head and went down. But the windlass and a small piece of the bow still remained, held by the anchors and the men clung to this.

Meanwhile the beach was a sight to behold, heaped with deal plank for miles.

By evening the storm abated somewhat and a rescue party contrived, at much risk, to reach the wreck and bring ashore the exhausted sufferers.

Soon after, in another gale, the last vestige of the old ship disappeared. Divers were brought over to try to raise her copper bottom, valued at $10,000. They could not do it; it is there yet, covered from sight by the drifting sand, and there it will probably remain until "the sea gives up its dead".

There are many Marcopolo relics around Cavendish to this day. George R. has the name-board on one of his barns and is therefore frequently referred to as "Marcopolo George". There are also many-gate posts of the enduring pitch-pine of her masts—two of them in our barnyard to this day.

Tonight I watched the flashing light on my mysterious headland and thought over all those "old, forgotten, far-off things", gleaming in "the light that never was on sea or land."

Friday, June 4, 1909
Cavendish, P.E.I.

Last night there was an eclipse of the moon. I had an hour of pure enjoyment watching it. I have always found a wonderful fascination in eclipses. No matter how many I have seen I am always just as interested in a new one as if I had never seen one before. To watch that strange dark shadow creeping over the brightness, slowly, steadily, relentlessly, until the whole disc is covered and glows redly through it, like the smouldering ember of a burned-out world! Then to see it retreating, vanquished, and the "orbed maiden" coming out radiantly and calmly from her ordeal by darkness! Oh, one feels, as Emerson says, that one has been present at the creation of light and of the world.

I have always loved the moon. I suppose everybody does. We owe far more to the sun; in fact for all practical and essential purposes, we could get along quite as well without the moon altogether, while the loss of the sun would mean the extinction of our very lives. Yet nobody feels any particular affection for the sun. It is the moon we love. Her cold, silvery light irradiates the pages of old romance. Her never ceasing changes have all the charm of variety in a beautiful woman. There is no more exquisite sight in the universe than a young moon in a sunset sky. I have seen some new moons setting over dark hills that I shall remember in the halls of eternity.

And the magic of moonlight—the evasive, white-woven enchantment of moonlight—ah, we have all been intoxicated with it now and again—we have all walked in a world of faery "with the moon's beauty and the moon's soft pace."

Saturday, June 5, 1909
Cavendish, P.E.I.

This afternoon I spent at Russell Macneill's. It is necessary that I do these things occasionally—and how I dislike them!

I dislike—as I have always disliked—the country custom of going somewhere to "spend the afternoon". It is very seldom that it is anything but dull; and at Russell's it is worse than dull. Russell is a typical "clodhopper". His wife is a stupid, petty-minded woman. They are people with whom I have nothing in common. Yet I have to visit them now and again, else they would be offended. And that would not do, grandmother has to get Russell to haul her coal for her and do various other things which Uncle John refused to do for her. Hence, for her sake, I have to keep on friendly terms with people in whose company I find not one spark of interest or congeniality—people who can talk nothing but gossip and not even entertainingly of that. For gossip is *sometimes* interesting, if it is skilfully and delicately handled; but when it is infused with misunderstanding and jealousy and spite—Good Lord, deliver us! It is dreadful to visit at a place where you have to say every word over to yourself before you utter it aloud to make sure it is harmless and won't involve you in mischief if reported elsewhere.

Saturday, June 25, 1909
Cavendish, P.E.I.
Tonight I had to go to a choir practice. I have been going to choir practices for six years and I do not think I have grumbled to you—or anyone about it. But tonight I *must* grumble—and so get those six years out of my system.

Choir practice is one of the most unpleasant duties I have to fulfil. Six years ago, when the former organist went away, I had to step into her place. I say *had* to. There was absolutely no one else in the church who could play the organ at that time and although I was bitterly averse to becoming organist I was urged by minister and choir until I was driven to consent.

I have always disliked the position. I have no real musical gift and so feel like "a square peg in a round hole". Still, the playing of simple hymns and Psalm tunes on Sunday does not demand any great talent and I do not so much dislike *that*. It is the choir practice I dislike. Some of the members of the choir are no friends of mine and I always feel the atmosphere disagreeable. Some of them are no friends of each other and are always getting slighted or offended. In the winter I have to walk long distances alone to the practices. Yes, I hate it all. I look forward to every practice night with aversion. It is so apt to be disagreeable in one way or another. Tonight it was especially so. Uncle John's daughter "Tot", an impudent, ill-bred girl, justly disliked by all the members of the choir was, as usual, a disturbing element and annoyed everybody.

July 11, 1909
Cavendish, P.E.I.
To-day I finished reading Keats' poems. I got the book in March and have been reading so many pages per day ever since. On the whole, I do not like Keats. Perhaps if I had known him in childhood I might have so grown up with him as to love him, tinging his lines with the hues of my own life as I lived it. But I did not and he comes to me too late.

It is not because I find his poems lacking in beauty that they leave me indifferent. They are, in reality, *too full of beauty*. One feels stifled in roses and longs for a breath of frosty air or the austerity of a mountain peak towering to the stars. There is little in Keats' poems except luscious beauty—so much of it that the reader is surfeited. At least, that is how they affected me....

August 1st, 1909
Cavendish, P.E.I.
This evening I spent in Lover's Lane. How beautiful it was—green and alluring and beckoning! I had been tired and discouraged and sick at heart before I went to it—and it rested me and cheered me and stole away the heartsickness, giving peace and newness of life.

I owe much to that dear lane. And in return I have given it love—and fame. I painted it in my book: and as a result the name of this little remote woodland lane is known all over the world. Visitors to Cavendish ask for it and seek it out. Photographs of its scenery have appeared in the magazines. The old lane is famous.

September 1, 1909
Cavendish, P.E.I.

My new book "Anne of Avonlea" came today. We very soon become used to things. When my first book came to me I was much excited and half intoxicated with joy. But the new book only interested me mildly. I liked its "get-up" and glanced over it with calm approval—and then went for a walk in the woods and thought no more about it.

I have dedicated it to my old teacher, Miss Gordon, in gratitude for her sympathy and encouragement in the old days. Whether she will ever see it or not I do not know for I have lost track of her. I have not heard from her for over three years and all my efforts to locate her present abode have been in vain.

September 4, 1909
Cavendish, P.E.I.

I have been reading Tennyson to-day. I like Tennyson, although I cannot think he is a supremely great poet. There is something lacking in him. He is very beautiful—not *too* beautiful, as Keats is—very graceful, in short, the Perfect Artist. But he seldom lets us *forget* the artist—we are always *conscious* of the art—we are never swept away by some splendid mountain torrent of feeling. Not he—he flows on serenely, between well-ordered banks and carefully laid out pleasaunces. And that is good. But an occasional bit of wild nature would make it better still. No matter how much one loves a garden one does not want to be cooped up in it *all* the time—one likes an excursion now and then to the waste places.

I detest Tennyson's *Arthur*! If I'd been *Guinevere* I'd have been unfaithful to him too. But not for *Lancelot—he* is just as unbearable in another way. As for *Geraint*, if I'd been *Enid* I'd have *bitten* him. These "patient Griseldas" of women deserve all they get!

Speaking to a friend once of Tennyson I said, "I *like* Tennyson because he gives me nothing but pleasure. I cannot *love* him because he gives me nothing but pleasure."

My friend did not understand the epigram. But it held truth. I love best the poets who *hurt* me—who offer me the roses of their thoughts with the sharp thorn among them, piercing to the bone and marrow. When in reading a poem I come across some line or couplet that thrusts itself into my heart with a stab of deadly pain—then is my soul knit unto the soul of that poet forevermore. Browning hurts me worse than any poet I have ever read—and so I love him most. Even Wordsworth, "as soft as evening in his favorite May", occasionally says something so vital and poignant that I am ready to cry out with the agony of it—and so I love him too, in spite of his much balderdash.

But I think I shall have some love for Tennyson after this—for today I read a verse in *In Memoriam* which I do not think I can ever have read carefully before—which scorched me with a sudden flame of self-revelation and brought to me one of those awful moments when we look into the abysses of our own natures and recoil in horror from the shapes of evil we see there—as if, while treading over garlands, we had inadvertently peeped into a foul nest of knotted snakes.

The verse was—

"Do we indeed desire the dead
Should still be near us at our side?
Is there no baseness we would hide,
No *inner vileness* that we dread?"

I stopped to repeat the question to myself and forced myself to answer it. Did I really wish *my* dead to be near me—at my side—*always*—to know all my thoughts and hear all my words and see all my deeds? No—no—no! A thousand shuddering times no! And in that admission was the shame and shrinking of the realization that I do or think things every day of my life which I would not be willing to have them know or share in.

Tuesday, Sept. 21, 1909
Cavendish, P.E.I.

This evening Oliver Macneill and I were walking in Lover's Lane under its whispering maple boughs and balsam breathing firs. The air was warm and wood-fragrant; the moonlight fell down through the boughs in splashes of silver. It was all very beautiful. But tonight I realized that I must walk no more in Lover's Lane with Oliver Macneill.

He is a second cousin of mine, home from Dakota on a visit. He came the first of the month and I have seen a good deal of him. There were a great many things in him I did not like, and several more that I laughed at but he was pleasant, companionable and, in some ways, interesting. It didn't occur to me that there was any danger in our friendship. I knew that he had recently divorced his wife on the ground of her unfaithfulness and that gossip reported him to be "looking for" another one—probably thinking that he might find a more satisfactory one among our simple unspoiled P.E.I. girls. And I knew that in the first week of our acquaintance he had shown some unmistakeable signs that he hoped to find her in me. But as I had snubbed all his advances and as he has since been paying marked attention to Campsie Clark I did not suppose there was any reason why I should not accept and enjoy the pleasant companionship which thus offered itself for a time in my lonely life.

But tonight I found that I was again playing with fire. Oliver Macneill told me he loved me and asked me to be his wife. Now, I would not marry Oliver Macneill for any inducement that could be offered to me—I do not feel the slightest wish or temptation to marry him. So our intercourse must cease. He is one of those impulsive, passionate men who rush to extremes in everything and a further indulgence in our companionship might bring real suffering into his life. I don't want to do this. His love, springing up thus suddenly in a few weeks, cannot as yet have taken much hold on his nature and he will soon forget me.

There is another reason—and a humiliating one—why I must put an end to our companionship. Tonight I realized clearly that Oliver Macneill is one of those men of whom I have met a few in my life—men who, without being able to inspire in me one spark of real love or even admiration, yet have the power to kindle in me a devastating flame of the senses. I have a horror of feeling thus towards any man I cannot marry. It seems to me a shameful, degrading, dangerous thing—and it is. Tonight I thrilled from head to foot under the caressing tones of Oliver's voice and his physical nearness to me as we walked in that shadowy lane. *He* did not know or suspect this—I succeeded in hiding it. But the very repression of such intense feeling made it burn more fiercely. I was ashamed of it—and yet, too, I knew there was in it

"The poison and the sting

Of things too sweet."

It *was* sweet, with all the deadly sweetness of the pleasures of sense, blent with the spiritual charm of the moonlight and the whispering shadows.

Oliver took my answer hardly and pleaded passionately, but I do not think there is much lasting harm done as far as he is concerned. I think he is a man who falls in love easily and quickly, loves wildly for the time being, and gets over it just as easily and quickly.

He is a curious compound psychologically—an odd mixture of the most contradictory characteristics.

And must not the same thing be said of myself? Do not extremes meet in my nature also? Can it be that the woman who stood on the shore last night and felt her very soul caught up to the seventh heaven in an unspeakable rapture of pure aspiration and unearthly joy be the same woman who walked in Lover's Lane tonight and burned with the wild flame of sense that scorched me? How can such things be? Is it because the higher the tree reaches towards the stars the deeper must its roots strike into the soil of earth? Perhaps that is the explanation.

October 13, 1909
Cavendish, P.E.I.
Today Oliver Macneill left on his return to Dakota.

These last three weeks have been a species of nightmare to me. There was no use in trying to avoid Oliver—he sought me out everywhere and came here almost every evening. I had to go out walking with him or he would have made a scene before anyone who happened to be about. He would not take no for an answer. I have never seen such a reckless, desperate man. I think he tried every possible means to induce me to marry him, even to trying to bribe me with his wealth—of which it seems he has a goodly share. He made all sorts of absurd propositions—if I would marry him and live with him three months out of the year I could go where I liked and live where I pleased the rest of the time! If I would be his wife for *one year* he would take himself out of my life at the end of the time etc.

At last, however, I convinced him that he was wasting his breath. He is gone—and the whirlwind of passion that has so suddenly swept over my life will speedily die away. I know that and am glad of it. Yet just at this moment there is something in me that is crying out for him with a hideous desire and longing. My higher self is thankful he is gone; but my lower self is writhing in agony and would leap up with a fierce joy if Oliver were at this instant to appear before me.

October 20, 1909
Cavendish, P.E.I.

Thank God, I am my own woman again—and wondering at myself! I feel as if some evil demon had been exorcised out of me. For the past week I have lived in an anguish of smothered emotion. And then, all at once, it was as if a fever left me—as if some unclean spirit had been cast out. On my bended knees this morning I prayed that nothing like this might ever enter my life again. It costs too much to conquer it. The crushing down of such powerful impulses does a violence to Nature which she is not slow to avenge. "Another such victory and I am undone."

November 7, 1909
Cavendish, P.E.I.

This evening I walked in Lover's Lane—and enjoyed it for the first time since Oliver Macneill went away. For some time after he left I could not go there. One evening I tried. I got as far as the fence by Mr. Webb's field and I had to turn back. A week later I made another attempt. This time I forced myself to go to the lane, for I knew that was the only way to exorcise the memories that were spoiling it for me. I went through it from end to end in the twilight. Every step was an anguish. Longing and loneliness possessed me.

But the next time was easier; and tonight the lane was my own again and there was nothing in my thoughts or feelings to come between me and the soul of the woods.

Sunday, Dec. 5, 1909
Cavendish, P.E.I.

....I am much better physically this fall than I have been for some time. I have been, as usual, much worried, overworked mentally by reason of having nothing to do but work, and at times very lonely. But so far this season I have had none of those terrible attacks of gloom and restlessness. In October I was in town and consulted Dr. Jenkins. I have been taking his medicine ever since and probably that is why I feel better. When I think of November last year I cringe. What a hideous month it was for me! I am very thankful indeed that this year has not repeated that experience.

Yet I dread the winter more than I can express. Grandmother is suffering so from rheumatism now. I feel so alone and helpless when I realize our position. Well, I suppose I have to live only one day at a time and one always seems able to do *that*. It is the "tomorrow" we can't live through! If I can only keep physically well and nervously unbroken I shall not mind anything else so much.

Thursday, Dec. 23, 1909
Cavendish, P.E.I.

So far this week has been a hard one. I must write a bit of a growl tonight to relieve my feelings. I fear I am going to be very nervous again this winter just as I was last.

I have been over-working of late. The Page Co. wish to bring out in book form a serial of mine which ran in a magazine last winter. It was called "Una Of The

Garden". But it was not long enough to please them, so I have had to re-write and lengthen it—a business I dislike very much. I began it in mid-November and as it had to be in the publishers' hands by New Year's I had to hurry. A fortnight ago I saw that I would not be able to finish it at my regular rate of progress, so I have been writing at it every spare minute since until I would fairly feel faint with fatigue. But I shall have it done on time. Its name is to be changed to "Kilmeny of the Orchard". It is a love story with a psychological interest—very different from my other books and so a rather doubtful experiment with a public who expects a certain style from an author and rather resents having anything else offered it.

Monday it snowed all day. I wrote from morning until bed-time. Tuesday it snowed all day, I wrote from morning until dark. Then I dressed and went with Alec and May Macneill to spend the evening with friends in Rustico. I was so tired I could not enjoy myself and as usual was worried about grandmother at home alone. We had an unpleasant drive home and I got snow-damp and chilly. I could not sleep when I went to bed and got up yesterday morning with a sore throat. It snowed all day and I wrote all day. My throat grew worse and at dark I had to drop my pen and lie down on the sofa. My head ached and I was feverish, and that feeling of dread and weariness I know so well again took possession of my mind. I hated the thought of going to bed. I knew I would not sleep and the thought of lying there in the darkness, feeling as I did, seemed unbearable. At last I resolved not to endure the darkness anyhow but to leave my lamp burning all night. I was afraid to do so, for grandmother often prowls about the house after night, to seek out the cause of mysterious noises she hears or fancies she hears, and if she were to discover my light burning would think it a dreadful extrava- gance or would think I was up to some unlawful doings—and would never be able to sleep in peace again. But last night I determined to risk it. It was well I did for I had a bad night, sleeping fitfully with oppressive dreams, and then waking up in mental and physical distress. At such times it was a great comfort to *see* my own dear room, with my pictures on the walls and my books on their shelves. I think I was a little light-headed with the fever of my cold, for it seemed to me that the *sight* of those familiar objects was all that kept me from falling into some horrible abyss of strangeness.

To-day it snowed all day. There is a great deal of snow down. No mail came. I wrote from nine o'clock in the morning until eight in the evening. My throat is still sore, but my headache is better and I hope I shall sleep tonight. But I am very tired and weary and sick at heart. Every morning I set my teeth to endure the day. Every evening I wonder how I am to face to-morrow. I am very morbid and nervous. I know it is mainly from lack of exercise and too-constant work. But what can I do? It is impossible to go walking in soft snow four feet deep. And if I don't work there is nothing to pass the time. I am so thankful I *can* work. I hope and pray *that* capacity may never be taken from me, for if it should be I would not be able to go on with life.

I have some lovely bulbs in flower. They are a great comfort and sweetness to me.

Christmas Eve 1909
Cavendish, P.E.I.

Christmas Eve! The very name seems like a mockery to me. A time of good-will and peace and rejoicing—and I feeling as I do! I must "write it out" before I go to bed, or I shall not sleep tonight—and I do want to sleep, for I haven't slept well this week and if I do not tonight what shall I do tomorrow—Christmas day?

As it was impossible to stir out I wrote all day. My throat is better but I am tired and spiritless. I forced myself to work because working is one degree *less hard* than not working. Of course I could not have done any original work but fortunately I had my *Kilmeny* manuscript ready to copy out and I wrote at it until my hand grew too stiff and tired to write more.

The mail came at dark—a heavy Christmas mail. It was full of Christmas boxes and greetings for me and the pleasure and excitement of these might have roused me out of my depression if a letter from Frede Campbell had not been among them, telling me of the serious illness of her father. Aunt Annie is as yet none too well, though better than last year; and I feel as if she and Uncle John Campbell were the only ones in the world to whom I can turn for any help in regard to grandmother.

My condition this evening alarms me—I feel so bitter and *vindictive*. I can't even cry—it would be a relief if I could. I know this is a morbid mood and not the real *me*—but it has me at grips for all that. I feel like a trapped creature, tortured by every movement, ready to bite savagely even at the hand of a deliverer.

In years past I asked of fate happiness and joy. Now all I ask is peace of mind and release from my load of care and worry. It is crushing the life out of me—and, worse still, it is making a bitter woman of me. I find myself tonight wishing that I had been born a hard, entirely selfish person, with no regard whatever for the feelings of others and no sense of duty or hesitancy in inflicting pain. That wish is dreadful. I *know* it—and I shall *feel* its dreadfulness when this black mood is past. But just now it is surging up in my soul and drowning out everything else.

I feel utterly *rebellious*. I feel tonight as if God were indeed the cruel tyrant of Calvin's theology, who tortures his creatures for no fault of their own at His whim and pleasure. I feel like shrieking at Him defiantly. "Why did you create me to suffer like this? Why did you thwart every wish and instinct and sensibility you implanted in me? I will not give you reverence or love any more than a creature strapped to the rack will love or reverence his tormentor."

Like Byron's *Cain*, I feel like saying that I could

"dare to look
The Omnipotent tyrant in the face and tell Him
His evil is *not* good."

In days to come I shall read over this record with horror. But it shall stand—I shall always let it stand to make me more gentle in my judgment of rash deeds in others, when I recall the fearful thoughts that surged into my own soul, like some foul brood engendered in darkness.

My common sense tells me that all this is mainly the result of a week's confinement to the house and distressing conditions in that house. Very true. If this had brought about physical illness my common sense would indicate the cause just as truly. But that would not remove the illness—or dull the pain—or assist recovery.

Saturday Night. Dec. 25, 1909
Christmas is over. I am glad!

Last night I could not get the sleep for which I hoped. I had a wild fit of crying after I went to bed. Then I spent the rest of the night in fitful doses made wretched by bad dreams and a terrible sense of physical oppression. This morning when I wakened I felt as if I *could not* get up. Up I did get, however. I felt badly until the middle of the forenoon, when the feeling of dread and "blackness" suddenly left me. I was better for the rest of the day. In the afternoon I went to William Laird's where I had been invited for tea. I did not feel like going but I forced myself to go because I thought it might be better for me.

I walked down over a very bad road, through a dead, stirless white world, under a chill gray sky. I cannot say I enjoyed myself. There was in my mind and soul something cold and hard and bitter that prevented that. And to compel oneself to talk and laugh and jest when feeling wretched is not pleasant. But still I felt better for going. The brood of black thoughts that had infested my heart scurried out of sight when laughter and companionship shed light on them, as rats will hide from the light. I felt as if I had been released from the grasp of an evil thing.

Sunday, Dec. 26, 1909
Cavendish, P.E.I.
We are in the grip of a terrible winter storm and will, I fear, be all drifted up by morning. I am suffering from a very severe cold. I can hardly breathe, my head aches and a hard tight cough racks me continually. It would not be much wonder if I were nervous and depressed but I am not. I certainly do not feel very cheerful but the "black mood " is not on me tonight.

I passed the day reading and writing letters.
"I sought for shelter from cold and snow
In the light and warmth of long ago"
by reading over the journal of my schooldays. Some days this has a bad effect on me but it did not have today. I found myself dwelling on what was bright and happy in those old years and the better and more lovable qualities in those with whom I lived and mingled. I have temporarily lost the power of lightening present ills by looking hopefully forward to the future. Somehow I cannot do that now. If life yet holds any good thing for me it can only be reached by a passage through pain and worry and anguish of parting such as in my present condition of nervous weakness I shrink from intolerably. "Forward tho' I canna see, I guess and fear." So it is easier to look backward to the sunny spots in the past.

Nevertheless, owing to my physical distress it has been a long day. This evening, as I paced the floor in the twilight, listening to poor grandmother groaning with rheumatism, I smiled rather grimly as I contrasted my lot with what the world doubtless supposes it to be. I am a famous woman; I have written two very successful books. I have made a good bit of money. Yet, partly owing to

Uncle John's behavior, partly to grandmother's immovable prejudices I can do *nothing* with my money to make life easier and more cheerful for grandmother and myself. And there is so much I *might* do if I could—fix up this old home comfortably, furnish it conveniently, keep a servant, travel a little, entertain my friends. But as it is I am as helpless as a chained prisoner.

I think I have coughed once for every sentence written here.

100. A little gate into Lovers' Lane
[Cavendish]

101. Oliver Macneill

102. My own dear room
[*Cavendish*]

1910

....I finished and sent off the *MS* of *Kilmeny* last week. I miss it for I cannot settle down to any work which requires concentrated thought. *Kilmeny* did not. I had merely to copy and amplify existing thoughts. I am making very poor progress with *The Story Girl*. The hours are rare when I am in a mood for creative work and I do not wish to spoil it by working at it when I cannot do my conception of it justice.

Tonight I feel that life is *too hard*—that I cannot endure it any longer.

Today I have spent on the sofa all the time I was not doing necessary work. I was too weary to lift my head. I lay there—and *thought* and *thought*. I seem to have been living over my whole past life today, from my earliest recollection. I have been haunted and tortured by old memories. I do not know which hurt the most—the pleasant ones or the unhappy ones. I think the former. My mood is very morbid. I wonder if it would do any good to write out all the recollections that have crowded into my thoughts today, like a series of pictures and sensations, at which I could not choose but look and which I could not choose but feel. Besides, I am always being bothered by publishers and editors for "information" regarding my childhood and "career", and it will be handy to have it all ready for them at the cost of copying out.

I have always had a somewhat remarkable memory—an advantage which, like everything else, has its shadow. I can remember when I was no more than twenty months old. As I have written before in this journal I remember seeing my mother in her coffin. She died on September 14, 1876, when I was 22 months old. But in July of that summer Uncle Leander and his family were here. One of them was my cousin Cassie, a child slightly older than myself. I remember sitting on the sofa in the room and seeing Cassie, in a white, embroidered dress, going through the hall door. I have three other memories, which I think must have antedated this, but I have no means of determining just how old I was at the several times. In the very nature of them, however, they must have belonged to the first dawning of consciousness. I think they occurred before I could talk. On one occasion I remember myself in father's arms, being carried about the sitting room to look at the pictures and other ornaments. On the mantel was a glass vase with a border of deep scallops. On these scallops were markings somewhat resembling a human face. As father held me up to see this it seemed to me that the face on one of the scallops made a hideous grimace at me. I was terrified beyond endurance. I broke out into screaming and would not be pacified. I remember that terror—and *feel* it—vividly at this very moment.

The second memory is similar in its nature. We had company to tea. I behaved badly in some fashion at the table and Aunt Emily took me away and shut me up alone in the parlor. It was very dusky for the slat blinds were down. I stood inside the door, a cold, terrified mortal, sobbing in fear and shame. Then it suddenly seemed to me that all the chairs in the room, headed by the big haircloth rocking chair, were dancing around the table in the centre, making faces at me as they passed me. Oh, the horror of it! I broke into frenzied screaming and I think someone came and took me out.

The third memory is of father taking me to town to be photographed. The photographer brought out a big fur robe to fling over the chair. Again I was terrified. I cried and screamed; nothing, not even the taking away of the fur, could pacify me. So no picture was taken of me that day. I am sure I could not *talk* at the time of these memories. I have no recollection of *saying* a word—only of things *seen* and sensations *felt*.

The first six years of my life are very hazy. I do not seem to have any *connected* memories of them. Here and there a picture-like scene stands out in vivid colors. Many of these are connected with visits to Grandfather Montgomery's place at Park Corner. They lived in the "old house" then—a most quaint and delightful old place as I remember it. I recall in particular a certain long "back hall", with cupboards on one side and a window on the other. At the end of this was a short flight of steps going up to a little private sitting room of Grandmother Montgomery's. Out of this another flight of steps led down to Grandmother's bedroom. "Grandmother" Montgomery was my father's stepmother. His own mother had died several years before. It was there, when I was about five or six that I had typhoid fever. I remember it very distinctly. The night before I took ill I was out in the kitchen with the servants. I was sitting before the stove—an old "Waterloo"— and the cook was "riddling" the fire with a long straight bar of iron used for that purpose. She laid it down on the hearth and I promptly picked it up, intending to do some "riddling" myself—an occupation I much liked, loving to see the glowing red embers fall down on the black ashes.

Alas, I picked the poker up by the wrong end! As a result my hand was terribly burned. It was my first initiation into physical pain—at least the first of which I have any recollection. I suffered horribly and cried bitterly, yet I took considerable satisfaction out of the commotion I had caused. For the time being I was splendidly, satisfyingly important. Grandfather scolded the poor, distracted cook. Father entreated that something be done for me; frenzied folks ran about suggesting and applying a score of different remedies. One of these—to hold the burned hand in a saucer of kerosene oil—made the burn far worse. Finally I cried myself to sleep, holding my hand and wrist in a pail of cold water—the only thing that gave me any relief.

In the morning I wakened with a headache. Father dressed me and carried me out to the breakfast-table. I could not eat and began to cry. They took me into the little bedroom off the sitting room and put me to bed. I remember nothing more of my hand. It was well long before I was. I had typhoid fever.

I do not know how long I was ill but I was very low and several times they thought I could not possibly recover. Grandmother Macneill was sent for and came up. I was so delighted to see her that the excitement increased my fever and after she had gone out father, thinking to calm me, told me that she had gone home. He meant well but it was an unfortunate statement. I believed it implicitly— too implicitly. When Grandmother came in again I could not be convinced that it was she. No, *she* had gone home. Consequently, this tall thin woman by the bed must be Mrs. Murphy, a woman who worked frequently at grandfather's and whom I did not like. Nothing could convince me as to the contrary. From that out, all through my illness, I would not suffer grandmother to approach me or do anything for me—no, she was Mrs. Murphy and I would not have her near me. This was put down to delirium but it does not seem to me that it was. I was quite conscious of everything else. It was rather the fixed impression made on my mind in its weak state by what father had told me. Grandmother had gone home, I reasoned. *Therefore*, the woman who looked like her *must* be someone else.

It was not until I was able to sit up that I got over this delusion. One evening it simply dawned on me that it really was grandmother. I was so happy and could not bear to be out of her arms. I remember stroking her face continually and saying in amazement and delight, "Why, you are *not* Mrs. Murphy after all—you are grandma."

Everybody seemed very glad when I recovered. I think it would have been much better for me if I had died then. How much suffering I would have been spared!

Typhoid fever patients were not dieted so strictly during convalescence in those days as they are now. I remember one day, long before I was able to sit up, that my dinner consisted of fried sausages—rich, pungent, savory, home-made sausages. I felt hungry and I ate ravenously. Of course, by all the rules of the game those sausages should have killed me. But they did not. These things are fated. I feel sure that nothing short of Predestination saved me from those sausages.

I remember a terrible fright I got the next summer. It was announced in a Charlottetown paper that a certain man who set up to be a prophet had predicted that the coming Sunday would be the judgment day. I believed this—or almost believed it—and my agony of mind was dreadful. I dared not ask the opinion of the "grown-ups" because I was almost as much afraid of being laughed at as I was of the Judgment Day. But all the Saturday before the fateful Sunday I vexed Aunt Emily to distraction by repeatedly asking her if we would go to Sunday School the next afternoon. Her impatient assurances that of course we would were a great comfort to me. If she really expected that there would be Sunday School she could not believe that the next day would see the end of the world. Nevertheless the next night and all Sunday was a period of intense wretchedness for me. Sleep was entirely out of the question. Might I not hear "the last trump" at any moment? I can laugh at it now—anyone would laugh. But it was real torture to a credulous child—just as real as mental agony in after life.

Sunday was even more interminable than Sundays usually were. But it came to an end at last and as its "low-descending sun" dimpled the purple sky line of the

Gulf I drew a long breath of relief. The beautiful green world of blossom and sunshine had not been burned up. It was going to last for awhile longer. But I have never forgotten the suffering of that Sunday.

The next summer I began to go to school. I had learned to read and write before going and was in the "second book" of the old *Royal Reader* series in vogue then. I had learned the "primer" at home, and then gone into the second reader thus skipping the "first" reader. When I went to school and found out that there was a "first" reader I felt greatly aggrieved to think I had never "gone through" it. I seemed to have missed something—to suffer, in my own estimation at least, a certain loss of standing because I had never had it. To this day there is a queer, absurd regret in my soul that I missed that first reader when all the other children had it.

However, there I was in the Second Reader; and I remember—with a little thrill to this day—the compliment the teacher paid me on my reading—the first compliment I have any recollection of receiving. We were standing up in the side aisle and our lesson was the immortal rhyme, "How Doth the Little Busy Bee". We all read in turn and then "the master" said of me, "This little girl reads better than any of you, although she is younger and has never been to school before." How my heart swelled! Truly, the trite old words of the trite old song are as true as most trite things are—"Kind words can never die".

I have no especial remembrance of my first day in school. Aunt Emily took me down to the schoolhouse—which was just outside our gate—and gave me into the charge of some of the "big girls" with whom I sat that day. The next morning I was late. Very shyly I slipped into the schoolroom and sat down beside one of the "big" girls—Pensie Macneill, I think. At once a wave of laughter rippled over the school.

I had come in with my hat on!

As I write, the fearful shame and humiliation I endured at that moment rushes over me again. I felt that I was a target for the ridicule of the universe. Never, I felt certain, could I live down such a terrible mistake. I crept out to take off my hat, a crushed morsel of humanity.

The big girls—they were ten years old and seemed all but grown-up to me—soon tired of my novelty and I gravitated down to my own age. That first summer I sat in the front seat with Maud Woodside. Minie—short for Jemima—Kesley also sat with us for a short time. We "did" sums and learned the multiplication table and wrote copies and read lessons and repeated spellings. At recesses we played for the most part in the "bush". I shall always be thankful that my school was near a grove—a spruce grove with winding paths and treasure trove of ferns and mosses and violets. It was a better educative influence in my life than the lessons learned at the desk in school. And there was a brook in it, too—a delightful brook with a big, deep clear spring where we went for buckets of water. It was a great treat to be allowed to "go for a bucket" of water.

We had playhouses in the bush—two or three girls sharing one between them. And great was the rivalry between the various establishments in broken dishes, mossed cupboards and stone seats. We picked gum, too, which the teacher remorselessly confiscated when he saw us chewing it. My first teacher was Kaye

Ross. I went to him only a few days as I had begun going near the close of the school year. He was followed by George Simpson who taught only till New Year's. I remember nothing at all of him and very little of his successor—a man named Lamont, who had red hair, *whiskers*—also red—and a *wife*. That a schoolmaster should have whiskers and a wife seemed two uncanny and unnatural things to those of us who were used to the beardless youths in their teens who had been the Cavendish pedagogues.

I remember very little of Mr. Lamont beyond his red side-whiskers and the fact that he tried to make me, a child of seven, learn off by heart the long complex formulas in the arithmetic. They were totally incomprehensible to me and he might as well have tried to make me memorize Greek. But at the time I supposed, with a seven-year-old's pathetic faith in the wisdom of grown-ups, that he was quite right in trying to make me learn them. But now I feel indignation and contempt for a man who would set a child a task so impossible—and useless if possible! I can't imagine what his motive was. No other teacher ever thought of such a thing. Even Lamont himself never asked any of the other children to do it.

In the winter following my seventh birthday Aunt Emily married and went away. I remember her wedding as quite an event, as well as the weeks of mysterious preparations beforehand and all the baking and "frosting" of cakes that went on. Aunt Emily was only a girl then but in my eyes she was as old as all the grown-ups. I had no conception of age then. Either you were grown-up or you were not—that was all there was about it.

The wedding was one of the good, old-fashioned sort—all the big "connection" on both sides being present, the ceremony at seven o'clock, supper immediately afterwards, dancing and games until the wee sma's, and another big supper at one o'clock. Aunt Emily was dressed in brown silk. A silk dress was a great rarity in those days and nobody expected to have more than one in a lifetime. My mother's was a bright green silk. To my mind it was very ugly; but I believe it was thought very handsome at the time. It was trimmed with bands of green satin and green fringe. And the skirt was very voluminous. Aunt Emily's, eight years later, was furnished out with pleatings and flounces and overskirt. And it had a train, with a white ruching sewed all around it! Of course she had a bonnet. Whenever a young girl was married in those days she immediately donned a bonnet, no matter if she were still in her teens. It was not until five years later that this fashion died out. I was about twelve when the last bride wearing a bonnet "appeared out" in Cavendish church. It was a bonnet of brown silk with "drab" bows and long satin ties. Aunt Emily's bonnet was of black jet with a white feather. It seems absurd enough now; yet those dressy little bonnets were very becoming to fresh young faces; and nothing is ridiculous when it is the custom!

Her bridesmaid was Grace Macneill, also arrayed in brown silk. Uncle John Montgomery was a great favorite of mine. He was a kind, generous, open hearted man. Aunt Emily's wedding was the last festivity in this old house. With her went all the social life that had ever centered here. Grandfather and grandmother were left to settle into the indifferent routine of age and I to grow up in that routine.

The next summer Mr. Lamont went away and William McKay came. I have very little recollection of the year he taught here, as far as school goes and, in spite of the fact that he boarded here for the first six months, I remember little of his personality. I could not have disliked him, however, or I should remember it. Neither could I have been much attracted to him. We "small fry" did not come in for much notice from the teachers then, so they made no great impression on us. He was a very dark, black-haired, thick-browed man, commonly known as "Bill Buffer", from the fact that his father who lived at Clifton was known as "Buffer" McKay—to distinguish him from the many other McKays there.

To digress for a moment—the subject of those McKays was a humorous one. I remember having heard that when father kept store at Clifton there was *twenty six* William McKay's on his books. To differentiate so many of the same name nicknames were resorted to, some of which were ludicrous enough. "Geordie Bain", "Geordie Squires", "Geordie Bush", "Geordie Creek" were all legally George McKay. Sandy Long Jim and Sandy Big Tom were others. They were never spoken of in any other way. It is a matter of record that a minister in Clifton once gravely called upon "Alexander Big Jim" to lead in prayer. And Alexander Big Jim as gravely complied. Nobody even smiled.

To return to our mutton—that is, the year Mr. McKay taught here. Time was then reckoned in Cavendish by the year of the reigning pedagogue, much after the fashion of ancient Rome with her consuls.

That was the summer the *Marcopolo* came ashore and the Nelson boys came here to board. It was a very happy summer for me. There was so much going on—so much excitement—that I was left pretty much alone and not teased or nagged. I had constant playmates, too, for the first time, and this was rare good fortune. I have described my life with the Nelson boys elsewhere in this journal, so there is no need to repeat it here. But those three years of their stay in Cavendish comprise the brightest and happiest memories of my childhood— unclouded memories, for we never had a quarrel in all those three years and we *did* have fun in abundance—simple, wholesome fun, with our playhouses and swings, our games in the beautiful summer twilights when we ranged happily through fields and orchards, or in the long winter evenings by the fire.

After Mr. McKay went away Mr. Fraser came. He was a boyish young fellow and boarded here. He was not a successful teacher for he could not control the big turbulent boys, as old as himself, who attended then. But we little folk loved him because he was so good and kind to us. Soon after he came he created an enormous sensation by offering prizes. How excited we all were! I made up my mind to win the prize in my class—offered to the one who was "head oftenest". I *did* win it and I have it yet. It was a volume of delightful fairy tales and even yet I can read them with pleasure.

Early in the winter following my ninth birthday I took a severe cold which settled on my lungs. I was miserable all winter and did not go to school. I was not allowed to go outside the door—somewhat different from the present day method of treating lung troubles!

Father was home that winter and spent much of his time here. His visits were periods of unclouded delight for me. He had come home from the West after a three year's absence and remained home till March, when he went west again leaving his native Island forever although he knew it not.

Apart from father my principal pleasures were dolls and books. Of dolls I had quite a family and I was very fond of playing with them. I had two "china" ones and three wax ones. One of the china ones had half her head broken off and the other had lost an arm. But how I loved them for their very misfortunes! One of the wax dolls was a small one I had found in my stocking on my sixth Christmas. The second was quite a large one which Mrs. Cunningham, the aunt of the Nelson boys, had sent me. I was very proud of her because she was so beautifully dressed in red cashmere trimmed with lace, but I never gave her as much love as I gave my broken china ones. The third was a huge doll as large as a baby, also the gift of Mrs. Cunningham. I was proud of this doll because of her size but I don't think I loved her at all. All my dolls had very fancy names but I have forgotten them all except that of the largest one which was called Roselle Heraldine. I had a little doll bedstead which father had given me, with a complete outfit of sheets, pillows and blankets. I learned to sew, making patchwork quilts for my dolls, and I had a goodly supply. Then I had a little china teaset and a tiny frying pan and a little iron, all of which were a great source of pleasure to me.

But I was always fonder of reading than of anything else. There were not a great many books in the house but, as we kept the post office, there were generally plenty of papers and a magazine or two. And what books we had were well and often read. There were two, red-covered "Histories of the World", with crudely colored pictures, which were a perennial delight to me. I fear that as histories they were not especially reliable but as story books they were very interesting. They began with Eden, went through "the glory that was Greece and the grandeur that was Rome" down to Victoria's reign. Then there was a book called "Little Katey and Jolly Jim" which was much to my taste and a missionary book dealing with the Pacific Islands. The pictures in this book of cannibal chiefs with their extraordinary hair arrangements had a great fascination for me. *Pilgrim's Progress* was read and re-read with never failing delight. Many a time did I walk the strait and narrow path with *Christian* and *Christiana*—although I never liked *Christiana's* adventures half so well as *Christian's*. For one thing there was such a crowd with *Christiana*; she had not half the fascination of that solitary intrepid figure who faced all alone the shadows of the dark valley and the encounter with *Apollyon*.

I am proud of liking *Pilgrim's Progress*; I am not quite so proud of the fact that I found just as much delight in reading Talmage's sermons. That was Talmage's palmy day. All the travelling colporteurs carried his books and a new volume of Talmage's sermons meant then pretty much what a "best seller" means now. It was not the religion in them which attracted me—though I liked that then, too— but his vivid word-paintings and dramatic climaxes. His sermons were as interesting as fiction. I couldn't read them with any patience now and Talmage is dead and discredited. But I owe him a very real debt of thanks for pleasure given to a child craving for the vividness of life.

There were not many novels to be had. Those were the days when novels were frowned upon. *Pickwick Papers*, *Zanoni*, and *Rob Roy* were almost the only novels in the house and I pored over them until I almost knew them by heart—I *did* know whole chapters of *Zanoni* by heart. Grandmother took a magazine called "Godey's Lady's Book" and its monthly advent was a great event. I remember the preposterous fashion plates of bustles and overskirts which I thought very wonderful and beautiful. I used to pore over them, imagining myself arrayed in them, and firmly determined to have something just like them when I grew up. Mrs. Cunningham sent Wellington a monthly magazine called "Wide Awake" which contained splendid stories. It possessed a distinct literary quality and was one of the best formative influences in my childhood. The serials in it, by the best writers of the day, were a never-failing delight and the illustrations were almost as good.

Wellington had won Hans Andersen's tales as a prize and they were rare food for my fancy. I had a few "Children's Books" which contained much good reading for a child. Fortunately I could read anything I liked over and over repeatedly, extracting fresh interest and sweetness from it every time. In the long winter evenings, when the fire was lighted in the sitting room, I sat and pored over my dear stories, while grandfather read his paper and grandmother knitted or sewed, and the boys studied their lessons by candle light out in the kitchen. They were very pleasant evenings and shine with a soft glow of beauty in my memory. But the thought of them hurts me unbearably in these sad moods of evenings so different. At 8 o'clock I was sent to bed in the bedroom off the sitting room. There I lay, pleasantly watching the light from the sitting room on the ceiling and dreaming waking dreams. For I had already begun to live that strange inner life of fancy which has always existed side by side with my outer life—a life into which I have so often escaped from the dull or painful real. It is one of the hardest things now, in these moods of nervous pain and sadness that overwhelm me that I cannot so escape, even for a time. The pain prevents the play of the imagination and holds me prisoner from that life of dream where I have roved in fairyland and had wonderful adventures and tasted strange sweet happiness unmarred by any cloud or shadow. Ah, yes, many a happy hour I spent, lying there on my pillows in the dim room. The memory brings bitter, stinging tears to my eyes as I write. It is not good to recall such things in my present mood of loneliness and soul-ache. "A sorrow's crown of sorrow is remembering happier things".

That winter I first began to keep a diary and write "pieces" on "letter bills" and in the little yellow notebooks sent out by a patent medicine firm—Dr. Pierce's of Buffalo fame, to be precise. I owe old Dr. Pierce a real debt of gratitude! As I had no place in which to lock them up then and as I was very much averse to their being seen I used to hide them on two little "shelves" formed by two boards which had been nailed across the underside of the ends of the room sofa. I fondly believed nobody knew of the existence of these shelves but myself. They were soon packed full of MSS. I wish heartily that I had those same MSS now. They would be invaluable to me. But every year, as I used to read them over, some seemed to my maturing intelligence too silly to be kept. I was ashamed of them and burned them—as when I was about fourteen I burned all the "note book" diaries I had kept—something I shall always regret having done. They were quaint little documents, as I remember them—quaint and naive and painfully truthful and sincere, whether I wrote of my own doings or of others. Poor little diaries, long ago ashes, what pages of a child's life you were—a little simple life of dreams and childish pleasures. Not quite as happy as childhood should be—and as it might so easily have been—but seeming very bright now to my backward-glancing eyes, so used to the dullness and dreariness of my present existence.

I suffered a good deal that winter from my "conscience spells". I have described them before. When they came on I discarded all books except the Bible, Talmage's sermons, and a certain slim little volume entitled "The Memoir of Anzonetta Peters". I shall never forget that book. It belonged to a type now vanished from the earth fortunately—but much in vogue at that time. It is the biography of a child who at five became "converted", grew very ill soon afterwards, lived a marvellous patient and saintly life for several years, and died after great suffering at the age of twelve.

I must have read that book a score of times if I did once. I don't think it had a good effect on me. For one thing it discouraged me horribly—for Anzonetta was so hopelessly perfect that I felt it was no use to try to imitate her. Yet I *did* try. She never seemed by any chance to use the ordinary language of childhood at all. She invariably responded to any remark, if it were only "How are you to-day, Anzonetta?" by quoting a hymn or Scripture verse. Anzonetta was a perfect library of hymns. She died to one, her last faintly whispered utterance being,

"Hark, they whisper! Angels say,

Sister spirit, come away."

I dared not make the attempt of using verses and hymns in current conversation. I had a wholesome conviction that I would be laughed at and moreover I doubted being understood. But I did my best—I filled my little "diary" of the time with them—I even went Anzonetta one better and wrote out whole hymns, whereas she seldom if ever went beyond two verses. My favorite hymn of that time was one descriptive of heaven with the refrain,

"But what must it be to be there?"

I remember writing under this hymn in my journal, "I wish I were in heaven now, with mother and George Whitefield and Anzonetta B. Peters".

But I did not really wish it. I hated the very thought of it. But I believed I *ought* to wish it and so I tried to!

In the spring my health improved and after the spring vacation I returned to school. Vacation came then in spring and fall—three weeks to each. Midsummer holidays were unknown, except perhaps a week at the first of July. Before Mr. Fraser came we had only every alternative Saturday as a holiday. During his term the trustees decided upon what many people considered a daring and dangerous innovation—they decreed that every Saturday should be a holiday.

School life begins to grow distinct and interesting in my memory that summer. The great events of the year were the two semi-annual "examinations", one at Christmas, one at the end of June. Then the trustees and the ministers came to examine the school. Mr. Fraser was the first teacher under whom I took written examinations. We looked upon these as serious and dreadful things. I am afraid we sometimes cheated a little in them to the extent of asking questions of each other. We were always put in separate seats and all the text books were given to the master. But there were such things as notes. I don't think it ever occurred to us—or ever was told us, that this was dishonorable. It seemed a quite justified evasion of what we then considered the useless tyranny of written examinations.

I was never allowed to "go barefoot" to school, and as all the other children went so I felt keenly that this was a humiliating difference between them and me. I wanted to be "like the rest". I think it would have been wiser if I had been allowed to "go barefoot". My pleadings availed not. At home it was permitted under protest; but in school I must always wear "buttoned boots". Not long ago a girl who went to school with me confessed that she had always envied me those "lovely buttoned boots". Human nature, I suppose—always desirous of what it has not got. There was I, aching to be barefoot like my mates; there were they, resentfully coveting my buttoned boots!

Another thing that worried me with a sense of unlikeness was the fact that I had to go home to dinner every day while the rest took their dinners. *This* was rank foolishness on my part. It was much better and nicer in every way that I was near enough the school to go home to a good warm dinner. But it did not seem half so interesting as taking lunch to school and eating it, sitting in groups on the play-ground or under the tree with a bottle of milk that had been kept cool and sweet in the brook water. Great was my delight on stormy winter days when I had to "take my dinner, too". I was "one of the crowd" then, not set apart in any lonely distinction of superior advantages.

I do not think that the majority of grown people have any real idea of the tortures sensitive children suffer over any marked difference between themselves and the other denizens of their small world. I remember one winter when I was sent to school wearing a new style of apron. I think still it was very ugly. Then I thought it hideous. It was a long, sack-like garment *with sleeves*. Those sleeves were the crowning indignity. Nobody in school had ever worn aprons with sleeves before. When I went to school one of the girls sneeringly remarked that they were "baby aprons". This capped all! I could not bear to wear them—but wear them I had to, until they were worn out. But the humiliation never grew less. To the end of their existence—and they *did* wear horribly well, never getting any fortunate rents or tears—those "baby" aprons marked for me the extreme limit of human endurance.

I had nothing else to complain of in regard to my clothes. I was always kept nicely dressed and my clothes were generally pretty and becoming, though occasionally a little old fashioned owing to grandmother's inability to adapt herself to changing modes. *Materially*, I was well cared for. *Mentally* I had the power of foraging for myself to a certain extent. It was *emotionally* and *socially* that my nature was starved and restricted.

Child life, in a country settlement, is necessarily simple and quiet—and this, with some modifications, is as it should be. Life in Cavendish was markedly so. Day school and Sunday School made up a child's life. At the time of which I write Sunday School was as much of a social function—to us—as a religious one. We thought, I regret to say, quite as much of displaying our own good clothes and seeing those of our friends as we did of our lessons. Yet the latter were not neglected. We were strictly made to learn our "golden texts", our catechism questions, and our "paraphrases" at home. I remember one thing that always puzzled me. The "Shorter Catechism" which was used in the "big" classes was five times as long as the one we used in our "little" classes!

The use of the Catechism has almost gone out in the Sunday Schools of the present day. This is deplored in some quarters but I think it is a good thing. I doubt if the memorizing of those dry formulas ever did anyone any real good. Certainly it never did me any. I did not understand the meaning of half I learned and it was never explained to me. Moreover, the Shorter Catechism teaches things that are no longer believed—and never should have been believed. When one comes to think of it it was a hideous thing to teach children the doctrines of "election" and "predestination". What a conception of God to implant in a child's mind! Fortunately I think it did not take any real hold on our minds. We did not comprehend the real meaning of the terrible answers we so glibly recited. The "catechism" was something that had to be learned, but its doctrines slipped over our minds like pebbles over ice, making little impression.

I was not fortunate in my Sunday School teachers. They were three old maids in succession and their personality was neither lovable nor helpful to a child. One of them, I remember, became insane a few years later and drowned herself. Yet she was a kind, gentle woman and I liked her the best of the three. One of them was the homeliest woman I ever saw with a face spotted with moles and a pendulous lower lip. None of them did anything to make Christianity beautiful or appealing or even clear to me. Indeed, they rather prejudiced me against it, since they were "Christians" and I somehow had the idea that to be a Christian meant to be as ugly and stupid and—and—well, as *unromantic* as those "good" women were. They made me feel—and I believe that this feeling is still firmly embedded in my subconscious mind—that *religion* and *beauty* were antagonists and as far as the poles asunder. They gave me the same feeling towards it as they did towards matters of sex—that it was something necessary but ugly—something you were really ashamed of, although you had to have it—or go to hell! As for "heaven", I don't remember that they ever discussed it but I thought it was a rather dull though gorgeous place where we did nothing but stand around and sing. Not even my dearly beloved "What must it be to be there" could counteract this impression. As for the personality and teachings of Christ, I had as little idea of their real meaning as the young heathen for whom I occasionally gave my "five cent pieces" or went around collecting with a "Mission Card".

But I liked going to Sunday School and would have been sorry to miss a day; and some of my sweetest memories are of those hours spent in the old church with my little mates, with our "testaments" and "lesson sheets" held primly in our cotton-gloved hands.

That was the summer of "Pussywillow and Catkin".

I have always been very fond of cats. I do not know how I came by the taste. Father hated cats, mother did not like them, and grandfather and grandmother detested them. They never liked to see me petting cats but did not actually forbid my having one. I had had several before this but I do not remember them very clearly. My cats had a precarious tenure of their lives. We had a dog "Gyp"—a nice old dog, with one very bad fault. He, too, hated cats and pursued them to the death. He killed several kittens for me. This summer when I got two kittens, a sweet little gray one and a white one spotted with black I determined to keep them shut up in the granary until they grew big enough to defend themselves. I called them by the names I had found in "The Letter Box" of "Wide Awake" and thought very beautiful and appropriate.

I fear my poor little pets had rather dull lives in the granary. They were well fed but did not grow rapidly. But they were a great pleasure to me and I loved them both—especially the gray Pussywillow—with all the devotion of my passionate little heart. For it is my doom to love whatever I care for with such intensity that there is as much pain as pleasure in my love. Catkin was a little too meek and pink-nosed to suit me but Pussywillow was the cutest little scrap of striped fur ever seen. By the fall they were allowed the run of the barns. But one bitter morning I found Pussywillow dying of poison, caused by eating a poisoned rat. My little pet died in my hands. Never shall I forget my agony!

It was the first time I *realized* death—the first time anything I really loved left me forever. At that moment the curse of the race came upon me—"death entered into my world"—and I turned my back on the Eden of childhood where everything had seemed everlasting. I was barred out of it forever by the fiery sword of that unforgettable and unforgotten pain. Yes, I feel that pain still as I write—the sickening soul convulsion and anguish with which I beheld my little pet's bright eyes glazing and its tiny paws growing stiff and cold. It is twenty five years since that day and the scar of that hurt is still on my soul.

I mourned my little gray playfellow longer and more bitterly than most human beings are mourned. I remember that I used to dream that it came back to life—and how bitter the awakening always was.

Catkin lived until the winter and then disappeared. I felt sorry over her loss but I had never loved her as I loved Pussywillow, and her loss was softened by the lingering hope that she was still living and would come back.

I decided that it was no use trying to "keep a cat" as long as Gyp was alive. Gyp lived until I was about twelve. Then he died and I grieved over that, too, for I was very fond of old Gyp. But the next spring I got a gray-and-white kitten whom I named Topsy—also after a cat in "Wide Awake". She grew up into a beautiful and intelligent cat and lived for seven or eight years. She finally "disappeared" the winter I was teaching in Bideford. One of her first "batch" of kittens was a handsome gray with white paws and breast. I kept him and named him Max. He was a dear cat but when he was about two years old he went away and never returned—the fate of so many roving Thomases. Since then I have had four pet cats—all grays, for I have come to think that the only real cat is a gray cat! The first was "Coco", a pretty light gray, whose name I changed to "Bobs" in a fit of hero worship during the Boer War. The second was Daffy, the First—a dark gray. Then came Daffy the Second—a silver gray, the dearest and handsomest cat I ever had. All these died of poison. When Daffy the Second died I felt almost as badly as I had felt over Pussywillow's death long ago. Now I have Daffy the Third whom I got as a kitten from Alec Macneill's. He is four years old, a very large, handsome fellow and stays home so closely that his days have been long in the land. I do not know what I would do without him. I would be ashamed to say just how much I love that cat. And he doesn't love me at all! There isn't a particle of affection in him. But he is so handsome that he is his own excuse for being and he knows more than would be wholesome in a human being but is quite lawful in a cat. He is fond of rocking chairs and cushions and has had a perfectly happy life, viewed from a cat's standpoint. Grandmother pets him almost as much as I do. Formerly she did not like my pets and seemed to resent the affection I gave them. But in these lonely, later years, neglected by her children, she seems to have changed in this respect and grown fond of the Daffies and almost indulgent to them. Well, there are many worse friends than the soft, silent, furry, cat-folk.

I like dogs also and would like to keep one but it is impossible under my present circumstances. There are so few things that are *not* impossible!

The summer after my ninth birthday Mr. Fraser went away and James McLeod reigned in his stead. He taught here for three years. We did not like him—at least, while he was here. He used to whip us very unmercifully. Everything was punished by a "cut" or so, across the palm, with a hardwood pointer. But he never wounded our souls with sarcasm and the physical pain was soon forgotten and forgiven. I cannot discover any bitterness in my soul towards him for it. He was a fairly good teacher in some respects. But I had not yet awakened to a love of study for its own sake. I learned my lessons because I had to and as I was quick of perception and retentive of memory this never meant much work to me; but I took no especial pleasure in it. My ambition was always awake however; it was a desirable thing to "keep head" and a terrible disgrace to "get down" in class.

As the school was large, "Jim"—we called him that behind his back—could not always overtake his classes. Consequently he often sent some of the older scholars to "hear" the second and third classes. This we thought a great pleasure. But we soon discovered that if "Jim" thought we *wanted* to hear a class we would not be asked to. At first he used to glance over the room and if he saw a pupil idling send him or her to take the class. But when he found that this was far from being considered a punishment he changed his tactics. For my own part, I invented a scheme which worked "like magic". When "Jim" called out the class I stopped work and gazed into vacancy. Then, when I caught his eye, I would snatch up my pencil and fall to "ciphering" furiously. "Jim" rarely failed to fall into the trap. Here was a pupil who was evidently *afraid* that she would be sent to hear a class for her sins. Consequently, that pupil must be sent and was. Trying to look cross and reluctant but inwardly jubilant I would go out to the aisle and proceed to "hear" the class.

Notwithstanding "Jim's" strictness, he could not be everywhere, or see everywhere, at once and we had much unlawful fun behind his back. A very fashionable game of the time was "knifey", played with a jack-knife on the sod of the playground. Amanda and I used to play it in school hours, with a huge pin on our laps or on the soft wood of our seat!

We had many games for recesses. "Ball" was the standard in spring and fall but the summer days were too hot for it. Then we played "Knifey", "Jackstones", "King, King, come along", "Bar on", "Stepstone", "Little Sally Water", "Oh, Love it is a dangerous game" and "Drop the handerchief". There was a large school and there were always enough children for real fun. In winter we played "Blind Man's Buff" in the school porch, or went coasting. We used to have some glorious coasts on the "school hill", Pierce Macneill's field and our "big hill field". Upsets added to the fun. How short the dinner hours seemed those days! The Nelson boys went away that winter and I missed them much. The following summer Uncle Leander's boys, Fred and Murray, came over for the first time. I looked forward to their coming with delight for I expected they would be Well and Dave over again. But I was disappointed. Not totally so in Fred. I rather liked him and in that and many following summers we were tolerably good friends, though we had plenty of quarrels. There were some very petty things about Fred, but on the whole we agreed. I never liked Murray. He was a selfish boy with a very exaggerated idea of the importance of Murray Macneill. Unless a girl bowed down to him and worshipped him he had no use for her. Unless you looked upon Murray as a wonder and flattered him unstintedly he did not care for you. I was much too independent for this; the frank comradeship which I had felt for Well and Dave and which was all I could offer him did not please him. So we were never friends; and in the course of a few years, during which I had found Murray out in various mean and petty deeds and speeches, I grew to dislike him heartily and had as little to do with him as I possibly could. We would have had very little company if it had not been for the frequent visits of my uncles and aunts. Grandfather and grandmother seldom went anywhere and rarely had anyone come here. I was never allowed to visit anywhere save at Pensie's and Amanda's. If we had not had the post office very few of our neighbors would ever have been in the house.

But the family visits were quite frequent in those days. Uncle John and Aunt Annie Campbell, Aunt Emily and Uncle John Montgomery often came. The former were my favorites. I was always glad to see them, all the more if Clara and Stella came too. Aunt Emily was less welcome for she generally thought it her duty to reform all my faults during her visit. And she was one of those unlucky people who rather make others worse than improve them, by arousing a sort of impatient contrariness in them. But I liked Uncle John Montgomery very much.

Uncle Chester, then a lawyer in Ch'Town and Aunt Hattie came out two or three times a year. I liked Uncle Chester fairly well but I disliked his wife. Aunt Hattie was a cold, selfish woman who lived only to be amused. Uncle Leander, and his family always came over from St. John N.B. in summer. His second wife, Aunt Annie, was a very sweet woman. Uncle Leander generally brought a supply of novels with him and I used to have a glorious reading debauch after his coming. I was never quite "at home" with any of them, except Aunt Annie's family, but still their coming was always welcome, as meaning brightness and excitement of a sort.

The summer of my twelfth year was, I think, the first summer we had midsummer vacation. I lived much outdoors in summer. We—the Nelson boys and I, and, later on, Fred and I—were very fond of going trouting up the brook in the woods. It was on one such expedition with Well and Dave, one exquisite summer evening that I had my first walk through Lover's Lane. I enjoyed its beauty to the full, little dreaming how much it was to mean to me in after years. The two bridges that crossed it were capital trouting places. And there was another spot equally good— the Birch Pool under the roots of an overhanging clump of white birches in a woodsy corner. We fished with hook and line, using worms for bait. Sometimes I managed to "put my worm on" for myself, but I expended a fearful amount of nervous energy in doing so. How I hated it! The Nelson boys always put the worms on for me but Uncle L's boys were not so nice about it. I preferred to go through the agony myself than have it done for me with some jibe about my sex. But I loved trouting and often made good catches. I remember the thrill of pride I felt one day when I caught quite a large trout—as large as some caught in the pond. Fred Macneill was with me and I felt that I went up ten percent in his estimation. He respected me much more thereafter. A girl who could catch a trout like that was not to be altogether despised.

Next to trouting berry-picking was my delight—and to pick berries in "Sam Wyand's" field was the crown of delight. This field was "away back" behind "Jimmy Laird's woods". It was a veritable "beauty spot", almost encircled with thick, rustling maple woods which were thickly carpeted with ferns. We went to it through wood lanes fragrant with June-bells, threaded with sunshine and shadow, banked by green mosses. We saw foxes and rabbits in their native haunts. And I have never heard anything sweeter than the whistling of the robins at sunset in the maple woods around that field. Oh, how the sweetness of those old days, when I was so near to nature, comes back to me as I write of them, and makes me homesick for them.

"Sam Wyand's field!" It was not a beautiful or romantic name in itself but it stands for exquisite beauty in my memory. The mere name calls up all the old loveliness connected with it—and I ache in every fibre of my lonely soul for the sweet, simple delights that were never marred or darkened by any past pain or fear of future shadow. To childhood, as to God, *all* is the present. There is neither past nor future.

That summer of my twelfth year was the summer Grandfather went to England to a great Exhibition held there. Uncle Chester went with him and Aunt Hattie and her baby stayed with us while they were away. I remember the delight and excitement when grandfather and uncle returned—the gifts and pictures and souvenirs they brought and the wonderful tales they had to tell. It was nice to have grandfather home again. In those days he was not so irritable and unreasonable as he became a few years later in the childishness of advancing age. There were many fine things about grandfather Macneill. He had a rich, poetic mind, a keen intelligence and a refined perception. He was a good conversationalist and a lover of nature. His faults were an irritable temper, a vanity that sometimes made him a little ridiculous and at other times smarted under imaginary slights, and, worst of all, an utter disregard of the feelings of other people—or, rather, a failure to realize that they had any feelings. He had no patience with anything that fell short of his ideals, and never seemed to have any conception how harsh and brutal were some of the things he said, especially to children. In some things he was very unreasonable and prejudiced. He was really very fond of and proud of all his grandchildren but he showed that fondness and pride in a very unwise manner. For example—he never said a kind or encouraging world to me; he said many sneering and unkind ones; and he constantly held up to me as paragons my other cousins. Consequently I believed for years that I was the only one of his grand-children that he disliked. Later in life I discovered that he was just the same to them—saying harsh or sarcastic things to them and praising me—a proceeding which naturally aroused their jealousy and tended to make them dislike me. If he had only reversed the process—at least to the extent of saying his kind things to our faces and holding his tongue to others about our faults—he would have been a much more lovable man and would have exercised a much stronger influence for good over us.

The winter I was twelve father wrote me that he was soon to be married again—to a Miss Mary McRae of Ontario. I was delighted over the news. I fondly believed that I would have a real mother to love and be loved by. The many stories I had read of "cruel stepmothers" had not infected my mind at all. I knew only one stepmother in real life—Uncle Leander's second wife. No mother could have been kinder and more affectionate than she was to the sons of her husband's first marriage. She furnished my conception of a stepmother, and I thought mine would be like her. After father's marriage I wrote her affectionate letters wherein I poured out my childish soul to her and sent her pressed flowers from my favorite haunts. When I afterwards came to know the sort of woman she was I smiled at myself for the sentiment I had lavished on a creation of my own fancy. Such a woman could care nothing for my poor tributes of ferns and Junebells. But I was blissfully ignorant of this as yet. It gave me exquisite joy to search the woodlands until I found something I deemed perfect enough to offer her and I fondly supposed that she would feel on receiving it the same joy I had felt in sending it.

That next summer James McLeod went away. All we girls cried ourselves half blind at his departure. All at once we discovered—or thought we did—that we were deeply attached to him. And truly, a tie of three years—three years is a long time in childhood—could not be broken without pain. But I think his affecting farewell speech, beginning "The time has come for us to part" had much to do with our lavish luxury of tears. Annie Stewart began to cry first and it spread from one to another like a swift infection, until we were all crying stormily. But our tears were quickly dried after all was over—as the tears of children ever are.

The trustees then engaged a "lady teacher". No "lady teacher" had ever reigned in Cavendish school before and wise heads were shaken in doubt over the experiment. "Izzie" Robinson was the one selected. There was some doubt for a time between her and another candidate; I remember that I was much delighted when Miss Robinson was chosen. I knew nothing of her; but her brother had once taught in Rustico and had been here once or twice to get his papers "signed" before grandfather, who was a J.P. On one occasion he had helped me with my geography lesson so nicely that I thought him "lovely". I argued that his sister would probably be just as nice. I was doomed to disappointment.

Miss Robinson came here to board—literally forced herself on us, indeed. Grandmother did not wish to take her and only yielded to much entreaty on Miss R's part. It was a pity she did so. Grandfather behaved very unwisely in regard to her—very childishly. Yet there was something to be said on his side, too. Miss Robinson was a very inferior person, with a very exaggerated notion of her own importance. She could not "take a joke" at all, resenting it as an insult to her dignity. Grandfather was fond—far too fond—of teasing people—"giving them bars", as he called it. If Miss Robinson had been a different type—for example, had she been like her successor, Miss Gordon—she might have taken this in good part and won grandfather over. But she did not. She betrayed her petulance and resentment, and Grandfather took a dislike to her. He was not to be blamed for that. But he was certainly blameworthy for the way he showed it. His "bars" became mordant and insulting. He and she were constantly bickering. Miss R. vented her dislike of Grandfather in all her dealings with me, especially in school. She never lost an opportunity of lashing me with sarcasm—often totally undeserved—before my mates. She was the only teacher I ever disliked—and I did dislike her intensely. She would stoop to the pettiest deeds and speeches. One example must suffice. It was characteristic of her whole demeanor towards me.

We were in the class, "analyzing" a poem, verse about. Clemmie Macneill was analyzing her verse. My turn was next and I was intent on the analysis of my verse, to have it in readiness; and, as was my custom in thinking over anything, I was gazing before me into space, seeing nothing of the objects before my eyes. Meanwhile—as I was told afterwards for I was quite unconscious of it at the time—Clemmie came to grief over the parsing of a word in her verse. Miss R. accordingly parsed it for her. Then, I suppose, she happened to encounter my probably puzzled gaze; and I, amid my wonder as to whether a certain clause were adverbial or adjectival, was suddenly recalled to a sense of my surroundings by this biting remark, delivered in such a tone as only "Izzie" Robinson could use. "Well, I suppose *you* think that isn't right, Maud. That is what your face says. You have *a very expressive face*." The venomous sneer of her last sentence is quite untransferable to paper.

I stared at the vulgar woman like one stunned, utterly ignorant what offence I had committed, unable even to say a word in my own defense. A giggle ran around the class at my expense. My soul burned within me over the cruel and wanton injustice of her attack—and it burns yet as I write. I should like to meet that woman to-day and tell her exactly what I think of her for uttering such a speech to a child who had not been doing or saying anything to provoke it. But this was only one of many such insults.

In March I went for a long visit to Aunt Emily in Malpeque. I had a very nice time and do not recall ever having been lonely or homesick. The Malpeque people were noted for their sociability; there was always plenty of company; Uncle John Montgomery was very kind and jolly; and Maggie Abbott, an orphan girl who had been brought up there, was my companion. Despite the difference in our ages—Maggie was 18—we were "chums". Maggie's parents belonged to a low and immoral class. But Maggie herself was a sweet-natured, pure-minded, sensitive girl. We had "great fun" together that winter and spring.

In May I came home to find, as before related, that Miss Robinson was gone, and I was not allowed to go to school. This was an unwise and undignified course of conduct on the part of my grandparents. It inflicted much needless suffering on me. Though I did not like Miss R. and though she would probably have treated me worse than ever, I still wished to go to school. I was interested in my studies. I was lonely and wanted the companionship of my mates. I was subjected to much mortification from the significant questions which were always being asked me. Altogether, that summer was a very unhappy one for me, made more so by a quarrel between Uncle John and Grandfather which lasted till the fall, when they were reconciled. Uncle John was wholly to blame in the affair and ran true to form in his behavior from start to finish. But grandfather's lack of tact precipitated the quarrel. It made us all terribly unhappy.

That summer I began to take music lessons. As we had no organ I used to go down to "Uncle Jimmie's", just across the road, and practice. My music teacher was a Miss Snowey, a very young girl who was not at all a good teacher although she had considerable natural talent. Later on, when father and grandmother between them gave me my organ, I took lessons from Mrs. Spurr. I liked the lessons and did not dislike practising. But now I think it was all rather a waste of time and money, because I had no real musical gift. And certainly, if I had never learned to play I would have been spared a good deal of annoyance and bother in later life when, by reason of being able to play a little, I have been forced or drawn into uncongenial and vexatious positions.

At the end of the school year in June Miss R. engaged to stay for another year—much to my despair. A year seems an eternity when one is twelve. It seemed to me that I could *not* bear another year of loneliness and exclusion from the world of my mates.

But in the autumn came good news. Miss R. was to leave at the New Year. Life grew roseate and hopeful again for me. The first day of the new teacher's advent found me in my old seat with Amanda, and oh, how happy I was! It makes my heart ache now in these hard days of monotonous pain and loneliness to remember how happy I could be and often was in those old days. I cannot conceive it possible that I could feel so now under any circumstances.

Hattie Gordon was a very different type of woman and teacher from Izzie Robinson. She was not faultless; but she was a lady, which Miss R. was not, and she had a certain stimulating personality which I have never found in any other teacher. She had the power of inspiring a love of study for its own sake and of making the dry bones of the school routine alive with interest.

What a worker she was! I realize that now, although at the time I took it as a matter of course. I owe her a great debt for the sympathy and encouragement she always showed me.

Miss Gordon was the first of our teachers to require the writing of compositions. Every week we of the advanced classes had to write one at home on a given subject, sometimes selected by ourselves, sometimes by the teacher. I revelled in this; but, naturally, most of the scholars detested it. The honor of writing the best compositions generally fluctuated between Nate Lockhart and myself. We had always had recitations on Friday afternoons and this—also dreaded by most of the pupils—was a great delight to me. With my flexible memory it was no trouble to learn a piece of poetry "off by heart" and it was a dramatic joy to recite it. Miss Gordon added to the ordinary recitations the variation of dialogues and songs, and we often had quite a little concert on Friday evenings, as well as much fun in preparing the dialogues. It was all very good training, too.

Miss Gordon it also was who organized a "Mayflower picnic" each spring. Delightful festivals they were. The school was large ranging from 40 to 50 pupils. This meant jollity and intellectual stimulus as well. The Cavendish school of today seems to me a very forlorn institution. I feel sorry for the few children who attend it. There are only about a dozen in the district and half of those are French. They never seem to have any of the real, good, wholesome "fun" school children should have. They never play games—there isn't enough of them. They never coast or play ball or build playhouses. And they don't learn as well or as much as we did, for there is no competition to inspire them.

The year I was fifteen—and when I found myself fifteen at last I thought I was grown up!—was in the main a happy one, at least in its earlier months. True, I had little social life. I was never allowed to visit anywhere except at Amanda's and Pensie's. That was one of the Literary Society's palmy winters but I was seldom permitted to attend a meeting. Now and then I was let go to one, under protest, and always enjoyed it hugely. Miss Gordon took an active interest in the Literary and encouraged her pupils to recite or read at its meetings. Finally I was asked to recite. I felt as I should now feel if I were asked to read before the crowned heads of Europe. I wished to recite because of the kudos of it—but I was very nervous and frightened. How anxiously I practised my selection—"The Child Martyr"— before my mirror! How excited I was when the night of the concert arrived! I remember every incident of that evening. How I trembled as I mounted the platform when my name was called out! How faint and faraway my voice sounded in my own ears! But, thanks to my faithful rehearsals it seemed to sound all right in other people's ears. Several of Miss Gordon's other pupils recited that night, too. I do not think we did her training any discredit. She was proud of us all and never hesitated to give her meed of commendation. I can see her yet, smiling on us, dressed in the brown velvet coat and smart little toque she wore that winter. She was considered to be very "dressy". We were always much interested then in what our teachers wore and how they dressed their hair. Miss Gordon had pretty hair, fair and wavy. Her face was not at all pretty but it was striking, and she had a peculiar and interesting smile. She had a very quick temper, easily roused by trifles, but she seldom voiced it. It was betrayed only in her suddenly crimsoning face and ominous silence. But it passed as quickly as it came. She was never sarcastic or vindictive. She made some mistakes as we all do, but they were not of the kind that last or rankle.

All that winter I was looking forward to going out to Prince Albert with Grandfather Montgomery. I was naturally much excited and delighted. I had never even been on a train. My heart thrilled at the idea of seeing father again; and at that time, filled with the impression made on my mind by my few trips to Ch'Town I thought it would be quite heavenly to live in a *town*.

We went in August. The journey out was an unqualified delight. I enjoyed every moment of it. But when I reached Prince Albert the glamor vanished. For the first few weeks I suffered from homesickness to a degree that makes me shudder even now. The discovery of what my stepmother was like naturally increased this. But in any case I should probably have suffered keenly, because it is my nature to love a spot where I have long lived very deeply and passionately and feel keen anguish when removed from it. Yet I did not dislike Prince Albert as a place to live in and after the first keen edge of my nostalgia wore away I liked it well enough.

I did not like the High School very well. Mr. Mustard was a very poor teacher.

The pupils—three girls and six boys—were an odd-chance medley. There was no system about our studies. I was far ahead of the other pupils in most of the branches, but far behind them in two or three I had never studied—book-keeping for instance. I do not think I learned one thing of any value at that school. But I might have got a teacher's certificate by spring if I could have gone regularly. But after Bruce was born I could not get there at all.

I disliked Mr. Mustard professionally and personally—or it might be more correct to say that I felt a contempt for him. It has always given me a disagreeable feeling to recall that he fell in love with me and suggested marriage. I did not, and do not, consider that it was at all a compliment. He was, as we girls bluntly said, "A ninny and a bore", and I resented his clumsy attentions far more bitterly than I would have resented his dislike.

I did not care for, or find much pleasure in, the society of my stepmother's people except her mother, Mrs. McTaggart, who was a dear old soul. Edith Skelton was a jolly companion and after she left the Pritchards were my friends and the only ones I cared much for. Laura's friendship meant a great deal to me that year. So did Will's. We had many happy and pleasant hours together, filled with the unthinking joy of youth. The few days I spent with Laura out on their farm were the brightest of my western sojourn.

In September I came home, travelling alone from Prince Albert to Ottawa—a girl of sixteen! I don't know how I dared do it. Yet I did not feel in the least dismayed or alarmed at the prospect when I set out. And I got along all right. I had plenty of spirit and dauntlessness then and I enjoyed my journey home.

Miss Gordon was still teaching in C. She got up another concert that fall and I, as well as some others of her former pupils, helped. It was a very pleasant affair all through and the concert was a success.

That winter grandmother went over to Park Corner for a week—the last time she ever went from home for more than a day. I kept house while she was away and it was not a pleasant experience in some respects for grandfather behaved in a fashion which I can only call absurd. He was always more irritable and unreasonable than usual when grandmother was away. He was lonely without her—which was natural but was no excuse for his outbursts of temper and his impatience with those who were trying to do their best. Nothing I did pleased him. If, by reason of inexperience, I made some little mistake he railed and sneered at me, as if I had done something really dreadful and inexcusable. I can never forget his tone, look and words on some occasions. When I try to recall him in his more amiable moods these more deeply branded impressions seem to obliterate all else. It was his *injustice* which ranked most deeply. When I really did wrong and was scolded for it, no matter how severely, I might feel badly at the time but it never left any bitterness. But to be stormed at or sneered at because of some trifling mistake or accident—for example, such as letting a bit of ham slip into the fire through the bars of a much delapidated old gridiron while turning it—*did* leave a bitterness that has never been effaced. I was glad indeed when grandmother came home.

Then I went over to Park Corner to give Clara, Stella and George music lessons. I did not dislike giving the girls lessons, but I could make nothing of George. He was a spoiled, headstrong, bad-tempered boy and these qualities had been intensified by his parents' unwise indulgence. However, this meant only two disagreeable hours a week and for the rest we all enjoyed ourselves heartily. Our amusements certainly seem to me now rather crude and frivolous but they satisfied at seventeen.

Clara, Stella and I were just at the age when the opposite sex are more interesting than they ever are before or after. We each had two or three "beaux" who "saw us home" from meetings, took us driving and kept up a not unfriendly rivalry with each other over our favors. I am very much afraid that we delighted in all this, and I blush to think how much we talked about those boys and how large a share "he said" and "he did" played in our conversation. We liked to be teased about them, too—oh, yes, we did! It was all very silly and harmless—if anything silly can really be harmless which I doubt. A wiser training and a different environment might have saved us from this silly age—but possibly not. I have since seen it manifested just as strongly in girls who had both advantages. It seems a sort of phase in natural development which few girls escape. At all events, we were in the thick of it that winter.

I came home early in June, was lonely for a week, then slipped back into my old groove once more. I had a pleasant summer though not without some troubled hours. In September I at last obtained grandmother's somewhat reluctant consent to study for P.W.C. and a teacher's certificate.

Selena Robinson taught here that year. She was a rather nice girl personally and we were chums. But she was a very poor teacher. Had I stayed home that year and studied by myself I would have got on just as well. I did not much enjoy going to school. It did not seem like Cavendish school to me. Very few of my old set were left. But outside of school I had a pleasant winter. The disagreeable things were obscured by the glitter of starry hopes; and I had a little circle of friends and duties which satisfied me then. The Literary Society and the Prayer Meeting were the only "social functions" and it was considered a great disappointment if a stormy night prevented one or the other. So I lived my double life, as it seems to me I have always done—as many people do, no doubt—the outward life of study and work and social intercourse and the inner one of dreams and aspirations.

In July I went to town to take the P.W.C. entrance exam. It was an anxious time. I was so sure that my whole future depended on it. And when it was over there was a more anxious time still—three weeks of waiting for the result. I was very dubious and the longer I waited the more dubious I became, until I felt sure that it was impossible that I could have passed. I was afraid I had failed in arithmetic— and arithmetic was one of the "vital" subjects. If you failed in it you did not "pass" no matter what your other marks were.

Then one day the long agony of suspense came to an end. The papers came out with the list of successful candidates and I had passed well up. What a relief it was! And what a happy girl went dancing to the shore that night! I do not think it would be possible to feel *now*, no matter under what circumstances, as I felt then. Only youth can feel so.

In September I went to P.W.C. It was, I believe, the happiest year of my life. Yet it was not all sunshine either. I had a very poor boarding house. That my room was bitterly cold and the table the poorest that could be imagined, the food of wretched quality, ill cooked and served, were the smallest of the evils. The MacMillan family were most vulgar and ill-bred people; the majority of their boarders belonged to their own class; the whole atmosphere of the place was the worst possible for a young girl in the formative period of her life.

These drawbacks, however, did not cloud my P.W.C. year very darkly. I was too young and inexperienced to realize what living in such an environment might mean, and the material hardships were borne patiently because I knew they were only temporary. It is wonderful how much difference it makes in the endurance of anything if we can believe that it is only temporary. Mary Campbell and I extracted endless fun out of our very tribulations. I remember Mary staggering across the room one day and pretending to faint because when we came home from college we discovered clean slips on our pillows—a *very* rare occurrence!

But there was nothing to mar the college side of my life. It was all a delight to me. I was happy every minute I spent in the old college, *except* when in the geometry class. I enjoyed my studies—and I studied hard. When the year drew to a close I was conscious only of regret.

They had a very barbarous custom in regard to exams at that time. Nowadays it is changed; but then the college exams and the "license" exams were entirely different things. At the end of the year we had a hard fortnight of college exams. Then, tired and fagged as we were, we had to go over the whole ground again in a breathless week of "license" exams.

The License exams that year were very hard—so hard that out of many candidates an absurdly small percentage passed. I shall never forget that anxious, driven week. But at last it was over; and how delightful and impossible it seemed to be free.

I came home but had a somewhat unhappy and anxious summer. It was so difficult to secure a school. The country was swarming with teachers especially the host of "third class" ones let loose by the failure of so many candidates, who would take any school gladly for no "supplement" at all. Unless you applied in person you had very little chance of getting a school. This I could never do, as grandfather would not assist me in any way to secure a school, even by so much as letting me have a horse to drive to a district. I had to depend on written applications. I sent out dozens of them and tasted each mail day the bitterness of repeated disappointment when no answer came from any.

It was the last of July before I finally got the Bideford school. What a relief it was to me! With what interest I looked forward to my work! It seemed a great thing to me then—much greater, I suppose, than it really was. With a heart full of courage and ambition I packed my trunks and went to Bideford.

My first week there was a miserable one. I was bitterly homesick; I was unsettled and worried about finding a boarding house; and I found it hard to get my school organized and in running order. I was assailed by a horrible suspicion that I was not going to like teaching, after all my struggles to become a teacher. I used to be so tired and discouraged every evening when I got home from school that I could not help crying for sheer sickness of heart.

But that passed; and with the exception of that week my year in Bideford was a happy and hopeful and enjoyable one. I worked very hard in my school. I was enthusiastic and had many "ideals"—which suffered a good deal from contact with the real; but I was never wholly false to them nor they to me.

I had a large—a too-large school—especially in summer. I had 21 in the primer class alone. But the majority of my pupils were nice and lovable. They liked me and I had the satisfaction of knowing that I was a successful "schoolmarm".

I was also fortunate in my boarding house. I had a comfortable room, good table, and refined companionship. Mrs. Estey was a dear. In spite of her sixteen years' seniority we were "chums". I did not like Mr. Estey. And to tell the plain truth I don't think his wife liked him either. But he was absent so often and so long on circuit visitations that he seemed to count for very little. He was inferior in every respect to Mrs. E. There seemed to be no affection or comradeship between them. They called each other "Mr." and "Mrs." Estey, even when alone and Mrs. Estey never seemed like herself in his presence. I had neither liking nor respect for him. He was a selfish, uncultured, high-tempered man who had had, and has since had, trouble on almost every circuit he ever was on. But he was, as I have said, away a great deal and Mrs. E. and I were very happy in his absence.

The worst drawback of the winter was the bad road I always had to school. A great deal of snow fell that winter. The road was never broken as all the travelling was by the river ice. I shall never forget some of those walks, especially when the spring thaws set in. I sometimes arrived at the school wet to the waist and had to spend the day in that condition.

Socially I had a nice time. Lou D. gave me plenty of pleasant drives and outings. But I have always been sorry that I went with him. I fear it did spoil his life. He was never married. I met him on the street in town last fall and hardly knew him, he looked so old and careworn. He walked out to Bertie's with me and when we parted at the gate he turned up his coat lapel and showed me under it a little "button pin" on which was a picture of myself copied from a photo I gave him when I left Bideford. I had not the heart to tell him that I objected to his wearing it even unseen. Yet I certainly did not like the idea. However, even if it were seen, nobody would recognize me by it now, so I suppose it does not matter. But it does matter that his life has been made unhappy through me.

But I could not foresee this in the Bideford days. I was only a careless young girl with a girl's liking for fun and frolic. It was country custom for the girls and boys to drive about with each other in friendly fashion and half the time it meant nothing. I do not now think it a good custom; but at the time I simply accepted it as a matter of course.

Yes, that Bideford year was a pleasant one, both as regards my school and my social life. It was, although I knew it not, the last happy year of my life.

From Bideford I went to Halifax for a year at Dalhousie College. I should have dearly loved to have taken the full Arts course. But that was out of the question. I could not afford it. So I had to content myself with a year in special courses.

Looking back on my life with the insight which comes from riper experience I think my going to Dalhousie was a mistake—a waste of time and money. I do not think I received any good whatever from that year as far as educational value went. But I did not see this at the time. I wished to go to Dalhousie for two reasons, of which perhaps the second was the more potent though kept very secret. In the first place, I thought a special course in English, languages etc. would help me in my ambitions to be a writer and also help me to obtain better schools; and in the second place I hoped that it might be possible to find some entrance into journalism while in Halifax—"get on a newspaper" or something of the sort. This hope was disappointed. No such opportunity came my way. And in regard to my classes at college I cannot see that I gained any good from them that I would not have gained just as effectually and much more cheaply in the solitude of some country school district with my books and my pen. If I had taken that money and taken a cheap little run over England and Scotland it would have been of far more value to me. But everybody of my home circle would have thought me crazy and extravagant to do that—I would have thought I was myself!

I did not quite like boarding at the Ladies' College. Accustomed as I had been for two years to much greater personal freedom I found the restrictions irksome and the unmitigatedly feminine atmosphere rather stifling. The girls who formed my immediate circle I liked passably well but I did not find in any of them a really congenial associate. Miss Clark was the only *real* friend I had there—the only one in whose society I felt really at home, or found any real satisfaction. Yet I enjoyed many things in that year. It is not because I did not enjoy it that I consider it a wasted year. It is simply because I do not think it advanced me in any way. But I have many pleasant memories of it—and that, after all, is no mean legacy for a year to leave.

When I came home I had another mortifying summer, vainly trying to get a school. I had hoped that my Dalhousie year would be of some assistance to me in this respect. But it was of no weight against the plethora of teachers who could make personal application. It was not until the fall that I obtained the Belmont school.

That year, even apart from my unhappy engagement to Edwin Simpson, was the hardest I ever lived. It was hard in almost every way a year could be hard. I did not like my school. The majority of the pupils were rough, ill-bred, ignorant little creatures whom it was neither a pleasure nor a satisfaction to teach. Of course there were a few exceptions but they were in truth very few. The school was large and the work very heavy. I had one pupil whom I had to take through the first year course of P.W.C., extra work which meant much extra toil and worry for me but, of course not a cent of extra pay—nor as the sequel showed, extra gratitude either.

I had very little social life. The Simpson, Campbell and Allan Fraser families were the only ones with whom it gave me any pleasure to associate. The rest of the Belmont people were of a very inferior caste. I had a poor boarding house, a cold room, poor table, rough, illiterate people. My health was not good. The days were a routine of drudgery. Yet my spirit did not fail me. I believed there must be something better further on and I struggled towards it.

In the spring came the agony of my mistaken engagement, swallowing up all other ills, as a dreadful physical pang blots out the consciousness of gnat stings. For a whole year I lived in such anguish of mind as I pray may never fall to my lot again. The memory of it has lost none of its keenness in all these years.

That year in Bedeque! What a strange year it was. A year of mad passion! And how I suffered! "To love where we esteem not", it is indeed torture. And yet—I am not sorry I had that love, in spite of all the suffering it brought me. I *cannot* be sorry. For all its pain there was in it, too, a wild potent sweetness that somehow means more to me in recollection than all the rest of the ordinary happiness of my life put together. It is a bitter thing to love vainly. But a drab life with no love in it—that would be the worst thing of all!

Monday, Feb. 7, 1910
Cavendish, P.E.I.

I wonder if anything could be offered me which would—supposing it were possible— induce me to live this past month over again. There are, perhaps, one or two things which might be potent enough. But even if I were offered the most intense and perfect happiness of my most daring dreams as a reward for enduring such another month I should hesitate to take the risk—because in all truth, I do not think I *could* live through it without going insane.

"That which I feared" has come upon me—I have had a month of nervous prostration—an utter breakdown of body, soul, and spirit. The hideous suffering of it, especially of the first fortnight, is something of which the mere remembrance curdles my blood. I thank God I do not come of a stock in which there is any tendency to insanity. If I had I believe that my mind would have given way hopelessly.

It came on very suddenly after my last entry. A new and dreadful worry which preyed on me for a week or two precipitated the crisis I suppose. At all events I broke down completely.

I could not sleep. For a week I hardly slept a moment. I can never forget the agony of those sleepless nights and the resulting days. For the ensuing fortnight I dozed fitfully. But this past week I have begun to sleep fairly well again.

The days were only one degree less hideous than the nights. I could not eat; every mouthful had to be forced down. I could not work or think or read or talk. I was possessed by a very fury of restlessness, only to be endured by walking the floor until my limbs failed from very exhaustion. Hitherto, when I have had similar though slighter nervous attacks I have been able to conceal my condition from grandmother. But this time it proved impossible and the resultant worry and alarm of the poor old soul was an added wretchedness to me.

I dreaded to see anyone coming to the house. When people came I had to hold myself still and talk to them—and I think death would have been easier. It was only by sheer will power that I could concentrate my mind sufficiently to understand what they were saying or make a coherent reply. Then when they had gone I was worse than ever.

Some days I would feel slightly better—so that I *could* compel myself to do such things as *had* to be done. Other days I could only walk the floor like one possessed of devils. Everybody noticed my wretched appearance but attributed it to the facial neuralgia from which I was indeed suffering severely enough but which seemed a very trifling ill compared to my nervous suffering.

I wanted to die and escape life! The thought of *having to go on living* was more than I could bear. I seemed to be possessed by a morbid dread of the future. No matter under what conditions I pictured myself I could only see myself suffering unbearably. I have heard *hell* defined as "a world from which hope was excluded". Then I was in hell for those three weeks. I had *no* hope. I could not realize any possible escape from suffering. It seemed to me that I must exist in that anguish forever. This is, I believe, a very common symptom of neurasthenia—and it is the hardest of all to bear. We can endure almost any pain if we can *hope* that it will pass. But when we are convinced that it will never pass it is unbearable.

I could not in a hundred pages detail all my sufferings during that awful time. I understand now what drives some people to suicide.

I went to Dr. Simpson and told him I was suffering from insomnia and nervousness. He gave me some medicine which has already helped me a good deal. The worry which precipitated the attack has also been partially removed and I feel that I am recovering. I can *work* again—oh, the blessedness of it. But I am far from well yet and some of my days are very miserable. Oh, if I could only see Frede for a few hours and "talk things out" with her. But she is away down at Cape Traverse this winter and I cannot see her.

I have come to the last page of this book, and I feel a curious regret as if I were parting from some real old friend and confidant. This book *has* been a friend to me. Without it I verily believe I should have gone under. It is a rather tragic volume. From cover to cover it gives a record of unhappiness. It began with my mistaken engagement to Edwin Simpson—who, by the by, oddly enough, is at present suffering from nervous prostration, also, as I heard recently.

Nearly thirteen years ago I began this volume of my journal. Now it is ended. They have been in most respects a hard thirteen years. Yet I have won literary success and fame in them; and hard as they have been they have been salutary in many respects. Perhaps in no other way could their lessons have been taught; perhaps had I been happier I had not climbed so high, lacking the spur of pain. But I *would* like a *little* happiness, just for a change. Whether it will ever be mine I do not know. Just now I am too discouraged to have any hope of it.

Good-bye old journal. You have been in all these long hard, lonely thirteen years almost my only comfort and refuge.

[THE END OF VOLUME 2]

103. The mantle in the old sitting room
[Cavendish]

104. A pensive Sunday School scholar
[LMM c.1884]

Notes

1889

September 22 A SIMPSON . . . A MACNEILL. Lucy Maud Montgomery's family tree shows evidence of Cavendish intermarriages: her mother, who was a Macneill, was related to the Simpsons, because her great-grandfather John Macneill (one of the first three men to settle in Cavendish) married the daughter of William Simpson (another of the three earliest settlers) and also through a series of intermarriages between Simpson and Macneill cousins. Lucy Maud Montgomery lived with her maternal grandparents, Alexander Macneill and Lucy Woolner Macneill. **October 22** MISS GORDON. L.M. Montgomery dedicated *Anne of Avonlea* (1909) to Hattie Gordon Smith, of New Perth, teacher at Cavendish from 1888 to 1892. **October 24** UNDINE (1811). A romance by Baron de la Motte Fouqué, about a fairy-child mysteriously introduced into a humble household. Nate was a nephew of Dr. A.J. Lockhart, a Nova Scotia educator and poet. PRAYER-MEETING. A Presbyterian mid-week service, with hymns and Bible readings. **November 13** CARRUTHERS. The Rev. James Carruthers was Minister of St. James Kirk, Charlottetown, 24 miles away. THE HALL. Cavendish Hall housed a lending library and a literary society (founded 1886) that offered community concerts and public lectures. **November 23** THE CHILD MARTYR. This recital piece by May Anderson tells of a Scottish child who guards her father's hiding place and dies to protect him; the poem appears in Shoemaker's *Best Selections*, a very popular compendium of performance pieces (Philadelphia: Penn, 1884). Most of the recitations mentioned in the journals can be found in this or comparable anthologies, or in the textbooks used in Prince Edward Island schools, e.g., the *Royal Reader* series (London: Nelson, 1876). **November 27** COURT. Mock-trial, with formal testimony, was a pedagogical device that Miss Gordon had learned at Prince of Wales College.

1890

February 17 SUPERSTITIONS. This courtship ritual implies that boys and girls in Prince Edward Island shake hands, British fashion; in the USA in the 1890s it would not be good form for women to shake hands. "ANGELS AND MINISTERS OF GRACE DEFEND US!" *Hamlet*, I,iv,39. **February 19** MRS. SPURR. The Baptist minister's wife; Nate Lockhart was her son by an earlier marriage. MONTREAL WITNESS. School essay contests ran annually in *The Montreal Witness and Canadian Homestead* (1845-1938), an evangelical, pro-Temperance, anti-Catholic weekly journal, edited in the 1890s by John Redpath Dougall. CAPE LEFORCE. On the Cavendish shore; see the entry for June 3, 1909. YANKEE STORM. In October 1851 a storm destroyed more than 70 American schooners near Cavendish. See

395

entry for June 3, 1909. Montgomery retold the story in *The Golden Road* (1913). THE MARCOPOLO. Fastest sailing vessel of her time, wrecked July 25, 1883. LMM's essay was published a year later in the Charlottetown *Patriot*, March 11, 1891, as "'The Wreck of the Marco Polo': in Canadian Prize stories Written for *The Montreal Witness*". The story is retold at length in the journal entry for June 3, 1909. **February 27** EIGHT-HAND REEL. Traditional Scottish country dance; the Baptist community in Cavendish would not have countenanced this party. JEW'S HARP. Small lyre-shaped instrument held to the mouth to make a twanging sound. **April 10** SANDSHORE. A localism for the white sea beaches. **April 18** RECIPROCITY. Reduction or abolition of import duties between Canada and the U.S.A. was a burning political issue. In the 1891 election, Conservatives (under John A. Macdonald) would attack Liberals (under Wilfrid Laurier) for urging reciprocal agreements, which they thought would lead to Canada's annexation by the United States. **April 22** GRANDPA MONTGOMERY. The Hon. Donald Montgomery (1808-93) was a political power in Prince Edward Island: a member of the provincial assembly (1838-62), he was Speaker during the early debates about Confederation. He became a member of the Canadian Senate in Ottawa after Confederation. **May 13** "MAYFLOWER PICNIC". A social outing to gather trailing arbutus or ground laurel: listed in the *Dictionary of Canadianisms* as "Maritimes, obs." **July 1** THE SWEDISH WEDDING MARCH. The fame of "the Swedish nightingale", Jenny Lind, had popularized Swedish music in this period. At Swedish weddings the Lutheran pastor led a dignified march and folkdance. "THE SHIP ON FIRE". This poem by Charles Mackay appears in Bell's *Standard Elocutionist* (London: Hodder and Stoughton, 1885) as a "Recitation for junior pupils". The exciting story is presented largely in dialogue. **July 26** HUNTER RIVER PEOPLE. From the nearest railway town, 17 miles inland. CAWNPORE. A section of Cavendish Beach, where there were fishing huts; it was named for a battle in the Indian Mutiny, 1857. **July 31** DEVEREUX. A gothic novel (1829) by Edward Bulwer-Lytton about young love and politics in Renaissance England. **August 8** ACADIA COLLEGE. A Baptist College at Wolfville, Nova Scotia. Nathan Lockhart was the only student from PEI among 33 freshmen. **August 9** PARK CORNER. A village 13 miles west of Cavendish. CLIFTON. Lucy Maud Montgomery's birthplace is now part of New London; the house where she was born was restored as a PEI Centennial project. SPIRITS OF THE DEPARTED. Stories of "hauntings" are featured in Montgomery's *Anne of Avonlea* (1909), *The Story Girl* (1911), and in many of her short stories. **August 11** KENSINGTON. The railway station nearest to Park Corner. The Island was over-endowed with railroads; railway debt had forced PEI to enter Confederation in 1873. SPECIAL. The railroad maintained elegant cars for use by senior politicians and company officials. SIR JOHN. Sir John A. Macdonald (1815-1891) Prime Minister, 1867-73, 1878-91; leader of the Conservative party since 1854. ST. LAWRENCE. One of the ferries from Summerside to Cape Tormentine. Train-cars were loaded onto the ferries crossing the Northumberland Strait. SALVATION ARMY BARRACKS. The Army had "invaded" the Maritimes in 1885; corps were established in both Charlottetown and Summerside in 1886. **August 12** ST. JOHN. The New Brunswick junction in the Halifax and Montreal routes of the Canadian Pacific Railway. "YANKEE".

American tourists were drawn to the Maritimes by interest in Longfellow's *Evangeline* (1847); in Montgomery's novels American ladies appear as elegant performers at summer hotel concerts. **August 13** ST. LAWRENCE HALL. Major hotel in Montreal, about to be outshone by the new palatial Windsor, built in 1890. ELECTRICITY. In 1885 electric lights came into use in Charlottetown, but the rest of the island had no electricity in 1891; some rural areas were still without electricity until after World War II. **August 14** STREET CAR. Tram lines had been laid in downtown Montreal streets by 1875. **August 15** LADIES PARLOR. An elegantly-furnished railway car, set aside as protection against smoking, spitting, and rough language. HIGH CHURCH. The Church of England was still considered the "Established" church in Canada: Presbyterians differed from Anglicans—particularly High Church Anglicans—on points of doctrine and ceremony. In PEI, in 1890, there were about 30,000 Presbyterians, 5,000 Anglicans. "BLOW SOFT O'ER CEYLON'S ISLE". A line in "From Greenland's Icy Mountains", a hymn by Bishop Reginald Heber (1783-1826). "THE CLOCKMAKER". T.C. Haliburton's satire, *The Clockmaker; or the Sayings and Doings of Sam Slick of Slickville*—published first in Halifax in 1836, with many British and American editions to follow—mocks Yankees and Canadian maritimers. **August 17** WINNIPEG. Capital of Manitoba, with a population of 25,000 in 1890. **August 18** REGINA. With a population of around 9,000 in 1890, Regina had been the seat of government of the Northwest Territories since 1885. (Saskatchewan did not become a province until 1905.) FATHER. Hugh John Montgomery had been a homestead inspector, auctioneer, real-estate salesman, and right-of-way purchaser for the Regina-Prince Albert Railway, in Battleford and Prince Albert since 1881. **August 20** DUCK LAKE. The end of a spur line north of Regina, giving access to the Northwest towards Edmonton; this town had been a rallying point for Louis Riel and Gabriel Dumont during the 1885 Rebellion. MR. MC TAGGART. Originally from Cannington, Ontario, John McTaggart was the stepfather of LMM's stepmother. PRINCE ALBERT. Founded in 1866 as a Presbyterian mission and a Hudson's Bay Company fort; the 1890 census showed a population of 1,090, not counting the Indian settlement to the west. BATTLEFORD. Small town at the end of another branch line running from Regina; LMM's father had been briefly transferred there from Prince Albert. **August 23** HIGH SCHOOL. In 1885 the Presbyterians had opened a non-denominational co-educational high school, whose building was destroyed by fire in the spring of 1890; temporary quarters in the Town Hall served LMM and her schoolmates. HIS WIFE. Mary Ann McRae, stepdaughter of John McTaggart. **September 1** MR. MUSTARD. John Alexander Mustard, from Scott Township, Ontario, a former schoolmate of LMM's stepmother, had graduated from the University of Toronto (B.A.) in 1889. TEACHER'S CERTIFICATE. With no normal school in the Territories, a student could go directly from school into teaching. **September 3** WILLIAM MC KENZIE (1849-1923). Railway magnate from Toronto, President of the Canadian Northern Railway; his family had come to Prince Albert for ceremonies on September 2, 1890, marking the opening of passenger service from Regina. He was the uncle of LMM's stepmother. In 1891 the family changed the spelling of their name to "Mackenzie". NITCHIE. An Algonkian Indian term, like the Ojibwa word "anishinabe": a friend; applied in a derogatory way to Indians. "Nitchie Joe" is the name of a character in the only story by Montgomery set in the prairies: "Tannis of the Flats", written in 1902 and published in the *Canadian Magazine* in 1914. It introduces a Métis family named Dumont. INDIAN BLOOD. Reference to the "detestable" half-breeds reveals lingering prejudice. In 1884 Louis Riel had come to Prince Albert at the invitation of the Scotch-Indians; but they did not join his force after the skirmish at Batoche. **September 19** BERTIE JARDINE. Son of Dr. Robert Jardine, M.A., D.D., the Presbyterian minister. FREEMASONS' ROOM. Like the Orange Lodges in Ontario, the Free Masons' secret society was connected with anti-Catholic sentiment. LMM's father belonged to the Kinnistine Masonic Lodge. **October 6** DOUGLAS MAVEETY. Son of J.D. Maveety, publisher of the Prince Albert *Times* since its founding in 1882; he had been drawn to Prince Albert by Charles Mair, exponent of "Canada First". **October 20** EDIE WENT. Edith Skelton returned to Battleford, leaving the Montgomerys without household help. **November 16** EVANGELINE. Longfellow's narrative poem about the expulsion of French-speaking Acadians from Grand-Pré (Nova Scotia) in 1755. At this time LMM wrote the Cape Leforce story: see the entry for December 7. **November 19** ELOCUTIONIST. Travelling performers of recitation pieces practised a complex rhetorical art—a major theatrical form in the 1890s. **December 1** BUFFALO COAT. Imitation buffalo robes were more common than coats made from real buffalo hides; the buffalo was disappearing from the Prairies by 1890. **December 5** WILLIE PRITCHARD. *Anne's House of Dreams* (1917) is dedicated to Willard's sister Laura Pritchard Agnew. **December 7** CHARLOTTETOWN PATRIOT. Founded in 1859 by a Laird from New Glasgow, 3 miles from Cavendish. Note the remarkable speed in publication and delivery: posted, accepted, edited, printed, and received in Saskatchewan all in three weeks. **December 10** "LEAVE HOPE BEHIND". Dante's *Inferno*, Canto III, line 9. "STAND UPON THE ORDER OF OUR GOING". *Macbeth*, III,ii,119. **December 14** "PANSY" BOOK. "Pansy"—Mrs. G.R. Alder—published a series of stories of child life, from 1876. 31 Pansy Books published by Lothrop were succeeded by 73 Pansy Series books, by Mrs. Alder and others, published by Ward, Lock; all preached missions, temperance, prayer.

1891

January 26 FATHER . . . AT A COUNCIL MEETING. Hugh John Montgomery had run against T. Agnew and F.C. Baker for his seat on Council; he became Chairman of the Board of Works. The Council erected a new Town Hall in 1891. **February 13** ON THE LIBERAL TICKET. The election of 1891 was called on Reciprocity. Hugh John Montgomery's affiliation with the Liberals was surprising, considering his father's political ties with the Conservatives and John A. Macdonald. **February 23** BARRACKS. Prince Albert was the district centre for the North West Mounted Police. CHUTE. A wooden structure for tobogganing, packed with snow and iced for speed; presumably decorated in the style popularized on Mount Royal in Montreal and at Rideau Hall in Ottawa. **March 7** ELECTION. Wilfrid Laurier cited the "rough and tumble politics" of Prince Albert in this election. **March 10** TEMPERANCE CONCERT. The Canadian Temperance League, incorporated in 1890, was mounting a vigorous campaign for "world prohibition, purity and peace". "THE CHRISTENING". A comic piece by E.J. Corbet: a young mother wants to call her son "Augustus Percival Guy", which leads Uncle Silas to shout "Jeehosophat!"—and this is how the minister christens the baby. **March 30** MR. STOVEL. Cyrus R. Stovel, a dental surgeon who married Mary McKenzie, half-sister of Mrs. McTaggart (mother of LMM's stepmother) and of William McKenzie. **April 6** PREDESTINATION. Presbyterians believed that because of the sinful nature of man, a just God could never forgive and save him, but a merciful God , by His mere will and pleasure, could elect a few persons to salvation; everyone is thus predestined to salvation or (more commonly) damnation. **April 20** THE CONVENT SCHOOL. St. Anne's Convent was the first high school in Prince Albert, opened in 1884. **April 23** JUDGE MC GUIRE. A long-lasting power in Prince Albert, who was still influential in 1913. **May 14** A VOLUNTEER. In 1885 a party of 95 volunteers and Mounties from Prince Albert had marched to Duck Lake to fight Riel and Dumont; 12 were killed and 11 wounded. **May 25** MAYOR JOHNSON. Mayor for one year only. **May 31** PARLIAMENT ADJOURNS. Sir John A. Macdonald had suffered a stroke, and no one knew when Parliament would adjourn; Macdonald died on June 6, 1891. "JUNE". Ten four-line stanzas, neatly rhymed, published in the *Patriot* on June 17, 1891. **June 6** KNOX COLLEGE. Presbyterian theological college in the University of Toronto. AN ARTICLE. Published as "A Western Eden" in the Prince Albert *Times* on June 17, 1891, it is a description of the Saskatchewan River, the modern Indian—facing extinction— and the hopeful future of the Prairies. **June 16** A TABLE RAP. Experimenting with "psychic phenomena", the group places fingers on a table and concentrates on willing it to lift and move. **June 18** "'TIS PLEASANT, SURE". Lord Byron, "English Bards and Scotch Reviewers" (1809), lines 51-2. **July 1** CORNERSTONE. The first Presbyterian church, built in 1872 and seating 120, was torn down in 1891. DOMINION DAY. On July 1 Canadians celebrate the Confederation of four provinces in 1867. EXCURSION DOWN THE RIVER. The Hudson's Bay Company had established steamboats on the Saskatchewan River in 1872. **July 5** MR. AGNEW. Andrew Agnew was the son of T.J. Agnew, whose ox-cart line preceded the railway as the main means of transport to Prince Albert. **July 24** TRAMS. The electric railway ran four miles from Prince Albert to Maiden Lake. **August 27** EDDIE JARDINE. Brother of Bertie and Arthur; he was on his way to school in Toronto. **August 29** FORT WILLIAM. Now part of Thunder Bay, Ontario; passengers boarded the Canadian Pacific steamship here for passage through Sault Ste. Marie to Owen Sound, where they entrained again. **August 31** THE "SOO". Sault Ste. Marie. **September 2** SIR RICHARD CARTWRIGHT (1835-1912). In 1891 Cartwright was the chief financial critic in the Liberal opposition (led by Laurier). **September 3** THE INTERCOLONIAL. Railway line from Ottawa to Montreal, now part of the Canadian Pacific Railway. **September 4** VICTORIA BRIDGE. This bridge in Montreal was opened in 1860 by the Prince of Wales. **November 7** VARIOUS PRINTED ARTICLES. These early productions are contained in a scrapbook that is now held at the Confederation Centre, Charlottetown. **November 19** NATE'S CLASS PICTURE. In his first year at Acadia University, Nate had had an "A"in every course and played on the football team. **December 4** "THE COUNTRY SCHOOL". A sprightly mini-drama in comic dialect by H. Bateman; found in

Shoemaker's *Best Selections*, 1884; also in the *5th Royal Reader*, prescribed for PEI schools. **December 19** "DIVISION" CHARTER. Banner of the Temperance movement. UNION JACK. The British flag was the flag of Canada until 1965. "NON SCHOLAE". Latin motto: "We learn not for school but for life." **December 22** SKETCH BOOK. *The Sketch Book of Geoffrey Crayon, Gent.* (1820), a collection of tales and sketches, in which Irving combines local colour with folklore. It had been presented to LMM by Dr. Stovel in August, along with a book of Emerson's *Essays*.

1892

January 10 EMERSON. Ralph Waldo Emerson's *Essays* (1841) includes rhapsodies on Nature and a philosophy of self-reliance. **February 13** PARCHESI. From the Hindu "pachisi": a board game similar to backgammon. **February 27** ROBERT ELSMERE. Bestseller (1888) by Mrs. Humphrey Ward preaching social Christianity and downplaying miraculous elements. EDWIN SIMPSON. From Belmont; he had been a teacher in Bideford and was now at school in Park Corner, preparing for college. LEM MCLEOD. The "Cove" McLeods were a large French River family. **March 10** JAMES MC INTYRE. Son of Mary (Montgomery) McIntyre; LMM's cousin, and nephew of the groom. **April 9** A HOOKING. A women's party or "bee" to work together on hooked rugs. **May 7** FACTORY BOYS. From Sawyer's lobster cannery at the mouth of the French River. **June 22** MONTANA. The fields were nicknamed for "wild west" States. **June 30** TO OREGON. Miss Gordon eventually settled in British Columbia. **July 17** SCHULTZ. (Sir) John Christian Schultz had been a prisoner of the Métis during the Red River Rebellion of 1869-70; he had been a main force in stirring the fury of Toronto Orangemen at the execution of Thomas Scott by Riel. **August 1** WELL AND DAVE. Wellington and David Nelson were the prototypes of Felix and Bev, the two Toronto cousins who come to live on a PEI farm in Montgomery's *The Story Girl* (1911) and *The Golden Road* (1913). In parts of this long journal entry, omitted here, LMM recalls happy times with the boys: building a playhouse, coasting, picking gum, playing ball, telling ghost stories, "making" money, and using stilts and bow-and-arrows. She recounted these details in a series of autobiographical articles entitled "The Alpine Path", published in *Everywoman's World* in 1917, and reprinted in book form as *The Alpine Path* (Toronto: Fitzhenry & Whiteside, 1974). **August 9** PRINCE OF WALES. The provincial training school for teachers had opened in Charlottetown in 1856; Prince of Wales College was established in 1860; the two were amalgamated in 1879. MISS WEST. This teacher was appointed to Cavendish school in 1892, but left after a few months owing to illness. **December 10** MAGIC LANTERN. Slides were projected onto a screen from a box containing a light.

1893

January 12 "SCOTTISH CHIEFS . . . EASY". Jane Porter's long-popular romance *Scottish Chiefs* (1810), based on the life of William Wallace; *Valentine Vox the Ventriloquist* (1840), a British adventure novel by Henry Cockton; *Mr. Midshipman Easy* (1836), a story of sea-life by Captain Frederick Marryat (who also wrote boys' books, including *The Young Settlers in Canada*). **June 30** ENTRANCE

EXAMS. Provincial examinations were set by the faculty of Prince of Wales College. **July 2** EPISCOPALIAN. Use of this term shows an American influence in the Island. In Quebec or Ontario St. Paul's and St. Peter's would be called "Anglican" or "Church of England". **July 4** PROFESSOR CAVEN. John Caven taught English and school management at Prince of Wales College. His opinions are probably those imputed in Montgomery's *Anne of Avonlea* to "Professor Rennie". Caven, who had been educated at Edinburgh and Rome, wrote extensively about PEI history. ARSENAULT. Joseph Octave Arsenault supervised practice teaching; in 1893 he became principal of the Model School, founded that year. **September 4** CHARLOTTETOWN. Capital of Prince Edward Island, founded 1750; its population in 1893 was 11,000. MRS. ALEXANDER MACMILLAN. *McAlpine's City Directory 1888* lists "Barbara McMillan, boarding house, 24 Hillsborough"—a house near the harbourfront, about 5 blocks from Prince of Wales College. **September 5** DR. ANDERSON. Alexander Anderson, Ll.D., Principal of the College and of the Provincial Normal school 1868-1902, taught Latin composition. ALL THE GIRLS. In the fall of 1893 there were 77 women and 99 men at PWC, which had been co-educational since 1879. Annual fees for the year were $10 for Charlottetown residents, $5 for country students. "FIRST CLASS". Third Class students attended only from August to December, studying English, History, Geography, Arithmetic, French, Chemistry, Agriculture, School Management, School Laws, Teaching, and Music; Second Class students took the same courses, except Music, for a full year and added Algebra, Geometry, Physics, Latin, and Scientific Temperance; First Class students normally attended for two years, adding Greek and Trigonometry, and doing advanced work in all subjects. **September 6** PROF. HARCOURT. George Harcourt, B.A.Sc., McGill University, was appointed in 1891 to teach Agriculture and Chemistry. SHAW. Herbert Shaw (of Brackley Point), B.Sc., McGill University, had been appointed in September to teach Geometry. FIRST CLASS ENGLISH. The curriculum included *The Merchant of Venice*, Scott's *Lay of the Last Minstrel*, Addison's *"Sir Roger de Coverley"*, Tennyson's *"Guinevere"*, Pope's *" 'Essay on Criticism'*, and Meiklejohn's *English Literature of the 18th and 19th centuries*, in addition to the Second Class list—*Paradise Lost*, Book I, and Macaulay's "Essay on Milton"—and the Third Class readings: *Macbeth*, Scott's *Lady of the Lake*, selections from Addison's *Spectator* essays, and Macaulay's *Lays of Ancient Rome*. **September 28** EXHIBITION. Established in 1879, the Charlottetown Exhibition had moved to grounds outside the city in 1890; at Queen Square, three blocks from the College, there were still horse and cattle parades and Scottish dancing at Exhibition time. THE LADIES' WORLD. Founded in New York in 1886, it was a respected magazine publishing good material and selling at 50¢ a year. LMM submitted a poem in seven stanzas of five lines each, rhymed a-b-a-b-b: a violet, seen trampled in a city street, brings memories of a woodland lane, blue skies and a blue-eyed friend; it was published in July 1894. **October 3** ZION CHURCH. Erected in 1860 on Grafton Street, one block west of Hillsborough, Zion Presbyterian resulted from the secession of a group of families from the Old Kirk of St. James, the Free Kirk, and the Athenaeum. With its frescoed ceilings, upholstered pews, and instrumental music, this was the stylish downtown church. The Rev. David Sutherland, the incumbent, was not related to LMM's

Sutherland cousins. WALLACE ELLIS. Originally "Wallace E . . ."; in the typescript copy of the journal LMM fills in the blank with "Ellis". FITZROY STREET. 187 Fitzroy is actually just one block north of the College buildings on Kent Street. **October 22** ROCKY POINT. Professor Caven published a poem about the old French Fort Lajoie, on Rocky Point at the mouth of Charlottetown harbour. MRS. YOUNG'S. "Fairholme", 230 Prince Street. BIG BRICK METHODIST. On Prince St., near Zion Church, the First Methodist Church was called by a contemporary satirist "The First Disorderist Church . . . where the preacher shouts, and the ladies exhibit their loud and extravagant fashions". **November 11** BUSINESS COLLEGE. Located on the second floor of the new Brown Block on Richmond Street. GOING OUT WEST. In 1891 the population of PEI had been 109,000; it was now declining because of migration to the Prairies. **November 27** "FROM GREENLAND'S ICY MOUNTAINS". A missionary hymn (1819), by Bishop R. Heber. MARY CAMPBELL AND . . . NORMAN. Cousins of LMM from Darlington; at Christmas, Norman went back to Darlington as a Third Class teacher, with 24 pupils, and returned the next year to finish his First Class training. **December 5** "JAG" ON. slang: drunk. **December 6** MADE IN GERMANY. Easily destroyed: the reputation for flimsiness probably reflects the opinion of imports from Germany, in which there had been a phenomenal rise in the 1890s.

1894

January 9 FRED WEST, B.A. Frederick West (brother of the Miss West who taught briefly at Cavendish), a graduate of Dalhousie University, had resigned in September from the faculty of PWC. **February 13** THE FAMOUS "BAD BOY". *A Bad Boy's Diary: By Little Georgie*, a comic novel (1880) by American author Metta Victoria (Fuller) Victor, attributed to Walter T. Gray, was the first of a very popular series. An earlier "bad boy" appeared in T.B. Aldrich's *The Story of a Bad Boy*, a bestseller of 1869. CONFAB. Slang for "confabulation": a chat. **February 15** TAL MACMILLAN. Talmage MacMillan of New Haven graduated with 88% and an Honor Diploma. "CHILDE HAROLD". *Childe Harold's Pilgrimage* (1812-18), a romantic travel poem by Lord Byron. **March 1** "COLLEGE RECORD". Hedley McKinnon of Charlottetown edited the school paper. LMM's contributions included "The Usual Way" (a spoof on schoolgirl studying—interrupted by gossip, candy, and talk of new hats and boys) and "Extracts from the Diary of a Second Class Mouse" (PWC as seen from a mouse's perspective). In the following year Edwin Simpson, Norman Campbell, and Cyrus Macmillan edited the *Record*. **April 2** JOHN RILEY. J.F. Reilly of Summerside appears second in the honor diploma list. **April 7** STUART SIMPSON, JIM STEVENSON. Boys from Bay View and New Glasgow, neighbouring villages to Cavendish. **May 2** B. FAYE MILLS. The two-week visit of this American evangelist dominated local newspapers. **May 24** "GRACIOUS QUEEN". Queen Victoria; her birthday is a national holiday in Canada. THE PARK. Victoria Park, on the harbour front, was a civic centre because of its cricket, football and baseball clubs, tennis courts, cycling paths, militia training grounds, and promenade. **May 29** EXAMS. Most exams ran four hours, except Greek (four-and-a-half hours) and Roman History (five hours). Immediately after completing college exams, Normal School students wrote for their teacher's licence three exams a day for five days. **May 31** PORTIA IN THE PLAY. LMM's essay on *The Merchant of Venice* suggests that Portia's wit, tact in handling suitors, and delicacy in love are less important than her intellectual power and eloquence. **June 8** OPERA HOUSE. The theatre was in the new Masonic Temple, which opened on October 25, 1893, on Grafton Street near Queen. HONOR LISTS. LMM had top marks in both English courses and in Agriculture; she tied for first place in School Management and in Essay-writing, and was in the top five in Teaching. CHALLIE. Challis: a very fine cotton or woollen fabric. **June 9** THE GUARDIAN. Both Charlottetown papers praised the essay and the performance. **June 16** CARTER'S. A general store on Queen Street. **July 14** "VANITY FAIR". Novel (1848), by William Makepeace Thackeray. **July 26** A SCHOOL. LMM went as a Second Class teacher to Bideford, with a supplement of $10, a school house allowance of $20, and contingent expenses of $20; her salary was $180 a year. BIDEFORD. A north-shore fishing village about 66 miles west of Cavendish in a protected bay famous for oysters. Founded in 1814 by William Ellis and his apprentices, Williams and England; in 1860 Alex Millar established the Bideford flour mill. These 4 families still dominated Bideford life in the 1890s. **July 28** DOMICILED. Consistently misspelled "domociled" throughout the journal. **July 31** MRS. ESTEY. Wife of the Methodist minister; it was she who put liniment into a cake by mistake—suggesting one of the adventures of Montgomery's "Anne" in *Anne of Green Gables*. **August 8** AN INDIAN. Micmac Indians inhabited villages on the North shore of PEI. **September 2** RUSSIA'S FOREIGN POLICY. Russian imperialism in this period was widely decried, e.g., by Kipling in *Letters of Marque* (1891). **September 18** "LOGOMACHY". A word game, ironically called "Methodist casino", since Methodists disapproved of all card games, including the then-popular Casino. **September 29** MACAULAY'S ESSAYS. Thomas Babington Macaulay (originally misspelled "McAulay") was the influential author of *The Lays of Ancient Rome* (1842) and *A History of England* (1849). "COCO". Kitten given to LMM by the Millars in September. "THE GLORY AND THE DREAM". From William Wordsworth's "Ode: Intimations of Immortality from Recollections of Early Childhood" (1807). **October 31** CAPTAIN RICHARDS. A wealthy shipowner and builder in Bideford. Captain Richards' home, built in 1864, was selected a hundred years later as the best house of its vintage in PEI. **November 5** "GUY FAWKES" NIGHT. Until well into the twentieth century Canadians lit bonfires to celebrate the defeat of the "Popish plot" of 1605 to overthrow the British government. ORANGE LODGE. Protestant fraternal society, very strong in rural Canada, commemorating the victories over the Irish in 1690 by King William III (of Orange). LEW DYSTANT. LMM changes the spelling to "Lou" on further acquaintance. **November 20** "CINDERELLA". LMM's scrapbooks show that she played one of the sisters; Edith England played Cinderella. "The Irish Love Letter" appears as "The Old Settler's Story" in the program preserved in her scrapbook. **December 6** "PROHIBITION". In 1901 Prince Edward Island would become the first province to legislate prohibition of sale of alcohol. In Island schools "Scientific Temperance" was an examination subject. **December 17** MY BASKET. Young women packed fancy food into decorated baskets for "basket socials"; an auction decided which man would buy each basket and claim its creator as a supper partner. **December 28** MASONIC SUPPER. The Freemasons' secret society owned the Hall or Temple, which was a centre of social activity in many villages.

1895

January 27 "SCARLET LETTER". *The Scarlet Letter* (1850), a novel by Nathaniel Hawthorne, set in a Puritan New England village. **March 14** "ON THE GULF SHORE". The Charlottetown scrapbook dated 1893-6 contains this poem, "by Maud Eglington", published in February 1895, and another published in the *Ladies' Journal*, July 1895, "When the Apple Blossoms Blow", by "Maud Cavendish". This Toronto magazine bought ten more poems and two stories from LMM before 1900. KISSING GAMES. Young people are paired by blind chance in games such as Spin the Bottle and Post Office. **April 12** GRAND DIVISION. Regional meeting of the "Sons of Temperance". "THE SCHOOLMASTER'S GUESTS". Recital piece by Will Carleton, in Bell's *Standard Elocutionist*: the district fathers dress down the young teacher—one of them is spokesman, the others mutter, "Them 'ere is my sentiments tew!". **April 20** HALIFAX LADIES' COLLEGE. A residential school in Halifax, Nova Scotia, founded in 1887, on Pleasant Street (now Barrington) at Harvey. DALHOUSIE. A university in Halifax, founded in 1818. In 1895 it granted degrees in Arts, Science, Engineering, Law and Medicine, and enrolment was just over 300. The University was housed in the Forrest Building, on College Street. **June 17** A STORY. "A Baking of Gingersnaps" by "Maud Cavendish", published July 1895. **June 28** "THE SCEPTRE IS DEPARTED FROM JUDAH". Genesis 49, 10: "The sceptre shall not depart from Judah". **July 2** CLASS-MEETING. Methodist Bible classes for young adults. S'SIDE. Entrance exams for PWC were held in several regional centres such as Summerside. LMM consistently uses capitals within the abbreviations, as in "S'Side", and "Ch'Town". **September 15** HALIFAX. The capital of Nova Scotia, and the cultural and financial centre of Canadian Maritime provinces; in 1895 it had a population of around 40,000. Halifax appears as "Kingsport" in Montgomery's *Anne of the Island* (1915). **September 17** PICTOU HARBOR. Ferry-boat terminus on north shore of Nova Scotia. STELLARTON . . . TRURO. The old Intercolonial line to Halifax. CALISTHENICS. Swedish-style gymnastic exercises were performed in most women's colleges. The LMM scrapbook has a cartoon— "Vassar, '94, doing calisthenics"—of two girls exercising, to the horror of an elderly aunt. **September 18** H.L.C. Halifax Ladies' College. In 1894-5 there were 92 students, most of them in the College's Conservatory of Music. MISS KER. The Principal of Halifax Ladies' College, a graduate of Girton College, Cambridge, England. **September 19** GLEES. College songs, sung by freshmen, in defiance of sophomores; see Montgomery's *Anne of the Island*. DR. FORREST. John Forrest, D.D., was President of Dalhousie from 1885 to 1911. THE PARK. Point Pleasant Park lies between the Northwest Arm and Halifax harbour. **September 25** ENGLISH PROFESSOR. Dr. Archibald McKellar MacMechan (1862-1935) was born in Berlin, Ontario, educated at the University of Toronto and Johns Hopkins University, and began teaching at Dalhousie in 1889. A scholar and essayist, he published many books, including editions of two works by Thomas Carlyle in 1896 and 1901, and *Headwaters of Canadian Literature* (1924), which became a landmark in nationalist appreciation. SACKVILLE COLLEGE. Mount Allison College, at Sackville, New Brunswick—now Mount Allison University. **October 3** POORHOUSE. A hostel for the indigent at the corner of Robie and South Streets. **October 12** "MOON OF FALLING LEAVES". See Isabella Valancy Crawford's poem "Malcolm's Katie" (1884), II, 61. UNITED SERVICE. Army and Navy team. **October 22** THE OPERA. LMM's Halifax scrapbook includes programs for *Olivette, Iolanthe, Billie Taylor, Faust,* and *The Beggar Student.* Operas were put on at the Academy of Music on Pleasant (Barrington) Street, near the HLC. **October 27** FORT MASSEY CHURCH. Presbyterian church (now a United church) at the corner of Queen and Tobin Streets. **December 1** PHILOMATHIC SOCIETY. A literary and philosophical society, founded 1891 ("philomath": a lover of learning); all faculty members were honorary members, and all past and present students could join for an annual fee of fifty cents. Montgomery's *Anne of the Island* cites ideas presented at the Philomathic as the best learning acquired at "Redmond". IAN MAC LAREN. Pen-name of John Watson, author of the bestseller *Beside the Bonnie Brier Bush* (1894). This novelist, and others of the sentimental Scottish school—e.g., S.R. Crockett and J.M. Barrie—created models of LMM's materials: daunting old ladies, dour old men, slim sprightly girls and serious youths, watchful neighbours, and genteel poverty. Y.M.C.A. The Young Men's Christian Association building was at the corner of Granville and Prince Streets. **December 12** THE SUBJECT. John Milton in his epic, *Paradise Lost* (1667), proposed to re-examine the story of man's first sin, and "to justify the ways of God to man". **December 23** DYSTANT . . . LEM'S. John and Lem were brothers of Lewis Dystant, of Ellerslie. Lem worked for the Halifax Bakery and Confectionery Company. "GREENBANK". The fortress on George's Island appears as "William's Island" in Montgomery's *Anne of the Island,* in a passage with interesting variations on this journal entry: "They all sat down in the little pavilion to watch the autumn sunset of deep red fire and pallid gold. To their left lay Kingsport, its roofs and spires dim in their shroud of violet smoke. To their right lay the harbour, taking on tints of rose and copper as it stretched out into the sunset. Before them the water shimmered, satin smooth and silver gray, and, beyond, clean shaven William's Island loomed out of the mist, guarding the town like a sturdy bull-dog. Its lighthouse beacon flared through the mist like a baleful star, and was answered by another in the far horizon" (chapter 6, "In the Park").

1896

January 11 CITADEL HILL. Historic site of the old fortress and barracks on the high mound at the centre of Halifax. **January 20** AENEID. Virgil's epic on the founding of Rome. Book V, dealing with the death of Aeneas's father, and with the burning of the ships at Troy, also describes manly sports—racing, archery, and wrestling. TITANIA. Queen of the fairies in Shakespeare's *A Midsummer's Night's Dream* (1596). ROMEO AND JULIET. Shakespeare's tragedy of star-crossed lovers (1595). "OLD MORTALITY". Walter Scott's novel (1816) about the Covenanters of Scotland. LAGGED. Slang: arrested. **February 15** EVENING MAIL.

One of four Halifax daily newspapers. **February 20** "OUR CHARIVARI" (originally misspelled "Charavari"). Like Montgomery's *The Golden Road* (1913), this story is written from the point of view of a young boy visiting his PEI family farm. "GOLDEN DAYS". A long-established juvenile magazine, published in Philadelphia, 1880-1907. LMM changed the order of her successes when she retold the story of this fortunate fortnight in *The Alpine Path* (see note on entry for August 1, 1892). **March 14** "THE EXPERIENCES OF A GIRL STUDENT". Published as "A Girl's Place at Dalhousie College", this essay quotes Tennyson's *Princess*, reviews the achievements of the 25 young women who had graduated from Dalhousie since 1881, and comments gracefully on the objects and values of a university education for working girls and for wives. **March 21** THE YOUTH'S COMPANION. The leading American magazine for young people; published in Boston, it had a circulation of 540,000 by 1900. "FISHER LASSIES". A poem in nine quatrains, perfectly rhymed, a-a-b-b, and signed "M.L. Cavendish", it offers a romanticized picture of girls—"joyous, lithe-limbed, as the sea-birds free"—waiting for their men to come in from the sea. The rhythm echoes the grimmer "Three Fishers Went Sailing", a popular recital song by Charles Kingsley. **April 2** "THE APPLE PICKING TIME". "By M.L. Cavendish", published in *Golden Days*, October 1, 1896. **April 17** SENIOR ENGLISH PAPER. LMM wrote on "Metre in Milton's *Comus*"; the thesis was an optional addition to senior English, to finish "with distinction". **April 25** GEORGE MUNRO. A generous benefactor of Dalhousie University, though not himself a Dalhousie graduate, Munro (1825-96) had endowed several professorships and provided scholarship funds. **July 8** GOLDEN DAYS. The magazine published "Our Practical Joke" in July 1896, and "A Missing Pony" in September 1896. **July 20** MC CLURE SYNDICATE. S.S. McClure, the founder of *McClure's Magazine* (1893), also started the first newspaper syndicate to reprint previously published material, including stories by well-known authors such as Kipling, Stevenson, and Rider Haggard. CHICAGO INTER-OCEAN. A solid, respectable, culturally significant magazine; in 1892 it pioneered the use of colour printing on rotary presses in its Sunday supplement. "In Spite of Myself" appeared in the issue of July 1896. **August 18** BELMONT. A village on Malpeque Bay about 40 miles from Cavendish. ED SIMPSON. Like Gilbert Blythe in *Anne of Green Gables*, Ed was helping a young lady he favoured to find a teaching job by recommending her for his own school. **August 20** THE OLD BLUE CHEST. This appears in Montgomery's *The Story Girl*. **October 21** MR. SIMPSON. Sam Simpson's father had married LMM's great-aunt. AUNT MARY LAWSON. Another great-aunt, sister of LMM's grandfather Alex Macneill; a favourite relative and a repository of family stories. *The Golden Road* (1913) is dedicated to her memory. "TOO MUCH OF THE ONE BREED". Samuel and Mrs. Simpson were first cousins. CENTRAL SIXTEEN. Central Lot 16 is a village inland from Bentick Cove. RICHMOND BAY. At the junction of the Grand River and Malpeque Bay. SECOND CLASS WORK. Like LMM when she studied Greek, Marie Munro intended to by-pass the Third Class work and enter PWC with advanced standing. **October 22** "HOBSON'S CHOICE". No choice at all: from an anecdote in *The Spectator*, 1712, about a liveryman named Hobson who made each customer take the horse nearest the door. **October 27** HYPERION TO A SATYR. *Hamlet*,

I,ii,140. YCLEPT. "Named"; an archaism, used mock-heroically. "OFF-THE-PARLOR". A small ground-floor bedroom, usually reserved for an elderly person. **November 4** "CABINED, CRIBBED, CONFINED". "cabin'd, cribb'd, confin'd", *Macbeth*, III,iv,24. **November 7** THE AMERICAN AGRICULTURIST. Founded in 1842 and published in New York, it became a weekly magazine in 1894. It published Montgomery's "Home from Town" in November 1896, and "Riding to Church" in February 1897. **December 7** I SAT OFF. In the typescript of the Journal, LMM changes this to "I went".

1897

February 3 MR. BAKER. A Baptist evangelist who had been preaching at the Grand Division (see note to journal entry of April 12, 1895). **February 7** IMMERSION. A Baptist conversion ceremony that entails plunging the whole person in water. **March 9** ARTHUR'S HOME MAGAZINE. With *Godey's Lady's Book* and *Paterson's*, one of a trio of bestselling women's magazines. Montgomery's "Strayed Allegiance" was published in the July 1897 issue (her "Goose Feud" had appeared in April). *Arthur's* ceased publication the next year. PHILADELPHIA TIMES. A reform paper, founded by A.K. McClure in 1878; it published Montgomery's "A Prize in Elocution" in March, "Extra French Exam" in May, and "Detected by the Camera" in June. "The Violet Challie Dress" appeared in August and "Gold Link Bracelet" in September. **March 15** CROQUINOLE. A game played with checkers on a round board. **April 9** MADE UP MY MIND. The typescript of the journal adds that the Campbells had objected to her intimacy with the Simpson family and put pressure on her to resign. MY WRITING. LMM now began recording in a literary scrapbook the writing and publication dates for all her poems and stories. She wrote the poems "From a Gable Window" and "The Light in Mother's Eyes" in April. CRIMPERS. Small irons for pleating. LAMBREQUIN. Short curtain across the top of a window. **April 15** LAURA. Laura Pritchard had married Andrew Agnew in Prince Albert on June 3, 1896. **June 30** CURTAIN ISLAND. Now called Courtin Island. LMM used this setting in "The Curtain Island Mystery", which was published in the *Star Monthly*, October 1902. SPARTAN BOY. Another legendary child martyr: rather than cry out and betray his family the boy let a fox gnaw his breast. ALBERTON. North-shore town, 40 miles west of Belmont, near the western tip of the Island. TEACHERS' CONVENTION. Professional development conference: a school holiday. DREE THIS WEIRD. Scottish dialect: "endure this fate". **October 7** "HARVEST IS ENDED". Compare "The harvest is past, the summer is ended, and we are not saved." *Jeremiah*, 8, 20. LOWER BEDEQUE. On the Dunk River, which empties into the Summerside Harbour bay, on the south shore of Prince Edward Island. The Indian name means "the hot place". CHRISTIAN ENDEAVOR SOCIETY. The first Young People's Society of Christian Endeavour, originally a youth movement in evangelical Protestant churches, was instituted in 1881 by Dr. F.E. Clark in Portland, Maine. An interdenominational and international World's Christian Endeavor Union was formed in 1895. "THE STORY OF AN AFRICAN FARM". An influential feminist book (1883) by Olive Schreiner; she also wrote *Women and Labour* (1911). WRITTEN A GREAT DEAL. LMM's scrapbook entitled "Stories and Poems late 1890s" includes sixty-nine items, such as

"Old Hector's Dog", "The Tree Lovers", "The Poplars at the Gate", "If Love should Come", "New Fashioned Flavoring", "Margaret Ann's Mother", "Which Dear Charmer", "Kismet", and "A Brave Girl". MUNSEY. *Munsey's Magazine*, founded in 1889, serialized the most popular writers; it paid ½¢ a word. LMM's poem in *Munsey's* was "If Love Should Come". "THE GATES AJAR". A long-time bestseller (1868) by Elizabeth Phelps; pious and sentimental treatment of a girl who has lost her lover in the Civil War. "THE LOVE LETTERS OF A WORLDLY WOMAN". Lucy Lane Clifford wrote this popular book (1891, London: Arnold); it went into many American editions (Chicago: Donahue; New York: Harper).

1898

January 22 MIRAMICHI. A fishing and ship-building region in New Brunswick. MR. CORNELIUS LEARD'S. The Leard family had been in the Bedeque district since 1823. "THE PLAY OF HAMLET". LMM misquotes Walter Scott: ". . . the tragedy of Hamlet, the character of the Prince of Denmark being left out." (*The Talisman*, 1825). **April 8** TELEGRAM. Telegram service had been established on the Island since 1853; the first trans-Atlantic telegraph message to America, sent from Ireland, was received in Charlottetown in 1858. MARAH. A lake of bitter waters; see Exodus 15,22. "WHO CAN CONCEIVE WHO HAS NOT PROVED". From Byron's 'To Emma" (1804). SOME SUCCESSES IN LITERATURE. In April 1898 the *Christian Herald* published Montgomery's "A Pastoral Call"; the *Philadelphia Times* published five other stories in 1898: "Brother's Queer Ruse", "Real Test of Friendship", "Courage for the Occasion", "A Lesson in Behavior", and "Story of a Ruby Ring". *Golden Days* published three stories; the *Family Herald* published "A Brave Girl" and "Jen's Device". Other work was published during 1898 in the *Sunday Republican, Illustrated Youth and Age, Pilgrim, Congregationalist, Springfield Sunday Republican, New England Farmer, Family Story Paper, Youth and Age*, and *The Churchman*. "THE QUICK OR THE DEAD". Amelie Rives' novelette, *The Quick or the Dead?* (1888), deals with the hysterical passion of a young widow, fighting against her growing love of a new suitor. "NIGHT AND MORNING". This novel (1841) by Bulwer Lytton centred on a lawsuit. GRANDFATHER'S . . . WILL. Alex Macneill left his property to his son John with the proviso that Mrs. Macneill have the use of the house for the rest of her life. **July 10** "A WINDOW IN THRUMS". An early sentimental novel (1889) by J.M. Barrie about a young man who sacrifices ambition for the sake of his old mother. "OPENING A CHESTNUT BURR". An evangelical novel (1874) by the Rev. E.P. Roe, that has a shipwreck as a sensational climax. ELLA WHEELER WILCOX. A popular and prolific writer of sentimental verse; her *Poems of Passion* (1883) was criticized for being "immoral" but was, in fact, rather ethereal. "QUO VADIS". This world bestseller (1897) by the Polish author Henry Sienkiewicz, was a trend-setter in historical romance. **October 8** "BUT YET I KNOW". From Wordsworth's "Ode: Intimations of Immortality Recollected from Childhood" (1807), on the consolations as well as the losses involved in maturing. CAVENDISH IS LOOKING. The rest of this long entry (omitted from these selections) describes the houses on the Cavendish road. On February 15, 1911, she would again describe this walk, with fuller details about the family in each of the houses. **December 31** BICYCLES. There had been a craze for bicycles in 1895. THE CHRISTIAN. A novel (1897) by Hall Caine, who wrote earnest, deeply religious fiction. THE MANXMAN. An earlier bestseller (1894) also by Caine. KIPLING'S "BALLADS". Rudyard Kipling's *Barrack-room Ballads* (1892).

1899
April 4 ANTHONY HOPE. The pen-name of Sir Anthony Hope Hawkins (1863-1933), bestselling author of *The Prisoner of Zenda* (1894), *Rupert of Hentzau* (1898), *The Dolly Dialogues* (1894), and other popular novels; his *Phroso* had appeared in 1897. "THE CHILDREN OF THE ABBEY". A highly coloured society romance (1796) by Regina Marie Roche. **May 1** "TOWER OF LONDON". A novel (1840) by W.H. Ainsworth, about Lady Jane Grey, Queen Mary, and Queen Elizabeth. ATLANTIC. The *Atlantic Monthly* (1857-) is an American magazine of literature, art, and politics. The March issue contained "An Evicted Spirit" by Marguerite Merington, the story of a mourning family, presented from the point of view of the dead child. LARES AND PENATES. Household gods (Latin): most dear possessions. **May 28** MARIE CORELLI. Bestselling English author of high-pitched romances, e.g., *The Sorrows of Satan* (1895). Lilith, the legendary first wife of Adam, was a demon, a vampire. WEYMAN. Stanley Weyman, author of *Under the Red Robe* (1894), another hectic bestseller. CROCKETT. S.R. Crockett, Scottish novelist who had shifted from sentimental novels in the Scottish dialect to historical adventure yarns. **July 24** TO CANVASS MAYFIELD. Canvassers called at every house on the road between Cavendish and Mayfield, the next village on the road to Charlottetown. Compare *Anne of Avonlea*, ch. 6. COMMUNION SUNDAY. In the Presbyterian church the sacrament was limited to members of the church who had been given cards in a pre-communion visitation by the elders. "'TWAS ON THAT NIGHT WHEN DOOMED TO DIE". This hymn by the Rev. J. Morison (1781) continues, "The saviour of the world took bread". "I KNELT DOWN". Compare *Anne of the Island*, ch. 40. **October 8** MARK TWAIN. *More Tramps Abroad* (1897) was an English version of Twain's autobiographical travel narrative, *Following the Equator* (1897).

1900
January 14 "THE LADY OF THE LAKE". Walter Scott's romantic poem (1810) portrays an innocent, isolated girl courted by a disguised king and a Highland chieftain, and contains sensitive descriptions of Trossach scenery. "RUPERT OF HENTZAU". Both in this novel (1898) and in the one to which it is a sequel, *The Prisoner of Zenda* (1894), Hope's hero renounces the chance to seize happiness for himself. THE TRANSVAAL WAR. Canada sent a contingent to South Africa during this conflict (1899-1902). VANITY FAIR. Contrast LMM's earlier comment on this novel in her entry of July 4, 1894. **May 1** "GOD IN CURSING GIVES US BETTER GIFTS". From Elizabeth Barrett Browning, "Aurora Leigh". NINETY-SIX DOLLARS AND EIGHTY-EIGHT CENTS. Half the salary of a second-class teacher in a country school. RACINE'S ATHALIE. A tragedy (1691) about the daughter of Jezebel and Ahab. "KING SOLOMON'S MINES". A popular romance (1885) by Rider Haggard set in South Africa. "THE KING'S MIRROR". One of Anthony Hope's annual best-sellers (1899). "FOUR GEORGES". *The Four Georges and William IV*, a four-

volume work (1884-1901), begun by Irish historian and novelist Justin M'Carthy, and completed by his son Justin Huntly M'Carthy. PARKMAN'S "WOLF AND MONTCALM". *Montcalm and Wolf* (1884), a sweeping history of the Seven Years' War and the Conquest, by American historian Francis Parkman. "THE LAST OF THE MOHICANS". The second (1826) of Fenimore Cooper's five novels about the American frontier. "ASCENT OF MAN". *The Ascent of Man* (1894) by the Scottish clergyman Henry Drummond, author of *Natural Law in the Spiritual World* (1883), presented a popularized and spiritualized version of evolution. "FARTHEST NORTH". An account (1897) of the Arctic by Norwegian explorer and statesman Fridtjof Nansen. **June 7** "ISABEL CARNABY". This novel (1898) by E.T. Fowler (The Honourable Ellen Thorneycroft) was published in London by Hodder & Stoughton and in New York by Appleton. "JANICE MEREDITH". A popular novel (1899) by Paul Leicester Ford. Four New York editions, by Dodd, Mead, Grosset & Dunlap, P.F. Collier, and A.P. Watt—all in 1899—were made possible by loose copyright laws, and suggest the urgent search among publishers for best sellers. ALCOTT STORIES. Some of LMM's stories come very close to Louisa May Alcott's: e.g., in Montgomery's "Her Pretty Golden Hair", published in the *Philadelphia Times*, 1898, a girl sacrifices her one beautiful feature to help family finances, as Jo does in Alcott's *Little Women* (1868). **August 5** I WROTE FOR PURE LOVE OF IT. This section of the entry (omitted here) continues with the details of early literary efforts. The account is transcribed with few changes into *The Alpine Path* (see note on entry for August 1, 1892). **October 7** UNDINE. See note on entry for October 24, 1889. **November 10** "A PAIR OF SLIPPERS". A sentimental poem about "grandmamma's" young days: LMM's entry for March 4, 1901 (omitted in these selections) records a request from Arthur Mason of Pittsfield, Mass., to set the verses to music; LMM's scrapbook contains a program from its premiere at a musicale in Pittsfield. **December 22** "GETTING ON PRETTY WELL". In 1900 LMM published "When the Fishing Boats Come in", "Evening Dreams", and other poems, and added *Good Housekeeping*, *Sports Afield*, and *Waverley* to the list of journals that had purchased her short stories.

1901

January 23 "THE QUEEN". Victoria ascended the throne in 1837. **March 2** A CERTAIN OLD SCREW. This is still shown to tourists at the Park Corner homestead of the Campbell family. **March 21** THE HOUSEHOLD. This cheap home monthly had developed into an excellent magazine. FIRST PRIZE. "Pennington's Girl" won a prize in *Ladies' Journal* in 1900; "A Homesick Heart" earlier won a $25 prize in the *Family Herald and Weekly Star*. **August 23** THE KIND OF JUVENILE STORY I LIKE. The bestselling book of 1900 was *The Wonderful Wizard of Oz*, by L. Frank Baum. The death of Lewis Carroll in 1898 had prompted various writings about children's books. The moral-hunting editors worked mostly for presses with religious affiliation, such as Judson's (the American Baptist Publishing Society of Philadelphia), which published Margaret Marshall Saunders' *Beautiful Joe* (1894). **November 13** SAND. Scottish dialect: strength, determination. "DAILY ECHO". The Halifax Chronicle Company put out the *Echo* as an afternoon paper. AUER LIGHTS. A beam directed across the presses to check the paper run.

W.C.A. Women's Christian Association. **November 14** WOOLNOUGH'S RES-
TAURANT. At 153 Hollis street. WINDSOR. A small town 40 miles from Halifax.
"AROUND THE TEA TABLE". For this column LMM produced items on fashion,
love-letters, hair styles, diet, handwriting, hymns, streetcars, slang, and photography. PRINCE STREET. It runs from Citadel Hill to the wharves. HALIGONIAN. A
native of Halifax. DOCTOR FELL. An allusion to a famous quatrain based on a
Latin epigram, written by Thomas Brown (1663-1704) when he was a youth: "I
do not like thee, Doctor Fell;/ The reason why I cannot tell . . ." MC LELLAN.
LMM changes this to McClellan in the typescript of her journals. **November 16**
EXHIBITION. The Halifax Exhibition Building and Grounds were on Windsor Street,
at the site of the present-day Halifax Forum. **November 18** MOLASSES "KISS".
Candy. PLYMOUTH BRETHREN. A fundamentalist Christian sect established c.1828
in Dublin and in 1830 in Plymouth, England; members considered the Scriptures
the only true guide. THE DELINEATOR. New York monthly fashion magazine
(1873-1937); in 1894 it began printing articles and fiction of interest to women
and became so successful that four foreign editions were published. SMART SET.
The Smart Set (1890-1930) was a New York monthly, founded by W.D. Mann as a
society journal; it grew into a witty literary journal, publishing many prominent
writers of the day. AINSLEE'S. London semi-monthly that grew out of the illustrated quarterly, the *Yellow Book*, in 1898 and published the most popular writers
of England and America. **November 23** UNIVERSALIST CHURCH. Universalist
Church of America, founded in Gloucester, Mass., in 1779; Universalists believe
that it is God's purpose to save every individual from sin through divine grace
revealed in Jesus Christ. ST. LUKE'S. Anglican Church on Morris Street, near the
corner of Church. ROYAL VISIT. King Edward VII's second son and daughter-in-
law (later King George V and Queen Mary) were on a global tour to celebrate the
establishment of the new British Commonwealth. BUNTING. Brightly coloured
fabric used for flags and for decorating public buildings. THE COMMON. A large
recreational area in the centre of Halifax. **December 12** BON MARCHE. A shop
on Pleasant Street, near the corner of Prince.

1902
January 20 FORT MASSEY. A Presbyterian church at the corner of Queen and
Tobin Streets. **February 1** RE-READING THE SCARLET LETTER. Other journal
entries (omitted here) show that during this time in Halifax LMM was also reading
more current and stylish books, including *The Witch of Prague* (1891) by F. Marion
Crawford, *What Maisie Knew* (1897) by Henry James, *Mrs. Halliburton's Troubles*
(1862) by Mrs. Henry Wood, and *The Little Minister* (1891) by J.M. Barrie.
March 29 "POT-BOILING" STUFF. At least thirty stories by LMM were accepted
for publication during this Halifax year. **May 1** 25 MORRIS. This central street
becomes University and leads to Dalhousie University. **May 4** A.P.A. American
Press Association: a wire service carrying international stories. **May 12** "A
BAD BOY'S DIRY". See note to entry for February 13, 1894. **June 2** JOSIAH
ALLEN'S WIFE. Pseudonym of Marietta Holley, the author of a series of comic dia-
lect books featuring the homely philosophizing of Josiah Allen's wife "Samantha":
Samantha on the Race Problem (1892) and others. **September 21** NORA
LEFURGEY. The young teacher came to board at the Macneill farm in February.

1903

April 12 "THE HOUSE OF SEVEN GABLES". *The House of the Seven Gables* (1851), a novel by Nathaniel Hawthorne. "ALHAMBRA". *The Alhambra* (1832), 41 sketches by Washington Irving, who had lived in the ancient Moorish palace in Granada, Spain, in 1829. ADAM BEDE. Novel (1859) by George Eliot. LMM misspells the author's name "Elliot". "THE RUBAIYAT". *The Rubaiyat of Omar Khayyam* (1859), a translation by Edward Fitzgerald of the quatrains of the 12th-century Persian poet. CO-OPERATIVE DIARY. LMM copied over 100 pages of this joint effort into her own journal. **August 16** EDWIN SIMPSON. Earlier summer entries record efforts to avoid meeting her former fiancé. **August 18** JOHN CLARKS AND ARTHUR SIMPSONS. LMM is inconsistent in her manner of referring to families collectively. The manuscript has "John Clarks' and Arthur Simpsons"; the typescript has "John Clark's and Arthur Simpsons"; compare the references to "Uncle Johns", implying reference to his family. **December 3** A CHECK. LMM's account books, now in the Library of the University of Guelph, record all payments for her stories and poems. ANOTHER SERIAL. "The Running Away of Chester" ran in *Boys' World* weekly from November 14, 1903 to December 26, 1903; "The Bitterness in the Cup" ran in *American Home*, December 1903 and January 1904. PRES. BOARD OF PUBLICATIONS. The Presbyterian Board of Publications was one of a group of church-related presses that had helped develop a number of popular authors.

1904

March 16 NOTHING NEW TO READ. Many entries of this period (omitted here) refer to the books LMM was currently reading: J.M. Barrie's *Tommy and Grizel* (1900), Jean Ingelow's *Dead Year* (1867), E.N. Westcott's *David Harum* (1898), and George DuMaurier's *Trilby* (1894). **November 14** EPHRAIM WEBER. LMM's letters to this correspondent have been published as *The Green Gables Letters*, edited by Wilfrid Eggleston (Toronto: Ryerson, 1960). GEO. B. MACMILLAN. Letters to this correspondent, discovered by Mollie Gillen, appear in *My Dear Mr.M.*, edited by F.W.P. Bolger and Elizabeth Epperley (Toronto: McGraw-Hill Ryerson, 1980).

1905

January 2 WHAT A STARVED CHILDHOOD. These reflections—which could mean that she had read three recent bestsellers about orphan children (*Lovey Mary* by Alice Hegan Rice in 1903. *Rebecca of Sunnybrook Farm* by Kate Douglas Wiggin in 1903, and *Freckles* by Gene Stratton Porter in 1904)—occur during the period in which LMM was probably writing *Anne of Green Gables*. "PEEP OF DAY" SERIES. Methodist Sunday school stories by Mrs. Favell Lee (Bevan) Mortimer, published from the 1830s on by the American Tract Society of Boston. **February 8** AN EASTER STORY. LMM published at least 32 stories in 1905. POINT LACE CENTREPIECE. A doily made entirely with a needle. SALAD DAYS. The mature Cleopatra's phrase for her youth, in *Antony and Cleopatra*, I,v,75. **March 3** MRS. BROWNING. Poet Elizabeth Barrett Browning (1806-61) author of *Sonnets from the Portuguese* (1850), *Aurora Leigh* (1857), and other works. **March 11** THE STRAIT. Strait of Northumberland: ferries to the mainland were blocked.

March 26 NO REAL COMPANION. Compare Montgomery's *Emily of New Moon* (1923). **May 20** "JUNGLE BOOKS". *The Jungle Book* (1894) and *The Second Jungle Book* (1895) by Rudyard Kipling contain stories about a child brought up by animals. PICKWICK PAPERS AND DAVID COPPERFIELD. *The Posthumous Papers of the Pickwick Club* (1837) and *David Copperfield* (1849-50), two novels by Charles Dickens. ELIZABETH AND HER GERMAN GARDEN. Published anonymously (1898) by novelist Elizabeth von Arnim. **July 30** UNCLE LEANDER'S FAMILY. Leander Macneill's illness, diagnosed as "paralysis agitans" (Parkinson's Disease), prevented his family from coming for the usual month-long visit and left LMM free for a summer of writing. It seems clear that this was the time she was completing *Anne of Green Gables*. AN OLD SCRAPBOOK. One of several formerly on display at LMM's birthplace, Clifton; now in the Archives of the Art Gallery at the Confederation Centre, Charlottetown. **August 11** EUGENE ARAM. Bulwer Lytton's novel (1832) of a murderer redeemed by love. **October 1** SWORD OF DAMOCLES. In classical mythology Damocles was forced by Dionysius to sit at a banquet, where a naked sword was suspended above his head by a single hair. **December 10** THE SAFE COMPASS. Evangelical stories by the Rev. Richard Newton, an American Episcopalian (New York: Carter, 1863). FRONTISPIECE. Illustration facing title page; LMM consistently misspells this word as "frontespiece". **December 24** BERTHA'S WEDDING DAY. A newspaper clipping in LMM's scrapbook notes that the Rev. Ewan Macdonald performed the ceremony.

1906

April 5 SIDNEY. Nova Scotia mining town. MABEL SAUNDERS. A cousin of Margaret Marshall Saunders, author of *Beautiful Joe* and a string of other bestselling children's stories. **October 12** EWAN MACDONALD. LMM misspells his name in this entry and errs regarding his age—he was 36, not 34. VALLEYFIELD. He was born in Bellevue, near Valleyfield in the east-central section of PEI, about 50 miles east of Cavendish near the Valleyfield River, which flows into Cardigan Bay. A newspaper item about his farewell reception speaks of his broad mind and vigorous heart—"an indefatigable worker and a genial companion". CARDIGAN. On the East coast of PEI. WHIST. A four-handed card game, the forerunner of bridge; trump is set by the dealer's last card, rather than by bidding. **November 20** "WHATEVER GODS THERE [*sic*] BE". Misquoted from "Invictus" (1888) by W.E. Henley. **December 2** EVERYBODY'S. New York magazine founded by Wanamaker's; it was one of the leading 10¢ general illustrated magazines, particularly noted for popular serials. THE FUTURE LIFE. The translation of a French dissertation (Paris, 1905) by Louis Lucien Bacle (pseudonym, Louis Elbe) based on "ancient wisdom and modern science" (Chicago: McClung, 1906, and London: Chatto, 1907).

1907

January 20 GIBBON'S "ROME". *The History of the Decline and Fall of the Roman Empire* (1776-88), a six-volume work by Edward Gibbon. **August 16** L.C. PAGE CO. This company had published Bliss Carman's poetry between 1902 and

1905 (collected in *The Pipes of Pan*, 1906) and also Charles G.D. Roberts' *Poems* (1907). BOBBS-MERRILL. In 1904 Bowen-Merrill, a famous house of bestsellers, became Bobbs-Merrill and took over the copyright from Hill, Reilly and Lee of *The New Wizard of Oz*, first published in 1900. MACMILLAN OF NEW YORK. This firm published the Number 1 book on the 1902 bestseller list, Owen Wister's *The Virginian*, and in 1903 Jack London's *The Call of the Wild*. LOTHROP, LEE, AND SHEPARD. Lothrop published the bestseller of 1900, Irving Bacheller's *Eben Holden*. HENRY HOLT. Publisher of *The Prisoner of Zenda*, 1894.

1908

January 12 MY NEW BOOK. *Anne of Avonlea* (1909). **May 3** BLOOMFIELD. Inland, on the railway line in the most westerly area of PEI, about 80 miles from Cavendish. SO HOPELESS, SO PLAYED-OUT. The entry continues with a long narrative of her early life similar to the reprise that concludes this volume of the Journals. **June 20** MY BOOK. LMM copied this passage, with some stylistic changes, into "The Alpine Path" (see note on entry for August 1, 1898). **July 16** "MERRY WIDOW" HAT. One with a wide curved brim, as worn in Franz Lehar's operetta, *The Merry Widow* (1905). **October 15** A "BEST SELLER". LMM's account book records sales in the first year, 1908, as follows: Canadian, 775; Australian, 500; English, 500; U.S., 18,286; total: 20,061. Sales would double in the second year. **November 10** WAVERLY . . . ROB ROY . . . THE TALISMAN . . . IVANHOE. Novels (1814, 1817, 1825, 1819) by Sir Walter Scott.

1909

February 20 BLISS CARMAN. Maritime poet turned transcendental philosopher; Carman wrote a book of essays, *The Making of Personality* (1908), with Mary Perry King. The only other Canadian poet named in the journals is Archibald Lampman: LMM quotes from "The Frogs" on May 27, 1900. "OF THE RACE THAT KNOWS JOSEPH". A common inversion of Exodus 1,8: "a new king over Egypt, which knew not Joseph". **March 16** SLEWS. Variant of "sloughs": deep mud or mire. **April 11** THE LONDON SPECTATOR. The *Spectator*, an intellectual weekly periodical started in 1828, had many notable contributors. **April 16** INTERNATIONAL COUNCIL OF WOMEN. Founded in 1888 in the United States as part of the suffrage movement. **June 1** ANDERSEN'S FAIRY TALES. Hans Christian Andersen's *Tales* (1835) was first translated into English in 1846. THE STORY GIRL. LMM weaves a collection of stories into this novel (1911), which was to become her favourite. THE "HONEY STEW" ABOUNDED. Several tales in *The Story Girl* feature ghosts and thrills. **June 3** SEVEN YEARS OLD. LMM's son, Dr. Stuart Macdonald, corrected this in the typescript to "8 years old". "O'ER THE FOAM". From Keats's "Ode to a Nightingale" (1819), lines 69-70. THE PLIMSOLL BILL. The Merchant Shipping Act of 1876 decreed that a mark on the hull should indicate the maximum loading-level of a ship: Samuel Plimsoll had agitated for this measure and designed the "Plimsoll line". DEAL PLANKS. Fir or pine sawed into 6-foot lengths. CHRISTIANIA. The former name of Oslo, the capital of Norway. "OLD, FORGOTTEN, FAR-OFF THINGS". For "old, unhappy, far-off things", from William Wordsworth's "The Solitary Reaper" (1805), line 19. "THE LIGHT

THAT NEVER WAS ON SEA OR LAND". From Wordsworth's "Elegiac Stanzas" (1805), line 15. UNCLE JIMMIE. James Macneill, older brother of Alex Macneill; village poet and eccentric. **July 11** KEATS' POEMS. The entry continues with a quotation from "Ode to a Nightingale" (1820). **September 4** TENNYSON . . . BROWNING. LMM had not included Browning in her list of favourite poets in college days. "DO WE INDEED DESIRE THE DEAD". From Tennyson's *In Memoriam A.H.H.* (1850), LI,1. **September 21** "THE POISON AND THE STING". From Adelaide Procter's poem "Per pacem ad lucem" (1892). **October 20** "ANOTHER SUCH VICTORY AND I AM UNDONE". Plutarch's *Lives*, Pyrrhus, 21. **December 23** CHANGED TO KILMENY. Kilmeny was a heroine of Scottish folklore; her story is told in James Hogg's *The Queen's Wake* (1813). **December 24** "DARE TO LOOK". Lord Byron's *Cain: A Mystery* (1821), I,138. **December 26** "FORWARD THO' I CANNA SEE". Robert Burns, "To a Mouse"(1787), line 46.

1910

January 7 "HOW DOTH THE LITTLE BUSY BEE". The first line of Isaac Watts' "Against Idleness and Mischief" (1715). THE SCHOOLHOUSE. A photo caption explains "Originally it had only two large low windows on each side and the roof was lower". THE WEE SMA'S. Scottish dialect: very early in the small hours of the morning. "DRAB". Light brown colour. JET. Polished black lignite used as beading. TO RETURN TO OUR MUTTON. Gallicism: to return to our subject. "LITTLE KATEY AND JOLLY JIM". Anonymous (London: Nisbet, 1865). PILGRIM'S PROGRESS. John Bunyan's allegory (1678) about Christian's travels from the city of destruction to the celestial city; in Part IV Christiana, her children, and her neighbour Mercy go on the same pilgrimage. TALMAGE. Thomas DeWitt Talmage published a very popular evangelical series, *Sermons, Delivered in the Brooklyn Tabernacle* (New York: Harper, 1872). COLPORTEURS. Book-hawkers, especially Bible salesmen. "GODEY'S LADY'S BOOK". Sentimental, moralistic stories, accompanied by hand-coloured illustrations of fashions, made *Godey's* the best-known women's magazine. It was published from 1830 to 1898, with minor changes. "WIDE AWAKE". Founded in 1875 by Daniel Lothrop, who also published *Pansy* and *Babyland*. "A SORROW'S CROWN OF SORROW". From Lord Tennyson's "Locksley Hall" (1842), line 76. "BUT WHAT MUST IT BE TO BE THERE?". From George Whitefield's *Hymn Book* (1753). GEORGE WHITEFIELD (1714-1770). He joined John Wesley's Methodist movement and became an extraordinarily effective evangelical preacher. CATECHISM QUESTIONS. The Presbyterian Shorter Catechism contained 107 questions and answers concerning doctrines and duties (the Anglican Church had 24), beginning with "Q: What is the chief end of man? A: To glorify God and to enjoy Him forever." "BOBS". Named for Lord Roberts, a British hero from the days of the Indian Mutiny, and Commander-in-Chief at Bloemfontein and Pretoria in the South African Boer War. GAMES. The list includes bouncing-ball games, circle games, permission games, and pursuit games. J.P. Justice of the Peace: lay magistrate, appointed to notarize deeds. VERSE ABOUT. Taking turns to read verses. SCHOOLMARM. An American derivative from "schoolma'am" ("schoolmadam"). **February 7** A NEW AND DREADFUL WORRY. Nothing in the journal, letters, or scrapbooks explains this phrase. CAPE TRAVERSE. On the South Shore; the nearest point to the mainland.

Omissions

All the entries that have been deleted, either in part or in total, are listed below. An asterisk after the date indicates that the deletion is only partial.

1890: Jan. 8; Feb. 25, Apr. 9; June 11; July 17; Sept. 4, 9, 27; Oct. 18; Nov. 12; Dec. 12; **1891**: Feb. 27; Mar. 30*; May 7, 14*; June 17; July 6, 8; Aug. 10, 12, 17, 23, 28; Sept. 3*, 13, 14, 19, 26; Oct. 8, 13, 16, 18, 19; Nov. 7*, 19*; **1892**: Jan. 9; Feb. 18, 28*; Mar. 4, 7*, 12*, 27; Apr. 27; May 2, 5, 6, 14, 18, 21, 22; June 1, 6, 29; July 1, 17*; Aug. 1*, 13, 27; Sept. 24, 29; Oct. 21; Nov. 4; Dec. 2, 4, 29; **1893**: Jan. 25, 26; Feb. 13, 17*; Mar. 3, 4, 8, 12; Apr. 4, 7, 11, 20, 23; May 1, 10, 16, 24; June 3, 8*, 16, 19, 24; July 3, 10, 20, 29; Aug. 16, 17, 21, 22, 26; Sept. 10, 27; Oct. 8; Nov. 9, 14, 18, 21, 26; Dec. 1, 4, 9, 10, 11, 17, 18, 19, 21, 27, 28, 31; **1894**: Jan. 5, 7, 10*, 25, 26, 28; Feb. 2, 5, 9; Mar. 1*, 6, 7, 10, 17, 18, 19, 20, 22, 23, 25, 26, 27, 28, 30, 31; Apr. 1, 6, 9, 11, 12, 13, 15, 16, 19, 22, 23, 24, 27, 28; May 1, 3, 12; June 12, 13, 14, 25, 28; July 1, 2, 5*, 8, 17; Aug. 1, 10, 13*, 16, 30; Sept. 4*, 8, 9, 10, 13, 15, 21; Oct. 1, 6, 7, 11, 12, 17, 24, 27, 30; Nov. 6, 11, 16, 27; Dec. 4, 9, 14, 16, 24; **1895**: Jan. 2, 7, 9, 12, 14, 24; Feb. 6, 11, 13, 25, 26; Mar. 3, 7, 20, 24; Apr. 1, 11, 28, 30; May 10, 13, 16, 19, 30; June 1, 2, 13, 19, 22, 27; July 13; Aug. 1, 11, 12; Sept. 5*, 16, 20, 21, 27, 28, 30; Oct. 6, 17, 20, 21; Nov. 22; Dec. 1*, 4, 8, 30, 31; **1896**: Jan. 1, 22, 25, 31; Feb. 3, 5, 7, 15*; Mar. 3, 7, 14*, 28; Apr. 5, 10, 28; May 1, 30; June 3, 8, 14; July 29; Aug. 1, 20*, 24, 28, 30; Sept, 8, 19, 29; Oct. 15, 27*, 28; Nov. 1, 7*, 13, 24; Dec. 2, 9, 17, 19, 21*; **1897**: Jan. 16, 25; Feb. 13; Mar. 22, 29; Apr. 5, 25*; May 3, 7, 21, 25; **1898**: Apr. 8*; Oct. 8*; **1899**: May 28*; **1900**: May 20*, 27; June 7*; Aug. 5*, 11; Oct. 7*, 8, 10, 11, 23; **1901**: Jan. 5, 14; Feb. 10, 22; Mar. 2*, 4, 21*; Apr. 14; May 12; Aug. 23*; Sept. 1, 9; Nov. 18*, 22, 23*, 28, 29; Dec. 17, 21, 27; **1902**: Jan. 21, 27; Feb. 8, 15, 22, 28; Mar. 1, 16, 31; Apr. 8*, 12; June 14, 30; July 31; Aug. 31; Sept. 29; Oct. 27; Dec. 10, 27; **1903**: Jan. 13; Feb. 2, 9, 21; Mar. 20; Apr. 30; May 2, 29; June 6, 30*; July 11, 19, 26; Aug. 10, 12, 15, 18; Sept. 10; Oct. 20, 31; Nov. 14, 19, 20; Dec. 27; **1904** Feb. 6, 20, 28; Mar. 11*; Apr. 9*, 19, 20, 30; May 5, 20, 29; July 3, 5; Oct. 5, 24, 30, 31; Dec. 20; **1905**: Jan. 17; Feb. 7; Mar. 16; Apr. 14; May 20*, 21; July 30*; Aug. 4, 6; Oct. 15*; Nov. 8, 12, 16; **1906**: Jan. 14, Feb. 1, 3*, 25; Mar. 2; Apr. 18*; May 13*; Nov. 4*, 6*, 11, 12; Dec. 4; **1907**: Jan. 27; Feb. 5*, 25*, 27; Mar. 10; Oct. 9*; Nov. 3, 13; Dec. 17*; **1908**: Jan. 12*; May 3*, 19; Sept. 1, 24; Nov. 3, 5, 11, 21; Dec. 13*, 20; **1909**: Jan. 31; Feb. 1, 16; Mar. 3, 31; Apr. 3, 11*, 18; May 1, 8, 14, 21; June 30; July 11*; Dec. 5*; **1910**: Jan. 1, 6*.

Index

Acadia College, 24, 34
Agnew, Andrew, 52, 56, 115
Alberton, PEI, 192-3
America Press Association, 281
Anderson, Professor Alex, 92, 93, 95-6, 103-4, 106, 112, 121, 137, 145, 155, 308
Andrews, Mrs. and Miss (Halifax boarding house), 280, 282; boarders: Colborne, Grant, McAfee, Pearson, 280
Anne of Avonlea, 331, 336, 338, 340, 358
Anne of Green Gables, 331, 335, 339, 350
Archibald, Rev. W.P., 8, 13, 80, 148, 161
Arsenault, Professor Joseph Octave, 91
Atlantic Monthly, 237
authors cited: Alcott, 251; Andersen, 375; Barrie, 148; Browning, Robert, 358; Browning, E.B., 304; Byron, 103-4, 158, 363; Caine, Hall, 230; Carman, Bliss, 347; Cicero, 145, 155; Crockett, 148; Eliot, George; 286; Emerson, 75, 356; Hawthorne, 286; Hope, Anthony, 247; Irving, 71, 75, 286; "Josiah Allen's Wife", 282; Keats, 357, 358; Kipling, 230, 306; Longfellow, 133, 158; Lytton, Bulwer, 24, 283; McLaren, Ian, 148; Milton, 149; Schreiner, Olive, 257; Scott, 342; Shakespeare, 102, 155; Tennyson, 133, 158, 358-9; Whittier, 158; Wordsworth, 358

Baptist Church, 89, 179, 189, 196-7, 283; in Belmont, 175; in Cavendish, 81, 336; in New Glasgow, 142
    preachers: Baker, 176, 178, 180-1, 186; Belyea, 317; Higgins, 182; Jackson, 237; McLeod, 178, 180; MacDougall, 283
    Young People's Union, 206, 209
Battleford, NWT (Sask.), 29, 51
Bay View, PEI, 230; Zella Clark, 14
Beaton, Archie, 252
Bedeque, 136, 201, 202, 205, 207-9, 219, 221, 226-7, 240, 391; LMM in, 201-27
    families: see Leard
    school, 203, 221
Belmont, 163, 168-9, 391, 171, 178, 181, 183, 193, 195, 201, 225, 391; LMM in, 163-95
    families: see Campbell, Fraser, Lyle, Simpson
    school, 164
Bideford, 115, 158, 379, 389, 390, 165, 168, 170, 171, 181, 225-6, 250, 261, 309; LMM in, 115-42

families: see Ellis, England, Estey, Dystant, Hayes, McArthur, Millar, Moore, Richards, Williams
    school, 116-17, 119, 120, 123, 125, 140-1
Bird Island, PEI, 118
Bloomfield, PEI, 334
Boer War, 247-8, 282, 379
books cited: *Adam Bede*, 286; *The Alhambra*, 286; Andersen's *Fairy Tales*, 351; *The Ascent of Man*, 250; *Athalie*, 249; *A Bad Boy's Diry*, 281; *Barrack-Room Ballads*, 230; *Black Douglas*, 238; *The Clockmaker*, 28; *The Children of the Abbey*, 235; *The Christian*, 230; *David Copperfield*, 306; *Devereux*, 24; *The Decline and Fall of the Roman Empire*, 329; *Elizabeth and Her German Garden*, 307; Macaulay's *Essays*, 120; *Eugene Aram*, 309-10; *Farthest North*, 250; *The Four Georges*, 250; *The Future Life*, 325; *Gates Ajar*, 197; *Hamlet*, 204, 208; *The Haunters and the Haunted*, 283; *The House of the Seven Gables*, 286; *The House of the Wolf*, 238; *Isabel Carnaby*, 251; *Ivanhoe*, 342; *Janice Meredith*, 251; *The Jungle Books*, 306; *The King's Mirror*, 250; *King Solomon's Mines*, 249; *The Lady of the Lake*, 247; *The Last Days of Pompeii*, 114; *The Last of the Mohicans*, 250; *The Law of Psychic Phenomena*, 317; *Little Katey and Jolly Jim*, 374; *The Love Letters of a Worldly Woman*, 198; *The Making of Personality*, 347; *The Manxman*, 230; *The Memoir of Anzonetta Peters*, 376; *Mr. Midshipman Easy*, 88; *More Tramps Abroad*, 242; *Night and Morning*, 221; *Old Mortality*, 155; *Opening a Chestnut Burr*, 223; *Pansy*, 37, 253; *Peep of Day*, 302; *Phroso*, 235; The Pickwick Papers, 306, 374; *The Pilgrim's Progress*, 374; *Poems of Passion*, 223; *The Quick or the Dead*, 220; *Quo Vadis*, 223; *Rob Roy*, 42, 374; *Robert Elsmere*, 77; *The Rubaiyat*, 286, 289; *Rupert of Hentzau*, 247; *The Safe Compass*, 312; *The Scarlet Letter*, 133, 278; *Scottish Chiefs*, 88; *The Sketch Book* (W. Irving), 71; *The Story of an African Farm*, 197, 247; *The Soul of Lilith*, 238; *Talisman*, 342; *Talmage's Sermons*, 376; *The Tower of London*, 237; *Undine*, 3, 253; *Valen-*

417